Course   **Corporate Responsibility
and Regulation**
Villanova School of Business
Summer Business Institute 2013

http://create.mcgraw-hill.com

ISBN-10: 1121502962   ISBN-13: 9781121502963

Contents

1. Philosophical Ethics and Business   1
2. Contractual Performance and Agency   49
3. Corporate Governance and Business Organizations   74
4. Corporate Governance   106
5. Corporate Social Responsibility   151
6. Financial and Securities Regulations   188
7. Contracts   227
8. Torts Affecting Business   272
9. Employment Laws   304
10. Discrimination in Employment   336
11. The American Legal System   376
12. Intellectual Property   426
13. International Law   462
A. Selected Sections of Article 2 of Uniform Commercial Code   495
B. Selected Sections of the Sarbanes-Oxley Act of 2002   501
C. Selected Sections of Securities Act of 1933   506
D. Selected Sections of Securities Exchange Act of 1934   508

Credits

1. Philosophical Ethics and Business: *Chapter 3 from Business Ethics: Decision-Making for Personal Integrity and Social Responsibility, Second Edition by Hartman, DesJardins, 2011* 1

2. Contractual Performance and Agency: *Chapter 9 from The Legal and Regulatory Environment of Business, 16th Edition by Reed, Pagnattaro, Cahoy, Shedd, Morehead, 2013* 49

3. Corporate Governance and Business Organizations: *Chapter 14 from The Legal and Regulatory Environment of Business, 16th Edition by Reed, Pagnattaro, Cahoy, Shedd, Morehead, 2013* 74

4. Corporate Governance: *Chapter 18 from Business, Government, and Society: A Managerial Perspective, Text and Cases, 13th Edition by Steiner, Steiner, 2012* 106

5. Corporate Social Responsibility: *Chapter 5 from Business, Government, and Society: A Managerial Perspective, Text and Cases, 13th Edition by Steiner, Steiner, 2012* 151

6. Financial and Securities Regulations: *Chapter 17 from The Legal and Regulatory Environment of Business, 16th Edition by Reed, Pagnattaro, Cahoy, Shedd, Morehead, 2013* 188

7. Contracts: *Chapter 6 from Law, Business, and Society, Tenth Edition by McAdams, Neslund, Zucker, 2012* 227

8. Torts Affecting Business: *Chapter 10 from The Legal and Regulatory Environment of Business, 16th Edition by Reed, Pagnattaro, Cahoy, Shedd, Morehead, 2013* 272

9. Employment Laws: *Chapter 21 from The Legal and Regulatory Environment of Business, 16th Edition by Reed, Pagnattaro, Cahoy, Shedd, Morehead, 2013* 304

10. Discrimination in Employment: *Chapter 20 from The Legal and Regulatory Environment of Business, 16th Edition by Reed, Pagnattaro, Cahoy, Shedd, Morehead, 2013* 336

11. The American Legal System: *Chapter 4 from Law, Business, and Society, Tenth Edition by McAdams, Neslund, Zucker, 2012* 376

12. Intellectual Property: *Chapter 11 from The Legal and Regulatory Environment of Business, 16th Edition by Reed, Pagnattaro, Cahoy, Shedd, Morehead, 2013* 426

13. International Law: *Chapter 12 from The Legal and Regulatory Environment of Business, 16th Edition by Reed, Pagnattaro, Cahoy, Shedd, Morehead, 2013* 462

A. Selected Sections of Article 2 of Uniform Commercial Code: *Chapter Appendix IV from The Legal and Regulatory Environment of Business, 16th Edition by Reed, Pagnattaro, Cahoy, Shedd, Morehead, 2013* 495

B. Selected Sections of the Sarbanes-Oxley Act of 2002: *Chapter Appendix V from The Legal and Regulatory Environment of Business, 16th Edition by Reed, Pagnattaro, Cahoy, Shedd, Morehead, 2013* 501

C. Selected Sections of Securities Act of 1933: *Chapter Appendix VI from The Legal and Regulatory Environment of Business, 16th Edition by Reed, Pagnattaro, Cahoy, Shedd, Morehead, 2013* 506

D. Selected Sections of Securities Exchange Act of 1934: *Chapter Appendix VII from The Legal and Regulatory Environment of Business, 16th Edition by Reed, Pagnattaro, Cahoy, Shedd, Morehead, 2013* 508

Chapter **3**

Philosophical Ethics and Business

Opening Decision Point

Executive Compensation: Needed Incentives, Justly Deserved, or Just Distasteful?

Perhaps no part of the financial market collapse of late 2008, and the government bailout that followed, caused as much public outcry as did the financial bonuses and compensation paid to senior executives of failed companies. American International Group (AIG) became the target of much of this criticism. Persuaded that AIG was "too big to fail," by March 2009 the U.S. federal government had committed $180 billion dollars to rescue AIG from bankruptcy. In early March of 2009, AIG announced that it was paying $165 million in bonuses to 400 top executives in its financial division, the very unit that was at the heart of the company's collapse.

AIG cited two major factors in the defense of these bonuses: they were owed as a result of contracts that had been negotiated and signed before the collapse, and they were needed to provide an incentive to retain the most talented employees at a time when they were most needed.

Critics claimed that the bonuses were an example of corporate greed run amok. They argued that contractual obligations should have been overridden and renegotiated at the point of bankruptcy. They also dismissed the effectiveness of the incentive argument since this supposed "talent" was responsible for the failed business strategy that led to AIG's troubles in the first place.

As part of the government bailout of AIG, Edward M. Liddy, an associate of Secretary of the Treasury Henry Paulson, was named CEO of AIG in September of 2008. Former CEO Martin Sullivan resigned earlier in the summer as AIG's financial troubles intensified, but he did not retire without first securing a $47 million severance package. In comparison, Liddy himself accepted a salary of $1, although his contract held out the possibility of future bonuses.

In testimony before the U.S. Congress soon after being named CEO, Liddy was asked to explain the expense of a recent AIG-sponsored retreat for AIG salespeople. The retreat cost AIG over $400,000 and was, in Liddy's words, a "standard practice within the industry." Six months later, when news broke about the $165 million bonus payments, Liddy—suggesting that the executives consider doing "the right thing" by returning the bonuses—described them as "distasteful."

Within months of taking office, the Obama administration took steps to limit executive compensation at firms that accepted significant government bailout money, including the retirement packages of the former CEOs of Citigroup, General Motors, and Bank of America. Announcing this action, Treasury Secretary Timothy Geithner observed that "this financial crisis had many significant causes, but executive compensation practices were a contributing factor."

- How would you describe the bonuses paid to AIG executives in March of 2009? Is it an ethical issue at all? Why or why not?
- Are there any facts that you would want to know before making a judgment?
- What alternatives to paying the bonuses would have been available to Edward Liddy?

(continued)

(concluded)

- Do you agree that AIG had an obligation to pay the bonuses? How strong is the duty to fulfill a contract, even one requiring payment of such bonuses? When should a contract be overridden by other concerns?
- Do you think the employees deserved the bonuses?
- How would you judge whether or not the bonuses were effective incentives?
- Do you agree with Liddy that they were "distasteful"? Is this judgment a matter of personal opinion and taste, or is it instead a reasonable and objective judgment?
- Who are the stakeholders in the decision to pay bonuses to AIG executives? How do their interests affect the contract between AIG and its employees?
- During the presidential debates in October 2008, then-candidate Barack Obama said that "the Treasury should demand that money back and those executives should be fired." Do you agree?
- Is executive compensation purely a private matter between an employer and employee, or should it be a matter of public concern and government policy?

 ## Chapter Objectives

After reading this chapter, you will be able to:

1. Explain the ethical theory of utilitarianism.
2. Describe how utilitarian thinking underlies economic and business decision making.
3. Explain how the free market is thought to serve the utilitarian goal of maximizing the overall good.
4. Explain some challenges to utilitarian decision making.
5. Explain principle-based, or deontological ethical theories.
6. Explain the concept of human rights and how they are relevant to business.
7. Distinguish moral rights from legal rights.
8. Explain several challenges to deontological ethics.
9. Describe and explain virtue-based theories of ethical character.

Introduction: Ethical Theories and Traditions

Consider the reasons that you or others offered to defend or criticize the payment of large bonuses to AIG executives. Upon reflection, these reasons fall into three general categories. Some reasons appeal to the *consequences* of paying the bonuses: they either will, or will not, provide incentives for producing good work and beneficial future consequences. Other reasons appeal to certain *principles:* one should not break a contractual promise, even if it has unpopular results; one should never benefit from serious harms that have been caused by one's own actions. Other reasons cite matters of *personal character:* accepting bonuses is greedy, or distasteful. Paying the bonuses that were due in the face of public criticism was courageous and had to be done as a matter of integrity.

As it turns out, the three major traditions of ethical theory that we shall rely on in this text are represented by these three categories. This should be no surprise since ethical traditions in philosophy reflect common ways to think and reason about how we should live, what we should do. Ethics of consequences, ethics of principles, and ethics of personal character are the traditions that will be introduced in this chapter.

Chapters 1 and 2 introduced ethics as a form of practical reasoning in support of decision making about how we should live our lives. Ethics involves what is perhaps the most significant question any human being can ask: How *should* I live my life? But, of course, this question is not new; every major philosophical, cultural, political, and religious tradition in human history has grappled with it. In light of this, it would be imprudent to ignore these traditions as we begin to examine ethical issues in business.

Nevertheless, many students think that discussions of ethical theories and philosophical ethics are too abstract to be of much help in business. Discussion of ethical "theories" often seems to be too *theoretical* to be of much relevance to business. Throughout this chapter, we hope to suggest a more accessible understanding of ethical theories, one that will shed some light on the practical and pragmatic application of these theories to actual problems faced by business people. (For an examination of the pragmatic application, see the reading by Norman Bowie at the end of this chapter, "It Seems Right in Theory but Does It Work in Practice?")

An ethical theory is nothing more than an attempt to provide a systematic answer to the fundamental ethical question: How should human beings live their lives? In many ways, this is a simple question that we ask, at least implicitly, every day. What am I going to do today, and why? Ethics can be understood as the practice of examining these decisions and thinking about answers to that question: Why?

Ethical theories attempt to answer the question of how we should live, but they also give *reasons* to support their answers. Ethics seeks to provide a rational justification for *why* we should act and decide in a particular prescribed way. Anyone can offer prescriptions for what you should do and how you should act, but a *philosophical* and reasoned ethics must answer the "Why?" question as well.

Many people and cultures across the world would answer this "why" question in religious terms and base their normative judgments on religious foundations. "You ought to live your life in a certain way because God commands it." The biggest practical problem with this approach, of course, is that people differ widely about their religious beliefs. If ethics is based on religion, and if different cultures have widely divergent religious beliefs, then it would seem that ethics cannot escape the predicament of relativism. (See the Decision Point "Who Is to Say What Is Right or Wrong" for more on ethical relativism.)

Unlike religious ethics which explains human well-being in religious terms, philosophical ethics provides justifications that must be applicable to all people regardless of their religious starting points. The justifications of philosophical ethics connect the "oughts" and "shoulds" of ethics to an underlying account of

Decision Point

Who Is to Say What Is Right or Wrong?

Are you an ethical relativist? Ethical relativism holds that ethical values are relative to particular people, cultures, or times. Relativism denies that there are can be any rationally justified or objective ethical judgments. When there are ethical disagreements between people or cultures, the ethical relativist concludes that there is not way to resolve that dispute and prove one side is right or more reasonable than the other.

Consider Edward Liddy's description of the AIG bonuses as "distasteful." Ordinarily, we think of matters of taste as personal, subjective things. You enjoy spicy Indian food, while I prefer simple Midwestern meat and potatoes. It is all a matter of personal taste. Liddy may have found the bonuses distasteful, but others find them well-deserved. Ethical relativists believe that ethical values are much like tastes in food; it all depends on, or it is all relative to, one's own background, culture, and personal opinions.

Do you believe that there is no way to decide what is ethically right or wrong? Imagine a teacher returns an assignment to you with a grade of "F." When you ask for an explanation, you are told that, frankly, the teacher does not believe that people "like you" (e.g., men, Christians, African Americans) are capable of doing good work in this field (e.g., science, engineering, math, finance). When you object that this is unfair and wrong, the teacher offers a relativist explanation. "Fairness is a matter of personal opinion," the professor explains. "Who determines what is fair or unfair?" you ask. Your teacher claims that his view of what is fair is as valid as any other. Because everyone is entitled to their own personal opinion, he is entitled to fail you since, in his personal opinion, you do not deserve to succeed.

- Would you accept this explanation and be content with your failing grade? If not, how would you defend your own, opposing view?
- Are there any relevant facts on which you would rely to support your claim?
- What values are involved in this dispute?
- What alternatives are available to you?
- Besides you and your teacher, are there any other stakeholders—people who are or should be involved in this situation?
- What reasons would you offer to the dean in an appeal to have the grade changed?
- What consequences would this professor's practice have on education?
- If reasoning and logical persuasion do not work, how else could this dispute be resolved?

human well-being. Thus, for example, "you should contribute to disaster relief because it will reduce human suffering" is a philosophical justification for an ethical judgment, whereas "you should contribute to disaster relief because God commands it, or because it will bring you heavenly rewards" are religious rather than philosophical justifications. (For a discussion on the application of relativism, oughts and shoulds to the particular concept of bribery, see the reading "Ethical Dimensions of Decision-Making in the Developing World: The Case of Bribery in Mauritus" by Geetanee Napal at the end of this chapter.)

Finally, ethical theories are not comprised of one single principle or framework. Ethical theories evolved over time and have been refined and developed by many different thinkers. The insights of an ethical theory prove to be lasting because they truly do pick out some important elements of human experience. To emphasize this fact, this chapter will refer to these theories more commonly as ethical "traditions."

This chapter will introduce three ethical traditions that have proven influential in the development of business ethics and that have a very practical relevance in evaluating ethical issues in contemporary business. **Utilitarianism** is an ethical tradition that directs us to decide based on overall *consequences* of our acts. **Deontological ethics** direct us to act on the basis of moral *principles* such as respecting human rights. **Virtue ethics** directs us to consider the *moral character* of individuals and how various character traits can contribute to, or obstruct, a happy and meaningful human life. The Caux Round Table (CRT) Principles for Responsible Business, included at the end of this chapter, provide an interesting blend of utilitarian, deontological, and virtue-based guidelines for business.

Utilitarianism: Making Decisions Based on Ethical Consequences

OBJECTIVE

The first ethical tradition that we shall examine, utilitarianism, has its roots in eighteenth and nineteenth century social and political philosophy, but its core idea is just as relevant in the twenty-first century. Utilitarianism's fundamental insight is that we should decide what to do by considering the *consequences* of our actions. In this sense, utilitarianism has been called a **consequentialist** approach to ethics and social policy: we should act in ways that produce better consequences than the alternatives we are considering. Much more needs to be said to turn this simple insight into an adequate ethical theory. The first, and most obvious, question is: What is meant by "better consequences"?

The most cogent answer to this question can be given in terms of the ethical values described in the previous chapters. "Better consequences" are those that promote human well-being: the happiness, health, dignity, integrity, freedom, respect of all the people affected. If these elements are basic human values, then an action which promotes more of them than the alternative action does is more reasonable from an ethical point of view. A decision that promotes the greatest amount of these values for the greatest number of people is the most reasonable decision from an ethical point of view.

Utilitarianism is commonly identified with the principle of "maximize the overall good" or, in a slightly different version, of producing "the greatest good for the greatest number." The ultimate ethical goal, according to utilitarians, is to produce the best consequences for all parties affected by the decisions. Decisions that accomplish this goal are the right decisions to make ethically; those that do not are ethically wrong.

The emphasis on the overall good, and upon producing the greatest good for the greatest number, make utilitarianism a social philosophy that opposes policies that aim to benefit only a small social, economic, or political minority. In this way, utilitarianism provides strong support for democratic institutions and policies. Government and all social institutions exist for the well-being of all, not to further the interests of the monarch, the nobility, or some small group of the elite. Likewise, the economy and economic institutions exist to provide the highest standard of living for the greatest number of people, not to create wealth for a few.

As another business-related example, consider the case of child labor, discussed in further detail in chapter 6. Utilitarian thinking would advise us to consider all the likely consequences of a practice of employing young children in factories. Obviously, there are some problematic consequences: children suffer physical and psychological harms, they are denied opportunities for education, their low pay is not enough to escape a life of poverty, and so forth. Many of the human values previously described are diminished by child labor. But these consequences must be compared to the consequences of alternative decisions. What are the consequences if children in poor regions are denied factory jobs? These children would still be denied opportunities for education; they are in worse poverty; and they have less money for food and family support. In many cases, the only alternatives for obtaining any income available to young children who are prohibited from joining the workforce might include crime, drugs, or prostitution. Further, we should consider not only the consequences to the children themselves, but to the entire society. Child labor can have beneficial results for bringing foreign investment and money into a poor country. In the opinion of some observers, allowing children to work for pennies a day under sweatshop conditions produces better overall consequences than the available alternatives. Thus, one might argue on utilitarian grounds that such labor practices are ethically permissible because they produce better overall consequences than the alternatives.

This example highlights several important aspects of utilitarian reasoning. Because utilitarians decide on the basis of consequences, and because the consequences of our actions will depend on the specific facts of each situation, utilitarians tend to be very pragmatic thinkers. No act is ever absolutely right or wrong in all cases in every situation; it will always depend on the consequences. For example, lying is neither right nor wrong in itself, according to utilitarians. There might be situations in which lying will produce greater overall good than telling the truth. In such a situation, it would be ethically justified to tell a lie.

Also, utilitarian reasoning usually supplies some support for competing available alternatives, e.g., ban child labor as harmful to the overall good or allow child labor as contributing to the overall good. Deciding on the ethical legitimacy of alternative decisions requires that we make judgments about the likely consequences of our actions. How do we do this? Within the utilitarian tradition, there is a strong inclination to turn to social science for help in making such predictions. After all, social science studies the causes and consequences of individual

---

Reality Check *Is Utilitarianism Egoistic?*

While the imperative to maximize pleasure or happiness sounds selfish and egoistic, utilitarianism differs from **egoism** in important ways. Egoism is also a consequentialist theory, but it focuses on the happiness of the individual. In other words, instead of determining the "greatest good for the greatest number," egoism seeks "the greatest good for me!"

Utilitarianism judges actions by their consequences for the general and overall good. Consistent with the utilitarian commitment to democratic equality, however, the general good must take into consideration the well-being of each and every individual affected by the action. In this way utilitarianism serves the ultimate goal of ethics: the impartial promotion of human well-being. It is impartial because it considers the consequences for everyone, not just for the individual. People who act in ways to maximize only their own happiness or the happiness of their company are not utilitarians, they are egoists.

---

and social actions. Who is better situated than a social scientist to help us predict the social consequences of our decisions? Consider the fields to which one might turn in order to determine the likely consequences of child labor. Economics, anthropology, political science, sociology, public policy, psychology, and medical and health sciences are some of the fields that could help determine the likely consequences of such practices in a particular culture.

In general, the utilitarian position is that happiness is the ultimate good, the only thing that is and can be valued for its own sake. Happiness is the best and most reasonable interpretation of human well-being. (Does it sound absurd to you to claim that unhappiness is good and happiness is bad?) The goal of ethics, both individually and as a matter of public policy, should be to maximize the overall happiness. (See Reality Check, "Is Utilitarianism Egoistic?")

Utilitarianism and Business

OBJECTIVE

We previously claimed that studying ethical theories had a practical relevance for business ethics. In fact, perhaps utilitarianism's greatest contribution to philosophical thought has come through its influence in economics. With roots in Adam Smith, the ethics which underlie much of twentieth century economics—essentially what we think of as the free market—is decidedly utilitarian. In this way, utilitarianism continues to have a very strong impact on business and business ethics.

Utilitarianism answers the fundamental questions of ethics—What should we do?—by reference to a rule: maximize the overall good. But another question remains to be answered: *How* do we achieve this goal? What is the best means for attaining the utilitarian goal of maximizing the overall good? Two answers prove especially relevant in business and business ethics.

OBJECTIVE

One movement within utilitarian thinking invokes the tradition of Adam Smith and claims that free and competitive markets are the best means for attaining utilitarian goals. This version would promote policies that deregulate private industry, protect property rights, allow for free exchanges, and encourage competition. In

Reality Check *Utilitarian Experts in Practice*

Consider how the Federal Reserve Board sets interest rates. There is an established goal, a public policy "good," that the Federal Reserve takes to be the greatest good for the country. (This goal is something like the highest sustainable rate of economic growth compatible with minimal inflation.) The Fed examines the relevant economic data and makes a judgment about the present and future state of the economy. If economic activity seems to be slowing down, the Fed might decide to lower interest rates as a means for stimulating economic growth. If the economy seems to be growing too fast and the inflation rate is increasing, they might choose to raise interest rates. Lowering or raising interest rates, in and of itself, is neither good nor bad; the rightness of the act depends on the consequences. The role of public servants is to use their expertise to judge the likely consequences and make the decision that is most likely to produce the best result.

such situations decisions of rationally self-interested individuals will result, as if lead by "an invisible hand" in Adam Smith's terms, to the maximum satisfaction of individual happiness.

In classic free market economics, economic activity aims to satisfy consumer demand. People are made happy—human welfare or well-being increases—when they get what they desire. Overall human happiness is increased therefore when the overall satisfaction of consumer demand increases. The law of supply and demand tells us that economies should, and healthy economies do, produce (supply) those goods and services that consumers most want (demand). Since scarcity and competition prevent everyone from getting all that they want, the goal of free market economics is to optimally satisfy, i.e., maximize, the satisfaction of wants (happiness). Free markets accomplish this goal most efficiently, according to defenders, by allowing individuals to decide for themselves what they most want and then bargain for these goods in a free and competitive marketplace. This process will, over time and under the right conditions, guarantee the optimal satisfaction of wants, which this tradition equates with maximizing overall happiness.

Given this utilitarian goal, current free market economics advises us that the most efficient means to attain that goal is to structure our economy according to the principles of free market capitalism. This requires that business managers, in turn, should seek to maximize profits. This idea is central to one common perspective on corporate social responsibility. By pursuing profits, business ensures that scarce resources are going to those who most value them and thereby ensures that resources will provide optimal satisfaction. Thus, competitive markets are seen as the most efficient means to the utilitarian end of maximizing happiness.

A second influential version of utilitarian policy turns to policy experts who can predict the outcome of various policies and carry out policies that will attain utilitarian ends. Because utilitarian reasoning determines what to do on the basis of consequences, reasonable judgments must take into account the likely consequences of our actions. But predicting consequences of human action can be studied and improved by careful observation. Experts in predicting such consequences, usually trained in the social sciences such as economics, political science, and public policy, are familiar with the specifics of how society works and they therefore are in a position to determine which policy will maximize the overall good. (See Reality Check, "Utilitarian Experts in Practice.")

This approach to public policy underlies one theory of the entire administrative and bureaucratic side of government and organizations. From this view, the legislative body (from Congress to local city councils) establishes the public goals that we assume will maximize overall happiness. The administrative side (presidents, governors, mayors) executes (administers) policies to fulfill these goals. The people working within the administration know how the social and political system works and use this knowledge to carry out the mandate of the legislature. The government is filled with such people, typically trained in such fields as economics, law, social science, public policy, and political science. This utilitarian approach, for example, would be sympathetic with government regulation of business on the grounds that such regulation will ensure that business activities do contribute to the overall good.

The dispute between these two versions of utilitarian policy, what we might call the "administrative" and the "market" versions of utilitarianism, characterize many disputes in business ethics. One clear example concerns regulation of unsafe or risky products. (Similar disputes involve worker health and safety, environmental protection, regulation of advertising, and almost every other example of government regulation of business.) One side argues that questions of safety and risk should be determined by experts who then establish standards that business is required to meet. Government regulators (for example, the Consumer Products Safety Commission) are then charged with enforcing safety standards in the marketplace. (See Decision Point, "Should Financial Markets Face Greater Government Regulation?")

The other side argues that the best judges of acceptable risk and safety are consumers themselves. A free and competitive consumer market will insure that people will get the level of safety that they want. Individuals calculate for themselves what risks they wish to take and what trade-offs they are willing to make in order to attain safety. Consumers willing to take risks likely will pay less for their products than consumers who demand safer and less risky products. The very basic economic concept of efficiency can be understood as a placeholder for the utilitarian goal of maximum overall happiness. Thus, market-based solutions will prove best at optimally satisfying these various and competing interests and will thereby serve the overall good.

Challenges to Utilitarian Ethics

OBJECTIVE

While the utilitarian tradition contributes much to responsible ethical decision making, it is not without problems. A review of some general challenges to utilitarianism can guide us in evaluating later applications of utilitarian decision making.

Decision Point   *Should Financial Markets Face Greater Government Regulation?*

In the aftermath of the financial meltdown of 2008–09, many people believe that a lack of regulation and oversight by government agencies such as the Federal Reserve Bank and the Securities and Exchange Commission (SEC) played a major role in causing the crisis. From this perspective, the financial crisis was hastened by more than two decades of U.S. public policy that moved away from regulation in the name of less government, fewer regulations, and a more free economy.

Critics argue that a deregulated market allowed a wide range of suspect financial practices that are associated with some of the largest business failures in world history. Weak or nonexistent government regulation failed to protect the economy from the "off-book partnerships" made famous by Enron; the sub-prime mortgages that led to the collapse of three of the largest investment banks in the world, Lehman Brothers, Bear Stearns, and Merrill Lynch; and credit-default swaps that were central to the problems of AIG. Of equal importance, failure to police mergers and acquisitions by enforcing anti-trust regulations created a number of firms that were judged to be "to big to fail," leading to huge government bailouts. Indeed, many critics claim that the deep recession of 2008–09 was directly related to the failure of unregulated markets in such fields as finance, real-estate, and the auto industry.

Defenders and critics of deregulation agree that a healthy and efficient economy is the best means for maximizing the overall social good. They disagree on whether a healthy economy is one that leaves the market free of government regulation, or one in which government regulators play an active role. Given that this issue isn't a simple matter of regulations or not, but involves a range of options along a continuum of less-to-more regulation, do you generally support more or less government regulation of economic markets?

- What facts are relevant in answering this question? Does it depend on the type of regulation or the industry being regulated?
- How would you decide if a regulation is successful? A failure?
- What values support a policy of deregulation? What values count against it?
- Other than the industry regulated, who are some other stakeholders that might be affected by government regulation?
- What might serve as an alternative to government regulations? Can professional codes and standards play a role?

A first set of problems concerns the need for utilitarian reasoning to count, measure, compare, and quantify consequences. If utilitarianism advises that we make decisions by comparing the consequences of alternative actions, then we must have a method for making such comparisons. In practice, however, some comparisons and measurements are very difficult.

For example, in principle, utilitarianism tells us that the interests of all stakeholders who will be affected by a decision ought to be included in calculating the consequences of a decision. But there simply is no consensus among utilitarians on how to measure and determine the overall good. Many business ethics issues highlight how difficult this could be. Consider the consequences of using non-renewable energy sources and burning fossil fuels for energy. Imagine trying to calculate the consequences of a decision to invest in construction of a nuclear power plant whose wastes remain toxic for tens of thousands of years. Consider how difficult it would be to calculate all the consequences of the decision faced by members of Congress to provide hundreds of billions of dollars to bailout companies that are "too big to fail."

A second challenge goes directly to the core of utilitarianism. The essence of utilitarianism is its reliance on consequences. Ethical and unethical acts are determined by their consequences. In short, the end justifies the means. But this seems to deny one of the earliest ethical principles that many of have learned: the end does not always justify the means.

This challenge can be explained in terms of ethical principles. When we say that the ends do not justify the means what we are saying is that there are certain decisions we should make or certain rules we should follow no matter what the consequences. Put another way, we have certain duties or responsibilities that we ought to obey even when doing so does not produce a net increase in overall happiness. Examples of such duties are those required by such principles as justice, loyalty, and respect, as well as the responsibilities which flow from our roles as a parent, spouse, friend, citizen, or professional.

Several examples can be used to explain why this is a serious criticism of utilitarian reasoning. Since utilitarianism focuses on the overall consequences, utilitarianism seems willing to sacrifice the good of individuals for the greater overall good. So, for example, it might turn out that the overall happiness would be increased if children were held as slave labor. Utilitarians would object to child labor, not as a matter of principle, but only if and to the degree that it detracts from the overall good. If it turns out that slavery and child labor increases the net overall happiness, utilitarianism would have to support these practices. In the judgment of many people, such a decision would violate fundamental ethical principles of justice, equality, and respect.

The ethical tradition that we will turn to in the next section argues that individuals possess certain basic rights that should not be violated even if doing so would increase the overall social happiness. Rights function to protect individuals from being sacrificed for the greater overall happiness. Thus, for example, it is often argued that child labor is ethically wrong in principle even if it contributes to the overall social good because it violates the rights of young children.

A similar example cites those principles that arise from commitments that we all make and the duties that flow from them. For example, as a parent we love our children and have certain duties to them. Violating such commitments and duties would require individuals to sacrifice their own integrity for the common good.

Such commitments and duties play a large role in business life. Contracts and promises are exactly the commitments that one ought to honor, even if the consequences turn out to be unfavorable. The defense of bonuses to AIG executives that cited the contractual duty to pay them is an example of this type of reasoning. The duties that one takes on as part of a professional role function in a similar way. Arthur Andersen's auditors should not have violated their professional duties simply to produce greater overall beneficial consequences. Lawyers have a duty not to help their clients find ways to violate the law, even if they are offered a high salary to do so. Teachers should not violate their professional duties by failing students whom they do not like. Aaron Feuerstein might claim that despite bad overall consequences, he had to remain loyal to his employees as a matter of principle. We will consider similar themes professional commitments and duties when later chapters examine the role of professional responsibilities within business institutions.

Nevertheless, utilitarian ethics does contribute to responsible decision making in several important ways. First, and most obviously, we are reminded of the significance of consequences. Responsible decision making requires that we consider the consequences of our acts. But, the shortcomings of utilitarian reasoning must also be kept in mind. It is difficult to know everyone who will be affected by our decisions and how they are impacted. Utilitarian reasoning demands rigorous work to calculate all the beneficial and harmful consequences of our actions. Perhaps more importantly, utilitarian reasoning does not exhaust the range of ethical concerns. Consequences are only a part of the ethical landscape. Responsible ethical decision making also involves matters of duties, principles, and personal integrity. We turn to such factors in the following sections.

Deontology: An Ethics of Rights and Duties

OBJECTIVE

Making decisions based upon the consequences certainly should be a part of responsible ethical decisions making. But this approach must be supplemented with the recognition that some decisions should be a matter of principle, not consequences. In other words, the ends do not always justify the means. But how do we know what principles we should follow and how do we decide when a principle should trump beneficial consequences? Principle-based, or "deontological" ethical theories, work out the details of such questions.

The language of "deontology" and "deontological ethics" is very abstract and is likely to strike many students as so much academic gobbledygook. But the idea behind this approach is commonsensical. Ethical principles can simply be thought of as a type of rule, and this approach to ethics tells us that there are some rules that we ought to follow even if doing so prevents good consequences from happening or even if it results in some bad consequences. Rules or principles (e.g., "obey the law," "keep your promises," "uphold your contracts") create **duties** that bind us to act or decide in certain ways. For example, there is an ethical rule prohibiting slave labor, even if this practice would have beneficial economic consequences for society.

What rules should we follow? Legal rules, obviously, are one major set of rules that we ought to follow. We have a duty to pay our taxes, even if the money might be more efficiently spent on our children's college education. We ought to stop at a red light, even if no cars are coming and I could get to my destination that much sooner. I ought not to steal my neighbor's property, even if he will never miss it and I will gain many benefits form it. Decision making within a business context will involve many situations in which one ought to obey legal rules even when the consequences, economic and otherwise, seem to be undesirable.

Other rules are derived from various institutions in which we participate, or from various social roles that we fill. As a teacher, I ought to read each student's research paper carefully and diligently, even if they will never know the difference and their final grade will not be affected. In my role as teacher and university faculty member, I have taken on certain responsibilities that cannot be abandoned whenever it is convenient for me to do so. As the referee in a sporting event, I have the duty to enforce the rules fairly, even when it would be easier not to do so. Similar rule-based duties follow from our roles as friends (do not gossip about your friends), family-members (do your chores at home), students (do not plagiarize), church member (contribute to the church's upkeep), citizens (vote), and good neighbors (do not operate your lawn mower before 8 A.M.).

There will be very many occasions in which such role-based duties arise in business. As an employee, one takes on a certain role that creates duties. Every business will have a set of rules that employees are expected to follow. Sometimes these rules are explicitly states in a code of conduct, other times in employee handbooks, still others are simply stated by managers. (See Reality Check, "Ethical Principles and the United Nations Global Compact.") Likewise, as a business manager, there are many rules one ought to follow in respect to stockholders, employees, suppliers, and other stakeholders.

Perhaps the most dramatic example of role-based duties concerns the work of professionals within business. Lawyers, accountants, auditors, financial analysts, bankers have important roles to play within political and economic institutions. Many of these roles, often described as "gatekeeper functions," insure the integrity and proper functioning of the economic, legal, or financial system. Chapter 2 introduced the idea of professional responsibilities within the workplace and this theme will be developed further in chapter 10.

The Enron and Arthur Andersen case provides a helpful example for understanding professional duties. While examining Enron's financial reports, the auditors at Arthur Andersen knew that diligent application of strict auditing standards required one decision, but that the consequences of this diligent application would be harmful to Arthur Andersen's business interests. A fair analysis of this aspect of the Enron–Arthur Andersen scandal would point out that Andersen's auditors failed their ethical duties precisely because they did not follow the rules governing their professional responsibilities and allowed beneficial consequences to override their professional principles. (See Reality Check, "Ethical Rules as a Check on Misguided Consequences.")

So far we have mentioned legal rules, organizational rules, role-based rules, and professional rules. We can think of these rules as part of a social agreement, or social contract, which functions to organize and ease relations between

Reality Check *Ethical Principles and the United Nations Global Compact*

Ethical principles and duties can often be found in corporate and professional codes of conduct. One example of such a code that has had worldwide impact is the U.N. Global Compact's code. The United Nations launched the U.N. Global Compact in 2000 as a means to encourage businesses throughout the world to commit to ethical business practices. Businesses joining the Global Compact commit to following ten fundamental ethical principles in the areas of human rights, labor, the environment, and anti-corruption. The United Nations describes its principles as follows:

The Global Compact asks companies to embrace,support and enact, within their sphere of influence, a set of core values in the areas of human rights, labour standards, the environment, and anti-corruption:

Human Rights

Principle 1: Businesses should support and respect the protection of internationally proclaimed human rights; and

Principle 2: make sure that they are not complicit in human rights abuses.

Labour Standards

Principle 3: Businesses should uphold the freedom of association and the effective recognition of the right to collective bargaining;

Principle 4: the elimination of all forms of forced and compulsory labour;

Principle 5: the effective abolition of child labour; and

Principle 6: the elimination of discrimination in respect of employment and occupation.

Environment

Principle 7: Businesses should support a precautionary approach to environmental challenges;

Principle 8: undertake initiatives to promote greater environmental responsibility; and

Principle 9: encourage the development and diffusion of environmentally friendly technologies.

Anti-Corruption

Principle 10: Businesses should work against corruption in all its forms, including extortion and bribery.

Since its founding in 2000, over 5,200 businesses in 130 countries have joined the Global Compact and committed to these principles. Included in this list are such well-known U.S. firms as Accenture, Alcoa, Campbell Soup, Coca-Cola, Deloitte Touche, Ford Motor Co., Gap, General Mills, Hewlett-Packard, Intel, JC Penny, KPMG, Levi Strauss, Merck, Microsoft, PepsiCo, Starbucks, Sun Microsystems, Dow Chemical, and Timberland.

Source: United National Global Compact, "The Ten Principles," http://unglobalcompact.org/AboutTheGC/TheTenPrinciples/index.html

---

individuals. No group could function if members were free at all times to decide for themselves what to do and how to act. By definition, any cooperative activity requires cooperation, i.e., requires rules that each member follows.

In the view of many philosophers, fundamental ethical duties must bind us in a stricter way than the way we are bound by contracts or by professional duties. You should not be able to "quit" ethical duties and walk away from them in quite the way that one can dissolve a contract or walk away from professional duties by quitting the profession. In the language of many philosophers, ethical duties should be **"categorical" imperatives** rather than hypothetical. Hypothetical duties would be like professional code of conduct that binds you *only if* you are a member of the profession. Categorical duties do not contain this "if" clause.

Reality Check *Ethical Rules as a Check on Misguided Consequences*

The Enron and Arthur Anderson case demonstrates one of the major vulnerabilities of the consequentialist approach. Utilitarians would rightfully point out that Andersen's auditors did not make decisions according to strict utilitarian ethical principles. The auditors calculated the consequences, but only those to their own firm and their own well-being. Had they truly calculated the *overall* consequences of their decisions, as utilitarianism requires, Andersen's auditors may very well have made the right ethical decision. Instead,

they thought only about the $100 million of business generated by Enron and decided to allow this influence to override their principles. But, this shows the difficulty in calculating consequences. Because it is so difficult to know all of the consequences of our actions, it will always be tempting to consider only the consequences to ourselves and our associates. To avoid the slide from utilitarian overall consequences to more solely individualistic, egoistic (and non-ethical) consequences, deontological ethics advises us to follow the rules, regardless of consequences.

I *should* or *must* (an imperative) obey a fundamental ethical rule *no matter what* (a categorical).

Human Rights and Duties

OBJECTIVE

Are there *any* such fundamental duties? Are there any rules we should follow, decisions we should make, no matter what the consequences? The foremost advocate of this tradition in ethics, the eighteenth century German philosopher Immanuel Kant, argued that, at bottom, there is essentially one fundamental moral duty, one categorical imperative: respect the dignity of each individual human being. A more simple way to say this is to say that every individual human being has a **human right** to be treated with respect.

Kant claimed that this duty to respect human dignity could be expressed in several ways. One version directs us to act according to those rules that could be universally agreed to by all people. (This is the first form of the famous "Kantian categorical imperative.") Another, less abstract version, requires us to treat each person as an end in themselves and never only as means to our own ends. In other words, our fundamental duty is to treat people as subjects capable of living their own lives and not as mere objects that exist for our purposes. To use the familiar subject/object categories from grammar, humans are subjects because they make decisions and perform actions rather than being objects that are acted upon. Humans have their own ends and purposes and therefore should not be treated simply as a means to the ends of others.

Since every person has this same fundamental duty towards others, each of us can be said to have fundamental human rights: the right to be treated with respect, to expect that others will treat us as an end and never as a means only, and to be treated as an autonomous person. I have the right to pursue my own autonomously chosen ends as long as I do not in turn treat other people as means to my ends and this right applies equally to each and every individual.

Such human rights, or moral rights, have played a central role in the develop-ment of modern democratic political systems. The U.S. Declaration of Indepen-dence speaks of "inalienable rights" that cannot be taken away by government. Following World War II, the United Nations created the U.N.'s Declaration of Human Rights as a means for holding all governments to fundamental standards of ethics. The reading "Business and Human Rights: A Not-So-New Framework for Corporate Responsibility" by Christine Bader and John Morrison, which follows this chapter, examines how the United Nations' Declaration of Human Rights might also provide a framework for understanding business' social responsibilities.

To return to an earlier example, this deontological or Kantian tradition in eth-ics would object to child labor because such practices violate our duty to treat children with respect. We violate the rights of children when we treat them as mere means to the ends of production and economic growth. We are treating them merely as means because, as children, they have not rationally and freely chosen their own ends. We are simply using them as tools or objects. Thus, even if child labor produced beneficial consequences, it would be ethically wrong because it violates a fundamental human right.

In this way, the concept of a human or moral right is central to the principle-based ethical tradition. The inherent dignity of each individual means that we can-not do whatever we choose to another person. Human rights protect individuals from being treated in ways that would violate their dignity and that would treat them as mere objects or means. Rights imply that some acts and some decisions are "off-limits." Accordingly, our fundamental moral duty (the "categorical imper-ative") is to respect the fundamental human rights of others. Our rights establish limits on the decisions and authority of others.

Consider how rights function relative to the utilitarian goal of maximizing the overall good. Suppose that you owned a local business and your local government decided that your property would make a great location for a city park. Imag-ine that you are the only person who disagrees. On utilitarian grounds, it might seem that your land would best serve the overall good by being used for a park. However, your property rights prevent the community from taking your land (at least without just compensation) to serve the public. A similar issue happens with the music and video downloads and file sharing. Some would argue on utilitarian grounds that the greatest happiness would be promoted by allowing unlimited free file-sharing of music and video files. Clearly, more people would get more of what they want and happiness would be optimized under such a scheme. But the owners of these files, those individuals and companies who have property rights over them, would claim that their rights should not be violated simply to produce greater overall consequences. For another example about conflicting rights, see the Decision Point, "Eminent Domain for the Public Good."

In summary, we can say that human rights are meant to offer protection of certain central human interests, prohibiting the sacrifice of these interests merely to provide a net increase in the overall happiness. The standard account of human rights offered through the Western ethical tradition connects basic human rights

Decision Point

Eminent Domain for the Public Good

Should the government be able to take private property as a means to increase the local tax base? In the summer of 2005, the U.S. Supreme Court decided that the city of New London, Connecticut, could legally exercise eminent domain by seizing private property as part of a plan to redevelop a waterfront area. The city argued that the private homes and property in the area would be better used if it were developed by private businesses as part of a more upscale residential and commercial project. The increased property values would create an increased tax base leading to increased public revenues and thereby providing greater good for a greater number of people. Citizens in the area who were to lose their homes argued that their rights were being violated. The Court, in *Kelso vs. New London,* concluded that their constitutional and legal rights were not violated. How would you have decided if you were on the Supreme Court and do you perceive a violation of ethical rights?

- What facts would you need to have in order to make a decision in this case?
- Other than the legal rights involved, what ethical values are involved in this case?
- Besides the homeowners, the city government, and the developers are there any other stakeholders who should be involved in this case?
- How do you think that the city decided that the beneficial consequences of this policy would outweigh the harmful consequences?
- What duties do city government officials have to individual homeowners and to the city as a whole ?

to some theory of a basic human nature. The Kantian tradition claims that our fundamental human rights, and the duties that follow from them, are derived from our nature as free and rational beings. Humans do not act only out of instinct and conditioning; they make free choices about how they live their lives, about their own ends. In this sense, humans are said to have a fundamental human right of autonomy, or "self-rule."

From these origins, we can see how two related rights have emerged as fundamental within philosophical ethics. If autonomy, or self-rule, is a fundamental characteristic of human nature, then the freedom to make our own choices deserves special protection as a basic right. But, since all humans possess this fundamental characteristic, equal treatment and equal consideration must also be fundamental rights. They are, according to much of this tradition, "natural rights" that are more fundamental and persistent than the legal rights created by governments and social contracts. (See the Reality Check, "Are Fundamental Human Rights Universally Accepted?")

Christine Bader has served as the Advisor to the U.N. Special Representative of the Secretary-General for business and human rights, and John Morrison has

Reality Check *Are Fundamental Human Rights Universally Accepted?*

In 1948, the United Nations adopted a Universal Declaration of Human Rights. Since that time, this Declaration has been translated into more than 300 languages and dialects. The Declaration contains thirty articles outlining basic human rights. In part, the declaration includes the following:

PREAMBLE

Recognition of the inherent dignity and of the equal and inalienable rights of all members of the human family is the foundation of freedom, justice and peace in the world.

Article 1.
All human beings are born free and equal in dignity and rights. They are endowed with reason and conscience and should act towards one another in a spirit of brotherhood.

Article 2.
Everyone is entitled to all the rights and freedoms set forth in this Declaration, without distinction of any kind, such as race, colour, sex, language, religion, political or other opinion, national or social origin, property, birth or other status.

Article 3.
Everyone has the right to life, liberty and security of person.

Article 4.
No one shall be held in slavery or servitude; slavery and the slave trade shall be prohibited in all their forms.

Article 5.
No one shall be subjected to torture or to cruel, inhuman or degrading treatment or punishment.

Article 9.
No one shall be subjected to arbitrary arrest, detention or exile.

Article 10.
Everyone is entitled in full equality to a fair and public hearing by an independent and impartial tribunal, in the determination of his rights and obligations and of any criminal charge against him.

Article 18.
Everyone has the right to freedom of thought, conscience and religion; this right includes freedom to change his religion or belief, and freedom, either alone or in community with others and in public or private, to manifest his religion or belief in teaching, practice, worship and observance.

Article 19.
Everyone has the right to freedom of opinion and expression; this right includes freedom to hold opinions without interference and to seek, receive and impart information and ideas through any media and regardless of frontiers.

Article 23.
(1) Everyone has the right to work, to free choice of employment, to just and favourable conditions of work and to protection against unemployment.
(2) Everyone, without any discrimination, has the right to equal pay for equal work.
(3) Everyone who works has the right to just and favourable remuneration ensuring for himself and his family an existence worthy of human dignity, and supplemented, if necessary, by other means of social protection.
(4) Everyone has the right to form and to join trade unions for the protection of his interests.

Article 25.
(1) Everyone has the right to a standard of living adequate for the health and well-being of himself and of his family, including food, clothing, housing and medical care and necessary social services, and the right to security in the event of unemployment, sickness, disability, widowhood, old age or other lack of livelihood in circumstances beyond his control.

Article 26.
(1) Everyone has the right to education.

been the Executive Director of the Institute for Human Rights and Business. Together, they have drafted a discussion, included at the end of this chapter that advocates for these fundamental human rights as an appropriate underlying framework for business' role in society, no matter what region or sector. Since there remains a gap in governance between what businesses are permitted to do according to the laws of the countries in which they operate and "permit-ted" to do according to a recognition of the fundamental rights discussed above, Bader and Morrison explain the U.N. Special Representative's framework for multinational corporations of "Protect, Respect, and Remedy." Consider the realistic corporate application of the rights protected under the U.N.'s Declara-tion of Human Rights (see Reality Check, "Are Fundamental Human Rights Universally Accepted?") under that framework (see the reading at the end of the chapter).

Moral Rights and Legal Rights

OBJECTIVE

It will be helpful at this point to distinguish between moral rights and legal rights. To illustrate this distinction, let us take employee rights as an example. Three senses of employee rights are common in business. First, there are those *legal* rights granted to employees on the basis of legislation or judicial rulings. Thus, employees have a right to a minimum wage, equal opportunity, to bargain collectively as part of a union, to be free from sexual harassment, and so forth. Second, employee rights might refer to those goods that employees are entitled to on the basis of contractual agreements with employers. In this sense, a particular employee might have a right a specific health care package, a certain number of paid holidays, pension funds, and the like. Finally, employee rights might refer to those moral entitlements to which employees have a claim independently of any particular legal or contractual factors. Such rights would originate with the respect owed to them as human beings.

To expand on this understanding, consider how legal and contractual rights interact. In general, both parties to an employment agreement bargain over the conditions of work. Employers offer certain wages, benefits, and working condi-tions and in return seek worker productivity. Employees offer skills and abilities and seek wages and benefits in return. Thus, employment rights emerge from contractual promises. However, certain goods are legally exempt from such nego-tiation. An employer cannot make a willingness to submit to sexual harassment or acceptance of a wage below the minimum established by law a part of the employment agreement. In effect, legal rights exempt certain interests from the employment contract. Such legal rights set the basic legal framework in which business operates. They are established by the legal system in which business operates and, in this sense, are part of the price of doing business. Consider your own perspective on this question in the Decision Point: "Do Employees Have Moral Rights?"

So, too, human rights lie outside of the bargaining that occurs between employ-ers and employees. Unlike the minimum wage, moral rights are established

Decision Point   *Do Employees Have Moral Rights?*

Employees certainly have legal rights, such as the right to be paid a minimum wage, to enjoy equal opportunity in the workplace, and to be free from sexual harassment. Many employees also have contractual rights, such as the right to an employer contribution to a retirement plan, health care, or certain number of vacation and sick days. But do employees really have rights against their employer that are not specified in the law or in the employment contract? Do employers have duties to their employees other than what is required by law and the employment contract? If every human has a right to health care, do employers have a moral duty to provide health insurance for every employee? Do employers have a duty to provide a just wage? Do employers have a duty to respect an employee's right to privacy?

and justified by moral, rather than legal, considerations. Moral rights establish the basic moral framework for legal environment itself, and more specifically for any contracts that are negotiated within business. Thus, as described in the United States Declaration of Independence, governments and laws are created in order to secure more fundamental natural moral rights. The rights outlined above in the excerpt from the United Nations fit this conception of fundamental moral rights.

Challenges to an Ethics of Rights and Duties

OBJECTIVE

So what rights do we have and what does that mean for the duties of others? In the U.S. Declaration of Independence, Thomas Jefferson claimed that we have "inalienable rights" to life, liberty, and the pursuit of happiness. Jefferson was influenced by the British philosopher John Locke, who spoke of "natural rights" to life, health, liberty, and possessions. The U.N. Universal Declaration of Human Rights (see the reality check) lists more than 26 human rights that are universal.

Acknowledging this diversity of rights makes it easy to understand the two biggest challenges to this ethical tradition. There appears to be much disagreement about what rights truly are basic human rights and, given the multiplicity of rights, it is unclear how to apply this approach to practical situations, especially in cases where rights seemingly conflict.

Take, for example, a possible right to health care. During debates over health care reform in the U.S. Congress in 2009, many claimed that humans have a right to health care. Other societies would seem to agree in that many countries have instituted national health plans to provide citizens with at least minimal health care. The U.N. Declaration would seem to agree, claiming that humans have a right "to a standard of living adequate for the health and well-being" and that this right includes medical care. But many disagree and point out that such a right would carry significant costs for others. If every human has a right to health care, who has the duty to provide it and at what costs? Does this mean that doctors and nurses can be required to provide free medical care? Does this right entail a right to the best treatment possible? To elective surgeries? To wellness care or nursing homes? To cosmetic surgery?

Critics charge that unless there is a specific person or institution that has a duty to provide the goods identified as "rights," talk of rights amounts to little more than a wish list of things that people want. What are identified as "rights" often are nothing more than good things that most people desire. But, if every human truly does have a right to a standard of living adequate for all the goods mentioned in Article 25 of the U.N. Declaration, who has the duty to provide them?

More relevant to business is the Declaration's Article 23 that everyone has a "right to work and free choice of employment." What would this mean to a business? Is it helpful to say that an employee's human rights are violated if they are laid-off during a recession? Who has the duty to provide jobs to every unemployed person? This same Article refers to a "right to just and favourable remuneration." But what is a just wage and who gets to decide?

The first major challenge to an ethics based on rights is that there is no agreement about the scope and range of such rights. Which good things qualify as rights, and which are merely things that people want? Critics charge that there is no way to answer this. Yet, unless there is some clear way to distinguish the two, the list of rights will only grow to unreasonable lengths and the corresponding duties will unreasonably burden everyone.

A second challenge also points to practical problems in applying a theory of rights to real-life situations. With a long list of human rights, all of which are claimed to be basic and fundamental, we need a practical guide to decide what to do when rights come into conflict. For example, how would we decide between one individual's right to medical care and the physician's right to just remuneration of her work? Suppose the person needing medical care could not afford to pay a just fee for the care?

Perhaps the most important such conflict in a business setting would occur when an employer's rights to property come into conflict with an employee's alleged rights to work, just wages, and health care. While the U.N. Declaration does not mention a right to property as a basic human right, many philosophers in the Western tradition agree with John Locke and include it among our natural rights. Granting economic rights to employee would seem to create numerous conflicts with the property rights of employers. Critics point out that the ethical tradition of rights and duties has been unable to provide a persuasive and systematic account for how such conflicts are to be resolved.

Virtue Ethics: Making Decisions Based on Integrity and Character

OBJECTIVE

For the most part, utilitarian and deontological approaches to ethics focus on rules that we might follow in deciding what we should do, both as individuals and as citizens. These approaches conceive of practical reason in terms of

Reality Check *Virtues in Practice*

The language of virtues and vices may seem old-fashioned or quaint for modern readers, but this was a dominant perspective on ethics in the western world for centuries. If you develop a list of adjectives that describe a person's character, you will find that the language of virtues and vices is not as outdated as it may seem.

The ancient Greeks identified four primary virtues: courage, moderation, wisdom, and justice. Early Christians described the three cardinal virtues of faith, hope, and charity. Boys Scouts pledge to be trustworthy, loyal, helpful, friendly, courteous, kind, obedient, cheerful, thrifty, brave, clean, and reverent.

According to ancient and medieval philosophers, the virtues represented a balanced mean, the "golden mean," between two extremes, both of which would be considered vices. Thus, for example, a brave person finds the balance between too little courage, which is cowardice, and too much courage, which would be reckless and foolhardy.

The virtues are those character traits or habits that would produce a good, happy, and meaningful life. Practicing such virtues and habits and acting in accord with one's own character is to live a life of integrity.

---

deciding how to act and what to do. Chapter 1 pointed out, however, that ethics also involves questions about the type of person one should become. Virtue ethics is a tradition within philosophical ethics that seeks a full and detailed description of those character traits, or virtues, that would constitute a good and full human life.

Virtues can be understood as those character traits that would constitute a good and meaningful human life. Being friendly and cheerful, having integrity, being honest, forthright and truthful, having modest wants, and being tolerant are some of the characteristics of a good and meaningful human life. (For additional qualities, see the Reality Check, "Virtues in Practice.") One can see virtue ethics at play in everyday situations:we describe someone's behavior as being out of character or describe someone as being a person of integrity. Perhaps the best place to see the ethics of virtue is in the goal of every good parent who hopes to raise happy and decent children.

To understand how virtue ethics differs from utilitarian and deontological approaches, consider the problem of egoism. As mentioned previously, egoism is a view which holds that people act only out of a self-interest. Many economists, for example, assume that all individuals always act out of self-interest; indeed, many assume that rationality itself should be defined in terms of acting out of self-interest. The biggest challenge posed by egoism and, according to some, the biggest challenge to ethics is the apparent gap between self-interest and altruism, or between motivation that is "self-regarding" and motivation that is "other-regarding." Ethics requires us, at least at times, to act for the well-being of others. Yet, some would claim that this is not possible. Humans only act from self-interested motives.

An ethics of virtue shifts the focus from questions about what a person should *do,* to a focus on who that person *is.* This shift requires not only a different view of ethics but, at least as important, a different view of ourselves. Implicit in this

Reality Check *Is Selfishness a Virtue?*

Does ethics demand that we sacrifice our own interests for others? If so, is this reasonable? Is it even possible?

The tension between ethics and self-interest has been central to philosophical ethics since at least the time of Socrates and Plato. Ethical responsibilities certainly seem to require that we sometimes restrict our own actions out of consideration for the interest of other people. Yet, some thinkers have concluded that such a requirement is unreasonable and unrealistic. It is unreasonable because it would be too much to ask people to act against their own self-interest; and it would be unrealistic because, in fact, it is simply part of human nature to be selfish.

Twentieth-century philosopher Ayn Rand argued that selfishness is a virtue. Rand denied that altruism, acting for the interests of others, was an ethical virtue. Altruism too easily makes people predisposed to sacrifice for others and ignores their own basic interests. Instead, she argued that ethically responsible people stand up for their own interests and should be motivated by a concern with their own interests. From this perspective, selfishness is a virtue; people who act out of a concern for their own interests will live more fulfilling and happy human lives.

This philosophical starting point has led many thinkers, including Rand herself, to adopt a political and social philosophy of libertarianism. This is the view that the fundamental right of individuals is the right to liberty, understood as the right to be free from interference by others. Libertarianism also provides philosophical support for free market capitalism and is often the ethical view implicit in the thinking of people in business. Free markets are the economic system that best serve the libertarian goal of protecting individual rights of liberty.

But even Rand recognized that selfishness in this philosophical sense was not the same as what is commonly understood as selfish behavior. Simply doing whatever one wants will not necessarily work for one's own self-interest. The behavior of the stereotypical selfish and self-centered person who is antagonistic to others is not likely to lead to a happy, secure, and meaningful life. Rand recognized that self-interest, properly understood, may sometimes demand that we restrict and regulate our own desires. Further, since the virtue of selfishness applies equally to all people, our own self-interest is limited by the equal rights of others.

Thus, Rand's version of libertarianism is not as extreme as it might first appear. No ethical tradition expects people to live a life of total self-sacrifice and self-denial. But even those who might be described as ethical egoists concede that rational self-interest does create ethical limits to our own actions and that narrowly selfish people are unethical.

distinction is the recognition that our identity as individuals is constituted in part by our wants, beliefs, values, and attitudes. A person's **character**—those dispositions, relationships, attitudes, values, and beliefs that popularly might be called a "personality"—is not some feature that remains independent of that person's identity. Character is not like a suit of clothes that you step into and out of at will. Rather, the self is identical to a person's most fundamental and enduring dispositions, attitudes, values, and beliefs.

Note how this shift changes the nature of justification in ethics. If, as seems true for many people, an ethical justification of some act requires that it be tied to self-interest, we should not be surprised to find that this justification often fails. Ethical controversies often involve a conflict between self-interest and ethical values. Why should I do the ethical thing if it would require me to give up a lot of money? For a personality that does not already include a disposition to be modest, the only avenue open for justification would involve showing how the disposition serves some other interest of that person. Why should an executive turn down a multi-million dollar bonus? The only way to answer this question appears to be to show how it would be in his self-interest to do so. But, this is at times unlikely. (See Reality Check, "Is Selfishness a Virtue?")

On the other hand, for the person already characterized by modest and unaffected desires, the question of justifying smaller salaries is less relevant. If I am the type of person who had moderate and restrained desires for money, then there is no temptation to be unethical for the sake of a large bonus. For many people, the "self" of self-interest is a caring, modest, unaffected, altruistic self. For these people, there simply is no conflict between *self*-interest and altruism.

The degree to which we are capable of acting for the well-being of others therefore seems to depend on a variety of factors such as our desires, our beliefs, our dispositions, and our values; in short, it depends on our character or the type of person we are. If people are caring, empathetic, charitable, and sympathetic, then the challenge of selfishness and egoism is simply not a factor in their decision making.

Virtue ethics emphasizes the more affective side of our character. Virtue ethics recognizes that our motivations—our interests, wants, desires—are not the sorts of things that each one of us chooses anew each morning. Instead, human beings act in and from character. By adulthood, these character traits typically are deeply ingrained and conditioned within us. Given that our character plays such a deciding role in our behavior, and given the realization that our character can been shaped by factors that are controllable (by conscious individual decisions, by how we are raised, by the social institutions in which we live, work, and learn), virtue ethics seeks to understand how those traits are formed and which traits bolster and which undermine a meaningful, worthwhile, and satisfying human life.

Virtue ethics can offer us a more fully textured understanding of life within business. Rather than simply describing people as good or bad, right or wrong, an ethics of virtue encourages a fuller description. For example, we might describe Aaron Feurestein as heroic and courageous. He is a man of integrity, who sympathizes with employees and cares about their well-being. Other executives might be described as greedy or ruthless, proud or competitive. Faced with a difficult dilemma, we might ask what a person with integrity would do? What an honest person would say? Do I have the courage of my convictions? In other words, you might consider someone you believe to be virtuous and ask yourself what that person would do in this situation. What would a virtuous person do?

Besides connecting the virtues to a conception of a fuller human life, virtue ethics also reminds us to examine how character traits are formed and conditioned. By the time we are adults, much of our character is formed by such factors as our parents, schools, church, friends, and society. But powerful social institutions such as business and especially our own places of employment and our particular social roles within them (e.g., manager, professional, and trainee) have a profound influence on shaping our character. Consider an accounting firm

Reality Check *Can Virtue Be Taught?*

Plato's famous dialogue the *Meno* opens with the title character asking Socrates this basic question: Can virtue be taught? If ethics involves developing the right sort of character traits and habits, as the virtue theorist holds, then the acquisition of those traits becomes a fundamental question for ethics. Can we teach people to *be* honest, trustworthy, loyal, courteous, moderate, respectful, and compassionate?

Meno initially cast the question in terms of two alternatives: either virtue is taught or it is acquired naturally. In modern terms, this is the question of nurture or nature, environment or genetics. Socrates' answer is more complicated. Virtue cannot simply be taught by others, nor is it acquired automatically through nature. Each individual has the natural potential to become virtuous, and learning from one's surroundings is a part of this process. But, ultimately, virtues must be developed by each individual through a complex process of personal reflection, reasoning, practice, and observation, as well as social reinforcement and

conditioning. Virtues are habits, and acquiring any habit is a subtle and complex process.

Parents confront this question every day. I know my children will lead happier and more meaningful lives if they are honest, respectful, cheerful, moderate and not greedy, envious, gloomy, arrogant, or selfish. Yet simply telling my children to be honest and to avoid greed is insufficient; nor can I remain passive and assume that these traits will develop naturally. Instilling these character traits and habits is a long-term process that develops over time.

Business institutions also have come to recognize that character formation is both difficult and unavoidable. Employees come to business with certain character traits and habits, and these can get shaped and reinforced in the workplace. Hire a person with the wrong character traits, and there will be trouble ahead. Designing a workplace, creating a corporate culture, to reinforce virtues and discourage vice is one of the greatest challenges for an ethical business.

that hires a group of trainees fully expecting that fewer than half will be retained and where only a very small group will make partner. That corporate environment encourages motivations and behavior very different from a firm that hires fewer people but gives them all a greater chance at long-term success. A company that sets unrealistic sales goals will find it creates a different sales force than one that understands sales more as customer service. Virtue ethics reminds us to look to the actual practices we find in the business world and ask what types of people are being created by these practices. Many individual moral dilemmas that arise within business ethics can best be understood as arising from a tension between the type of person we seek to be and the type of person business expects us to be. (See Reality Check, "Can Virtue Be Taught?")

Consider an example described by someone who is conducting empirical studies of the values found within marketing firms and advertising agencies. This person reported that, on several occasions, advertising agents told her that they would never allow their own children to watch the very television shows and advertisements that their own firms were producing. By their own admission, the ads for such shows aim to manipulate children into buying, or getting their parents to buy, products that had little or no real value. In some cases, the ads promoted beer drinking and the advertisers themselves admitted, as their "dirty little secret," that they were intended to target the teenage market. Further, their own research evidenced the success of their ads in increasing sales.

Independent of the ethical questions we might ask about advertising aimed at children, a virtue ethics approach would look at the type of person who is so able to disassociate oneself and one's own values from one's work, and the social institutions and practices that encourage it. What kind of person is willing to subject others' children to marketing practices that they are unwilling to accept for their own children? Such a person seems to lack even the most elementary form of personal integrity. What kind of institution encourages people to treat children in ways that they willingly admit are indecent? What kind of person does one become working in such an institution?

A Decision-Making Model for Business Ethics Revisited

This chapter provided a detailed introductory survey of ethical theory. While some of these topics might appear esoteric and too abstract for a business ethics class, they have a very practical aim. Understanding the philosophical basis of ethics will enable you to become more aware of ethical issues, better able to recognize the impact of your decisions, and more likely to make better informed and more reasonable decisions. In addition, the theories allow us to better and more articulately explain why we have made or wish to make a particular decision. While a statement such as "we should engage in this practice because it is right" might seem a bit vague or unpersuasive, an alternate explanation such as "we should engage in this practice because more people will be better off than harmed if we do so" could be tremendously effective and convincing. When a decision leader asks you why you support or oppose a specific proposal, your response now has comprehensive substance behind it and will therefore be more sophisticated, credible and influential.

These ethical theories and traditions also provide important ways in which to develop the decision-making model introduced in chapter 2. These ethical theories, after all, provide systematic and sophisticated ways to think and reason about ethical questions. We now can offer a more detailed version of our decision-making model, one in which ethical theories are integrated into an explicit decision procedure. The decision-making process introduced here aims, above all else, to help you make ethically responsible business decisions. To summarize, we review that decision-making process in more detail below. (See the following Reality check, "Nash's 12 Questions" for an alternative decision-making model.)

1. **Determine the facts.** Gather all of the relevant facts. It is critical at this stage that we do not unintentionally bias our later decision by gathering only those facts in support of one particular outcome.
2. **Identify the ethical issues involved.** What is the ethical dimension? What is the ethical issue? Often we do not even notice the ethical dilemma. Avoid normative myopia.
3. **Identify stakeholders.** Who will be affected by this decision? What are their relationships, their priorities to me, and what is their power over my decision

Reality Check *Nash's 12 Questions*

There is nothing magical about the decision-making model that we introduce here. This is simply one way to frame the many factors involved in responsible decision making. There are other models that can work just as well. One such model, proposed by philosopher Laura Nash, suggests asking oneself 12 questions prior to reaching a decision in an ethical dilemma:

1. Have you defined the problem accurately?
2. How would you define the problem if you stood on the other side of the fence?
3. How did the situation occur in the first place?
4. Who was involved in the situation in the first place?
5. What is your intention in making this decision?
6. How does this intention compare with likely results?
7. Who could your decision or action injure?
8. Can you engage the affected parties in a discussion of the problem before you make your decision?
9. Are you confident that your decision will be as valid over a long period as it seems now?
10. Could you disclose without qualms your decision or action to your boss, your CEO, the board of directors, your family, or society as a whole?
11. What is the symbolic potential of your action if understood?
12. Under what conditions would you allow exceptions to your stand?[1]

or results? Who has a stake in the outcome? Do not limit your inquiry only to those stakeholders to whom you believe you owe a duty; sometimes a duty arises as a result of the impact. For instance, you might not necessarily first consider your competitors as stakeholders; however, once you understand the impact of your decision on those competitors, an ethical duty may arise

4. **Consider the available alternatives.** Exercise "moral imagination." Are there creative ways to resolve conflicts? Explore not only the obvious choices, but also those that are less obvious and that require some creative thinking or moral imagination to create.

5. **Consider how a decision affects stakeholders.** Take the point of view of other people involved. How is each stakeholder affected by my decision? Compare and weigh the alternatives: ethical theories and traditions can help here.
   a. Consequences
      i. beneficial and harmful consequences
   b. Duties, rights, principles
      i. What does the law say?
      ii. Are there professional duties involved?
      iii. Which principles are most obligatory?
      iv. How are people being treated?
   c. Implications for personal integrity and character
      i. What type of person am I becoming through this decision?
      ii. What are my own principles and purposes?
      iii. Can I live with public disclosure of this decision?

Opening Decision Point Revisited
Executive Compensation

In early June 2009, the U.S. Treasury Department appointed Kenneth Feinberg to oversee compensation packages that are offered to executives at firms that received significant government bailout money. The companies included AIG, CitiGroup, Bank of America, and General Motors. In making the announcement, Treasury Secretary Timothy Geithner said "The financial crisis had many significant causes, but executive compensation practices were a contributing factor. Incentives for short-term gains overwhelmed the checks and balances meant to mitigate against the risk of excessive leverage."

Feinberg was immediately dubbed the first ever "compensation czar" and critics saw this appointment as a first step towards government wage controls. Defenders saw this as long-overdue and a necessary step to bring fairness to executive compensation and hoped that this practice would extend beyond only those firms receiving government funding.

- What consequences, good and bad, short- and long-term, can you reasonably foresee from this appointment?
- What principles might be cited to defend this position? What principles might it violate?
- What would be the virtues necessary for someone to be a good compensation czar? What vices would make such a person bad in this position?
- Should government set a "maximum wage" limit in the way that it sets a minimum wage?

6. **Guidance.** Can you discuss the case with relevant others; can you gather additional opinions or perspectives? Are their any guidelines, codes, or other external sources that might shed light on the dilemma?
7. **Assessment.** Have you built in mechanisms for assessment of your decision and possible modifications? Are they necessary? Make sure that you learn from each decision and move forward with that increased knowledge; you may face similar decisions in the future or find it necessary to make changes to your current situation.

Questions, Projects, and Exercises

1. Using the distinction between theoretical reason and practical reason introduced in chapter 1, identify which of your other business courses have practical goals. Which courses aim to help student learn how to make responsible decisions about what they should do and how they should act? Can you identify the values that are either implicitly or explicitly taught in these classes?
2. What makes a decision or issue *ethical*? How would you explain the differences between ethical/non-ethical, and ethical/unethical?

3. What ethical issues or dilemmas have you ever experienced in the workplace? How were they resolved? Are there any ethical issues or dilemmas presently being discussed at your school?

4. Are there some ethical values or principles that you believe are relative to one's own culture, religion, or personal opinion? Are there some that you believe are not? What makes them different?

5. Do an Internet search on international human rights and/or fundamental moral rights. Can you make the argument that any moral rights are universally acknowledged?

6. Why might the political goal of economic growth be considered a utilitarian goal?

7. Some political philosophers understand the ethical foundations of legislatures to be utilitarian, while the ethical foundation of the judiciary is deontological. How would you explain this distinction?

8. Do people have a right to do whatever they want? If not, in what sense can people have a right to liberty or personal freedom?

9. The right of private property is often described as a "bundle" of rights. What rights are involved in ownership of property?

10. Relying on the description of virtue ethics, how would you describe Aaron Feuerstein's character? What type of person would make the decision he made?

11. Can such character traits as honesty, loyalty, trustworthiness, compassion, and humility be taught? Do people learn to be selfish, greedy, aggressive, or do these traits come naturally?

12. Do professionals such as accountants and lawyers have duties and obligations that other people do not? From where would such duties come?

Key Terms

After reading this chapter, you should have a clear understanding of the following Key Terms. The page numbers refer to the point at which they were discussed in the chapter. For a more complete definition, please see the Glossary.

autonomy, *p. 112*	deontological ethics, *p. 100*	moral rights, *p. 114*
categorical imperative, *p. 109*	duties, *p. 107*	rights, *p. 114*
character, *p. 118*	egoism, *p. 102*	utilitarianism, *p. 100*
consequentialist theories, *p. 100*	ethical relativism, *p. 99*	virtue ethics, *p. 100*
	human rights, *p. 110*	

End Note

1. Laura Nash, "Ethics without the Sermon," *Harvard Business Review,* 56, no. 6 (1981): 80–81.

Readings

Reading 3-1: "Business and Human Rights: A Not-So-New Framework for Corporate Responsibility," by Christine Bader and John Morrison, *p. 125*

Reading 3-2: "The Caux Principles for Responsible Business," Caux Round Table, *p. 130*

Reading 3-3: "Ethical Dimensions of Decision-Making in the Developing World: The Case of Bribery in Mauritus," by Geetanee Napal, *p. 132*

Reading 3-4: "It Seems Right in Theory but Does It Work in Practice," by Norman E. Bowie, *p. 137*

Reading **3-1**

Business and Human Rights: *A Not-So-New Framework for Corporate Responsibility*

Christine Bader and John Morrison

Using human rights to understand, guide, and regulate business is a relatively recent phenomenon, one that at first might seem counterintuitive. The modern international human rights system is based on the Universal Declaration of Human Rights (UDHR), which was agreed to in 1948 by the world's governments to hold each other to account after the atrocities of World War II. The UDHR says nothing about companies;[1] nor do the International Covenants that followed to provide more detail on what the UDHR intended. For business to embrace human rights would seem to contradict the notion, most famously articulated by Milton Friedman, that "there is one and only one social responsibility of business: to use its resources and engage in activities designed to increase its profits so long as it stays within the rules of the game, which is to say, engages in open and free competition without deception or fraud."[2]

However, human rights are a compelling proposition for the globalising economy. While corporate social responsibility (CSR)—a term used to capture any form of corporate engagement on social issues—is increasingly popular, it is culturally relative: There are no universal CSR principles, beyond what a particular company operating in a particular area decides for itself.

Human rights, however, as embodied in the UDHR, is the single statement of societal values for all people of the world, irrespective of nationality, religion, gender or ethnicity. A global set of principles is of great utility for companies that transcend national borders and strive for legitimacy in the global marketplace.

This article recounts the recent history of business and human rights, with particular attention to two initiatives: a United Nations (UN) mandate on business and human rights and the Business Leaders Initiative on Human Rights (BLIHR). It asserts that human rights provide the right framework for considering business's role in society, no matter what region or sector.

In the 1990s, apparel and footwear companies (notably, Nike and the clothing line by U.S. television celebrity Kathie Lee Gifford) came under fire for having their products made in factories in the developing world where workers were paid poorly, subject to terrible working conditions, and sometimes physically abused. At the same time, companies in the oil, gas, and mining sectors were accused of supporting human rights abuses committed by the governments of the countries in which they were operating. Ken Saro-Wiwa was a Nigerian activist executed after leading protests against the environmental damage that Shell's operations allegedly caused in his country; some observers believe that Shell could have prevented the execution by arguing that Saro-Wiwa was entitled to his freedom of speech. A few years later, BP (formerly British Petroleum) was accused of supporting a rogue, violent element of the Colombian military that was perpetrating abuses in the name of protecting company facilities.

By the end of the decade, the companies under fire and some of their peers came together with human rights groups and other interested parties to develop codes of conduct for their respective industries. Some of these multi-stakeholder initiatives, most notably the Fair Labor Association and the Voluntary Principles on Security & Human Rights, still exist today and continue to attract new members.[3]

In the first decade of the new century, human rights discussions spread into other business sectors. In 2003 a number of banks, under fire for funding projects with adverse human rights impacts, launched the Equator Principles, a set of social and environmental standards that the banks agreed to adhere to for certain kinds of loans.[4]

In 2004, Yahoo! complied with a request from the Chinese government to hand over information about one of its users, journalist Shi Tao—which enabled authorities to find and jail him. In 2006, Google launched Google.cn, its search engine supported by servers in China—and in doing so agreed to censor search results. Those companies followed suit of the aforementioned industries by entering into multi-stakeholder discussions on a code of conduct, resulting in the establishment of the Global Network Initiative in 2008.[5]

Virtually all businesses can impact human rights. These impacts can of course be positive: The jobs that companies provide can lead to stronger realization of a great range of rights, including the right to work, right to an adequate standard of living and right to own property. As people achieve greater economic freedom, they are poised to demand and achieve greater fulfillment of other rights, such as the right to education and the right to participate in cultural life and in government.

But as the aforementioned examples show, business can also infringe on human rights. So what should company responsibilities be with respect to human rights?

There have been attempts to saddle companies with all of the same responsibilities as governments. This is not appropriate: Governments are held accountable by their constituents, for example through elections. In contrast, company executives answer to their directors and shareholders—who are likely to be far removed from the people who their business is affecting. What recourse is available for victims of corporate-related abuse? They can try to sue the company—that is, if they can afford a lawyer, if there is a court that will accept both the case and the company as being in its jurisdiction. Or they can try to mount a public campaign to try to embarrass the company into behaving differently—but that's rarely effective for redressing actual harm.

During his term as UN Secretary-General, Kofi Annan often expressed belief in the power of business to be a force for good. He established the UN Global Compact, an initiative in which companies commit to implementing ten principles upholding social and environmental standards; he made it clear that business has a role to play in the achievement of the Millennium Development Goals, eight ambitious targets for reducing global poverty by 2015.[6]

In 2005, Annan appointed Harvard professor John Ruggie to be UN Special Representative of the Secretary-General for business and human rights. Ruggie was charged with bringing clarity to what had become quite a polarized debate: Some campaigning organizations wanted an international treaty on corporate responsibility; some business interests were adamant that no new standards were necessary; and most governments were largely disengaged.

Ruggie's first task was to better understand the problem he was meant to address: What human rights abuses have been linked to corporations: in what industries, in what countries, and what rights have been at stake? What have the UN treaty bodies, the divisions of the UN whose job it is to interpret human rights conventions, said about corporations? What jurisprudence is there about business and human rights? What rights do companies themselves recognize and how, through their own policies and practices? What is the cause of this rapid growth in alleged corporate-related abuses?[7]

Over the past few decades, companies have globalized while governments are confined by state borders. A computer hardware company with headquarters in the U.S. could be importing iron from South America to make equipment assembled in east Asia that will be shipped to European consumers who call helpdesks in south Asia. One product—and yet, if the iron ore mine is using forced labour, or the manufacturing facility bans independent trade unions, it is likely that no one will be penalized. U.S. courts would consider the mine and assembly operations distinct legal entities, subject only to local courts; the South American country might be reluctant to pursue charges for fear of tainting its reputation as an attractive place for foreign investment; and some governments restrict union activity.

This misalignment between global companies and national legal systems leads to governance gaps that enable human rights abuses to take place. Indeed, Ruggie's research and reports from others showed that the worst cases of corporate-related human rights harm occur disproportionately in low income countries; in countries that often had just emerged from or still were in conflict; and in countries where the rule of law was weak and levels of corruption high—in otherwise, where governance was likely to be the weakest.

Eventually it became clear to Ruggie, through extensive global consultations and research, that what was needed was an overarching framework for business and human rights, based on some fundamental principles that everyone agreed, upon and within which principles and specific guidance could be further developed. Ruggie presented that framework to the UN Human Rights Council in 2008, with the title of "Protect, Respect, Remedy".

The first pillar of the framework, "Protect", emphasizes the duty of governments to protect against human rights abuses by third parties, including business. International law clearly states that governments have a duty to protect people within their territory or jurisdiction against human rights abuses by non-State actors, including by business. States must take all necessary steps to protect against such abuse, including preventing, investigating, and punishing the abuse, and provide access to redress when abuses occur.

The second pillar of the framework, "Respect", affirms the corporate responsibility to respect human rights: in other words, not to infringe on the rights of others, and to demonstrate that respect through ongoing human rights due diligence. The responsibility to respect is not a Ruggie invention:

It is recognized by organizations like the International Labor Organization, the Organization of Economic Cooperation and Development, and the world's largest employer groups such as the International Chamber of Commerce and the International Organisation of Employers.[8] Companies increasingly recognize their responsibility to respect through their own public statements and by joining initiatives such as the Global Compact.

The third pillar of the framework, "Remedy", underscores the need for more effective access to remedies for victims of corporate-related abuse. Even with the best intentions by governments and companies, disputes over corporate impact on human rights are likely to occur, and as mentioned earlier, people seeking redress currently have few good options. In addition, effective grievance mechanisms can not only help solve issues when they arise, but can also provide feedback to a company that shows where it might need to change practices—and most importantly, catch problems before they escalate to abuses.

The Human Rights Council unanimously endorsed the "Protect, Respect, Remedy" framework, making it the first substantive policy statement on business and human rights by a UN body, and extended Ruggie's mandate so that he can develop more specific recommendations within each pillar. But one group of leading multinational companies had already begun exploring what the responsibility to respect means for them.

Following the 2002 World Summit on Sustainable Development in Johannesburg, a small group of people including Anita and Gordon Roddick, co-founders of The Body Shop International plc, the cosmetics company known for its activist stances against animal testing and for fair trade, realized that there was no equivalent to the Business Leaders Initiative on Climate Change for social issues. In May 2003, the Business Leaders Initiative on Human Rights (BLIHR)[9] was founded by seven companies: ABB, Barclays, MTV Europe, National Grid, Novartis Foundation for Sustainable Development, Novo Nordisk and The Body Shop International. Mary Robinson, former President of Ireland and UN High Commissioner for Human Rights, became BLIHR's Honorary Chair.[10]

During 2004, Hewlett-Packard Company, StatoilHydro and Gap Inc. joined the initiative. In 2006, Alcan Inc., AREVA, Ericsson and General Electric joined; and in August 2007, The Coca-Cola Company brought the total number of BLIHR companies to thirteen.

BLIHR's primary purpose was to find practical ways of implementing the Universal Declaration of Human Rights and to inspire other businesses to do the same. With that two-pronged mission, BLIHR's work evolved into two streams: a toolbox of practical materials to aid the integration of human rights into business; and a soapbox, by which BLIHR members would promote greater awareness of human rights with other companies in their respective industries and beyond.

During its first three years, BLIHR worked to understand how human rights can be applied in specific companies, and what sorts of tools and information might be needed to do so. In 2006, BLIHR produced a guide for integrating human rights into business, based on standard business management systems, in partnership with the Global Compact and the UN High Commissioner for Human Rights. Central to this guide and the BLIHR toolbox is a matrix enabling business to map their existing policy and practice against the Universal Declaration of Human Rights and associated covenants.

BLIHR's work is part of a flurry of activity in recent years by a wide variety of organizations that have developed materials and programs to improve business's impact on human rights. These initiatives generally fall into one of three categories:

1. Principles: A number of organizations have developed general principles, sometimes for a particular industry or topic, meant to enable companies to state their commitment to human rights at a very high level as a first step. Examples include the UN Global Compact and the UN Principles for Responsible Investment.[11]

2. Procedures: Some initiatives have gone to the next level of granularity by developing more specific tools to help companies manage human rights. This includes guidance on assessing human rights impacts, for example from the Danish Institute for Human Rights's Human Rights and Business Project.[12]

3. Monitoring and Reporting: Some organizations have focused on assessing and reporting on these processes once they're in place. Most prominent in this area has been the Global Reporting Initiative.[13]

BLIHR companies tested many of these tools and participated in many related initiatives, and in doing so demonstrated that embracing human rights can result in better management of risk to their business and the people their business affects; more informed decision-making; and stronger relationships with stakeholders. BLIHR concluded in 2009 as it was never meant to be a permanent initiative, but as one of its founding members put it, a "strong shot of coffee". Members of the BLIHR community are continuing to evangelize for business and human rights, within their industries and more broadly.

Some skeptics of the business and human rights movement claim that it is solely a Western phenomenon. However, there are several indications that countries outside of North America and Europe are viewing business through a human rights lens:

- South Africa's post-apartheid constitution explicitly holds companies accountable for the full range of civil, political, economic, social and cultural rights. National human rights institutions in Kenya, Malawi, Zambia, Uganda and Ghana are increasingly turning their attention to business, and companies in Darfur are being scrutinized over whether they are exacerbating conflict there.

- In India, a growing number of domestically-owned companies expanding abroad are increasingly engaged in human rights as they seek to find a more objective framework for applying traditional Indian values in other cultures. The Global Business Initiative on Human Rights[14] (part of BLIHR's legacy) and Partners In Change co-hosted a meeting of 40 Indian companies in New Delhi in November

2009 where human rights was seen as a key facet of operating internationally.

- The Chinese government passed new laws in 2007 strengthening labor rights, and has been outspoken in promoting CSR with its companies. The Shenzen Stock Exchange encourages companies to release social responsibility reports along with their annual reports.[15]

Both the business community and the human rights community have a vested interest in universalism. Companies that operate globally often lament the inconsistency of laws, standards, and enforcement across jurisdictions. The expectation that companies respect human rights is a universal norm, espoused by citizens all over the world. The global financial crisis that began in 2008 demonstrated that universal frameworks are necessary—and that human rights and business are inextricably linked.

The UN "Protect, Respect, Remedy" framework is one step towards strengthening global governance. There has already been considerable uptake of the framework by both companies and governments, as the BLIHR companies began to demonstrate.

It is important not to overstate success to date: Only a few hundred companies—of the hundreds of thousands of multinationals, never mind small to medium-sized enterprises—have human rights policies. Few management education programs train future business leaders on human rights, and indeed few corporations proactively seek human rights expertise—until disaster strikes.

However, it is clear that human rights are an enduring framework with powerful application to the role of business in society—all over the world. The next few years will see continued application of the framework, and hopefully continuous improvement in our understanding and management of business's impacts on society.

End Notes

1. The UDHR does, however, call on "all organs of society" in its preamble, which is often interpreted to include business. However, this is a moral statement and not one with legal effect.

2. Friedman, M., "The Social Responsibility of Business is to Increase its Profits," *The New York Times Magazine* (September 13, 1970).

3. See Fair Labor Association, http://fairlabor .org/ and International Business Leaders Forum, Business for Social Responsibility, "Voluntary Principles on Security and Human Rights," http:// voluntaryprinciples.org/ (accessed November 10, 2009).

4. Equator Principles, http://www.equator-principles.com/ (accessed November 10, 2009).

5. Global Network Initiative (2008), http:// globalnetworkinitiative.org/ (accessed November 10, 2009).

6. See United Nations Global Compact, http:// www.unglobalcompact.org/ and United Nations Millennium Development Goals, http://www .un.org/millenniumgoals/ (accessed November 10, 2009).

7. All materials related to John Ruggie's mandate are archived at the Business & Human Rights Resource Centre web portal, http://www .business-humanrights.org/ (accessed November 7, 2009).

8. See, e.g., "Joint initial views of the International Organisation of Employers (IOE), the International Chamber of Commerce (ICC) and the Business and Industry Advisory Committee to the OECD (BIAC) to the Eighth Session of the Human Rights Council on the Third report of the Special Representative of the UN Secretary-General on Business and Human Rights" (May 2008), http://www.business-humanrights.org/SpecialRepPortal/Home/ ReportstoUNHumanRightsCouncil/2008 (accessed November 7, 2009).

9. www.blihr.org

10. Business Leaders Initiative on Human Rights, http://blihr.org/ (accessed November 10, 2009).

11. Principles for Responsible Investment, http:// www.unpri.org/ (accessed November 10, 2009).

12. Danish Institute for Human Rights, http://www
.humanrights.dk/business (accessed November
10, 2009).

13. Global Reporting Initiative, http://www
.globalreporting.org/Home (accessed November 10, 2009).

14. www.global-business-initiative.org.

15. For this and other examples, see Rug-
gie's Corporate Law project, described at
http://www.business-humanrights.org/
SpecialRepPortal/Home/Materialsbytopic/
Corporatelaw/CorporateLawTools (accessed
November 7, 2009).

Reading **3-2**

The Caux Principles for Responsible Business[1]

The Caux Round Table (March 2009)

Introduction

The Caux Round Table (CRT) Principles for
Responsible Business set forth ethical norms for
acceptable businesses behavior.

Trust and confidence sustain free markets and
ethical business practices provide the basis for
such trust and confidence. But lapses in business
integrity, whether among the few or the many,
compromise such trust and hence the ability of
business to serve humanity's needs.

Events like the 2009 global financial crisis have
highlighted the necessity of sound ethical practices
across the business world. Such failures of governance and ethics cannot be tolerated as they seriously
tarnish the positive contributions of responsible
business to higher standards of living and the
empowerment of individuals around the world.

The self-interested pursuit of profit, with no
concern for other stakeholders, will ultimately
lead to business failure and, at times, to counterproductive regulation. Consequently, business
leaders must always assert ethical leadership
so as to protect the foundations of sustainable
prosperity.

It is equally clear that if capitalism is to be
respected, and so sustain itself for global prosperity, it must be both responsible and moral. Business
therefore needs a moral compass in addition to its
practical reliance on measures of profit and loss.

The CRT Principles

The Caux Round Table's approach to responsible
business consists of seven core principles as detailed
below. The principles recognize that while laws and
market forces are necessary, they are insufficient
guides for responsible business conduct.

The principles are rooted in three ethical foundations for responsible business and for a fair and functioning society more generally, namely: responsible
stewardship; living and working for mutual advantage; and the respect and protection of human dignity.

The principles also have a risk management
foundation—because good ethics is good risk management. And they balance the interests of business
with the aspirations of society to ensure sustainable
and mutual prosperity for all.

The CRT Principles for Responsible Business
are supported by more detailed Stakeholder Management Guidelines covering each key dimension
of business success: customers, employees, shareholders, suppliers, competitors, and communities.

Principle 1–Respect Stakeholders Beyond Shareholders

- A responsible business acknowledges its duty to
contribute value to society through the wealth
and employment it creates and the products and
services it provides to consumers.

- A responsible business maintains its economic health and viability not just for shareholders, but also for other stakeholders.
- A responsible business respects the interests of, and acts with honesty and fairness towards, its customers, employees, suppliers, competitors, and the broader community.

Principle 2–Contribute to Economic, Social and Environmental Development

- A responsible business recognizes that business cannot sustainably prosper in societies that are failing or lacking in economic development.
- A responsible business therefore contributes to the economic, social and environmental development of the communities in which it operates, in order to sustain its essential 'operating' capital—financial, social, environmental, and all forms of goodwill.
- A responsible business enhances society through effective and prudent use of resources, free and fair competition, and innovation in technology and business practices.

Principle 3–Respect the Letter and the Spirit of the Law

- A responsible business recognizes that some business behaviors, although legal, can nevertheless have adverse consequences for stakeholders.
- A responsible business therefore adheres to the spirit and intent behind the law, as well as the letter of the law, which requires conduct that goes beyond minimum legal obligations.
- A responsible business always operates with candor, truthfulness, and transparency, and keeps its promises.

Principle 4–Respect Rules and Conventions

- A responsible business respects the local cultures and traditions in the communities in which it operates, consistent with fundamental principles of fairness and equality.
- A responsible business, everywhere it operates, respects all applicable national and international laws, regulations and conventions, while trading fairly and competitively.

Principle 5–Support Responsible Globalisation

- A responsible business, as a participant in the global marketplace, supports open and fair multilateral trade.
- A responsible business supports reform of domestic rules and regulations where they unreasonably hinder global commerce.

Principle 6–Respect the Environment

- A responsible business protects and, where possible, improves the environment, and avoids wasteful use of resources.
- A responsible business ensures that its operations comply with best environmental management practices consistent with meeting the needs of today without compromising the needs of future generations.

Principle 7–Avoid Illicit Activities

- A responsible business does not participate in, or condone, corrupt practices, bribery, money laundering, or other illicit activities.
- A responsible business does not participate in or facilitate transactions linked to or supporting terrorist activities, drug trafficking or any other illicit activity.
- A responsible business actively supports the reduction and prevention of all such illegal and illicit activities.

End Note

1. The Caux Round Table, http://www.cauxroundtable.org/index.cfm?&menuid=8 (March 2009).

Reading **3-3**

Ethical Dimensions of Decision-Making in the Developing World: *The Case of Bribery in Mauritius*

Geetanee Napal

Introduction

The developing world faces the problem of corruption, bribery being the most common form of corruption. To some people, the practice of bribery provides an easy way out and is viewed as acceptable (Select Committee on Fraud and Corruption, 2001), as distinct from being accepted as an inevitable practice, with a feeling of resignation. This paper is based on the results of a survey run in Mauritius, a developing nation, the objective of which was to determine how ethical dimensions (moral, cultural and duty) impact on decision making in a developing nation and draw general conclusions for the developing world.

In designing the survey, emphasis was laid on ethical issues likely to be encountered in the business sector in a developing nation that is, direct corruption in the form of bribery. For analytical purposes, a multi-dimensional ethics scale was used to assess the impact of moral, cultural and duty factors on the ethical perceptions of business people. Respondents were asked to rate the action likely to be adopted in specific hypothetical ethical dilemmas, using each of the normative philosophy scales developed by Reidenbach and Robin (1988) and consisting of three major dimensions that is, a moral equity dimension, a contractualism dimension and a relativism dimension (Kujala, 2001).

The paper starts with a discussion of the relevant literature, followed by a brief description of the research environment and an overview of the survey findings.

Corruption in Business

Corruption constitutes a serious problem for many countries around the globe. A corrupt setting is referred to as a system characterised by flawed governance, corruptible individuals and authoritarian regimes (Segal, 1999). Various authors acknowledge the presence of corruption in all types of society, in both developed and developing countries including France, Italy, Belgium, The Netherlands, America, Russia, Japan, Hong Kong, Singapore, Malaysia, China, India, Korea (Brown and Cloke, 2006; Leisinger, 1999; Matland, 1998; O'Donnell, 1997; Ng, 2006; Priem et al. 1998; Rabe, 1999; Scanlan, 2004; Toye and Moore, 1998). In certain contexts corruption is culturally accepted and is encouraged by the traditional offering of gifts or bribes to officials. Corruption can take the form of abuse of authority and manipulation of resources. In some places, such acts take place on a large scale amongst powerful political leaders and business executives. There is the perception that ruling parties hold monopoly power and there is no political will to fight corruption in developing nations. Amongst the factors that account for corruption are low wages, abuse of power and problems caused by colonialism. Where corruption prevails resources are misallocated, authorities are undermined and both public and private sector development tend to suffer.

Common forms of corruption include bribery and extortion. Extortion can take the form of either gifts or favours as a condition to the execution of public duty or the abuse of public funds for one's own benefit. Bribery is the act of accepting gifts or favours offered, the objective being to induce the person to give special consideration to the interests of the donor. Some cultures condone the act of bribery as long as it brings in opportunities. Bribery involves "the payment or remuneration of an agent of some organisation to do things that are inconsistent with the purpose of his or her position or office. Good examples of such act include paying a judge to be partial to your case, paying a policeman to forego giving you a speeding ticket, or paying a buyer to use your company's services" (Adams and Maine, 1998: 49). The concept of bribery has for long dominated the world of business. Bribery is a form of corruption and constitutes a key issue that business executives often face in the context of global ethics. To some cultures however, giving presents and gratifications to government officers is an indispensable courtesy and a normal way of doing business. As such, bribery is not always considered as an offence.

Cross-Cultural Issues

Unethical practices and corruption in business predominate in various sectors of developing economies. These act as barriers to development and limit the potential to offer an acceptable quality of life to the people of these countries. Corruption takes the form of bribes and illegal payments in the context of trade, aid and investment flows between countries. It can entail preferential access to trading opportunities, favouritism in the processing of investment proposals and kickbacks derived from the abuse of international procurement procedures with serious economic repercussions.

In India for example, corruption has taken such a wide dimension that it has become an industry; 'like an industry it seeks to create a public demand' (Alatas, 1999, p. 57). Opportunities to corrupt exist in various sectors of the Indian economy, including the education sector. The admission to university represents a good example: while eighty percent admission to the tertiary education institution is on merit, the remaining twenty percent is officially reserved for citizens who have represented the state. On the job market, young and ambitious candidates offer money and get appointed. It is common habit for politicians and influential people to place their friends or relations in advertised jobs and get 'rewarded' for such practices.

Similarly in China, people have little faith in social justice and the fairness of society. In an opinion poll, 64.3 percent of respondents held that an honest person would always be at a disadvantage. In 1995, President Jiang Zemin's anti-corruption campaign targeted 'the very top of the party and its commercial princes'. China experienced numerous major corruption scandals, which gave the Chinese population the impression, that some of the government and the Communist party were under the influence of "an all-powerful syndicate of free-booting racketeers" (Van Kemenade, 1998, p. 20). China was in close competition with Indonesia for the first place as the most corrupt country in Asia (Transparency International Corruption Index 1995, Germany). On a scale of one to ten, ten corresponding to high levels of corruption, China's score exceeded eight. In some cases, corrupt individuals got promoted to senior positions for purely political reasons (Van Kemenade, 1998). This trend characterises the developing world in general. In Africa for example, corruption is viewed as part of the culture.

It is common practice for government officials to negotiate for bribes prior to awarding licences or signing loan agreements or authorizing development projects (National Integrity Systems, Transparency International, Country Study Report, Zambia, 2003). In some African states, investigations on corruption are viewed as harassment of the people. Employees of institutions like the Police Service, the Judiciary, the Revenue Authority or the Passports Office expect bribes to do their work and to overlook regulations or to influence a judgement in favour of the donor of the bribe. As a result, the quality of service rendered is lowered and citizens lose confidence in national institutions. The major causes of corruption include wide discretionary powers vested in public officials, poor conditions of service in the public service, weak systems of internal control, the absence of a code of conduct in the public sector, weak enforcement of anti-corruption legislation, socio-cultural norms associated with an individualistic culture that favours loyalty to one's friends and family members and unethical political leadership.

Is It Right to Bribe?

Donaldson and Werhane (1996) question the practice of bribery: "Is it morally right to pay a bribe to gain business?" If specific norms permit bribery in a particular country, then the practice of bribery is culturally or traditionally acceptable in that country. It is a fact that in some contexts, the laws of relativism condone bribery (De George, 1999). Sometimes personal values tend to supersede corporate values when one is involved in ethical dilemmas (Badaracco and Webb, 1995).

Bribery is subject to varying interpretations worldwide. Bribe payers may defend themselves by associating their actions with utilitarian principles, namely that "the good outweighs the bad" (De George, 1999: 73). If one were to base oneself on deontology to question the 'ethics' behind bribery, the outcome would be different as the objective is to consider the act of bribery itself. Deontology focuses on one's duty or obligation to explore the motives behind particular alternatives.

Bribery is a common feature of business as there is a perception that it has a positive impact through the 'grease effect', i.e. bribing a bureaucrat as a means to bypass red tape and act as an incentive to make civil servants more productive (Leff, 1964). A similar argument was put forward recently by Blackburn et al. (2006) namely that corruption could be growth-enhancing if it helps circumvent heavy and unnecessary regulations in the bureaucratic process. Laczniak and Murphy (1993) focus on situations where the payment of bribes may be of direct benefit to businesses, in the context of international trade. This gives bribe-payers access to profitable contracts over competitors. There is evidence that large bribes are paid in order to get access to foreign contracts or to avail of tax incentives. However, some authors are of the opinion that the use of bribes as speed-money in a bureaucratic setting is self-defeating (Kauffman and Wei, 2000). In fact, there is little evidence of positive effects of corruption in countries with red tape (Ades and di Tella, 1997). Can one justify having recourse to bribes as a means to overcoming institutional rigidities that stand in the way of progress?

Business conducted through unethical procedures remains a dangerous practice (Rossbacher, 2006). After all, the costs associated with corruption have to be borne by the State. Corruption alters the composition of government expenditure thereby hindering productive activities and negatively impacting on economic and social development (Tanzi and Davoodi, 1998; Mauro, 1998; Gupta et al, 2001). The results of empirical studies show that corruption reduces the effectiveness of aid-funded projects and further weakens political support for and within donor countries (Brautigam, 1992; Harriss-White and White, 1996). Even petty corruption, as judged by sums of money changing hands, contributes to a pervasive syndrome of problems that keeps developing nations poor (Galtung, 1997; Hancock, 1989; Khan, 1996). Unethical conduct usually starts in a mild form but spreads quite fast, eventually leading to systemic corruption (Leisinger, 1999). Often, nothing is done to stop this unhealthy pattern of behaviour so that it progressively becomes entrenched in the system. In the long run, it gets more difficult to eliminate this culture of corruption. As this trend is pursued, corruption impairs the rule of law and weakens the foundation on which economic growth depends, thereby undermining development.

Corrupt economies tend to lose out on the world market. The stability of a corrupt regime only consolidates and intensifies corruption. Any government who becomes the ally of corruption would only convert such stability into an obstructive and destructive force inimical to economic growth and development. In some places, corrupt financial or economic practices of extensive dimension are culturally accepted (Tanzi, 1998; Alatas, 1999; Chakraborty, 1997). Business enterprises themselves with some highly honourable exceptions, often consider corrupt practices to be part of the normal business process (Rossbacher, 2006).

Many developing nations illustrate the type of corruption referred to as the abuse of trust in the interest of personal and private gain. On the one hand there are corruptible individuals and on the other, there are socially powerless people who, by their condition, are tempted to 'seek opportunities' by having recourse to illicit activities. This explains the culture of bribery that characterises some societies. The Mauritian experience shows that corruption can take the form of abuse of authority, manipulation of resources, both in the public and private sectors (Ribouet, 2007; Thanay, 2007). In addition to instances of petty corruption, large-scale corruption prevails in specific sectors. Officials involved in development projects, procurement and the privatisation of state-owned enterprises, amongst other activities are often involved in grand corruption. People are more likely to be punished for petty corruption while no sanction is imposed on the socially powerful found guilty of grand corruption. It is a fact that corruption is associated on the one hand with government and politics and on the other, with business and the way businesses and states interact.

The following sections give an overview of the research setting, methodology and the survey conducted amongst Mauritian employees of the service sector namely from consultancy businesses, the financial services sector and the hospitality industry. The hypothetical situations presented to participants refer to clear cases of corruption, with different degrees of ethical consequence.

Research Setting

Mauritius is a developing island nation in the Indian Ocean, independent in its government since 1968. Originally claimed by the Dutch, its history includes 100 years of French rule, followed by a century of British rule. Relative to land area, it is one of the most densely populated countries on earth—has a population of more than 1.2 million people—and has one of the most diverse populations on the globe, with residents of Indian, Chinese, European and African descent in the country. Over the decades, many other subcultures have emerged including Franco-Mauritian, Anglo-Mauritian, Hindu, Muslim and Creole subcultures.

According to the latest household budget survey, the average annual income in this nation is 122,000 rupees, equivalent to less than $4,100 US or £2,800 per year. Consequently, there is a tendency to associate corruption with low income although recent corruption scandals proved the contrary. The evidence shows that high-level officials seek financial security through illicit transactions and this is confirmed by the findings of the Select Committee on Fraud and Corruption, 2001. Anti-corruption strategies formulated by the previous regime, upon winning the 2000 elections, included the introduction of anti-corruption legislation and the creation of a totally independent and empowered institution to fight corruption. In spite of these initiatives however, Mauritius has been unable to control corruption. The current regime, in their electoral campaign that preceded the general elections of 2005, strongly emphasized their intention to combat corruption, but again there has been no concrete action. It is quite common for political people to focus on how endangering corruption is, but they only do so as Opposition members. Efforts to develop the economy have sometimes been obstructed by piecemeal approaches that have jeopardized national integrity through an increase in corrupt practices associated with a lack of transparency and accountability. The country has a history of corruption and has recently faced a number of high-profile cases of corruption, in both the public and private sectors. Mauritius has consistently scored between 4.1 and 5.0 out of 10 on the Corruption Perceptions Index of Transparency International from 1998 to 2007 (on a scale of 0–10, 0 being most corrupt and 10 being cleanest). Yet, every government denies the validity of the Corruption Perceptions Index, stating that it is based on perceptions and therefore does not reflect reality.

What seem to predominate in Mauritius are socio-cultural norms related to the individualistic culture that favours loyalty to one's close relations and unethical political leadership. The weakness of pressure groups, inclusive of the media in developing nations means that business people do not feel compelled to observe or respect standards of ethics as is the case in first-world countries, hence the prevalence of corruption.

Methodology

Scenarios representing acts of bribery were presented to the sample population. Respondents were asked to rate the action likely to be adopted, using the normative philosophy scales developed by Reidenbach and Robin (1988). Based on a content analysis of five theories of ethics namely, justice, deontology, relativism, utilitarianism and egoism an eight-item multidimensional ethics scale (*fair, just, moral, acceptability to family, cultural acceptability, traditional acceptability, violates an unspoken promise and violates an unwritten contract*) was developed. These eight items were condensed into three dimensions that is, moral equity, contractualism and relativism dimensions (Kujala, 2001).

Summary of Survey Findings

The scenarios constituting the survey can be described as follows: Scenario 1 involves corruption on a small scale while Scenario 3 presents a more serious issue where the objective is to evade the payment of a licence. On the other hand, Scenario 2 carries even more significant ethical consequences as a convicted individual uses his power to bribe the judiciary to rule in his favour.

Petty corruption in the form of a speed-up gratuity can take the form of either gifts or favours as a condition to the execution of public duty. In Scenario 1, the bribe payer offers a speed-up gratuity to local authorities to get a building permit or to empower the authorities and hasten procedures. Participants drew a distinction between moral (fair, just, acceptable to family) and cultural dimensions (culturally acceptable, traditionally acceptable), hence condemning the act of bribe offer, considered as an illicit activity. Results show that the cultural acceptability of offering a bribe as a speed-up gratuity is a powerful predictor of whether or not people would rate such act as ethical.

Scenario 2 refers to an accused party who decides to bribe the best judges to give him a 'fair' trial. There is an allegation of criminal behaviour against an individual who corrupts the judiciary to avoid punishment. If he succeeds in his attempt to 'clear' his name, he would constitute an exception to the basic rule that condemns crime. If participants perceive the accused person as innocent, they may consider the act of bribe offer as an initiative undertaken to do justice to the latter. The moral issue here is the act of bribing the judiciary. Respondents view bribery at such a level as widely practised and accepted. The notion of bribery was associated with culture, implying that the cultural acceptability of bribing the judiciary is a powerful predictor of whether people would evaluate such a choice as 'ethical'.

Scenario 3 presents another instance of bribery. It involves the evasion of payment of a municipality licence. In many countries, such act is considered as a criminal offence leading to heavy fines and imprisonment. On the other hand however, some people may regard the practice of bribery as justifiable if they believe that paying a larger sum in the form of licence constitutes a 'waste of money'. The results indicate that the cultural acceptability of offering bribery to evade the payment of a licence is a powerful predictor of whether people would consider such act as right.

In earlier studies conducted in the United States of America, participants gave priority to duty concepts as they evaluated the ethicality of the scenarios. In the present study, the relativistic scales were rated as more significant than the duty/contractualism scales as respondents evaluated each scenario. Participants were all from the business sector, which could explain the association of moral factors with relativistic ones. Had we sampled a population of students following a 'Business Ethics' course or young graduates for instance, the outcome might have been different. In this case, participants might have clearly distinguished between notions of morality and culture, rather than demonstrate a strong reliance on cultural factors. One could also expect greater reliance on duty factors in explaining ethical perceptions.

Conclusion

The results give evidence of a strong cultural factor that explained the responses to the scenarios and confirm that moral evaluations are specific to situations. While earlier studies emphasized the idea of implicit contract and promise as being inherent in the evaluation of an ethical problem, this theory does not hold in the case of a developing nation. In two of the scenarios (Scenarios 1 and 3), participants made a clear distinction between the moral and relativistic scales. This is probably because the hypothetical situations involved more serious unethical conduct like the payment of bribery or tax evasion. The consequences associated with bribery are more serious that is, they carry higher risks. From the findings of Scenario 2, we conclude that although bribery constitutes an unethical practice, in that particular case it has been condoned culturally. The survey findings relate closely to what the existing literature states that is, the laws of relativism condone bribery in some contexts (De George, 1999; Donaldson and Werhane, 1996).

One of the most significant findings of this study is the importance of the relativistic factor in explaining ethical judgments. This result has never emerged in earlier applications of the R & R scale in the United States of America. Although universal rules condemn tax evasion, bribery, crime and unethical conduct in general, our results give evidence that developing countries interpret universal rules differently. This confirms that the model of ethical decision making in a developing nation is different from the one used in the developed world. It can be said that these survey results emphasise the strength of the cultural/relativistic dimension on ethical thinking in a developing country, reflecting the state of emerging economies with an individualistic culture.

Reference

Note: Notes and references removed for publication here, but are available on the book website at www .mhhe.com/busethics2e.

Reading **3-4**

It Seems Right in Theory but Does It Work in Practice?[1]

Norman E. Bowie

It is not uncommon for business people, including business executives, to find the conclusions of an ethical theory as it applies to a case in business to be persuasive, but nonetheless not accept the conclusions because to do so would be impractical from a business point of view. Thus it might be right in theory but it is not practical in business. There are three great traditions in ethical theory, the virtue theory of Aristotle, the duty theory of Immanuel Kant, and the utilitarianism of Jeremy Bentham and John Stuart Mill. In recent times these traditions have been supplemented by other theories such as feminist ethics. It seems to me

that if ethical theory is to serve as a foundation for business ethics, it must be the case that these traditional theories are not only persuasive as theories but also can be applied practically to actual business practice. In this essay, I will try to show how the fundamental principles of Kant's ethical theory are both theoretically persuasive and practical in a business context.

Before proceeding it is important to note that the question I am addressing is not strictly an ethical question. After all under our starting assumption business people have already agreed that as a matter of ethical theory, they are persuaded by the answer the ethical theory gives to the case at hand. They just don't think that doing what the ethical theory requires is possible in a business context. What the business person seems to want is for an answer that is both ethically justified and prudent from a business perspective. For Kant showing that something is ethically required is sufficient since morality always trumps prudence. Although Kantians may accept the moral answer as definitive for action, business people will not. If acting morally undermines my business, why should I be moral? That is the question that a business person is like to ask.

Framing the issue as ethics vs. business is an example of what R. Edward Freeman calls "the separation thesis." By the separation thesis he means the thesis that ethical concerns and business concerns are in two separate realms. Freeman argues that business and ethics are always intertwined in business activity. A manager should strive to make business decisions that are both ethically sound and sound in business terms. In what follows I will show how Kant's theory enables managers to make decisions that are sound from both an ethical and a business point of view.

Business Decisions Should Not Be Self Defeating

Kant's fundamental moral principle is the categorical imperative. Kant's moral imperative is categorical because it always holds—there are no "ifs, and, or buts." The classic statement of the categorical imperative is "One must always act on that maxim that one can will to be a universal law." What does Kant mean here? An illustration regarding stealing should help. Why is stealing even when one is in difficult financial circumstances wrong? Suppose one is in difficult financial circumstances and is tempted to steal? If one should decide to steal what is the principle (maxim) for such an action? It must be that "it is morally permissible for me to steal when I am in financial difficulty." Kant now requires that on the basis of rational consistency we must make my maxim

"it is ok for me to steal when I am in financial difficulty" into a universal principle, "it is morally permissible for any person in financial difficulty to steal." After all what applies in one case must apply in all similar cases. However, the universal maxim that would permit stealing is self-defeating. An important point of a system of property rights is that it assumes that property rights are morally protected even if others might need the property more. To accept a maxim that permits stealing is to undermine the very system of property rights—the very property rights that the thief must presuppose in order to be a thief.

If this seems too abstract consider the rule of lining up. Suppose one is in a hurry and wonders if it would be morally permissible to cut in line? The maxim for that action would be "it is morally permissible to cut in line when one is in a hurry." However, the universal version of that maxim is that "It is morally permissible for anyone to cut in line when he or she is in a hurry." But that maxim is self-defeating. If anyone could cut in line when he or she was in a hurry, the very notion of lining up would make no sense. A similar argument shows that lying or the breaking of contracts is wrong.

Kant's reasoning shows why free riding is wrong. A free rider benefits when others follow the rule, but the free rider does not. If everyone behaved as the free rider (if the free riding maxim were made universal), there could be no free riding because you would no longer have the rule. Universal free riding on a rule makes the rule nugatory. Put it another way, the free rider is not making a contribution to the institution that relies on the contributions of those participating in the institution— a contribution the free rider agreed to make when he or she participated in the institution. Now if a maxim permitting free riding were universalized, the institution itself would be undermined.

Kant's reasoning here is highly practical in business. After the collapse of the communist economic system in Russia, one of the tasks Russia had was to establish a stock market. However, the companies that were listed on the stock market did not give out accurate financial information. In other words these companies were not transparent and there was no regulatory apparatus in place to make them transparent. But a stock market can only exist if there is a reasonable amount of transparency regarding the financials of the listed companies. Thus the initial attempts at a stock market fell short; the stock market in Russia only came into existence when a number of companies were able to establish themselves as truth tellers about their financial condition.

Poland had a similar difficulty in establishing a national banking system. The first attempt to establish a national bank failed because people did not pay back their loans. If enough people fail to pay their loans, the bank cannot stay in business.

Kant's reasoning is also relevant when one examines the string of financial scandals in the United States culminating in the subprime lending crisis of 2007–2008. The categorical imperative shows why breaking a promise is wrong. If a maxim that permitted promise breaking were made universal, then promises would have no point. A promise breaker can only succeed if most people keep their promises. If anyone could break his or her promise whenever it was convenient, then no one would make promises. The breaking of contracts is also wrong for the same reason.

Financial market work best when there is maximum transparency. The greater the amount of knowledge, the easier it is to assign risk. Increasing transparency makes markets more efficient. Thus participants in the financial markets support rules that increase transparency. What contributed to the Enron debacle was the fact that off balance sheet entities were created that hid Enron's risks. Once the risks came to light, Enron collapsed very quickly. Something similar happened in the subprime mortgage crisis. Mortgages with varying degrees of risk were bundled together in ways that made in very difficult to determine the underlying value of the assets behind the mortgages. Once the housing market turned and prices began to fall, investors began to worry about the risk but were unable to determine what their risks were. What amounted to a run on the bank occurred with

the firm Bear Stearns. It was widely rumored that Lehman Brothers and even Merrill Lynch might go under. Only action by the Federal Reserve provided sufficient capital to prevent a financial collapse. Nonetheless financial institutions lost hundreds of billions of dollars. Financial markets require transparency. Universalizing actions that undermine transparency undermine financial markets. When a tipping point is reached, financial markets freeze up and cease to function. Participants in markets are morally required to support transparency.

Both academics and practitioners concerned with corporate strategy have discovered the role of trust as a significant element of competitive advantage. Let us define a trusting relationship as one where those in the relationship will not take undue advantage of opportunistic situations. In business, relationships built on trust provide competitive advantage in two basic ways. First, within a firm, trusting relationships make the firm more efficient. For example, when there is trust between employers and employees, there is less monitoring, some behavior may not need to be monitored at all and there is less need for detailed information. The relation between an employer and an employee can be a mentoring relationship rather than simply a monitored relationship. As a result teamwork is more easily achieved. All of this creates a competitive advantage for those companies that pursue enlightened human resource management based on trust.

Another way of illustrating the competitive advantage of trust relationships is to look at a common management problem. With a commission system, sales people are given incentives to sell as much of a product as they can without regard to the ability of the manufacturing unit of the business to manufacture the product in a timely manner. If a manager wants to build a cooperative relation between sales and manufacturing, then he or she must think carefully about the use of commissions as a way to reward sales. Yet another illustration is provided by a long standing tradition in American business to separate the design process from manufacturing. Thus engineers create prototypes that are then given to manufacturing to produce. However, since there was no communication between design and manufacturing, inevitably there are "bugs" that need to be worked out. Working out the bugs is an unnecessary transaction cost that could be greatly mitigated or even avoided if engineering and manufacturing worked together through both the design and the manufacturing stage. The Japanese auto manufacturers learned this early and the efficiencies that resulted helped Japan seize extensive market share at the expense of American automobile manufacturers.

It may seem that these arguments are purely consequentialist. They are consequentialist but not purely so. Consider the following argument that shows the power of Kant's categorical imperative here.

1. A business that fails to be competitive will go out of business.
2. A person or group of persons who start a business and invest in it, do not want it to go out of business.
3. Building relationships of trust are necessary if the business is to be competitive.
4. Therefore intentional actions that fail to develop these trust relationships involve the business people in self-defeating actions. The actors both want the business to survive and by consciously failing to take the actions necessary for it to survive, they show that they do not want it to survive and that is surely self-defeating behavior.

Thus Kant's categorical imperative shows that trusting relationships are required on both utilitarian grounds and on Kantian grounds as well.

Business Decisions Should Not Violate the Humanity of a Person

Kant's ethical theory involves more than a formal test that ethical decisions should not be self-defeating. After all suppose that treating employees simply as a cost and thus as interchangeable with capital and machinery gave business a competitive advantage. Using an argument similar to the one

I used for trusting relationships I could show that such treatment of people would be morally required. But, according to Kant, treating employees in that way would be immoral.

Kant has a second formulation of the categorical imperative which says, "Act so that you treat humanity, whether in your own person or in that of another, always as an end and never as a means merely." To act in accord with this formulation of the categorical imperative, one must treat persons with respect. Why? Because persons have a dignity that Kant said was beyond price. That is why Kant would not permit employers to treat employees as if they were simply on a par with capital or machinery—as if they were mere factors of production.

Kant argued that only human beings were free and that as a result of being free, they could act rationally by which Kant meant that could act according to laws of their own making. As free and rational creatures, they could also be held responsible for their actions. Since persons can be held responsible, they can be held subject to moral law. It is the fact that persons are free, rational, responsible beings capable of acting morally that gives them the dignity that is beyond price.

Kant believed that each of us recognizes that we have dignity that is entitled to respect. Indeed in contemporary society, failure to respect a person can easily result in the disrespected person acting angrily or even violently against those who show disrespect. Since each of us feels entitled to respect and is justified in this feeling, then as a matter of logic each of us must respect those who are like us, namely we must respect other persons. Since the obligation of respect is a matter of consistency, the first and second formulations of the categorical imperative are linked.

The obligation to respect persons has direct application to business and business ethics. Management actions that coerce people or deceive them do not treat employees with respect. Coercion is a direct denial of autonomy and deception also robs a person of his or her freedom since alternatives that would be available to a person are kept off the table. The courts have recognized that coercion is a serious violation of ethics. In the classic case of Henningsen vs. Bloomfield Motors the court voided standardized warranties that limited liability in the light of injury from defective automobiles. The court said, "The warranty before us is a standardized form designed for mass use. It is imposed on the automobile consumer. He takes it or leaves it. No bargaining is engaged in with respect to it."

The court must have reasoned that the take it or leave it alternative is analogous to the demand of the armed robber, "your money or your life." Although there is a choice here, it is a coerced choice.

Certain business practices support respecting the humanity of a person. Open book management is a technique that in effect turns everyone in the business into a chief finance officer (CFO). Under this technique all employees receive all the numbers that are relevant to the business. In this way they understand the business and are better able to act for the longer term success of the business. Open book management has a number of devotees and is increasingly adopted. Open book management in conjunction with other enlightened management practices empowers employees and empowerment is one way of showing that the employee is respected. Another way to show respect for employees is to provide them with meaningful work. Empowerment is one of the characteristics of meaningful work. A complete list of the characteristics of meaningful work is beyond the scope of this essay, but suffice it to say, if employees believed their work was meaningful, some popular phrases or references would not be so ubiquitous. There would not be as many references to TGIF or to Monday as blue Monday or Wednesday as hump day (half way to TGIF). Empowered employees who believe they are making a contribution to the public good through their work are highly motivated and contribute mightily to the success of the business enterprise. What is right in ethical theory in this case contributes to successful business practice.

Business Should Be Seen as a Moral as well as an Economic Community

If employees deserve a kind of respect that capital and machinery does not, then what should a business look like from the point of view of a Kantian? Kant's third formulation of the categorical imperative helps us understand what such a business should look like. Kant says that we should act as if we were a member of an ideal kingdom of ends in which we were both subject and sovereign at the same time. Substitute "moral organization" for "ideal kingdom of ends." How should such an organization be run? Well if the rules for running the organization are to be morally justified, they would have to be rules that everyone in the organization could accept. In that way each person would be both subject and sovereign with respect to the rules.

Kant's ideas here are a moral challenge to hierarchical theories of management—a challenge to a management philosophy that says to the employee, "Yours is not to question why, but simply do or die." Kant's moral theory is also a challenge to the pervasive doctrine of employment at will—a doctrine which says that you can be fired for any reason, good, bad, or morally unjustifiable reason. For Kant unjustifiable actions cannot be moral actions. What Kant's third formulation requires is that employees have a say in the organization's rules and procedures. The work of psychologists has shown that Kant's moral demands are sound from a practical point of view. Some of the pioneering work here has been done by Chris Argyris one of the most consistent critics of hierarchical management. Employees who are given a say are more highly motivated employees and highly motivated employees contribute to the bottom line of the business. Also teamwork and cooperation, which are so highly valued in today's organization, require that members of the organization have voice in how the organization is run and in the decisions it makes.

Also a Kantian who views the organization from the perspective of an ideal kingdom of ends will not treat the organization as a mere instrument for their own personal use. If the individuals in an organization view it purely instrumentally, these individuals are predisposed to behave in ways that harm organizational integrity. The insight of the contemporary Kantian John Rawls that organizations are social unions constituted by certain norms is useful here. Organizations are not mere instruments for achieving individual goals. To develop this notion of a social union, Rawls contrasts two views of how human society is held together: In the private view human beings form social institutions after calculating that it would be advantageous to do so; in the social view human beings form social institutions because they share final ends and value common institutions and activities as intrinsically good. In a social union, cooperation is a key element of success because each individual in a social union knows that he cannot achieve his interests within the group by himself. The cooperation of others is necessary as it provides stability to the organization, enables it to endure, and enables individuals both to realize their potential and to see the qualities of others that lead to organizational success. Rawls's notion of a social union has much in common with Kant's ideal kingdom of ends.

This analysis can be applied directly to the issue of excessive executive compensation and to the endless chain of corporate scandals from 2001 to the 2007–2008 sub-prime mess. Many have reacted to the recent wave of corporate scandals by saying that executives are overly greedy: a character flaw.

But why have some executives become greedy? The explanation is in the distinction between viewing an organization as merely an instrument to satisfying one's individual needs and seeing an organization as a social union. If the organization is seen as a means to personal enrichment and not seen as a cooperative enterprise of all those in the organization, it should come as no surprise that the executives of such an organization feel entitled to the rewards. Psychological theorists have shown that people tend to take credit when things go well and blame bad luck or circumstances beyond one's control when things go badly. Thus a CEO takes all the credit when an organization performs well but blames the general economy or other factors when things go poorly. This human tendency is predictable when executives look at organizations instrumentally.

Conclusion

This essay provides a brief tour through Kantian ethical theory and shows how it is both theoretically sound and practical. At least with Kantian ethics there need be no divergence between good theory and sound practice.

End Note

1. The ideas in the essay are adapted from my book *Business Ethics: A Kantian Perspective,* Blackwell Publishers 1999.

9 Contractual Performance and Agency

Learning Objectives

In this chapter you will learn:

9-1. To understand how courts interpret contracts.

9-2. To identify when contract performance duties arise.

9-3. To understand how contractual duties are discharged.

9-4. To understand that nonperformance of contracts results in a breach unless performance is excused.

9-5. To predict the consequences of a breach of contract.

9-6. To describe the authority of agents to act on behalf of a principal in contracts and beyond.

In the preceding chapter, you studied the basics of contract terminology and classifications. You learned about the essential elements and form required to create a valid, enforceable contract. Finally, you read about how contracts impact third parties.

In this chapter, your study of contracts continues as you learn about the performance of contracts and the consequences of breach. In addition, you will learn the basic principles of agency authority related to contracts and other legal contexts. These topics are of critical importance to businesspeople. After studying this chapter, you should have answers to the following questions:

- Are there rules that businesspeople should know that determine what contract language means?

PART 3 Legal Foundations for Business

- How do parties (and courts) decide if promises in a contract have been fully performed?
- What happens if a contract is not fully performed?
- What authority do agents have to bind a party to a contract?

>> Interpretation of Contracts

If each party is satisfied with the other's performance under a contract, there is no problem with interpreting the contract's terms. But when disagreement about what a term means, or whether additional promises were made, interpretation often becomes necessary. How do we decide who is right?

One of the most important contract interpretation principles is that courts decide what a contract means. The meaning of a contract is a "question of law," which means that a judge makes the final determination. However, depending on the circumstances and issues, that determination may require factual information from the parties or other witnesses. To guide their interpretation, courts use established rules designed to reduce ambiguity in a predictable manner. Understanding these rules can ensure that a contract is not interpreted differently than you predict.

1. RULES OF INTERPRETATION

In the interpretation of contract terms, handwriting is the best evidence of intention.

Common words are given their usual meaning. "A rose is a rose is a rose," said the poet, and a court will interpret this common word to refer to a flower. If the meaning of the word is clear on the face of the contract, courts will usually reject a party's attempt to reinterpret it later. However, if there is evidence that a word has a particular *trade usage,* courts will give it that meaning. In a contract in the wine trade, the term *rose* would not refer to a flower at all but to a type of wine.

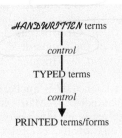

Many businesses today use printed form contracts. Sometimes the parties to one of these printed contracts type or handwrite additional terms. What happens when the typed or handwritten terms contradict the printed terms? What if the printed terms of a contract state "no warranties," but the parties have written in a 90-day warranty? In such a case, courts interpret handwritten terms to control typed terms and typed terms to control printed ones. The written warranty will be enforced since the writing is the best evidence of the parties' true intention.

Another rule is that when only one of the parties drafts (writes) a contract, courts will interpret ambiguous or vague terms against the party that drafts them. Courts often apply this rule to the adhesion contracts discussed in Chapter 8 as well as insurance contracts and interpret the contract to give the non-drafting party the benefit of the doubt when deciding the meaning of a confusing term or phrase.

Case 9.1 illustrates how important a court's interpretation of contractual language is in determining the rights of the parties.

case **9.1** >>

CITIBANK, N.A. v. MORGAN STANLEY & CO. INTERNATIONAL, PLC
724 F. Supp. 2d 398 (S.D.N.Y. 2010).

The following case involves one of the most complex transactions in modern business, the credit default swap. This is an agreement in which one party promises to cover the losses of another in the event of a default on credit extended for a security. In exchange for this promise, the other makes payments, similar to an insurance contract. The losses covered can be quite large, and the consequence of default can be severe on the party offering coverage. As you probably know, credit default swaps played a significant role in the recent financial crises. However, at base, credit default swaps are contracts. When there is a dispute as to the meaning of the agreement, courts must use the same rules of contract interpretation that apply in more mundane situations.

The specific question before the court was whether Citibank breached the terms of a credit default swap it entered into with Morgan Stanley & Co. Internationals, PLC (MSIP) in 2006. In order to insure against losses from $366 million extended as credit to another firm called Capmark, Citibank entered into a default swap with MSPI for a payment of approximately $750,000. When Capmark defaulted in 2008, Citibank acted by liquidating Capmark's security to make up for the original debt. However, the liquidation fell short by over $246 million. According to the default swap agreement, MSIP was liable for the shortfall. MSIP argued that it was not liable for that amount because Citibank liquidated the security without first obtaining MSIP's consent as required by the contract. To determine whether consent was necessary, the court considered the terms of the credit default swap contract.

SCHEINDLIN, J.: This dispute can be resolved by reference solely to the contractual documents properly considered by the Court on this motion—the Indenture, Credit Agreement, and Swap with MSIP's admissions. Allegations and evidence extrinsic to the contractual documents, therefore, have not been considered . . .

It is undisputed that the consent rights MSIP asserts Citibank violated derive exclusively from section 6(d) of the Swap Confirmation. . . . MSIP

argues that when Citibank ordered liquidation of the Capmark VI CDO, Citibank provided a "consent of or with respect to" the Revolving Facility, thereby implicating MSIP's rights under section 6(d). Citibank counters that it did not provide a consent under section 6(d) but rather issued a "direction" pursuant to the Indenture. . . . Thus, the parties' cross motions boil down to whether Citibank's conduct implicated MSIP's consent rights under section 6(d).

MSIP admits that Citibank, in its role as Administrative Agent of the Revolving Facility, *directed* the Trustee to liquidate the Collateral. . . . Nonetheless, MSIP cites to section 6.07 of the Credit Agreement and argues that Citibank, in its role as Lender to the Revolving Facility, provided a consent pursuant to section 6(d).

MSIP argues that because this provision requires the Administrative Agent (i.e., Citibank) to obtain "authorization" before ordering the liquidation of the Capmark VI CDO, Citibank was required to *authorize* itself to take such action. Thus, according to MSIP, when Citibank caused the Trustee to liquidate the Collateral, it occurred in two separate steps: *First,* Citibank, as Lender, *authorized* itself, as Administrative Agent, to direct the Trustee. *Second,* Citibank, as Administrative Agent, *directed* the Trustee to undertake the liquidation. MSIP further argues that because the definition of "consent" in section 6(d) includes "authorisation," . . . when Citibank, as Lender, *authorized* the liquidation of the Capmark VI CDO, Citibank provided the *consent* that triggered MSIP's rights under section 6(d).

Even assuming that section 6.07 is applicable—a point Citibank does not concede . . .—MSIP's linguistic gymnastics and strained reasoning is not persuasive. First, I reject MSIP's focus on Citibank's two roles under the Credit Agreement. That Citibank was required to consent to or authorize its own action makes no sense. Because Citibank was always the sole Lender to the Revolving Facility, Citibank was always the only principal for which it was acting as Administrative Agent. Thus, under the circumstances, Citibank was simultaneously sole Lender, Controlling Class, and Administrative Agent. As such, MSIP's admission that Citibank

[continued]

directed the liquidation as Administrative Agent is tantamount to an admission that Citibank did nothing but issue a direction, which is fatal to MSIP's position.

Nor do I accept MSIP's attempt to read "direction" to fall within the definition of "consent" by way of "authorization" and "authorisation." Not only is "direction" conspicuously absent from the plain terms of section 6(d), "direction" is also not included within the definition of "consent" found in the Master Agreement. The fact that "consent" includes "authorisation" under the Master Agreement does not mean or imply that every method of "authorisation" is a "consent." Indeed, the plain language of section 6.07 makes clear that "authorization" may be effected by either a consent *or* a direction.

Furthermore—and as section 6.07 itself demonstrates—the contractual documents at issue here repeatedly distinguish between the words "direction" (or "direct") and "consent." . . . This is not surprising given that the two words have different meanings: while "consent" is a word of acquiescence, "direction" is a word of action. . . . Similarly, "authorization" and "direction" are also utilized differently in the contracts . . . —a distinction recognized in New York law.

If these highly sophisticated parties truly intended "consent" to include "direction" via "authorization" or "authorisation", they could and would have so provided. To merge these terms as if they were one would render meaningless the distinction between them.

In sum, Citibank's issuance of a direction under the Indenture did not implicate MSIP's consent rights under section 6(d) of the Swap Confirmation. Therefore, Citibank was permitted to direct the liquidation of the Capmark VI CDO without acquiring MSIP's prior written consent. MSIP's attempt to introduce ambiguity where there is none cannot prevent this result.

For the reasons stated above, Citibank's motion for judgment on the pleadings and for dismissal of MSIP's original counterclaims is granted. MSIP's motion for judgment on the pleadings is denied. . . .

>> CASE QUESTIONS

1. What obligation did MSIP argue Citibank breached, and what did MSIP believe should be the result?
2. What evidence did the court use to determine the meaning of the contract?
3. Why did the court find MSIP's suggested interpretation unpersuasive?
4. How could the parties have drafted an agreement that required MSIP's explicit consent before liquidation?

2. THE PAROL EVIDENCE RULE

The parol evidence rule prohibits testimony about the oral negotiation that results in a written contract; thus, read the contract before signing.

Like the statute of frauds, the **parol evidence rule** influences the form of contracts. This rule states that parties to a complete and final written contract cannot introduce oral evidence in court that changes the intended meaning of the written terms.

The parol evidence rule applies only to evidence of oral agreements made at the time of or prior to the written contract. It does not apply to oral modifications coming after the parties have made the written contract (although the statute of frauds may apply).

Suppose that Chris Consumer wants to testify in court that a merchant of an Ultima washing machine gave him an oral six-month warranty on the machine, even though the $450 written contract specified "no warranties." If the warranty was made after Chris signed the contract, he may testify about its existence. Otherwise, the parol evidence rule prevents him from testifying about an oral agreement that changes the terms of the written contract.

An exception to the parol evidence rule allows evidence of oral agreement that merely explains the meaning of written terms without changing the terms. Also, oral evidence that changes the meaning of written terms can be given if necessary to prevent fraud.

>> Performance

LO 9-2

The fundamental reason any of us enter into a contract is to assure the performance of the promise made or to secure the performance of the action desired. What we want is the other party's **duty of performance.** In turn, they want this same duty to be performed by us. An extremely high percentage of contracts are performed in such a way that makes the contracting parties happy. Thus, the most simple (and realistic) statement concerning performance of contracts is that it typically happens. When the parties perform, the obligations of the contract are discharged. A party to a contract is **discharged** when that party is relieved from all further responsibility of performance.

However, not all contractual obligations are fully performed. When less than full performance occurs, a number of legal issues arise. For example, a complete lack of performance results in a breach of the contract. As summarized in Figure 9.1, less than full performance results in issues about the level of performance and excuses for nonperformance. As you study this figure and read the next sections, keep in mind that contracting parties ultimately arrive at one of two conclusions: (1) they are discharged from the obligation to perform further or (2) they are liable for breaching the contract.

3. CONDITIONS OF PERFORMANCE

Parties typically put conditions in their contracts to clarify when performance is due. While conditions reflect the creativity of the contracting parties, classifications of conditions usually take three forms.

If something must take place in the future, before a party has a duty to perform, it is a **condition precedent.** For example, a building developer may contract to buy certain land "when the city annexes it." The annexation is a condition precedent to the developer's duty to purchase the land. Parties should think through their business environment and state clearly the conditions governing their performance. For example, in a supplier-customer contract, the parties should state whether payment by the customer is a condition precedent for the seller to deliver or is delivery by the seller a condition precedent for payment.

A **condition subsequent** excuses contractual performance if some future event takes place. A marine insurance policy might terminate coverage for any shipping losses "if war is declared." This is a condition subsequent. Another typical example of this type of condition is the requirement that an insured motorist or homeowner must notify the insurance company

As an employee, you usually have a responsibility to work for a certain amount of time (equivalent to a pay period) before your employer is obligated to pay you. You are entitled to be paid before working the next period. The performance of work is a condition to be paid, and receiving your pay is a condition for you to continue working. Do you see how contractual conditions govern performance?

270   **PART 3**   Legal Foundations for Business

Figure 9.1 Contractual performance flow chart

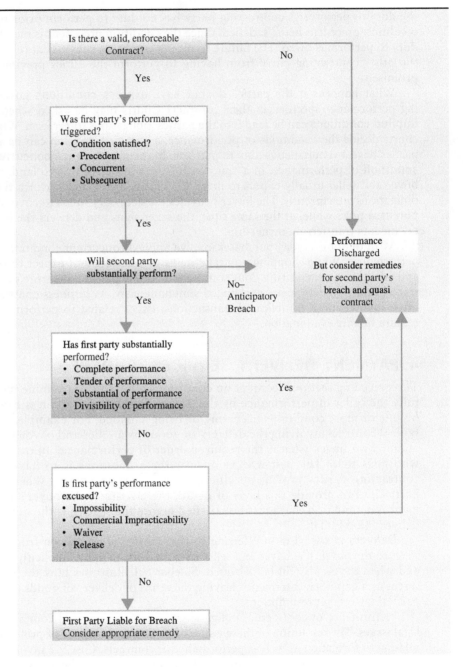

of a claim (from a car accident or homeowner's loss) within a short time period (five days perhaps) of the claim arising from the accident of the loss. Failure to provide this notice relieves the insurance company of its duty to provide coverage.

The distinction between conditions precedent and conditions subsequent can appear quite subtle. The key difference is found in the timing of the duty to perform. A contracting party has no duty to perform prior to a condition precedent being satisfied. Once the condition precedent is met, the duty to perform is owed. The failure to meet a condition subsequent relieves the other contracting party from having to perform the duties previously promised.

What happens if the parties do not have **express conditions** governing performance specified in their contract? Courts may be asked whether **implied conditions** can be read into the parties' obligations to perform. When courts decide the conditions of performance, a common decision can be the parties have a simultaneous duty to perform. In essence, there is a **concurrent condition** of performance. In a contract for the transfer of title to land, the buyer and seller usually expect to meet at a closing event and perform their obligations concurrently. The buyer provides the necessary funds to cover the purchase price while, at the same time, the seller signs and delivers the legal documents transferring ownership.

Most of our everyday purchases involve implied concurrent conditions of performance. While shopping you take items to a cashier and expect to pay and take the items with you. Your contractual duty to pay and the store's contractual duty to deliver are exchanged simultaneously. As business contracts often involve more complicated transactions, issues related to performance require further examination.

> Employers required to notify their insurance companies of claims by employees should provide this notice when an employee files a claim of discrimination with the EEOC.

4. PAYMENT, DELIVERY, SERVICES TENDERED

The preceding sections' content on conditions allows us to examine more fully the order of performance by the parties. Performance often is based on one or more conditions occurring or being satisfied. For example, in a typical contract involving the delivery of goods by a seller and payment of money by a buyer, what is the required order of performance? In essence, who goes first? The best way to answer these questions is to have the contracting parties provide specific guidance in the contract. When the parties fail to provide this level of detail, the law states the buyer's payment is a condition that must be satisfied before the seller has the duty to deliver (§2-511(1)).

Delivery is a legal term referring to the transfer of possession from the seller to the buyer. The buyer and seller may presume to know implicitly how and when the goods will be delivered. Sidebar 9.1 illustrates how the UCC serves as a gap-filler, thereby not leaving the terms of delivery of goods to the parties' uncertain presumptions.

Performance of contractual obligations presents parties and courts with legal issues. The resolution of these issues often requires analysis of principles relating to formation as well as performance of contracts. Case 9.2 involves a typical business transaction. Notice how the court examines the questions of which party made the offer and which one accepted it. The conclusion of this formation issue impacts which party has failed to perform.

The UCC provides valuable guidance to performance issues in contracts for the sales of goods. However, when a contract involves the performance of services, the parties to the contract should take time to provide specific conditions. If their agreement lacks specificity, reasonableness needs to

>> *sidebar* 9.1

Terms of Delivery in the UCC

Suppose your company sells office equipment to a buyer. Further suppose that the contract carefully describes the equipment and the purchase price. However, the contract provides no specific guidance as to when or where the equipment is to be delivered.

The UCC permits and encourages the enforceability of this contract by providing a series of gap-filling provisions. In essence, if the parties fail to write clear instructions on delivery of the equipment, the UCC controls.

The seller's obligation is to tender delivery of the goods, and the buyer's duty is to accept and pay for them (§2-301). The phrase *tender of delivery* means the seller must make the goods available to the buyer. If, as in our example, the contract makes no statement about delivery, the presumption is the buyer must make arrangements to pick up the goods at the location the seller designates (§2-503(1)).

Many buyers may not want to assume the burden of picking up the goods at the seller's location.

Thus, it is common for the buyer and seller to agree the goods will be shipped to the buyer. If the contract does not provide additional details, how does the seller satisfy its obligation to ship the goods? The UCC states the seller satisfies its obligation to ship goods once they are transferred to the shipper for transportation (§2-504). If the goods are damaged in transit, the liability rests on the buyer, not the seller.

To avoid the assumption of risk, experienced buyers may insist on what is called a destination contract. This contract requires the seller to get the goods shipped and delivered to a specific place of business designated by the buyer. The risk of loss for damage to the goods remains with the seller until the goods safely arrive at the buyer's destination (§2-310(1)(b)).

Do you now see why negotiation over the terms of performance, such as shipment and delivery, should be so important to your company?

govern the relationship and performance. For example, let's assume your manufacturing company hires software consultants to oversee the installation and implementation of new programs that hopefully will enhance your overall efficiency. The contract specifies the date for the completion of this work by the consultants; however, the contract does not provide a beginning date.

 case 9.2 >>

VENTURE MEDIA LIMITED PARTNERSHIP v. COLT PLASTICS COMPANY, INCORPORATED
168 F. 3d 484 (4th Cir. 1999)

PER CURIAM: . . . Venture sells cosmetic products through direct-response marketing. Colt manufactures and sells plastic containers for cosmetic products.

In 1994, Venture approached Colt seeking to purchase plastic containers for its line of cosmetic products. Meetings were held between representatives of both Colt and Venture. . . . When all of these issues were settled, Venture began placing orders with Colt.

In its business, Colt uses a number of forms including a Quotation/Proposal Form (Proposal Form) and an Invoice Form (Invoice). . . .

[continued]

Between 1994 and September 1995, Venture ordered from Colt, and Colt manufactured and shipped, plastic containers for Venture's cosmetic products. . . . Venture placed orders with Colt using a purchase order. After manufacturing and shipping the plastic containers requested in the various purchase orders, Colt sent an Invoice to Venture requesting payment. The Invoice stated that payment was "due 30 days from the Invoice date," and "amounts 30 days past due [were] subject" to twelve percent annual interest. This period of time passed with the two companies transacting without incident.

However, in August and early September 1995, Venture felt as if there were problems. The deliveries were arriving late, and Colt refused to increase Venture's line of credit. To resolve these issues, Venture requested a meeting with Colt. At this meeting, Colt assured Venture it would resolve the concerns raised by Venture.

Based on these assurances, on September 21, 1995, Venture sent a purchase order to Colt for plastic containers totaling $339,996.25. The purchase order specified exact quantities, exact prices for each quantity, and the total price. In addition, the purchase order explicitly specified the location where the products should be shipped and stated: "Please notify us immediately if this order cannot be shipped complete on or before 11/03/95." Colt never sent an acknowledgment to Venture but began to manufacture the plastic containers requested in the purchase order.

Between late February and early March 1996, Colt shipped plastic containers aggregating $47,922.18 to Venture in a series of shipments. Colt also sent Invoices for each shipment to Venture. Venture never paid Colt for these deliveries and did not give notice to Colt of any defects in the delivered goods within the thirty-day period required by the Proposal Form. Colt continued to manufacture plastic containers totaling $122,799.59 after the deadline date for delivery specified in Venture's purchase order. Because of the outstanding balance owed by Venture, Colt never shipped these plastic containers to Venture. Colt sold what it could of these products to third parties, but because these plastic containers were specially manufactured for Venture, they were difficult to sell on the open market. Consequently, Colt continues to hold in its inventory $108,793.84 in plastic containers manufactured for Venture.

On December 30, 1996, Venture filed this suit against Colt in the Circuit Court of Maryland for Baltimore County alleging breach of contract. . . . Colt removed the case to the United States District Court for the District of Maryland based on diversity jurisdiction. Colt filed a counterclaim alleging breach of contract and seeking $47,922.18 plus interest for the plastic containers sent to Venture and $108,793.84 for the plastic containers specially manufactured for, but not sent to Venture.

Both parties moved for summary judgment with respect to all claims. The district court granted Colt's motion for summary judgment, and therefore, entered judgment in favor of Colt on Venture's claims and on Colt's counterclaim. . . . On appeal, Venture contends the district court erred when it granted summary judgment in favor of Colt. . . .

The parties agree that a contract existed for the sale of plastic containers amounting to $339,996.25, but vigorously dispute which terms control the sale. According to Venture, a $339,996.25 contract for plastic containers was formed when it sent its purchase order to Colt and Colt began to manufacture the plastic containers. Venture further maintains that Colt breached the contract by: (1) delivering defective plastic containers; (2) delivering damaged plastic containers; (3) failing to deliver the plastic containers by the agreed upon dates; (4) failing to extend Venture a volume purchase discount; and (5) failing to extend Venture's line of credit. In response, Colt contends that a $339,996.25 contract for plastic containers was formed when Colt sent its Proposal Form to Venture and Venture sent its purchase order to Colt. According to Colt, Venture breached the contract when it failed to make payment for the plastic containers that were manufactured and delivered to Venture. Colt further maintains that it never breached its contract with Venture because the plain language of the Proposal Form disposes of Venture's breach of contract allegations.

The district court granted summary judgment in favor of Colt on Venture's breach of contract claim, concluding that a contract was formed when Colt sent the Proposal Form to Venture and Venture sent the purchase order for $339,996.25 of plastic containers to Colt. Further, the district court concluded that Venture breached the contract when it failed to make payment for the plastic containers that Colt manufactured and delivered to Venture. Finally, the district court concluded that Colt did not breach its contract with Venture because the plain language of the Proposal Form was dispositive of Venture's breach of contract allegations. . . .

Under Maryland common law, an offer is "a expression by the offeror . . . that something over which he at least assumes to have control shall be done or happen or shall not be done or happen if the conditions stated in the offer are complied with." An offer must be definite and certain. Further, the intention of the parties is one of the primary factors when deciding whether an offer was made. Therefore, the facts and circumstances of each particular case are crucial.

[continued]

In this case, Colt's Proposal Form was an offer. From 1994 through September 1995, Venture placed purchase orders with Colt for various plastic containers. Throughout this period, Colt sent numerous Proposal Forms to Venture. The Proposal Form explicitly sought acceptance by means of a purchase order. In conformity with this condition, Venture placed all of its orders by means of purchase order. Venture always abided by Colt's terms and never objected to them. Accordingly, we agree with the district court that Colt's Proposal Form was an offer made to Venture.

The Code states that once a certain and definite offer is made, acceptance may be made in any manner that is reasonable. However, an offeror may be particular about the appropriate means of acceptance. Here, Colt's Proposal Form was explicit: the proposal "may be accepted only by written purchase order." Venture abided by this requirement when it submitted its purchase order on September 21, 1995, accepting Colt's offer, thus creating a binding contract between the two companies under the terms of Colt's Proposal Form.

Having determined that Colt's Proposal Form constituted a valid offer and Venture's purchase order constituted a valid acceptance, thereby creating an enforceable contract, we agree with the district court that the contract's terms are dispositive of Venture's breach of contract claim. Accordingly, for the reasons stated above, the district court appropriately granted summary judgment in favor of Colt on Venture's breach of contract claim.

Turning to Colt's counterclaim for breach of contract, the district court awarded Colt $47,922.18 plus $7,524.50 in interest for the plastic containers Colt manufactured and shipped to Venture. Because Venture accepted the shipment, did not object to the quality, and did not make payment, Colt was entitled to summary judgment on its counterclaim for these damages. Further, because the explicit terms of the Invoices sent to Venture by Colt allow interest at a twelve percent annual rate beginning sixty days after the date the Invoice was due, the district court correctly awarded the sales price and interest to Colt in the total amount of $55,446.68.

Colt is also entitled to damages for the plastic containers that it manufactured specifically for Venture. The aggregate contract price for these plastic containers is $122,799.59. Colt has sold some of these containers on the open market but still has $108,793.84 of the plastic containers manufactured for Venture in its inventory. The district court correctly awarded this amount to Colt.

We conclude that the district court properly granted summary judgment in favor of Colt on Colt's counterclaim for breach of contract. The district court properly awarded Colt: (1) $55,446.68 (sales price and interest) for the plastic containers delivered to Venture; and (2) $108,793.84 for the plastic containers that Colt specially manufactured for Venture and has been unable to sell on the open market. . . .

For the reasons stated herein, the judgment of the district court is

Affirmed.

>> CASE QUESTIONS

1. In what businesses are Venture and Colt involved?
2. According to the court, who is the offeror and the offeree in this case?
3. What are the actual offer and acceptance in this factual situation?
4. How does the answer to the preceding question impact the conclusion of which party is entitled to a finding in its favor?
5. Which party is liable to the other?

One party's tender of performance may satisfy a required condition leading to the other party's duty to perform.

Reasonable standards should govern your company and these consultants. Hopefully, effective negotiation will overcome the lack of direction in the contract. The concept of tendering performance may help. To **tender performance** means to offer to perform. When the consultants offer to send a team to your plant next week, they are tendering performance. A reasonable response is to permit this work to begin by allowing the consultants access to your facility. Once work begins, the contract's provisions on when payment is owed will govern your performance.

5. SUBSTANTIAL PERFORMANCE

Beyond the order of performance as determined through conditions, the degree or amount of performance can become an issue. A party to a contract may not always perfectly perform the duties owed. The more complex a contract is, the more difficult it is for a party to complete every aspect of performance. Courts generally recognize three levels of performance. These levels are summarized in Sidebar 9.2.

>> *sidebar* 9.2

Levels of Performance

1. *Complete Performance* recognizes that a contracting party has fulfilled every duty required by the contract. Payment of money, for example, is a contractual duty of performance that a party can perform completely. A party that performs completely is entitled to a complete performance by the other party and may sue to enforce this right.

2. *Material Breach* is a level of performance below what is reasonably acceptable. A party that has materially breached a contract cannot sue the other party for performance and is liable for damages arising from the breach.

3. *Substantial Performance* represents a less-than-complete performance. However, the work done is sufficient to avoid the claim of a breach. A party who substantially performs may be entitled to a partial recovery under the contract.

Substantial performance is a middle ground between full performance and a breach due to nonperformance. Substantial performance is much more than some performance. It is even greater than significant performance. A very typical example when substantial performance is applicable occurs in service-oriented contracts. The consultants in the software installation/implementation contract should recover for work performed even if the entire contract is not completed on time.

Likewise, a construction contractor who gets a home built but has not finished all the landscaping and finishing details by the due date is not denied a financial recovery. This builder can recover under the contract but remains liable for any damages to the homeowner for delays. It would be unfair, from the legal perspective, to allow the homeowner to refuse to pay the builder because a deadline is missed.

> Substantial performance is close to, but less than, full performance. Some or even significant performance may not satisfy the requirement of substantial performance.

6. DIVISIBILITY OF PERFORMANCE

Up to this point, we have assumed a contract specified aspects of performance by one party followed by the next party's performance. Alternatively, a contract may call for both parties to perform concurrently. It is possible, and indeed quite common, for a contract to be divided into segments or installments. An employment contract is a good example. One party (the employee) performs services for a period of time followed by the other party (the employer) paying the wages that are due. This pattern of recurring conditions precedent allows the employment contract to be divided into parts. This contract is considered to be divisible, typically into segments timed as pay periods.

Many contracts that at first glance appear divisible actually are not. While our consulting contract example may look to be divided into monthly or quarterly periods, the manufacturer would have a good argument that it wants the installation and implementation of the software complete. A portion of the work is not what is desired. The contract calls for all the work to be done. Thus, this contract is not divisible. Similarly most construction contracts are viewed as a whole and not as divisible into installments. The fact that the contract may call for payment to be forthcoming following certain benchmarks are met does not make the contract divisible.

With respect to performance, the benefit of divisibility is to view the duty to perform as a series of smaller contracts. This may reduce the amount of disputes (numbers of them and the dollar figures involved) that arise due to nonperformance of the contract.

> *The divisibility or entirety of a contract helps determine when performance of duties should occur.*

>> Excuses for Nonperformance

Generally speaking, in contracts the party who refuses to perform a promise can expect to be sued for breaching the agreement. Even beyond the special situations related to performance presented in the previous sections, the law may provide for nonperforming with a valid excuse. If such an excuse for nonperformance exists, there can be no legitimate claim of a breach. The next sections of this chapter present material relevant to most business contracts.

Prior to studying these topics, it is important to revisit the fact there are many ways to discharge a party's obligation under a contract. The most common ways to achieve a discharge follow:

> *Remember, a discharge relieves a party from the obligation to perform contractual promises.*

1. Complete performance of the contract.
2. Tendering performance if that tender is rejected.
3. Substantial performance.
4. Performance of part of a divisible contract.

In addition, a legitimate excuse for nonperformance can result in a party being discharged from contractual performance.

7. IMPOSSIBILITY OF PERFORMANCE

A party's nonperformance is excused because of **impossibility of performance.** This may occur because of the death of an essential party, the destruction of essential materials, or the subject matter of the contract becomes illegal.

If the subject matter of the contract is destroyed, the contract becomes impossible to perform. When a contract exists for the sale of a building, and the building burns, the seller is discharged from performance. Likewise, when there is a contract for personal services, and the party promising the services becomes ill or dies, the party receives discharge from performances.

> *Impossibility of performance is less likely to occur compared to impracticability.*

The party that promises performance that becomes illegal is also discharged because of impossibility of performance. Mere increased difficulty or reduced profitability, however, does not constitute impossibility of performance.

8. COMMERCIAL IMPRACTICABILITY

Under the UCC a party to a sale-of-goods contract receives discharge from performance because of **commercial impracticability** (§2–615). The *impracticability* standard is not as difficult to meet as the *impossibility* standard. What constitutes impracticability of performance depends upon the circumstances of the situation. For instance, a manufacturer may be discharged from an obligation to make goods for a buyer when the manufacturer's major source of raw materials is unexpectedly interrupted. But if the raw materials are reasonably available from another supplier, the manufacturer may not receive discharge because of impracticability.

9. WAIVER OR RELEASE

A party may be excused from not performing contractual obligations by the other party to the agreement. When a party intentionally relinquishes a right to enforce the contract, a **waiver** occurs. When a party announces the other party does not have to perform as promised, a **release** exists. The distinction between a waiver and a release is not important when examining the resulting discharge of the contract. Nonperformance of the contract is forgiven and there is no liability for a breach of contract.

To gain some clarity regarding these closely related terms, focus on the timing of the nonperformance. Waivers generally occur after a contracting party fails to perform. In this situation, nonperformance by one party may cause the other party to waiver its right to enforce the contract. The waiver typically is unilateral. The nonbreaching party grants the waiver. A landlord may waive the right to collect a late payment fee when the rent is only two days overdue.

Releases usually occur before a contracting party fails to perform. A release often takes the form of a negotiated contract. The release is bargained for and is supported by consideration. A borrower may seek the lender's release to avoid having to make an interim payment. This borrower may have to agree to pay the entire debt before its original due date to get the lender's release from the interim payment.

>> Breach of Contract

A party that does not live up to the obligation of contractual performance is said to breach the contract. There are several remedies or solutions available for a breach of contract. These include the following:

- Negotiated settlement
- Arbitration
- Various awards, including compensatory, consequential, liquidated, and nominal damages
- Specific performance
- Rescission

You contract with *P* to paint your house for $2,000. *P* does not complete the job, and you hire *R* and pay $3,000. You are entitled to $1,000 from *P* as compensatory damages.

Figure 9.2 *Remedies for breach of contract*

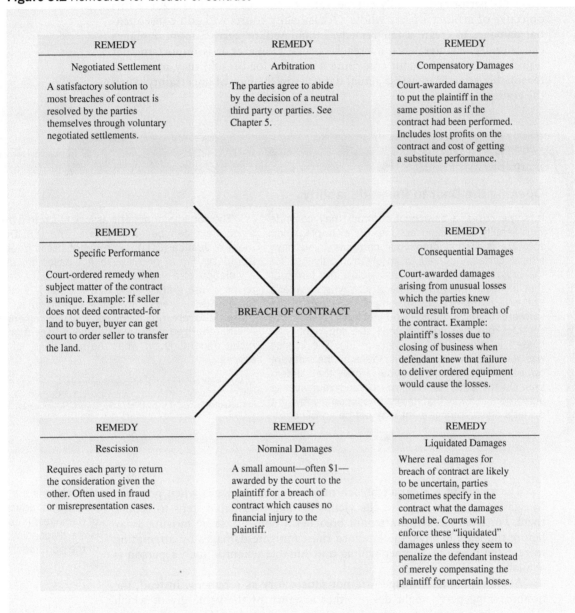

Figure 9.2 provides a summary of these remedies for breach of contract. Note that the choice of one remedy may exclude others. For example, if one choses rescission, one cannot also make a claim for damages.

Awarding money damages is the more common way courts provide remedies to nonbreaching parties. The theory behind such awards rests in putting the damaged person in the same financial position as if the contract was fully performed. Usually compensatory damages suffice to achieve this objective of making a party whole. Occasionally courts will add consequential damages to create a fair remedy. Liquidated, or agreed-upon, damages can simplify disputes when a breach occurs. However, it is important that liquidated damages cannot constitute a penalty for breach; they must be a reasonable attempt to assess actual damages in the face of uncertainty when the contract is formed.

>> *sidebar* 9.3

Opening the Door to Related Liability

In some cases, a breach of contract may coincide with liability for related actions. For example, when software is loaded onto your computer, you have almost certainly agreed to an electronic license for the program's copyright. If you violate the terms of that license in a way that impacts a copyright owner's exclusive rights—e.g., by making more copies of the software than permitted—you not only breach the contract, but also infringe upon the copyright (discussed in more detail in Chapter 11). The license was your relief from copyright claims by the software owner, and by breaching it you remove that protection. On the other hand, if you breach your license agreement in a way that has no impact on a copyright owner's rights, infringement may not be an issue.

The liability for actions associated with a breach of contract can be quite severe. The U.S. Department of Justice (DOJ) has brought cases under the Computer Fraud and Abuse Act based in part on a violation of a website's terms of use. In general, terms of use grant access to a website in exchange for the user agreeing to follow certain rules. When those rules are not followed, the user is engaged in unauthorized access. Criminal prosecution may result depending on what the user does with that access.

Sources: *MDY Indus., LLC v. Blizzard Entertainment, Inc.*, 629 F.3d 928 (9th Cir. 2010); Nick Akerman, "When a Breach of Contract is Evidence of Computer Fraud," *The National Law Journal*, November 29, 2010.

The victim of a contract breach must mitigate damages when possible. Mitigating damages requires the victim to take reasonable steps to reduce them. For example, when a tenant breaches a house lease by moving away before the lease expires, the landlord must mitigate damages by attempting to rent the house to another willing and suitable tenant if such a person is available.

At times, money damages are not satisfactory as a remedy. Instead, the nonbreaching party might desire either a return of the value given, which involves the equitable remedy of rescission or restitution. Or a party might request an order that the breaching party specifically perform the contractual promise made, which is known as specific performance.

Efficient Breach Should you always perform your contractual obligations if at all possible? Scholars have long debated whether performance of contractual duties should be predicated on more than economic benefit. One school of thought suggests that if one monetarily compensates the non-breaching

Mitigation is the purposeful reduction of damages; it usually is the responsibility of the nonbreaching party.

party according to the contract terms, nothing more is required. You may be able to breach, fully compensate the nonbreaching party, and still end up better off. That scenario is termed an efficient breach, because all parties end up either indifferent or in a better position than if the contract was performed. But another view argues that one is morally obligated to carry through on one's promises.

Mortgage contracts provide a current context for considering the issue of efficient breach. This is discussed in sidebar 9.4 below.

>> sidebar 9.4

Walking Away from a Mortgage

In essence, a mortgage is a contract. In such an arrangement, a bank or other lender (mortgagee) has provided the funds for purchasing property (a home) in exchange for the homeowner's (mortgagor) agreement to make payments with interest. Property is pledged as security for the loan. In a "title" state, the lender actually holds the deed until the mortgage is paid, but in a "lien" state, the lender merely has a right to obtain title if payments are not made. In either case, the failure to make payments on a mortgage—a breach of contract—can result in a "foreclosure" wherein the lender takes ownership of the property. In some states, the mortgagor has no further obligation after the mortgagee forecloses.

In a strong economy, when home prices rise, making payments on a mortgage seems like a good economic arrangement for all involved. However, in a bad economy, home prices may fall so quickly that a mortgagee's payments will cover only the inflated portion of the loan for many years. Such a mortgage is said to be "underwater," with the property being worth far less than the amount owed to the lender. When this happens, a homeowner may be inclined to simply walk away from the mortgage, permitting the lender to take over the property and recoup only a part of the amount loaned. To many, this makes economic sense, at least from the perspective on the homeowner. But is it morally wrong?

Consider whether it is acceptable to walk away from a mortgage that is substantially underwater. What would be the impact on the housing market if many people did this? Try to imagine arguments for both sides.

LO 9-6

>> Agency Law in Contracts and Other Contexts

Business organizations cannot accomplish anything without the assistance of individuals. An accounting firm does nothing as an organization. The work of the firm is done through the accountants and other employees. Likewise, a local restaurant provides food through the work of servers, cooks, managers, and other employees. In both cases, those employees undertake acts that implicate contract, tort, or criminal law.

The people who get the work done are called *agents,* and the principles presented below are referred to as *agency law.* The actions of agents can have significant consequences to business organizations. The concepts presented in the next four sections form the fundamentals of agency relationships in the transaction of everyday business.

10. TERMINOLOGY

The application of agency law involves the interaction among three parties. Although individuals usually are these parties, agency relationships can involve business organizations. Figure 9.3 illustrates a three-step approach to understanding how the law views the purpose of agency relationship.

First, a **principal** interacts with someone (or some organization) for the purpose of obtaining that second party's assistance. This second party is the **agent.** Principals hire agents to do tasks and represent them in transactions. All employees are agents of the employer/principal, but not all agents are employees. For example, a principal may hire an **independent contractor** to perform a task. Principals do not directly control independent contractors and independent contractors generally work for more than one principal. Examples of independent contractors include attorneys (other than in-house counsel), outside accountants and subcontractors hired to perform construction projects. The nature of their relationship with the principal determines whether employees or independent contractors have authority to contractually bind the principal.

Next, the agent (on behalf of the principal) interacts with a **third party.** Third, the usual legal purpose of the agent is to create a binding relationship between the principal and third party. Typically, the agent wants Step 3 to involve the understanding that any liability created by Steps 1 and 2 is replaced by the new principal–third party relationship. To accomplish this substitution, the agent must remember to comply with the following duties owed to the principal:

> Organizations deal with third parties through the actions of agents.

- A duty of loyalty to act for the principal's advantage and not to act to benefit the agent at the principal's expense.
- A duty to keep the principal fully informed.
- A duty to obey instructions.
- A duty to account to the principal for monies handled.

In studying the law of agency, keep in mind that the employer/business organization is the principal and the employee is the agent. Whether employee conduct creates liability for the employer is the usual agency issue facing businesses. Such issues may involve either contracts or torts.

11. CONTRACTUAL LIABILITY FROM AN AGENT'S ACTS

How is a company bound in a contract? For an employee to bind the employer to a contract negotiated with a third party, the employer must

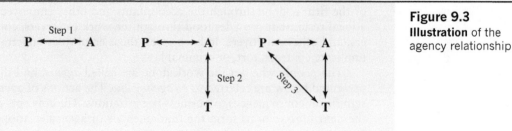

Figure 9.3
Illustration of the agency relationship

282 **PART 3** Legal Foundations for Business

have authorized the employee's actions. Contractual authority can take the following forms:

- Actual authority.
- Expressed, written authority.
- Implied authority.
- Apparent authority.

Only when one of these types of authority is present will the principal and the third party become contractually bound.

Specific instructions, whether spoken or written, given by an employer to an employee create actual authority.

Actual Authority A simple example helps illustrate the concept of actual authority. Suppose, as an owner of a restaurant, you hire Alex to be an evening manager. You discover that the restaurant is running low on coffee. You write a note to your friend, Terry, the manager of the local grocery store. In this note, you ask Terry to allow Alex to charge $100 worth of coffee to your restaurant's account at the grocery store. You give this note to Alex with instructions to purchase the coffee and deliver the note to Terry. If Terry allows Alex to charge $100 worth of coffee, is your restaurant liable to pay $100 to the grocery store? The answer is yes, because Alex had **actual authority,** which was expressed in writing.

Now suppose a week later, you send Alex to the same grocery store to buy pound cake and yogurt. This time you call Terry on the phone and ask that Alex be allowed to charge the cost of the cake and yogurt. Once again, your restaurant is contractually liable to pay for this purchase since Alex was actually authorized to contract through your expressed oral statement to Terry.

>> *sidebar* 9.5

Can Electronic Agents Make Contracts?

In the current business environment, it is common for contracts to be formed electronically. Agency law is not necessarily involved in such agreements. For example, agency may not arise as an issue if a live party accepts a browse-wrap or click-wrap agreement. This is because, although the contract is offered electronically, a person generated it originally. However, what happens if the computer providing the contract can change the terms in accordance with customer input. Or consider the case of an electronic contract that is accepted by a computer program (often referred to as a "bot") on behalf of its creator. Can a contract be formed by these electronic agents?

In general, the answer to the above questions is yes. As a result of recent federal and state legislation, the law supports the ability of electronic agents to bind their live principals. The federal Electronic Signatures in Global and National Commerce Act (ESIGN) provides that a contract may not be denied legal effect "solely because its formation, creation, or delivery involved the action of one or more electronic agents so long as the action of any such electronic agent is legally attributable to the person to be bound." The Uniform Electronic Transactions Act (UETA), adopted by 48 states, provides that "A contract may be formed by the interaction of electronic agents of the parties, even if no individual was aware of or reviewed the electronic agents' actions or the resulting terms and agreements."

Implied Authority   What if, sometime later, you and your co-owner are out of town and Alex is in charge of the restaurant for the evening. Alex, realizing that the tuna salad is in short supply, goes to Terry's grocery store and charges to the restaurant $60 worth of tuna fish. Upon your return, you find a bill from Terry for this purchase. Legally, do you have to pay it? Yes. This time Alex's actions contractually bind the restaurant to Terry since Alex had **implied authority** to do what was necessary for the restaurant's benefit. This implied authority arises from the position Alex holds as evening manager and by the history of the express authority situations.

> Implied authority can be inferred from the acts of an agent who holds a position of authority or who had actual authority in previous situations.

Apparent Authority   Finally, suppose that you terminate Alex's employment. In retaliation, Alex goes to Terry's grocery store and charges a variety of groceries that are consistent with the food your restaurant serves. When you get the bill from Terry, is the restaurant liable? Answer—yes. Even though Alex lacks any actual (expressed or implied) authority, your failure to notify Terry of Alex's termination left Alex with **apparent authority.** Due to the history of Alex's representing your restaurant, it is reasonable for Terry to assume that this incident is one more in the series of Alex's properly charging items to the restaurant's account. To prevent this unwanted liability from occurring, you should have let Terry know that Alex is no longer employed. This notice destroys the existence of apparent authority.

> Remember to notify third parties if an agent no longer works for you; this notice is essential to cut off apparent authority.

It should be noted that in this last scenario, involving the existence of apparent authority, you would have a claim against Alex for the monies you had to pay Terry. Alex's liability to you arises because Alex breached the duty of loyalty owed to the restaurant.

The basic concepts of agency law apply to the operation of business organizations. Sometimes the law provides technical rules, such as those applicable to how partners can bind their partnership. One such special rule is worthy of mention. A partner in a **trading partnership,** that is, one engaged in the business of buying and selling commodities, has the implied authority to borrow money in the usual course of business and to pledge the credit of the firm. A partner in a **nontrading partnership,** such as an accounting or other service firm, has no implied power to borrow money. In the latter case, such authority must be actual before the firm will be bound.

Ratification   What happens when an agent enters into a contract without proper authority? Although the agent does not have the power to bind the principal, the contract may become binding if ratified. **Ratification** occurs when a principal voluntarily decides to honor an agreement, which otherwise would not be binding due to an agent's lack of authority. Returning to the example of the restaurant's evening manager Alex, suppose Alex enters into a contract on behalf of the restaurant to purchase $100,000 worth of kitchen equipment. If Alex had no authority to bind the restaurant, yet you realize that this is a great deal, you could ratify the contract, and follow through with the transaction.

12. TORT LIABILITY FROM AN AGENT'S ACTS

The legal elements of a tort are discussed later, in Chapter 10. For the purpose of this discussion, you should know that a tort is a breach of a duty that causes injury to a person or their property. If you drive your car onto the sidewalk and hit a pedestrian, you are personally liable for the tort of negligence due to your poor driving. Now, suppose the driver was your employee delivering items from your business. Can the injured victim collect damage from you and your business? The answer is found in agency law.

An agent who causes harm to a third party may create legal liability owed by the principal to the third party. The legal test for imposing this "vicarious liability" depends on whether the agent was acting within the scope of employment when the tort occurred. Any time an employee is liable for tortious acts in the *scope of employment,* the employer is also liable. This is because of the tort doctrine of **respondeat superior** ("let the master reply").

The reason for *respondeat superior* is that the employee is advancing the interests of the employer when the tortious act occurs. If the employee is not doing the work, the employer would have to do it. Therefore, the employer is just as liable as the employee when the employee acts tortiously in carrying out the work. In a sense, the employer has set the employee in motion and is responsible for the employee's acts.

Most *respondeat superior* cases involve employee negligence. Note, however, that the employer is strictly liable once the employee's fault is established. And it does not matter that the employer warned the employee against the tortious behavior.

Some *respondeat superior* cases involve an employee's intentional tort. If a store's service representative strikes a customer during an argument over the return of merchandise, the store will be liable under *respondeat superior.* But if the argument concerns football instead of the return of merchandise, the store will not be liable. The difference is that the argument over football is not within the scope of employment.

Usually, the only defense the employer has to the strict liability of *respondeat superior* is that the employee was outside the scope of employment. Sometimes this defense is made using the language **frolic and detour.** An employee who is on a frolic or detour is no longer acting for the employer. If, for example, an employee is driving to see a friend when an accident occurs, the employer is not liable.

An employer who must pay for an employee's tort under *respondeat superior* may legally sue the employee for reimbursement. In practice, this seldom happens because the employer carries insurance. Occasionally, an insurer who has paid a *respondeat superior* claim will sue the employee who caused the claim.

The type of business organization in existence determines the extent of responsibility for agents' torts. In essence, partners are liable for all transactions entered into by any partner in the scope of the partnership business and are similarly liable for any partner's torts committed while she or he is acting in the course of the firm's business. Each partner is in effect both an agent of the partnership and a principal, being capable of creating both contract and tort liability for the firm and for copartners and likewise being responsible for acts of copartners. Generally, shareholders of corporations and members of LLCs are protected from tort liability that exceeds the amount of their investment.

Do know when agents are and are not acting within the scope of employment.

An agent on a frolic and detour leaves the scope of employment, and the principal is not liable for the agent's actions.

13. CRIMINAL LIABILITY

As with torts and contracts, agents can impose criminal liability on business organizations. There are a variety of ways businesspeople and their organizations can be found criminally responsible. The issue of holding businesses criminally liable has been emphasized by the scandals in the beginning of this century. The repercussions of Enron, WorldCom, Tyco, and others are still being felt. And recent cases like the one involving the Galleon Group demonstrate that the emphasis continues.

>> Additional Thought On Contracts

Before concluding your study of contracts, the point made at the beginning of Chapter 8 should be reemphasized. Understanding contracts is critical because they are the key to transacting business. Having an appreciation for contract law may make you a more effective negotiator in some instances. However, as your career advances and you get involved in more complicated business transactions, you will work closely with lawyers to create contractual documentation. Sidebar 9.6 offers some concluding guidance on how to maintain a balanced relationship with your lawyer. Remember, your goal should always be to create contracts that enhance your business activities.

>> *sidebar* 9.6

Suggestions for Businessperson/Lawyer Relationship on the Drafting of Contracts

- Contracts are business documents; they should be in writing whenever possible.
- Use plain English.
- Tell story of relationship; provide timeline of obligations.
- Avoid legalese (whereas; party of the first part, etc.); be careful with "and," "or," "before," "on," "after," "each," "every," etc.
- There should be a flow from section to section.
- Create clear definitions, if necessary.
- Proofread carefully.
- Ask questions about language or issues you do not understand.
- Consistently redraft to update.

>> Key Terms

Actual authority 282	Condition precedent 269	Frolic and detour 284
Agent 281	Condition subsequent 269	Implied authority 283
Apparent authority 283	Delivery 271	Implied conditions 271
Commercial impracticability 277	Discharge 269	Impossibility of performance 276
Concurrent condition 271	Duty of performance 269	Independent contractor 281
	Express conditions 271	

Nontrading partnership 283
Parol evidence rule 268
Principal 281
Ratification 283

Release 277
Respondeat superior 284
Substantial performance 275
Tender performance 274

Third party 281
Trading partnership 283
Waiver 277

>> Review Questions and Problems

Interpretation of Contracts

1. *Rules of Interpretation*

   Gus contracts to buy a used car from Cars Galore, Inc. The printed contract specifies "no warranties." But Gus and the sales manager of Cars handwrite into the contract a 90-day guarantee on the transmission. If the transmission fails after 60 days, is there a warranty protecting Gus? Explain.

2. *The Parol Evidence Rule*

   Caryn negotiates to buy 50 washers and 50 dryers from the "We-Clean-It Company." These machines are going into laundermats that Caryn operates with her family. Because these machines will be heavily used, Caryn got the company to agree to a one-year warranty instead of the standard 90-day warranty. Following the negotiation, Caryn signs a written contract. Only later, Caryn realizes there is no warranty provision in the written contract. What should Caryn do to be able to enforce the original extended warranty agreement?

Performance

3. *Conditions of Performance*

   (a) Why are conditions important in understanding how and when contracts are performed?

   (b) List the three types of conditions that are most common in contractual performance.

4. *Payment, Delivery, Services Tendered*

   (a) Explain the role of tender of performance.

   (b) What is the impact of one party tendering its performance?

5. *Substantial Performance*

   Ace Contracting constructs an office building for Realty Enterprises. Realty's tenants quickly find a number of minor problems with the plumbing and insulation of the new building. When Realty contacts Ace about bringing its work up to standard, Ace promises to correct the problems, but never does.

   (a) Can Realty rescind the contract?

   (b) What are Realty's legal remedies?

6. *Divisibility of Performance*

   Why is an employment contract usually viewed as being divisible while a construction contract is not considered divisible?

Excuses for Nonperformance

7. *Impossibility of Performance*

   To be a legitimate excuse for nonperformance, impossibility must be real and absolute. What are three examples of factual situations involving real impossibility of performance?

8. *Commercial Impracticability*

   A tripling of prices by an illegal cartel of uranium producers caused Westinghouse Electric Corp. to default on uranium delivery contracts to a number of utility companies. The companies sued and Westinghouse settled. If the case had gone to trial, what defense might Westinghouse have raised to excuse its nonperformance under the contracts?

9. *Waiver or Release*

What do waivers and releases have in common?

Agency Law in Contracts and Other Contexts

10. *Terminology*

(a) What are the names given to the three parties typically involved in an agency relationship?

(b) Describe the general purpose of the agency relationship.

11. *Contractual Liability*

For several years, Albert acted as a collection agent for Paulette. Recently, Paulette revoked Albert's authority to collect payments from customers. However, neither Paulette nor Albert told any customers of Albert's termination. Yesterday, Theresa, one of Paulette's customers, paid Albert the money owed to Paulette. Albert never gave this money to Paulette. Is Theresa liable to pay Paulette? Why or why not?

12. *Tort Liability from an Agent's Acts*

Tammy was shopping in Save-a-Lot Grocery Store when Stewart, an employee, brushed Tammy's ankle with a grocery cart. A short time later, while still shopping, Tammy told Stewart that he should say "Excuse me," and then people would get out of his way. Stewart then punched Tammy in the face, knocking her to the floor. If Tammy sues Save-a-Lot, what legal issue must be addressed to determine whether Save-a-Lot is liable?

13. *Criminal Liability*

Describe how business organizations can be found criminally responsible for their actions. What is the way such organizations are punished?

business >> *discussions*

As a new sales representative for Misco Equipment Corporation, you take a customer out to dinner. Before dinner is over, you have shaken hands on a deal to sell the customer nearly a half-million dollars' worth of industrial equipment. In writing up the formal contract the next morning, you discover that you misfigured the equipment's price. Your error could cost Misco $60,000. You telephone your customer and explain the situation.

Is the "deal" you made an enforceable contract?

Does the mistake you made permit you to get out of an enforceable contract?

What do you think will happen in this situation?

14 Corporate Governance and Business Organizations

Learning Objectives

In this chapter you will learn:

14-1. To describe the factors to consider when deciding on the form of organization.

14-2. To contrast the basic organizational forms that businesses select to conduct business.

14-3. To compare the hybrid organizational forms businesses may utilize to take advantage of attributes of various basic structures.

14-4. To understand the complexity of making a decision on the organizational form and recognize trends in managing organizations.

Have you ever thought about how businesses are organized? Why is one business a partnership and another a corporation? How do these businesses get transactions completed through someone other than the owner? There must be some legal principles at work because you know you do not have to deal with the owner of the clothing store when you make a purchase. A multinational company transacts business all over the world and its shareholders (owners) are not parties to its contracts.

Previous chapters discuss legal issues related to various business transactions. In this chapter, we focus on how these transactions are accomplished and the selection of which organizational form is best to complete such transactions. As

425

you begin the study of this chapter, ask yourself, How does a company enter into a contract? How does an organization become liable to its customers, shareholders, or other parties. The answers to these questions depend on how the business is organized. In addition, to understand the material in this chapter, the material on agency in Chapter 9 is important. It provides a helpful foundation for the following.

In the chapter, you will examine the factors that should be considered when deciding the most appropriate organizational form. You also will review the various choices of organizations used to conduct business. Prior to this examination and review, a quick introduction to the forms of organizations is presented.

LO 14-1 1. FORMS OF BUSINESS ORGANIZATIONS

People conduct business using a number of different organizational forms. The law recognizes three basic forms and several hybrid forms that contain attributes of two or more basic forms. These various forms are listed in Sidebar 14.1.

>> *sidebar* 14.1

Possible Forms of Business Organizations

The three basic forms include:

- Sole proprietorships
- Partnerships
- Corporations

The hybrid forms include:

- Limited partnerships
- S corporations
- Limited liability companies
- Limited liability partnerships

The issue of which organizational form is best usually involves closely held businesses; publicly held businesses typically are corporations.

Two terms are important as they relate to the number of owners of a business organization. Some organizations are owned by only a few persons. Such organizations are said to be **closely held**. Family-owned and family-operated businesses are common examples of closely held organizations. Other businesses may be owned by hundreds, if not thousands, of persons. These organizations are **publicly held** ones. Examples of publicly held businesses include those whose stock is traded on a public exchange.

You should understand that the decision of selecting an appropriate organizational form usually is limited to those situations involving the few owners of a closely held business. When a business is publicly held by a large number of owners, the form of organization usually is a corporation. The reason for this corporate form being used is that shareholders can transfer their ownership without interfering with the organization's management.

>> Factors to Consider When Selecting a Business's Organizational Form

Significant factors to consider in selecting the best organizational form for a particular business activity include:

- The cost of creating the organization.
- The continuity or stability of the organization.
- The control of decisions.
- The personal liability of the owners.
- The taxation of the organization's earnings and its distribution of profits to the owners.

In the following sections, each of these factors is defined so that you can more easily apply their meaning in Sections 7 through 12.

2. CREATION

The word *creation* means the legal steps necessary to form a particular business organization. At times, a businessperson may be concerned with how much it will cost to have each form established. Usually, the cost of creation is not a major factor in considering which form of business organization a person will choose to operate a business. The most significant creation-related issues are how long it will take to create a particular organization and how much paperwork is involved.

The issues when considering methods of creating business organizations usually are time and money.

3. CONTINUITY

Another factor to consider when selecting the best organizational form for a business activity is the continuity of the organization. How does an organization's existence relate to its owners? By this question the meaning of the word *continuity* becomes associated with the stability or durability of the organization.

The crucial issue with this continuity factor is the method by which a business organization can be dissolved. A **dissolution** is any change in the ownership of an organization that changes the legal existence of the organization. In essence, the questions become: Is the organization easily dissolved? What impact does a dissolution of the organizational form have on the business activity of that organization?

The death, retirement, or withdrawal of an owner creates issues of whether an organization and its business will continue.

4. MANAGERIAL CONTROL

The factor of control concerns who is managing the business organization. Often this issue is of vital importance to the owners. The egos of businesspeople can cause them to insist on equal voices in management. As you study this factor under each organizational form, keep in mind the difficulties that can arise when a few strong-willed business owners disagree with one another. Usually when people are excited about getting started in a business

Don't assume you and your co-owners have to be equal in all aspects; voice in management can be decided among you.

opportunity, no one takes time to discuss methods of resolving potential deadlocks. The failure to consider how to overcome disputes involving managerial control can cause business activities to suffer and the organization to fail. Therefore, consideration of potential conflict and mechanisms to resolve disputes are essential to consider when selecting a form for a business venture.

5. LIABILITY

Do always examine how liability passes from the organization to the owner.

When considering the liability factor, you should ask yourself: To what degree is the owner of a business personally liable for the debts of the business organization? Additionally, you may ask: When is the owner liable under the law for harm caused by the business organization? Generally, businesspeople want to limit their personal liability. Although there are organizations that appear to accomplish this goal, you will see that such appearances might be misleading when actually conducting business transactions. For this reason, this liability factor is very important and deserves significant consideration as it relates to each of the organizational forms presented below.

6. TAXATION

Remember a single tax is not always better than a double tax.

This factor often is viewed as the most critical when selecting the form of business organization. At issue is: How is the income earned by the business taxed? How is the money distributed to the business owners taxed? Is it possible that owners may have to pay taxes on money that is attributed to them as income but which they have not actually received? The answers to these questions provide much needed guidance when deciding which form of organization is best suited for a business's operation.

People have stated that the double taxation of corporate income should be avoided by selecting a different form of organization. As you will see, there are specific advantages to creating the organizational forms that are "single taxed." However, advantages also exist when an organization is subject to the supposed "double tax."

LO 14-2

>> Selecting the Best Organizational Form

The following six sections apply the various factors to consider when deciding which organizational form is best for a particular business activity. Following these sections is a brief discussion on how to make a good decision when selecting the best organizational form.

7. SOLE PROPRIETORSHIPS

When considering the five factors introduced above, it has been said that the **sole proprietorship** has many virtues. However, the use of this business organization is very limited because multiple owners cannot create a proprietorship. Depending on the factual situation presented, greater continuity, less liability, and more flexible tax planning may be required than those afforded by the law of the sole proprietorship.

A sole proprietorship is the easiest and least expensive business organization to create. In essence, the proprietor obtains whatever business licenses

CHAPTER 14 Corporate Governance and Business Organizations   429

Figure 14.1   *Corporate Form Selection Factors*

Form	Creation	Continuity	Control	Liability	Taxation
Sole Proprietorship	No formal documentation—business licenses only	So long as proprietor desires, but no transfer to others	Total control by proprietor	Personal obligation for all debts and liabilities	All business income subject to personal taxation
Partnership	Automatic based on business conduct; modified by agreement	Dissolved whenever one partner withdraws	Each partner has equal voice; modified by agreement	Personal obligation for all debts and liabilities; joint and several liability	All business income subject to personal taxation, divided equally
Corporation	Incorporators apply for state charter with articles of incorporation	Perpetual, so long as it can conduct business	Managed by officers, appointed by directors, who are elected by shareholders	Shareholder obligations limited to investment, absent other commitments	Corporate income taxed; shareholders taxed only on income distributed
Limited Partnership	Partnership agreement and certificate filed in public office where business is conducted	Dissolved when general partner withdraws	General partners have total control	Personal obligation for general partners; limited partners obligated for investment	All business income subject to personal taxation
S Corporation	Incorporators apply for state charter with articles of incorporation	Perpetual, so long as number of shareholder limited	Managed by officers, appointed by directors, who are elected by shareholders	Shareholder obligations limited to investment, absent other commitments	All business income subject to personal taxation
Limited Liability Company or Partnership	Organizers file articles of organization with state official	Dissolved when member withdraws, but may be continued by those remaining	Equal management by members unless manager designated	Members are agents, but liable only for investment	All business income subject to personal taxation

Source: Delaware Division of Corporations, Legal Business Structure Table, http://revenue.delaware.gov/services/
Business_Tax/business_structures_table.pdf

are necessary and begins operations. Legally, no formal documentation is
needed. The ease of (perhaps the lack of) the steps used to create a proprietorship makes it an attractive alternative when beginning a new business venture. However, as the other factors might dictate, a business may shift away
from the proprietorship form as it becomes more successful.

A proprietorship's continuity is tied directly to the will of the proprietor.
In essence, the proprietor may dissolve his or her organization at any time
by simply changing the organization or terminating the business activity.

Do It! this phrase
describes how a
proprietorship is
formed.

The fact that the propreitorship's business activity may be more stable than the proprietor's willingness to remain actively involved in the business indicates that the sole proprietorship is a less desirable organizational form. Ownership of a sole proprietorship cannot be transferred.

The sole proprietor is in total control of his or her business's goals and operations. While the proprietor has complete responsibility for the business's success or failure, the owners of all other organizational forms usually share control to some degree. As long as this control issue is carefully thought out, there can be real value in having more than one voice in control of managing a business enterprise.

A sole proprietor is personally obligated for the debt of the proprietorship. Legally speaking, this owner has <u>unlimited liability</u> for the obligations of this type of business organization. The business organization's creditors can seek to hold the proprietor personally liable for 100 percent of the debts and legal obligations that the proprietorship cannot satisfy. The desire to avoid the potentially high risk of personal liability is an important reason why other organizational forms might be viewed as preferable to the proprietorship.

A sole proprietorship is not taxed as an organization. All the proprietorship's income subject to taxation is attributed to the proprietor. The initial appearance of this tax treatment may appear favorable because the business organization is not taxed. However, the individual proprietor must pay the applicable personal tax rate on the income earned by the proprietorship whether the proprietor actually receives any of the income from the organization or not. If the organization retains its profits for business expansion purposes instead of distributing this money to the proprietor, that owner still must pay taxes on the income made by the proprietorship.

> A sole proprietorship may appear to have many advantages; sharing responsibility and liability with others are not among them.

8. PARTNERSHIPS

Whenever two or more people wish to own a business together, a partnership is a possible organizational form. In general, a **partnership** is an agreement between two or more persons to share a common interest in a commercial endeavor and to share profits and losses. The word *persons* in the previous sentence should be interpreted broadly enough to allow business organizations, as well as individuals, to form a partnership. For example, two or more individuals, an individual and a corporation, a partnership and a corporation, or any combination of these entities may agree to create a business organization called a partnership.

Due to the potentially complex relationships established through a partnership, factors to consider when studying the appropriateness of this organizational form are presented under subheadings that correspond to the factors presented above.

Creation When compared to other forms of business organizations (other than the sole proprietorship), a partnership is easily formed. The cost of forming a partnership is relatively minimal. In addition, the creation of a partnership is made easier since it does not need to get permission from each state in which it does business.

The key to a partnership's existence is satisfying the elements of its definition:

1. Two or more persons.
2. A common interest in business.
3. Sharing profits and losses.

If the parties conduct their affairs in such a way as to meet these definitional elements, a partnership exists regardless of whether the persons involved call themselves partners or not. Sidebar 14.2 presents issues related to the existence and naming of a partnership.

Don't operate a business with one or more co-owners without a carefully drafted partnership agreement; unresolved issues lead to major legal problems.

>> *sidebar* 14.2

Formation and Naming of a Partnership

Since the existence of a partnership is based on the partners' agreement, it is possible that this agreement is implied from the conduct or actions of the parties. Partners should never rely on implied agreements. Rather, their agreement should be explicitly stated among the parties and drafted into a formal document. The formal agreement is called the **articles of partnership.**

Since a partnership is created by agreement, the partners select the name of the partnership. This right of selection is subject to two limitations in many states. First, a partnership may not use any word in the name, such as "company," that would imply the existence of a corporation. Second, if the name is other than that of the partners, the partners

must give notice as to their actual identity under the state's **assumed-name statute.** Failure to comply with this disclosure requirement may result in the partnership being denied access to courts, or it may result in criminal actions being brought against those operating under the assumed name.

An example of these naming concepts could arise in the creation of a partnership to conduct business as a consulting firm. If the firm's name is a listing of your surname and those of your partners, your identities are clear via your firm's name. However, if you called your partnership "We are the Best Consulting," you and your partners would need to comply with any applicable assumed-name statute.

Continuity A general partnership is dissolved any time there is a change in the partners. For example, if a partner dies, retires, or otherwise withdraws from the organization, the partnership is dissolved. Likewise, if a person is added as a new partner, there is a technical dissolution of the organization. Therefore, it generally is said that the partnership organization is easily dissolved. Even if the partnership agreement provides that the partnership will continue for a stated number of years, any partner still retains the power to dissolve the organization. Although liability may be imposed on the former partner for wrongful dissolution in violation of the agreement, the partnership nevertheless is dissolved.

A dissolution does not necessarily destroy the business of a partnership. Dissolution is not the same thing as terminating an organization's business activity. Termination involves the winding up or liquidating of a business; dissolution simply means the legal form of organization no longer exists. Sidebar 14.3 addresses how parties might prevent dissolution from destroying a partnership's business success.

>> *sidebar* 14.3

Anticipating a Partnership's Dissolution—Buy and Sell Agreements

To prevent problems that may arise when a partner dies or withdraws from a partnership, the articles of partnership should include a **buy and sell agreement.** This agreement, which should be entered into when the business entity is created, provides for the amount and manner of compensation for the interest of the deceased or withdrawing owner.

Buy and sell agreements frequently use formulas to compute the value of the withdrawing partner's interest and provide for the time and method of payment. In the case of death, the liquidity needed is often provided by the cash proceeds from life insurance taken out on the life of the deceased and made payable to the business or to the surviving partners. Upon payment of the amount required by the buy and sell agreement to the estate of the deceased, the interest of the deceased ends, and all the surviving partners can continue the business, as members of a new partnership.

Don't rely on partners having an equal voice in managing the organization; negotiate how to share this managerial responsibility.

Managerial Control In a general partnership, unless the agreement provides to the contrary, each partner has an equal voice in the firm's affairs. Partners may agree to divide control in such a way as to make controlling partners and minority partners. The decision of who has what voice in management is of crucial importance to the chances of the business's success and to the welfare of the partners' relationship with each other. The possibility of a deadlock among partners is very real, especially when there are only a few partners and there are an even number of them. Care should be taken to design mechanisms to avoid or at least handle the disputes that will arise when partners share managerial control. A written partnership agreement should provide specific language governing issues of managerial control.

Liability All partners in a general partnership have unlimited liability for their organization's debts. These partners' personal assets, which are not associated with the partnership, may be claimed by the partnership's creditors. From a creditor's perspective, this personal liability of each partner extends to the organization's entire debt, not just to a pro rata share. These partners are **jointly and severally liable** for the partnership's obligations. For example, assume that a general partnership has three partners and that it owes a creditor $300,000. If it is necessary to collect the debt, this creditor can sue all three partners jointly for the $300,000. As an alternative, the creditor can sue any one partner or any combination of two for the entire $300,000. Among the partners, anyone who has to pay the creditor more than her or his pro rata share of the liability usually can seek contribution from the remaining partners.

Taxation Like proprietorships, partnerships are not a taxable entity. The fact that this type of organization pays no income tax does not mean that the profits of the partnership are free from income tax. A partnership files an information return that allocates to each partner his or her proportionate share of profits or losses from operations, dividend income, capital gains or losses, and other items that would affect the income tax owed by a partner.

Partners then report their share of such items on their individual income tax returns, irrespective of whether they have actually received the items.

This aspect of a partnership is an advantage to the partners if the organization suffers a net loss. The pro rata share of this loss is allocated to each partner, and it can be used to reduce these partners' personal taxable income. However, by this same reasoning, a partnership is a disadvantage if the organization retains any profits made by the organization for the purpose of expansion. Suppose a partnership with three equal partners has $30,000 in net income. If the partnership keeps this money, there still is a constructive distribution of $10,000 to each partner for tax purposes. Assuming that these partners are in a 28 percent personal income tax bracket, they each would have to pay $2,800 in taxes even though they actually received nothing from the partnership.

> A partnership does not pay taxes; this may be a benefit or detriment to the partners depending on whether the organization makes or loses money and whether it distributes or retains any profits made.

concept >> *summary*

Advantages and Disadvantages of Partnerships

The basic law relating to partnerships is found in the Uniform Partnership Act., a state law that can exist in slightly different forms in different states. As articulated in the act, the partnership form of organization generally has the following advantages:

1. A partnership is easily formed because it is based on a contract among persons.
2. Costs of formation are not significant.
3. Partnerships are not a tax-paying entity.
4. Each partner has an equal voice in management, unless there is a contrary agreement.
5. A partnership may operate in more than one state without obtaining a license to do business.
6. Partnerships generally are subject to less regulation and less governmental supervision than are corporations.

Offsetting these advantages, the following aspects of partnerships have been called disadvantages:

1. For practical reasons, only a limited number of people can be partners.
2. A partnership is dissolved anytime a partner ceases to be a partner, regardless of whether the reason is withdrawal or death.
3. Each partner's liability is unlimited, contrasted with the limited liability of a corporate shareholder.
4. Partners are taxed on their share of the partnership's profits, whether the profits are distributed or not. In other words, partners often are required to pay income tax on money they do not receive.

9. CORPORATIONS

The third basic organizational form that might be used to operate a business is the corporation. A **corporation** is an artificial, intangible entity created under the authority of a state's law. A corporation is known as a **domestic corporation** in the state in which it is incorporated. In all other states, this corporation is called a **foreign corporation.** A corporation created under the authority of a foreign country may be called an **alien corporation,** though it is generally treated the same as a foreign corporation under the law. As a creature of state legislative bodies, the corporation is much more complex to create and to operate than other forms of businesses. These legal complexities associated with the corporation are presented in a way that parallels the preceding section so that comparisons with partnerships can be easily made.

Do check the website of your state's authority responsible for issuing corporate charters. In most states, this authority is under the secretary of state.

Creation   A corporation is created by a state issuing a **charter** upon the application of individuals known as **incorporators.** In comparison with partnerships, corporations are more costly to form. Among the costs of incorporation are filing fees, license fees, franchise taxes, attorneys' fees, and the cost of supplies, such as minute books, corporate seals, and stock certificates. In addition to these costs of creation, there also are annual costs in continuing a corporation's operation. These recurring expenses include annual reporting fees and taxes, the cost of annual shareholders' meetings, and ongoing legal-related expenses. Sidebar 14.4 describes the process of incorporation.

>> *sidebar* 14.4

Steps in Creation of a Corporation

The formal application for a corporate charter is called the **articles of incorporation.** These articles must contain the proposed name of the corporation. So that persons dealing with a business will know that it is a corporation, the law requires that the corporate name include one of the following words or end with an abbreviation of them: "corporation," "company," "incorporated," or "limited." In addition, a corporate name must not be the same as, or deceptively similar to, the name of any domestic corporation or that of a foreign corporation authorized to do business in the state to which the application is made. The corporate name is an asset and an aspect of goodwill. As such, it is legally protected.

In addition to the proposed corporate name, the articles of incorporation usually will include the proposed corporation's period of duration, the purpose for which it is formed, the number of authorized shares, and information about the initial corporate officials.

Once drafted, these papers are sent to the appropriate state official (usually the secretary of state), who approves them and issues a corporate charter. Notice of this incorporation usually has to be advertised in the local newspaper in order to inform the public that a new corporation has been created. The initial board of directors then meets, adopts the corporate bylaws, and approves the sale of stock. At this point, the corporation becomes operational.

If a corporation wishes to conduct business in states other than the state of incorporation, that corporation must be licensed in these foreign states. The process of qualification usually requires payment of license fees and franchise taxes above and beyond those paid during the initial incorporation process. If a corporation fails to qualify in states where it is conducting business, the corporation may be denied access to the courts as a means of enforcing its contracts.

The separation of the corporate organization's existence from its owners' willingness to remain associated with it is viewed as a major advantage to the corporation's stability.

Continuity   In contrast to a partnership, a corporation usually is formed to have perpetual existence. The law treats a corporation's existence as distinct from its owners' status as shareholders. Thus, a shareholder's death or sale of her or his stock does not affect the organizational structure of a corporation. This ability to separate management from ownership is an often cited advantage of the corporation.

Although the sale of stock by a major shareholder or the shareholder's death has no legal impact on the organization's existence, this event may have a very real adverse impact on that corporation's ability to do business. The shareholder may have been the driving force behind the corporation's success. Without this shareholder, the corporation's business may fail.

Managerial Control In the corporate form of organization, the issue of control is complicated by three groups. First, the **shareholders** elect the members of the board of directors. These **directors** set the objectives or goals of the corporation, and they appoint the officers. These **officers**, such as the president, vice president, secretary, and treasurer, are charged with managing the daily operations of the corporation in an attempt to achieve the stated organizational objectives or goals. Thus, which one of these three groups really controls the corporation?

To answer this question effectively, you must realize that the issue of who controls a corporation varies depending on the size of the ownership base of the organization. In essence, matters of managerial control require us to examine the publicly held corporation as distinct from the closely held corporation.

>> *sidebar* 14.5

Why Are So Many Companies Incorporated in Delaware?

If you look for the state of incorporation for a large company, there is a good chance that you will discover it is Delaware. In fact, by the state's own estimate, more than 50 percent of publicly traded companies and 63 percent of Fortune 500 companies are incorporated in Delaware. You may find this surprising considering the state's relatively small population and geographic size. There must be a reason that so many companies choose Delaware.

Several factors have been suggested to explain Delaware's success as an incorporating forum. One of the most frequently cited is the state's stable legal environment. This includes Delaware's respected judiciary, and in particular the Court of Chancery, which is highly experienced in deciding issues related to the state General Corporation Law. Additionally, the legislature is generally believed to be supportive of business interests. There is no income tax for businesses that do not operate in Delaware (though there is a franchise tax). And the state Division of Corporations makes the process of incorporation simple and efficient.

Sources: Delaware Division of Corporations, http://corp.delaware.gov/; Theodore Eisenberg & Geoffrey Miller, *Ex Ante Choices of Law and Forum: An Empirical Analysis of Corporate Merger Agreements*, 59 Vand. L. Rev. 1975 (2006).

Publicly Held Corporations In very large corporations, control by management (a combination of the directors and officers) is maintained with a very small percentage of stock ownership through the use of corporate records and funds to solicit proxies. Technically, a **proxy** is an agent appointed by a shareholder for the purpose of voting the shares. Management can, at corporate expense, solicit the right to vote the stock of shareholders unable to attend the meetings at which the directors of the company are elected. An outsider must either own sufficient stock to elect the directors or must solicit proxies at his or her own expense. The management of a large corporation usually can maintain control with only a small minority of actual stock ownership.

During the first years of this century, we have seen evidence of the negative aspects arising from a few shareholders, who also serve as officers and directors, controlling large, publicly held corporations. The lack of sufficient review and influence from those called "outside directors" contributed to corporate scandals that shocked the public confidence in business and the economy. You should appreciate that limiting the role of corporate governance to only a few people can lead to massive fraud. Despite legal requirements designed to increase the influence of corporate directors, all accounting records are not perfect.

Closely Held Corporations   Unlike the situation with a large, publicly held corporation, one shareholder (or at least a small group of shareholders) may be able to control a closely held corporation. This can result because this individual (or the group) can own an actual majority of the issued shares. This majority can control the election of a board of directors. In fact, the shareholders with the largest amount of stock are often elected to this board of directors. The directors, in turn, elect officers, who again may be the shareholders with the largest interests. In a very real sense, those who own a majority of a closely held corporation can rule with near-absolute authority.

What are the rights of those who do not possess control in a closely held corporation—the so-called minority interest? To a large degree, the owners of the minority interest are subject to the decisions of the majority. The majority may pay themselves salaries that use up profits and may never declare a dividend. However, the minority interest is not without some rights, because the directors and officers stand in a fiduciary relation to the corporation and to the minority shareholders if the corporation is closely held. This relation imposes a duty on directors to act for the best interests of the corporation rather than for themselves individually.

If the majority is acting illegally or oppresses the rights of the minority shareholders, a lawsuit known as a **derivative suit** may be brought by a minority shareholder on behalf of the corporation. Such suits may seek to enjoin the unlawful activity or to collect damages for the corporation. For example, contracts made between the corporation and an interested director or officer may be challenged. If a suit is brought, the burden is on the director or officer (who may be the majority shareholder) to prove good faith and inherent fairness in such transactions.

The basic difficulty of owning a minority interest in a closely held corporation arises from the fact that there is no ready market for the stock should the shareholder desire to dispose of it. Of course, if there is a valid buy and sell agreement, then there is a market for the stock. Thus, as with partnerships, buy and sell agreements are absolutely essential in closely held corporations.

Liability   The legal ability to separate a corporation's shareholders from its managers means that the owners are liable for the debts of the corporation only to the extent of those shareholders' investment in the cost of the stock. Thus, corporate shareholders are said to have **limited personal liability.**

The generalization that the investors in a corporation have limited liability but those in a partnership have unlimited liability is too broad and needs qualification. To be sure, someone investing in a company listed on the New York Stock Exchange will incur no risk greater than the investment, and the concept of limited liability certainly applies. However, if the company

Do realize that any minority ownership interest in a corporation provides you with very little influence.

Your status as a shareholder in a closely held corporation probably limits your liability for torts; you likely forgo your limited liability for contracts by cosigning your corporation's contracts.

is a small, closely held corporation with limited assets and capital, it will be difficult for it to obtain credit on the strength of its own net worth. As a practical matter, shareholders will usually be required to add their own individual liability as security for borrowing. For example, if the XYZ Company seeks a loan at a local bank, the bank often will require the owners, X, Y, and Z, to personally guarantee repayment of the loan.

This is not to say that shareholders in closely held corporations do not have some degree of limited liability. Shareholders have limited liability for contractlike obligations that are imposed as a matter of law (such as taxes). Liability also is limited when the corporate obligation results from torts committed by company employees while doing company business.

Even in these situations, the mere fact of corporate existence does not guarantee the shareholders will have liability limited to their investment. When courts find that the corporate organization is being misused, the corporate entity can be disregarded. This has been called **piercing the corporate veil.** When this veil of protection has been pierced, the shareholders are treated like partners who have unlimited liability for their organization's debts.

The **alter-ego theory,** by which the corporate veil can be pierced, may also be used to impose personal liability upon corporate officers, directors, and stockholders. If the corporate entity is disregarded by these officials themselves, so that there is such a unity of ownership and interest that separateness of the corporation has ceased to exist, the alter-ego theory will be followed and the corporate veil will be pierced.

Simply alleging that a person is the sole owner of a corporation engaged in wrongful activity will not result in a piercing of the corporate veil. This conclusion is appropriate when the owner has respect for the existence of the organization. In Case 14.1, note the number of factors that must be considered before the corporate veil is pierced.

> The phrases *limited liability* and *unlimited liability* are overly simplistic; an understanding of a business owner's liability goes beyond these simple terms.

 case 14.1 >>

ALLI, v. U.S.
83 Fed. Cl. 250 (2008)

This case involves Dr. Alli and his spouse, property owners who sued the U.S. Department of Housing and Urban Development (HUD) for failure to pay housing assistance for residents of three apartment complexes. The owners held the apartment complexes through a business organization called BSA Corporation. HUD counterclaimed that the Allis breached the agreement for housing assistance due to multiple health and safety violations. Moreover, HUD argued that the Allis were personally liable for the violations, which compelled HUD to pay for relocation of the affected residents.

Among other issues, the court was required to determine whether to strip away the liability protection of the Allis' corporation and "pierce the corporate
veil." The court investigated the extent to which the corporate form was merely used as a shield for illegal activity.

ALLEGRA, J.: The three housing properties at issue were acquired by one or more of plaintiffs in the 1980s with varying degrees of assistance from HUD. In 1983, the Allis, doing business as BSA Associates, acquired the Pingree/Gladstone property (Pingree) through a HUD auction and with financing provided by a HUD mortgage. In 1989, Dr. Alli, doing business as BSA Associates, acquired the Riverside property (Riverside) in like fashion and with similar HUD financing. That same year, BSA Corp. (with Dr. Alli as

[continued]

signatory) acquired the Collingwood/Kirkwood property (Collingwood), again with financing through a HUD mortgage. Each of these properties participated in the Section 8 housing program. . . .

In its counterclaims, defendant [HUD] has asserted three breach of contract claims—one each for Pingree, Riverside, and Collingwood—attributable to plaintiffs' failure to maintain the property in good repair and condition so as to provide decent, safe and sanitary housing. For Pingree and Riverside, defendant seeks $110,096.45 and $79,675, respectively—its cost of relocating families from the properties to safe housing. For Collingwood, defendant seeks $90,646.40 for the cost of moving families to safe housing, $18,128.80 for foreclosures costs, and $1,112,173.45 for the cost to HUD of providing basic services, security, and repairs while acting as mortgagee-in-possession of Collingwood.

Defendant must carry the burden of proof on its counterclaims. . . . Based on the record, the court finds that defendant has done so, demonstrating that plaintiffs breached the HAP contracts in failing to maintain the properties in a safe, decent and sanitary state. . . .

The next question is who is liable for the damages caused by these breaches. Defendant asserts that the Allis should be jointly and severally liable for these damages. As to Collingwood, that means that the court must decide whether the corporate veil of BSA Corp. should be disregarded and liability imposed directly upon Dr. Alli and his wife. "The concept of 'piercing the corporate veil' is equitable in nature," the Federal Circuit has stated, and "courts will pierce the corporate veil 'to achieve justice, equity, to remedy or avoid fraud or wrongdoing, or to impose a just liability.' . . . Because BSA Corp. was incorporated under the laws of Michigan, the court applies that law in deciding whether the corporate veil should be pierced.

. . . Michigan courts often have employed the following tripartite formula:

First, the corporate entity must be a mere instrumentality of another entity or individual. Second, the corporate entity must be used to commit a fraud or wrong. Third, there must have been an unjust loss or injury to the [party seeking to pierce the veil].

. . . In considering the first of these prongs—whether the corporation is a mere instrumentality—courts have examined *inter alia* the adequacy of the corporation's capitalization, the commingling of funds, the diversion of corporate assets for personal use, a failure to comply with the formalities of corporate organization, and domination and control over the corporation by another person or entity. . . .

In general, then, under Michigan law, when the notion of a corporation as a legal entity is used to defeat public convenience, justify a wrong, protect fraud or defend a crime, that notion may be set aside and the corporation treated as being one with its shareholders. . . . As the Sixth Circuit once commented:

Michigan appears to follow the general rule that requires demonstration of patent abuse of the corporate form in order to pierce the corporate veil. There must be such a unity of interest and ownership that the separate personalities of the corporation and its owner cease to exist, and the circumstances must be such that adherence to the fiction of separate corporate existence would sanction a fraud or promote an injustice.

United States v. Cordova Chem. Co., 113 F.3d 572, 580 (6th Cir. 1997) (en banc), *vacated on other grounds, sub nom., United States v. Bestfoods,* 524 U.S. 51, 118 S. Ct. 1876, 141 L. Ed. 2d 43 (1998) . . . Other cases emphasize that while there must be some misuse of the corporate form to trigger piercing, that misuse need not necessarily constitute fraud. . . .

In the case *sub judice,* the Allis were the sole owners of BSA Corp., which they purportedly hired to manage their properties and which purportedly owned Collingwood. Every indication is that this corporation was a mere instrumentality that the Allis relied upon when it served their purposes and ignored when it did not. They commingled their funds with those of the corporation—indeed, at trial and in his earlier deposition, Dr. Alli admitted that he and his wife provided interest-free loans to BSA Corp. and, at other times, deposited their personal funds into accounts supposedly controlled by the corporation. The Allis certainly treated the assets of the corporation as if their own—on June 30, 1992, for example, they entered into a deed of trust, as individuals, that encumbered the Collingwood property in exchange for two loans of $250,000 and $75,000, respectively. They provided no evidence to indicate that the proceeds from these loans were used to maintain or improve Collingwood—in fact, BSA Corp. never requested HUD's approval of the loans, as would have been required under the Collingwood regulatory agreement. Periodically, thereafter, the Allis took funds from the Collingwood project account to make payment on these loans and to pay for personal expenses. Accordingly, there is clear proof that BSA Corp. was a merely instrumentality here, disregarded when it served the Allis' purposes, thereby satisfying one of the requirements for piercing the corporate veil. . . .

The other requirements under Michigan law for piercing the corporate veil are satisfied here, as well. First, BSA Corp. certainly was wielded by the Allis to

[continued]

commit a wrong—the failure to maintain the buildings in question in safe, decent and sanitary condition, consistent with BSA Corp.'s contractual obligations. And this entire opinion is a testament to magnitude and seriousness of this wrong. Second, every indication is that the failure to pierce the veil of this thinly-capitalized corporation would lead the United States to suffer an unjust loss. Defendant is seeking well in excess of $1 million in its counterclaims, insofar as it relates to Collingwood, with the majority of those costs associated with HUD's taking over as mortgagee-in-possession. The record suggests that BSA Corp. lacks the funds to pay a judgment of even a fraction of that magnitude. Accordingly, the court concludes that the circumstances here are appropriate for allowing defendant to pierce the corporate veil and hold Dr. Alli and his wife personally liable for any damages arising under the Collingwood counterclaim. . . .

Picture again these unpleasant images. A bathroom with an umbrella hanging upside-down to catch water leaking through a gaping hole in the ceiling. Other erstwhile bathrooms with exposed and deteriorating floor boards; buckled, molded and mildewed tiling, some with empty holes where plumbing once existed. Kitchens with broken and missing counters, cabinetry with no doors (some dangling from the walls), roach-infested and rusted refrigerators, and other nonfunctional appliances. Plastered walls and tiled ceilings in dimly-lit hallways, so dilapidated, water-damaged and partially-collapsed as to appear cave-like. Outside doors left off their hinges, cracked masonry, and roofs and flashing no longer impermeable, all exposing residents to the elements. A basement filled with feces and vermin, the latter an army so plentiful that those who enter unprotected immediately become infested. And, at least on one January day, elderly and little children huddled in coats and blankets around open ovens trying to keep warm in sub-freezing temperatures. Scenes from a dystopian novel about a post apocalyptic world? No, we now know that these graphic pictures are of the dwellings at issue in this case.

Even these soul-chilling images cannot quite capture the pernicious conditions and degradation reflected by the record—predicaments and experiences that, nonetheless, formed the essence of the everyday existence of the tenants who lived in the affected properties. Faced with overwhelming evidence, the court is convinced that plaintiffs failed to comply with their solemn contractual obligations to maintain and operate the properties in question so as to provide decent, safe and sanitary housing—and that HUD was correct in finally calling them to task.

As such, the court finds that plaintiffs have not met their burden of proof in establishing that defendant breached the HAP contracts and regulatory agreements at issue. On its counterclaim, defendant has borne its burden of establishing that plaintiffs breached the very same agreements. Defendant also has demonstrated that the corporate veil of BSA Corp. should be pierced and that Dr. Alli and his wife, therefore, should be liable for any damages owed with respect to the Collingwood property. . . .

>> CASE QUESTIONS

1. On what basis were Dr. Alli and his wife claiming they were not personally liable for the conditions in the apartment complexes that lead to the HUD expenditures?
2. What wrong did HUD suggest the corporate form was being used to commit? Why is this element important?
3. What conduct led the court to conclude that piercing the corporate veil was appropriate?

Taxation   Corporations must pay income taxes on their earnings. Sidebar 14.6 on the next page sets forth these tax rates. The fact that there is a separate corporate income tax may work as an advantage. For example, if the corporation makes a profit that is to be retained by the corporation to support growth, no income is allocated to the shareholders. These shareholders will not have their personal taxable income increased, as would a partner in a similar situation. In addition, the corporate rate may be lower than the individual rates.

>> *sidebar* 14.6

Corporate Tax Rates*

>> INCOME	>> TAX RATE
$0–$50,000	15%
$50,000–$75,000	25%
$75,000–$10,000,000	34%
over $10,000,000	35%

*In addition to these rates, there are excess taxes when corporate taxable income exceeds $100,000. These taxes increase again if corporate taxable income exceeds $15,000,000.
Source: 26 U.S.C. §11.

"The United States may soon wind up with a distinction that makes business leaders cringe—the highest corporate tax rate in the world. . . . But by taking advantage of myriad breaks and loopholes that other countries generally do not offer, United States corporations pay only slightly more on average than their counterparts in other industrial countries."

David Kocieniewski,
The New York Times,
May 2011

Ways corporate shareholders might avoid paying two taxes on the business's income and dividend payments:
Reasonable salaries.
Reasonable expense accounts.
Reasonable loans from shareholders.
Reasonable accumulation of earnings. Subchapter S election.

But corporations also have tax disadvantages. Suppose a corporation suffers a loss during a given tax year. The existence of the corporate tax works as a disadvantage, since this loss cannot be distributed to the shareholders in order to reduce their personal tax liability. Indeed, a net operating loss (NOL) to a corporation can be used only to offset corporate income earned in other years. And the allocation of such a loss can be carried back only for two years and carried forward for 20 years. Under the American Recovery and Reinvestment Act of 2009, small businesses can take advantage of additional years to carry back losses. (*Note:* There are many different rules concerning specialized carryover situations. The Internal Revenue Code should be examined prior to relying on the general rule just stated.)

Perhaps a greater disadvantage of the corporate tax occurs when a profit is made and the corporation wishes to pay a dividend to its shareholders. The money used to pay this dividend will have been taxed at the corporate level. It is then taxed again because the shareholder must take the amount of the dividend into his or her own personal income. Although the rate of this second tax is reduced to 15 percent, as a part of a 2003 tax reduction, the existence of the second tax is potentially significant in selecting the best organizational form for a business. This situation has been called the **double tax** on corporate income. A similar situation of double taxation occurs when a corporation is dissolved and its assets are distributed to shareholders as capital gains. Yet, as the discussion next indicates, the double tax may not be as big a disadvantage as it appears at first.

Avoiding Double Taxation   Corporations have employed a variety of techniques for avoiding the double taxation of corporate income. First, reasonable salaries paid to corporate officials may be deducted in computing the taxable income of the business. Thus, in a closely held corporation in which all or most shareholders are officers or employees, this technique may avoid double taxation of substantial portions of income. As might be expected, the Internal Revenue Code disallows a deduction for excessive or unreasonable compensation and treats such payments as dividends. Therefore, the determination of the reasonableness of corporate salaries is often a tax problem in that form of organization.

Second, corporations provide expense accounts for many employees, including shareholder employees. These are used to purchase travel, food, and entertainment. When so used, the employee, to some extent, has compensation that is not taxed. In an attempt to close this tax loophole, the law limits deductions for business meals and entertainment to 50 percent of the cost. Meal expenses and entertainment are deductible only if the expenses are directly related to or associated with the active conduct of a trade or business. For a deduction, business must be discussed directly before, during, or directly after the meal. Additionally, meal expenses are not deductible to the extent the meal is lavish or extravagant. Thus, the use of the expense account to avoid taxation of corporate income is subject to numerous technical rules and limitations.

Third, the capital structure of the corporation may include both common stock and interest-bearing loans from shareholders. For example, assume that a company needs $100,000 cash to go into business. If $100,000 of stock is issued, no expense will be deducted. However, assume that $50,000 worth of stock is purchased by the owners and $50,000 is lent to the company by them at 10 percent interest. In this case, $5,000 interest each year is deductible as an expense of the company and thus subject to only one tax as interest income to the owners. Just as in the case of salaries, the Internal Revenue Code has a counteracting rule relating to corporations that are undercapitalized. If the corporation is undercapitalized, interest payments will be treated as dividends and disallowed as deductible expenses.

The fourth technique for avoiding double taxation, at least in part, is simply not to pay dividends and to accumulate the earnings. The Internal Revenue Service seeks to compel corporations to distribute those profits not needed for a business purpose, such as growth. When a corporation retains earnings in excess of $250,000, there is a presumption that these earnings are being accumulated to avoid a second tax on dividends. If the corporations cannot rebut this presumption, an additional tax is imposed.

Fifth, a corporation may elect to file under Subchapter S of the Internal Revenue Code. This election eliminates the corporate tax; this subject is discussed further in Section 11 of this chapter.

concept >> *summary*

Advantages and Disadvantages of Corporations

The usual advantages of the corporate form of organization include the following:

1. This form is the best practical means of bringing together a large number of investors.
2. Control may be held by those with a minority of the investment.
3. Ownership may be divided into many unequal shares.
4. Shareholders' liabilities are limited to their investments.
5. The organization can have perpetual existence.
6. In addition to being owners, shareholders may be employees entitled to benefits such as workers' compensation.

Among the frequently cited disadvantages of the corporate organization are the following:

1. The cost of forming and maintaining a corporation, with its formal procedural requirements, is significant.
2. License fees and franchise taxes often are assessed against corporations but not partnerships.
3. A corporation must be qualified in all states where it is conducting local or intrastate business.
4. Generally, corporations are subject to more governmental regulation at all levels than are other forms of business.
5. Corporate income may be subject to double taxation.

10. LIMITED PARTNERSHIPS

A limited partnership basically has all the attributes of a partnership except that one or more of the partners are designated as **limited partners.** This type of partner is not personally responsible for the debts of the business organization. However, these limited partners are not permitted to be involved in the control or operations of the limited partnership. The management is left in the hands of one or more **general partners** who remain personally liable for the organization's debts.

The attributes of a general partnership and a corporation that combine to make the limited partnership an attractive alternative form of business organization are discussed under the subheadings that follow.

Creation   Like a general partnership, a limited partnership is created by agreement. However, as in the case of a corporation, state law requires that the contents of a certificate must be recorded in a public office so that everyone may be fully advised as to the details of the organization. This certificate contains, among other matters, the following information: the name of the partnership, the character of the business, its location, the name and place of residence of each member, those who are to be the general partners and those who are to be the limited partners, the length of time the partnership is to exist, the amount of cash or the agreed value of property to be contributed by each partner, and the share of profit or compensation each limited partner shall receive.

The limited partnership certificate is required to be recorded in the county where the partnership has its principal place of business. An additional copy has to be filed in every community where the partnership conducts business or has an office. Whenever there is a change in the information contained in the filed certificate, a new certificate must be prepared and recorded. If an accurate certificate is not on record and the limited partnership continues its operation, the limited partners become liable as general partners. Substantial compliance with all the technical requirements of the limited partnership law is essential if the limited partners are to be assured of their limited liability.

The terms of the limited partnership agreement control the governance of the organization. These terms should be read carefully and understood by all general and limited partners before the agreement is signed. Failure of the parties to state their agreement clearly may result in a court's interpreting the limited partnership agreement.

> Limited partnerships are complex organizations that have been used to raise money for real estate investments and management of complex entities, such as professional sports teams.

Continuity   The principles guiding partnerships also apply to limited partnerships if there is a change in the general partners. A limited partner may assign his or her interest to another without dissolving the limited partnership.

Managerial Control   In a limited partnership, the general partners are in control. Limited partners have no right to participate in management. The impact of this relationship on the operations of a limited partnership is discussed in detail in the next subsection.

Liability   The true nature of the limited partnership being a hybrid is in the area of owners' liability. Traditionally, the general partners in a limited partnership have unlimited liability. However, the limited partners are not personally liable for the partnership's debts. These limited partners' liability typically will not exceed the amount of their investments.

Under the Revised Uniform Limited Partnership Act (RULPA), a limited partner's surname may not be used in the partnership's name unless there is a general partner with the same name. If a limited partner's name is used in the firm's name, that partner will become personally liable to unsuspecting creditors.

Limited partners also may not participate in the management of the limited partnership. Under the RULPA, a limited partner who participates in the organization's management becomes liable as a general partner if a third party had knowledge of the limited partner's activities. Sidebar 14.7 lists actions by a limited partner that are not considered participation in management.

>> sidebar 14.7

Actions by Limited Partner

Limited partners do not lose the benefit of limited personal liability when performing the following:

- Acting as an agent or employee of the partnership.
- Consulting with or advising a general partner.
- Acting as a guarantor of the partnership's obligations.
- Inspecting and copying any of the partnership's financial records.
- Demanding true and full information about the partnership whenever circumstances render it just and reasonable.

- Receiving a share of the profits or other compensation by way of income.
- Approving or disapproving an amendment to the partnership's certificate.
- Voting on matters of fundamental importance such as dissolution, sale of assets, or change of the partnership's name.
- Having contribution returned upon dissolution.

---

11. S CORPORATIONS

Beginning in 1958, the federal government permitted shareholders of certain corporations to unanimously elect to have their organization treated like a partnership for income tax purposes. This election is made possible through the language of subchapter S of the Internal Revenue Code. Today, organizations that are subject to this election often are referred to simply as **S corporations.**

The S corporation has all the legal characteristics of the corporation previously discussed in this chapter. The one exception to this similar treatment is that shareholders in the S corporation are responsible for accounting on their individual income tax returns for their respective shares of their organization's profits or losses. In essence, these shareholders can elect to have their business organization treated, for tax purposes, as if it were a partnership. Through this election, the shareholders avoid having a tax assessed on the corporate income itself. Even though the S corporation does not pay any taxes, like a partnership, it must file an information return with the Internal Revenue Service.

S corporations cannot have more than 100 shareholders, each of whom must elect to have the corporate income allocated to the shareholders annually in computing their income for tax purposes, whether actually paid out or not. Only individuals are eligible to elect under subchapter S. Therefore, other forms of business organization, such as partnerships, limited partnerships, or corporations, cannot be shareholders in an S corporation.

Do remember the limitation on the number of shareholders in an S corporation reduces it as an option for many business ventures.

In addition to the limitations just stated, there are many technical rules of tax law involved in S corporations. However, as a rule of thumb, this method of organization has distinct advantages for a business operating at a loss because the loss is shared and immediately deductible on the returns of the shareholders. It is also advantageous for businesses capable of paying out net profits as earned. In the latter case, the corporate tax is avoided. If net profits must be retained in the business, subchapter S tax treatment is disadvantageous because income tax is paid on earnings not received, and there is a danger of double taxation to the individual because undistributed earnings that have been taxed once are taxed again in the event of the death of a shareholder. Thus, the theoretical advantage of using an S corporation to avoid double taxation of corporate income must be carefully qualified.

>> *sidebar* 14.8

Nonprofit Corporations

Depending on the purpose of your organization, you may find that creating a nonprofit corporation instead of one of the above forms is a better choice. A nonprofit corporation must file articles of incorporation with the state, it is run by a board of directors and has limited liability, just like a traditional corporation. However, a nonprofit does not return a profit to its owners. Rather, it must return any profits made to the organization to be used for future operations. Importantly, a nonprofit can have paid employees, the payment to whom is considered an expense. Many different types of businesses are run as nonprofits, including charities, religious organizations, museums, and even universities.

One critical attribute for many nonprofits is tax-exempt status. In addition to eliminating tax liability, such status permits donors to deduct contributions from their taxes. The U.S. Internal Revenue Service must approve exempt status, and many nonprofits file under section 501(c)(3) of the IRS code. Similar filings must be made with the relevant state. Yearly filings to the IRS are required, and organizations that do not comply or meet the exemption requirements may have their status revoked. In 2011, the IRS announced that it was revoking the tax-exempt status of 275,000 nonprofits, shrinking the sector by 17 percent. This action demonstrates the diligence that is required if a corporation is to effectively operate as a nonprofit.

Sources: National Council of Nonprofits, www.councilofnonprofits.org; IRS, Tax Information for Charitable Organizations, www.irs.gov/charities/charitable/; Stephanie Strom, "I.R.S. Ends Exemptions for 275,000 Nonprofits," *The New York Times*, June 8, 2011.

---

12. LIMITED LIABILITY ORGANIZATIONS

The **limited liability company** is a relatively new organizational alternative. In 1977, Wyoming was the first state to pass a law permitting the creation of this type of business organization.

Over the last two decades, the growth of LLPs and LLCs has made these organizational forms very popular for closely held businesses.

In 1988, the Internal Revenue Service ruled that limited liability companies (LLCs) would be treated as nontaxable entities, much like partnerships, for federal income tax purposes. Following this ruling, states rushed to pass legislation authorizing businesspeople to operate their businesses as LLCs. In essence, its owners have more flexibility than with the S corporation while not having to struggle with the complexities of the limited partnership.

A variation of the LLC is known as the **limited liability partnership.** This organization often is used by professionals, such as doctors, lawyers, and accountants. In the true sense of a hybrid, an LLC and an LLP have characteristics of both a partnership and a corporation.

The growing popularity of these forms of business organizations requires a careful examination of various factors. The focus of the following subheadings is on the LLC.

Creation   An LLC is created through filings much like those used when creating a corporation. **Articles of organization** are filed with a state official, usually the secretary of state. Instead of "incorporators," the term **organizers** is used. The name of any LLC must acknowledge the special nature of this organizational form by including the phrase "limited liability company," or "limited company," or some abbreviation, such as "LLC" or "LC." An LLC created in a state other than the one in which it is conducting business is called a foreign LLC. Like a foreign corporation, this LLC must apply to the state to be authorized to transact business legally. An LLC also must file annual reports with the states in which it operates.

Continuity   The owners of LLCs are called **members** rather than shareholders or partners. Membership in LLCs is not limited to individuals. Unlike in the S corporation, a business organization can be an owner in any LLC. The transferability of a member's interest is restricted in the fashion of a partner as opposed to the free transferability of a corporate shareholder. Anytime a member dies or withdraws from the LLC, there is a dissolution of the business organization. However, the business of a dissolved LLC is not necessarily adversely impacted if the remaining members decide to continue business. Either as provided in the articles of organization or by agreement of the remaining members within 90 days of the withdrawing member's disassociation, the business of the LLC may be continued rather than wound up.

Managerial Control   The managerial control of an LLC is vested in its members, unless the articles of organization provide for one or more **managers.** Regardless of whether members or managers control the LLC, a majority of these decision makers decide the direction of the organization. In a few situations enumerated in the state law authorizing LLCs, unanimous consent of the members is required for the organization to make a binding decision. Similarly to partners in a partnership, members of LLCs make contributions of capital. They have equal rights to share in the LLC's profits and losses, unless these members have agreed otherwise. When a member is in the minority with respect to decisions being made on behalf of the LLC, that dissenting member may have rights very much like a dissenting shareholder in a corporation. These rights include bringing a derivative lawsuit against the controlling members of the LLC. Ultimately, a dissenting member has the right to sell the membership interest to the other members of the LLC.

>> *sidebar* 14.9

Fiduciary Duties in LLCs

It is a standard proposition that corporate officers and directors owe fiduciary duties of care and loyalty to shareholders. Do managers of limited liability companies owe similar duties to members? Surprisingly, this is an area of law that is still being developed. Some states treat LLC fiduciary duties similar to those owed in corporations, while others apply the rules for partnership. Fiduciary duties are clearly spelled out in some state statutes, while others are silent. In some cases, different duties are triggered in a "manager managed" LLC versus one that is "member managed." Delaware provides an especially strong mechanism for limiting fiduciary duties by permitting their contractual elimination in the LLC agreement. Courts are still working out what the above statutory language means in the context of this relatively new form of business organization. It is an important issue. In deciding what state is best for LLC organization and what language to include in the agreement, the desired nature of fiduciary duties should be considered.

Source: Sandra K. Miller, *What Fiduciary Duties Should Apply to the LLC Manager After More Than a Decade of Experimentation?* 32 J. Corp. L. 565 (2007).

Liability   For liability purposes, members do act as agents of their LLC. However, they are not personally liable to third parties. Thus, these members have attributes of both partners and shareholders with respect to liability.

Taxation   Finally, state laws and the IRS recognize LLCs as nontaxable entities. Although the LLC appears to have many advantages, do not forget that careful analysis is needed in every situation to determine whether this type of tax treatment is in the members' best interests.

LO 14-4   >> Operating the Organization

With an understanding of the various organizational forms and the factors businesspeople need to consider when deciding how to do business, we are ready to focus on making the decision as to which form of organization is most appropriate for conducting business. Following the next section, this chapter concludes with some thoughts on trends in operating business organizations.

13. MAKING THE DECISION

Don't assume there is an easy answer to which organizational form is best; careful analysis and consultation with experts help businesspeople make wise decisions in the selection process.

There usually is no absolutely right answer to the question, Which organizational form is best for a particular business's operation? Hopefully the preceding sections have presented you with some helpful background material to consider when this important decision is made.

The criteria used to select a form of organization needs to be reviewed periodically. This review should be done in consultation with close advisers such as attorneys, accountants, bankers, and insurers. These people weigh the factors and costs involved and then select the most suitable organizational form for the business's needs at that time. Because this selection process balances advantages against disadvantages, the decision often is to choose the least objectionable form of organization.

Today, the growth in limited liability partnerships and limited liability companies could lead you to think these are the best options for your business activities. While one of these forms may be best, a careful analysis will consider the various factors discussed in this chapter.

It is not unusual for the growth in a business to be reflected in changes in organizational forms as a part of a life cycle. For example, business activity could begin through the efforts of a sole proprietor. As the business grows and investors join the business, the organizational form could shift to a partnership or limited partnership (depending on the active or passive nature of the investor). An alternative to the partnership or limited partnership could be a limited liability organization. As the business matures and prepares to conduct a public offering of its stock, the corporate form becomes the most feasible organization.

14. TRENDS IN MANAGING THE ORGANIZATION

In the wake of the recent financial crises, a great deal of public attention has focused on the management of publicly held corporations. In the next chapter, you will study the Dodd-Frank Wall Street Reform and Consumer Protection Act (Dodd-Frank Act), which includes corporate governance reform among its many provisions. Subsequent chapters address other legal issues important to governance, such as competition laws and securities and financial regulations. Since control of business organizations is a major topic in this chapter, three important trends merit consideration here.

A first significant trend in corporate governance relates to shareholders becoming increasingly active. For example, shareholders have asked for more say in the level of executive compensation. There is concern that such compensation is excessive in some cases and insufficiently scrutinized by the board of directors. The recent Dodd-Frank Act seeks to provide shareholders with the ability for greater oversight or "**say-on-pay**" by requiring periodic, nonbinding shareholder votes on compensation. Another issue for shareholders has been the difficulty in influencing the composition of the board of directors. The Dodd-Frank Act addresses this issue as well by mandating rules that permit shareholders to include their own board candidates in proxy materials. In addition, fewer firms have staggered terms of service for their boards of directors, which increases the ability of shareholders to reform leadership. One may conclude that, in the current business environment, corporate boards are now more likely to engage shareholders in governance decisions.

A second trend is the continued definition of the nature of corporate personhood. As described above, corporations are considered legal persons under the law. They undertake activities like individuals, such as buying and selling property. In addition, corporations incur liability for their actions, such as manufacturing defective products. Thus, in many cases, corporations and individuals reasonably have an equal claim to rights and protections under the law. For example, in *Citizens United v. Federal Election Commission,* 130 S. Ct. 876 (2010), the Supreme Court affirmed a corporation's speech protections under the Constitution's First Amendment by striking down a federal law that limited spending on political advertising. On the other hand, a federal circuit court in *Kiobel v. Royal Dutch Petroleum Co.,* 621 F.3d 111 (2d Cir. 2010), recently determined that corporations are not subject to the same liability as individuals for violations of international law under the Alien Tort Statute.

> "Congress gave shareholders a new 'say on pay' over executive compensation. And the returns are in: At 98.5% of companies, the answer was yes."
>
> **Jessica Holzer,**
> ***The Wall Street Journal,* July 8, 2011.**

To be sure, it is not always obvious when corporations should be treated identically to individuals. Recently, as detailed in Case 14.2 below, the U.S. Supreme Court addressed the question of whether corporations possess personal privacy rights as defined by the federal Freedom of Information Act.

case 14.2 >>

FEDERAL COMMUNICATIONS COMMISSION v. AT&T INC.
131 S. Ct. 1177 (2011)

AT&T voluntarily disclosed to the Federal Communications Commission (FCC) that it might have overcharged the government for telecommunications and information services related to a program designed to enhance access to schools and libraries. The FCC investigated, and AT&T provided various documents in response. AT&T eventually agreed to pay the government $500,000 to settle the case.

When a trade association representing some of AT&T's competitors requested the company's documents through a Freedom of Information Act (FOIA) request, AT&T objected on the basis that it would constitute a violation of personal privacy. However, the FOIA's "personal privacy" exemption to making records public had never been applied to corporations. Although corporations are considered legal persons, it was not clear under the statute that the broad legal definition of "person" applied here. Thus, the Court was required to determine when corporate "persons" have "personal privacy" rights protected by the FOIA.

ROBERTS, C.J.: The Freedom of Information Act requires federal agencies to make records and documents publicly available upon request, unless they fall within one of several statutory exemptions. One of those exemptions covers law enforcement records, the disclosure of which "could reasonably be expected to constitute an unwarranted invasion of personal privacy." . . . The question presented is whether corporations have "personal privacy" for the purposes of this exemption. . . .

AT&T relies on the argument that the word "personal" in [the FOIA exemption] incorporates the statutory definition of the word "person." . . . The Administrative Procedure Act defines "person" to include "an individual, partnership, corporation, association, or public or private organization other than an

agency." . . . Because that definition applies here, the argument goes, "personal" must mean relating to those "person[s]": namely, corporations and other entities as well as individuals. This reading, we are told, is dictated by a "basic principle of grammar and usage." . . .

We disagree. Adjectives typically reflect the meaning of corresponding nouns, but not always. Sometimes they acquire distinct meanings of their own. The noun "crab" refers variously to a crustacean and a type of apple, while the related adjective "crabbed" can refer to handwriting that is "difficult to read,"; . . . "corny" can mean "using familiar and stereotyped formulas believed to appeal to the unsophisticated," . . . which has little to do with "corn," . . .; and while "crank" is "a part of an axis bent at right angles," "cranky" can mean "given to fretful fussiness,". . . .

Even in cases such as these there may well be a link between the noun and the adjective. "Cranky" describes a person with a "wayward" or "capricious" temper . . . which might bear some relation to the distorted or crooked angular shape from which a "crank" takes its name. That is not the point. What is significant is that, in ordinary usage, a noun and its adjective form may have meanings as disparate as any two unrelated words. The FCC's argument that "personal" does not, in fact, derive from the English word "person," but instead developed along its own etymological path . . . simply highlights the shortcomings of AT&T's proposed rule.

"Person" is a defined term in the statute; "personal" is not. When a statute does not define a term, we typically "give the phrase its ordinary meaning." . . . "Personal" ordinarily refers to individuals. We do not usually speak of personal characteristics, personal effects, personal correspondence, personal influence, or personal tragedy as referring to corporations or other artificial entities. This is not to say that corporations do

[continued]

not have correspondence, influence, or tragedies of their own, only that we do not use the word "personal" to describe them.

Certainly, if the chief executive officer of a corporation approached the chief financial officer and said, "I have something personal to tell you," we would not assume the CEO was about to discuss company business. Responding to a request for information, an individual might say, "that's personal." A company spokesman, when asked for information about the company, would not. In fact, we often use the word "personal" to mean precisely the *opposite* of business-related: We speak of personal expenses and business expenses, personal life and work life, personal opinion and a company's view. . .

AT&T dismisses these definitions, correctly noting that "personal"—at its most basic level—simply means "[o]f or pertaining to a particular person.". . . The company acknowledges that "in non-legal usage, where a 'person' is a human being, it is entirely unsurprising that the word 'personal' is used to refer to human beings.". . . But in a watered-down version of the "grammatical imperative" argument, AT&T contends that "person"—in common *legal* usage—is understood to include a corporation. "Personal" in the same context therefore can and should have the same scope, especially here in light of the statutory definition. . . .

The construction of statutory language often turns on context, . . . which certainly may include the definitions of related words. But here the context to which AT&T points does not dissuade us from the ordinary meaning of "personal." We have no doubt that "person," in a legal setting, often refers to artificial entities. The Dictionary Act makes that clear . . . But AT&T's effort to ascribe a corresponding legal meaning to "personal" again elides the difference between "person" and "personal." . . .

Regardless of whether "personal" can carry a special meaning in legal usage, [HN7] "when interpreting a statute . . . we construe language . . . in light of the terms surrounding it." . . .

AT&T's argument treats the term "personal privacy" as simply the sum of its two words: the privacy of a person. Under that view, the defined meaning of the noun "person," or the asserted specialized legal meaning, takes on greater significance. But two words together may assume a more particular meaning than those words in isolation. We understand a golden cup to be a cup made of or resembling gold. A golden boy, on the other hand, is one who is charming, lucky, and talented. A golden opportunity is one not to be missed. "Personal" in the phrase "personal privacy" conveys more than just "of a person." It suggests a type of privacy evocative of human concerns—not the sort usually associated with an entity like, say, AT&T. . . .

AT&T contends that this Court has recognized "privacy" interests of corporations in the Fourth Amendment and double jeopardy contexts, and that the term should be similarly construed here. . . . But this case does not call upon us to pass on the scope of a corporation's "privacy" interests as a matter of constitutional or common law. The discrete question before us is instead whether Congress used the term "personal privacy" to refer to the privacy of artificial persons in FOIA Exemption 7(C); the cases AT&T cites are too far afield to be of help here.

. . . AT&T has given us no sound reason in the statutory text or context to disregard the ordinary meaning of the phrase "personal privacy." . . .

We reject the argument that because "person" is defined for purposes of FOIA to include a corporation, the phrase "personal privacy" in Exemption 7(C) reaches corporations as well. The protection in FOIA against disclosure of law enforcement information on the ground that it would constitute an unwarranted invasion of personal privacy does not extend to corporations. We trust that AT&T will not take it personally.

>> CASE QUESTIONS

1. Why did AT&T believe that it had rights of personal privacy under FOIA?
2. How did the Court interpret the phrase "personal privacy?" What sources and rules did it apply?
3. Does the Court's decision mean that corporations are no longer "legal persons"?
4. Does the Court's decision mean that corporations have no privacy or secrecy rights?

A third trend is the increased focus on legal liability for directors and officers. Although officers and directors are liable for their own intentional criminal and tortious acts, they have traditionally faced little personal risk for harms committed by the company.[1] The business judgment rule provides protection from liability to shareholders for business decisions, and corporations are generally obligated to indemnify directors and officers for third-party harm resulting from company business. In addition, it is common for corporations to purchase director and officer (D&O) insurance policies that provide expanded coverage for the actions of corporate leadership.

However, the recent financial crisis and other incidents of corporate malfeasance have created more support for increased director and officer accountability. Sidebar 14.10 addresses some specific developments in this regard.

>> *sidebar* 14.10

Increased Scrutiny of Directors and Officers

In order to ensure that corporate executives do not profit from misstated finances, the Dodd-Frank Act requires companies to have a policy for "clawing back" compensation that should not have been awarded. This is broader than a similar provision in the Sarbanes-Oxley Act, which was triggered only by misconduct. In addition, the SEC has demonstrated an increased willingness to pursue directors of public companies for knowingly permitting violations of U.S. securities laws. The application of the "Responsible Corporate Officer Doctrine"—a provision that imposes strict (unintentional and non-negligent) executive liability in certain federally regulated fields like healthcare—may also be on the rise. However, regardless of the increased scrutiny, some argue that the liability risks of serving as a corporate officer or director are still small in comparison to the advantages.

Sources: Michael W. Peregrin, "No D.&O. Liability Risk? Wouldn't That be Nice," *The New York Times Dealbook*, June 16, 2011; Steven M. Davidoff, "Despite Worries, Serving at the Top Carries Little Risk," *The New York Times Dealbook*, June 7, 2011.

"Federal prosecutors officially adopted . . . a softer approach that, longtime white collar lawyers and former federal prosecutors say, helps explain the dearth of criminal cases despite a raft of inquires into the financial crisis."

Gretchen Morgenson & Louise Story, *The New York Times*, July 7, 2011.

In a counter-trend, criminal prosecutions for corporate wrongdoing may be declining due to the increased use of "deferred prosecution agreements" (DPA) by the federal government. A DPA is used to encourage self-reporting and remediation of illegal acts before a criminal case is commenced. This alternative avoids some of the harsh consequences that can accompany prosecutions while still addressing the crime itself. The use of DPAs increased after the government's case against accounting firm Arthur Andersen. The firm was initially convicted for its role in destroying documents related to its client, Enron. Its conviction was eventually overturned, and Arthur Andersen was severely damaged, unable to continue its operations as one of the country's largest accounting firms. If the government had used a DPA instead, many believe, the firm might still be around and the employees who had nothing to do with the alleged crime would not have suffered. Despite the advantages, there is some concern that the overuse of DPAs could lead to an

[1]Martin Petrin, *The Curious Case of Directors' and Officers' Liability for Supervisions and Management: Exploring the Intersection of Corporate and Tort Law*, 59 Am. U. L. Rev. 1661 (2010).

overly lenient environment for addressing corporate malfeasance. Coupled with the Supreme Court's recent narrowing of the federal "honest services" law to incidents of bribery and kickbacks in *Skilling v. U.S.*, 130 S. Ct. 2896 (2010), the future may yield fewer corporate criminal cases.

We encourage you to use what you learn in this chapter to stay current in this area of operating and managing business organizations.

>> Key Terms

Alien corporation 433	Domestic corporation 433	Manager 445
Alter-ego theory 437	Double tax 440	Member 445
Articles of incorporation 434	Foreign corporation 433	Officer 435
Articles of organization 445	General partner 442	Organizer 445
Articles of partnership 431	Incorporator 434	Partnership 430
Assumed-name statute 431	Jointly and severally	Piercing the corporate
Buy and sell agreement 432	liable 432	veil 437
Charter 434	Limited liability	Proxy 435
Closely held 426	company 444	Publicly held 426
Corporation 433	Limited liability	S corporation 443
Derivative suit 436	partnership 445	Say-on-pay 447
Director 435	Limited partner 442	Shareholder 435
Dissolution 427	Limited personal liability 436	Sole proprietorship 428

>> Review Questions and Problems

1. *Forms of Business Organizations*

    (a) What are the three traditional business organizations and the four hybrid forms?

Factors to Consider When Selecting a Business's Organizational Form

2. *Creation*

    Relative to other factors discussed in this chapter, how important is the factor of creation?

3. *Continuity*

    Why does dissolution of a business organization not necessarily impact that organization's business activities?

4. *Managerial Control*

    Why should business owners take time to discuss the control each will exert over the organization's activities?

5. *Liability*

    What is meant by the phrase liability of a business organization as compared to the liability of the owners?

6. *Taxation*

    Why is taxation an important element to consider when selecting the appropriate organization for your business activities?

Selecting the Best Organizational Form

7. *Sole Proprietorships*

    What are the limitations of the sole proprietorship?

8. *Partnerships*

   Terry is the senior partner in an accounting firm. One of Terry's partners performs an audit. The audited firm sues Terry, as the senior partner, for alleged errors in the audit. If Terry is found liable, can Terry sue to collect a pro rata share of this liability from the other partners? Why or why not?

9. *Corporations*

   (a) Who controls the closely held corporation? Explain.

   (b) Describe five techniques that a corporation might use to avoid the double taxation of corporate profits.

10. *Limited Partnerships*

    Laura and Gary have formed a limited partnership, with Gary agreeing to be the general partner. This partnership has purchased supplies from Sam. Sam has received a promissory note signed on behalf of the partnership as payment. If the partnership is unable to pay this note, can Sam hold Gary personally liable? Explain.

11. *S Corporations*

    (a) Although it is technically a corporation, the S corporation has the attributes of which business organization when considering the taxation factor?

    (b) What is the implication of this treatment if the S corporation has a profitable year but does not distribute dividends to its shareholders?

12. *Limited Liability Organizations*

    What is the advantage of this organizational form compared to the S corporation?

Operating the Organization

13. *Making the Decision*

    Albert and Barbara wish to enter into the business of manufacturing fine furniture. Which form of business organization would you recommend in each of the following situations? Explain each of your answers.

    (a) Barbara is a furniture expert, but she has no funds. Albert knows nothing about such production, but he is willing to contribute all the money needed to start the business.

    (b) The furniture-manufacturing process requires more capital than Albert or Barbara can raise together. However, they wish to maintain control of the business.

    (c) The production process can be very dangerous, and a large tort judgment against the business is foreseeable.

    (d) Sales will be nationwide.

    (e) A loss is expected for the first several years.

14. *Trends in Managing the Organization*

    Detail three trends in the law related to corporate governance. Discuss whether you believe these trends, taken together, reflect an increase or decrease in legal risk associated with managing the organization.

business >> *discussions*

1. You and two of your college roommates have discussed plans to open a restaurant. You intend to attract college-age students who are health- and fitness-minded to your restaurant. You and your co-owners agree that each will invest equally in terms of time and money. However, in addition to contributions made by each of you, another $700,000 is essential for the restaurant to succeed.

> What type of organization is best suited for this business activity?
> Who will manage the restaurant during times that you and your co-owners are not present?
> What liabilities do you and your co-owners face?

2. Three years following your graduation with a business degree, you and three classmates began operating a consulting business. Your firm specializes in offering support related to payroll-and account-management computer applications. So far, your firm has relied on the four of you as its only consultants. A potential major client requests that your firm make a proposal for a year-long project. This project would result in your firm hiring several additional consultants and support staff. Because of the length of time and financial commitment this project may take, you and your co-owners take time to address the following questions:

> How would your firm conduct business on such a large scale?
> How could you limit potential liability for and by various consultants?
> Which form of business organization is best suited to meet the needs of your growing firm?.

Chapter **Eighteen**

Corporate Governance

Mark Hurd

Mark Hurd arrived as the chief executive officer at Hewlett-Packard in 2005. The company's board of directors, a body of strong and conflicted personalities, had just fired Carly Fiorina, the first woman ever to lead a corporation as big as HP. Her dual sins were trying to dominate the board and allowing the stock price to languish. Her story is the subject of the case study at the end of this chapter.

Hurd got along with the board and got results. He was diligent and relentless, dictating a regimen of cost-cutting, wringing waste from every department, forcing managers to justify every dollar in their budgets. Soon he eliminated 14,500 jobs, about 10 percent of the company's workforce. His severities were resented by some, but share prices climbed. He also had strategic vision. Major acquisitions moved HP into growing markets. He acquired Electronic Data Systems (EDS), then shed another 24,600 workers in the consolidation. He acquired 3Com, then Palm Inc. In five years he turned HP into the world's largest information technology company. Its share price, shown in Figure 18.1, more than doubled.

Then, on June 29, 2010, Hurd opened a letter from celebrity lawyer Gloria Allred. It accused him of sexually harassing an HP marketing contractor named Jodi Fisher by touching her body suggestively and speaking of intimate personal matters. It also said he had breached his duty of confidentiality in telling her about HP's pending purchase of EDS in 2008. An eight-page chronology of his contacts with Fisher was enclosed. The letter ended with an offer to settle. He immediately gave it to an HP attorney, who forwarded it to the board of directors.[1]

In 2007 Hurd had begun a series of "executive summits" held around the world to meet important customers. An assistant recommended Jodi Fisher as a consultant who could help at the events by briefing him on people, making introductions, and steering him around the room. Her qualifications were elusive. After graduating from Texas Tech University with a political science degree, she moved to Los Angeles seeking her fortune as an actress. Her subsequent portfolio included nude *Playboy* photos, roles in a string of erotic films such as "Intimate Obsession" and "Blood

---

[1] Robert A. Buth, Ben Worthen, and Justin Scheck, "Accuser Said Hurd Leaked an H-P Deal," *The Wall Street Journal*, November 6–7, 2010, p. A1.

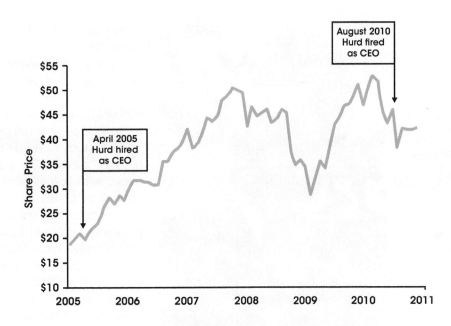

FIGURE 18.1
Hewlett-Packard Share Price: 2005–2011

Source: Yahoo! Finance, Historical Prices.

Dolls," and a reality television show appearance. Along the way, she married, divorced, and managed apartments.[2]

Hurd first interviewed Fisher in Los Angeles. Then she was flown to Denver, where they had a three-hour dinner. He hired her and between 2007 and 2009 they worked a dozen meetings together at luxury hotels around the world. Often they dined after the day's event. She was paid between $1,000 and $10,000 each time.

The 10 members of HP's board were concerned about the letter. That weekend they conducted a conference call to talk with him. Hurd said he and Fisher had dined several times but were not closely acquainted. He denied any sexual relationship with her.[3] Later she would say the same. He assured them her accusations were false. Some directors had done searches of her name, discovering her background in adult films. Hurd said he was unaware of this. The board was supportive. It wanted to keep a talented chief executive.

Shortly, Hurd suggested to the board that HP pay to settle the allegations. It did not agree. It also was unsure of its obligation to disclose events to shareholders. If the tale of a CEO and an adult actress came out, tabloid journalism would damage HP's reputation. That could affect the share price. If the claims were groundless, however, was there any duty to reveal them?

The board also hired a law firm to investigate Hurd's actions. That investigation revealed a series of prevarications. While Hurd had denied a close relationship with Fisher, a different picture emerged. The two had often dined together. They met at times when she did not work at an HP event. One night HP flew Fisher to a luxury hotel in Boise, Idaho, where she and Hurd had dinner. They watched a football game

---

[2] Alexandra Berzon, Ellen Byron, and Ben Worthen, "Far From H-P, A Job in Jersey," *The Wall Street Journal,* August 12, 2010, p. B1.

[3] Robert A. Guth, "Former H-P CEO Defends His Acts," *The Wall Street Journal,* October 19, 2010, p. B3.

632   Chapter 18   *Corporate Governance*

Mark Hurd, chief executive officer, chairman of the board, and president of Hewlett-Packard is shown here speaking at a 2010 company event.
Source: AP Photo/Danny Johnston.

in the bar, then in his room. The next day Hurd met with some local officials, but Fisher was not present. Hurd told the investigators that he liked to relax with Fisher at the end of the day. She made him feel uplifted. It was, he told investigators, a "very close personal relationship."[4]

Also, study of Hurd's computer revealed he had viewed 30 pornographic Web pages with scenes from her films. An examination of his expense reports found that six times he dined with Fisher but the notations recorded his bodyguard as the dinner companion. Hurd said his assistant filled out the reports and often put the bodyguard's name in when she was unsure who was present.

At this point Hurd's support on the board ebbed. Some directors favored firing him, but at least two holdouts wanted to avoid losing such an effective CEO. If the sexual harassment claims were groundless, the rest was of small concern. The directors scheduled a meeting with Gloria Allred to review the allegations. Hurd offered to repay the company for contested expense claims amounting to about $20,000. This was a minor amount to him and to the company. Since arriving he had received $146 million in compensation.

Other directors were unpersuaded. "He lied to my face and he's lying to you," one said.[5] He had violated HP's conduct code, which requires "uncompromising integrity" from every employee in a "company known for its ethical leadership." Part of the code sets forth a "Headline Test," to distinguish right from wrong by asking how actions would look if they came out in a news story or were reviewed by respected colleagues. It also admonishes employees to "[c]reate business records that accurately reflect the truth."[6] At HP a fabricated expense account was grounds for firing.

Early in August, Hurd reached an undisclosed financial settlement with Fisher that prohibited her from discussing the allegations. She released a statement saying there were many inaccuracies in her letter. Hurd explained he had settled because the amount was small compared with going to court.[7] The board was furious. Now it would have no chance to hear from Fisher and her lawyers. Hurd's remaining supporters gave up and agreed to a unanimous vote calling for his resignation. He complied.

---

[4] Guth, Worthen, and Scheck, "Accuser Said Hurd Leaked an H-P Deal," p. A10.

[5] Lucille S. Salhany, quoted in ibid., p. A10.

[6] Hewlett-Packard Company, *Our Standards of Business Conduct* (Palo Alto, CA: Hewlett-Packard Company, 2010 revision), front cover and pp. 3, 8, and 11.

[7] Guth, "Former H-P CEO Defends His Acts," p. B3.

His severance package was worth approximately $40 million. HP's share price dropped 14 percent over the next weeks and did not fully recover for six months. Fisher released a statement that she was "saddened" by his downfall.[8]

Not everyone agreed with the decision. A *Wall Street Journal* columnist called Hurd's offenses "piddling."[9] A *Los Angeles Times* business writer suggested "maybe it's the board that should have gone, not Hurd."[10] Larry Ellison, founder and CEO of Oracle Corporation, spoke for many.

> The HP board just made the worst personnel decision since the idiots on the Apple board fired Steve Jobs many years ago . . . In losing Mark Hurd, the HP board failed to act in the best interest of HP's employees, shareholders, customers and partners.[11]

Ellison then hired Hurd as a co-president of Oracle. HP filed a trade secrets lawsuit because Hurd had signed a confidentiality agreement. He was intimately familiar with the pricing details and component costs of HP products in areas where HP and Oracle directly competed. To settle the suit, Hurd waived his rights to $14 million of stock options in his severance package. He stayed at Oracle.

The Mark Hurd story is a story of corporate governance in action. The duty of every company's board is to watch over management in the interest of shareholders. What was the board's duty here, to maximize shareholder wealth or to uphold the integrity of management? In this chapter we define corporate governance and explain how it works. We also discuss its flaws. An unusual part of the Mark Hurd story is that, unlike many corporate boards, this one had the courage to fire a CEO. As we will show, many do not.

WHAT IS CORPORATE GOVERNANCE?

corporate governance
The exercise of authority over members of the corporate community based on formal structures, rules, and procedures.

Corporate governance is the exercise of authority over members of the corporate community based on formal structures, rules, and procedures. This authority is based on a body of rules defining the rights and duties of shareholders, boards of directors, and managers. These parties form a power triangle, shown in Figure 18.2, that controls the corporation. Steady tension exists between them, and the rules are designed to align their interests, distribute power, and settle disputes. The rules come from multiple sources, including state charters, state and federal laws, stock exchange listing standards, and corporate governance policies.

Corporate governance practice has changed dramatically over time. From the rise of market economies in the early 1700s until the mid-1800s most companies were small and run by their owners. However, with industrial capitalism some small companies grew very large and could no longer be capitalized or managed by one or two owner-proprietors. Soon ownership was dispersed in a stockholder

---

[8] Quoted in Ben Worthen and Joann S. Lublin, "Mark Hurd Neglected to Follow H-P Code," *The Wall Street Journal,* August 9, 2010, p. B1.

[9] Holman W. Jenkins, Jr., "The Mark Hurd Show," *The Wall Street Journal,* August 18, 2010, p. A15.

[10] Michael Hiltzik, "Ouster of HP Chief Has Look of Panic," *Los Angeles Times,* August 11, 2010, B6.

[11] Quoted in Ashlee Vance, "Oracle Chief Faults H.P. Board for Forcing Hurd Out," *The New York Times on the Web,* August 10, 2010.

FIGURE 18.2

The Power Triangle
Corporate governance is the exercise of authority over members of the corporate community. It is based on rules that define power relationships between shareholders, boards of directors, and managers.

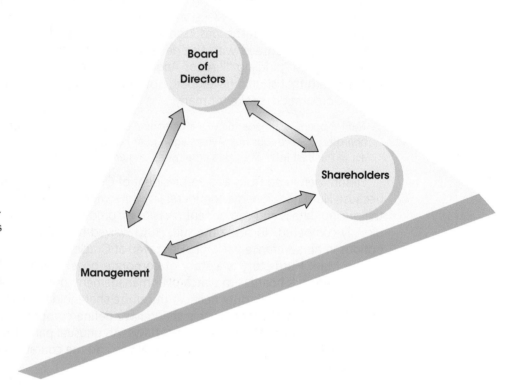

multitude where each person had only a small, fractional investment and most had little knowledge of the business. In this situation, power passed to expert managers who ran companies for the unorganized, inarticulate crowd of owners.

With the transition, boards of directors formed to monitor management for the shareholders. Shareholders were largely unqualified to manage what they owned. Hired managers had the competence to run a complex corporation, but they needed day-to-day freedom from a crowd of meddling owners. Yet they still needed supervision, because as salaried employees they lacked the same incentive to maximize profits as the owners. They might even be tempted to make their continued employment and larger salaries the top priority. It became the board's job to balance, mediate, and reconcile the competing powers and interests of owners and managers. Thus emerged the basic structure of modern corporate governance.

THE CORPORATE CHARTER

corporate charter
A document issued by a state government to create a corporation.

A *corporate charter* is the document that creates a corporation. Charters are also called articles of incorporation. U.S. corporations are chartered by the state in which they incorporate.[12] All 50 states and the District of Colombia charter corporations. When a corporation is formed in a state, it is then governed by that

[12] A few quasi-public enterprises chartered by the federal government, such as the Tennessee Valley Authority, are exceptions.

state's laws. At the Constitutional Convention of 1787, the founders debated a federal chartering power but decided that state controls were appropriate to regulate the more geographically limited corporate activity of that era. Their judgment was eventually outdated. As corporations expanded in size and power, states were unable to control their excesses and, as we will see, the federal government has slowly added layers of corporate law above state laws. However, all corporations are still chartered by a state.

Corporate charters specify the purpose of the corporation, usually "any lawful act for which a corporation may be organized," and specify basic rights and duties of stockholders, directors, and officers. Fundamentally, they lodge control over the enterprise in stockholders who own shares of stock with voting rights in corporate matters. State corporation laws then give directors a *fiduciary responsibility* to shareholders, that is, as the entity entrusted with oversight of the owner's property, they are legally bound to care for that property in the owner's interest. They are responsible for appointing the managers who run the day-to-day affairs of the company.

Charters may also include provisions about numbers of shares and classes of stock authorized, dividends, annual shareholder meetings, the size of boards, and procedures for removing directors. They are brief documents, usually no more than 10 or 20 pages even for the largest companies. They are supplemented with *bylaws,* or rules the company writes to clarify in detail how broad provisions of its charter will work. These bylaws resolve such ordinary matters as who presides over shareholder meetings and whether directors can hold a meeting over the telephone.

States compete to attract the incorporation fees and tax revenues of corporations. For more than a century tiny Delaware has been the victor in this competition. It charters about half of all public corporations in the United States. About 17 percent of its state tax revenues, far more than any other state, come from chartering fees. Although costs of incorporating in Delaware are high, its corporate laws are friendly toward directors and managers. To maintain its addiction to corporate tax revenue the state has repeatedly innovated more flexible and enabling rules. Other states must match or approach its standards to remain competitive.

Delaware refuses to be underregulated. For example, when the personal liability of directors began to expand in the 1980s, several states experimented with tentative limits to such exposure. Delaware reacted by limiting director liability for all but the most witless and negligent acts. Within a year, 35 states matched its leniency.[13] In this race to the bottom "no one in Delaware is willing to play hare while some other state tortoise gains ground."[14] In addition, Delaware also has a special Chancery Court that handles only business cases and is very friendly to boards and managers. It is expensive and difficult for all but the wealthiest shareholders of a Delaware corporation to prevail in a lawsuit against directors or managers.

fiduciary responsibility
The legal duty of a representative to manage property in the interest of the owner.

bylaws
Rules of corporate governance adopted by corporations.

---

[13] Roberta Romano, "The States as a Laboratory: Legal Innovation and State Competition for Corporate Charters," *Yale Journal on Regulation,* Summer 2006, p. 212.

[14] Delaware attorney Lawrence A. Hamermesh, quoted in Mark J. Roe, "Delaware's Shrinking Half-Life," *Stanford Law Review,* December 2009, p. 129.

Shareholder activists, who believe that boards and top executives have too much power in corporate governance, are provoked by Delaware. They lobbied North Dakota to pass a new, model law with provisions that strengthen the powers of stockholders and make boards more independent of management.[15] Corporations such as Whole Foods Markets that emphasize social responsibility in their strategies have been pressured to reincorporate in North Dakota. There has been no rush.

POWER IN CORPORATE GOVERNANCE: THEORY AND REALITY

The legal line of power in state charters and incorporation laws runs from the state, to shareholders, to directors, to managers. However, this legal theory diverges from the reality as widely practiced. The theory is shown on the left side of Figure 18.3. The reality, as shown on the right, is that CEOs often dominate boards of directors and both together dominate shareholders.

Stockholders

Stockholders are said to be owners of corporations. However, rather than owning an identifiable part or fraction of the corporation as property they own only a

FIGURE 18.3   **Flow of Authority in Corporate Governance**

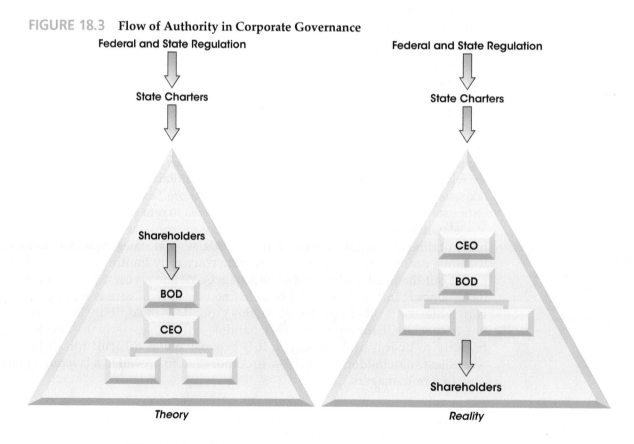

[15] The Publicly Traded Corporations Act (2007).

stock certificate. Owning this certificate gives them certain limited, but important, rights. A basic reason their rights are limited is that under state laws common stockholders are free of liability for the corporation's actions, therefore, their control of those actions is diminished.

Stockholders' rights are given in corporate charters, bylaws, and state and federal laws. Their basic entitlements are to (1) sell their stock, (2) vote to elect directors and on other corporate issues, (3) receive information about the corporation, (4) receive dividends, (5) sue the corporation if directors and officers commit wrongful acts, and (6) acquire residual assets in case of bankruptcy, but only after payment of creditors and bondholders.

If stockholders are dissatisfied with corporate management, they can sell their shares. Otherwise, they influence management by voting in corporate elections. In large public companies stockholders receive notice of elections to be held at annual meetings. Such elections typically ask for a vote on director nominees, management's choice of auditors, charter amendments or changes in bylaws, stock issuances, and nonbinding resolutions. Stockholders are invited to attend an annual meeting and vote their shares. Or, if they do not attend, they can fill out a ballot-like *proxy card* that gives management the authority to cast votes for them as they indicate. The proxy card is accompanied by a *proxy statement* with legally mandated information about the matters up for a vote, including biographies of director nominees and their qualifications, a detailed analysis of executive compensation, and the text of other proposals.

The annual meeting itself is a formal, ritualized event usually held in the spring. Its purpose is to allow voting and interaction between stockholders, directors, and officers. A typical meeting has several parts, a business meeting where agenda items are raised and voting results announced, a presentation by the chief executive about the company's outlook, and a question-and-answer session for stockholders. When the floor is opened for questions at a big company meeting, meaningful exchanges are rare. A few stockholders may praise the CEO for doing a good job. Activists, who have purchased a few shares to gain entry, harangue management for irresponsible behavior. Most are respectful, but some are not. At a recent Chevron Corp. meeting an energy activist started a protest chant and was arrested.[16] Every spring a few others require security escorts to leave. Employees may rise to express grievances. At one FedEx meeting a freight handler stated that while the company was making millions of dollars in profits he and others were not paid enough to "have a decent life."[17]

proxy card
A form stockholders mark giving management the right to vote their shares as indicated. It is also called simply a proxy or a proxy form.

proxy statement
A booklet of information sent to stockholders before annual votes on directors, executive pay, and other matters.

Shareholder Resolutions

Shareholders, either individuals or funds, can propose resolutions for a vote at the annual meeting. These resolutions are printed in the proxy statement. Securities

[16] John Letzing, "Activist Faces Charges in Chevron Outburst," *The Wall Street Journal,* September 29, 2010, p. B4.

[17] Comments of Ray Mercado, FedEx Corp., *FedEx 2010 Shareowners Meeting Transcript,* September 27, 2010, pp. 10–11.

and Exchange Commission (SEC) regulations set forth the requirements they must meet, including the following.[18]

- Sponsors must own $2,000 or more of the company's shares for at least one year.
- They may not submit more than one resolution a year.
- The resolution cannot exceed 500 words and must be sent to the company for approval at least 120 days before the annual meeting.
- The shareholder must appear at the meeting to present the resolution.
- The resolution must get 3 percent of the vote to be resubmitted the next year, 6 percent to be resubmitted a third year, and 10 percent for the fourth year and after.

Under SEC rules, a company can reject a proposed resolution for any of 13 reasons. For example, it can reject a proposal if it is a personal grievance, contains false or misleading statements, or deals with matters beyond the company's influence. The SEC must approve each rejection. In 2009 a Catholic investor group wanted to introduce a proposal about sensitivity to American Indian peoples at the FedEx annual meeting. The resolution required FedEx to "identify and dissociate with any names, symbols and imagery that disparage American Indian peoples" and to report on whether its diversity training for management was "sensitive to Native American rights, histories and cultures." FedEx contacted the SEC, seeking to omit the proposal because it dealt with "ordinary business operations." Proposals can be excluded under this exception if they constitute shareholder micromanagement of fundamental, day-to-day tasks in running the company. FedEx argued this one sought oversight of advertising and training, both "ordinary" functions that shareholders were unqualified to oversee. The SEC agreed and the proposal was omitted.[19]

Each year hundreds of shareholder resolutions qualify to appear on proxy statements. In 2010, 507 resolutions were voted on. Most, 342, wanted corporate governance reforms such as allowing shareholders to convene special meetings, splitting the chairman and CEO positions, and forcing managers to hold stock awards until two years after their employment ended. Ninety got a majority of votes cast. Another 165 resolutions focused on social issues, including concerns such as political spending, carbon emissions, toxic chemicals, diversity, and animal welfare. There was little support for them. Only two had a majority vote, both requesting the company prepare a report on sustainability.

Almost universally, shareholder proposals are followed by the statement, "The Board of Directors recommends a vote AGAINST this proposal." This is accompanied by an explanation of why the board urges rejection. Its opposition is usually fatal. Even when a proposal receives a majority vote, it is not binding. However, its success puts pressure on the company and often results in change.

---

[18] "Shareholder Proposals," 17 CFR §240.14a-8 (2011).

[19] Securities and Exchange Commission, Office of Chief Counsel, Division of Corporation Finance, FedEx Corporation No Action Letter, July 14, 2009.

Assessing Shareholder Influence

Although in theory shareholders have the voting power to influence or even re-place management, they rarely exercise it. First, corporate elections are not fully democratic. They have several elements of democracy. Shareholders are at liberty to vote. Their votes count equally.[20] And the majority rules. However, as in old-style communist elections there is often no contest. Directors usually run unop-posed. Stockholders can vote for or against them (or abstain), but they cannot vote for another candidate. Stockholders can submit nominees to board nominating committees, but the directors do not have to pick them. Occasionally a large share-holder tries to challenge the election of one or more directors, but this is hugely expensive and rarely successful.

Management also has other advantages. It is united, while stockholders are fragmented. Among such a large group of passive individuals it is hard for oppo-sition to coalesce. Most shareholders follow management's voting recommenda-tions. And as proxies come in, management can see how the vote is going and, if necessary, call on large shareholders, including brokers or pension funds, to change their votes. In sum, the influence of shareholders is very weak. In 1949 one perceptive investor summed up the contradiction of stockholder power this way. The words are as apt today as then.

> In legal rights and legal machinery . . . stockholders as a class are king. Acting as a majority they can hire and fire managements and bend them completely to their will. Though ownership may be widely scattered, there is no legal obstacle to many stockholders' joining forces so as to create an effective majority voice on any issue that may arise . . .
>
> [I]n practice . . . the stockholders are a complete washout. As a class they show neither intelligence nor alertness. They vote in sheep-like fashion for whatever the management recommends and no matter how poor the management's record of accomplishment may be.[21]

FEDERAL REGULATION OF GOVERNANCE

For more than 150 years state incorporation statutes, laws, and court decisions defined the requirements of corporate governance. At first this worked well. Most corporations were small. Their activities were confined within state boundaries. However, in the late 1800s and early 1900s mergers and firm growth created much larger firms that served national markets. These firms required more capital. Be-fore the 1890s only a small number of very wealthy individuals held stock. But larger firms issued stock freely and their ownership was dispersed among small investors in many states.

---

[20] An exception is when companies have dual classes of stock. An example is Ford Motor Company, where members of the Ford family own Class B shares, which are given greater weight than common shares in company elections.

[21] Benjamin Graham, *The Intelligent Investor* (New York: HarperCollins, 2005), p. 207. Originally published in 1949.

Now both business activity and stock ownership crossed state lines. State corporation laws proved less and less adequate for oversight, especially since corporations sought charters in those states with the most flexible and permissive rules. Perhaps the greatest defect of state governance laws was inability to prevent fraud and manipulation in national capital markets.[22]

This deficiency eventually had catastrophic consequences. Prosperity in the 1920s led to a stock market boom. After 1927, buying in then-unregulated securities markets reached a frenzy. Entrepreneurs set up hollow empires of companies just to issue stock. Brokers allowed investors with very modest incomes to buy shares on margins as low as 10 percent. The buyers often knew little or nothing about the companies behind their shares. When a speculative bubble burst in October 1929, prices collapsed in days of extreme panic. People lost their savings. The nation advanced into depression.

In response to this catastrophe the federal government intervened to protect stockholders and bring integrity to capital markets. Congress passed the Securities Act of 1933 requiring companies to register securities and provide financial statements and other information to buyers before their sale. It then passed the Securities Exchange Act of 1934 giving birth to a regulatory agency, the Securities and Exchange Commission that would police securities markets. The 1934 law also required companies to file periodic reports, including annual reports called 10-Ks, quarterly reports called 10-Qs, and reports known as 8-Ks that quickly update investors on significant events such as votes in annual meetings.

These initial statutes added a layer of governance law above state laws. Since then, this layer has expanded. The Securities and Exchange Commission (SEC) is an independent regulatory commission with five members, one of whom serves as chairman, appointed by the president for five years. Since 1934 Congress has passed 38 more statutes adding to the SEC's powers. It now has a staff of 3,500 and an annual budget of approximately $900 million. Other entities, including the Treasury Department and the Federal Reserve System, also regulate securities markets.

Despite proliferation, federal and state governance laws have not always been a match for situations that arise. The stories of Enron and Lehman Brothers teach how governance reforms still play catch-up with governance abuses.

Enron Corp.

Spectacular business scandals are recurrent in American history. However, not since the epic corporate misdeeds of the 1930s had there been such a wave of business scandals as at the turn of the twenty-first century. Enron's amazing disintegration in 2001 was the supernova in a field of frauds where executives looted shareholder wealth while directors slept. In multiple instances corporate governance failed.

Enron was an energy company headquartered in Houston, Texas, and incorporated in Oregon. Until the 1990s it was a staid natural gas, oil, and electricity

---

[22] Jack B. Jacobs, "The Reach of State Corporate Law Beyond State Borders: Reflections Upon Federalism," *New York University Law Review,* November 2009, pp. 1151–55.

producer. Then it radically changed its business model to become the world's largest online energy trading company. Its apparent success earned the admiration of investors, academics, and the public.

As it grew it created a structural maze of limited partnerships and other financial entities, numbering in the hundreds, to carry out exotic financial transactions. It all seemed to work. Enron's profits went from $1 million in 1996 to $1.1 billion in 2000. Investors, few of whom understood the puzzling structure and hedging activities, romanticized its prospects and drove share prices skyward. They delighted in a 1,415 percent return between 1990 and 2000, a period ending in speculative frenzy as the stock shot from $19.10 in 1999 to a high of $90.80 in 2000.

This bright picture clouded late in 2001 when the company announced a $554 million after-tax charge against revenues. Soon it revised its financial statements from 1997 to 2001, reducing net income more than $1 billion. The reason was it had reported false income from suspicious trading arrangements. Markets turned against Enron. It could not borrow to meet its obligations and late in 2001 it filed for bankruptcy. About $60 billion in market value was wiped out.

Enron had a board of distinguished directors (see the box on the next page). Following the bankruptcy it set up a special committee to investigate its actions. One focus was on a series of off-balance-sheet partnerships created by Andrew S. Fastow, the company's chief financial officer. The board had approved them although they created a conflict of interest.[23] In some partnerships Fastow was both a manager for Enron and an investor in an outside entity that engaged in financial transactions, such as the buying and selling of assets, with Enron. Which interest would be his priority, Enron's or his own? Unfortunately, Fastow was using the partnerships to enrich himself.

Another problem was that the partnerships concealed Enron's true financial state. Accounting rules were that if an outside investor, here Fastow, put in 3 percent or more of the capital in a partnership, the corporation, even if it provided the other 97 percent, did not have to declare it a subsidiary. Therefore, its assets and debt could be withheld from the corporation's balance sheet.[24] Using this loophole, Enron's directors eventually approved removing almost half Enron's assets from its balance sheet, hiding losses and debt totaling hundreds of millions of dollars.

The directors recognized it was a conflict of interest for Fastow to be an outside investor in the partnerships, but rationalized it was a modest risk considering the great possible gain for Enron. They thought it could be handled with controls specified by the board. They were mistaken. Their policy gave a green light to expansion of the partnerships beyond anything they ever envisioned. In fact, this partnership proliferation exposed the company to fatal risks. Simultaneously, Fastow orchestrated side deals netting him more than $30 million as an individual.

---

[23] William C. Powers, Jr., chair; Raymond S. Troubh; and Herbert S. Winokur, Jr., *Report of Investigation by the Special Investigative Committee of the Board of Directors of Enron Corp.,* February 1, 2002. Powers was dean of the University of Texas School of Law. Powers and Troubh were appointed to the board after the committee was formed. Winokur had been a member of the board at the time of bankruptcy.

[24] John R. Emshwiller and Rebecca Smith, "Murky Waters: A Primer on Enron Partnerships," *The Wall Street Journal,* January 21, 2002, p. C14.

Enron's Board of Directors

In 2001, the year that Enron filed for bankruptcy, its board consisted of the 14 members below, including one female, one black, and two Asian directors. Two members, Lay and Skilling, were officers of Enron. The other 12 were nonemployee directors.

ROBERT A. BELFER, 65
Chairman and CEO
Belco Oil & Gas Corp.

NORMAN P. BLAKE, JR., 59
Chairman, President, and CEO
Comdisco, Inc.

RONNIE C. CHAN, 51
Chairman
Hang Lung Group

JOHN H. DUNCAN, 73
Investor

DR. WENDY L. GRAMM, 56
Director, Mercatus Center Regulatory Studies
Program, George Mason University and wife of
U.S. Senator Phil Gramm (R-Texas)

DR. ROBERT K. JAEDICKE, 72
Professor (Emeritus) of Accounting
Stanford University

KENNETH L. LAY, 58
Chairman of the Board

CHARLES A. LeMAISTRE, 77
President (Emeritus)
University of Texas M.D. Anderson Cancer Center

JOHN MENDELSOHN, 64
President
University of Texas M.D. Anderson
Cancer Center

PAULO V. FERRAZ PEREIRA, 46
Executive Vice President
Group Bozano

FRANK SAVAGE, 62
Chairman
Alliance Capital Management International

JEFFREY K. SKILLING, 47
President and CEO
Enron Corporation

JOHN WAKEHAM, 68
United Kingdom Secretary of State (ret.) and
former Member of Parliament

HERBERT S. WINOKUR, JR., 57
Chairman and CEO
Capricorn Holdings, Inc

In the previous year, each nonemployee director received an average cash payment of $79,107, including an annual fee and additional fees for attending meetings or chairing one of the five board committees (executive, audit, finance, compensation, or nominating). In addition, each nonemployee director received grants of Enron stock and stock options valued at $836,517. At the time of the 2001 annual shareholders' meeting the nonemployee directors owned a total of $670 million in Enron shares. The 14 directors also served on the boards of 25 other companies.

Source: Enron Corp., *Proxy Statement,* March 27, 2001, pp. 1–12.

Controls on Fastow were never properly implemented. The board's audit committee was supposed to conduct annual reviews of all partnerships, but it failed to probe deeply into the bizarre transactions being generated. The board also made Enron's chief accounting officer responsible for reviewing and approving all transactions between the company and its partnerships. The review was inadequate because, said the investigating committee, top management was "not watching the store."

Indeed, a fundamental cause of the catastrophe was a change in culture wrought by the two top officers, Chairman of the Board Kenneth L. Lay and CEO Jeffrey K. Skilling. They fostered and permitted a freewheeling climate that tolerated junior officers engaging in illegal activities. Enron became the classic illustration of a Wild West corporate culture characterized by reckless financial deals, avarice, and deceit. It lacked an emphasis on integrity. With Lay as its chairman and Skilling a member, the board failed in its duty to maintain norms of ethics and compliance.

The investigative committee absolved Enron's board of sole blame for the bankruptcy, but accused it of failing to exercise its oversight responsibility. It found that board members "were severely hampered by the fact that significant information was withheld from them," but also that the board "did not fully appreciate the significance of some information that came before it."[25] Partnership arrangements involving substantial sums and risk were presented to the board and it failed to give them the scrutiny they deserved. Some intricate deals received only 10 or 15 minutes of attention. Fastow's first partnership was one of six agenda items in a board meeting that lasted just an hour. One director attended by calling in from a pay phone in Virginia and could not clearly hear the discussion.[26] While the investigating committee felt the board could not be faulted for not acting if it had no or insufficient information, it could be faulted for limited scrutiny and probing.

An investigation by the U.S. Senate was harder on the board. Interviews with board members revealed many conflicts of interest. For example, Enron was paying director John Wakeham $6,000 a month in consulting fees. The current and prior presidents of the M.D. Anderson Cancer Center in Texas were both board members. In the previous five years Enron and Ken Lay had given $600,000 to this institution. Director Wendy Gramm's husband, Senator Phil Gramm, received campaign contributions from Enron.[27] These and several other financial ties undermined the independence of the directors.

The Senate investigation also concluded that the board had authorized excessive compensation of Enron executives. One year the board approved a compensation plan in which executives received $430 million in bonuses when the company's

[25] Powers, Troubh, and Winokur, *Report of the Special Investigative Committee of the Board of Directors of Enron Corp.,* pp. 159 and 148.

[26] The director was Wendy Gramm. In John Gillespie and David Zweig, *Money for Nothing* (New York: Free Press, 2010), pp. 67–68.

[27] Report of the Permanent Subcommittee on Investigations, Committee on Governmental Affairs, U.S. Senate, *The Role of the Board of Directors in Enron's Collapse,* 107th Congress, 2nd Session, Report 107-70, July 8, 2002, pp. 54–56.

entire net income was only $975 million. In 2000 Ken Lay earned $140 million. One of his subordinates received $265 million in the same year. The board also approved a line of credit for Lay, who withdrew $77 million in cash from Enron, then replaced it with Enron stock! Overall, concluded the Senate report, "the Enron Board failed to provide the prudent oversight and checks and balances that its fiduciary obligations required and a company like Enron needed."[28]

In 2006, a federal jury found Lay and Skilling guilty of conspiracy and fraud in the Enron collapse. Jurors believed both had lied publicly about the company's financial health while all along profiting from the sale of millions of shares of their Enron stock.[29] Lay's death voided his conviction, but Skilling was sentenced to 24 years and four months in jail. Fastow pleaded guilty to conspiracy and fraud charges. Because of his willingness to testify against former top executives he was given a comparatively light six-year sentence. None of Enron's outside directors faced criminal indictments. However, 10 members of the board agreed to pay $13 million from their own pockets to settle a civil suit by Enron employees charging they had failed in their oversight of company retirement plans.[30]

Other Failures of Governance

The failures of the Enron board were echoed in other fraud scandals at about the same time. Among the most prominent are these.

- At Tyco International the board slumbered while CEO L. Dennis Kozlowski took as much as $125 million in corporate funds for his personal use and conspired with his CFO Mark H. Swartz to misrepresent the company's financial condition and boost its stock price. On conviction for grand larceny, falsifying accounting records, and conspiracy, both received prison sentences of 8 to 25 years. Kozlowski was ordered to pay $97 million in restitution and a $70 million fine. His wife visited him only once in prison, coming to tell him she wanted a divorce.[31] Tyco's directors, who failed to exercise adequate oversight, suffered no formal penalty.

- At Adelphia Communications the directors dozed as founder John J. Rigas and his son Timothy concealed $2.3 billion in off-balance-sheet debt, stole $100 million from the company, and lied to investors about its financial condition. At sentencing, the judge told the elder Rigas that he had "set Adelphia on a track of lying, of cheating, of defrauding," then heard Rigas respond that "in my heart and conscience, I'll go to my grave really and truly believing I did nothing."[32] He was sentenced to 15 years in federal prison, his son Timothy to 20 years, and another son, John, Jr., to 10 months' home confinement. The Adelphia directors were never penalized for their limp oversight.

---

[28] Ibid., p. 59.

[29] *United States v. Jeffrey K. Skilling and Kenneth W. Lay,* Cr. No. H-04-025, S. Dist. Tex. (2006).

[30] *Newby, et al., v. Enron Corp.,* 235 F. Supp. 2d 594 (2002).

[31] Steve Dunleavy, "On Her First Prison Visit, My Wife Told Me, 'I Want a Divorce' Koz," *New York Post,* October 30, 2006, p. 6.

[32] Quotations are in Dean Starkman, "Rigases Given Prison Terms," *The Washington Post,* June 21, 2005, p. D1.

- At WorldCom, in a story told more fully in Chapter 7, the board napped while CEO Bernard J. Ebbers and CFO Scott D. Sullivan concealed falling revenues and rising expenses in an $11 billion accounting fraud. Ebbers was sentenced to 25 years in prison, Sullivan to 5 years. Accused of negligent oversight, 11 WorldCom directors agreed to pay 20 percent of their aggregate net worth, about $20.3 million, in restitution to defrauded investors.[33] As with the Enron directors, this came from their own pockets.

Each of these corporations declared bankruptcy. Jobs and life savings were lost. In each case the directors failed in their duty to protect shareholders from self-interested, predatory managers. Their failure inspired a range of corporate governance reforms aimed at sharpening boardroom vigilance. The centerpiece was the Sarbanes-Oxley Act of 2002.

The Sarbanes-Oxley Act

Sarbanes-Oxley Act of 2002
A statute enacted to prevent financial fraud in corporations. It mandated stricter financial reporting and greater board oversight.

On signing the *Sarbanes-Oxley Act of 2002* into law President George W. Bush said it embodied "the most far-reaching reforms of American business practice since the time of Franklin Delano Roosevelt."[34] There was little disagreement. The law's primary focus is on accounting rules. It also puts devices in place to hold management responsible for accurate financial reports and it increases the oversight responsibilities of boards of directors. Here are its main provisions.

- It creates a Public Company Accounting Oversight Board to oversee accounting firms and improve the accuracy of their audits.
- Audit firms are prohibited from doing consulting work for corporations while also auditing their books. Audit firms must rotate every five years. This broke a long-standing conflict of interest situation where auditors were tempted to please their clients in order to pursue lucrative consulting contracts.
- Companies must tell whether they have a code setting forth "standards of honesty and ethical conduct" for senior financial officers or, if not, why not.
- Every board of directors must create an audit committee to oversee the firm's accounting policies and controls. It must consist of independent directors who do not receive fees from the company other than their director's compensation. One member of this committee must be a "financial expert."
- The CEO and the CFO must sign and certify the accuracy of annual and quarterly financial reports. If the statements are false, they face criminal penalties up to $5 million and 20 years in prison.
- Companies must reveal off-balance-sheet transactions such as those used by Enron.
- Boards of directors are prohibited from approving personal loans for company executives.
- Directors (and managers) are subject to heavy penalties. Civil violations can lead to fines of up to $100,000. Criminal violations can lead to fines of up to $50 million and lengthy prison terms.

---

[33] Daniel Akst, "Fining the Directors Misses the Mark," *The New York Times*, August 21, 2005, sec. 3, p. 6.
[34] Quoted in Stephen M. Bainbridge, "The Creeping Federalization of Corporation Law," *Regulation*, spring 2003, p. 28.

The business community complained that the law was burdensome. A 2005 survey found the average cost of implementing it in 90 companies ranged from a few hundred thousand dollars for small firms to $7.8 million for the largest.[35] Large corporations now spend millions of dollars a year in complying and complain that its costs may exceed its benefits.[36]

Enron's failure shook up the governance system everywhere. Corporate groups, accountants, credit rating agencies, securities analysts, and stock exchanges all came out with sets of reforms to strengthen boards. The New York Stock Exchange is an example. It maintains rules that all listed companies must follow. Soon after the enactment of Sarbanes-Oxley it revised these rules to conform with and go beyond the new law. It required a majority of independent directors on the boards of all listed companies. In addition, it required every board to have three committees—audit, compensation, and governance (or nominating)—each composed entirely of independent directors.

Did all this rulemaking work to awaken and empower boards? The answer is no. While it may have prevented an unknown number of frauds and scandals, it failed to prevent widespread board somnolence, a curiosity at the center of a near systemwide financial collapse in 2008. The story of Lehman Brothers is exhibit A.

Lehman Brothers

Lehman Brothers Holdings began in 1850 as a cotton broker and grew into the nation's fourth-largest investment bank. Since 1994 it had been run by a CEO named Richard S. Fuld, Jr. Intense, intimidating, and impatient, Fuld had a confrontational manner and, according to one colleague, gave off "little physical cues" hinting any disagreement could turn to physical violence.[37] Once, when a manager asked him to wait, he cleared the person's desk with a sweep of his hand. Fuld referred to Lehman as "the mother ship" and demanded total loyalty. He saw each day, each situation as a battle. You were either on the team or off it. In keeping with this worldview, he made Lehman stock a large part of compensation and required employees to hold it as long as five years before selling. This motivated everyone so long as the stock price rose.

In 2006, Fuld decided that the way to keep share prices rising was to make Lehman grow faster. He introduced an aggressive strategy requiring more risk and increased leverage on capital. Lehman invested its assets in subprime mortgages, commercial real estate, high-yield bonds, leveraged loans, and mortgage-backed securities. This reduced its liquidity and raised firmwide risk. It did grow, to $691 billion in assets by 2007. Its leverage ratio eventually reached 39 to 1, that is, it had borrowed $39 for every dollar in its accounts.

---

[35] Deborah Solomon, "At What Price?" *The Wall Street Journal,* October 17, 2005, p. R3.

[36] One 2007 survey found average annual compliance costs of $5 million and only 31 percent of directors of surveyed firms who thought benefits exceeded costs. Korn/Ferry Institute, *34th Annual Board of Directors Study* (New York: Korn/Ferry International, 2007), p. 16.

[37] Anonymous, quoted in Steve Fishman, "Burning Down His House," *New York Magazine,* December 8, 2008, p. 1.

Richard S. Fuld at a 2010 hearing of the Financial Crisis Inquiry Commission where he testified on the bankruptcy of Lehman Brothers. Source: AP Photo/ Carolyn Kaster.

To fund its operations, Lehman depended on borrowing tens of billions of dollars each day in financial markets. Its ability to do so turned on the confidence of others in its liquidity. When the subprime mortgage crisis materialized in 2007, lenders began to lose confidence in Lehman and required more collateral, even for routine financing. To shore up confidence Lehman resorted to an accounting trick its employees called "Repo 105." Ordinarily, Lehman raised cash using *repurchase agreements* in which it sold assets to a counterparty and agreed to repurchase them in the next 24 to 72 hours. During these brief, routine financing transactions the assets stayed on Lehman's balance sheet. But with the Repo 105 technique, Lehman sold assets equal to 105 percent or more of the cash it received, which, under a strained interpretation of accounting rules, allowed it to treat the asset transfer as a sale.

repurchase agreement A financing transaction in which one firm lends assets to another firm in exchange for cash with a simultaneous agreement to purchase the assets back.

Using Repo 105, Lehman briefly removed up to $50 billion of assets from its balance sheet precisely at the end of the first and second quarters in 2008, allowing it to reduce its net leverage ratio from 13.9 to 12.1. With this sleight of hand Lehman ended reporting periods with a stronger-looking, but misleading, balance sheet. It was not a clear violation of accounting rules, yet Lehman never disclosed its use to lenders, investors, analysts, or its own board of directors. Thus, it concealed the firm's real debt level from interested parties. Not everyone at Lehman accepted the legitimacy of Repo 105. Some of its accountants called it a gimmick. A senior vice president wrote to the firm's controller complaining of "balance sheet manipulation" and reported the use of Repo 105 to Lehman's external auditor Ernst & Young.[38] Nobody acted.

Repo 105 was not enough to save Lehman Brothers. In September 2008, as credit markets began to freeze, another investment bank, Bear Stearns, almost failed and was rescued at the last minute by a government-arranged merger with JP Morgan Chase. Attention then turned to Lehman Brothers, which was viewed as the next most vulnerable investment bank. It faced a run on its assets, was no longer able to borrow, and filed for bankruptcy September 15. It set a new record for the size of a bankruptcy, besting WorldCom and, before it, Enron.

Lehman's bankruptcy caused panic in the markets. That day the Dow Jones average fell 504 points. The next day insurer AIG faced imminent collapse. Prime Fund, a money market fund that held Lehman's notes, was no longer able to maintain its shares at $1 of face value. Both had to be bailed out by an infusion of billions of dollars from the Federal Reserve System. And within a month Congress passed an emergency rescue plan, the $700 billion Toxic Assets Relief Program intended to shore up the nation's "too-big-to-fail" institutions. Fuld would later argue that "Lehman's demise was caused by uncontrollable market forces," but admit that "I, myself, did not see the depth and violence of the crisis. I did not see the contagion. I believe we made poor judgments . . ."[39]

Lehman's shareholders lost almost everything. Its stock fell from a high of $62.19 that January to $3.65 at bankruptcy, a 94 percent decline. Where was the firm's board of directors, the entity charged with monitoring management for them? Lehman had an 11-member board including 10 independent directors and one insider, Richard Fuld, who was both chairman of the board and CEO (see the box). Fuld dominated the selection of directors, and they were a congenial group, unlikely to challenge him. There was little board turnover. And directors were generous in compensating Fuld. Between 2000 and 2008 his average pay was $46 million a year.[40]

Only 1 of the 10 outside directors, Jerry A. Grundhofer, had any recent banking experience and he had served only for five months. Another, 80-year-old Henry Kaufman, had retired from investment banking 20 years earlier. Others included current and retired executives from nonfinancial industries. It was not a group selected for keen insight into financial transactions.

During the year preceding bankruptcy the board met eight times and its members earned between $325,038 and $397,538. The directors were informed that Lehman was taking increased risk to create firm growth. At every board meeting they received a risk report, including a numeric representation of the firm's "risk appetite." Managers told the board they were taking precautions to monitor and limit overall risks. They did not, however, fully inform it about all

[38] *Report of Anton R. Valukas, Examiner, In re Lehman Brothers Holdings Inc.,* Chapter 11 Case No. 08-13555, S. Dist. N.Y., March 11, 2010, vol. 1, p. 21.

[39] Testimony of Richard S. Fuld before the Financial Crisis Inquiry Commission hearing on "Too Big to Fail: Expectations and Impact of Extraordinary Government Intervention and the Role of Systemic Risk in the Financial Crisis," Washington, DC, September 1, 2010, p. 203.

[40] Scott Thurm, "Oracle's Ellison: Pay King," *The Wall Street Journal,* July 27, 2010, p. A16.

Lehman Brothers' Board of Directors

These were the 11 members of the Lehman Brothers board of directors in 2008 when the firm filed for bankruptcy. Only Richard S. Fuld was a Lehman Brothers executive. The other 10 were nonemployee directors who qualified as independent under the rules of the New York Stock Exchange.

MICHAEL L. AINSLIE, 64
Private Investor and Former President and
Chief Executive Officer of Sotheby's Holdings

JOHN F. AKERS, 73
Retired Chairman of International Business
Machines Corporation

ROGER S. BERLIND, 77
Theatrical Producer

THOMAS H. CRUIKSHANK, 76
Retired Chairman and Chief Executive Officer of
Halliburton Company

MARSHA JOHNSON EVANS, 60
Rear Admiral, U.S. Navy (Retired)

RICHARD S. FULD, JR., 61
Chairman and Chief Executive Officer,
Lehman Brothers Holdings Inc.

SIR CHRISTOPHER GENT, 59
Non-Executive Chairman of GlaxoSmithKline Plc.

JERRY A. GRUNDHOFER, 63
Chairman Emeritus and Retired Chief Executive
Officer of U.S. Bancorp

ROLAND A. HERNANDEZ, 50
Retired Chairman and Chief Executive Officer of
Telemundo Group, Inc.

HENRY KAUFMAN, 80
President of Henry Kaufman & Company, Inc.

JOHN D. MACOMBER, 80
Principal of JDM Investment Group

In the previous year, each nonexecutive director received an annual cash retainer of $75,000 plus fees for chairing and attending meetings of board committees. Each also received grants of Lehman Brothers stock or stock options valued at $245,038. The 10 nonexecutive directors served on the boards of 16 other companies.

Source: Lehman Brothers Holdings Inc., *Proxy Statement,* March 5, 2008, pp. 6–18.

the dangers. For example, they neglected to mention periodic shortcomings in liquidity tests. And they failed to inform the directors that the firm sometimes exceeded its risk limits. At one board meeting, when the firm had exceeded these limits, the CFO edited a standard chart to remove the risk appetite numbers that ordinarily appeared.[41]

Another time, Lehman's president told a manager not to give the board much detail about risky subprime mortgages because the directors were "not

[41] *Report of Anton R. Valukas, Examiner, In re Lehman Brothers Holdings Inc.,* Chapter 11 Case No. 08-13555, S. Dist. N.Y., March 11, 2010, vol. 1, pp. 21 and 141.

sophisticated."[42] The board did have a risk committee, but it met only twice in the year before Lehman's bankruptcy. It was chaired by the octogenarian Henry Kaufman. Its other members included a retired admiral who had been head of the Girl Scouts, the retired chairman of IBM, a theatrical producer, and the retired chairman of a Spanish-language television company. It was not a group with much background for judging such esoterica as the single tranche collateralized debt obligations that Lehman used to hedge risks.

Lehman's management made serious errors of judgment. Senior officers, including Fuld, certified deceptive financial statements based on accounting tricks. The board failed to detect trouble and rein in extreme risk. Corporate governance let the firm's shareholders down. Although Lehman's headquarters were in New York, it was incorporated in Delaware. A special examiner appointed by the court in Lehman's bankruptcy case found that neither company officers nor directors had breached their fiduciary duty to shareholders under Delaware law. They were protected by its lenient "business judgment" rule, which rejects personal liability absent "reckless indifference," "deliberate disregard," or actions "without the bounds of reason."[43]

Since Lehman had risk policies in place and the directors had discussed risk, their bank accounts were safe from angry shareholders. However, as a group, directors and managers lost considerable wealth. Fuld was Lehman's largest individual shareowner with 12.6 million shares. He held them until the end and, based on price decline from a 2008 high, lost approximately $738 million. The directors held a combined 1.1 million shares that lost about $60 million in value.

The Dodd-Frank Act

Dodd-Frank Act
A statute to reform financial regulation and prevent a recurrence of the 2007–2008 financial crisis.

In the aftermath of Lehman's failure and the financial disaster in its wake, Congress responded with another repair statute, the 849-page *Dodd-Frank Wall Street Reform and Consumer Protection Act of 2010* (the Dodd-Frank Act). At its core it was a huge dose of new financial regulations targeting root causes of the recent crisis. It mandated five new agencies and 330 new rulemakings.[44] There were new powers over banks and financial markets, restraints on risk-taking, limits on hedging and the use of novel financial products, mortgage lending reforms, and strengthened mortgage lending criteria.

While the law's main focus was financial reform, it did not neglect governance failures observed at Lehman and other companies that survived the crisis only with government assistance. The public believed investment bankers were overpaid, and so the Dodd-Frank Act moved to strengthen checks on executive compensation.

- At least once every three years companies have to submit their executive compensation packages to a stockholder vote. The stockholders may approve or disapprove; however, the vote is not binding.

[42] Ibid., p. 90.

[43] Ibid., pp. 47–48 and pp. 54–55.

[44] Curtis W. Copeland, *Rulemaking Requirements and Authorities in the Dodd-Frank Wall Street Reform and Consumer Protection Act,* Congressional Research Service, Report No. R414722, November 3, 2010, p. 8.

- If an executive is entitled to special compensation in case of merger, buyout, or other change of control, the stockholders must have a chance to vote their approval or disapproval. Again, the vote is not binding.
- All members of the board committee that sets executive compensation must be "independent," that is, free of any conflict of interest coming from any paid connection to the company apart from being a director.
- In proxy statements companies must disclose the relationship between executive compensation and their financial performance, including changes in stock values. They must also disclose the ratio of the median pay of all the firm's employees to that of the chief executive.
- If a company issues an accounting restatement, it must recoup any compensation paid to an executive based on financial performance.

It is too early to tell whether and how these requirements will affect executive pay. They attempt to empower stockholders, a notoriously apathetic lot. An additional effort to strengthen stockholders is a requirement that they can submit the names of director nominees and have them included in the proxy materials sent out by companies. This is a big change. In the past shareholders who wanted to run a board candidate had to contact other shareholders at their own very high expense. Now, the company would be forced to put opposition names on its own proxy forms. However, implementation of this procedure is uncertain. When the SEC wrote a new rule giving stockholders who owned 3 percent of the companies' shares access to the proxy, big corporations sued to stop it.[45] They feared that dissident groups, for example, union pension funds or activist coalitions, would be empowered to undermine and distract management by triggering election battles.

BOARDS OF DIRECTORS

The stories of the boards at Enron and Lehman Brothers are singular, but they illustrate widespread tendencies and shortcomings. In fact, the boards of American corporations are marbled with pathologies that enervate them in performance of their watchdog function.

They are often hand-picked by powerful CEOs who fill them with friends and retired CEOs having reputations for congeniality. They depend on management for information and allow management to control agendas. They are unwilling to confront CEOs to whom they owe their selection and compensation. In the harmonious board cultures of most corporations, an abrasive director faces ostracism. Not all directors work hard. Some see their service as largely honorific. Others who are top executives at other companies are preoccupied. A few divide their attention by serving on too many other boards. Many CEOs see their boards as

---

[45] Securities and Exchange Commission, "Facilitating Shareholder Director Nominations; Proposed Rule," 74 FR 29024, June 18, 2009.

unproductive; in a recent survey only 16 percent rated them "highly effective."[46] One described his board as "an aquarium full of dead fish."[47]

Despite pronounced flaws, governance reforms are having an effect. Today boards of directors are in transition, evolving from a collegial, largely honorific group to an assertive watchdog of management. The transition is incomplete, perhaps even preliminary, but that is the direction of change.

Duties of Directors

State incorporation laws require boards of directors. They impose two lofty duties on them, first, to represent the interests of stockholders by conducting a profitable business that enhances share value, and second, to exercise due diligence in supervising management. Directors violate these duties if they put their own self-interest ahead of the shareholders or if they are unreasonably neglectful in their oversight. In practice, directors do not make day-to-day management decisions. Instead, they exercise a very broad oversight, taking responsibility for "the overall picture, not the daily business decisions, the forest, not the trees."[48]

Here is a short list of specific board functions.

- Approve the issuance of securities and the voting rights of their holders.
- Review and approve the corporation's goals and strategies.
- Select the CEO, evaluate his or her performance, and remove that person if necessary.
- Give advice and counsel to management.
- Create governance policies for the firm, including compensation policies.
- Evaluate the performance of individual directors, board committees, and the board as a whole.
- Nominate candidates for election as directors.
- Exercise oversight of ethics and compliance programs.

Board Composition

The average board has 11 members and this has not changed for many years. Most state incorporation laws require a minimum of three, but companies typically have between 7 and 15. The number is often specified as a range in corporate charters. For example, in its Delaware charter Walt Disney Corporation specifies a board of "not less than nine directors or more than twenty-one."[49] Directors are elected by shareholders, usually for terms of one year. Under Delaware law, once

[46] The 2009 National Association of Corporate Directors *Public Company Governance Survey,* cited in Beverly Behan, "Wise Counsel? How to Get Your Board Back on Track," *The Conference Board Review,* Summer 2010, p. 46.

[47] Anonymous, quoted in Ibid., p. 44.

[48] Robert A. G. Monks and Nell Minow, *Corporate Governance,* 3rd ed. (Malden, MA: Blackwell Publishing, 2004), p. 201.

[49] *Restated Certificate of Incorporation of the Walt Disney Company,* Office of the Secretary of State of Delaware, November 17, 1999, Article V(1).

elected they cannot be removed by their fellow directors. Some have terms of two or three years. In such cases only half or a third of the directors are elected each year. Some shareholders dislike such staggered terms, arguing that they insulate directors from frequent accountability.

Directors are most often current or retired executives of other corporations who are sought out for their business acumen. Others include former government officials, politicians, athletes, entertainers, and university presidents or professors. There is growing but limited demographic diversity. In a survey of the largest 100 public corporations 16 percent of directors were female and 15 percent were minorities. Directors are also older; 42 percent were 65 or over.[50] Those who are officers of the company are *inside directors*. They usually come from the ranks of top executives. Those who are not employed by the company are *outside directors*. These directors are also called nonexecutive directors. When outside directors have no important business dealings with the company other than being on its board, they are called *independent directors*.

Standards of independence have tightened. Since recent regulatory and listing rules require a majority of independent directors on the full board and on several committees, they now dominate in numbers. The typical board of 11 has only 1 inside director, the CEO, usually acting as chairman of the board. Overall, outside directors now hold 87 percent of board seats and insiders only 13 percent.[51] The average director serves on only one or two boards; less than 2 percent serve on five or more.[52]

Boards do much of their work in committees. Federal law and stock exchange rules mandate at least three, each composed entirely of independent directors. An *audit* committee oversees auditing and financial reports and assesses financial risks in the company's strategy. A *compensation* committee reviews the performance of top executives and sets their compensation. It also sets the director's pay. The average director of a large public company puts in about 20 hours a month and earns $213,000 a year in retainers and company stock. Shareholders do not approve director's pay packages.[53] And a *nominating* committee identifies candidates for election to the board. Additional committees sometimes found are executive, corporate governance, finance, succession planning, sustainability, science and technology, and investment committees. Board committees usually have three to five members.

inside directors
Directors who are employees of the company.

outside directors
Directors who are not company employees.

independent directors
Outside directors of a corporation who, aside from their directors' duties, do not have business dealings with it that would impair their impartiality.

Board Dynamics

The average board meets eight times a year, although many meet monthly. In advance, the directors receive "board books" of materials, often voluminous, for their review. Then they travel to corporate headquarters. The day before the meeting is occupied with committee meetings, most of which last two to four hours, followed in the evening by a dinner for directors and company executives.

[50] Korn/Ferry Institute, *The Korn/Ferry Market Cap 100: Board Leadership at America's Most Valuable Public Companies* (New York: Korn/Ferry, 2010), pp. 10–12.

[51] PwC, *Annual Corporate Directors Survey: The 2010 Results* (New York: PwC, 2010), p. 30.

[52] Ibid., p. 32.

[53] Colin Leinster, "Are Board Members Paid Enough? 'Definitely Not,'" *Corporate Board Member,* Third Quarter 2010, at www.boardmember.com; and Robert C. Pozen, "A New Model for Corporate Boards," *The Wall Street Journal,* December 30, 2010, p. A15.

The full board meets the next day for an average of four to six hours.[54] Agendas include committee reports, mandatory governance matters, and presentations by company executives. Sometimes a favored senior manager comes to give a Power-Point presentation. Much is routine. The agenda is often crowded and rushed, leaving no time for probing discussions of strategy or risks.[55] In a recent survey a majority of directors said they would like "much more" time devoted to these two subjects.[56] Even if there is meaningful dialogue, conflict and discord are rare. For example, Enron directors who had served for many years described an atmosphere of amity and consensus. They recalled only two instances of a dissenting vote.[57]

The chairman of the board presides over meetings. At most companies this title is held by the CEO, giving him or her a dual role. From this position CEOs can dominate their boards by deciding what information to circulate and by fixing agendas. CEO influence often extends to the selection of supportive directors. In the past CEOs simply suggested new names to compliant boards that then approved nominees who were virtually assured of election by shareholders. Stock exchange rules now require that names be approved by nominating committees of independent directors. These committees have the power to hire search firms to find candidates. However, the CEO is still a source of nominations; few boards will act on a nominee over the objection of a CEO, giving the CEO, in effect, a veto power.

In 2003 the New York Stock Exchange modified its listing standards to require that independent directors meet regularly absent members of management. This is intended to allow outside directors to express concerns that might be suppressed for reasons of collegiality or intimidation in the presence of management. Most large company boards elect a *lead director* from the ranks of independent outside directors to create agendas and preside over such sessions. In practice, however, a lead director operating in the shadow of a combined chairman and CEO lacks substantial power to reshape a board.[58]

Advocates of greater board independence believe that a better solution for strengthening the board is to split the roles of chairman and CEO. They argue that if the board is supposed to appoint, monitor, evaluate, and compensate the CEO it is a conflict of interest to put the CEO in charge. Having a chairman other than the chief executive would diminish that conflict even if the CEO still sat on the board. Thus, many companies have separated the two roles, appointing a *nonexecutive chairman* to lead their boards. Most still combine the two roles, but the trend is toward a split. After the financial crisis in 2008, given the example of Richard S. Fuld's reign over a

lead director
An independent director who presides over meetings of nonmanagement directors.

nonexecutive chairman
A chairman of the board who is not an executive of the corporation.

---

[54] Ibid., pp. 8 and 14.

[55] Gillespie and Zweig, *Money for Nothing,* pp. 107–08.

[56] PwC, *Annual Corporate Directors Survey: The 2010 Results,* pp. 8–9.

[57] Report of the Permanent Subcommittee on Investigations, Committee on Governmental Affairs, U.S. Senate, *The Role of the Board of Directors in Enron's Collapse,* p. 8.

[58] Ira M. Millstein and Stephen Davis, eds., *Chairing the Board: The Case for Independent Leadership in Corporate North America,* Policy Briefing No. 4, Millstein Center for Corporate Governance and Performance, Yale School of Management, 2009, p. 20.

weak Lehman Brothers board, Congress stopped short of requiring separation, but the Dodd–Frank Act requires companies to tell their shareholders once a year why they choose to combine or separate the two roles.[59]

Management often opposes separation. One fear is compromising clarity in the chain of command. According to Jack Welch, former chairman and CEO of General Electric, splitting the roles encourages "decision shopping" by managers who seek out the leader most likely to support them. "When there are two bosses," he says, "you can often get two messages, and that's too bad."[60] It can also be harder for the CEO to make quick decisions if the chairman must be consulted. Another fear is that split roles might threaten a collegial board environment by provoking "mindless animosities and ego contests" between the two leaders.[61] To avoid this, advocates of separation advise that the chairman be someone without ambition to run the company, perhaps a retired chief executive. Despite doubts and resistance, the trend is to move to nonexecutive chairmen; about 40 percent of companies on the Standard & Poor's 500 index have done so.[62]

EXECUTIVE COMPENSATION

Top executives are not simply given paychecks. Instead they are compensated using arcane schemes, mysterious in their complexity that can baffle untutored bystanders. When the schemes are well devised, pay follows performance. When poorly devised they result in excessive pay unrelated to performance. In this section we discuss the components, dynamics, and problems of executive compensation.

Components of Executive Compensation

The pay of top corporate officers is set by the board of directors. In keeping with stock exchange rules, each board must have a compensation committee composed entirely of independent directors. Its members, of course, may be cronies of the CEO. Nevertheless, the committee must create a defensible written plan. At most companies the compensation scheme reflects three beliefs. First, to attract and retain managerial talent, compensation must be competitive. Second, it should be based on both individual and company performance. And third, it should align the interests of executives with the interests of shareholders. These goals are typically achieved using some combination of the following elements.

Base Salary

The annual base salary is usually set near the median salary for leaders of similar firms. At Sherwin-Williams, for example, the salaries of the top five executives are based on a survey of the base salaries of executives with similar

59 Section 972, "Disclosures Regarding Chairman and CEO Structures," 15 USC 78a, sec. 14B.

60 Jack Welch and Suzy Welch, "A Week of Blows to Business," *BusinessWeek,* May 18, 2009.

61 Millstein and Davis, *Chairing the Board,* p. 19.

62 Joann S. Lublin, "Chairman-CEO Split Gains Allies," *The Wall Street Journal,* March 30, 2009, p. B4.

stock option
The right to buy shares of a company's stock at a fixed or *grant price* in the future and under conditions determined by the board of directors.

grant price
The price at which a specified number of shares can be purchased in the future by executives who hold options.

vesting date
The date when stock options can be exercised by purchasing shares at the grant price.

expiration date
A future date, after the vesting date, when shares can no longer be bought at the grant price.

performance shares
Shares of company stock awarded after a fixed period of years if individual and company performance goals are met.

responsibilities at 18 peer companies, all similarly sized industrial firms.[63] Companies use such peer group comparisons as a measure of the market for executive talent. Base salaries for CEOs stay around $1 million, the amount that the Internal Revenue Service allows as tax deductible.[64] At Sherwin-Williams the CEO received $1.3 million in 2009. Its other top executives received between $488,000 and $733,000.

Annual Cash Incentives

Most large companies make an annual bonus part of the compensation package. Criteria for earning the bonus vary. At McGraw-Hill the CEO's incentive pay is based on meeting net income (weighted 75 percent) and revenue (weighted 25 percent) goals.[65] At Abbott Laboratories the CEO's yearly bonus is based on whether the company hits multiple financial goals including profitability, sales, returns, and earnings per share. This resulted in an award of $3.9 million in a recent year.[66] Annual cash incentives are typically based on meeting financial targets. If targets are missed bonuses go down and, when companies do poorly, the bonus columns in compensation tables often contain goose eggs.

Long-Term Stock-Based Incentives

Compensation in stock is designed to align managers' incentives with the interests of stockholders. There are several frequently used types of stock awards.

First, *stock options* give an executive the right to buy the company's stock at a fixed or *grant price* in the future and under conditions determined by the board of directors. Options are usually priced at the closing market price on the day they are granted. The holder of the options then can buy these shares from the company at a specified future date, called the *vesting date*. The holder must buy them before a later *expiration date* when the options can no longer be exercised. At Johnson & Johnson, for example, options vest and can only be exercised (purchased) three years after they are granted and must be exercised within 10 years or they expire.[67] Thus, if Johnson & Johnson grants 1,000 options to an executive at $70 a share and the price rises to $100 after five years, the executive may buy them from the company for $70,000, then sell them for $100,000, making a $30,000 profit (minus taxes and fees). However, if after three years the shares have fallen to $50, they are said to be "under water" and they are worthless. The executive will not exercise the options.

Second, *performance shares* are shares awarded after a fixed period of years only if individual or company performance goals are met. These shares may be awarded in part or not at all depending on how closely performance matches goals. Typically, the time from grant to award is at least three years. General Electric awards its top executives "performance share units" that convert into shares of GE stock after five years. Half the shares are awarded if cash flow from operating activities grows

---

[63] Sherwin-Williams Company, *Proxy Statement*, March 9, 2007, pp. 24–25.

[64] See 26 USC §162(m)(1) 2010.

[65] McGraw-Hill Companies, *Proxy Statement*, March 23, 2010, p. 38.

[66] Abbott Laboratories, *Proxy Statement*, March 15, 2010, pp. 14 and 18.

[67] Johnson & Johnson, *Notice of Annual Meeting and Proxy Statement*, March 17, 2010, p. 29.

an average of 10 percent a year during the interim.[68] The other half of the shares are awarded if total return to shareholders exceeds that of the Standard & Poor's 500 index. If these goals are not met, the "units" are canceled, unlike options that can be exercised any time between vesting and expiration.

Third, *restricted stock* is a grant of stock with restrictions on transaction that are removed when a specified condition is met. Usually, the recipient receives dividends and can vote the shares but cannot sell them until the restriction is lifted. Any specified condition can be a restriction. Often, it is tenure at the company. In this way, restricted stock is used to lock in promising talent or key executives. If, for example, the shares vest in 10 years, then the executive must stay on the job that long to realize their value.

IBM uses restricted stock to retain the loyalty of its "senior leadership team" in what it believes is a highly competitive market for executive talent. Awards are typically for five years and are forfeited if the person leaves. In 2010 the top five most compensated executives at IBM held a little more than 14 million restricted stock units worth approximately $2.2 billion.[69] At ExxonMobil 50 to 75 percent of senior executive's pay is in restricted shares. Of these, half are restricted for 5 years and half for 10 years or until the executive retires, whichever is *later*. If the person leaves, the grants are canceled. Its compensation committee argues for such lengthy time restrictions because in the oil and gas industry the wisdom of investments may not be known for many years.[70] Unlike stock options, restricted shares are not worthless if their market price is below the grant price when they vest.[71]

Options, performance shares, and restricted stock are all used to create a long-term performance incentive. They also align manager and shareholder interests by promoting stock ownership of top executives.

Retirement Plans

Companies provide generous pensions for top executives. Each year they credit pension funds with a sum calculated as a percent of the person's salary. This sum is held by the company to cover future pension payments; however, it is reported as part of the executive's total compensation. For large companies with highly paid CEOs the increased value of a pension can be significant. In a recent year it added $1.9 million for Samuel J. Palmisano of IBM, $1.9 million for Jeffrey Immelt of GE, and $4.4 million for Andrew Liveris of Dow Chemical Company.

Perquisites

Acknowledging the needs and lifestyles of top executives, companies often provide extra benefits. Among the most common are annual physical exams, travel on

---

restricted stock
A grant of stock with restrictions. It cannot be sold until certain conditions are met, most often the lapse of time or meeting a performance goal.

---

[68] Performance share units granted after 2009 convert if adjusted cumulative industrial cash flow from operating activities is $70 billion or higher. General Electric Company, *Notice of 2010 Annual Meeting and Proxy Statement*, March 9, 2010, p. 24.

[69] IBM *Notice of 2010 Annual Meeting and Proxy Statement*, March 8, 2010, p. 44.

[70] ExxonMobil Corp., *Notice of 2010 Annual Meeting and Proxy Statement*, April 13, 2010, pp. 29–30.

[71] As an example, suppose a manager is awarded both options and restricted stock on a day when shares sell at $20. Five years later, on a day when the price is $18, both the options and the restricted shares vest. The options are worthless, because to exercise them the manager must buy the shares at $20. The restricted stock, on the other hand, is transferred to the manager at its current value. It can be sold immediately for $18 a share.

FIGURE 18.4 **How Emerson Electric Uses Elements of Compensation**

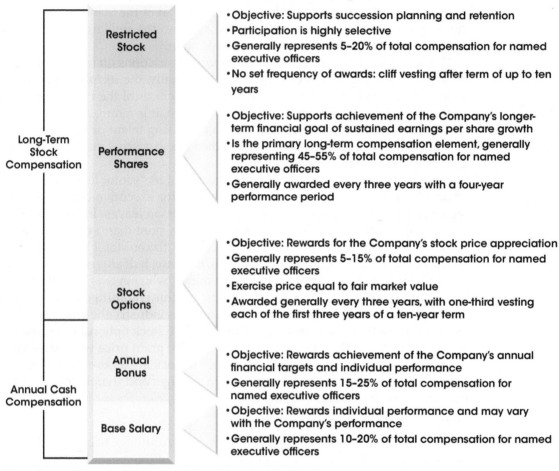

Source: Emerson Electric Co., *Definitive Proxy Statement*, December 10, 2010, p. 18.

company jets, home alarm systems, bodyguards, leased autos, club memberships, personal financial planning, and life and health insurance. SEC rules require that the dollar value of such extras be disclosed to shareholders. A few examples of reported perks are $38,272 in premiums on a medical plan with no deductibles or co-payments for the chief executive at TRW Automotive, $49,440 for a "weekend driver" for Martha Stewart at Martha Stewart Living Omnimedia, $391,000 for personal financial planning for the CEO of Occidental Petroleum, and $3.7 million to a division president at Microsoft for a loss on the sale of his home when he relocated.[72]

At each company, compensation committees choose among these basic elements of executive pay, picking combinations that fit their compensation philosophy. Figure 18.4 shows how Emerson Electric Co. uses a flexible combination of

[72] Joann S. Lublin, "Shareholders Hit the Roof Over Home-Loss Subsidies," *The Wall Street Journal*, October 25, 2010, p. B1; and Daniel Fisher, "The Perk Game," *Forbes*, June 7, 2010, p. 36.

pay elements to reward and retain its top executives. Each executive is compensated based on factors such as level of responsibility, promise, performance, and length of service.

Although the base pay of top executives can be generous, astronomical payouts are usually the fruition of earlier incentive awards. With stock-based awards the bonanza can come as long as 10 years after the shares are awarded, sometimes making it seem that compensation is out of step with current performance.

Problems with CEO Compensation

There are multiple shortcomings of CEO compensation. Here are some of the most important.

First, critics are outraged by extraordinary payouts. The perception of widespread, excessively generous remuneration is an old story. President Franklin D. Roosevelt railed against the "entrenched greed" of executives. Yet pay in his era was modest compared with today. For example, in 1929 Eugene G. Grace, president of Bethlehem Steel, the highest-paid top executive, received a salary of $12,000 and a bonus of $1.6 million. Translated into current dollars this is $20 million. If that sum astonished the nation, it would no longer. The highest paid executive in the decade 2000 to 2010, Larry Ellison, the CEO of Oracle, averaged $184 million a year and took home $700 million in 2001 alone.[73] In 2009 average CEO pay at 456 of the largest companies was $7.23 million and eighteen companies went over the $20 million mark.[74]

The source of outrage about CEO pay is a sense of unfairness. In 2010 the average S&P 500 CEO made 267 times the wages of the least-paid company worker.[75] The CEO is only one person, but hundreds or thousands of employees labored to make the firm profitable. Usually, however, CEO pay is determined by market forces in the competition for managerial talent.[76] And most managers never get the dramatically high salaries that attract criticism. Indeed, some argue that more than a few top executives are underpaid. This is especially true in smaller businesses. However, spectacular excesses define public perception of pay in corporate America.

Second, compensation is not always aligned with performance. While total compensation is higher in larger firms and mostly follows share price performance, there are notable exceptions. Between 2000 and 2009 Barry Diller of IAC/InterActive and Expedia.com received $1.1 billion while the share price declined 12 percent. Over the same years Richard D. Fairbank of Capital One Financial received $569 million while the share price declined 14 percent. From 1999 to 2009 John T. Chambers of Cisco Systems received $393 million while the share price

---

[73] Thurm, "Oracle's Ellison: Pay King," p. A16.

[74] Joann S. Lublin, "Paychecks for CEOs Climb," *The Wall Street Journal*, November 15, 2010, p. A1; and Joann S. Lublin, "A Closer Look at Three Big Paydays," *The Wall Street Journal*, November 15, 2010, p. B5.

[75] Rana Foroohar, "Stuffing Their Pockets," *Newsweek*, September 13, 2010, p. 20.

[76] Steven N. Kaplan, "Are U.S. CEOs Overpaid?" *Academy of Management Executive*, May 2008.

declined 29 percent.[77] Robert Nardelli, who abruptly resigned as CEO of Home Depot in 2007, received exit pay of $210 million on top of his previous year's pay of $33 million. Nardelli, who was reputed to be a despot, failed over six years to raise the company's share price.

Nevertheless, defenders of CEO compensation say many large compensation packages are justified by stockholder gains. This clearly applies to former CEOs Lee Raymond of ExxonMobil and Jack Welch of General Electric. The price of their companies' stock rose significantly over long periods while they were in office. Steven Jobs of Apple received more than $700 million in compensation over the past decade, most in the vesting of restricted shares, but in that time shareholder value increased more than 1,000 percent. Arguably, these executives, and others, devised and executed the strategies responsible for rising equity. Their achievements were rewarded accordingly.

Third, some compensation committees fail to design and execute adequate compensation plans. Such plans are a complex mixture of art and science involving many choices and judgments.[78] Not a few committees choose badly. For example, when they base salaries and bonuses on median levels in a group of peer companies they often choose larger peers. Compensation tends to increase with company size. Since most committees set executive compensation at or above the median in the peer group, choosing larger peer companies increases pay. One study of 429 firms found that more than 96 percent set their CEO's median salary and bonus at or above the peer group benchmark. Because firms chose larger companies in their peer groups, this had the effect of raising chief executive total compensation an average of $1,191,020 over what it would have been if peer groups contained similarly sized companies.[79]

An example is Tootsie Roll Industries, which uses a peer group of 16 companies, all larger than Tootsie Roll, most substantially (see the box). Four have between 20 and 30 times Tootsie Roll's revenues. Using median compensation in the peer group as one element of compensation, Tootsie Roll paid its 90-year-old CEO Melvin Gordon $2.6 million in 2009.[80] Its board has only five directors, including Melvin Gordon and his wife, President Ellen Gordon, who was paid $2.5 million. The remaining three independent directors sit on the compensation committee.

Some compensation committees fall under the spell of a powerful CEO. Imagine a situation in which a committee with a well-constructed compensation plan is approached by such a CEO during a recession. The CEO's pay, which is based on incentives to achieve revenue growth, has fallen. "I'm working harder than ever," argues the CEO. "The economy is beyond my control and I deserve more than the current plan allows." The committee then gives in, making a onetime departure

[77] Thurm, "Oracle's Ellison: Pay King," p. A16.

[78] Robin A. Ferracone, *Fair Pay, Fair Play: Aligning Executive Performance and Pay* (San Francisco: Jossey-Bass, 2010), p. 35.

[79] Michael Faulkender and Jun Yang, "Inside the Black Box: The Role and Composition of Compensation Peer Groups," *Journal of Financial Economics,* May 2010, p. 268.

[80] Tootsie Roll Industries, Inc., *Proxy Statement,* March 26, 2010, pp. 11 and 16.

Tootsie Roll Industries Peer Group

Tootsie Roll Industries uses a study of compensation levels in other companies as a basis for determining the compensation of its top executives. In 2009 it picked these 16 companies as its peers in the snack and confectionary industries. Tootsie Roll had revenues of $496 million.

Peer Company	Annual Revenues (in millions)
Campbell Soup Company	$7,586
Dean Foods Company	$11,158
Del Monte Foods Company	$3,627
Diamond Foods, Inc.	$571
Flowers Foods, Inc.	$2,601
General Mills, Inc.	$14,691
H. J. Heinz Company	$10,148
Hershey Company	$5,299
J&J Snack Foods Corp.	$653
Kellogg Company	$12,587
Lancaster Colony Corp.	$1,051
Lance, Inc.	$918
McCormick & Company, Inc.	$3,192
Ralcorp Holdings, Inc.	$2,892
The J. M. Smucker Company	$3,758
TreeHouse Foods, Inc.	$1,512

Source: Tootsie Roll Industries, *Proxy Statement*, March 26, 2010, p. 11 and Tootsie Roll Industries, *Annual Report*, Form 10-K, March 1, 2010, exhibit 13, p. 2.

from its formal plan, and approves an award of several million stock options, currently of modest value, to the unhappy CEO. Years down the road, when the economy is better, this exception might result in princely sums that are wildly inconsistent with current performance. If pay is to correlate with performance, compensation policies must not only be designed well, but they must be consistently implemented.

Fourth, executives can manipulate their compensation. When annual salary and bonus are based on accounting measures such as net income, the CEO can take actions to maximize short-term profits. When compensation is based on stock options, the CEO can delay taking profits until a future year when options vest. Another problem with options has been *backdating*, or setting the exercise price of options at the price on a date before the date they were granted. As explained, an option gives the owner the right to buy stock in the future at a set price. Normally that price is the closing stock market price on the day of the grant. Backdating occurs when the company, at the time of the grant or retroactively, fixes the grant

backdating
Setting the exercise price of stock options at the price on a date before the date they were granted.

Backdating: A Hypothetical Example

1. On June 1, 2008, a CEO gets an option grant to purchase 1,000 shares of his company's stock which can be exercised in two years. The shares are priced at $30, the closing price on the New York Stock Exchange that day.

2. On June 1, 2010, when the options vest, the stock is selling for $29 a share. At this point the stock option is worthless.

3. The company decides to backdate the options to May 1, 2008, when the shares closed at $22.

4. The executive now decides to exercise the options, buying 1,000 shares from the company at $22 for $22,000, then selling them on the open market for $29 a share or $29,000. This nets a profit before taxes and brokerage fees of $7,000.

5. The value of the options is reported by the corporation as a cost, reducing net income. The lost value, in theory, reduces shareholder value.

date as a past date when the price of the stock was lower. In plain terms, companies search the past for troughs in share prices, then pretend the options were granted at these low points (see the above box).

A statistical analysis of options published in *The Wall Street Journal* found that at some companies they were granted repeatedly on days when share prices hit historic lows.[81] One example was a striking series of favorable coincidences at UnitedHealth Group, where 12 separate option grants went to William W. McGuire, its chairman and chief executive, on days when the stock fell to yearly or quarterly lows. According to the *Journal*, the odds against picking this series of dates by chance were 1 in 200 million, lower than the odds for winning the Powerball lottery. Further investigation found that over time McGuire received 44 million options, most of which were illegally backdated. He was forced to resign and return more than $600 million to the company.[82]

And fifth, disclosures of compensation policy are difficult to understand. Companies must disclose their compensation plans and the annual compensation of the top five executive officers to shareholders. They do this in the proxy statements mailed before annual meetings. The sections on compensation are lengthy. An average "discussion and analysis" is 25 to 30 pages of challenging prose filled with charts, columns of figures, and footnotes that invite a magnifying glass. IBM's most recent compensation discussion covered 53 pages with 30 charts and tables.

These discussions became more complex in 2006 when the SEC imposed more than 100 pages of new rules for their contents.[83] Although the rules were

[81] Charles Forcelle and James Bandler, "The Perfect Payday," *The Wall Street Journal*, March 18, 2006, p. A1.

[82] Eric Dash, "Former Chief Will Forfeit $418 Million," *The New York Times*, December 7, 2007, p. C1.

[83] See Securities and Exchange Commission, "Executive Compensation and Related Person Disclosure; Final Rule and Proposed Rule," 71 FR 53158, September 8, 2006; Securities and Exchange Commission, Executive Compensation Disclosure; Interim Final Rule," 71 FR 78338, December 29, 2006; and subsequent conforming amendments, RIN 3235-AI80.

intended to give stockholders more "clear, concise and meaningful information," they may have had a reverse effect.[84] Most companies now design their discussions to satisfy regulators rather than as a communication to the average shareholder, who might be inclined to stop reading after sentences such as the following.

> *United States Steel* The 2006 performance award vested in 2009 at a rate of 53.84 percent of the target based upon U.S. Steel's total shareholder return ranking at nearly the 27th percentile of the peer group for the preceding three-year performance period.[85]

> *Target Corporation* The amounts reported have been adjusted to eliminate service-based forfeiture assumptions and exclude reversals of amounts expensed but not reported in prior years' Summary Compensation Tables, both of which are used for financial reporting purposes.[86]

> *Suncor Energy* Cash payments are provided for annual remuneration during the notice period, for ESP options which, but for the Termination Event, would have become exercisable during the notice period, and for PSUs and RSUs that would pay out during the notice period based on a performance factor calculated at the date of termination, if applicable.[87]

Despite such examples, there is also some clarity in compensation discussions. A required "summary compensation table" gives the sum of annual salaries, bonuses, stock awards, pension value, and perquisites. However, a CEO's true compensation is a stream of value extending into the future that expands or contracts depending on periodic vesting of stock awards, the market value of those shares, incentive payments based on future corporate performance, and unusual events such as hostile mergers, which can trigger special "golden parachutes" for ousted executives. In such a living equation, a precise dollar figure for compensation is an elusive, moving target.

CONCLUDING OBSERVATIONS

In this chapter we discuss how shareholders, boards of directors, and managements interact in an imperfect system of corporate governance. Shareholders have the power to control managers, but they are scattered, passive, and largely absent any influence in practice. Boards of directors exist to monitor management for the shareholders, but they are frequently watchdogs without a bark, content to rubber-stamp the actions of management. Fortunately, most of the time management is trustworthy and proficient, giving stockholders a fair return on their investment.

[84] Securities and Exchange Commission, "Executive Compensation and Related Person Disclosure," 71 FR 53158, September 8, 2006, at 53160.

[85] United States Steel Corporation, *Notice of Annual Meeting of Stockholders and Proxy Statement,* April 27, 2010, p. 57.

[86] Target Corporation, *Proxy Statement,* April 23, 2009, p. 35.

[87] Suncor Energy Inc., *2010 Management Proxy Circular,* p. 29.

Recently, as in the cases of Enron and Lehman Brothers, failures of governance have had awful consequences. As in the past, Congress responded with new rules to strengthen governance by making directors more independent of management and giving shareholders a more powerful voice. So the governance system is evolving. Its formal checks and balances, having been slightly recalibrated, may now better protect corporate stakeholders.

High Noon at Hewlett-Packard

In the beginning there was a garage. As legend has it, this humble structure in Palo Alto, California, gave birth to giant Hewlett-Packard Company. It was there that Bill Hewlett and David Packard, both recent graduates of Stanford University, spent years tinkering before coming up with their first successful product, a precision oscillator. The two partners went public with their company in 1949.

As it grew they ran it using a homegrown philosophy called the HP Way. At its core the HP Way emphasized the worth of each employee. It inspired a nonhierarchical, decentralized, and participative company in which the creativity of each scientist and engineer was freed.

For many years Hewlett-Packard was the bright star in the Silicon Valley firmament. But as the twentieth century approached, it no longer blazed with innovation. Its aging co-founders' hands had lifted from the controls. Despite booming markets, its earnings were lackluster, its share price stagnant. Eventually, its board of directors saw the need for a new CEO.

CARLY FIORINA

The choice was Carleton S. Fiorina, called Carly by friends and associates. Fiorina was the first woman to head a corporation as large as Hewlett-Packard. She came from a position as a group president at Lucent Technologies. Her mandate from the HP board was to shake things up.

Immediately, Fiorina was a celebrity. It frustrated her when the media categorized her as "Carly Fiorina, female CEO" and reporters focused on her as a woman rather than on her mission at HP.[1]

> From the first . . . both the language and the intensity of the coverage were different for me than for any other CEO. It was more personal, with much

commentary about my personality and my physical appearance, my dress, my hair or my shoes . . . There was a persistent rumor . . . that I'd built a pink marble bathroom in my office.[2]

She learned that her actions would be interpreted through a gender lens. After taking the helm at HP in 1999 she was called both a "bimbo" and a "bitch" in Silicon Valley chat rooms. When male CEOs fired people, they were called firm and commanding; she was labeled vengeful. Such interpretations made her job "infinitely more difficult."[3]

Fiorina believed that HP had been poorly managed for years. She set to work galvanizing its managers. One problem was that in the HP culture, decisions were decentralized. This was faithful to the HP Way, which taught that employees were the primary source of wisdom. But it slowed operations. Fiorina began to restructure processes so that everything went through her.

The first sign of trouble came in November 2000, when Lewis Platt, the former CEO who continued as chairman of the board, requested that Fiorina leave a board meeting so the other directors could talk.[4] He told them she was moving too fast with her plans for change.

Although the board affirmed its support for her, Fiorina was troubled. She responded by regularly inviting the directors to management meetings and setting up a Web site where they could find any data available to other HP employees. At board meetings she started going around the table asking each director to speak and state what action they would take on important issues. After each meeting she summarized points of agreement and disagreement in writing,

[1] Carly Fiorina, *Tough Choices: A Memoir* (New York: Portfolio, 2006), p. 171.

[2] Ibid., p. 172.

[3] Ibid., p. 173.

[4] Platt's resignation as CEO had been amicable. He would resign as chairman and retire from the company on December 31, 1999. Fiorina was then elected chairman.

EXHIBIT 1

The Hewlett-Packard Board in 1999

When Carly Fiorina arrived at Hewlett-Packard this was the board of directors. There were 13 members, 9 outside directors and, including herself, 4 inside directors. Four of the outside directors were related to the cofounders by birth or marriage. The board had five committees: Audit, Compensation, Executive, Finance and Investment, and Organization Review and Nominating. Each director was paid a $100,000 retainer, of which 75 percent was paid in HP stock. Individual directors were paid $5,000 for serving as committee chairs and a fee of $1,200 for each full board meeting attended.

Philip M. Condit, 57
Chairman and CEO, Boeing Company

Patricia C. Dunn, 46
Chair, Barclays Global Investors

John B. Fery, 69
Retired Chairman and CEO, Boise Cascade

Carleton S. Fiorina, 45
CEO, Hewlett-Packard Company

Jean-Paul G. Gimon, 63
General Representative, Credit Lyonnais and son-in-law of HP cofounder William R. Hewlett

Sam Ginn, 62
Chairman, Vodafone AirTouch

Richard A. Hackborn, 62
Retired Executive Vice President, Hewlett-Packard

Walter B. Hewlett, 55
Chairman, The William and Flora Hewlett Foundation

George A. Keyworth, 60
Chairman, Progress & Freedom Association

Susan Packard Orr, 53
Chair, The David and Lucile Packard Foundation

David Woodly Packard, 58
Founder, Packard Humanities Institute

Lewis E. Platt, 58 (Chairman)
Former CEO, Hewlett-Packard

Robert P. Wayman, 54
Executive Vice President and Chief Financial Officer, Hewlett-Packard

along with action steps. This detail mentality may have irritated some directors.

TENSION ON THE BOARD

Fiorina had a strong view about the board's role in corporate governance. The directors were there to watch over management. Their duty was to see the big picture and ensure that major strategies were aligned with the stockholders' interests. However, the day-to-day work of running the enterprise was management's job—her job.

> The management team's job is to manage the company and produce results. A board meets six or eight times a year and cannot possibly know enough of the details of a business to manage it. And yet a board must represent the company's owners and this means knowing enough to ask the right questions.[5]

[5] Fiorina, *Tough Choices*, p. 210.

As time went on, she believed that some influential board members failed to draw a line between their broad oversight role and her daily management role. One was Richard Hackborn, a retired HP executive who had worked closely with the co-founders over the years. Another was George Keyworth, a former science adviser to President Ronald Reagan with a doctorate in physics. Both were technologists who, she felt, lacked appreciation for problems of execution. They were filled with suggestions and sometimes wanted to change projects and budgets in midstream. They met with employees. They even suggested that Fiorina fire certain managers.

Among other ideas, they proposed the acquisition of Compaq Computer Corporation. This was an opportunity to expand market share and achieve operating economies, but the combination would be difficult. It would require laying off tens of thousands of people in both companies and blending distinctive cultures.

After considerable debate, the full HP board unanimously agreed to the $22 billion acquisition. Just before the announcement in late 2001, HP's intentions were leaked to the media, obviously by a well-informed insider. Now HP was placed on the defensive. Reaction in the business press and among investors was immediately hostile due to the conventional wisdom that such huge combinations usually failed. HP's share price fell. The identity of the leaker was never discovered.

Then board member Walter Hewlett, the co-founder's son, surprised Fiorina by changing his mind and opposing the acquisition. He was soon joined by David Packard, son of the other co-founder. Together, the two controlled more than 16 percent of HP shares. Both disliked the dilution of their ownership in the company that would come from issuing millions of new shares for the acquisition.

Hewlett stopped attending board meetings and, with Packard, launched a battle to garner enough votes to stop the deal. He persuaded one board member, Sam Ginn, to change his mind. Ginn then came to a board meeting and pressed the other directors to reverse course. They held firm. Finally, after a bitter fight, HP's shareholders approved the acquisition by a slight 3 percent margin.[6] The merger was completed;

Carly Fiorina discusses the plan to buy Compaq at a 2001 news conference. Source: © AP Photo/Paul Sakuma.

however, a consequence of the internecine battle was that investors remained skeptical about it for years.

Fiorina's problems with the board continued. As time passed, expectations from the Compaq merger were far from being met. Earnings targets were missed. HP's share price languished. The board was unhappy. Fiorina continued to believe that the board was intruding on her role as chief executive by nosing into operational details.

A change on the board came when two CEOs, Sam Ginn and Phil Condit, retired in early 2004. That left only two other CEOs with operating experience. These were the kind of board members most valued by Fiorina because she felt that they respected her management prerogatives. It proved difficult to recruit others in their mold, however, because after the passage of the Sarbanes-Oxley Act in 2002 the leaders of large corporations cut back on outside board memberships to focus more on time-consuming governance requirements in their own firms.

Then there was the abrasion of the board's technology committee. It was formed in 2002 at the suggestion

---

[6] A week after the meeting Walter Hewlett filed a lawsuit in the Delaware Chancery Court alleging that HP had bought the vote of Deutsche Bank. In April, the court dismissed the lawsuit and Hewlett did not further contest the vote.

of director Tom Perkins. Perkins had moved to the HP board from the Compaq board in 2001. He was a formidable presence, combining a long history at HP with a keen mind for strategy. He had been hired by Hewlett and Packard in 1957 and ran the company's research labs for more than a decade until they put him in charge of the new computer division. Perkins built the HP computer business, then left in 1972 to co-found what became the nation's leading venture capital firm, Kleiner, Perkins, Caufield & Byers.

This partnership provided seed capital for Silicon Valley start-ups. Its spectacular successes were Genentech, AOL, Netscape, Amazon, and Google. Perkins became a billionaire, soon adopting an extraordinary lifestyle of mansions and fast cars. His sailing ship, the *Maltese Falcon* is, at 289 feet, the longest private yacht in the world. After his first wife died of cancer, he married, then divorced, celebrity romance novelist Danielle Steel. According to Perkins, they remain deeply in love, but they cannot live together because "it would be easier to merge General Motors and General Electric. You know, we lead big, complicated lives."[7]

Perkins was joined on the technology committee by George Keyworth and Dick Hackborn, the inventor of laser printing. All three were fascinated with scientific details and soaring possibilities for new products. All three were dominating directors. Under their lead, the committee began to function as a board-within-a-board. It often met the day before a regular board meeting, and its agenda ranged over all aspects of HP's business. It was a breeding ground for projects and suggestions. Most of them were rejected by Fiorina, who believed that the "disruptive" technologists lacked appreciation for the obstacles to achieving financial results from their ideas. In her view, "They thought because they understood technology, they understood everything."[8] As their suggestions were spurned, the committee members grew restive.

Another conflict also arose. The technologists became impatient with director Patricia Dunn's leadership of the audit committee. Dunn was a determined force. The proof was in her career. She grew up in Las Vegas, where her mother was a model and showgirl and her father booked entertainment at hotels. When she was 11, her father died. When the time for college

HP Director Tom Perkins at the window of his San Francisco office in 2006. Source: © AP Photo/Eric Risberg.

came, she won a scholarship to the University of Oregon, but had to drop out and work as a cook and housekeeper to support herself and her mother. Later she attended the University of California, Berkeley on a scholarship, making a daily three-bus commute and graduating with a journalism degree.[9]

Soon she took a temporary secretarial position at Wells Fargo Bank in San Francisco. After the bank was acquired by Barclays Global Investors, she rose to become that company's CEO from 1995 to 2002. She came to the HP board in 1998. In 2001 she was diagnosed with breast cancer and a year later with melanoma, causing her to step down as CEO. She retained her position as chairman of the board at Barclays.

On the audit committee she focused on governance procedures. She was methodical and organized. Keyworth and others saw an obsession with details that blocked her appreciation of the big picture. Her strength was the minutia of legal compliance, not the spirited, freewheeling strategy debate the technologists thrived on. They worried that the board was moving in the wrong direction. It needed an infusion of imagination.

Perkins felt it had become what he called a "compliance board," or a board focused on obeying laws

---

[7] "Conversation with Tom Perkins," *The Charlie Rose Show,* December 5, 2007, transcript, p. 12.

[8] Fiorina, *Tough Choices,* p. 280.

[9] George Anders and Alan Murray, "Inside Story of Feud That Plunged HP into Crisis," *The Sunday Times,* October 15, 2006, p. B18.

and rules, where meeting time was consumed with boring hours of reports by lawyers and committees. In contrast, Perkins wanted a "guidance board," or a board of knowledgeable insiders and industry experts that takes an active role in the company, not only reviewing strategy, but becoming deeply involved in its management.[10] A compliance board plodded along checking boxes. A guidance board could better jolt HP from its slumber.

Perkins and his technology committee colleagues wanted to add Silicon Valley friends with scientific and entrepreneurial backgrounds to the board. Fiorina resisted these nominations. She continued to favor candidates with big-company operating experience, ideally, CEOs of other large corporations who were more likely to share her view that the board should stay at arms' length from management. Tension over the role of the board and its composition hung in the air. It did not ease when Tom Perkins retired in 2003 after reaching the mandatory retirement age for HP directors of 72.

Over the next year the directors grew more troubled by Fiorina's performance. Revenues and profits were climbing, largely because the Compaq merger made HP much bigger. However, the merger was not living up to expectations. Fiorina continued to be a media celebrity. She frequently traveled for speeches and appearances. Keyworth, Dunn, and others believed she was distracted from, even unattracted to, the relentless, draining hard work of running a big company. Her subordinates were frustrated. Talented managers were quitting. HP had lost market share in computers to Dell and in network servers to both Dell and IBM. Its profit margins in key business segments were falling. HP's share price was just over $40 when Fiorina was named CEO in 1999. Through 2004 it traded below $20. She had centralized management so that almost every decision went through her, and she resisted efforts by board members to reach into the management process. She failed to communicate with them except at regularly scheduled meetings. They regarded her as imperious.[11]

Late in the year, Keyworth led a movement to bring Perkins back, arguing that the board needed another member with technology expertise. He told Fiorina that Perkins missed being on the board. She countered that his return was a breach of HP's governance policy. In the post-Enron climate of reform, disregard of the retirement rule would look bad. Moreover, what the board really needed was another big-company chief executive with operating expertise. Yet in a momentary lapse of resolve, she agreed to Perkin's return. It was a slip she would regret.

FIORINA'S FALL

Perkins was invited to attend a January 2005 board meeting as a visitor. His official reappointment would take longer to meet the letter of HP's governance policy. However, several members requested that the board vote immediately to appoint him. Fiorina countered that his formal confirmation must wait. He had not studied statements of operating results that needed approval that day. If all voting directors were not well versed on the financials, requirements of the Sarbanes-Oxley Act would be sacrificed. She got her way.

Although not yet officially appointed, Perkins nevertheless stayed in the meeting and was immediately outspoken. He suggested specific actions, including acquisition of another software firm and altering the roles of certain top executives. Fiorina rebuffed the advice, telling Perkins and his allies that it was her prerogative as CEO to make such decisions. According to Perkins, "She made it very clear . . . that our opinions were less than welcome on operational and organizational specifics."[12]

As the meeting wore on, the board proposed a reorganization to delegate some of Fiorina's duties to other executives. She opposed the plan. If the board held her accountable for results, then it should let her make her own decisions about how to achieve them. But by the end of the meeting she had agreed to combine two product groups under a new manager and yielded to ground rules for evaluating other changes over the coming months.

Days later, *The Wall Street Journal* published a front-page story about the meeting quoting "people close to the situation," phrasing that could refer only to two or more directors.[13] According to the article,

---

[10] Tom Perkins, "The 'Compliance' Board," *The Wall Street Journal,* March 2, 2007, p. A11.

[11] Anthony Bianco, *The Big Lie: Spying, Scandal, and Ethical Collapse at Hewlett-Packard* (New York: Public Affairs, 2010), pp. 105–06.

[12] Tom Perkins, *Valley Boy: The Education of Tom Perkins* (New York: Gotham Books, 2007), p. 4.

[13] Pui-Wing Tam, "Hewlett-Packard Board Considers a Reorganization," *The Wall Street Journal,* January 24, 2005, p. A1.

the HP board was still supportive of Fiorina, but very concerned about the company's ragged financial performance, an exodus of managers to competing firms, and weak market performance. Of Fiorina, one source said she "has tremendous abilities," but "she shouldn't be running everything every day. She is very hands on and that slows things down."[14]

"It is hard to convey how violated I felt," said Fiorina.[15] This leak was a profound breach of confidentiality. If directors are to fulfill their oversight role, they must be able to trust the others present. If they fear that remarks will become public they might not engage in the open, honest, and unreserved deliberations that best serve stockholders. She immediately convened a conference call with the entire board. After scolding them for the breach, she asked the board's nominating and governance committee to investigate. It engaged an attorney to interview each board member, not only to ask about the leak, but to solicit their views about the overall effectiveness of the board and how to improve its functioning.

Fiorina was certain that Tom Perkins and his technology committee friend Keyworth were the leakers because they were the ones pushing hardest for the reorganization described in the article.[16] In the investigation, only Perkins admitted speaking to a reporter, insisting that he had not initiated the story, but responded only when he was called to confirm its contents. He claimed he had only tried to ward off some damaging details. No other director admitted involvement. The attorney's report also described the board as "dysfunctional" due to personality conflicts and the tendency of a few dominating members to divert the agenda to long discussions on side topics.

After this, the directors stopped communicating with Fiorina. A special February 8 board meeting was set up in a hotel to keep it out of the media. When Fiorina arrived Patricia Dunn immediately called the group to order, though Fiorina, as chairman of the board, would ordinarily preside. Dunn asked if Fiorina had anything to say. Fiorina read a 30-minute statement defining and defending her role as CEO. It was met with silence. According to Dunn, "The basic message the board took from it was, 'You guys don't

know what you're doing.'"[17] She was asked to leave the room.

After she left, the directors broke into "turbulent" debate, with Perkins and Keyworth pushing hard for her removal.[18] Three hours later, a majority formed behind Fiorina's immediate replacement. She was summoned. On her return, only two board members remained at the conference table, Dunn and Robert Knowling, the retired CEO of Simdesk Technologies. "The Board has decided to make a change," said Knowling. "I'm very sorry, Carly."[19] She left with a bonus package of $21 million, HP shares worth $18.2 million, and a pension of $200,000 a year.[20] Yet in that hour her star fell to earth. She felt devastated.[21]

PATRICIA DUNN ASCENDANT

In the following days, the board named Robert P. Wayman, HP's long-time chief financial officer, to be interim CEO and picked Patricia Dunn to be its non-executive chairman. In this position Dunn would preside at board meetings but would not play an active role in managing the company. Separation of the board chairmanship from the CEO position was Tom Perkins' idea and reflected his belief that a strong board should not be dominated by the same person who is the company's top manager. It also gave the board more power over management.

Dunn's influence had risen during the period when Perkins and Keyworth emerged as the leading antagonists toward Fiorina. At first Dunn was neutral, but at some point she moved over to join the two in their campaign for change.[22] In addition, Dunn had been diagnosed the year before with advanced ovarian cancer and endured surgery and chemotherapy. Both Perkins and Keyworth had lost wives to cancer. They were sympathetic and liked her fortitude. Perkins even proposed that Dunn receive an

[14] Ibid., p. 1.

[15] Fiorina, *Tough Choices,* p. 290.

[16] James B. Stewart, "The Kona Files," *The New Yorker,* February 19–26, 2007, p. 155.

[17] Quoted in Bianco, *The Big Lie: Spying, Scandal, and Ethical Collapse at Hewlett-Packard,* p. 120.

[18] Perkins, *Valley Boy,* p. 6.

[19] Fiorina, *Tough Choices,* p. 303.

[20] Pui-Wing Tam and Joann S. Lublin, "H-P Gave Fiorina $1.57 Million in Bonus Payments Last Year," *The Wall Street Journal,* February 14, 2005, p. B2; and Carol J. Loomis, "How the HP Board KO'd Carly," *Fortune,* March 7, 2005, p. 99.

[21] Fiorina, *Tough Choices,* p. 303.

[22] Stewart, "The Kona Files," p. 156.

EXHIBIT 2

The Hewlett-Packard Board in Early 2005

This is the board that fired Carly Fiorina on February 8. One director, Sanford Litvak, had abruptly resigned on February 2. He was replaced on February 7 by Tom Perkins. Since 1999 the board had shrunk to nine members due largely to resignations by representatives of the Hewlett and Packard families in protest over the Compaq merger. Finding replacements in the new governance climate created by the Sarbanes-Oxley Act proved difficult. By now each director was paid a $200,000 retainer. The board had voted in 2004 to double its compensation. Directors who chaired committees were paid an additional $10,000.

Lawrence T. Babbio, Jr., 60
Vice Chairman and President, Verizon Communications

Patricia C. Dunn, 51 (Non-executive Chairman)
Chair, Barclays Global Investors

Richard A. Hackborn, 67
Retired Executive Vice President, Hewlett-Packard

George A. Keyworth, 65
Chairman, Progress & Freedom Association

Robert E. Knowling, Jr., 49
Former Chairman and CEO, Simdesk Technologies

Thomas J. Perkins, 73
Partner, Kleiner Perkins Caufield & Byers

Robert L. Ryan, 61
Senior Vice President and CFO, Medtronic

Lucille S. Salhany, 58
President and CEO, JHMedia

Robert P. Wayman, 59
Interim CEO, Hewlett-Packard

additional $100,000 for serving as chairman. She declined to accept it.

The immediate task for the board was to find a new CEO. Dunn, Perkins, and Keyworth headed the search. Within two months they hired Mark Hurd from NCR Corporation. Meanwhile, seven directors had approached Dunn, telling her that identifying the source of leaks and ending them was critical to maintaining trust and integrity on the board. All told, there had been 10 unauthorized leaks. They asked her to make renewed investigation a top priority.[23] She opened a new one and named it Project Kona after a spot in Hawaii where she and her husband own a vacation home.

[23] U.S. House of Representatives, Subcommittee on Oversight and Investigations of the Committee on Energy and Commerce, *Hewlett-Packard's Pretexting Scandal,* 109th Congress, 2d Sess., September 28, 2006, pp. 90, 129.

As the investigation began, other events eroded the comity between Dunn and Perkins. Perkins believed that since he had initiated her elevation to the chairmanship she would be deferential toward him. In this he erred. Early on he came to a board meeting with a sweeping agenda of strategy issues he wanted discussed. Dunn, however, had retreated into her armor of focus on details. She announced her discovery of many inconsistencies between HP's director's handbook and its bylaws. The meeting would be about harmonizing the two. Perkins was taken aback. This button-down approach assaulted his venture capitalist DNA. He had not even read the handbook and had no intention ever of doing so.

Vacancies existed on the board. As chairman of the nominating and governance committee Perkins found nominees, but Dunn was lukewarm. Again a difference of philosophy was the cause. Perkins submitted the names of Silicon Valley comrades who shared his values. Dunn wanted top executives from large, established corporations. When she suggested the president of PepsiCo, Perkins mocked him as "Sugar Daddy."[24]

Other abrasions angered Perkins, including a comment by Dunn in the presence of Hewlett-Packard managers that his new novel, *Sex and the Single Zillionaire,* was not her kind of reading.[25] The two frequently quarreled. However, he thought they had an agreement that if the leak investigation bore fruit, the matter would be handled by the two of them talking privately with the offending director. He wanted to extract an apology and a promise never again to talk with the press, then close the matter and go on. Again, he misjudged.

In the background, the leak investigation continued. One day the head of the Boston security firm told Dunn and HP's general counsel that his investigators had gotten the phone numbers of reporters who had written stories based on leaks. They were now going to obtain phone records using a technique called "pretexting." Investigators would call phone companies, pretending to be the reporters, and ask for records of their calls. Then they would get the directors' phone records the same way and check for calls back and forth. The HP counsel asked if this was legal. The security firm manager said yes. When the phone records were obtained, however, no evidence incriminated any director. The investigation had failed.

Nothing further was done until early in 2006 when another leak appeared. A CNET reporter published a story about the company's annual management retreat in January 2006. In it "a source" was quoted as saying that "[b]y the time the lectures were done at 10 p.m., we were pooped and went to bed."[26] The story also revealed that HP was considering certain kinds of software acquisitions.

Because of this new leak, Dunn launched a second round of investigation labeled Kona II. This time it was run by an HP lawyer with in-house investigators. Again, pretexting was used to obtain the phone records of both reporters and HP directors.

Patricia Dunn at a 2005 news conference. Source: © AP Photo/Paul Sakuma.

Comparing these phone records, they discovered two brief calls between Dawn Kawamoto, the reporter who wrote the January story, and director George Keyworth.

Trying to catch the conspirators in the act, they launched a sting operation. They fabricated a disgruntled HP manager who sent Kawamoto fake e-mails offering to reveal something sensational. A tracking program was embedded, so that if she sought to forward them to Keyworth or another director for confirmation the investigators would know. However, she simply invited the employee to call her. The HP investigators also staked out the homes of Kawamoto and Keyworth. No contact between them was observed.

In weekly meetings the investigative team kept Dunn informed. Questions about the legality of the tactics being used were raised by former police officers in HP's security department, but company attorneys told Dunn that all actions were legal. She said, "Throughout the process I asked and was assured—by both H-P's internal security department and the company's top lawyers, both verbally and in writing—that the work being undertaken to investigate and discover these leaks was legal, proper and consistent with the H-P way of performing investigations."[27]

[24] Stewart, "The Kona Files," p. 157.

[25] Tom Perkins, *Sex and the Single Zillionaire* (New York: Harper, 2007). Perkins had given Dunn an early draft of the book.

[26] Dawn Kawamoto, "HP Outlines Long-Term Strategy," CNET News.com, January 23, 2006.

[27] Patricia Dunn, "The H-P Investigation," *The Wall Street Journal,* October 11, 2006, p. A14.

Dunn and Perkins continued to abrade each other. After the regular board meeting in March, Dunn requested that Perkins and two others remain in the meeting room for a moment. The two disagree on what happened next. According to Perkins, Dunn told the others that he was out to get her and burst into tears. Dunn denies the statement, saying she told Perkins that his disruptive outbursts in meetings were counterproductive.[28]

Results of the leak investigation were revealed at the May 18, 2006, board meeting. That morning, just before the board convened, director Robert Ryan, an executive with Medtronic, who was now chair of the audit committee, met with Keyworth. When asked about Kawamoto's CNET article, Keyworth admitted to having lunch with her and discussing the retreat. He considered it a friendly lunch, not a press contact, and said he was surprised by the article. He felt that it was positive and harmless and told Ryan that if anyone had just asked him, he would have divulged the conversation. He was amazed to learn that this piece was the focus of a major investigation.

Meanwhile, Dunn took Perkins aside moments before the meeting and informed him about Keyworth. When she said the matter had to go before the full board, he was startled and irate. In the meeting, Ryan summarized a report from the HP lawyer in charge of the investigation. Keyworth was contrite. "I apologize for any discussion I had with the reporter in question that may have resulted in any of my colleagues on this board losing trust with me."[29] He added, "I would have told you all about this. Why didn't you ask? I thought I was just helping the company through a rough patch with the press. Aren't directors supposed to do that?"[30] He was asked to leave the room.

With Keyworth outside, Perkins spoke up. He argued that his friend's intention was innocent and the leak inconsequential. He believed that once again Dunn was focused on the trivia of process, "the 'sin' of the leak itself," rather than its substance.[31] When a motion was made to ask for Keyworth's resignation, Perkins grew "incandescent," and directed most of his fury at Dunn. After 90 minutes of dispute a vote was taken by secret ballot. The motion passed. At

that, Perkins said simply, "I resign," and walked out.[32] When Keyworth reentered he was asked to resign, but refused, noting that he had been elected by HP share owners and his legal obligation was to serve until they removed him.

THE END OF DUNN

It was Perkins' final meeting as an HP director, but he was not through with the company. He sought to have the minutes of the meeting rewritten to include his remarks that the investigatory tactics were illegal. When he discovered that his home telephone records had been deceitfully obtained, he wrote a letter to the board saying the investigation had violated the law. He demanded that it forward a copy of the letter to the Securities and Exchange Commission. When his demands were rejected, he instructed his lawyer to contact not only the SEC, but U.S. Attorney's offices in Manhattan and San Francisco, the California Attorney General, the Federal Communications Commission, and the Federal Trade Commission. This caused an explosion in the press, removing the cloak from an investigation that could not survive the light.

Within months, Dunn agreed to step down as chairman. Individual board members told her they did not believe she was involved in anything improper or illegal. But she had become a lightning rod for criticism of HP and its board.

CEO Mark Hurd and other directors urged her to remain on the board as a member. Soon, however, it was plain that she would be a major distraction. Finally, the board asked her to resign and she did so on September 22. She was asked not to speak at the press conference where her retirement was announced. Two HP attorneys who played a leading role in the investigations also resigned.

The next week, Dunn testified at a congressional hearing where she was flayed by members of the House Committee on Energy and Commerce. "What were you thinking?" asked Rep. John Dingell (D-Michigan).[33] "[I]s all of this really the HP way?" inquired Rep. Jan Schakowsky (D-Illinois).[34] In her testimony Dunn repeatedly fell back on assurances by

28 Stewart, "The Kona Files," p. 162.

29 Ibid, p. 163.

30 Perkins, *Valley Boy*, p. 15.

31 Ibid., p. 15.

32 Ibid., p. 16.

33 U.S. House of Representatives, Subcommittee on Oversight and Investigations of the Committee on Energy and Commerce, *Hewlett-Packard's Pretexting Scandal*, p. 13.

34 Ibid., p. 96.

HP lawyers and managers that the investigation was legal, at one point saying, "I do not accept personal responsibility for what happened."[35]

On October 4, she was charged by the State of California with four felony counts of wire fraud, identity theft, and conspiracy, charges that carried a potential sentence of 12 years in a state prison. Three investigators were also charged. All pleaded not guilty. Dunn's defense was that she had consistently questioned investigation tactics and been assured that they were legal. Therefore, state prosecutors could not prove she intended to commit a crime, a necessary factor for conviction. Moreover, no federal or state law was specific in making pretexting a crime.[36] Five months later a California Superior Court judge dropped the case against her and agreed to dismiss charges against the others in exchange for 96 hours of community service.[37] Dunn's health was a factor in the judge's decision, but the main reason was the tenuous nature of the charges.

Whether Dunn intended to commit a crime or not, Perkins is convinced that she pursued the investigation on the likelihood that he and Keyworth would be incriminated and forced to resign, thereby removing two of her political enemies. He states that at one point he decided to seek her resignation as chair, but claims he was talked out of it by Keyworth.[38] In the end he brought her down, doing on the outside what he did not do on the inside. His actions put Hewlett-Packard at the center of a scandal, made it the subject of late-night jokes, and ended careers. As a director, he was unruly, challenging, and stubborn. Those who would condemn him, however, should entertain this question. What would happen if he were put in a time machine and returned to the 1990s for service on Enron's board?

Questions

1. Over the time covered here, did Hewlett-Packard's board of directors fulfill its duties to the company's share owners? Explain how it met or did not meet basic duties.

2. What different perspectives on the role of the board are revealed in this story?

3. Was Carly Fiorina treated fairly by the board? Why or why not?

4. Were the leak investigations overseen by Patricia Dunn useful and important? Were they ethical?

5. Should George Keyworth have been asked to resign? Why or why not?

6. How do you appraise the behavior of Tom Perkins? Was he a model director or a renegade?

7. What actions could have been taken to improve the functioning of the HP board?

8. Did gender play any role in the fortunes of Fiorina and Dunn?

[35] Ibid., p. 120.

[36] As a result of the scandal, Congress passed the Telephone Records and Privacy Protection Act of 2006 (P. L. 109-476) to criminalize pretexting. More than a dozen states have passed similar laws.

[37] Matt Richtel, "H.P. Chairwoman and 3 Others Cleared in Spying Case," *The New York Times,* March 15, 2007, p. C1.

[38] Perkins, *Valley Boy,* p. 15.

Chapter **Five**

Corporate Social Responsibility

Merck & Co., Inc.

Corporate social responsibility takes many forms. The following story stands out as extraordinary.

For ages, river blindness, or onchocerciasis (on-ko-sir-KYE-a-sis), has tortured humanity in tropical regions. Its cause is a parasitic worm that, in its adult form, lives only in humans. People are infected with the worm's tiny, immature larvae when bitten by black flies that swarm near fast-moving rivers and streams. These larvae settle in tissue near the bite and form colonies, often visible lumps, where adults grow up to two feet long. Mature worms live for 7 to 18 years coiled in these internal nodes, mating, and releasing tens of thousands of microscopic new larvae that migrate back to the skin's surface, causing welts, lumps, and discoloration along with a persistent itch that drives some sufferers to suicide. Eventually, the parasites move to the eyes, causing blindness. The cycle of infection is renewed when black flies take a blood meal from an infected person, ingesting tiny larvae, then bite an uninfected person, passing on the parasite.

People suffer in many ways. For Amarech Bitena of Ethiopia, the cost of river blindness is a broken heart. The parasites came in childhood. Now, at 25, her skin is hard and dark, her vision blurred. She has not married. "When I think about the future," she says, "I feel completely hopeless. . . . My vision can't be restored. My skin is destroyed. I would have liked to be a doctor."[1] Almost 18 million people suffer from onchocerciasis in tropical areas of Africa, South America, and Yemen.[2] About 500,000 have impaired vision and 270,000 are blind. It saps economies by enervating workers and driving farmers from fertile, riverside land.

Until recently, no treatment for river blindness existed, and little was done. It is only one of many tropical diseases affecting millions in developing nations. Critics said that big drug companies ignored these epidemics to focus on pills for the diseases of people in rich nations. Years ago the World Health Organization began pesticide spraying to kill the black fly, but it was a frustrating job. Winds carry flies up to

---

[1] Claudia Feldman, "River Blindness: A Forgotten Disease," *The Houston Chronicle,* October 9, 2005, p. 5.
[2] "Fighting River Blindness and Other Ills," *The Lancet* 374, no. 9684 (2009), p. 91.

In countries ravaged by river blindness, the blind sometimes hold sticks and follow the lead of children. Merck commissioned this bronze sculpture for the lobby of its New Jersey headquarters, where top executives pass by each day. It symbolizes Merck's commitment to make medicine for the good of humanity. Because of Merck's unprecedented donation of a river blindness drug, such scenes are no longer common. Source: Photo courtesy of Merck & Co., Inc.

100 miles from breeding grounds. And scientists estimate that the breeding cycle must be suppressed for at least 14 years to stop reinfections.

In 1975 scientists at Merck & Co. discovered a compound that killed animal parasites. By 1981 they had synthesized it and marketed it for deworming dogs, cattle, sheep, and pigs. Ivermectin, as it was called, was a blockbuster hit and would be the best-selling veterinary drug worldwide for two decades. Merck's researchers had a strong hunch it also would be effective in humans against *Onchocerca volvulus,* the river blindness parasite.[3]

Merck faced a decision. It would be very expensive to bring a new drug to market and manufacture it. Yet people with the disease were among the world's poorest. Their villages had no doctors to prescribe it, no drugstores to sell it. Should Merck develop a drug that might never be profitable?

George W. Merck, son of the firm's founder and its leader for 32 years, once said: "We try never to forget that medicine is for the people. It is not for the profits. The profits follow, and if we have remembered that, they have never failed to appear."[4] This advice was still respected at Merck; it lived in the corporate culture. Merck's scientists were motivated by humanitarian goals and restraining them was awkward. The decision to go ahead was made. The cost would be $200 million.

Clinical trials of ivermectin confirmed its effectiveness. A single yearly dose of 150 micrograms per kilogram of body weight reduced the burden of tiny worms migrating through the body to near zero and impaired reproduction by adult parasites, alleviating symptoms and preventing blindness.[5]

Eventually, it became clear that neither those in need nor their governments could afford to buy ivermectin. So in 1987 Merck committed itself to manufacture and ship it at no cost to where it was needed for as long as it was needed to control river blindness. The company asked governments and private organizations to help set up distribution.

Since then, Merck has given away more than 2.5 billion tablets in 37 countries at a cost of $3.9 billion. Estimates are that treatment has prevented 40,000 cases of blindness each year; returned to use 62 million acres of farmland, an area the size of Michigan; and added 7.5 million years of adult labor in national workforces.[6] A study

---

[3] David Bollier, *Merck & Company* (Stanford, CA: Business Enterprise Trust, 1991), p. 5.

[4] Roy Vagelos and Louis Galambos, *The Moral Corporation* (New York: Cambridge University Press, 2006), p. 171.

[5] Mohammed A. Aziz, et al., "Efficacy and Tolerance of Ivermectin in Human Onchocerciasis," *The Lancet,* July 24, 1982.

[6] "Merck MECTIZAN® Donation Program: Priorities and Goals," at www.merck.com, accessed December 8, 2009.

of economic effects for two areas in Africa estimated $573 million in net benefits over 40 years.[7]

By 2012 the transmission of onchocerciasis in six Latin American countries is predicted to end. No end is in sight for Africa, but infection rates are falling in the most afflicted areas. In Benin, for example, infection rates in 51 areas ranged from 25 percent to 98 percent in the mid-1990s. Now the highest rate anywhere in the country is 3 percent.[8]

For a drug company to go through the new drug development process and then give the drug away is unprecedented. Merck's management believes that although developing and donating ivermectin has been expensive, humanitarianism and enlightened self-interest vindicate the decision. Few corporations have such singular opportunities to fight evil as did Merck, but every corporation must fulfill a range of obligations to society and many can apply unique commercial competencies to global problems. In this chapter we define the idea of social responsibility and explain how it has expanded in meaning and practice over time. The next chapter explains more about the management methods corporations use to execute social actions.

THE EVOLVING IDEA OF CORPORATE SOCIAL RESPONSIBILITY

corporate social responsibility
The duty of a corporation to create wealth in ways that avoid harm to, protect, or enhance societal assets.

Corporate social responsibility is the duty of a corporation to create wealth in ways that avoid harm to, protect, or enhance societal assets. The term is a modern one. It did not enter common use until the 1960s, when it appeared in academic literature. It often goes by other names, including its abbreviation CSR, corporate citizenship, stakeholder management, sustainability, and, in Japan, *kyosei*, a word that translates as "living and working together for the common good." Whatever it is called, there is no precise, operational meaning. It is primarily a political ideology, because its central purposes are to control and legitimize the exercise of corporate power. As an ideology, it is a worldview of how a corporate should act. In addition, it can be defined more narrowly as a management practice, specifically as the use of special tools and procedures to make a corporation responsible. This practical aspect is the subject of the next chapter.

The fundamental idea is that corporations have duties that go beyond lawful execution of their economic function. Here is the reasoning. The overall performance of a firm must benefit society. Because of market imperfections, the firm will not fulfill all its duties, and may breach some, if it responds only to market forces. Laws and regulations correct some shortcomings, more in developed countries, fewer in less developed. Beyond the law, firms must voluntarily take additional actions to meet their full obligations to society. What additional actions must they take? These have to be defined in practice by negotiation with stakeholders and they change over time.

Advocates of social responsibility, who occupy a very broad middle band of the political spectrum, justify it with three basic arguments. First, it is an ethical duty

[7] H. R. Waters, et al., "Economic Evaluation of Mectizan Distribution," *Tropical Medicine and International Health,* April 2004, p. A16.
[8] "Benin: The End of River Blindness," *Africa News,* May 8, 2008.

124 Chapter 5 *Corporate Social Responsibility*

FIGURE 5.1 **The CSR Spectrum**

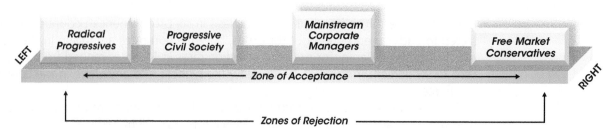

to promote social justice. A timeless principle is that power should be used fairly. If it harms or fails society, it is badly used. Second, social responsibility is practical. It has concrete benefits. It motivates employees and creates loyal customers. It leads to innovative products and strategies. It strengthens surrounding communities. It protects reputations and avoids regulation. In short, there is a "business case" beyond ethical duty. Third, it is necessary because other forces do not force full responsibility on corporations, particularly multinational corporations that operate across borders in a global arena of weak governance.

Opponents of corporate social responsibility are found toward the left and right edges of the political spectrum shown in Figure 5.1. On the far left, it is seen by radical Progressives as an insufficient doctrine, one that substitutes only poorly for tougher laws and regulations, allowing corporations to form a smoke screen of virtue behind which their "inviolable core" of profit seeking behavior is untouched.[9] On the far right, it is seen as a pernicious doctrine, draining and enervating the strength of the corporate institution. Conservative economists see it as an unwarranted cost. It creates administrative expenses, distracts executives, confuses economic goals with other goals, and subtracts from social welfare when the corporation is less efficient.[10] Corporations are owned by shareholders and the primary responsibility of managers is acting lawfully to maximize profits for them, thereby producing maximum value and surplus wealth for society.

Conservatives see capitalism as a natural, venerable, practical, and beneficent institution that has developed over centuries and led to rising global prosperity. They dislike CSR for thwarting natural market dynamics. They reject the agenda of corporate social responsibility, seeing it as centered in progressive ideology and based, therefore, on the goals of a movement at heart dubious of capitalism. Markets, not politics, should direct corporations. When markets fail, they should be corrected by the policies of representative government, not by unelected executives or activists.

Between these fringes there is wide acceptance of CSR. More moderate progressives are willing to work with responsible corporations. And corporate managers occupy a middle ground. Most now accept the idea as a practical necessity even as they often harbor doctrinal reservations. Years ago, most managers were on the

---

[9] Marjorie Kelly and Allen L. White, "From Corporate Responsibility to Corporate Design," *Journal of Corporate Citizenship*, spring 2009, p. 25. See also Subhabrata Bobby Banerjee, *Corporate Social Responsibility: the Good, the Bad and the Ugly* (Cheltenham: Edward Elgar Publishing, 2007).

[10] See, for example, "The Good Company: A Survey of Corporate Social Responsibility," *The Economist*, January 22, 2005.

right side of this spectrum. Why did they move left? As we will explain, the doctrine of corporate responsibility has evolved over time to require more expansive action by companies largely because stakeholder groups gained more power to impose their agendas, but also because the ethical and legal philosophies underlying it matured to support broader action by managers. In fact, corporate social responsibility is a profoundly durable and successful ideology. All through an era when free market principles were ascendant, it coiled more and more tightly around the corporation to restrain excesses and direct behavior to the public good. The story of corporate social responsibility begins with Adam Smith.

Social Responsibility in Classical Economic Theory

Throughout American history, classical capitalism, which is the basis for the market capitalism model in Chapter 1, has been the basic inspiration for business. In the classical view, a business is socially responsible if it maximizes profits while operating within the law, because an "invisible hand" will direct economic activity to serve the good of the whole.

This ideology, derived from Adam Smith's *Wealth of Nations,* is compelling in its simplicity and its resonance with self-interest. In nineteenth century America, it was elevated to the status of a commandment. However, the idea that markets harness low motives and work them into social progress has always attracted skeptics. Smith himself had a surprising number of reservations about the market's ability to protect human welfare.[11] Today the classical ideology still commands the economic landscape, but, as we will see, ethical theories of broader responsibility have worn down its prominences.

The Early Charitable Impulse

The idea that corporations had social responsibilities awaited the rise of corporations themselves. Meanwhile, the most prominent expression of duty to society was the good deed of charity by business owners.

Most colonial era businesses were very small. Merchants practiced thrift and frugality, which were dominant virtues then, to an extreme. Benjamin Franklin's advice to a business acquaintance reflects the penny-pinching nature of the time: "He that kills a breeding sow, destroys all her offspring to the thousandth generation. He that murders a crown, destroys all that it might have produced, even scores of pounds."[12] Yet charity was a coexisting virtue, and business owners sought respectability by giving to churches, orphanages, and poorhouses. Their actions first illustrate that although American business history can be pictured as a jungle of profit maximization, people in it have always been concerned citizens.[13]

Charity by owners continued in the early nineteenth century and grew as great fortunes were made. Mostly, the new millionaires endowed social causes as

---

[11] Jacob Viner, "Adam Smith and Laissez-Faire," *Journal of Political Economy,* April 1927.

[12] In "Advice to a Young Tradesman [1748]," in *The Autobiography of Benjamin Franklin and Selections from His Other Writings,* ed. Nathan G. Goodman (New York: Carlton House, 1932), p. 210. A crown was a British coin on which appeared the figure of a royal crown.

[13] Mark Sharfman, "The Evolution of Corporate Philanthropy, 1883–1952," *Business & Society,* December 1994.

126   Chapter 5   *Corporate Social Responsibility*

Andrew
Carnegie
(1835–1919).
Source: The
Library of
Congress.

individuals, not through the companies that were the fountainheads of their wealth.

One of the earliest was Steven Girard, a shipping and banking tycoon. When he died in 1831, the richest person in the nation, he made generous charitable bequests in his will, the largest of which was $6 million for a school to educate orphaned boys from the first grade through high school.[14] This single act changed the climate of education in the United States because it came before free public schooling, when a high school education was still only for children of the wealthy.

Following Girard, others donated generously and did so while still living. John D. Rockefeller systematically gave away $550 million over his lifetime. Andrew Carnegie gave $350 million during his life to social causes, built 2,811 public libraries, and donated 7,689 organs to churches. He wrote a famous article titled "The Disgrace of Dying Rich" and argued that it was the duty of a man of wealth "to consider all surplus revenues . . . as trust funds which he is called upon to administer."[15]

social
Darwinism
A philosophy of the late 1800s and early 1900s that used evolution to explain the dynamics of human society and institutions. The idea of "survival of the fittest" in the social realm implied that rich people and dominant companies were morally superior.

However, Carnegie's philosophy of giving was highly paternalistic. He believed that big fortunes should be used for grand purposes such as endowing universities and building concert halls such as Carnegie Hall. They should not be wasted by paying higher wages to workers or giving gifts to poor people; that would dissipate riches on small indulgences and would not, in the end, elevate the culture of a society. Thus, one day when a friend of Carnegie's encountered a beggar and gave him a quarter, Carnegie admonished the friend that it was one of "the very worst actions of his life."[16]

In this remark, Carnegie echoed the doctrine of *social Darwinism*, which held that charity interfered with the natural evolutionary process in which society shed its less fit to make way for the better adapted. Well-meaning people who gave to charity interfered with the natural law of progress by propping up failed examples of the human race. The leading advocate of this astringent doctrine, the English philosopher Herbert Spencer, wrote the following heartless passage in a best-selling 1850 book.

---

[14] The school became known as Girard College, which one of the authors of this book, George Steiner, attended. It still exists in Philadelphia.

[15] Andrew Carnegie, *The Gospel of Wealth* (Cambridge, MA: Harvard University Press, 1962), p. 25; originally published in 1901.

[16] Quoted in Page Smith, *The Rise of Industrial America*, vol. 6 (New York: Penguin Books, 1984), p. 136.

Herbert Spencer (1820–1903). Spencer attempted a synthesis of human knowledge based on the unifying idea of evolution. When he visited the United States in 1882 a grand dinner attended by 200 leading Americans was held for him at Delmonico's in New York. Source: © Hulton-Deutsch Collection/CORBIS.

It seems hard that a laborer incapacitated by sickness from competing with his stronger fellows should have to bear the resulting privations. It seems hard that widows and orphans should be left to struggle for life or death. Nevertheless, when regarded not separately, but in connection with the interests of universal humanity, these harsh fatalities are seen to be full of the highest beneficence—the same beneficence which brings to early graves the children of diseased parents and singles out the low-spirited, the intemperate, and the debilitated as the victims of an epidemic. [17]

Spencer approved of some charity, though only when it raised the character and superiority of the giver. Still, the overall effect of Spencer's arguments was to moderate charity by business leaders and retard the growth of a modern social conscience.

More than just faith in markets and social Darwinism constrained business from undertaking voluntary social action. Charters granted by states when corporations were formed required that profits be disbursed to shareholders. Courts consistently held charitable gifts to be *ultra vires,* that is, "beyond the law," because charters did not expressly permit them. To use company funds for charity or social works took money from the pockets of shareholders and invited lawsuits. Thus, when Rockefeller had the humanitarian impulse to build the first medical school in China, he paid for it out of his own pocket; not a penny came from Standard Oil. Although most companies took a negative view of philanthropy, by the 1880s the railroads were an exception. They sponsored the Young Men's Christian Association (YMCA) movement, which provided rooming and religious indoctrination for rail construction crews. Yet such actions were exceptional.

As the twentieth century approached, classical ideology was still a mountain of resistance to expanding the idea of business social responsibility. A poet of that era, James Russell Lowell, captured the spirit of the day.

> *Not a deed would he do,*
> *Nor a word would he utter*
> *Till he'd weighed its relations*
> *To plain bread and butter.*[18]

Social Responsibility in the Late Nineteenth and Early Twentieth Centuries

Giving, no matter how generous, was a narrow kind of social responsibility often unrelated to a company's impacts on society. By the late 1800s it was growing apparent to the business elite that prevailing doctrines used to legitimize business defined its responsibilities too narrowly. Industrialization had fostered social

---

[17] Herbert Spencer, *Social Statics* (New York: D. Appleton and Company, 1890), p. 354; first published in 1850.

[18] "A Fable for Critics," *The Complete Poetical Works of James Russell Lowell,* Cabinet Edition (Boston: Houghton, Mifflin and Company, 1899), p. 122.

problems and political corruption. Farmers were in revolt. Labor was increasingly violent. Socialism was at high tide. Average Americans began to question unfettered laissez-faire economics and the doctrine of social Darwinism.

As Rockefeller, Carnegie, and other barons of wealth gave away large sums, public doubt about their motives grew. They were accused of cloaking their greed with gifts that confused the eye, diverting it from the coarse origins of their money. As one of Carnegie's workers asked, "What use has a man who works twelve hours a day for a library, anyway?"[19] Thus the criticism that corporate responsibility is a smoke screen first emerged in this bygone era. It has never lost a following.

By now, business feared a growing clamor for more regulation. It was terrified of socialist calls for appropriation of assets. So it sought to blunt the urgency of these appeals by voluntary action.

During the Progressive era, three interrelated themes of broader responsibility emerged. First, managers were *trustees* that is, agents whose corporate roles put them in positions of power over the fate of not just stockholders, but also of others such as workers, customers, and communities. This power implied a duty to promote the welfare of each group. Second, managers had an obligation to *balance* these multiple interests. They were, in effect, coordinators who settled competing claims. Third, many managers subscribed to the *service principle*, a near-spiritual belief that individual managers served society by making each business successful; if they all prospered, the aggregate effect would eradicate social injustice, poverty, and other ills. This belief was only a fancy reincarnation of classical ideology. However, many of its adherents conceded that companies were still obligated to undertake social projects that helped, or "served," the public.[20] These three interrelated ideas—trusteeship, balance, and service—expanded the idea of business responsibility beyond simple charity. But the type of responsibility envisioned was still paternalistic, and the actions of big company leaders often showed an underlying Scroogelike mentality.

One such leader was Henry Ford, who had an aptitude for covering meanness with a shining veneer of citizenship. In the winter of 1914 Ford thrilled the public by announcing the "Five-Dollar Day" for Ford Motor Co. workers. Five dollars was about double the daily pay for manufacturing workers at the time and seemed very generous. In fact, although Ford took credit for being big-hearted, the $5 wage was intended to cool unionizing and was not what it appeared on the surface. The offer attracted hordes of job seekers from around the country to Highland Park, Michigan. One subzero morning in January, there were 2,000 lined up outside the Ford plant by 5:00 a.m.; by dawn there were 10,000. Disorder broke out, and the fire department turned hoses on the freezing men.

The few who were hired had to serve a six-month apprenticeship and comply with the puritanical Ford Motor Co. code of conduct (no drinking, marital discord, or otherwise immoral living) to qualify for the $5 day. Many were fired on pretexts

trustee
An agent of a company whose corporate role puts him or her in a position of power over the fate of not just stockholders, but also of others such as customers, employees, and communities.

service principle
A belief that managers served society by making companies profitable and that aggregate success by many managers would resolve major social problems.

---

[19] Quoted in Margaret F. Byington, *Homestead: The Households of a Mill Town* (Philadelphia: William F. Fell Co., 1910), p. 178.

[20] Rolf Lunden, *Business and Religion in the American 1920s* (New York: Greenwood Press, 1988), pp. 147–50.

Inventor and industrialist Henry Ford (1863–1947). The public made him a folk hero and saw him as a generous employer. But he manipulated workers to lower costs. Source: The Library of Congress.

before the six months passed. Thousands of replacements waited outside each day hoping to fill a new vacancy. Inside, Ford speeded up the assembly line. Insecure employees worked faster under the threat of being purged for a younger, stronger, lower-paid new hire. Those who hung on to qualify for the $5 wage had to face greedy merchants and landlords in the surrounding area who raised prices and rents.

Ford was a master of image. In 1926 he announced the first five-day, 40-hour week for workers, but with public accolades still echoing for this "humanitarian" gesture, he speeded up the line still more, cut wages, and announced a program to weed out less-efficient employees. These actions were necessary, he said, to compensate for Saturdays off. Later that year, Ford told the adulatory public that he had started a program to fight juvenile delinquency. He proposed to employ 5,000 boys 16 to 20 years old and pay them "independence wages."[21] This was trumpeted as citizenship, but as the "boys" were hired, older workers were pitted against younger, lower-paid replacements.

A few business leaders, however, acted more consistently with the emerging themes of business responsibility. One was General Robert E. Wood, who led Sears, Roebuck and Company from 1924 to 1954. He believed that a large corporation was more than an economic institution; it was a social and political force as well. In the Sears *Annual Report* for 1936, he outlined the ways in which Sears was discharging its responsibilities to what he said were the chief constituencies of the company—customers, the public, employees, suppliers, and stockholders.[22] Stockholders came last because, according to General Wood, they could not attain their "full measure of reward" unless the other groups were satisfied first. In thought and action, General Wood was far ahead of his time. Nevertheless, in the 1920s and after that, corporations found various ways to support communities. Organized charities were formed, such as the Community Chest, the Red Cross, and the Boy Scouts, to which they contributed. In many cities, companies gave money and expertise to improve schools and public health. In the 1940s corporations began to give cash and stock to tax-exempt foundations set up for philanthropic giving.

1950 to the Present

The contemporary understanding of corporate social responsibility was formed during this period. An early and influential statement of the idea was made in 1954 by Howard R. Bowen in his book *Social Responsibilities of the Businessman*.[23] Bowen said that managers felt strong public expectations to act in ways that went beyond profit-maximizing and were, in fact, meeting those expectations. Then he laid out the basic arguments for social responsibility: (1) managers have an ethical

---

[21] Keith Sward, *The Legend of Henry Ford* (New York: Rinehart & Company, 1948), p. 176.

[22] James C. Worthy, *Shaping an American Institution: Robert E. Wood and Sears, Roebuck* (Urbana: University of Illinois Press, 1984), p. 173.

[23] Howard Bowen, *Social Responsibilities of the Businessman* (New York: Harper, 1954).

duty to consider the broad social impacts of their decisions; (2) businesses are reservoirs of skill and energy for improving civic life; (3) corporations must use power in keeping with a broad social contract, or lose their legitimacy; (4) it is in the enlightened self-interest of business to improve society; and (5) voluntary action may head off negative public attitudes and unwanted regulations. This book, despite being almost 60 years old, remains an excellent encapsulation of the current ideology of corporate responsibility.[24]

Not everyone accepted Bowen's arguments. The primary dissenters were conservative economists who claimed that business is *most* responsible when it makes money efficiently, not when it misapplies its energy on social projects. The best-known advocate of this view, then and now, is Nobel laureate Milton Friedman.

> There is one and only one social responsibility of business—to use its resources and engage in activities designed to increase its profits so long as it stays within the rules of the game, which is to say, engages in open and free competition, without deception or fraud. . . . Few trends could so thoroughly undermine the very foundations of our free society as the acceptance by corporate officials of social responsibility other than to make as much money for their stockholders as possible. This is a fundamentally subversive doctrine.[25]

Friedman argues that managers are the employees of a corporation's owners and are directly responsible to them. Stockholders want to maximize profits, so the manager's sole objective is to accommodate them. If a manager spends corporate funds on social projects, he or she is diverting shareholders' dollars to programs they may not even favor. Similarly, if the cost of social projects is passed on to consumers in higher prices, the manager is spending their money. This "taxation without representation," says Friedman, is wrong.[26] Furthermore, if the market price of a product does not reflect the true costs of producing it, but includes costs for social programs, then the market's allocation mechanism is distorted.

The opposition of Friedman and other adherents of classical economic doctrine proved to be a principled, rearguard action. In theory the arguments were unerring, but in practice they were inexpedient. When the great tides of consumerism, environmentalism, civil rights, and feminism rose in the 1960s, leftist critics wanted to control rip-offs, pollution, employment discrimination, and other perceived excesses of capitalism with new regulations. In this power struggle Friedman's position seemed cold and indifferent, an abstract calculus aloof from costs in flesh and blood. It incited critics and invited retaliation and more regulation should the business community openly agree. Moreover, the idea that corporations could undertake expanded social responsibility was useful for business. If corporations volunteered to do more it would calm critics, forestall regulation,

[24] See, for example, Rosabeth Moss Kanter, *Supercorp* (New York: Crown Business, 2009), the result of three years of research and 350 interviews in 20 countries by the author and her team, leading to the discovery that "vanguard," or socially progressive, companies accept Bowen's basic arguments.

[25] *Capitalism and Freedom* (Chicago: University of Chicago Press, 1962), p. 133.

[26] "The Social Responsibility of Business Is to Increase Its Profits," *The New York Times Magazine*, September 13, 1970, p. 33.

and preserve their legitimacy. Not surprisingly, Friedman's view was decisively rejected by business leaders, who soon articulated a new vision.

In 1971 the Committee for Economic Development, a prestigious voice of business, published a bold statement of the case for expansive social responsibility. Society, it said, has broadened its expectations outward over "three concentric circles of responsibilities."[27]

- An *inner circle* of clear-cut responsibility for efficient execution of the economic function resulting in products, jobs, and economic growth.
- An *intermediate circle* encompassing responsibility to exercise this economic function with a sensitive awareness of changing values and priorities.
- An *outer circle* that outlines newly emerging and still amorphous responsibilities that business should assume to improve the social environment, even if they are not directly related to specific business processes.

Classical ideology focused solely on the first circle. Now business leaders argued that management responsibilities went further. The report was followed in 1981 by a *Statement on Corporate Responsibility* from the Business Roundtable, a group of 200 CEOs of the largest corporations. It said:

> Economic responsibility is by no means incompatible with other corporate responsibilities in society . . . A corporation's responsibilities include how the whole business is conducted every day. It must be a thoughtful institution which rises above the bottom line to consider the impact of its actions on all, from shareholders to the society at large. Its business activities must make social sense.[28]

Friedmanism
The theory that the sole responsibility of a corporation is to optimize profits while obeying the law.

After these statements from top executives appeared, the range of social programs assumed by business expanded rapidly in education, the arts, public health, housing, the environment, literacy, employee relations, and other areas. However, although the business elite formally rejected *Friedmanism*, corporate cultures, which change only at glacial rates, still promoted a single-minded obsession with efficiency and financial results. The belief that a trade-off existed between profits and social responsibility was (and still is) widespread and visible in corporate actions.

BASIC ELEMENTS OF SOCIAL RESPONSIBILITY

The three elements of social responsibility are market actions, externally mandated actions, and voluntary actions. Figure 5.2 illustrates the relative magnitude of each, how that magnitude has changed over historical eras, and how change will progress if the trend toward expansion of the idea of corporate responsibility continues. To be socially responsible, a corporation must fulfill its duties in each area of action.

Market actions are responses to competitive forces in markets. Such actions have always dominated and this will continue. When a corporation responds to

---

[27] Committee for Economic Development, *Social Responsibilities of Business Corporations* (New York: CED, 1971), p. 11.

[28] *Statement on Corporate Responsibility* (New York: Business Roundtable, October 1981), pp. 12 and 14.

132 Chapter 5 *Corporate Social Responsibility*

FIGURE 5.2
Motives for Social Responsibility and Their Evolving Magnitudes

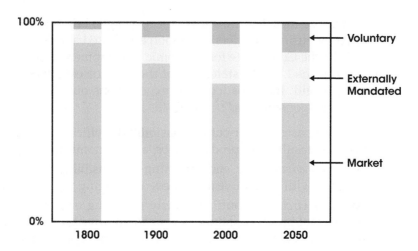

markets, it fulfills its first and most important social responsibility. All else pales before its economic impact. Recently the giant Unilever Group cooperated with Oxfam International, a confederation of progressive NGOs fighting world poverty, to study the overall impact of its branch company in Indonesia. Oxfam is suspicious of corporations and had "ruthlessly challenged" Unilever's profit-seeking actions.[29] Yet the final report detailed a wondrous economic effect in a country where half the population lives below $2 a day.

Unilever Indonesia (UI) is the 13th-largest company in the country. Like its global parent, it sells personal and home products such as Kleenex, Pepsodent, and Lux soap, along with a variety of foods. Over five years ending in 2006, UI made a net profit of $212 million. But the surprise was that its operations created total monetary value of $633 million along its *value chain*. A value chain is the sequence of coordinated actions that add value to a product or service. For Unilever it includes economic actors outside the corporation in both its backward supply chain and forward distribution channels.

Of the $633 million total, only 34 percent was captured by UI; the rest went to others: 4 percent to farmers for their crops, 12 percent to several hundred suppliers, 6 percent to product distributors, and 18 percent to as many as 1.8 million retailers, among them tiny shops and street vendors selling "sachets," or small packets of Unilever products made especially for low-income consumers who could not afford regular sizes. From its share, UI put the majority back into the Indonesian economy, reinvesting 25 percent in its local business, giving 30 percent to the government in taxes, and paying 7 percent in dividends to Indonesian shareholders.[30] Unilever Indonesia employed about 5,000 workers, but the study found that the entire value chain created 300,764 full-time jobs, an important contribution in a nation with more than 9 percent unemployment.

value chain
The sequence of coordinated actions that add value to a product or service.

[29] Jason Caly, *Exploring the Links Between International Business and Poverty Reduction: A Case Study of Unilever in Indonesia* (Eynsham, UK: Oxfam GB and Unilever PLC, 2005), p. 10.

[30] The other 38 percent was paid as dividends to overseas shareholders. Figures in this paragraph are from ibid., pp. 14, 82, and 83.

Figures such as these illustrate how the greatest positive impact of a corporation on society is economic and why maximizing that impact is a corporation's greatest social responsibility. From the study, Oxfam concluded that tremendous potential for poverty alleviation existed in UI's routine profit-seeking actions. It absolved Unilever of draining Indonesian society by profiting on the backs of poor people.

Mandated actions are those required either by government regulation or civil regulation. Government, or public, regulation is rooted in the authority of the state and its mandates are enforceable by law. Government mandates have multiplied rapidly in developed countries. *Civil regulation* is regulation by nonstate actors based on social norms or standards enforced by social or market sanctions. Civil regulation, sometimes called private regulation, has many faces. It is imposed when activists, consumers, investors, lenders, shareholders, or employees make demands on a company and failure to comply will lead to reputational or financial damage. Such mandates are enforced by the power of the market, not the power of law.[31] As we will see later in this chapter, mandates based on civil regulation are now expanding rapidly in the global economy.

The third element is *voluntary actions* that go beyond those compelled by law or regulation. Some voluntary actions can be called "legal plus" because they exceed required mandates. After the deadly Bhopal, India, gas leak in 1984, the subject of a case study in Chapter 11, the chemical industry introduced plant safety standards that went beyond the requirements of any nation. Other actions are unrelated to mandates, but respond to public consensus. Charitable giving, which is expected of every corporation though not legally required, is an example. Still other actions may be strategic initiatives where the firm seeks to profit from solving a social problem as does GE when it sells energy-saving hybrid locomotives.

civil regulation
Regulation by nonstate actors based on social norms or standards enforced by social or market sanctions.

GENERAL PRINCIPLES OF CORPORATE SOCIAL RESPONSIBILITY

What must a corporation do to be socially responsible? Many actions are possible. One meticulous study classified CSR into seven main areas with 31 categories containing 147 specific CSR activities.[32] Each company must choose a range of appropriate economic, mandated, and voluntary actions to fulfill its total obligations to society. No precise formula determines these choices. However, the following broad principles are widely accepted.

- *Corporations are economic institutions run for profit.* Their greatest responsibility is to create economic benefits. They should be judged primarily on economic criteria and cannot be expected to meet purely social objectives without financial incentives. Corporations may incur short-run costs on social initiatives that promise long-term benefits. And they should seek ways to solve social problems at a profit.

[31] See David Vogel, "The Private Regulation of Global Corporate Conduct," in Walter Mattli and Ngaire Woods, eds. *The Politics of Global Regulation* (Princeton, NJ: Princeton University Press, 2009).

[32] Ashridge Centre for Business and Society, *A Catalogue of CSR Activities* (Berkhamsted: Ashridge Centre for Business and Society, 2005). The areas are (1) leadership, vision, and values, (2) the marketplace, (3) the workforce, (4) supply chain activities, (5) stakeholder engagement, (6) the community, and (7) the environment.

- *All firms must follow multiple bodies of law*, including (1) corporation laws and chartering provisions, (2) the civil and criminal laws of nations, (3) legislated regulations that protect stakeholders, and (4) international laws, including treaties and trade agreements.

- *Managers must act ethically.* They must respect the law and, in addition, conform their behavior to ethical principles; model ethical values such as integrity, honesty, and justice; and set up codes, policies, and procedures to elevate behavior within the firm.

external cost
A production cost not paid by a firm or its customers, but by members of society.

- *Corporations have a duty to correct adverse social impacts they cause.* They should try to internalize negative *external costs*, or adverse costs of production borne by society. A factory dumping toxic effluent into a stream creates costs such as human and animal disease imposed on innocents, not on the company or its customers. Increasingly, this duty to correct radiates outward to include taking responsibility for adverse impacts along global supply chains.

- *Social responsibility varies with company characteristics* such as size, industry, products, strategies, marketing methods, locations, internal cultures, and external demands. Thus, a global pharmaceutical company such as Merck has a far different impact on society than a local insurance company, so its responsibilities are different and greater.

- *Managers should try to meet legitimate needs of multiple stakeholders.* Although corporations have a fiduciary duty to shareholders, it is not legally required, desirable, or possible, to manage solely in their interest. Consumers, employees, governments, communities, and other groups also have important claims on the firm.

- *Corporate behavior must comply with an underlying social contract.* To understand this contract and how it changes, managers can study the direction of national policies and global norms as evidenced in legislation, regulations, treaties, conventions, trade agreements, and public opinion.

- *Corporations should be transparent and accountable.* They should publicly report on their social performance in addition to their financial performance. This social reporting should cover major social impacts and, like financial reporting, be verifiable; that is, audited and checked by independent parties.

ARE SOCIAL AND FINANCIAL PERFORMANCE RELATED?

Scholars have done at least 127 studies to see if companies that are more socially responsible are also more profitable.[33] Most report a positive correlation between responsibility and profitability. Yet many have mixed, inconclusive, or negative findings. A review of 95 such studies over 30 years found that a majority (53 percent) showed that socially responsible behavior was related to higher profits. However, 24 percent found no relationship, 19 percent a mixed relationship, and 5 percent a negative relationship.[34]

[33] Joshua Daniel Margolis and James Patrick Walsh, *People and Profits: The Search for a Link between a Company's Social and Financial Performance* (Mahwah, NJ: Lawrence Erlbaum, 2001), p. 394.
[34] Ibid., p. 10.

Inconsistent results from study to study are not surprising given the difficult problems of method that researchers face. To begin, if social performance is defined as including economic performance, then any effort to separate the two elements to assess their relationship is doomed. Even if social performance is not defined to include economic performance, profit or loss does not solely depend on virtue, being also determined by market forces oblivious to the grade in a CSR report card. Also, no fixed, neutral definition of social responsibility exists, making it impossible objectively to rank corporations as more or less responsible. Many studies have used corporate responsibility ratings done by progressive analysts who evaluate companies based on whether they fulfill the left's social agenda. Others rely on rankings of reputation made by executives of Fortune 500 companies, who have a more conservative perspective.

As opposed to the subjectivity of a corporation's social performance it might seem that financial performance can be gauged more objectively, but there are many ways to measure profitability. Should researchers use accounting measures such as net income or market measures such as stock price appreciation?

In the above review of 95 studies, the authors report that researchers drew on 27 information sources to rate social performance and used 70 methods to calculate financial performance. This makes it difficult to compare the findings of one study to the findings of others. However, a fresh analysis of 52 studies took advantage of a statistical technique that allows correlations in individual studies to be compared. The authors found that the overall correlation between social and financial performance was "moderately positive," rising to "highly positive" for some combinations of performance measures.[35] Still, confounding results persist. A more recent study looked at companies that made *Business Ethics* magazine's annual list of 100 top corporate citizens four years in a row. It found that most were less profitable than direct competitors in their industries, suggesting to the authors that "higher profitability is associated with less corporate social responsibility."[36]

Overall, the majority of academic studies find that companies rated as notably responsible are at least as profitable, and often more so, than companies rated as less responsible. However, the results are mixed and there are such significant methodological questions that reservations are warranted. The best conclusion is that socially responsible behavior contributes to better financial performance for some companies, but evidence that it does so broadly for most companies is weak. If the evidence were stronger, there would be little need for activists and NGOs to force a CSR agenda on hesitant corporations.

CORPORATE SOCIAL RESPONSIBILITY IN A GLOBAL CONTEXT

In the early twenty-first century the doctrine of corporate responsibility is widely accepted in industrialized nations. Although its early development was strongest in the United States, sometime in the 1990s leadership passed to Europe, where

[35] Marc Orlitzky, Frank L. Schmidt, and Sara L. Rynes, "Corporate Social and Financial Performance: A Meta-Analysis," *Organization Studies* 24, no. 3 (2003).

[36] Arthur B. Laffer, Andrew Coors, and Wayne Winegarden, *Does Corporate Social Responsibility Enhance Business Profitability?* (San Diego: Laffer Associates, 2005), p. 5.

welfare state systems have nurtured some of the most powerful social justice NGOs and consumers are more inclined to purchase goods from companies they see as responsible. Until this time American corporations took the lead in evolving voluntary responses to societal demands because, relative to Europe, American markets were more laissez-faire and government regulation was looser, leaving more of the company's total responsibility in the voluntary category.

In Europe, social welfare states intervened more in markets and mandated extensive protections for workers, consumers, and the natural environment. While American companies volunteered to give health benefits to workers and make recyclable products, for example, their counterparts in the European Union were legally required to do so. So European companies never needed the spectrum of voluntary social actions that American companies did. Then, in the 1990s, Europe reacted to the rise of global competition, engaging with neoliberal ideas, deregulating markets, grinding away protections for workers, and shrinking other legal mandates on companies. In response, leading activist groups pressured firms to engage in more voluntary CSR activity and the stronger social welfare expectations in European nations gave birth to a robust, creative, and expansive design of corporate responsibility that now dominates and defines Western practice.

Corporate responsibility has strong roots elsewhere in both the developed and developing world and, as in Europe, its practice often diverges from the U.S. experience. In Japan, for example, it means paternalism toward workers and there is little tradition of philanthropy. In Australia voluntary CSR is actively encouraged by the government. In India it has risen on the teaching of Mohandas Gandhi that those who accumulate wealth hold it in trust for society.

Global CSR is now defined and dominated by the progressive ideology of Western civil society and the practices of Western multinationals. It has little foundation in some rapidly growing non-Western nations and as their businesses gain power in the world economy the consequences for CSR practice are unknown. The primary mystery is China, where a communist regime plans economic growth as it smothers dissent. Chinese corporations respond to social interests as directed by this unrepresentative, one-party government, and they adopt voluntary codes, standards, and social programs mainly to ease access into Western export markets. Although Confucian ethics teach harmony and reciprocity as central virtues and the basis of Buddhism is the interdependence of a person with the larger community and with nature, the Western idea of stakeholder engagement is lifeless in a Stalinist world.[37]

THE PROBLEM OF CROSS-BORDER CORPORATE POWER

While there is no consensus on the meaning and extent of CSR from nation to nation, the idea has taken on new and novel international dimensions in response to economic globalization. As governments deregulated markets and lowered

[37] See, for example, Po Keung Ip, "Is Confucianism Good for Business Ethics in China," *Journal of Business Ethics* 82 (2008); and "From CSR in Asia to Asian CSR," in Jem Bendell, Chew Ng, and Niaz Alam, "World Review," *Journal of Corporate Citizenship,* Spring 2009, pp. 19–22.

trade barriers in the 1980s, cross-border trade and investment began a steep rise. Dominant corporations grew larger and more active. As they did, critics and observers perceived the exercise of too much power and too little restraint, particularly of Western corporations in developing nations.

The perception that transnational corporations elude proper controls is rooted in a group of observations. First, international law, as found in treaties, conventions, and trade agreements, is weak in addressing social impacts of business. It strongly protects commercial rights, but norms protecting labor, human rights, nature, indigenous cultures, and other social resources are far less codified. Second, transnational corporations are subject to uneven regulation in developing nations, where institutions may be rudimentary and enforcement feeble. Some governments have overly bureaucratic agencies riddled with corruption. And some are undemocratic, run by elites that siphon off the economic benefits of foreign investment and neglect public needs. Third, in adapting to global economic growth, corporations use strategies of joint venture, outsourcing, and supply chain extension that create efficiencies, but sometimes also distance them from direct accountability for social harms. And fourth, significantly more government regulation of transnational firms is unlikely. No global government exists and no nation-state has the power (or the wish) to regulate international commerce. Developing nations fear, correctly, that stricter rules will deter foreign investment.

In a world where regulation is uneven, some corporations, such as Merck, have operated with high standards across nations. But others have compromised their standards in permissive host country environments. By the early 1990s, critics of multinational corporations began calling for new standards of responsibility. One by-product of globalization was the growing number, international reach, and networking of nongovernmental organizations (NGOs). Many of these groups developed a close association with the United Nations (UN), which, besides its peacekeeping function, promotes international human rights and interests of poorer, developing nations in the global South. During the 1990s, coalitions of NGOs pushed for a series of conferences sponsored by the UN for member nations. Conferences were held on environmental sustainability (Rio de Janeiro, 1992), population (Cairo, 1993), human rights (Vienna, 1994), social development (Copenhagen, 1995), and gender (Beijing, 1995).

THE RISE OF NEW GLOBAL VALUES

A defining moment came at the Rio conference on sustainability in 1992, when NGOs arrived demanding regulation of corporations. Their agenda failed, in part because the philosophy of economic liberalization driving the world economy was inhospitable to restrictions on business and in part because corporations and business groups that lobbied against regulation promoted an expanded, international doctrine of voluntary corporate responsibility. NGOs, unable to secure the hard regulations they wanted, were forced to work with business groups in developing new, innovative CSR mechanisms.

soft law
Statements of philosophy, policy, and principle found in nonbinding international conventions that, over time, gain legitimacy as guidelines for interpreting the hard law in legally binding agreements.

In hindsight, these conferences led to several important changes in the operating environments of multinational corporations. First, they generated a series of declarations, resolutions, statements of principle, guidelines, and frameworks under UN auspices that shaped international norms for the conduct of both nations and corporations. These documents created what international legal scholars call *soft law*. In the realm of international law, hard law, found mainly in treaties, creates binding rights, prohibitions, and duties. While soft law creates no binding obligations or duties for corporations, if its contents are widely accepted as expressing international norms it can, over time, become the basis for interpreting treaties. Second, the conferences provided occasions for NGOs to interact and develop influence strategies for confronting corporations. And third, they set the stage for further, this time global, expansion of the CSR ideology.

GLOBAL CORPORATE RESPONSIBILITY

The new, global dimension of CSR makes it the duty of a multinational corporation voluntarily to compensate for international and developing country regulatory deficits. It should do this, first, by extending its home country standards outward to its foreign operations and to its supply chain, and, second, by following a growing body of international norms enforced by various mechanisms of civil regulation. This new dimension of CSR flourishes because it has value across much of the CSR political spectrum. It appeals to activists as a substitute for the new laws they would prefer but cannot get and as a way to overcome the failure of weak governments to fight human rights abuses, corruption, ecological insult, and poverty. It also appeals to enlightened corporations as a way to forestall more traditional and formal regulation and to placate belligerent NGOs. As a result, the world seethes with activity pushing the idea along.

Figure 5.3 shows the range of entities and elements in an evolving system of global CSR. This system, solidifying now out of a less mature patchwork, organizes values, principles, rules, institutions, and management tools in support of voluntary corporate actions. Simultaneously, it has grown into a framework of civil regulation that can often command corporate behavior. We illuminate its structure by discussing the elements set forth in Figure 5.3, moving clockwise from the top right. In subsequent chapters we discuss some of them at greater length.

norm
A standard that arises over time and is enforced by social sanction or law.

principle
A rule, natural law, or truth used as a standard to guide conduct.

Development of Norms and Principles

A *norm* is a standard that arises over time and, as agreement on it becomes widespread, is enforced by social sanction or law. It is similar to a *principle*, which is a rule, natural law, or truth used as a standard to guide conduct. The norms and principles that direct global CSR are derived in part from timeless accretions of civilization, but international conventions to codify and interpret them are increasingly influential. The United Nations is a ringleader. An early codification of norms is the *Universal Declaration of Human Rights,* adopted by the UN in 1948,

FIGURE 5.3
**A Global
System of
CSR Activity**

FIGURE 5.3
**A Global
System of
CSR Activity**

which spells out a "common standard" of "inalienable rights," that are specified in 30 articles.[38] The rights in this document are now widely accepted and it is the foundation for many of the human rights standards in corporate and NGO conduct codes. It requires, for example, equal rights for men and women, and corporations following such codes must meet this standard, often by imposing it on suppliers in less developed nations where no legislation requires it.

A second milestone in the development of norms is the *Tripartite Declaration of Principles concerning Multinational Enterprises and Social Policy*, adopted by an agency of the UN in 1977. The Tripartite Declaration, so-called because unions, governments, and industry collaborated in its creation, came in response to the rising power of multinational corporations in the 1960s. It sets forth a long list of "guidelines" related to worker rights, for example, that multinational corporations should not offer wages and benefits less than those offered for comparable work elsewhere in a country.[39] Over the years, the *Tripartite Declaration* has been accepted

[38] *Universal Declaration of Human Rights,* G.A. res. 217 A (III), UN Doc. A/810, December 10, 1948, Preamble.

[39] *Tripartite Declaration of Principles concerning Multinational Enterprises and Social Policy,* 3rd ed. (Geneva: International Labour Office, 2001), p. v and p. 7, para. 33. First edition published in 1977.

as a foundational statement and it now is the basis for most international labor codes. As new norms solidify, additions are made, most recently a new entry in 2006 suggesting that multinational corporations had a duty to abolish child labor.

At the leading edge of emerging norms is a draft compilation of *Norms on the Responsibilities of Transnational Corporations,* advanced by the UN Human Rights Commission in 2004 and discussed for several years before dying in what has been called a "train wreck" of polarized arguments.[40] The *Norms* would obligate multinational corporations to protect a lengthy list of "universal" rights of peoples, consumers, workers, and the environment. The corporation "shall not use forced or compulsory labour," nor "shall [it] . . . advertise harmful or potentially harmful products" and it "shall generally conduct [its] activities in a manner contributing to the wider goal of sustainable development."[41] It requires transnational corporations to adopt internal rules for compliance, submit to monitoring by the UN in which NGOs would participate, and make "prompt reparation" for injuries due to lack of compliance. Nations would be asked to pass laws to legalize enforcement of the *Norms.*

The draft is an exceptionally aggressive document that advances past the edge of international consensus on corporate responsibility. Nations were skeptical of giving corporations the legal authority to enforce "universal," meaning Western, human rights standards in countries with diverging values. Corporations, with some exceptions, were bitterly hostile to the imposition of new duties and exposure to new liabilities. For now the *Norms* are moribund, but time is their ally.

Landmark statements of norms and principles such as these arise from the steady accretion of innumerable international charters, declarations, conventions, multilateral agency policies, and treaties on labor, human rights, corruption, migratory birds, and other issues that, by their sheer numbers, promote broad acceptance of progressive, developed-country values as universal norms. These norms are the basis for proliferating codes of conduct that target corporate behavior.

codes of conduct
Formal statements of aspirations, principles, guidelines, and rules for corporate behavior.

multistakeholder initiative
A code-based form of civil regulation created by some combination of corporate, government, NGO, or international organization actors.

Codes of Conduct

Codes of conduct are formal statements of aspirations, principles, guidelines, and rules for corporate behavior. They arise from many sources. Corporations write them. In addition, there are hundreds of codes created by industry associations, NGOs, governments, and international organizations such as the UN. Many codes result from collaborative processes by multiple parties; these are called *multistakeholder initiatives.* Any large multinational corporation will follow more than one code. It will have its own code or codes and, in addition, will be a signatory of multiple codes developed by other actors, likely including an industry code and specialized codes focused on labor, human rights, environmental

[40] Spoken remarks of J. Ruggie, the Secretary General's Special Representative on Business and Human Rights, quoted in David Kinley, Justine Nolan, and Natalie Zerial, "The Politics of Corporate Social Responsibility: Reflections on the UN Human Rights Norms for Corporations," *Company and Securities Law Journal* 25, no. 1 (2007), p. 31.

[41] *Norms on the Responsibilities of Transnational Corporations and Other Business Enterprises with Regard to Human Rights,* U.N. Doc. E/CN.4/Sub.2/2003/12/Rev.2 (2003), secs. D(5), F.(13), and G.(14).

protection, corruption, and other matters. Here are examples of codes from different sources.

- Samsung Electronics Company has a *Global Code of Conduct* based on five aspirational principles: legal and ethical behavior, a "clean organization culture" (which means a culture free of discrimination, sexual harassment, insider trading, and similar misbehaviors), respect for stakeholders, care for the environment, and social responsibility. Brief, descriptive statements in each category give more specific guidance to employees.[42]
- The *Electronic Industry Code of Conduct* is intended to protect the safety and rights of workers in overseas plants that do computer assembly and component manufacturing. The 11-page code requires participants, who sign on voluntarily, to "go beyond legal compliance" in enforcing its standards for labor, health and safety, environmental protection, and ethical behavior.[43] It explicitly incorporates standards in the *Universal Declaration of Human Rights* and other codifications of international norms.
- In the 1990s a small band of activists within Amnesty International UK, a human rights NGO, began to work with companies, resulting in a checklist of human rights principles that evolved into a code titled *Human Rights Guidelines for Companies*. Although no companies adopted the Guidelines in their entirety, their appearance altered a widespread belief of executives at that time that only governments, not corporations, had responsibility for human rights. They were the template for a wave of changes written into corporate codes and policies.[44]
- The Ethical Trading Initiative is an alliance of companies, unions, and NGOs based in the United Kingdom. It has a *Base Code* setting standards for working conditions in overseas supplier firms. Its 50 member companies agree to conform their own codes to the *Base Code*, apply the standards across their international supply chains to almost 40,000 contractors with 8.6 million workers, and allow independent monitoring for compliance. Although the entity can discipline and even expel member companies for noncompliance, it does not publicly report such actions or any information about individual companies.

No matter what the source of a code, the target is the corporation. A code's effectiveness depends on how the corporation carries it out. Codes written by corporations themselves often lack rigor. Codes created by other parties usually require companies to sign compliance agreements that require some form of monitoring, and these are more effective, if uneven in result, leading to a growing focus on ways of monitoring corporations to verify code compliance.

---

[42] Samsung Electronics Co., *Global Code of Conduct* (Seoul, Korea: Samsung, 2006).

[43] Electronic Industry Citizenship Coalition, *Electronic Industry Code of Conduct,* v3.0 (2009), p. 1, at www.eicc.info/EICC%20CODE.htm.

[44] Sir Geoffrey Chandler, "The Amnesty International UK Business Group," *The Journal of Corporate Citizenship,* Spring 2009, p. 33.

Reporting and Verification Standards

sustainability reporting
The practice of a corporation publishing information about its economic, social, and environmental performance.

There is growing demand for accurate information about CSR performance. This has led more companies to issue public reports that describe and measure their actions, a practice often called *sustainability reporting*. The reports take many forms. Information may be part of the annual report or appear in separate publications. It is costly to collect data and compile such reports, but they have benefits. They protect corporate reputation and they are a management tool for measuring performance and progress.

Two problems with sustainability reporting are, first, that defining and measuring social performance is difficult and, second, that the reports are not comparable from company to company. But uniformity is growing. In 2000, an organization in the Netherlands, the Global Reporting Initiative (GRI), released a model reporting framework that lists specific performance indicators and methods for doing the reports. Adoption of the GRI format has been so rapid that now 77 percent of the 250 largest global corporations are using it.[45]

Because of deep cynicism about corporate candor, institutions that independently verify reports have arisen. A nonprofit group, AccountAbility, has created a widely used "assurance standard" for independent parties that audit corporate reports for reliability. Reporting is further discussed in Chapter 6.

Certification and Labeling Schemes

Labels are symbols displayed on or with a product to certify that it, or its production process, meets a set of social or environmental criteria. Such schemes try to create a market for social responsibility by influencing consumers to prefer marked products. Criteria for labels are set by the labeling body, which is often a cooperative project of industry, NGOs, unions, and governments. Certified companies must usually allow independent auditors to inspect and monitor their activities. Typically the process is funded with licensing fees paid by producers, importers, and retailers. Here are several examples from dozens of such schemes.

- The *Kimberley Process Certification Scheme* is a device to stop the flow of so-called "blood" diamonds, which are rough diamonds from parts of Africa where sales to exporters fund civil wars and rebellions. Its governing body consists of 74 member nations, including all major diamond producing and importing nations, representatives from the diamond industry, and human rights groups. Each participating country is required to enforce trade rules. Companies export diamonds only in sealed, tamper-proof containers tagged with compliance certificates. Smuggling around the scheme persists, but after its inception in 2003 the share of "blood diamonds" in world markets dropped from 15 percent to 0.1 percent.[46]

- The *Forest Stewardship Council* sets standards to certify that forests are managed sustainably and certifies to mills, wholesalers, and retailers that wood

[45] KPMG, *International Survey of Corporate Responsibility Reporting 2008* (Amstelveen, the Netherlands: KPMG, 2008), p. 35.

[46] These percentages are in Vivienne Walt, "Diamonds Aren't Forever," *Fortune*, December 11, 2006, p. 89; and "Kimberley Process: Frequently Asked Questions," at www.kimberleyprocess.com/faqs/index_en.html, accessed December 5, 2009.

they buy is responsibly grown and harvested. It is an international body with 800 members, including timber companies, foresters, and NGOs ranging from Greenpeace Russia to the East Sepik Council of Women in Papua New Guinea. Members make decisions in a fastidiously democratic assembly where weighted counting gives the global North and South each 50 percent of votes. Because the Council's standards are high, it must compete with rival and less costly forest certification schemes created by industry that confuse consumers who are largely ignorant of differences between standards. The Council certifies only 5 percent of the world's timber harvest.[47]

fair trade
The idea that ethical consumers will pay a premium for commodities from producers in developing nations who use sustainable methods.

- Many certifications promote *fair trade*, or the idea that small, marginal producers in Africa, Asia, and Latin America should be paid a "fair," that is, a stable, guaranteed, and sometimes above-market price for crops so they can make a living and engage in sustainable farming practices. *Transfair USA*, a coalition of religious, human rights, labor, and consumer groups, offers the trademarked *Fair Trade Certified* term and logo on agricultural products such as coffee, tea, cocoa, honey, rice, and flowers exported to the United States. With coffee, for example, it audits sales of beans by farmers to companies. Its black-and-white logo depicting a farmer in front of a globe certifies that coffee farmers were paid a guaranteed minimum price.

Management Standards

management standard
A model of the methods an organization can use to achieve certain goals.

A *management standard* is a model of the methods an organization can use to achieve certain goals. The use of quality standards is widespread. Now, actors in the global CSR network have established standards for social responsibility or elements of social responsibility such as health and safety or environmental protection.

- The *EcoManagement and Audit Scheme* (EMAS) is a standard that rises above legal requirements for environmental performance in European nations that already have some of the world's strictest regulations.[48] Companies that join this voluntary initiative must reduce emissions, energy use, and waste beyond legal requirements. They also agree to publish regular statements of their environmental performance and have them checked for accuracy by outside auditors. More than 4,000 firms participate. They are allowed to use the EMAS logo in ads that make green claims for their products. EMAS is run by representatives of governments, industries, unions, and NGOs.

- The *International Organization for Standardization* (ISO), which has already created widely used standards in other areas, for example, ISO 9000 on quality and *ISO 14000* on the environment, is developing a broad new social responsibility standard named *ISO 2600* intended to set forth underlying principles, core subjects, and methods for integrating social performance in the plans, systems, and processes of organizations. The standard is now in draft form.[49]

[47] Tom Arup, "Timber Standard Pleases Union but Fails to Impress Greens," *Sydney Morning Herald,* November 30, 2009, p. 2.

[48] The standard is set forth in "Regulation (ED) No. 761/2001 of the European Parliament and of the Council of 19 March 2001," *Official Journal of the European Communities,* April 24, 2001, p. L114/1.

[49] International Organization for Standardization, *Draft International Standard ISO/DIS 2600: Guidance on Social Responsibility* (Geneva: ISO, 2009).

Social Investment and Lending

· Equity capital and borrowing are critical to corporate financial strategies. Knowing this, actors in the international CSR movement have tried to introduce social criteria into capital markets. Initiatives such as these threaten to raise the cost of capital for corporations that dodge evolving norms.

• Under the auspices of the United Nations, a coalition of institutional investors and civil society groups created a set of voluntary *Principles for Responsible Investment*. Its signatories, about 560 banks, pension funds, hedge funds, and insurers with, collectively, $18 trillion in assets, must consider a company's environmental, social, and governance performance when they evaluate investments.[50] They also must accept a duty to pressure corporations in the direction of responsible behavior.

• The *FTSE4Good Global Index* is intended to set the world standard for those wanting to invest in companies following "good standards of corporate responsibility." The index was started by a British company in 2001. Scanning a universe of about 2,000 companies on 23 world stock exchanges, it first excludes companies producing tobacco, nuclear weapons, nuclear power, and major weapons systems. From what remains, it includes approximately 650 companies that meet somewhat stringent criteria for the practice of CSR. Since its inception it has delisted more than 200 companies for lapses in meeting its standards.

Government Actions

Governments advance corporate responsibility mainly with binding national regulation. Some also promote voluntary actions. European nations lead. The European Commission and European Parliament generate a stream of communications and reports encouraging codes, labels, and forums. The Belgium government set up the *Belgium Social Label*, a brown-and-blue cartoon of a person with arms uplifted in exultation, presumably because the company that made the product saw to it that its entire production chain followed basic International Labor Organization standards. Sweden requires its 55 state-owned companies to produce a yearly sustainability report based on Global Reporting Initiative guidelines. Denmark requires several thousand companies to report annually on their efforts to reduce environmental impacts.

Elsewhere there is also encouragement. The United States does far less than most European governments, but one study found 50 federal activities that could be classified as promoting CSR.[51] However, most were awards or programs with tiny budgets. In Australia the legislature published a study of global CSR initiatives and recommended "greater uptake" of the idea by Australian companies.[52]

[50] PRI, "New Data Signals Growing 'Culture Change' Amongst Significant Portion of Global Investors," media release, July 16, 2009, p. 1.

[51] General Accountability Office, *Globalization: Numerous Federal Activities Complement U.S. Business's Global Corporate Social Responsibility Efforts*, GAO-05-744, August 2005.

[52] Parliamentary Joint Committee on Corporations and Financial Sectors, *Corporate Responsibility: Managing Risk and Creating Value* (Canberra: Senate Printing Unit, Parliament House, June 2006).

Although the governments of developing nations where human rights abuses, corruption, and ecosystem destruction are targeted sometimes resist or ignore efforts to impose Western-based schemes of civil regulation, the Chinese commission that manages state-owned firms for the central government recently issued a set of CSR guidelines for the companies it oversees. Calling CSR "an unavoidable pathway" that "has become a key criteria worldwide," these guidelines call on the firms to "develop in a people-centered, scientific way and make profits," and emphasize energy conservation, philanthropy, and jobs creation as core CSR duties.[53] Since the commission appoints, removes, disciplines, and sets the salaries of managers at state-owned firms, the guidelines are unlikely to be ignored. Some companies have already set up internal "CSR work commissions" to implement them.

Civil Society Vigilance

NGOs watch multinational corporations and police actions they see as departing from emerging global norms. A direct action campaign by experienced activists is unpleasant and, if it carries any element of validity, very dangerous to brand reputation. The abiding threat of attack inspires entry into various code, labeling, reporting, and standards schemes.

- The force behind the Electronic Industry Code of Conduct noted earlier is the Catholic Agency for Overseas Development. When the group issued a report on "computer factory sweatshops" and began a "Clean Up Your Computer" campaign, it galvanized Hewlett-Packard, IBM, Dell, and others in the industry to create a protective code of conduct.[54]

- In 2000, the Rainforest Action Network (RAN) began a campaign against Citigroup, alleging that the bank's loans funded socially and environmentally disruptive pipelines, mines, dams, and other projects in developing countries. RAN was the sharp edge of a coalition of more than 100 NGOs opposed to bank lending that failed to take deforestation, pollution, and disruption of indigenous peoples into account. Three years of artful attack on the bank's reputation and harassment of its executives went by until Citigroup tired. Working with other banks it adopted industry lending guidelines based on sustainability guidelines then in use by the World Bank. Today, largely due to pressure by RAN, 69 of the world's largest banks, making 95 percent of the world's private development loans, subscribe to these "voluntary" principles, now called the *Equator Principles*.[55] The *Principles* divide projects into high, medium, and low social and environmental risk and compel borrowers to meet standards for ecological protection and to consult with native peoples. In effect, this is a global environmental regulatory scheme for the banking, mining, forestry, and energy industries.

---

[53] State-Owned Assets Supervision and Administration Commission, *CSR Guideline for State-Owned Enterprises (SOE)*, January 4, 2008, trans. Guo Peiyuan, 1(a) and 1(d).

[54] CAFOD, *Clean Up Your Computer: Working Conditions in the Electronics Sector* (London: CAFOD, January 2004); and Peter Burrows, "Stalking High-Tech Sweatshops," *BusinessWeek,* June 19, 2006, p. 62.

[55] International Finance Corporation, Treasury Department, *Funding Operations* (Washington, DC: World Bank Group, July 2009), slide 5.

ASSESSING THE EVOLVING GLOBAL CSR SYSTEM

In sum, a perceived shortage of regulation over multinational corporations has been countered mainly by action within civil society to create private regulatory schemes. Elements of civil society, often working through the United Nations, came together on statements and conventions that congealed global norms, raising expectations of corporate behavior and opening miscreants to the reputation risks of activist "name and shame" campaigns. As this dynamic unfolded over 20 years, regulatory leadership flowed from nations to other actors, particularly to multiparty alliances combining NGOs, UN agencies, unions, and corporations. These bodies, novel at first, but now duplicating endlessly, direct corporate adherence to the CSR standards they create using tools such as codes, labels, audits, and certifications. So prolific is the device that one or more standards are now established for almost every industry and commodity.

The growth of civil regulation invites reflection. First, it reveals that for much of civil society constructive engagement with corporations has become more important than hostility and attack. There is a realization that business has unique organizational and financial capacities that can be brought to bear on global problems. Second, the multinational corporation is slowly and reluctantly being redefined as a stakeholder entity. In the new world of international civil regulation it has duties toward the environment, human rights, and social development as real as its duties to shareowners. Third, civil regulation is a pragmatic solution to the regulatory vacuum. It has partially, but not fully, compensated for lack of binding global regulation. Though piecemeal, experimental, partial, and subject to enforcement failures it is a forceful presence.

Finally, because it is an extra-state phenomenon, civil regulation raises issues of representation. Conservatives find the new system undemocratic because it relies heavily for monitoring and compliance on progressive NGOs that are self-constituted communities of belief, unelected and not clearly or formally representative even of their membership rolls, let alone of the people in developing countries affected by transnational corporations.[56] Goals are dominated by the muses/anxieties of Western activists.

CONCLUDING OBSERVATIONS

In this chapter we focused on defining and explaining the idea of corporate social responsibility and its evolution. Figure 5.4 summarizes this evolution.

Historically, corporations have been motivated primarily by profit. However, as they have grown in size and power they have been exhorted and pressured to alter this single-minded focus. This is because (1) the ideology of corporate social responsibility has gradually evolved an expanded ethical duty and (2) the power of stakeholders to enforce this duty has increased.

[56] Larry Cata Backer, 'Multinational Corporations, Transnational Law: The United Nations' Norms on the Responsibilities of Transnational Corporations as a Harbinger of Corporate Social Responsibility in International Law," *Columbia Human Rights Law Review,* Winter 2006, pp. 386–88.

FIGURE 5.4   **The Evolution of Corporate Social Responsibility**
Although the term corporate social responsibility is of relatively recent use, the idea it represents has been under construction for more than two centuries. These timelines show how its elements have evolved.

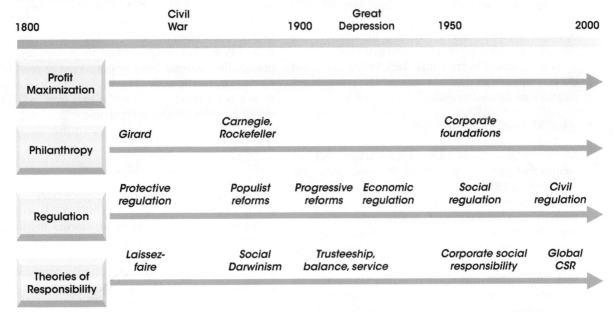

Doubts about CSR remain. In the progressive community there is cynicism about its limits. On the conservative side, elaborate CSR schemes might just be abandoned, replaced by nothing, allowing the natural grace of laissez-faire room to work. Debates over its proper nature will continue. Yet no radical changes are likely; the evolved CSR ideology that now exists is entrenched. No corporation of any size can afford to ignore the range of social obligations beyond market activity. In the next chapter, we will discuss specific management practices used to carry out corporate responsibility.

Jack Welch at General Electric

In April 1981 John Francis "Jack" Welch, Jr., became chief executive officer of General Electric. He held the position for 20 years until retiring in September 2001. During that time, he transformed GE, turning a solidly profitable manufacturing company into an exceptionally profitable conglomerate dominated by service businesses. If you had invested $100 in GE stock when Welch took the reins and held it for 20 years, it would have been worth $6,749.

Welch is lauded for his creative management style and became a national business hero. A fawning *BusinessWeek* article called him "America's #1 Manager."[1] *Fortune* magazine gushed that GE under Welch was "the best-managed, best-regarded company in America."[2] Yet the intense, aggressive Welch made fortunes for GE shareholders using methods that had mixed impacts on employees, unions, communities, other companies, and governments. As a result, not everyone sees the GE performance as a

[1] John A. Byrne, "Jack: A Close-Up Look at How America's #1 Manager Runs GE," *BusinessWeek*, June 8, 1998, p. 91.

[2] Jerry Useem, "It's All Yours, Jeff. Now What?" *Fortune*, September 17, 2001, p. 64.

model for corporate social responsibility. Upon Welch's retirement, the *Multinational Monitor,* a progressive magazine founded by Ralph Nader, devoted an entire issue to making "The Case Against GE." The lead editorial branded Welch as a corporate titan opposed to rules of society and said his actions were "disastrous" for workers and communities.[3]

Did General Electric under Jack Welch carry out the full range of its duties to society? Did it fall short? Readers are invited to decide.

JACK WELCH RISES

Most top executives come from backgrounds of wealth and privilege. Jack Welch is an exception. He was born in 1935 to working-class Irish parents in a small Massachusetts town. His father was a quiet, passive man who endured as a railroad conductor punching tickets on commuter trains. Welch's mother was a dominating woman who caused her husband to wilt but instilled a powerful drive in her son. Welch was an outstanding student at the University of Massachusetts at Amherst and went on to get a doctorate in chemical engineering at the University of Illinois.

After graduating, he started working at a GE plastics factory in 1960. His tremendous energy and ambition were very apparent. He was so competitive in weekend softball games that his aggressive play alienated co-workers and he stopped going. After one year, he threatened to quit when he got the same $1,000 raise as everyone else. His boss cajoled him into staying and as the years and promotions flashed by he never again wavered.

As he rose, Welch exhibited a fiery temperament and expected those around him to share his intensity. He was blunt, impatient with subordinates, and emotionally volatile. He loved no-holds-barred discussions in meetings but frequently put people on the spot, saying, "My six-year-old kid could do better than that."[4] With every promotion, he sized up his new staff with a cold eye and purged those who failed to impress him. "I'm the first to admit," he says, "I could be impulsive in removing people during those early days."[5]

This was just preparation for the big leagues to come. GE had a polished corporate culture reflecting the Eastern establishment values of its leadership over many decades. Welch did not fit. He was impatient, frustrated by the company's bureaucracy, and lacking in deference. With this mismatch GE might have repulsed Welch at some point, but his performance was outstanding. Several times he got mixed reviews for a promotion, but because of exemplary financial results he was never blocked. In 1981 he took over as CEO of one of America's singular companies.

THE STORY OF GENERAL ELECTRIC

The lineage of General Electric goes back to 1879 when Thomas Alva Edison (1847–1931), with the backing of banker J. P. Morgan, started the Edison Electric Light Company to make lightbulbs and electrical equipment. Although Edison was a great inventor, he was a poor manager and the company lost ground. So in 1892 Morgan took charge, engineering a merger with a competitor and plotting to reduce Edison to a figurehead in the new company.

Morgan disposed of Edison's top managers and dropped the word Edison from its name so that the firm became simply General Electric Company. Morgan sat as a commanding figure on the new company's board. Although Edison was also a director, he attended only the first meeting and never returned.[6]

After the merger, GE built a near-monopoly in the incandescent bulb market. Over the years, great things emerged from the company. Early in the twentieth century, its motors worked the Panama Canal locks, powered battleships, and ran locomotives.[7] GE's research labs bred a profusion of new electrical appliances, including fans, toasters, refrigerators, vacuum cleaners, ranges, garbage disposals, air conditioners, and irons. At first these new inventions were very expensive, but as more people purchased them, production costs fell and they became commodities within the reach of every family. By 1960 GE was credited with a remarkable list of other inventions, including

[3] "You Don't Know Jack," *Multinational Monitor,* July–August 2001, p. 5.

[4] Jack Welch, *Jack: Straight from the Gut* (New York: Warner Books, 2001), p. 43.

[5] Ibid., p. 43.

[6] Thomas F. O'Boyle, *At Any Cost: Jack Welch, General Electric, and the Pursuit of Profit* (New York: Knopf, 1998), p. 55.

[7] For more on the early history of GE see John Winthrop Hammond, *Men and Volts: The Story of General Electric* (Philadelphia: J. B. Lippincott, 1948).

the X-ray machine, the motion picture with sound, fluorescent lighting, the diesel-electric locomotive, the jet engine, synthetic diamonds, the hard plastic Lexan, and Silly Putty.[8]

As it added manufacturing capacity to build these inventions, GE grew. By 1981, when Jack Welch took the reins, the company had $27 billion in revenues and 404,000 employees. It was organized into 50 separate businesses reporting to a layer of six sector executives at corporate headquarters in Fairfield, Connecticut, who in turn reported to the CEO. To make it run, a large, almost imperial staff of researchers and planners created detailed annual plans setting forth revenue goals and other objectives for each business.

THE WELCH ERA BEGINS

Welch believes that managers must confront reality and adapt to the world as it is, not as they wish it to be. As he studied GE's situation in the early 1980s, he saw a corporation that needed to change. GE's manufacturing businesses were still profitable, but margins were shrinking. The wages of American workers were rising even as their productivity was declining. International competition was growing, particularly from the Japanese, who had cost advantages because of a weak yen. Although GE seemed healthy at the moment, ominous forces were gathering. In addition, Welch saw GE bloated with layers of bureaucracy that infuriated him by slowing decisions and frustrating change. The company, as currently operated, could not weather the competitive storms ahead. It would have to change.

Welch articulated a simple guiding vision. Every GE business would be the number one or number two player in its industry. If it failed this test it would be fixed, closed, or sold. In addition, Welch said all GE businesses would have to fit into one of three areas—core manufacturing, technology, or services. Any business that fell outside these three hubs was a candidate for sale or closure. This included manufacturing businesses that could not sustain high profit margins.

In the next five years, Welch executed his strategy by closing 73 plants, selling 232 businesses, and eliminating 132,000 workers from GE payrolls.[9] As he conformed GE to his vision, he also bought hundreds of

Jack Welch (1935–). Source: © Bob Daemmrich/CORBIS.

other businesses large and small. Within GE businesses he eliminated jobs through attrition, layoffs, and outsourcing. In the largest acquisition of that period, Welch acquired RCA in 1985. RCA was a giant electronics and broadcasting conglomerate with a storied history as the company that had developed radio technology. After paying $6.7 billion for RCA, Welch chopped it up, keeping NBC and selling other businesses one by one, in effect, destroying the giant company as an organizational entity. As jobs vanished, Welch got the nickname "Neutron Jack," comparing him with a neutron bomb that left buildings standing but killed everyone inside.

Welch also attacked the GE bureaucracy. One problem was its size. There were too many vice presidents, too many layers, and too many staffs with authority to review and approve decisions. A second problem was the bureaucratic mentality in which headquarters staff practiced a "superficial congeniality" that Welch interpreted as smiling to your face and getting you behind your back.[10] He demolished the hierarchy by laying

[8] Thomas F. O'Boyle, "'At Any Cost' Is Too High," *Multinational Monitor*, July–August 2001, p. 41.

[9] Frank Swoboda, "GE Picks Welch's Successor," *Washington Post*, November 28, 2000, p. E1.

[10] Welch, *Jack*, p. 96.

EXHIBIT 1

**The Vitality
Curve**

Source: *Jack:
Straight from the Gut*
by Jack Welch with
John A. Byrne.
Copyright © 2001
by John F. Welch,
Jr. Foundation. By
permission of
Grand Central
Publishing. All
rights reserved.

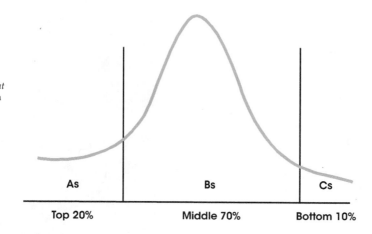

off thousands of central staff in strategic planning, personnel, and other areas. Then he set out to change GE's culture by promoting the notion of a "boundary-less" organization, or one in which ideas were freely exchanged so that organizational learning could rapidly occur. Welch compared GE to an old house:

> Floors represent layers and the walls functional barriers. To get the best out of an organization, these floors and walls must be blown away, creating an open space where ideas flow freely, independent of rank or function.[11]

Later, Welch introduced the practice of "workout" sessions in which employees in every GE business had an opportunity to confront their bosses to express frustration with bureaucratic practices and suggest more efficient alternatives. Managers in these sessions sat in front of a room filled with subordinates and had to agree or disagree on the spot to carry out suggestions. Thousands of such sessions were held to drive out the bureaucratic mentality.

Welch also used Crotonville, the company's training center on the Hudson River, to meet with managers and instill his vision. He invited candid discussions, and gradually the company culture became more informal and open.

DIFFERENTIATION

Welch is convinced that having the right people in management positions is the single most important cause of success in a business. Early in his career, he developed a colorful vocabulary to differentiate

between players. Inept managers were "turkeys" and "dinks," standouts were called "all-stars." As CEO he reinforced strategic initiatives with a system of "differentiation" that generously rewarded managers who achieved performance goals and got rid of those who missed them. In this system, every year each GE business was forced to evaluate its managers and rank them on a "vitality curve" that differentiated among As, Bs, and Cs. The As were committed people, filled with passion for their jobs, who took initiative and exceeded performance goals. They had what Welch called "the four Es of GE leadership":

> very high *energy* levels, the ability to *energize* others around common goals, the *edge* to make tough yes-and-no decisions, and finally, the ability to consistently *execute* and deliver on their promises.[12]

The vitality curve was Darwinian. The As were the top 20 percent, Bs were the middle 70 percent, and Cs were the bottom 10 percent (see Exhibit 1). The As received salary increases, promotions, and stock options. Welch followed their careers closely. He kept large loose-leaf notebooks containing evaluations of the top 750 of GE's 4,000 managers. Bs were considered vital to the success of the company and were coached so that some would become As. Cs were not worth wasting time on and were dismissed. The process was repeated annually, and each time the bottom 10 percent had to go. The curve applied to every GE business. No business leader could claim that his or her group was an exception, though some tried. Filling the A, B, and C categories forced difficult decisions. If 20 managers were evaluated, 2 had

---

[11] Welch, *Jack,* p. 162.

[12] Welch, *Jack,* p. 158.

to be placed at the bottom and their careers at GE ended. After several years of getting rid of low performers, the leaders of GE businesses resisted classifying anyone as a C, but Welch was relentless. If they didn't identify the bottom 10 percent, he refused to carry out stock option and salary recommendations for the entire group until they did. In this way, the bar of performance was continually raised.

Welch compared people to plants. "If they grow, you have a beautiful garden," he said. "If they don't, you cut them out."[13] He disagreed with those who found the system heartless:

> Some think it's cruel or brutal to remove the bottom 10 percent of our people. It isn't. It's just the opposite. What I think is brutal and "false kindness" is keeping people around who aren't going to grow and prosper . . . The characterization of a vitality curve as cruel stems from false logic and is an outgrowth of a culture that practices false kindness.[14]

AN ASSESSMENT OF THE WELCH YEARS

With Jack Welch at the helm GE sustained exceptionally high rates of profitability, and shareholders were enriched. Even with five stock splits, earnings per share rose from $0.46 in 1981 to $1.07 in 2000, his last full year as CEO, and total return on GE shares averaged 21.5 percent.[15] In 2000 GE reported a net operating margin of 19 percent and earned 27 percent on invested capital.[16] These are high figures for a large multinational corporation.

Welch also reshaped GE. He continuously bought and sold businesses both large and small. During his last four years alone he made more than 400 acquisitions. One underlying reason for the increasing profitability of GE is that through this churning of businesses GE's center of gravity shifted from manufacturing to services. The GE he inherited earned 85 percent of its revenues from manufacturing; the GE he created got 70 percent of its revenues from services.[17]

Welch wrung profits from GE by creating a performance culture. Managers were energized. Plants grew more efficient. For instance, when Welch became CEO, GE's locomotive plant in Erie, Pennsylvania, needed 7,500 hourly employees to make 350 locomotives a year. By 2000 productivity had improved so much that only 4,000 workers could make 900 locomotives a year.[18]

The story of the Welch years has the elements of legend. An ambitious son of working-class parents rises through hard work to command a mighty company, inspire managers everywhere, and become rich along with other company shareholders. To reward Welch for the shower of wealth he created, in his last year the GE board awarded him a special bonus bringing his yearly compensation to $174 million.[19] At this time he held more than 22 million shares of GE stock and options worth almost $1 billion, as shown in Exhibit 2. This is astronomical compensation for one person, but his $972 million in stock is only four-hundredths of 1 percent of the $460 billion in equity value created during his tenure.

Exhibit 2 shows how directors shared in the GE equity windfall. When they joined the board, each outside (nonemployee) director was given 5,000 shares of GE stock and a $150,000 life insurance policy. Thereafter, each year directors were given $75,000, $2,000 for each of the 10 meetings they were required to attend, and options on 18,000 more shares of GE stock. If they retired at age 65 with five years of service, they were eligible to receive the $75,000 annual retainer for life. There were other rewards. One GE business sold diamonds and directors could buy them at cost for their personal use or for spouses. The year that Welch retired, the group purchased $975,595 worth of diamonds and must have looked very good at the kinds of parties to which laid-off workers were not invited.[20]

While the board feted Welch, not everyone saw his leadership as something to admire or emulate. Early in his career, he was compared to a speedboat

---

[13] Quoted in Carol Hymowitz and Matt Murray, "Raises and Praise or Out the Door—How GE's Chief Rates and Spurs His Employees," *The Wall Street Journal,* June 21, 1999, p. B1.

[14] Welch, *Jack,* p. 162. See also Jack and Suzy Welch, "The Case for 20-70-10," *BusinessWeek,* October 2, 2006, p. 108.

[15] Swoboda, "GE Picks Welch's Successor," p. E1; Julie Schlosser, "Jack? Jack Who?" *Fortune,* September 17, 2001, p. 52.

[16] General Electric Company, *GE Annual Report 2000* (Fairfield, CT: General Electric Company, 2001), p. 42.

[17] James Flanigan, "New Boss's Challenge: To Keep GE Together," *Los Angeles Times,* August 26, 2001, p. C1.

[18] "Dignity and Defiance: An Interview with John Hovis," *Multinational Monitor,* July–August 2001, p. 35.

[19] *General Electric Company, Notice of 2001 Annual Meeting* and *Proxy Statement,* March 9, 2001, pp. 22 and 27.

[20] Ibid., p. 14.

EXHIBIT 2   The 2001 GE Board of Directors: Market Value of Total Holdings in GE Stock (shaded entries are inside directors)

Director	Value	Director	Value
James I. Cash Professor, Harvard Business School	$3,719,059	Sam Nunn Former U.S. Senator from Georgia	$4,516,975
Silas S. Cathcart CEO, Illinois Tool Works(ret.)	$34,601,060	Roger S. Penske Chairman, Penske Corp.	$6,844,896
Paolo Fresco Chairman, Fiat	$111,700,043	Frank H. T. Rhodes President Emeritus, Cornell University	$10,931,672
Ann M Fudge Vice President, Kraft Foods	$1,667,828	Andrew C. Sigler CEO, Champion International (ret.)	$5,820,301
Claudio X. Gonzalez CEO, Kimberly-Clark de Mexico	$9,871,797	Douglas A. Warner Chairman, J. P. Morgan Chase & Co.	$8,323,021
Andrea Jung CEO, Avon Products	$2,733,352	Dennis. D. Dammerman Chairman, GE Capital	$187,238,259
Kenneth G. Langone CEO, Invamed Associates	$14,805,848	Jeffrey R. Immelt President, General Electric	$130,853,846
Rochelle B. Lazarus CEO, Ogilvy & Mather Worldwide	$877,690	John F. Welch, Jr. Chairman and CEO, General Electric	$972,022,731
Scott G. McNealy CEO, Sun Microsystems	$2,089,684	Robert Wright Vice Chairman of GE, President, NBC	$229,777,982
Gertrude Michelson Former Senior V.P., Macy's	$14,381,950		

Source: General Electric Company, *Proxy Statement*, March 9, 2001, p. 12. Total holdings include common stock, option holdings, deferred compensation, restricted stock units, and stock appreciation rights.

going down a narrow canal, leaving considerable turbulence in its wake.[21] His detractors say that once Welch was at the master controls of GE he piloted the mammoth organization through global straits the same way. There is no denying that he created wealth. But what were the costs to people, communities, and society? The flaws in the Welch performance, according to critics, include the following.

Loss of Jobs

Early on, Welch was caricatured as a ruthless job cutter. When he became CEO in 1981, the corporate culture reinforced loyalty. People went to work at GE

directly out of college, stayed for 40 years, retired in communities of GE people, and attended GE alumni clubs until rigor mortis set in.

As Welch remodeled GE there were mass layoffs. Within a few years, one of every four employees was gone. Welch believed that the idea of loyalty in GE's culture retarded change, so he rooted it out. At meetings he told employees it was out of fashion. He instructed staff never to use the word *loyalty* in any company handbook or other document. He wanted all GE managers to prove their value every day and said people who knew they could be fired worked harder.

In the Welch years there was tumultuous change in the workforce. No total number exists for workers who lost jobs. When he took over there were 404,000 GE employees; when he left there were 313,000. In

[21] O'Boyle, *At Any Cost*, p. 59.

between, tens of thousands came and went. Union leaders estimate that in his last 15 years GE eliminated 150,000 jobs in the United States through layoffs, subcontracting, and outsourcing to foreign countries.[22] Welch expressed his feelings about these layoffs in his memoirs:

> Removing people will always be the hardest decision a leader faces. Anyone who "enjoys doing it" shouldn't be on the payroll and neither should anyone who "can't do it." I never underestimated the human cost of those layoffs or the hardship they might cause people and communities.[23]

Welch stressed globalization of production to lower costs. Many jobs still existed, but they left the United States. In 1985 the electrical worker's union had 46,000 members working at GE, but by 2001 the number had declined to 16,000. Ed Fire, the union's president, estimates that two-thirds of the 30,000 lost jobs were simply transferred to low-wage countries.[24] GE eliminated additional jobs in the United States by pressuring suppliers to migrate along with it. After moving production to Mexico, for example, GE Aircraft Engines held a conference for supplier companies and told them to cut costs by moving their facilities (and jobs) to Mexico's low-wage labor market or face inevitable loss of their GE business.[25] Says Fire:

> GE is the quintessential American corporation that has engaged in what has been referred to as the "race to the bottom"—finding the lowest wages, the lowest benefit levels and most intolerant working conditions . . . I don't think they have given enough consideration to the consequences, particularly the human consequences, of the decisions they make. In my opinion, the decisions are designed too much to increase the company's profitability at the expense of the employees.[26]

A Flawed Evaluation System

The vitality curve rating method is controversial. Critics argue that forced ranking hurts the morale of employees who are not placed on top. At first, GE ranked employees in five categories instead of three, but it was soon discovered that everyone who failed to land in the top category was demoralized. Hence, three categories were combined into one to create the "vital" 70 percent of Bs in the middle. Disheartening classifications as 2s, 3s, and 4s were abolished.

The system can also hurt teamwork by pitting people against each other. It may encourage backstabbing behavior. Its inflexibility produces unfair results when high-performing and low-performing units must classify managers the same way. The bottom 10 percent in an outstanding business may be better than middle- or top-ranked managers on a weaker team. If the axing of the bottom 10 percent goes on for many years, people who were once in the middle range may find themselves lopped off. Of course, the curve calls the recruiting system into question if recent hires are lost.

Forced ranking was just one source of pressure on GE managers, who were expected to meet high profit goals and knew that if there were too many mistakes or misjudgments Welch would get rid of them. His confrontational style reduced some to tears. He reportedly believed that overweight people were undisciplined. Some GE businesses hid these people when he visited for fear they would catch Welch's eye and lose their jobs. One large manager trying to save his career had surgery to staple his colon.[27] Working at GE was also hard on marriages because of the long hours required to be a player. Welch himself divorced in 1987 and remarried in 1990.

Because of Welch's status as a management icon, his approach to forced ranking has spread widely, imposing the practice on many managers at other corporations. Even small businesses have picked up the idea. The manager of a Fifth Avenue clothing store once took Welch aside and explained that he had 20 sales workers. "Mr. Welch," he asked, "do I really have to let two go?" "You probably do," replied Welch, "if you want the best sales staff on Fifth Avenue."[28]

---

[22] "GE Fast Facts," GE Workers United, May 7, 2001, at www.geworkersunited.org/news/fast_facts.asp.

[23] Welch, *Jack*, p. 128.

[24] Ed Fire, president of the International Union of Electronic, Electrical, Salaried, Machine and Furniture Workers–Communications Workers of America, the Industrial Division of CWA, "Resisting the Goliath," *Multinational Monitor*, July–August 2001, p. 31.

[25] Robert Weissman, "Global Management by Stress," *Multinational Monitor*, July–August 2001, p. 20.

[26] Fire, "Resisting the Goliath," pp. 31 and 33.

[27] O'Boyle, *At Any Cost*, p. 76.

[28] Welch, *Jack*, p. 434.

No Diversity at the Top

Using the vitality curve Welch created a high-performance management team, but failed to create diversity. The year before Welch retired *The New York Times* reported that although women and minorities were 40 percent of GE's domestic workforce, white men dominated its top leadership. The paper ran a photo collage of the top 31 executives, including heads of the 20 businesses responsible for 90 percent of corporate earnings. All were male and all but one were white.[29]

Diversity was never a priority for Welch. Later, he would explain why not. "Winning companies are meritocracies . . . [that] practice differentiation" and "this is the most effective way for an organization to field the best team." He argued, "Quotas artificially push some people ahead, independent of qualifications" and that slows the rise of star performers, puts "unprepared people" into important jobs, and "doesn't do much for results."[30] In the subhead for its story *The New York Times* challenged Welch with this question: "Can Only White Men Run a Model Company?"

Pollution in the Hudson River

For 35 years several GE manufacturing plants in New York released polychlorinated biphenyls (PCBs) into the Hudson River. They followed permits that set release levels and stopped in 1977 when PCBs were outlawed because of evidence they were toxic to humans and animals. PCBs cause cancer in test animals and probably cause cancer and other illnesses in humans.

More than 100,000 pounds of PCBs released by GE still lay on the riverbed. Although the biggest deposits were covered by new sediments, slowing their release into the river, the fishing industry had been destroyed, fish were unsafe for children or women of childbearing age to eat, and the chemicals gradually spread downstream from hot spots of contamination, flowing down 200 miles of river to the ocean, from there migrating around the planet.

The Environmental Protection Agency (EPA) studied the river, concluding that dredging the bottom was necessary to remove the dangerous deposits. This would be expensive, and GE was liable for the cost. Welch objected. During his last year as CEO he ordered an extensive campaign of radio and print ads in the Hudson River region to convince residents that dredging would be an ineffective nuisance. It succeeded in dividing them to such an extent that people began to shop only at stores where the owners supported their position and children teased classmates over their parents' views.[31] GE hired 17 lobbyists, including a former senator and six former House members, to fight an extended political battle against the cleanup.[32] Eventually, the company agreed on a cleanup plan, but only after Welch retired.[33]

The GE Pension Fund

During Welch's tenure the GE pension fund covered approximately 485,000 people, including 195,000 who were retired. As the stock market rose in the 1990s, the fund also rose, and by 2001 it totaled $50 billion. Its liabilities, the future payments it must make to retirees, were only $29 billion, leaving a surplus of $21 billion. GE's retirees and their unions requested increased benefits and cost-of-living increases for pensioners, but the company rejected their demands. By law, it did not have to meet more than the original obligations.

Welch understood that there were several benefits in leaving the pension plan overfunded. First, it generated bottom-line profits. Under accounting rules, a company can put interest earned by the pension fund on the balance sheet as revenue, and during the Welch years these earnings increased GE's net by as much as 13.7 percent.[34] Second, these "vapor profits" increased the income of top GE executives, whose bonuses were tied to corporate profits. And third, the excess funding made it easier for GE

[29] Mary Williams Walsh, "Where G.E. Falls Short: Diversity at the Top," *The New York Times,* September 3, 2000, sec. 3, pp. 1 and 13.

[30] Jack Welch with Suzy Welch, *Winning* (New York: HarperCollins, 2005), p. 346.

[31] John Glionna, "Dredging Up Ill Will on the Hudson," *Los Angeles Times,* October 1, 2001, p. A17.

[32] Charlie Cray, "Toxins on the Hudson," *Multinational Monitor,* July–August 2001.

[33] "GE's New Image: The Company Offers to Cooperate in Dredging the Hudson of PCBs," *The Times Union,* April 11, 2002, p. A12.

[34] Rob Walker, "Overvalued: Why Jack Welch Isn't God," *The New Republic,* June 18, 2001, p. 22. See *GE Annual Report 2000,* Notes to Consolidated Financial Statements, 6, "Pension Benefits."

to acquire companies with underfunded pension plans. This eased deal making, but involved sharing funds set aside for GE workers and retirees with people who got a windfall coming in after careers in other companies.

After being pressured by unions and pensioners, GE announced increases of 15 to 35 percent in 2000. But since 1965 prices had risen by 60 percent, so retirees were still losing ground.[35] Helen Quirini, 81, was part of a group protesting GE's failure to be more generous. After working 39 years at a GE factory, one year less than Welch's 40-year tenure, she retired in 1980 and was receiving $737 a month, or $8,844 a year. She believed that GE management was "out all the time trying to figure out how to screw us" using "accounting gimmicks."[36]

Welch's GE pension is $357,128 a month. Court documents filed in proceedings when Welch divorced his second wife in 2002 revealed that he spent an average of $8,982 a month on food and beverages, slightly more than Helen Quirini's yearly pension income.[37] A 1996 retention agreement between Welch and the GE board also granted him nonmonetary perquisites in retirement. He got lifetime use of a spacious apartment owned by GE at the Trump International Hotel and Tower on Central Park West in New York, including a cook, a housekeeper, and a wait staff plus flowers, laundry, dry cleaning, newspaper and magazine subscriptions, and front-row seats at sporting and entertainment events.[38] He was allowed unlimited use of GE's corporate jets. Criticism of these arrangements arose when they were detailed during the divorce. Although he felt there was nothing improper, he elected to pay GE "between $2 and $2.5 million a year" for continued use of the apartment and the planes.[39]

Criminality at GE

Pressure for performance tempts employees to cut corners. Welch knew this and tried to fuse high performance and integrity in the GE culture.[40] In his own words:

> If there was one thing I preached every day at GE, it was integrity. It was our No. 1 value. Nothing came before it. We never had a corporate meeting where I didn't emphasize integrity in my closing remarks.[41]

Yet during his tenure, GE committed a long string of civil and criminal transgressions. The *Multinational Monitor* compiled a "GE Rap Sheet," listing 39 law violations, court-ordered remedies, and fines in the 1990s alone.[42] Many are for pollution hazards from GE facilities. Others are for consumer fraud, including a $165,000 fine for deceptive advertising of lightbulbs and a $100 million fine on GE Capital for unfair debt-collection practices. Still others are for defense contracting fraud, including a $69 million fine for diverting fighter contract funds to other purposes and other fines for overcharging on contracts.

Since GE is such a large company, technical violations of complex regulations and incidents of wrongdoing by individual managers are inevitable. The *Multinational Monitor* sees "a consistent pattern of violating criminal and civil laws over many years."[43] The key question is whether GE's malfeasance increased because of relentless performance pressure on its managers.

THE WELCH ERA AND WHAT FOLLOWED

General Electric in the Welch era fulfilled its primary economic responsibilities to society. It was remarkably profitable. It paid taxes. Shareholders, including pension and mutual funds, were enriched. Many of its directors and managers became multimillionaires

---

[35] "GE Pension Fund Story: Workers Pay, GE Benefits," GE Workers United, April 1, 2001, at www.geworkersunited.org/pensions/index.asp?ID_61.

[36] Vincent Lloyd, "Penny Pinching the Retirees at GE," *Multinational Monitor,* July–August 2001, p. 23.

[37] "Here's the Retirement Jack Welch Built: $1.4 Million a Month," *The Wall Street Journal,* October 31, 2002, p. A1.

[38] Geraldine Fabrikant, "G.E. Expenses for Ex-Chief Cited in Filing," *The New York Times,* September 6, 2002, p. C1.

[39] Jack Welch, "My Dilemma and How I Resolved It," *The New York Times,* September 16, 2002, p. A14.

[40] For a description of his efforts see a book by GE's senior vice president for public affairs during the Welch years, Ben W. Heineman, Jr., *High Performance with High Integrity* (Boston: Harvard Business Press, 2008).

[41] Welch, *Jack,* pp. 279-80.

[42] "GE: Decades of Misdeeds and Wrongdoing," *Multinational Monitor,* July–August 2001, p. 26.

[43] Ibid., p. 30.

in GE stock. Welch believed he was acting for the greater good.

> I believe social responsibility begins with a strong, competitive company, only a healthy enterprise can improve and enrich the lives of people and their communities . . . That's why a CEO's primary social responsibility is to assure the financial success of the company. Only a healthy, winning company has the resources and the capability to do the right thing.[44]

In September 2001 Welch was succeeded by a new CEO, Jeffrey Immelt, a carefully groomed Harvard MBA drawn from GE's stable of stars. The new leader proved to have different values. Shortly after taking over he reversed Welch's two decades of opposition to cleaning up the Hudson River and agreed to a cleanup that would cost GE more than $1 billion.[45] He retained the ranking process for managers, but loosened rigid Welch-era guidelines. Now the bottom 10 percent could be 5 percent or 15 percent, but did not have to be exactly 10 percent. He joined the board of directors of Catalyst, a New York organization that promotes progress of women in management through research about sexism. And he appointed a new vice president for corporate citizenship.

But his real love was the environment. In 2002 a Catholic group filed a shareholder's proposal asking the company to measure its global warming gas emissions. It got only 20 percent of the vote at the annual meeting, but Immelt ordered an inventory anyway, then, over objections by subordinates who doubted global warming, pledged to cut GE's emissions. In 2005 Immelt launched GE's "eco-imagination" initiative based on a strategy of profiting from efforts to stop climate change. It focused the corporation on energy-saving, less polluting technologies, moving it into solar panels, wind turbines, coal gasification, recyclable plastics, and hybrid locomotives. Again, some hard-bitten, profit-focused managers resisted, but Immelt pushed on.

Immelt was more visibly alert to GE's social and environmental impacts than Welch. By 2008 the company was the second most socially responsible company among the largest 100 global corporations in one

[44] Welch, *Jack*, pp. 381–82.
[45] See the story of "The Majestic Hudson River," in Chapter 13.

prominent ranking by NGOs.[46] Yet for shareholders, his leadership was bad news.

If you had invested $10,000 in GE on the day Welch retired in 2001, counting dividends your investment shrank to $4,648 at the end of 2010, a loss of 54 percent. It was, of course, a difficult period. Four days after Immelt took over terrorists in jets with GE engines destroyed World Trade Center buildings insured by GE, leading to a global recession. Late in 2008 a global financial crisis caused the stock market to plummet. Nevertheless, over Immelt's tenure, GE underperformed the Dow Jones Industrial Index, a benchmark of large peer corporations. If you had put $10,000 into the Dow the day Welch retired you would have had $11,578 at the end of 2010, even with GE weighing down the index, a meager return for nine years, but 82 percent better than GE's return alone.

Questions

1. Corporate social responsibility is defined in Chapter 5 as the corporate duty to create wealth by using means that avoid harm to, protect, or enhance societal assets. Did GE in the Welch era fulfill this duty? Could it have done better? What should it have done?

2. Does GE under Welch illustrate a narrower view of corporate social responsibility closer to Friedman's view that the only social responsibility is to increase profits while obeying the law?

3. How well did GE conform with the "General Principles of Corporate Social Responsibility" set forth in the section of that title in the chapter?

4. What are the pros and cons of ranking shareholders over employees and other stakeholders? Is it wrong to see employees as costs of production? Should GE have rebalanced its priorities?

5. Was GE a more socially responsible corporation in the Welch era or the Immelt aftermath? In which era did it give the most benefit to society? What lesson(s) can be learned from the differences?

[46] This was the "Accountability Rating 2008: Full G100 Ranking," by the AccountAbility and Two Tomorrows networks, at http://www.accountabilityrating.com/latest_overview.asp. Vodafone was ranked first.

17 Financial and Securities Regulations

▢ Learning Objectives

In this chapter you will learn:

17-1. To understand the meaning of the term *securities* and to apply the broad scope of the securities laws and regulations.

17-2. To analyze the differences between a public offering and subsequent securities transactions.

17-3. To apply ways in which the laws cover these differences.

17-4. To evaluate when and why private individuals and organizations make claims to enforce securities laws.

17-5. To evaluate how state regulations add to the requirements of proper securities transactions.

17-6. To understand why the Sarbanes-Oxley Act was passed and evaluate its effectiveness.

17-7. To remember the complexity of the Dodd-Frank Wall Street Reform and Consumer Protection Act.

Chapter 14 examines how business activity can be organized. That chapter focuses on how the concept of corporate governance relates to the creation and management of business organizations. One way to view this chapter is as a continuation of those topics. The phrase corporate governance as used in this chapter relates to government regulation of the ownership of business organizations. Indeed, of all the topics covered in this text, enforcement and revisions of securities regulations are the principal means used by the federal and state government to create and restore investor confidence following scandals involving Enron, WorldCom, Tyco, Adelphia, HealthSouth, and other major corporations in 2000 and 2001. Financial reforms also followed the economic collapse in 2008, which was caused by the failure or near-failure of Lehman Brothers, Merrill Lynch, AIG, JP Morgan, Chase, Bank of America, Wachovia, and other financial institutions.

Your reading and study of this chapter will expose you to numerous examples as to how businesspeople are required to manage their organizations. This chapter also acquaints you, as a potential investor, with the laws protecting you and your fellow investors.

As you study this chapter, remember that the regulation of securities began as part of the program to help the United States overcome the great depression of the early 1930s. You should also realize that these securities laws are designed to give potential investors sufficient information so that they can make intelligent investment decisions based on factual information rather than on other less certain criteria. Although federal securities laws are 80 years old, their application is at the heart of corporate governance during the first years of the twenty-first century. Table 17.1 provides a chronological summary of various securities laws covered in this chapter.

table 17.1 >> Laws Regulating Securities Transactions

Statute	Summary of Major Provisions
Securities Act of 1933	• Disclosure law governing initial sale of securities to public.
	• Defines the term *security*.
	• Creates liability for false or misleading registration statement (Section 11).
	• Creates liability for failure to file a registration statement (Section 12[1]).
	• Creates liability for false or misleading prospectus (Section 12[2]).
	• Creates liability for fraudulent communications used in the offer of sales of securities (Section 17[a]).
Securities Exchange Act of 1934	• Created Securities and Exchange Commission.
	• Governs exchanges of securities beyond the initial sale.
	• Creates liability for fraudulent manipulation of securities' value (Section 10[b]).
	• Creates liability for short-swing profits made by insiders (Section 16).
	• Creates liability for false or misleading filings with the SEC (Section 18).
	• Creates liability for fraudulent transactions related to tender offers (Section 14[e]).
Insider Trading and Securities Fraud Enforcement Act of 1988	• Provides for recovery of triple damages in civil actions against user of nonpublic information.
	• Increases criminal sanctions for use of nonpublic information.
Securities Enforcement Remedies Act of 1990	• Increases civil fines for violations of securities laws.
	• Prohibits an individual's service as an officer or director.
Private Securities Litigation Reform Act of 1995	• Clarifies that individuals and organizations can sue primary parties, but not secondary parties, for securities violations.
	• Requires pleading of specific allegations of wrongdoing.

table 17.1 >> Laws Regulating Securities Transactions—*(Continued)*	
Statute	**Summary of Major Provisions**
State blue sky laws	• Impose another level of securities regulations beyond federal laws.
	• Govern intrastate securities transactions not regulated by federal laws.
Sarbanes-Oxley Act of 2002	• Increases budgetary support to Securities and Exchange Commission.
	• Creates Public Company Accounting Oversight Board.
	• Changes membership requirements of corporate audit committees.
	• Requires CEOs to certify financial statements.
	• Increases criminal penalties for fraud and false statements.
Dodd-Frank Wall Street Reform and Consumer Protection Act of 2010	• Enhances consumer protection.
	• Ends "Too Big to Fail" bailouts.
	• Reforms Federal Reserve.
	• Creates mortgage reforms.
	• Regulates various financial instruments and organizations.
	• Reforms SEC and investor protection.
	• Creates several new administrative oversight agencies.

Before we examine any of the laws in depth, the next two sections present introductory materials on the meaning of the term *security* and the role of the federal Securities and Exchange Commission.

1. WHAT IS A SECURITY?

LO 17-1

Because the objective of securities laws is to protect uninformed people from investing their money without sufficient information, the term **security** has a very broad definition. Indeed, the federal securities laws provide the following definition:

> "Security" means any note, stock, treasury stock, bond, debenture, evidence of indebtedness, certificate of interest or participation in any profit-sharing agreement, collateral-trust certificate, preorganization certificate or subscription, transferable share, investment contract, voting-trust certificate, certificate of deposit for a security, fractional undivided interest in oil, gas, or other mineral rights, or in general, any interest or instrument commonly known as a "security," or any certificate of interest or participation in, temporary or interim certificate for receipt for, guarantee of, or warrant or right to subscribe to or purchase, any of the foregoing.[1]

[1] *15 U.S.C.A. §77b(1). This definition is a part of the 1933 Securities Act. It is virtually identical to the definition of security found in the 1934 Securities Exchange Act.*

As this definition indicates, the word *security* includes much more than corporation stock. Historically, the Supreme Court has held that a security exists when one person invests money and looks to others to manage the money for profit. On the basis of this statement, courts seek positive answers to the following three questions when determining whether a person has purchased a security:

1. Is the investment in a common business activity?
2. Is the investment based on a reasonable expectation of profits?
3. Will these profits be earned through the efforts of someone other than the investor?

This three-prong analysis permits courts to find the sale of oil-well interests, the syndication of racehorses, and shares of limited partnerships are securities. The *Howey* case involved the sale of orange trees in a Florida orchard. The Howey-in-the-Hills Services Company offered buyers of trees a management service contract whereby Howey provided care for the trees and harvesting of the fruit. When the investors did not receive the return they expected, Howey was held liable for failing to comply with securities laws.[2]

2. SECURITIES AND EXCHANGE COMMISSION

The **Securities and Exchange Commission (SEC)** is an administrative agency created in 1934 that is responsible for administering the federal securities laws. The SEC consists of five commissioners appointed by the president for five-year terms. In addition to these commissioners, the SEC employs staff personnel such as lawyers, accountants, security analysts, security examiners, and others.

The SEC has both quasi-legislative and quasi-judicial powers. Under its quasi-legislative power, it has adopted rules and regulations relating to financial and other information that must be furnished to the Commission. Other rules prescribe information that must be given to potential investors. The SEC also regulates the various stock exchanges, utility holding companies, investment trusts, and investment advisers. Under its quasi-judicial power, the SEC also is involved in a variety of investigations.

>> The Securities Act of 1933: Going Public

The **Securities Act of 1933** is a disclosure law with respect to the initial sale of securities to the public. This law makes it illegal to use the mails or any other means of interstate communication or transportation to sell securities without disclosing certain financial information to potential investors. The following sections discuss several aspects of the act in detail, including who is regulated, what documents are required, when criminal and civil liability exist, and what defenses are available. As you read, remember that this law applies only to the initial sale of the security. Subsequent transfers of securities are governed by the Securities Exchange Act of 1934, discussed in Sections 7 through 11 of this chapter.

In essence, the 1933 Securities Act requires the disclosure of information to the potential investor or other interested party. The information given must

[2]*SEC v. W. J. Howey Co.,* 66 S. Ct. 1100 (1946).

not be untrue or even misleading. If this information is not accurate, liability is imposed upon those responsible.

The act recognizes three sanctions for violations:

- Criminal punishment.
- Civil liability, which may be imposed in favor of injured parties in certain cases.
- Equitable remedy of an injunction.

Proof of an intentional violation usually is required before criminal or civil sanctions are imposed. Proof of negligence will, however, support an injunction.

3. PARTIES REGULATED

The Securities Act of 1933 regulates anyone who is involved with or who promotes the initial sale of securities. Typically, these parties who must comply with the disclosure requirements of the 1933 Act fall into one or more of four roles.

An **issuer** is the individual or business organization offering a security for sale to the public. An **underwriter** is anyone who participates in the original distribution of securities by selling such securities for the issuer or by guaranteeing their sale. Often securities brokerage firms or investment bankers act as underwriters with respect to a particular transaction. A **controlling person** is one who controls or is controlled by the issuer, such as a major stockholder of a corporation. Finally, a **seller** is anyone who contracts with a purchaser or who is a motivating influence that causes the purchase transaction to occur.

Whenever you operate a business, you and your co-owners must understand the requirements of the 1933 Securities Act. Your organization clearly is an issuer. You and your co-owner clearly are controlling persons. Whether you also are an underwriter or seller or both will depend on the factual situation and relationships you create with other individuals or firms to promote and sell stock in your organization. Regardless of whether you occupy one or more of these roles, you must comply with the 1993 Act or face significant liability.

> Parties subject to the 1933 act include issuers, underwriters, controlling persons, and sellers.

4. DOCUMENTS INVOLVED

In regulating the initial sales of securities, the Securities Act of 1933 is viewed as a disclosure law. In essence, this law requires that securities subject to its provisions be registered prior to any sale and that a prospectus be furnished to any potential investor prior to any sale being consummated. Thus, an issuer of securities who complies with the federal law must prepare:

- A registration statement
- A prospectus

Registration Statement In an attempt to accomplish its purpose of disclosure, the Securities Act of 1933 contains detailed provisions relating to the registration of securities. These provisions require that a **registration statement** be filed with the SEC. The statement includes a detailed disclosure of financial information about the issuer and the controlling individuals involved in the offering of securities for sale to the public.

With respect to the filing of the registration statement, the law describes selling activities permitted at the various stages of the registration process.

> Three time periods involved in the registration process are the prefiling period, the waiting period, and the posteffective period.

This procedure and its time frame are a primary reason why you and your co-owner described in the Business Discussions cannot begin business immediately.

During the **prefiling period,** it is legal for the issuer of a security to engage in preliminary negotiations and agreements with underwriters. It is illegal to sell a covered security during this period. Offers to sell and offers to buy securities also are prohibited during this prefiling period.

After the registration statement is filed, a **waiting period** commences. This period typically lasts 20 days. During this time, the SEC staff investigates the accuracy of the registration statement to determine whether the sale of the securities should be permitted. During the waiting period, it is still illegal to sell a security subject to the act. However, it is not illegal to solicit a buyer or receive offers to buy. Since contracts to sell are still illegal, offers cannot be accepted during the waiting period. However, during these waiting periods, sellers may solicit offers for later acceptance.

Many solicitations during the waiting period are made in advertisements called **tombstone ads.** These ads are brief announcements identifying the security and stating its price, by whom orders will be executed, and from whom a prospectus may be obtained. Solicitations may also be made during the waiting period by use of a statistical summary, a summary prospectus, or a preliminary prospectus. These techniques allow dissemination of the facts that are to be ultimately disclosed in the formal prospectus.

A registration becomes effective at the expiration of the waiting period, 20 days after it is filed, unless the SEC gives notice that it is not in proper form or unless the SEC accelerates the effective date. Any amendment filed without the commission's consent starts the 20-day period running again. The end of the waiting period is the beginning of the **posteffective period.** During this period, contracts to buy and sell securities are finalized.

Prospectus   During the posteffective period, securities may be sold. A **prospectus** must be furnished to any interested investor, and it must conform to the statutory requirements. Like the registration statement, the prospectus contains financial information related to the issuer and controlling persons. Indeed, the prospectus contains the same essential information contained in the registration statement. The prospectus supplies the investor with sufficient facts (including financial information) so that he or she can make an intelligent investment decision. The SEC has adopted rules relating to the detailed requirements of the prospectus. The major requirements are detailed facts about the issuer and financial statements, including balance sheets and statements of operations of the issuer.

Don't rely on the prospectus as assurance the investment will make money.

Theoretically, any security may be sold under the act, provided the issuser and others follow the law and the rules and regulations enacted under it are followed. The law does not prohibit the sale of worthless securities. An investor may "foolishly" invest his or her money, and a person may legally sell the blue sky if the statutory requirements are met. In fact, the prospectus must contain the following in capital letters and boldface type:

THESE SECURITIES HAVE NOT BEEN APPROVED OR DISAPPROVED BY THE SECURITIES AND EXCHANGE COMMISSION NOR HAS THE COMMISSION PASSED UPON THE ACCURACY OR ADEQUACY OF THIS PROSPECTUS. ANY REPRESENTATION TO THE CONTRARY IS A CRIMINAL OFFENSE.

The SEC has alternative processes to this formal registration process for companies that sell securities to institutional investors. Rule 144A is an example of an SEC-approved regulation allowing sale of securities to investors such as pension funds. Under this Rule, the securities are labeled as restricted. All other provisions of the securities law, such as those related to any fraudulent transactions, remain applicable to transactions involving these restricted securities.

5. LIABILITY

Under the federal Securities Act of 1933, both criminal and civil liability may be imposed for violations. Criminal liability results from a willful violation of the act or fraud in *any* offer or sale of securities. Fraud occurs when any material fact is omitted, causing a statement to be misleading. The penalty is a fine of up to $10,000 or five years in prison or both.

Civil liability under the 1933 Act usually involves a buyer of securities suing for a refund of the investment. This liability on the issuer, controlling person, underwriter, and seller is significant because the investors' money typically is lost at the time of these civil claims.

Three sections of the Securities Act of 1933 directly apply to civil liability of parties involved in issuing securities:

- Section 11 deals with registration statements.
- Section 12 relates to prospectuses and oral and written communication.
- Section 17 concerns fraudulent interstate transactions.

Section 11: Registration Statement The civil liability provision dealing with registration statements imposes liability on the following persons in favor of purchasers of securities:

1. Every person who signed the registration statement.
2. Every director of the corporation or partner in the partnership issuing the security.
3. Every person who, with his or her consent, is named in the registration statement as about to become a director or partner.
4. Every accountant, engineer, or appraiser who assists in the preparation of the registration statement or its certification.
5. Every underwriter.

These persons are liable if the registration statement:

- Contains untrue statements of material facts.
- Omits material facts required by statute or regulation.
- Omits information that if not given makes the facts stated misleading.

This last situation describes the factual situation of a statement containing a half-truth, which has the net effect of being misleading. The test of accuracy and materiality is as of the date the registration statement becomes effective.

> "In 2006, for example, for the first time, more equity financing was raised in private transactions under the SEC's Rule 144A ($162 billion) than was raised in IPOs on the NYSE, Nasdaq, and the Amex combined ($154 billion)."
>
> **–Peter J. Wallison, "Capital Complaints," The Wall Street Journal, March 20, 2007.**

The issuer and experts assisting must make sure the registration materials are truthful and not misleading.

A plaintiff-purchaser need not prove reliance on the registration statement in order to recover the amount of an investment. All the plaintiff has to show is omitted or misleading information in the registration statement. A defendant can defend the suit by proving actual knowledge of the falsity by the purchaser. Knowledge of the falsity by a defendant need not be proved. However, a defendant's reliance on an expert such as an accountant is a defense. For example, a director may defend a suit on the basis of a false financial statement by showing reliance on a certified public accountant. This reliance exception logically does not apply to the issuer. Because the issuer provides information to the expert, the issuer should not be allowed to rely on the expert's use of the inaccurate information.

Section 12: Prospectus and Other Communications

This section of the 1933 Act is divided into two parts. The first subsection of Section 12 imposes liability on those who offer or sell securities that are not registered with the SEC. This liability exists regardless of the intent or conduct of those who fail to comply with the registration requirements. Thus, liability traditionally has been imposed against violators even though they lacked any wrongful intent. The Supreme Court has held that a defendant is free from liability if the plaintiff is equally responsible for the failure to file the registration statement.

Plaintiffs can recover for harm done by false or misleading information in a prospectus even if the prospectus is not read or reviewed.

The second subsection of Section 12 imposes liability on sellers who use a prospectus or make communications (by mail, telephone, or other instrumentalities of interstate commerce) that contain an untrue statement of material facts required to be stated or necessary to make statements not misleading. As under Section 11, the plaintiff does not have to prove reliance on the false or misleading prospectus or communication. Nor does the plaintiff have to establish that the defendant intended the deception.

Purchasers of such securities may sue for their actual damages. If the purchaser still owns the securities and he or she can prove a direct contractual relationship with the seller, the remedy of rescission and a refund of the purchase price is also available.

Section 17: Fraudulent Transactions

This provision concerning fraudulent interstate transactions prohibits the use of any instrument of interstate communication in the offer or sale of any securities when the result is:

1. To defraud.
2. To obtain money or property by means of an untrue or misleading statement.
3. To engage in a business transaction or practice that may operate to defraud or deceive a purchaser.

The requirement that a defendant-seller must act with the intent (**scienter**) to deceive or mislead in order to prove a Section 17 violation has caused much controversy over the years. The Supreme Court has resolved this issue by holding that a plaintiff must prove the defendant's intent to violate 1. However, no proof of the defendant's intent is required to find a violation of 2 or 3. The Court's decision is limited to when the plaintiff is seeking an injunction, because Section 17 does not explicitly provide for the private remedy of monetary damages.

6. DEFENSES

The Securities Act of 1933 recognized several defenses that may be used to avoid civil liability. Among the most important defenses are:

- Materiality.
- The statute of limitations.
- Due diligence.

Materiality   A defendant in a case involving the 1933 Act might argue that the false or misleading information is not *material* and thus should not have had an impact on the purchaser's decision-making process. Determining whether or not a particular fact is material depends on the facts and the parties involved.

The SEC and the courts have attempted to define materiality. The term *material* describes the kinds of information that an average prudent investor would want to have so that he or she can make an intelligent, informed decision whether or not to buy the security. A material fact is one that if correctly stated or disclosed would have deterred or tended to deter the average prudent investor from purchasing the securities in question. The term does not cover minor inaccuracies or errors in matters of no interest to investors. Facts that tend to deter a person from purchasing a security are those that have an important bearing upon the nature or condition of the issuing corporation or its business.

Statute of Limitations   The statute of limitations is a defense for both civil and criminal liability. The basic period is one year. The one year does not start to run until the discovery of the untrue statement or omission. Or it does not start to run until the time such discovery would have been made with reasonable diligence. In no event may a suit be brought more than three years after the sale.

Sarbanes-Oxley does not increase the statute of limitations under the 1933 Act.

A defense similar to the statute of limitations is also provided. The 1933 Act provides that if the person acquiring the security does so after the issuer has made generally available an earnings statement covering at least 12 months after the effective date of the registration statement, then this person must prove actual reliance on the registration statement.

Due Diligence   A very important defense for experts such as accountants is the **due diligence defense.**

To establish this defense, the expert must prove that a reasonable investigation of the financial statements of the issuer and controlling persons was conducted. As the result of this investigation, an expert exercising due diligence must prove that there was no reason to believe any of the information in the registration statement or prospectus was false or misleading.

In determining whether or not an expert, such as an accountant, has made a reasonable investigation, the law provides that the standard of *reasonableness* is that required of a prudent person in the management of his or her own property. The burden of proof of this defense is on the expert, and the test is as of the time the registration statement became effective. The due diligence defense, in effect, requires proof that a party was not guilty of fraud or negligence.

concept >> *summary*

Liability under the Securities Act of 1933

>> SECTION 11

Purpose: Creates liability for false or misleading registration statements.

Plaintiff's case: Not required to prove defendant's intent to deceive or plaintiff's reliance on documents.

Defendant's defenses: Proof of no false or misleading information; proof that plaintiff knew of false or misleading nature of information; except for issuers, proof of reliance on an expert (attorney or accountant).

>> SECTION 12

Purpose: (1) Creates liability for failing to file a required registration statement; (2) creates liability for false or misleading prospectus.

Plaintiff's case: Not required to prove defendant's intent to deceive or plaintiff's reliance on documents.

Defendant's defenses: For (1), plaintiff equally at fault for failing to file a registration statement; for (2), same as Section 11 defenses.

>> SECTION 17

Purpose: In an interstate transaction, it is unlawful to

(1) employ any device, scheme, or artifice of fraud;

(2) obtain money or property by untrue statement or omission of material fact;

(3) engage in events that operate or would operate as fraud or deceit.

Plaintiff's case: For (1), required to prove defendant's intent to deceive; for (2) and (3), not required to prove intent to deceive.

Defendant's defenses: For (1), proof of no intent to deceive and proof of good faith; for (2), proof of no material misstatement or omission; for (3), proof of no involvement in unlawful activities.

>> CRIMINAL LIABILITY

$10,000 fine or 5 years in prison or both.

>> Securities Exchange Act of 1934: Being Public

Whereas the Securities Act of 1933 deals with original offerings of securities, the **Securities Exchange Act of 1934** regulates transfers of securities after the initial sale. The 1934 Act, which created the Securities and Exchange Commission, also deals with regulation of securities exchanges, brokers, and dealers in securities.

The Securities Exchange Act makes it illegal to sell a security on a national exchange unless a registration is effective for the security. Registration under the 1934 Act differs from registration under the 1933 Act. Registration under the 1934 Act requires filing prescribed forms with the applicable stock exchange and the SEC.

Provisions relating to stockbrokers and dealers prohibit the use of the mails or any other instrumentality of interstate commerce to sell securities unless the broker or the dealer is registered. The language is sufficiently broad to cover attempted sales as well as actual sales. Brokers and dealers must keep detailed records of their activities and file annual reports with the SEC.

The SEC requires that issuers of registered securities file periodic reports as well as report significant developments that would affect the value of the security. For example, the SEC requires companies to disclose foreign payoffs or bribes to obtain or retain foreign business operations. Businesses must disclose their minority hiring practices and other social data that may be of public concern. Business has been forced by the SEC to submit certain shareholder proposals to all shareholders as a part of proxy solicitation. When a new pension law was enacted, the SEC required that financial reports disclose the law's impact on the reporting business. The SEC requires more complete disclosure of executive compensation packages.

The SEC's activity concerning information corporations must furnish to the investing public is almost limitless. With the actions of the PCAOB, SEC regulations are of paramount significance to all persons concerned with the financial aspects of business. This area of regulation directly affects the accounting profession. Since the SEC regulates financial statements, it frequently decides issues of proper accounting and auditing theory and practices.

> Sarbanes-Oxley, through the PCAOB and SEC regulations, impacts the accounting and audit practices.

The following sections examine how the Securities Exchange Act of 1934 affects the businessperson, the accountant, the lawyer, the broker, and the investor. These sections cover some fundamental concepts of this law, such as civil liability in general and insider transactions in particular, as well as criminal violations and penalties under the 1934 Act.

7. SECTION 10(b) AND RULE 10b-5

Most of the litigation under the Securities and Exchange Act of 1934 is brought under Section 10(b) of the act and Rule 10b-5 promulgated by the SEC pursuant to the act. Section 10(b) and Rule 10b-5 declare that it is unlawful to use the mails or any instrumentality of interstate commerce or any national securities exchange to defraud *any person* in connection with the *purchase or sale* of any security. Sidebar 17.1 contains the actual language of this section and rule.

>> *sidebar* 17.1

Language of Section 10(b) of the 1934 Act and SEC's Rule 10b-5

Section 10(b) states:

It shall be unlawful for any person, directly or indirectly, by the use of any means or instrumentality of interstate commerce or of the mails, or of any facility of any national securities exchange—

(b) To use or employ, in connection with the purchase or sale of any security registered on a national securities exchange or any security not so registered, any manipulative or deceptive device or contrivance in contravention of such rules and regulations as the [SEC] may prescribe.

Rule 10b-5, adopted by the SEC in 1942, states:

It shall be unlawful for any person, directly or indirectly, by the use of any means or instrumentality of interstate commerce, or of the mails or of any facility of any national securities exchange,

(a) To employ any device, scheme, or artifice to defraud,

(b) To make any untrue statement of a material fact or to omit to state a material fact necessary in order to make the statements made, in the light of the circumstances under which they were made, not misleading, or

(c) To engage in any act, practice, or course of business which operates or would operate as a fraud or deceit upon any person, in connection with the purchase or sale of any security.

Common issues regarding litigation under Section 10(b) and Rule 10b-5 include the following:

- Who is liable?
- What can be recovered by the plaintiff, and does the defendant have the right to seek contribution from third parties?
- When is information material to the transaction?
- Where does the law apply?

LO 17-4   *Liability*   Recently, the Supreme Court used Case 17.1 as a means to emphasize there is a limited answer to the question who is liable. While many cases clarify that parties directly connected to the sale of securities are liable, the following case focuses on the liability of third parties.

---

case 17.1 >>

STONERIDGE INVESTMENT PARTNERS, LLC, PETITIONER v. SCIENTIFIC-ATLANTA, INC., ET AL.
128 S. Ct. 761 **(2008)**

Charter Communications operates cable companies throughout the United States. Both Scientific-Atlanta and Motorola supply Charter with digital cable converter boxes that Charter provides to its customers. In 2000, Charter became concerned that it would not meet cash flow projections causing it to miss the financial estimates Wall Street established. To remedy this shortfall, Charter arranged to overpay Scientific-Atlanta and Motorola by the amount of $20 for each converter box. This deal was conditioned on these companies purchasing advertising from Charter in the amount equal to the overpayment. While these transactions had no economic impact, Charter recorded the advertisement purchases as revenue and capitalized the purchases of the converter boxes. This scheme allowed Charter to fool its auditor and to create financial statements that appeared to meet expectations by increasing its cash flow by about $17 million.

Purchasers of Charter stock, upon discovering this fraud, sued Charter, Scientific-Atlanta, and Motorola under the 1934 Securities Exchange Act. The latter two companies asked the District Judge to dismiss these claims since the companies were not parties to any securities fraud and are not subject to a private cause of action under the securities laws. The District Court and the Eighth Circuit Court of Appeals ruled

in favor of Scientific-Atlanta and Motorola finding there was not a private right of action against these third parties since they did not make a public misstatement and did not fail to disclose required information. The Supreme Court granted certiorari to address the conflict among the appellate courts concerning when third parties are liable under the 1934 Securities Exchange Act.

KENNEDY, J.: . . . Though the text of the Securities Exchange Act does not provide for a private cause of action for §10(b) violations, the Court has found a right of action implied in the words of the statute and its implementing regulation. In a typical §10(b) private action a plaintiff must prove (1) a material misrepresentation or omission by the defendant; (2) scienter; (3) a connection between the misrepresentation or omission and the purchase or sale of a security; (4) reliance upon the misrepresentation or omission; (5) economic loss; and (6) loss causation.

. . . [I]n §104 of the Private Securities Litigation Reform Act of 1995 (PSLRA), [Congress] directed prosecution of aiders and abettors by the SEC.

The §10(b) implied private right of action does not extend to aiders and abettors. The conduct of a secondary actor must satisfy each of the elements or

[continued]

preconditions for liability; and we consider whether the allegations here are sufficient to do so.

The Court of Appeals concluded petitioner had not alleged that respondents engaged in a deceptive act within the reach of the §10(b) private right of action, noting that only misstatements, omissions by one who has a duty to disclose, and manipulative trading practices . . . are deceptive within the meaning of the rule. . . . Conduct itself can be deceptive, as respondents concede. In this case, moreover, respondents' course of conduct included both oral and written statements, such as the backdated contracts agreed to by Charter and respondents.

A different interpretation of the holding from the Court of Appeals opinion is that the court was stating only that any deceptive statement or act respondents made was not actionable because it did not have the requisite proximate relation to the investors' harm. That conclusion is consistent with our own determination that respondents' acts or statements were not relied upon by the investors and that, as a result, liability cannot be imposed upon respondents.

Reliance by the plaintiff upon the defendant's deceptive acts is an essential element of the §10(b) private cause of action. It ensures that, for liability to arise, the requisite causal connection between a defendant's misrepresentation and a plaintiff's injury exists. . . . We have found a rebuttable presumption of reliance in two different circumstances. First, if there is an omission of a material fact by one with a duty to disclose, the investor to whom the duty was owed need not provide specific proof of reliance. Second, under the fraud-on-the-market doctrine, reliance is presumed when the statements at issue become public. The public information is reflected in the market price of the security. Then it can be assumed that an investor who buys or sells stock at the market price relies upon the statement.

Neither presumption applies here. Respondents had no duty to disclose; and their deceptive acts were not communicated to the public. No member of the investing public had knowledge, either actual or presumed, of respondents' deceptive acts during the relevant times. Petitioner, as a result, cannot show reliance upon any of respondents' actions except in an indirect chain that we find too remote for liability.

Invoking what some courts call "scheme liability," petitioner nonetheless seeks to impose liability on respondents even absent a public statement. In our view this approach does not answer the objection that petitioner did not in fact rely upon respondents' own deceptive conduct.

Liability is appropriate, petitioner contends, because respondents engaged in conduct with the purpose and effect of creating a false appearance of material fact to further a scheme to misrepresent Charter's revenue. The argument is that the financial statement Charter released to the public was a natural and expected consequence of respondents' deceptive acts; had respondents not assisted Charter, Charter's auditor would not have been fooled, and the financial statement would have been a more accurate reflection of Charter's financial condition. . . .

In effect petitioner contends that in an efficient market investors rely not only upon the public statements relating to a security but also upon the transactions those statements reflect. Were this concept of reliance to be adopted, the implied cause of action would reach the whole marketplace in which the issuing company does business; and there is no authority for this rule.

. . . It was Charter, not respondents, that misled its auditor and filed fraudulent financial statements; nothing respondents did made it necessary or inevitable for Charter to record the transactions as it did. . . .

Were we to adopt this construction of §10(b), it would revive in substance the implied cause of action against all aiders and abettors except those who committed no deceptive act in the process of facilitating the fraud; and we would undermine Congress' determination that this class of defendants should be pursued by the SEC and not by private litigants. . . .

The §10(b) private cause of action is a judicial construct that Congress did not enact in the text of the relevant statutes. Though the rule once may have been otherwise, it is settled that there is an implied cause of action only if the underlying statute can be interpreted to disclose the intent to create one. . . .

Concerns with the judicial creation of a private cause of action caution against its expansion. The decision to extend the cause of action is for Congress, not for us. Though it remains the law, the §10(b) private right should not be extended beyond its present boundaries. . . .

Secondary actors are subject to criminal penalties and civil enforcement by the SEC. The enforcement power is not toothless. Since September 30, 2002, SEC enforcement actions have collected over $10 billion in disgorgement and penalties, much of it for distribution to injured investors. And in this case both parties agree that criminal penalties are a strong deterrent. In addition some state securities laws permit state authorities to seek fines and restitution from aiders and abettors. All secondary actors, furthermore, are not necessarily immune from private suit. The securities statutes provide an express private right of action against accountants and underwriters in certain circumstances, and the implied right of action in §10(b) continues to cover secondary actors who commit primary violations.

Here respondents were acting in concert with Charter in the ordinary course as suppliers and, as

[continued]

matters then evolved in the not so ordinary course, as customers. Unconventional as the arrangement was, it took place in the marketplace for goods and services, not in the investment sphere. Charter was free to do as it chose in preparing its books, conferring with its auditor, and preparing and then issuing its financial statements. In these circumstances the investors cannot be said to have relied upon any of respondents' deceptive acts in the decision to purchase or sell securities; and as the requisite reliance cannot be shown, respondents have no liability to petitioner under the implied right of action. This conclusion is consistent with the narrow dimensions we must give to a right of action Congress did not authorize when it first enacted the statute and did not expand when it revisited the law.

Affirmed.

>> CASE QUESTIONS

1. What is the relationship between Charter, Scientific-Atlanta, and Motorola?
2. How did Scientific-Atlanta and Motorola assist Charter in creating fraudulent financial statements?
3. Why did the Supreme Court agree with the lower courts that Scientific-Atlanta and Motorola are not subject to the claims of shareholders under the 1934 Securities Exchange Act?

This decision appears to restrict plaintiffs' ability to recover against auditors, banks, and other parties associated with major scandals. Prior to this ruling, there have been significant settlements reached with auditors involved in some of the largest corporate scandals in history. Table 17.2 highlights a few of these largest settlements.

Damages A plaintiff in a suit under Rule 10b-5 must prove damages. The damages of a defrauded purchaser are actual out-of-pocket losses or the excess of what was paid over the value of what was received. Courts in a few cases have used the *benefit of the bargain* measure of damages and awarded the buyer the difference between what he or she paid and what the security was represented to be worth. A buyer's damages are measured at the time of purchase.

As Sidebar 17.2 illustrates, a buyer must allege specific damages due to the seller's fraud. An allegation of fraud and a drop in stock price is not enough to prove the case.

table 17.2 >> Largest Settlements of Securities Cases against Auditors

Year	Auditing Firm	Case	Amount
2000	Ernst & Young	Cendant Shareholders	$335 million
2008	Ernst & Young	Cendant Corp.	$300 million
2007	PWC	Tyco	$225 million
2006	Deloitte & Touche	Adelphia	$210 million

Source: David Reilly and Nathan Koppel, "Cendant Case Costs Ernst Almost $300 Million More," *The Wall Street Journal*, February 16–17, 2008.

>> *sidebar* 17.2

Proof of Loss Due to Fraud

Shareholders of Dura Pharmaceuticals, Inc., sued the company and its directors and officers for violations of the 1934 Securities Exchange Act. These plaintiffs claim they paid an artificially high price for the stock because Dura executives misrepresented that the Food and Drug Administration (FDA) would approve Dura's application to sell a new asthmatic spray. During the time in question, Dura's stock declined in price rapidly when it announced its sales projection would not be met. Later, when Dura announced that the FDA would not approve its new asthmatic spray, the stock declined again. However, within a week, Dura stock had regained much of that lost value.

The shareholder plaintiffs simply alleged they had lost money due to the inflated price of the stock and the misrepresentation by the Dura executives. The Supreme Court held that these simple allegations were not enough to establish the loss of value due to the fraud. More specific proof of the loss caused by the fraud is required.

Source: *Dura Pharmaceuticals, Inc. v. Broudo*, 125 S. Ct. 1627 (2005).

Computation of a defrauded seller's damages is more difficult. A defrauding purchaser usually benefits from an increase in the value of the securities, while the plaintiff seller loses this increase. Courts do not allow defrauding buyers to keep these increases in value. Therefore, the measure of the seller's damages is the difference between the fair value of all that the seller received and the fair value of what he or she would have received had there been no fraud. A fraudulent buyer loses all profits flowing from the wrongful conduct.

Plaintiffs under Rule 10b-5 are also entitled to consequential damages. These include lost dividends, brokerage fees, and taxes. In addition, courts may order payment of interest on the funds. Punitive damages are not permitted as they are in cases of common law fraud based on state laws. This distinction results from the language of the 1934 Act, which limits recoveries to actual damages.

The issue of whether a defendant who is liable under Section 10(b) can seek contribution from third parties was not resolved until 1993. In Sidebar 17.3, the Supreme Court concludes that a right of contribution does exist in Section 10(b) private actions.

>> *sidebar* 17.3

Right to Contribution from Others

To settle a securities lawsuit by its shareholders, Wausau Insurance agreed to pay $13.5 million. Following this settlement, Wausau filed a lawsuit against the attorneys and accountants involved in the public offering. These defendants sought dismissal of this complaint on the grounds that there is no right of contribution under §10(b). The Supreme Court concludes that there is a private right of contribution in §10(b) of the 1934 Act and in Rule 10b-5. Those charged with liability in a §10b-5 action have a right of contribution against other parties who have joint responsibility for the violation.

Source: *Musick, Peeler & Garrett v. Wausau Ins.*, 113 S. Ct. 2085 (1993).

Materiality Section 10(b) and Rule 10b-5 are usually referred to as the *antifraud provisions* of the act. A plaintiff seeking damages under the provisions must establish the existence of a material misrepresentation or omission made in connection with the purchase or sale of a security and the culpable state of mind of the defendant. Materiality under the 1934 Act is the same as materiality under the 1933 Act. However, liability under Rule 10b-5 requires proof of the defendant's intent to deceive. Proof of the defendant's simple negligence is not enough to establish liability. The plaintiff also must establish that the defendant's practice is manipulative and not merely corporate mismanagement.

The concept of fraud under Section 10(b) encompasses not only untrue statements of material facts but also the failure to state material facts necessary to prevent statements actually made from being misleading. In other words, a half-truth that misleads is fraudulent. Finally, failure to correct a misleading impression left by statements already made, or silence where there is a duty to speak, gives rise to a violation of Rule 10b-5 because it is a form of aiding and abetting the deception.

Another issue impacting materiality relates to when the plaintiff brings the complaint. The Supreme Court looks at when the potentially misleading statements are made and whether the plaintiff did know or should have known the statements were misleading. This examination is further described in Sidebar 17.4.

>> *sidebar* 17.4

Statute of Limitations for Fraud Claims

Merck & Co. manufactured and marketed the drug Vioxx, a painkiller used to reduce arthritis pain. In 1999, the Food and Drug Administration approved Vioxx as a prescription drug. Shortly after Vioxx was introduced, reports arose questioning whether taking Vioxx increased the risk of heart attack. Merck officials issued many statements and reports that promoted the virtues of Vioxx and downplayed any negative side effects. On October 9, 2001, *The New York Times* reported that Merck "had reexamined its own data and found no evidence that Vioxx increased the risks of heart attacks."

Despite these reassurances, Merck stock price rose and fell depending on the nature (good or bad) of news reported about Vioxx. Finally, on September 30, 2004, Merck withdrew Vioxx from the market.

Based on the uncertainty surrounding Vioxx, many lawsuits were filed against Merck. Included in these cases was one filed on November 6, 2003. A group of shareholders sued Merck, alleging that company officials had engaged in securities fraud under §10(b) by falsely and deceptively denying the risks associated with Vioxx. The defendants sought to

have this case dismissed as being filed too late under the applicable statute of limitations.

Upon its review, the Supreme Court concludes that the applicable statute of limitations, in this case, is two years. The Court also finds the limitations period "begins to run once the plaintiff did discover or a reasonable diligent plaintiff would have discovered the facts constituting the violation—whichever comes first." The Court also concludes the element of scienter (intention to defraud) by the defendant may be considered when determining whether the plaintiff knew or should known the fraud occurred. The element of scienter typically will delay the beginning of the statute of limitations running since the defendant is attempting to hide the fraud.

Based on the facts presented, the Court decides that statute of limitations has not run out since the plaintiffs could not have reasonably known before November 6, 2001 (two years prior to the lawsuit being filed) that Merck officials engaged in the alleged fraud.

Source: *Merck & Co. v. Reynolds*, 130 S. Ct. 1784 (2010).

One of the most difficult issues concerning materiality arises in preliminary merger negotiations. How should management respond when asked about merger possibilities? Should management reveal information about merger possibilities even when the likelihood of an actual merger is very slight? The Supreme Court uses an objective-person case-by-case analysis to determine whether information about potential mergers is material and thus required to be disclosed. The Court said, "materiality depends on the significance the reasonable investor would place on the withheld or misrepresented information."

International Application The application of §10(b) and Rule 10b-5 to international securities transaction appears to depend on the nationality of the purchaser and seller of the securities as well as the location of the actual sales transaction. Case 17.2 discusses the factual situation involving international sellers and buyers on foreign exchanges.

 case 17.2 >>

MORRISON v. NATIONAL AUSTRALIA BANK LTD.
130 S. Ct. 2869 (2010)

The National Australia Bank Limited (National or Bank) is the largest bank in Australia. Its common shares are traded on the Australian Stock Exchange and other foreign securities exchanges, but this stock is not listed for sale on any exchange in the United States. What is listed on the New York Stock Exchange is National's American Depositary Receipts (ADRs). An ADR represents the right to receive specified shares of a foreign stock.

In February 1998, National purchased a Florida corporation known as HomeSide Lending, Inc. This corporation made money through its mortgage-servicing rights. In essence, HomeSide earned profits by collecting mortgage payments. The key to HomeSide's success related to mortgages being paid over time. Any early payment of mortgages reduced HomeSide's profits as it reduced its income stream.

Between 1998 and 2001, National's annual reports included the success of HomeSide. However, National announced it was writing down the value of HomeSide's assests by $450 million in July 2001 and by another $1.75 billion in September 2001. The reason for these adjustments was due to very low interest rates causing many borrowers to refinance existing mortgages. The early payoff due to the refinanced mortgages hurt HomeSide's income.

A group of Australian investors filed a complaint in the United States District Court for the Southern District of New York alleging that the officers of National and HomeSide violated §10(b) of the 1934 Securities

Exchange Act. The basis of this complaint is that the officers misrepresented the calculation of HomeSide's value without considering the reduced income from its mortgage-servicing rights. The plaintiffs' complaint sought to have a class-action declared by the judge to protect investors against this fraud.

National, Homeside, and their officers successfully had the complaint dismissed since the District Court found it lacked jurisdiction to hear the case. The plaintiffs argued that HomeSide was a Florida corporation and investors had purchased National ADRs via the New York Stock Exchange. The District Judge found there was no jurisdiction because the acts in the United States were "at most, a link in the chain of an alleged overall securities fraud scheme that culminated aboard." On appeal, the Second Circuit affirmed the dismissal of the complaint. Certiorari was granted.

SCALIA, J.: We decide whether §10(b) of the Securities Exchange Act of 1934 provides a cause of action to foreign plaintiffs suing foreign and American defendants for misconduct in connection with securities traded on foreign exchanges. . . .

Rule 10b–5, the regulation under which petitioners have brought suit, was promulgated under §10(b), and does not extend beyond conduct encompassed by §10(b)'s prohibition. Therefore, if §10(b) is not extraterritorial, neither is Rule 10b–5.

[continued]

On its face, §10(b) contains nothing to suggest it applies abroad:

It shall be unlawful for any person, directly or indirectly, by the use of any means or instrumentality of interstate commerce or of the mails, or of any facility of any national securities exchange . . . [t]o use or employ, in connection with the purchase or sale of any security registered on a national securities exchange or any security not so registered, . . . any manipulative or deceptive device or contrivance in contravention of such rules and regulations as the [Securities and Exchange] Commission may prescribe.

Petitioners and the Solicitor General contend, however, that three things indicate that §10(b) or the Exchange Act in general has at least some extraterritorial application. First, they point to the definition of "interstate commerce," a term used in §10(b), which includes "trade, commerce, transportation, or communication . . . between any foreign country and any State." But we have repeatedly held that even statutes that contain broad language in their definitions of "commerce" that expressly refer to "*foreign* commerce" do not apply abroad. The general reference to foreign commerce in the definition of "interstate commerce" does not defeat the presumption against extraterritoriality.

Petitioners and the Solicitor General next point out that Congress, in describing the purposes of the Exchange Act, observed that the prices established and offered in such transactions are generally disseminated and quoted throughout the United States and foreign countries. The antecedent of such transactions, however, is found in the first sentence of the section, which declares that "transactions in securities as commonly conducted upon securities exchanges and over-the counter markets are affected with a national public interest." Nothing suggests that this *national* public interest pertains to transactions conducted upon *foreign* exchanges and markets. The fleeting reference to the dissemination and quotation abroad of the prices of securities traded in domestic exchanges and markets cannot overcome the presumption against extraterritoriality.

Finally, there is §30(b) of the Exchange Act, which *does* mention the Act's extraterritorial application: "The provisions of [the Exchange Act] or of any rule or regulation thereunder shall not apply to any person insofar as he transacts a business in securities without the jurisdiction of the United States," unless he does so in violation of regulations promulgated by the Securities and Exchange Commission "to prevent . . . evasion of [the Act]." (The parties have pointed us to no regulation promulgated pursuant to §30(b).) The Solicitor

General argues that this exemption would have no function if the Act did not apply in the first instance to securities transactions that occur abroad.

We are not convinced. In the first place, it would be odd for Congress to indicate the extraterritorial application of the whole Exchange Act by means of a provision imposing a condition precedent to its application abroad. And if the whole Act applied abroad, why would the Commission's enabling regulations be limited to those preventing "evasion" of the Act, rather than all those preventing "violation"? The provision seems to us directed at actions abroad that might conceal a domestic violation, or might cause what would otherwise be a domestic violation to escape on a technicality. At most, the Solicitor General's proposed inference is possible; but possible interpretations of statutory language do not override the presumption against extraterritoriality.

The Solicitor General also fails to account for §30(a), which reads in relevant part as follows:

It shall be unlawful for any broker or dealer . . . to make use of the mails or of any means or instrumentality of interstate commerce for the purpose of effecting on an exchange not within or subject to the jurisdiction of the United States, any transaction in any security the issuer of which is a resident of, or is organized under the laws of, or has its principal place of business in, a place within or subject to the jurisdiction of the United States, in contravention of such rules and regulations as the Commission may prescribe. . . .

Subsection 30(a) contains what §10(b) lacks: a clear statement of extraterritorial effect. Its explicit provision for a specific extraterritorial application would be quite superfluous if the rest of the Exchange Act already applied to transactions on foreign exchanges—and its limitation of that application to securities of domestic issuers would be inoperative. Even if that were not true, when a statute provides for some extraterritorial application, the presumption against extraterritoriality operates to limit that provision to its terms. No one claims that §30(a) applies here. . . .

In short, there is no affirmative indication in the Exchange Act that §10(b) applies extraterritorially, and we therefore conclude that it does not.

Petitioners argue that the conclusion that §10(b) does not apply extraterritorially does not resolve this case. They contend that they seek no more than domestic application anyway, since Florida is where HomeSide and its senior executives engaged in the deceptive conduct of manipulating HomeSide's financial models. . . . This is less an answer to the presumption against extraterritorial application than it is an assertion—a quite

[continued]

valid assertion—that that presumption here (as often) is not self-evidently dispositive, but its application requires further analysis. For it is a rare case of prohibited extraterritorial application that lacks *all* contact with the territory of the United States. But the presumption against extraterritorial application would be a craven watchdog indeed if it retreated to its kennel whenever *some* domestic activity is involved in the case. . . .

We think that the focus of the Exchange Act is not upon the place where the deception originated, but upon purchases and sales of securities in the United States. Section 10(b) does not punish deceptive conduct, but only deceptive conduct "in connection with the purchase or sale of any security registered on a national securities exchange or any security not so registered." Those purchase-and-sale transactions are the objects of the statute's solicitude. It is those transactions that the statute seeks to regulate; it is parties or prospective parties to those transactions that the statute seeks to protect. And it is in our view only transactions in securities listed on domestic exchanges, and domestic transactions in other securities, to which §10(b) applies.

The primacy of the domestic exchange is suggested by the very prologue of the Exchange Act, which sets forth as its object "[t]o provide for the regulation of securities exchanges . . . operating in interstate and foreign commerce and through the mails, to prevent inequitable and unfair practices on such exchanges. . . ." We know of no one who thought that the Act was intended to regulate *foreign* securities exchanges—or indeed who even believed that under established principles of international law Congress had the power to do so. The Act's registration requirements apply only to securities listed on national securities exchanges.

With regard to securities *not* registered on domestic exchanges, the exclusive focus on *domestic* purchases and sales is strongly confirmed by §30(a) and (b), discussed earlier. The former extends the normal scope

of the Exchange Act's prohibitions to acts effecting, in violation of rules prescribed by the Commission, a transaction in a United States security on an exchange not within or subject to the jurisdiction of the United States. And the latter specifies that the Act does not apply to "any person insofar as he transacts a business in securities without the jurisdiction of the United States," unless he does so in violation of regulations promulgated by the Commission "to prevent evasion [of the Act]." Under both provisions it is the foreign location of the transaction that establishes (or reflects the presumption of) the Act's inapplicability, absent regulations by the Commission. . . .

Finally, we reject the notion that the Exchange Act reaches conduct in this country affecting exchanges or transactions abroad. . . . Like the United States, foreign countries regulate their domestic securities exchanges and securities transactions occurring within their territorial jurisdiction. And the regulation of other countries often differs from ours as to what constitutes fraud, what disclosures must be made, what damages are recoverable, what discovery is available in litigation, what individual actions may be joined in a single suit, what attorney's fees are recoverable, and many other matters. . . .

Section 10(b) reaches the use of a manipulative or deceptive device or contrivance only in connection with the purchase or sale of a security listed on an American stock exchange, and the purchase or sale of any other security in the United States. This case involves no securities listed on a domestic exchange, and all aspects of the purchases complained of by those petitioners who still have live claims occurred outside the United States. Petitioners have therefore failed to state a claim on which relief can be granted. We affirm the dismissal of petitioners' complaint on this ground.

Affirmed.

>> CASE QUESTIONS

1. What is the nationality of the plaintiffs? Of the defendant?
2. What issue does the Supreme Court address in this case?
3. What conclusion does the Court reach?
4. Which arguments do the plaintiffs/petitioners present in support of the extraterritorial application of §10(b)?
5. How does the Court respond to these arguments?

As the result of this *Morrison* decision, an interesting situation would involve an American investor who buys a foreign stock on a foreign exchange. Would §10(b) of the Securities Exchange Act of 1934 protect this investor? While this question is not specifically addressed, it can be argued that *Morrison's* transactional test would seem to deny this American investor a basis for a claim.

8. INSIDER TRANSACTIONS

Section 16, one of the most important provisions of the Securities Exchange Act of 1934, concerns insider transactions. An **insider** is any person who:

- Owns more than 10 percent of any security.
- Is a director or an officer of the issuer of the security.

The SEC defines an officer for insider trading purposes as the executive officers, accounting officers, chief financial officers, and controllers. The SEC also examines the individual investor's function within the company rather than the title of the position held.

Section 16 and SEC regulations require that insiders file, at the time of the registration or within 10 days after becoming an insider, a statement of the amount of such issues of which they are the owners. The regulations also require filing within 10 days after the close of each calendar month thereafter if there has been any change in such ownership during such month (indicating the change). Sarbanes-Oxley shortens the time period for filing information about insider transactions. Now, these filings with the SEC must be made electronically within two business days of the insider's transaction.

The reason for prohibiting insiders from trading for profit is to prevent the use of information that is available to an insider but not to the general public. Because the SEC cannot determine for certain when nonpublic information is improperly used, Section 16 creates a presumption that any profit made within a six-month time period is illegal. These profits are referred to as **short-swing profits.** Thus, if a director, officer, or principal owner realizes profits on the purchase and sale of a security within a six-month period, the profits legally belong to the company or to the investor who purchased it from or sold it to an insider, resulting in the insider's profit and the investor's loss. The order of the purchase and sale is immaterial. The profit is calculated on the lowest price in and highest price out during any six-month period. Unlike the required proof of intent to deceive under Section 10(b), the short-swing profits rule of Section 16 does not depend on any misuse of information. In other words, short-swing profits by insiders, regardless of the insiders' states of mind, are absolutely prohibited.

While the SEC enforces the requirements of Section 16 that insiders file certain documents, the SEC does not enforce the provision that prohibits insiders from engaging in short-swing profits. This provision of Section 16 is enforced by civil actions filed by the issuer of the security or by a person who owns a security of the issuer.

9. NONPUBLIC INFORMATION

The SEC's concern for trading based on nonpublic information goes beyond the Section 16 ban on short-swing profits. Indeed, a person who is not technically an insider but who trades securities without disclosing nonpublic information may violate Section 10(b) and Rule 10b-5. The SEC takes the position that the profit obtained as the result of a trader's silence concerning information that is not freely available to everyone is a manipulation or deception prohibited by Section 10(b) and Rule 10b-5. In essence, the users of nonpublic information are treated like insiders if they can be classified as tippees.

A **tippee** is a person who learns of nonpublic information from an insider. In essence, a tippee is viewed as a temporary insider. A tippee is liable for the use of nonpublic information because an insider should not be allowed to do indirectly what he or she cannot do directly. In other words, a tippee is liable for trading or passing on information that is nonpublic.

The use of nonpublic information for financial gain has not been prohibited entirely. For example, in one case, a financial printer had been hired to print corporate takeover bids. An employee of the printer was able to deduce the identities of both the acquiring companies and the companies targeted for takeover. Without disclosing the knowledge about the prospective takeover bids, the employee purchased stock in the target companies and then sold it for a profit immediately after the takeover attempts were made public. He was indicted and convicted for having violated Section 10(b) and Rule 10b-5. The Supreme Court reversed, holding that the defendant had no duty to reveal the nonpublic information, since he was not in a fiduciary position with respect to either the acquiring or the acquired company.

In another case the U.S. Supreme Court further narrowed a tippee's liability. The Court ruled that a tippee becomes liable under Section 10(b) only if the tipper breaches a fiduciary duty to the business organization or fellow shareholders. Therefore, if the tipper communicated nonpublic information for reasons other than personal gain, neither the tipper nor the tippee could be liable for a securities violation.

These two Supreme Court cases have made it more difficult for the SEC to control the use of nonpublic information. However, the SEC has successfully argued that a person should be considered to be a temporary insider if that person conveys nonpublic information that was to have been kept confidential. This philosophy has become known as the **misappropriation theory** of insider trading. Case 17.3 approves the misappropriation theory.

 case 17.3 >>

UNITED STATES v. O'HAGAN
117 S. Ct. 2199 (1997)

GINSBURG, J.: . . . Respondent James Herman O'Hagan was a partner in the law firm of Dorsey & Whitney in Minneapolis, Minnesota. In July 1988, Grand Metropolitan PLC (Grand Met), a company based in London, England, retained Dorsey & Whitney as local counsel to represent Grand Met regarding a potential tender offer for the common stock of the Pillsbury Company, headquartered in Minneapolis. Both Grand Met and Dorsey & Whitney took precautions to protect the confidentiality of Grand Met's tender offer plans. O'Hagan did no work on the Grand Met

representation. Dorsey & Whitney withdrew from representing Grand Met on September 9, 1988. Less than a month later, on October 4, 1988, Grand Met publicly announced its tender offer for Pillsbury stock.

On August 18, 1988, while Dorsey & Whitney was still representing Grand Met, O'Hagan began purchasing call options for Pillsbury stock. Each option gave him the right to purchase 100 shares of Pillsbury stock by a specified date in September 1988. Later in August and in September, O'Hagan made additional purchases of Pillsbury call options. By the end

[continued]

of September, he owned 2,500 unexpired Pillsbury options. . . . O'Hagan also purchased, in September 1988, some 5,000 shares of Pillsbury common stock, at a price just under $39 per share. When Grand Met announced its tender offer in October, the price of Pillsbury stock rose to nearly $60 per share. O'Hagan then sold his Pillsbury call options and common stock, making a profit of more than $4.3 million.

The Securities and Exchange Commission (SEC or Commission) initiated an investigation into O'Hagan's transactions, culminating in a 57-count indictment. The indictment alleged that O'Hagan defrauded his law firm and its client, Grand Met, by using for his own trading purposes material, nonpublic information regarding Grand Met's planned tender offer. . . .

A divided panel of the Court of Appeals for the Eighth Circuit reversed all of O'Hagan's convictions. Liability under §10(b) and Rule 10b-5, the Eighth Circuit held, may not be grounded on the "misappropriation theory" of securities fraud on which the prosecution relied. . . .

Decisions of the Courts of Appeals are in conflict on the propriety of the misappropriation theory under §10(b) and Rule 10b-5. . . . We granted certiorari and now reverse the Eighth Circuit's judgment. . . .

In pertinent part, §10(b) of the Exchange Act provides:

> It shall be unlawful for any person, directly or indirectly, by the use of any means or instrumentality of interstate commerce or of the mails, or of any facility of any national securities exchange— . . .
>
> (b) To use or employ, in connection with the purchase or sale of any security registered on a national securities exchange or any security not so registered, any manipulative or deceptive device or contrivance in contravention of such rules and regulations as the [Securities and Exchange] Commission may prescribe as necessary or appropriate in the public interest or for the protection of investors.

The statute thus proscribes (1) using any deceptive device (2) in connection with the purchase or sale of securities, in contravention of rules prescribed by the Commission. The provision, as written, does not confine its coverage to deception of a purchaser or seller of securities; rather, the statute reaches any deceptive device used in connection with the purchase or sale of any security.

Pursuant to its §10(b) rulemaking authority, the Commission has adopted Rule 10b-5, which, as relevant here, provides:

> It shall be unlawful for any person, directly or indirectly, by the use of any means or instrumentality of interstate commerce, or of the mails or of any facility of any national securities exchange,
>
> (a) To employ any device, scheme, or artifice to defraud, [or] . . .

> (c) To engage in any act, practice, or course of business which operates or would operate as a fraud or deceit upon any person, in connection with the purchase or sale of any security.

. . . Under the "traditional" or "classical theory" of insider trading liability, §10(b) and Rule 10b-5 are violated when a corporate insider trades in the securities of his corporation on the basis of material, nonpublic information. . . .

The "misappropriation theory" holds that a person commits fraud "in connection with" a securities transaction, and thereby violates §10(b) and Rule 10b-5, when he misappropriates confidential information for securities trading purposes, in breach of a duty owed to the source of the information. Under this theory, a fiduciary's undisclosed, self-serving use of a principal's information to purchase or sell securities, in breach of a duty of loyalty and confidentiality, defrauds the principal of the exclusive use of that information. In lieu of premising liability on a fiduciary relationship between company insider and purchaser or seller of the company's stock, the misappropriation theory premises liability on a fiduciary-turned-trader's deception of those who entrusted him with access to confidential information.

The two theories are complementary, each addressing efforts to capitalize on nonpublic information through the purchase or sale of securities. The classical theory targets a corporate insider's breach of duty to shareholders with whom the insider transacts; the misappropriation theory outlaws trading on the basis of nonpublic information by a corporate "outsider" in breach of a duty owed not to a trading party, but to the source of the information. The misappropriation theory is thus designed to protect the integrity of the securities markets against abuses by outsiders to a corporation who have access to confidential information that will affect the corporation's security price when revealed, but who owe no fiduciary or other duty to that corporation's shareholders.

In this case, the indictment alleged that O'Hagan, in breach of a duty of trust and confidence he owed to his law firm, Dorsey & Whitney, and to its client, Grand Met, traded on the basis of nonpublic information regarding Grand Met's planned tender offer for Pillsbury common stock. This conduct, the Government charged, constituted a fraudulent device in connection with the purchase and sale of securities.

We agree with the Government that misappropriation, as just defined, satisfies §10(b)'s requirement that chargeable conduct involve a "deceptive device or contrivance" used "in connection with" the purchase or sale of securities. We observe, first, that misappropriators, as the Government describes them, deal in deception. A fiduciary who "[pretends] loyalty to the principal while secretly converting the principal's information for personal gain," "dupes" or defrauds the principal. . . .

[continued]

Deception through nondisclosure is central to the theory of liability for which the Government seeks recognition. As counsel for the Government stated in explanation of the theory at oral argument: "To satisfy the common law rule that a trustee may not use the property that [has] been entrusted [to] him, there would have to be consent. To satisfy the requirement of the Securities Act that there be no deception, there would only have to be disclosure." . . .

[F]ull disclosure forecloses liability under the misappropriation theory: Because the deception essential to the misappropriation theory involves feigning fidelity to the source of information, if the fiduciary discloses to the source that he plans to trade on the nonpublic information, there is no "deceptive device" and thus no §10(b) violation—although the fiduciary-turned-trader may remain liable under state law for breach of a duty of loyalty.

We turn next to the §10(b) requirement that the misappropriator's deceptive use of information be "in connection with the purchase or sale of [a] security." This element is satisfied because the fiduciary's fraud is consummated, not when the fiduciary gains the confidential information, but when, without disclosure to his principal, he uses the information to purchase or sell securities. The securities transaction and the breach of duty thus coincide. This is so even though the person or entity defrauded is not the other party to the trade; but is, instead, the source of the nonpublic information. A misappropriator who trades on the basis of material, nonpublic information, in short, gains his advantageous market position through deception; he deceives the source of the information and simultaneously harms members of the investing public.

The misappropriation theory targets information of a sort that misappropriators ordinarily capitalize upon to gain no-risk profits through the purchase or sale of securities. . . .

The misappropriation theory comports with §10(b)'s language, which requires deception "in connection with the purchase or sale of any security," not deception of an identifiable purchaser or seller. The theory is also well-turned to an animating purpose of the Exchange Act: to insure honest securities markets and thereby promote investor confidence. Although informational disparity is inevitable in the securities markets, investors likely would hesitate to venture their capital in a market where trading based on misappropriated nonpublic information is unchecked by law. An investor's informational disadvantage vis-à-vis a misappropriator with material, nonpublic information stems from contrivance, not luck; it is a disadvantage that cannot be overcome with research or skill.

In sum, considering the inhibiting impact on market participation of trading on misappropriated information, and the congressional purposes underlying §10(b), it makes scant sense to hold a lawyer like O'Hagan a §10(b) violator if he works for a law firm representing the target of a tender offer, but not if he works for a law firm representing the bidder. The text of the statute requires no such result. The misappropriation at issue here was properly made the subject of a §10(b) charge because it meets the statutory requirement that there be "deceptive" conduct "in connection with" securities transactions. . . .

. . . [T]he misappropriation theory, as we have examined and explained it in this opinion, is both consistent with the statute and with our precedent. Vital to our decision that criminal liability may be sustained under the misappropriation theory, we emphasize, are two sturdy safeguards Congress has provided regarding scienter. To establish a criminal violation of Rule 10b-5, the Government must prove that a person "willfully" violated the provision. Furthermore, a defendant may not be imprisoned for violating Rule 10b-5 if he proves that he had no knowledge of the rule. . . .

The Eighth Circuit erred in holding that the misappropriation theory is inconsistent with §10(b). The Court of Appeals may address on remand O'Hagan's other challenges to his convictions under §10(b) and Rule 10b-5. . . .

Reversed and remanded.

>> CASE QUESTIONS

1. What was O'Hagan accused of doing that was illegal?
2. What is the theory that the SEC argues is the basis of O'Hagan's wrongdoing?
3. How did the trial court and the appellate court rule in this case?
4. What reasons did the Supreme Court give for finding that the misappropriation theory is appropriate?
5. According to the Supreme Court, when and against whom did the misappropriation occur?

The SEC continues to focus its enforcement efforts on the misuse of non-public information at all levels of transactions. The SEC's efforts are aided by the fact that the civil penalty for gaining illegal profits with nonpublic information is three times the profits gained. In addition, controlling persons who fail to prevent these violations by employees may be civilly liable for the greater amount of triple damages or $1,000,000.

The penalties were increased to their current levels by the Insider Trading and Securities Fraud Enforcement Act of 1988. This law also provides that suits alleging the illegal use of nonpublic information may be filed within a five-year period after the wrongful transaction. This period, being substantially longer than the one year/three years limitation periods for other federal securities violations, illustrates the emphasis Congress has placed on preventing trading on nonpublic information.

Don't be tempted to take advantage of nonpublic information if you are an insider within your company.

10. ADDITIONAL CIVIL LIABILITY

In 1990, Congress expressed its concern for enforcement of the securities laws. In that year, the Securities Enforcement Remedies Act became law. This legislation provides that civil fines of up to $500,000 per organization and $100,000 per individual may be imposed and collected by the courts. In addition, an individual found to have violated the securities laws may be prohibited by the court from serving as an officer or director of a business organization. These fines and this prohibition from service can be utilized, at the judge's discretion, when a party in a civil case is found to have violated the securities laws. There does not have to be any proof of a criminal violation for these fines to be imposed.

Furthermore, Section 18 of the Securities Exchange Act of 1934 imposes liability on a theory of fraud on any person who shall make or cause to be made any false and misleading statements of material fact in any application, report, or document filed under the act. This liability favors both purchasers and sellers. A plaintiff must prove that the defendant knowingly made a false statement, that plaintiff relied on the false or misleading statement, and that plaintiff suffered damage.

Two distinctions between this section of the 1934 Act and Sections 11 and 12 of the 1933 Act are noteworthy. First, the requirement that an intent to deceive be proven under Section 18 means that the defendant's good faith is a defense. Good faith exists when a person acts without knowledge that the statement is false and misleading. In other words, freedom from fraud is a defense under an action based on Section 18. There is no liability under this section for simple negligence. Second, the plaintiff in a Section 18 case must prove reliance on the false or misleading filing. The simple fact that the filing is inaccurate is not sufficient. In a Section 11 or 12 case under the 1933 Act, the plaintiff does not have to establish reliance.

The Sarbanes-Oxley Act extends the statute of limitations for civil actions under the 1934 Act. Lawsuits must be filed within two years of the time the wrong was discovered (or should have been) and at least within five years of the wrongful act. The expansion of civil liability under the 1934 Act encourages settlement in many cases. Although the number of class-action securities

"Securities fraud class-actions settlements in the U.S. rose 39 percent to more than $3.8 billion in 2009."

Margaret Cronin Fisk, *Bloomberg.com,* **March 24, 2010**

table 17.3 >> Largest Securities Class-Action Settlements (2005–2007)		
Dollar Amount of Settlement	**Company**	**Year**
$7.2 billion	Enron	2006
$6.2 billion	WorldCom	2005
$3.2 billion	Tyco	2007

cases increased due to the 2008 market decline, the largest settlements come from the accounting scandals uncovered in 2000 and 2001. Table 17.3 summarizes some of these larger civil settlements.

11. CRIMINAL LIABILITY

The 1934 Act provides for criminal sanctions for willful violations of its provisions or the rules adopted under it. Liability is imposed for false material statements in applications, reports, documents, and registration statements. In response to the corporate scandals occurring during the beginning of the twenty-first century, Congress in 2002 increased the criminal penalties for violating the Securities Exchange Act of 1934. An individual found guilty of filing false or misleading documents with the SEC may be fined up to $5,000,000 and imprisoned for up to 20 years. A business organization found guilty of filing with the SEC false or misleading documents may be subject to a fine up to $25,000,000. An individual guilty of securities fraud may face a prison sentence of up to 25 years. These increased sanctions emphasize the seriousness with which all businesspeople must treat compliance with securities regulations.

The penalties are not theoretical. Sixteen officials from Enron have pled guilty and face a variety of prison terms. The CEO of WorldCom has been convicted and sentenced to 25 years in prison. The names of other former executives became commonly known because serious prison sentences get the public's attention. Whether these examples serve as deterrents for future fraudulent behavior remains to be seen.

Criminal liability is an important consideration for officers and directors as well as for accountants. Accountants have been found guilty of a crime for failure to disclose important facts to shareholder-investors. Compliance with generally accepted accounting principles is not an absolute defense. The critical issue in such cases is whether the financial statements as a whole fairly present the financial condition of the company and whether they accurately report operations for the covered periods. If they do not, the second issue is whether the accountant acted in good faith. Compliance with generally accepted accounting principles is evidence of good faith, but such evidence is not necessarily conclusive. Lack of criminal intent is the defense usually asserted by accountants charged with a crime. They usually admit mistakes or even negligence but deny any criminal wrongdoing. Proof of motive is not required.

As with issues of civil liability, most cases involving potential criminal liability are litigated under Section 10(b) and Rule 10b-5.

concept >> *summary*

Securities Exchange Act of 1934

>> SECTION 10(B)

Purpose: Creates liability for use of mail or any instrumentality of interstate commerce to defraud any person in connection with the purchase or sale of any security.

Plaintiff's case: Proof of defendant's intent to deceive through use of false information or nondisclosure of truthful information; plaintiff's reliance on fraudulent documents; and damages.

Defendant's defenses: No actual fraud was involved; only aided or abetted fraud; information was not material.

Civil liability: Person in violation of §10(b) is liable for actual damages, court costs, and reasonable attorney fees.

>> SECTION 16(B)

Purpose: Creates strict liability for any insider making a profit on issuer's securities during any six-month period.

Plaintiff's case: Proof of the short-swing nature of the profitable transaction.

Defendant's defenses: Proof of no short-swing transaction; good faith (lack of intent) is no defense.

Civil fines: Up to three times the illegal profits; ban from service as director or officer.

>> SECTION 18

Purpose: Imposes liability for fraudulently filing false or misleading documents with the SEC or any exchange.

Plaintiff's case: Proof of defendant's intent to make false or misleading documents filed; plaintiff's reliance on documents filed; and damages.

Defendant's defenses: Freedom from fraud; good faith—no intent to defraud; no reliance by plaintiff on documents filed.

>> CRIMINAL LIABILITY

For securities fraud: Up to 25 years in prison.

For false or misleading documents filed: $5,000,000 fine or 20 years in prison or both per individual; $25,000,000 fine per organization.

For trading on nonpublic information: $1 million fine or 10 years in prison or both per individual; $10 million fine per organization.

>> Other Considerations

In addition to understanding the historical nature of securities laws, every businessperson and investor should be familiar with two additional topics. First, in the next section, we present materials related to private parties suing to enforce the federal securities laws. Second, in the last section of this chapter, you should gain an understanding of how states also regulate the issuance and sale of securities.

12. PRIVATE SECURITIES LITIGATION REFORM ACT OF 1995

In 1994, the Supreme Court held that liability under Section 10(b) and Rule 10b-5 did not extend to parties aiding and abetting the primary violator.[3] The following year, Congress passed and President Clinton signed the **Private Securities Litigation Reform Act (PSLRA).** The law made it clear the Court's decision would not be expanded. Indeed, the PSLRA clarified that only the SEC can

"Congress amended the securities laws in 1995 to allow the Securities and Exchange Commission to bring actions against secondary violators that aid and abet securities fraud. Congress wisely declined to extend that right to private parties, out of concern of abusive securities litigation."

—Paul S. Atkins, "Stoneridge and the Rule of Law," The Wall Street Journal, January 25, 2008.

[3]*Central Bank of Denver, N.A. v. First Interstate Bank of Denver, N.A., 114 S.Ct. 1439 (1994).*

table 17.4 >> Number of Federal Securities Fraud Class Actions (filed each year)	
Year	**Number of Cases**
2000	216
2001	180
2002	224
2003	192
2004	228
2005	182
2006	119
2007	177
2008	223
2009	168
2010	176

Source: Stanford Law School Securities Class Action Clearinghouse in cooperation with Cornerstone Research. Retrieved from http://securities.stanford.edu/clearinghouse.research/2010_YIR/Cornerstone_Research_ Filing_2010_YIR.pdf.

pursue claims against third parties not directly responsible for the securities law violation. This part of the law helps form the basis for the decision in Case 17.1.

The PSLRA requires any private plaintiff to allege with specificity the scienter, or intent, of a company or its executives when filing a claim under Section 10(b) and Rule 10b-5. A plaintiff "must plead facts rendering an inference of scienter at least as likely as any plausible opposing inference."[4]

Congress, through the PSLRA, limits the amount of damages private plaintiffs can recover and restricts attorney fees. This law also provides requirements for the appointment of lead plaintiffs in securities class-action cases. Even with these restrictions, there are many securities class-actions filed each year. Table 17.4 details the number of these cases during this century. While it appears the amount of securities litigation is declining, new scandals and crises provide opportunities for more cases. Currently, the subprime mortgage crisis creates potential litigation.

13. STATE BLUE SKY LAWS

LO 17-5

Throughout their history, state regulations regarding securities laws commonly have been referred to as **blue sky laws**—probably because they were intended to protect the potential investor from buying "a piece of the attractive blue sky" (worthless or risky securities) without financial and other information about what was being purchased. The blue sky laws can apply to securities subject to federal laws as well as to those securities exempt from the federal statutes. It is clearly established that the federal laws do not preempt the existence of state blue sky laws. Due to their broad application, any person associated with issuing or thereafter transferring securities should survey the blue sky laws passed by the various states.

[4]*Tellabs, Inc. v. Mabor Issues & Rights, Ltd., 127 S.Ct. 2499 (2007).*

Although the existence of federal securities laws has influenced state legislatures, enactment of blue sky laws has not been uniform. Indeed, states typically have enacted laws that contain provisions similar to the antifraud provisions, the registration of securities provisions, the registration of securities brokers and dealers provisions, or a combination of these provisions of the federal laws. To bring some similarity to the various blue sky laws, the Uniform Securities Act was proposed for adoption by all states beginning in 1956. Since that time, the Uniform Securities Act has been the model for blue sky laws. A majority of states have used the uniform proposal as a guideline when enacting or amending their blue sky laws.

Registration Requirements   Despite the trend toward uniformity, state laws still vary a great deal in their methods of regulating both the distribution of securities and the practices of the securities industry within each state. For example, state regulations concerning the requirements of registering securities vary widely. Some states require *registration by notification,* other states require *registration by qualification.* Registration by notification allows issuers to offer securities for sale automatically after a stated time period expires unless the administrative agency takes action to prevent the offering. This is very similar to the registration process under the Securities Act of 1933. Registration by qualification usually requires a more detailed disclosure by the issuer. Under this type of regulation, a security cannot be offered for sale until the administrative agency grants the issuer a license or certificate to sell securities.

In an attempt to resolve some of this conflict over the registration procedure, the drafters of the Uniform Securities Act may have compounded the problem. This act adopts the registration by notification process for an issuer who has demonstrated stability and performance. Registration by qualification is required by those issuers who do not have a proven record and who are not subject to the Securities Act of 1933. In addition, the Uniform Securities Act created a third procedure—*registration by coordination.* For those issuers of securities who must register with the SEC, duplicate documents are filed with the state's administrative agency. Unless a state official objects, the state registration becomes effective automatically when the federal registration statement is deemed effective.

Exemptions   To further compound the confusion about blue sky laws, various exemptions of the securities or transactions have been adopted by the states. Four basic exemptions from blue sky laws have been identified. Every state likely has enacted at least one and perhaps a combination of these exemptions. Among these common four are the exemption:

1. For an isolated transaction.
2. For an offer or sale to a limited number of offerees or purchasers within a stated time period.
3. For a private offering.
4. For a sale if the number of holders after the sale does not exceed a specified number.

The second type of exemption probably is the most common exemption, because it is part of the Uniform Securities Act. Nevertheless, states vary on whether the exemption applies to offerees or to purchasers. There also is great variation on the maximum number of such offerees or purchasers involved.

That number likely ranges between 5 and 35, depending on the applicable blue sky law. The time period for the offers or purchases, as the case may be, also may vary; however, 12 months seems to be the most common period.

Usually the applicable time limitation is worded to read, for example, "*any* 12-month time period." In essence, this language means that each day starts a new time period running. For example, assume a security is exempt from blue sky registration requirements if the issuer sells (or offers to sell) securities to no more than 35 investors during any 12-month period. Furthermore, assume the following transactions occur, with each investor being a different person or entity:

- On February 1, 2011, issuer sells to 5 investors.
- On June 1, 2011, issuer sells to 10 investors.
- On September 1, 2011, issuer sells to 10 investors.
- On December 1, 2011, issuer sells to 5 investors.
- On March 1, 2012, issuer sells to 5 investors.
- On May 1, 2012, issuer sells to 10 investors.

Only 30 investors are involved during the 12-month period following February 1, 2011. However, 40 investors are purchasers during the 12 months following June 1, 2011. Therefore, this security and the transactions involved are not exempt from the blue sky law. Civil as well as criminal liability may result for failure to comply with applicable legal regulations.

Although blue sky laws may cause confusion because of their variation, ignorance of the state legal requirements is no defense. This confusion is aggravated when the businessperson considers the further applicability of federal securities laws. To diminish this confusion, any person involved in the issuance or subsequent transfer of securities should consult with lawyers and accountants as well as other experts who have a working knowledge of securities regulations.

>> Sarbanes-Oxley Act of 2002

LO 17-6

When the collapse of Enron was followed by the even larger accounting fraud and bankruptcy of WorldCom, congressional response was passage of the **Sarbanes-Oxley Act of 2002.** This law is named for its sponsors—Senator Paul Sarbanes, a Democrat from Maryland, and Representative Michael Oxley, an Ohio Republican. The Sarbanes-Oxley Act receives mixed reviews; however, most businesspeople agree it has overwhelming positive impacts on the way business is conducted and audited.

> Sarbanes-Oxley is "the most significant change to securities law since they were put into effect in the mid-1930s"
>
> **–Dennis M. Nalley Chairman of Price- waterhouse Coopers**

14. REVITALIZATION OF SEC

Through the Sarbanes-Oxley Act of 2002 and in response to the corporate scandals of the first few years of this century, Congress increased the authority it delegated to the SEC. A primary way of accomplishing this reinvigoration of a 70-year-old agency was to increase its budget. Because the budget is not controlled solely by Congress, there initially was some controversy with the Bush Administration as to the amount of the increase. The proposed increase of more than 75 percent of the SEC budget was not accomplished in one year; however, the SEC's increased budget has led to a more active SEC.

> "Our goal is to effectively balance the goal of providing shareholders with timely disclosure of accurate and complete compensation information with the need to prevent strategic company information from being revealed to competitors and damaging a company."
>
> **–John J. Castellani**
> **President of Business**
> **Roundtable**

Sarbanes-Oxley (SOX) increases the SEC's power over many of the governance issues discussed in Section 13 of this chapter. The following are among the new or proposed rules issued by the SEC in the past several years:

- The need for public companies to have a majority of independent directors on their boards.
- The focus on the agency's effort to collect civil damages against executives and their company so long as the shareholder's value will not be harmed.
- The increase in emphasis on how the Internet can assist shareholders in expressing their views through voting and other communications.
- The disclosure of executive compensation, including severance packages and other perks such as stock options, travel benefits, club memberships, and retirement plans. These disclosures cover the CEO, CFO, and the three other highest paid executives.

15. ACCOUNTING REFORMS

Sarbanes-Oxley creates the Public Company Accounting Oversight Board (PCAOB). This Board consists of five members appointed by the SEC commissioners. The PCAOB reports to the commissioners. Congress viewed accounting firms as a major contributor to the corporate scandals involving Enron, WorldCom, HealthSouth, Tyco, and others. This view is based, in part, on the role that the Arthur Andersen accounting firm played with Enron and WorldCom.

See case 15.3 clarifying the appointment and removal process of PCAOB members.

The PCAOB is given oversight of accounting firms that audit public companies. One of the first steps required of accounting firms was the separation of the auditing and consulting functions. The belief is that firms tainted their independence in the auditing function because they made so much more money consulting with these same corporate clients. This separation of the auditing and consulting functions is the reason why Arthur Andersen consultants formed a separate organization, which is now called Accenture. The management consulting services of PricewaterhouseCoopers (PWC) were sold to IBM, so that PWC can concentrate on its tax and audit practices.

The PCAOB requires that auditing firms refrain from conducting a variety of nonauditing services. These services include bookkeeping, system designs and implementation, appraisals and valuations, actuarial services, human resources functions, and investment banking.

The effectiveness of the role of PCAOB is still being determined. Some critics question the Sarbanes-Oxley Act for not making this Board truly an independent agency. Others believe that having the Board report within the SEC strengthens the new and existing administrative structure. In the years ahead, it will be interesting to observe the PCAOB's role in governing the effectiveness of public accounting firms.

16. CORPORATE GOVERNANCE

Over time, this area of regulation may be the major contribution of the Sarbanes-Oxley Act. Although other parts of the law get more attention because of the financial impact (see the next section of this chapter), restructuring how corporations govern themselves and the governance requirements required by the SEC and the PCAOB are of critical importance. Under this heading, several items relate to the audit of public companies.

Sarbanes-Oxley focuses on increasing the independence of the auditors. Congress seeks to ensure that auditors maintain the trust of the public and the corporate shareholders and not the loyalty of the corporate officers and directors. This effort principally is oriented to the public company's audit committee. Each member of this committee must be independent from the control of the company. No longer may a public company place its finance officer or other employee on the audit committee.

Further, at least one member of the audit committee has to be a financial expert. To qualify as a financial expert, it must be shown that through experience or education this person has an understanding of generally accepted accounting practices (GAAP), financial statements, audits of public companies, internal audit controls, and the functions of an audit committee.

Sarbanes-Oxley requires that the auditor report to this independent audit committee. The auditor should not have a close working relationship with the company's CFO, accounting staff, and other company officials. In addition, the audit partner of the auditing firm must rotate off the engagement every five years. Auditors also must preserve audit records for seven years.

> These legal requirements allow the audit firm to do what it historically did—review the company's finances and ensure accuracy.

17. FINANCIAL STATEMENTS AND CONTROLS

These requirements of the Sarbanes-Oxley Act have been the most controversial. One of the major reasons for the controversy is the cost associated with complying with these provisions. Section 302 of the law requires CEOs and CFOs to certify the accuracy of the quarterly and annual financial statements filed with the SEC. These officials also must certify the existence of internal financial controls. These controls are subject to an independent auditor's review, in the same manner that the financial statements must be audited. The certification of internal financial controls is mandated by Section 404 of Sarbanes-Oxley.

The Big Four accounting firms commissioned a study of the cost of implementing Section 404 certification of internal financial controls. This study divided companies into large ones with over $700 million in market capitalization and into smaller ones with between $75 million and $700 million in market capitalization. Table 17.5 shows this study's first-year cost of compliance.

Because the compliance costs issue creates political debate, the SEC extended the beginning date of compliance for smaller companies to 2008. The SEC also offered guidelines to reduce the burden on larger companies in certifying internal reporting controls. These actions and the repetitive nature of complying with Section 404 seem to bring down the compliance costs. Each year since 2004, larger companies find efficiencies related to Section 404 certification.

> The requirements of Section 404 "offered us an opportunity to look at our processes and in many cases improve them. We found our people really benefited from understanding the processes. It has made Staples a better company."
>
> **–John J. Mahoney**
> **CFO of Staples**

table 17.5 >> Cost of Section 404 Compliance in First Year

	Smaller Companies	Larger Companies
Average cost of Section 404 compliance	$1.5 million	$7.3 million
Average company revenues	$324 million	$7.9 billion
Cost as % of revenues	0.46%	0.09%

Source: CRA International Study, December 2005, commissioned by Deloitte & Touche LLP, Ernst & Young LLP, KPMG LLP, and Pricewaterhouse Coopers LLP.

> "Nearly 70% of the executives said auditors had reduced the number of 'key controls' they examined last year. Auditors were more likely to take a risk-based approach, to rely on the work of others and to use their own judgment in evaluating the effectiveness of the company's controls"
>
> **–Judith Burns, "Sarbanes-Oxley Costs For Compliance Declines," The Wall Street Journal, April 29, 2008.**

Other evidence that Sarbanes-Oxley is having a positive impact is found in the number of restatements of financial reports. During 2007, there were fewer restatements than in 2006. This was the first year to show a decline since Sarbanes-Oxley was enacted. Other good news was that the amount or severity of the average restatement also declined. These trends indicate that the impact of Sarbanes-Oxley is positive.

An additional provision of Sarbanes-Oxley emphasizes the importance of accurate financial records. Despite the fact that corporate scandals caused shareholders to lose billions of dollars, corporate executives received millions in bonuses and incentive payments. Sarbanes-Oxley provides that whenever there is a restatement of the company's financial condition, executives must return any bonuses paid as a result of the incorrect financial statements. The law also prohibits personal loans from the company to its executives.

18. SECURITIES FRAUD

Through Sarbanes-Oxley, Congress strengthened the punishment for committing securities fraud. In Section 11 of this chapter, you see the serious sanctions imposed on those guilty of fraud. In those sections we will revisit how Sarbanes-Oxley increases these potential sentences. In Section 10, you see how Sarbanes-Oxley increases the statute of limitations in civil cases.

Other provisions of this law create the crime of conspiring to commit securities fraud. As discussed in Chapter 13, the proof needed to establish a conspiracy often is less than the proof required to prove the underlying crime.

Finally, Sarbanes-Oxley provides protections for whistleblowers so that individuals are more willing to report the corruption that can lead to major scandals. Audit committees are required to adopt procedures ensuring that whistle-blowers' reports are taken seriously. Whistleblowers that suffer retaliation are able to recover civil damages and can be reinstated if terminated improperly. Under Sarbanes-Oxley, employees and employers must realize there are limitations to these protections, as discussed in Sidebar 17.5.

>> *sidebar* 17.5

Limitation of Whistleblower Protection

Two employees of Boeing were fired after the company learned these individuals had reported possible defects with the company's internal controls to a newspaper reporter. Following their termination, the employees filed a lawsuit seeking reinstatement and back pay based on the Sarbanes-Oxley Act whistleblower protection (Section 806).

Both the District Court and the Ninth Circuit Court of Appeals ruled in favor of Boeing, finding that Sarbanes-Oxley did not protect these employees since their activity as a "whistleblower" was to a newspaper reporter. Employees seeking protection of the whistleblower provision of Sarbanes-Oxley must report alleged fraud or securities violations to one of the three sources listed in the law. These sources are a federal administrative or law enforcement agency, Congress, or the employee's supervisor.

In essence, these courts find that a company's policy to prevent employees from sharing information with a newspaper reporter outweighs the employees' right to "blow the whistle" in a manner not recognized by Section 806 of the Sarbanes-Oxley Act.

Source: *Tides v. The Boeing Co.,*—644 F.3d 809 (9th Cir. 2011).

concept >> *summary*

Sarbanes-Oxley Act of 2002

>> INCREASED AUTHORITY TO SEC

- Mandates budgetary increases for SEC.
- Increases power of SEC over many of governance matters.
- Since 2002, SEC enforcement much more active.

>> ACCOUNTING REFORMS

- Creates Public Company Accounting Oversight Board.
- Oversight of auditing of public companies.
- Requires separation of auditing and consulting functions within accounting firms.

>> CORPORATE GOVERNANCE

- Increases independence of auditors.
- Requires audit committees to be independent with at least one member being a financial expert.
- Audit partner must rotate off engagement after five years.

- Auditors must preserve audit records for seven years.

>> FINANCIAL STATEMENTS AND CONTROLS

- CEO and CFO must certify accuracy of financial statements.
- Also must certify existence of internal financial controls.
- Internal financial controls are subject to audit, just like financial statements.
- When restatement is made, executives must return any bonuses paid on incorrect financial statements.

>> SECURITIES FRAUD

- Creates crime of conspiring to commit securities fraud.
- Increases criminal sentences in securities fraud cases to 20 years.
- Lengthens statute of limitation in civil cases.
- Protects whistleblowers.

>> Dodd-Frank Wall Street Reform and Consumer Protection Act of 2010

LO 17-7

Following the near collapse of the United States economy in the autumn of 2008 and the lingering adverse impact throughout 2009, Congress passed financial reforms in 2010. President Obama signed what has been called the most extensive reforms since the New Deal, and this massive bill became law on July 21, 2010. The changes in this law are summarized in Table 17.6. While it will take several years to see the full impact of the Dodd-Frank Act, this list demonstrates the extensive nature of these reforms.

There are numerous examples, in our history, when Congress created an administrative agency to ensure that the details contained in the legislation would be carried out. Chapter 15 discusses the principles of this form of government regulation, and we see the specifics of this policy in Chapter 16 (FTC and antitrust laws), this chapter (SEC and securities regulations), Chapter 18 (various agencies and consumer protection), Chapter 20 (EEOC and employment discrimination), Chapter 21 (various agencies and employment laws), and Chapter 22 (NLRB and labor laws).

What is striking about the Dodd-Frank Act is the way it addresses so many issues of reform. To accomplish its broad goals, Congress authorizes

table 17.6 >> Major Provisions of Dodd-Frank Wall Street Reform and Consumer Protection Act

- Enhances consumer protection
- Ends policy on "Too Big to Fail" bailouts
- Reforms Federal Reserve
- Creates mortgage reforms
- Regulates trading of derivatives
- Regulates hedge funds
- Regulates credit rating agencies
- Controls executive compensation and corporate governance
- Reforms regulations of banks and thrifts
- Regulates insurance industry
- Limits credit card interchange fees
- Reforms SEC and investor protections
- Regulates securitizations
- Regulates municipal securities
- Provides financial assistance to overcome mortgage crisis
- Disclosures to SEC of payments to U.S. or foreign governments related to commercial development of oil, natural gas, or minerals
- Disclosures to SEC concerning manufacturing of products derived from minerals from the Congo
- Limits U.S. loans to foreign governments unlikely to repay

Source: http://banking.senate.gov/public/_files/070110_Dodd_Frank_Wall_Street_Reform_comprehensive_summary_Final.pdf.

"The Financial Stability Oversight Council . . . proposed rules as to which large financial companies that were not banks would be regulated by the Federal Reserve because they constituted a potential threat to the nation's financial system's stability based on their size."

Edward Wyatt,
New York Times,
January 18, 2011

the creation of many new administrative organizations. Many of these new entities are housed within existing organizations. The following list highlights some of the new agencies:

- Consumer Financial Protection Board—CFPB (independent within Federal Reserve)
- Financial Stability Oversight Council—FSOC (independent)
- Federal Insurance Office—FIO (Treasury)
- Office of Financial Research—OFR (FSOC)
- Offices of Minority and Women Inclusion (within Bank and Securities Regulators)
- Office of Housing Counseling (HUD)
- Office of Credit Ratings (SEC)
- Investment Advisory Committee (SEC)
- Office of Investor Advocate (SEC)

What is most important to remember about these financial reforms is that Congress feels responsibility to react or respond to crises when they arise.

The effectiveness of these reforms will take many years to see since the full implementation of the Dodd-Frank Act is scheduled over many years. History tells us that despite Congress's response to the 2008 financial recession with all these proposed reforms, another crisis will likely lead to more regulation.

One example of how this complex is being implemented in stages concerns the whistleblower provisions. In 2011, the SEC approved final regulations allowing whistleblowers to report violations directly to the SEC. Businesses argued that the SEC should require employees to use a company's internal reporting systems in order to be protected by the Dodd-Frank Act. The SEC did not adopt this approach; however, employees who first use a company's internal processes are entitled to potentially higher financial reward. Such employees might be entitled to a reward of up to 30 percent of any recovery in excess of $1 million. Employees reporting directly to the SEC will receive less of a reward.

> "The Dodd-Frank bill requires the SEC to do more than 100 new rules, create 5 new offices, and conduct more than 20 studies and reports, which require significant use of staff resources and money."
>
> **Lynn Turner, former Chief Accountant for the SEC.**

>> Key Terms

Blue sky laws 569
Controlling person 547
Due diligence defense 551
Insider 562
Issuer 547
Misappropriation theory 563
Posteffective period 548
Prefiling period 548
Private Securities Litigation Reform Act (PSLRA) 568

Prospectus 548
Registration statement 547
Sarbanes-Oxley Act of 2002 571
Scienter 550
Securities Act of 1933 546
Securities and Exchange Commission (SEC) 546
Securities Exchange Act of 1934 552

Security 545
Seller 547
Short-swing profits 562
Tippee 563
Tombstone ad 548
Underwriter 547
Waiting period 548

>> Review Questions and Problems

1. *What Is a Security?*

   W.J. Howey Company and Howey-in-the-Hills Service, Inc., are Florida corporations under common control and management. Howey Company offers to sell to the public its orange grove, tree by tree. Howey-in-the-Hills Service, Inc., offers these buyers a contract wherein the appropriate care, harvesting, and marketing of the oranges would be provided. Most of the buyers who sign the service contracts are nonresidents of Florida who have very little knowledge or skill needed to care for and harvest the oranges. These buyers are attracted by the expectation of profits. Is a sale of orange trees by the Howey Company and a sale of services by Howey-in-the-Hills Service, Inc., a sale of a security? Why or why not?

2. *Securities and Exchange Commission*

   (a) When was this administrative agency created?

   (b) What types of regulatory authorities does the SEC have at its disposal?

The Securities Act of 1933: Going Public

3. *Parties Regulated*

   Who are the four types of parties governed by the 1933 Securities Act?

4. *Documents Involved*

    (a) What are the two important documents required by the Securities Act of 1933?

    (b) Under the provisions of the federal Securities Act of 1933, there are three important time periods concerning when securities may be sold or offered for sale. Name and describe these three time periods.

5. *Liability*

    To secure a loan, Rubin pledges stock that he represents as being marketable and worth approximately $1.7 million. In fact, the stock is nonmarketable and practically worthless. He is charged with violating the Securities Act of 1933. He claims that because no sale occurred, he is not guilty. Is he correct? Why or why not?

6. *Defenses*

    What are three defenses that might be used by a party charged with violating the Securities Act of 1933?

Securities Exchange Act of 1934: Being Public

7. *Section 10(b) and Rule 10b-5*

    (a) Section 10(b) of the Securities Exchange Act of 1934 and Rule 10b-5 are of fundamental importance in the law of securities regulations. What is the main purpose of this section and rule?

    (b) Do you suppose that an oral promise made and not performed can be the basis of arguing a party is guilty of defrauding another under §10(b) and Rule 10b-5?

8. *Insider Transactions*

    Donna, a corporate director, sold 100 shares of stock in her corporation on June 1, 2007. The selling price was $10.50 a share. Two months later, after the corporation had announced substantial losses for the second quarter of the year, Donna purchased 100 shares of the corporation's stock for $7.25 a share. Are there any problems with Donna's sale and purchase? Explain.

9. *Nonpublic Information*

    Eric Ethan, president of Inside-Outside Sports Equipment Company, has access to information which is not available to the general investor. What standard should Eric Ethan apply in deciding whether this information is so material as to prevent him from investing in his company prior to the information's public release?

10. *Additional Civil Liability*

    What is the purpose of Section 18 of the Securities Exchange Act of 1934?

11. *Criminal Liability*

    What are the dollar amounts related to fines and what are the number of years related to prison terms for those that violate the Securities Act of 1934?

Other Considerations

12. *Private Securities Litigation Reform Act of 1995*

    (a) What is the purpose of the PSLRA?

    (b) List four ways Congress accomplishes this purpose.

13. *State Blue Sky Laws*

    Why is it important for businesspeople to understand the role of state blue sky laws in addition to federal securities regulations?

Sarbanes-Oxley Act of 2002

14. *Revitalization of SEC*

    What was the primary way the Sarbanes-Oxley Act increased the authority and capabilities of the SEC?

15. *Accounting Reforms*

    List and describe two major developments designed to allow auditors to focus on their review of, and not service to, public companies.

16. *Corporate Governance*

Some commentators state that the concept of independence is the most important aspect of Sarbanes-Oxley. How is independence required and why is it critical to corporate governance?

17. *Financial Statements and Controls*

Describe the Sarbanes-Oxley provisions that require certification of financial statements and internal financial controls.

18. *Securities Fraud*

In what three ways did the Sarbanes-Oxley Act strengthen the enforcement of securities fraud?

business >> *discussions*

1. Two former roommates from college contact you about an opportunity to make big money. Their idea is to start a business to market a new video game system (the computer science major developed the software, the engineer created the hardware). They estimate it will take $5 million to $10 million to begin production, and they want to raise money by selling shares in the company to investors. They think their product is superior, and they are aware of the time factor. They want to get started as soon as possible. Your field of expertise is securities marketing.

Can the three of you just begin advertising for investors?
What steps must be followed to comply with the law?
How much time is needed before potential investors can be approached legally?

2. You and a former classmate started a computer software company five years ago. Originally, the two of you were the owners and only employees. The foundation of your company was your combined expertise in creating custom-designed applications addressing the human resource needs of your clients. As your company grew, you added programmers that now allow your business to provide a greater array of computer applications. You and your co-owner decide to raise capital by making a public offering of stock. In preparation for going public, you visit with several of your most valuable clients about investing in your company.

What concerns should you have regarding these conversations?
Is there anything about your expectations of the company's future performance you must or must not share?

3. You and two partners operate a graphics design and printing company. The success of this business relates to the high-quality service and products you provide to your clients. To move to the next level requires a considerable financial investment in computer software and hardware. You and your partners are considering forming a corporation and offering to sell stock to the public. You anticipate raising at least $40 million in new capital. As you ponder these moves, you seek answers to the following questions:

What requirements of the Sarbanes-Oxley Act will you have to meet?
What is involved in offering a new company's stock for sale to the public?
Are there aspects of doing business as a publicly traded company that are different from operating as a partnership?

CHAPTER SIX

Contracts

After completing this chapter, students will be able to:

1. Explain the importance of contracts to a capitalist, free market system.

2. Determine whether the Uniform Commercial Code or common law governs a contract dispute.

3. Identify the elements of a legally enforceable contract.

4. Classify a contract as bilateral or unilateral; express or implied; executory or executed.

5. Distinguish between valid, unenforceable, void, and voidable contracts.

6. Describe the elements of a valid offer.

7. Describe the elements of a valid acceptance.

8. Explain the significance of consideration as an element of a legally enforceable contract.

9. Compare and contrast the rights and duties arising in contractual assignment and delegation.

10. Compare and contrast different types of third-party beneficiaries to a contract.

11. Explain how a contract may be discharged.

12. Describe the remedies available for breach of contract.

Preface: The Role of Contracts in a Complex Society

A capitalist, free market system cannot operate effectively and fairly without a reliable foundation in contract law. At the practical level, all buyers and sellers must have confidence that the deal they are about to make will be completed as specified or that they will have a remedy available if it is not completed. Otherwise, the legal risk in making deals would act as a drag on the commercial process, reducing certainty and depreciating the extraordinary efficiency of the free market. At the philosophical level, the fundamental point of a contract regime is personal freedom. Contract law gives each of us a reliable mechanism for freely expressing our preferences in life. From buying a tube of toothpaste, a car, or a house, to paying tuition, to accepting an employment offer, to franchising a business, to borrowing millions of dollars, to adopting a child, and so on, the direction and value of our lives are shaped and protected to a significant degree by our contractual choices. To a considerable extent, we define ourselves as persons by the contractual choices we make, and contract law protects those choices. The indispensable role of contract law is revealed in the remarkable Facebook story that follows.

Who Owns Facebook?

Mark Zuckerberg, Facebook CEO, developed the fabulously successful social network while still a student at Harvard. At this writing in 2011, however, Zuckerberg's continuing ownership of the company is being challenged on the basis of a document alleged to be a contract signed by Zuckerberg. Paul Ceglia, an entrepreneur and accused felon, has sued Facebook and Zuckerberg claiming that he and Zuckerberg entered into a contract in 2003 that entitles Ceglia to a 50 percent share in the company. A photocopy of the document has been filed with Ceglia's lawsuit. Facebook has said the alleged contract is a forgery, and Zuckerberg has said that he is confident that he never signed any such contract.

Ceglia says the document turned up when he was looking through some old files to find assets to pay customers of his failed wood pellet business, an enterprise that is the subject of fraud charges filed against Ceglia. The document, Ceglia alleges, is a "Work for Hire" contract signed by Zuckerberg when he was an 18-year-old Harvard freshman. The alleged contract shows Ceglia agreeing to pay Zuckerberg $1,000 to write computer code for Street Fax, a company Ceglia was creating. That portion of the deal appears to be unchallenged at this writing. The document also refers to a $1,000 investment by Ceglia in a project repeatedly labeled "The Face Book" or, in one instance, "The Page Book." Ceglia claims a partnership arose from these dealings entitling him to a 50 percent share in Facebook. Ceglia also claims to have e-mail evidence supporting his claim. Facebook has indicated in court that Zuckerberg did sign a contract with Ceglia and did work for Ceglia but did not sign over any interest in Facebook. Indeed, Facebook claims that Zuckerberg could not have transferred a share in Facebook to Ceglia because he did not conceive of the Facebook project until the following year. Facebook presumably will try to establish that the document and the Zuckerberg signature are forgeries and failing that likely will rely on New York's six-year statute of limitations. Of course, if those strategies fail, a settlement could be the eventual resolution of this extraordinary case. [For the alleged Ceglia–Zuckerberg contract, see: "Work for Hire Contract" at **http:// www.businessinsider.com/mark-zuckerbergs-facebook-contract-with-paul-ceglia**]

Zuckerberg received better news on another legal front when a court refused to throw out a 2008 settlement between Zuckerberg and his college business partners, twins Cameron and Tyler Winklevoss. The twins' battle with Zuckerberg over the rights to the Facebook idea was the subject of the 2010 movie, *The Social Network*. The twins claim Zuckerberg stole their social networking idea. Zuckerberg denied that accusation, but the parties reached a settlement of about $65 million in 2008. The twins sued, however, to have the settlement overturned on the grounds that Facebook had not provided accurate valuation information during the settlement process. A court of appeals panel in 2011 rejected the twins' request. They have discontinued the appeals process at this writing.

At the same time, Boston software developer Wayne Chang is suing the Winklevoss twins for breach of contract, among other claims. Chang believes he is entitled to a share of the Winklevoss–Zuckerberg settlement (currently valued at around $160 million) based on a partnership and other understandings he claims to have entered with the twins during their Harvard years to create and operate a social networking site named ConnectU.

[For a Fox News account of Paul Ceglia's contracts-based claim for partial ownership of Facebook, see **www.youtube.com/watch?v=CQ9vDJWAeQQ** or for a humorous, animated overview of the Paul Ceglia–Mark Zuckerberg contracts dispute see **www. wellsvilledaily.com/features/x328920403/VIDEO-Animation-of-Ceglias-Facebook-lawsuit-against-Zuckerberg**]

Sources: Bob Van Voris, "Facebook Claimant Says He Owns 50%, Has E-Mails as Proof," *Bloomberg Businessweek,* April 12, 2011 [**http://www.businessweek.com**]; "Boston Developer Wants Cut of Winklevoss Twins' $65-Million Facebook Settlement," *Los Angeles Times,* May 12, 2011 [**http://latimesblogs.latimes.com/technology/2011/05/boston-developer-wants-cut-of-winklevoss-twins-65-million-facebook-settlement.html**]; Alice Gomstyn and Ki Mae Heussner, "Paul Ceglia: Facebook Claim Stemmed from Arrest," ABC News, August 2, 2010 [**http://abcnews. go.com**]; and Henry Blodget, "Analyzing the Facebook Contract: Is Mark Zuckerberg Screwed?" *Business Insider,* July 23, 2010 [**http://www.businessinsider.com**].

Part One—Building a Binding Contract

Introduction

We make promises as a matter of routine in our lives. Some of those create binding contracts; some do not. You promise, for example, to meet a friend after class, but you break your promise. Have you breached a contract such that you could be sued in court? Doubtless your answer is "no" and, barring unusual circumstances, you would be correct. But why? Thus, the central question in this chapter is the following: Under what circumstances do promises become enforceable contracts? For the most part, the answer to that question has been provided by court decisions (the common law) accumulating over the many centuries of evolving contract law stretching from the ancient Middle East to England and across the Atlantic to America. Those centuries of decisions provided a substantially fair, consistent, and predictable body of contract law; particularly in a culture where the parties normally dealt with each other face-to-face; often as acquaintances. As business transactions became more complicated, the parties more and more distant from each other and the comparative power between individuals and corporations evermore unbalanced, the need for government intervention increased. State legislatures began to impose new rules on what had been purely private transactions. Look, for example, at state and federal regulation of employment contracts/relationships governing working conditions such as hours of work, safety on the job, break time, etc. (as explained in detail in Chapter 12). State laws and court decisions resulted, to some extent, in a confusing, inefficient patchwork of laws that didn't conform to the reality of complex, contemporary business practice. As a result, the states developed the Uniform Commercial Code, a body of rules to govern commercial law across America.

> Have you breached a contract?

The Uniform Commercial Code

The National Conference of Commissioners on Uniform State Laws (NCCUSL) and the American Law Institute (ALI) developed, for state-by-state approval, the Uniform Commercial Code (UCC), a body of rules designed to render commercial law consistent across the 50 states. The UCC has been adopted in 49 states, and Louisiana has adopted portions of it. With a set of uniform, predictable rules, business can be practiced with confidence and minimal legal confusion.

The UCC is divided into a series of articles addressing the multitude of potential problems that arise in complex commercial practice. For our purposes the most important of those articles is Number 2, Sales, which governs all transactions involving the *sale of goods.* Section 2-105 of the UCC defines goods as tangible, movable, things. Hence cars, clothing, appliances, and the like are covered. Real estate, stocks, bonds, money, and so forth are not covered. Nor are contracts for services governed by the UCC. Of course, many transactions involve both goods and services. Characteristically, in determining whether the UCC applies, the courts have asked whether the dominant purpose of the contract is to provide a service or to sell a good. Appendix B, at the back of the text, sets out the complete Article 2.

The first question, then, in contract disputes is whether the UCC or the common law governs the situation. Throughout this chapter, you should remember that the UCC is always controlling (1) if the transaction is addressed by the UCC—that is, it involves a contract for the sale of goods—and (2) if a UCC rule applies to the issue in question. On the other hand, the judge-made, common law of contracts continues to govern transactions (1) not involving the sale of goods or (2) involving the sale of goods but where no specific UCC provision applies. Increasingly, in non-UCC cases, the courts are analogizing to UCC reasoning to render their judgments; that is, the common law is borrowing or absorbing UCC principles. This chapter, while focusing primarily on the common law of contracts, will introduce the role of the sales article in the practice of business. At this writing, NCCUSL/ALI–recommended revisions to the sales article are being considered by the various state legislatures, most of which seem reluctant to make major changes. Article 2A of the UCC governs *leases* of goods. In essence, Article 2A mimics the sales article except that it governs leases of goods rather than sales. Because of space constraints, Article 2A will not receive further attention in this text.

What Is a Contract?

Legally enforceable contracts must exhibit all of the following features:

1. **Agreement**—a meeting of the minds of the parties based on an offer by one and an acceptance by the other. The determination as to whether the parties have actually reached agreement is based on the *objective* evidence (the parties' acts, words, and so on) as a "reasonable person" would interpret it rather than on an effort to ascertain the subjective or personal intent of the parties.

2. **Consideration.** The bargained-for legal value that one party agrees to pay or provide to secure the promise of another.

3. **Capacity.** The parties must have the legal ability to enter the contract; that is, they must be sane, sober, and of legal age.

4. **Genuineness of assent.** The parties must knowingly agree to the same thing. Their minds must meet as evidenced by the objective evidence. If that meeting does not occur

because of mistake, fraud, or the like, a contract does not exist because the parties' assent was not real.

5. **Legality of purpose.** The object of the contract must not violate the law or public policy.

Contracts embracing these five features are enforceable by law and hence are distinguishable from unenforceable promises. As explained later, some contracts must be in writing to be enforceable.

Classification of Contracts

Contracts fall into a series of sometimes overlapping categories. Understanding those categories helps reveal the rather well-ordered logic of our contract system (see Figure 6.1).

Contract Formation

1. **Bilateral and unilateral contracts.** A *bilateral contract* emerges from a situation in which *both* parties make promises. A *unilateral contract* ordinarily involves a situation in which one party makes a promise and the other *acts* in response to that promise. For example, in beginning to establish your new restaurant you promise a college friend that if he completes his degree, you will hire him. He can accept your offer/promise by the act of completing college.

FIGURE 6.1
Classification of Contracts

Contract Formation
1. Bilateral/unilateral
   a. Bilateral contract—a promise for a promise.
   b. Unilateral contract—a promise for an act.
2. Express/implied
   a. Express contract—explicitly stated in writing or orally.
   b. Implied-in-fact contract—inferred from the conduct of the parties.
   c. Quasi-contract—implied contract created by a court to prevent unjust enrichment.

Contract performance
1. Executory contract—not yet fully performed.
2. Executed contract—fully performed by all parties.

Contract enforceability
1. Valid contract—includes all of the necessary ingredients of a binding contract.
2. Unenforceable contract—contract exists, but a legal defense prevents enforcement.
3. Void contract—no contract at all.
4. Voidable contract—one party has the option of either enforcing or voiding the contract.

2. **Express and implied contracts.** When parties overtly and explicitly manifest their intention to enter an agreement, either in writing or orally, the result (if other requirements are fulfilled) is an express contract. For example, in managing your department at an insurance firm, you sign a form contract with a local computer store ordering a new computer. In turn, the supplier's signature on the form creates an express, bilateral agreement.

If, on the other hand, you ask your local computer service to take a look at a machine that is down and one of the service's technicians does so, you have probably entered an *implied-in-fact contract*. A court would infer a promise by you to pay a reasonable price in return for the service's promise to make a commercially reasonable effort to repair the computer. The contract is inferred on the basis of the facts—that is, by the behavior of the parties.

Suppose in managing your insurance department you have received payment for insurance that was, in fact, issued by a rival firm. In these circumstances, it would be unfair for you to be able to keep the unearned money so the courts construct an implied-in-law or quasi-contract permitting the actual insurer to collect the money. This unusual situation in which the court infers the existence of a contract is employed only when necessary to prevent *unjust enrichment* (as would have been the case if you were to collect an insurance premium without having issued a policy).

Contract Performance

1. **Executory contracts.** A contract is labeled *executory* until all parties fully perform.

2. **Executed contracts.** When all parties have completed their performances, the contract is *executed.*

Contract Enforceability

1. **Valid contracts.** A valid contract meets all of the established legal requirements and thus is enforceable in court.

2. **Unenforceable contracts.** An unenforceable contract meets the basic contractual requirements but remains faulty because it fails to fulfill some other legal rule. For example, an oral contract may be unenforceable if it falls in one of those categories of contracts, such as the sale of land, which must be in writing (see the Statute of Frauds later in this chapter).

3. **Void contracts.** A void contract is, in fact, no contract at all because a critical legal requirement is missing; usually it is either an agreement to accomplish an illegal purpose (such as to commit a crime) or an agreement involving an incompetent (such as an individual judged by a court to be insane). In either case what is otherwise an enforceable contract is in fact void.

4. **Voidable contracts.** A voidable contract is enforceable but can be canceled by one or more of the parties. The most common voidable contracts are those entered by minors who have the option, under the law, of either disaffirming or fulfilling most contracts (explained later).

Can I Change My Mind?

Australian Vin Thomas placed his 1946 World War II Wirraway plane for sale on eBay. The plane reportedly is one of only five in the world still flying. Peter Smythe, also of Australia, matched the $128,640 reserve price moments before the online auction ended in 2006. Thomas then declined to convey the airplane to Smythe apparently because Thomas had already agreed to sell the plane to another party for $85,800 more than Smythe's bid. The case involved, among others, a pair of issues frequently arising in contracts law disputes: (1) Did the facts (the eBay auction) create a contract? (2) Can Thomas change his mind about selling the plane to the highest bidder?

Answer those questions according to the U.S. contract law that follows.

The Agreement: Offer

Characteristically, an offer consists of a promise to do something or to refrain from doing something in the future. A valid offer must include all of these elements:

1. Present *intent* to enter a contract.
2. Reasonable *definiteness* in the terms of the offer.
3. *Communication* of the offer to the offeree.

Intent

Assume that you are the purchasing manager for a trucking firm, and you need a small used van to do some local light hauling. Because time is of the essence, you decide to bypass the normal bidding process and go directly to the local dealers to make a quick purchase. At the first lot you find a suitable van. In discussing it, the sales manager says, "Well, we don't usually do this, but since you've been such a good customer, I'll tell you, we paid $10,000 for this one so I guess we are gonna need about $11,000 to deal with you." You say, "Fine. That's reasonable. I'll take it." The manager then says, "Now wait a minute, I was just talking off the top of my head. I'll have to punch up the numbers to be sure."

Do you have a deal at that point? The core question is whether the sales manager made an *offer.* Normally, language of that kind has been treated by the courts as preliminary negotiation lacking the necessary *intent* to constitute an offer. Of course, if no offer exists, you cannot accept, and no contract can emerge absent further negotiation.

Gambling

In 2006, Troy Blackford, a Des Moines, Iowa truck driver, won $9,387 gambling at Prairie Meadows casino. Blackford tried to collect the winnings, but his request was denied by the casino. Officials said that he had been banned from the casino since 1996, and the ban had not been lifted. (In the 1996 episode, Blackford had punched a slot machine and was belligerent with casino security.) Blackford sued the casino.

1. What was the central issue in the case? Explain.
2. Decide the case. Explain.

Source: Blackford v. Prairie Meadows Racetrack & Casino, 778 N.W.2d 184 (Ia. S.Ct. 2010).

> Suppose you were responding to an ad that said, "2007 full-size Ford cargo van, $20,000." Is that ad language an offer such that you can accept by promising to pay $20,000?

Advertisements The question of intent sometimes arises with advertisements. In buying the van for your business, suppose you were responding to an ad that said, "2007 full-size Ford cargo van, $20,000." Is that ad language an offer such that you can accept by promising to pay $20,000? Ordinarily, ads do not constitute offers, but rather are treated by the courts as *invitations to deal.* Were an ad actually treated as an offer, it would put the seller in the commercially impracticable position of being required to provide the advertised product at the advertised price to everyone who sought one, regardless of available supply. Presumably, that open-ended duty was not the seller's intent when issuing the ad. It follows then that the buyer, in responding to an ad, is technically making an offer, with the seller free to accept or decline.

On the other hand, courts have held that some ads do manifest a present intent to make an offer. The critical terms in those ads must be highly specific and complete, leaving nothing open for negotiation.

A Jet Fighter from Pepsi?

A 1995 Pepsico promotion offered merchandise in exchange for points earned by buying Pepsi-Cola. The television ad showed a teenager modeling some of the available merchandise. A Pepsi T-shirt was displayed for 75 points and a leather jacket for 1450 points. At the end of the ad, a U.S. Marine Corps Harrier "jump jet" landed outside a school, and the boy said, "Sure beats the bus." The ad said the jet was redeemable for 7 million points. John D.R. Leonard, at the time a 21-year-old business student in Seattle, Washington, joined five investors in writing a check to Pepsi for $700,008.50 and demanded the 7 million Pepsi points. Pepsi returned the check and said it had no intention of giving Leonard the $24 million jet. Leonard sued. Who wins? Explain.

Source: *John D.R. Leonard v. Pepsico,* 210 F.3d 88 (2d Cir. Ct. App. 2000).

[For a video of the ad, see **http://www.stcl.edu/faculty-dir/ricks/casebook/pepsi1.wmv.** Other versions of the ad can be found at pepsi2 and pepsi3]

Definiteness

Suppose you have completed a management training program for a "big box" retailer. In your first assignment as an assistant manager, your boss asks you to seek bids and make the other arrangements (subject to her approval) to resurface the store's large asphalt parking lot. You secure bids, and the lowest bidder offers to complete the work "later this summer" for $120,000. You briefly explain the offer to your boss, who tells you to take care of all the details. You are busy with other matters and you put off the parking lot project for a couple of weeks. When you get back to the contractor, he says, "Sorry, man, we hadn't heard from you, and we got another deal." Can you hold that contractor to his initial offer?

One of the requirements of a binding offer is that all of its critical terms must be sufficiently clear that a court can determine both the intentions of the parties and their duties. Clearly, in the asphalt case, many critical details—such as precisely when the work would be done, the quality of the surfacing material, its thickness, and the like—had not been established. Consequently, no offer existed. In a contract for the sale of goods, UCC 2-204 relaxes the definiteness standard by providing that "one or more terms" may be missing but the court can find a contract, nonetheless, where (1) "the parties have intended to make a contract" and (2) "there is a reasonably certain basis for giving an appropriate remedy." Under the UCC, the courts can actually fill in missing terms such as specifying a reasonable price where the contract had omitted a stipulation. The following case involving Mariah Carey, the pop music star, demonstrates some of the problems that can arise when an understanding is indefinite.

LEGAL BRIEFCASE

Vian v. Carey   1993 U.S. Dist.
Lexis 5460 (U.S. Dist. Ct. S.D.N.Y. 1993)

Judge Mukasey

Defendant Mariah Carey is a famous, successful and apparently wealthy entertainer. Plaintiff Joseph Vian was her stepfather before she achieved stardom, but at the start of this litigation was in the process of becoming divorced from defendant's mother. He claims defendant agreed orally that he would have a license to market singing dolls in her likeness. . . . Plaintiff claims that he and Carey had an oral contract for him to receive a license to market "Mariah dolls." These dolls would be statuettes of the singer and would play her most popular songs. Plaintiff claims that the contract was in consideration of his financial and emotional support of defendant, including picking her up from late-night recording sessions, providing her with the use of a car, paying for dental care, allowing her to use his boat for business meetings and rehearsals, and giving her various items, including unused wedding gifts from his marriage to her mother, to help furnish her apartment.

The alleged basis of the oral contract is that on at least three occasions, twice in the family car and once on Vian's boat, Vian told Carey, "Don't forget the Mariah dolls," and "I get the Mariah dolls." According to Vian, on one occasion Carey responded "okay" and on other occasions she merely smiled and nodded. Although Carey admits Vian mentioned the dolls two or three times, she testified that she thought it was a joke. For 30 years plaintiff has been in the business of designing, producing, and marketing gift and novelty items. Although it is not clear from the evidence the parties have submitted, it will be assumed that the alleged contract was formed after defendant turned 18. Under New York law, an oral agreement can form a binding contract. . . . In determining whether a contract exists, what matters are the parties' expressed intentions, the words and deeds that constitute objective signs in a given set of circumstances.

Therefore, the issue is whether the objective circumstances indicate that the parties intended to form a contract. Without such an intent, neither a contract nor a preliminary agreement to negotiate in good faith can exist. In making such a determination, a court may look at "whether the terms of the contract have been finally resolved." In addition, a court may consider "the context of the negotiations." Plaintiff has adduced no evidence that defendant ever intended by a nod of her head or the expression "okay" to enter into a complex commercial licensing agreement involving dolls in her likeness playing her copyrighted songs. The context in which this contract between an 18-year-old girl and her stepfather allegedly was made was an informal family setting, either in the car or on plaintiff's boat, while others were present. Vian's own version of events leads to the conclusion that there was no reason for Carey to think Vian was entirely serious, let alone that he intended to bind her to an agreement at that time. He admits he never told her he was serious. The objective circumstances do not indicate that Carey intended to form a contract with plaintiff. Although plaintiff's five-page memorandum of law fails to raise the possibility, plaintiff also has not shown that Carey intended to be bound to negotiate with plaintiff at some later date over the licensing of "Mariah dolls."

There can be no meeting of the minds, required for the formation of a contract, where essential material terms are missing. Thus, even if the parties both believe themselves to be bound, there is no contract when "the terms of the agreement are so vague and indefinite that there is no basis or standard for deciding whether the agreement had been kept or broken, or to fashion a remedy, and no means by which such terms may be made certain."

. . . The word "license" was not even used. As defendant points out, no price or royalty term was mentioned, nor was the duration or geographic scope of the license, nor was Carey's right to approve the dolls. Plaintiff admits he would not have gone ahead without defendant's approval, thus conceding the materiality of that term.

* * * * *

In sum, plaintiff has not raised a triable issue of fact as to the existence of a contract. Defendant's motion for summary judgment is granted.

Questions

1. Why did the court find for Carey?

2. As noted in the text, in UCC cases judges fill in contract terms where the parties clearly intended a deal. Should the court here fill in the missing terms to provide the necessary definiteness? Explain.

3. Pilgrim Village Company had employed Petersen as a construction manager at a specified annual salary and "a share of the profits." Petersen worked at salary for several years and then asked for a 10 percent share of the profits. The company refused, and Petersen sued seeking "some share of the profits." How should the court rule on Petersen's claim? Explain. See *Petersen v. Pilgrim Village,* 42 N.W.2d 273 (Wis. S.Ct., 1950).

Communication

As explained, an effective offer must be the product of a present intent, it must be definite, and it must be communicated to the offeree. Communication of an offer expresses the offeror's intent to make that offer. Suppose a friend tells you that your neighbor has offered to sell his classic jukebox for $10,000. You call your neighbor and say, "I accept. I'll be right over with the $10,000." Do you have a deal? No. The owner did not communicate the offer to you. The fact that it was not communicated to you may suggest that your neighbor does not want to sell or does not want to sell to you.

Duration of an Offer   Communication of an offer affords the offeree the opportunity to create a contract by accepting that offer, but how long does that opportunity last? Here are some general rules:

1. The offeror may revoke the offer anytime prior to acceptance. (Some exceptions are explained later.) Normally, revocation is effective on receipt by the offeree. Under common law the offeror has the right to revoke at any time prior to acceptance, even if he or she expressly promised to keep the offer open for a specified period.
2. The offer may specify that it is open for an express period (such as 10 days).
3. Where a time limit is not specified in the offer it will be presumed to be open for a reasonable period.
4. An offer expires if rejected or on receipt of a counteroffer.

Irrevocable Offers

Some kinds of offers may not be revoked. We will note three of them.

1. **Option contracts.** When an offeror promises to keep an offer open for a specified period and, in return, the offeree pays consideration (usually money), the parties have created an option contract, which is a separate agreement and is enforceable by its terms. For example, a friend has offered to sell to you his customized car that you have long cherished, but you want to think about it for a few days. You might enter an option contract with your friend under which you pay $100 for the seller's promise to keep the offer open for seven days. You are under no obligation to buy the car, but the seller is under a binding obligation not to withdraw the offer or sell to another during the seven days.
2. **Firm offers.** Under the UCC, if the owner of that customized car is a dealer (a merchant) and he made a written, signed offer to sell that car (a good) to you, indicating that his offer would remain open for seven days, he is bound to that promise whether you paid consideration for it or not. That situation is labeled a firm offer as specified in UCC 2-205, which also provides that such offers will be kept open for a reasonable period if the agreement does not mention a time, but that period cannot exceed three months.
3. **Offers for unilateral contracts.** A problem sometimes arises when the offeror attempts to revoke a unilateral offer after the offeree has begun to perform. For example, your neighbor invites you to rake her leaves for $10, and then, when you are virtually done, she yells from the doorway, "Oh, sorry, I changed my mind. You go home now." Historically, the offeror (the neighbor, in this case) was free to revoke at any time; but the modern position holds that the offeror normally cannot revoke if the offeree (you) has commenced performance. If that performance is then completed (you ignore your

neighbor's admonition to go home, and you finish the raking), the offeror (your neighbor) is bound to perform fully is bound to perform fully by paying the $10.

The Agreement: Acceptance

Suppose you are in training with a large real estate firm and your boss has authorized you to enter negotiations to buy a parcel of farmland that your company hopes to develop for housing. After preliminary discussions, you extend a written offer to the owner indicating, among other terms, that your company is willing to pay $10,000 per acre for a 10-acre parcel. Assume the owner responds by writing, "I accept your offer at $10,000 per acre, but I need to keep the two-acre homesite." The offeree has used the word *accept,* but does the response constitute a legally binding *acceptance?*

The general rule is that an effective acceptance must be a mirror image of the offer; that is, ordinarily its terms must be the same as those in the offer. Here the offeree has changed the terms of the offer and in so doing has issued a *counteroffer,* thus extinguishing the original offer.

Communication of Acceptance

An offer may be accepted only by the offeree—that is, the person to whom the offer was directed. Because unilateral offers are accepted by performance, no communication of acceptance beyond that performance ordinarily is necessary. In the case of a bilateral contract (a promise for a promise), acceptance is not effective until communicated.

Broadly, acceptance can be accomplished by a "yes" communicated face-to-face, by a nod of the head or some other appropriate signal, by telephone, or by other unwritten means, unless the law of the state requires writing in that particular kind of transaction.

Mailbox   Confusion sometimes arises when the parties are not dealing face-to-face. In general, acceptance is effective upon dispatch by whatever mode of communication has been explicitly or implicitly authorized by the offeror. This well-settled position is labeled the *mailbox rule* and means, among other things, that an acceptance is effective when sent even if never received. [For one professor's review of the mailbox rule and related rules, see **http://www.tomwbell.com/teaching/KMailbox.pdf**]

Authorization   The offeror controls the acceptance process and may specify an exclusive manner in which an acceptance must be communicated. If so, a contract is not created if the acceptance is communicated in anything other than the stipulated fashion. Traditionally, if the offeror did not give an *express authorization* to a means of communication, an acceptance by the same or faster means than that used by the offeror was implied. *Implied authorization* might also arise from such factors as prior dealings between the parties and custom in their industry.

Modern View   Under the UCC the rules have relaxed a bit. If no specific instructions for acceptance are included in the offer, the offeree is free to accept in any reasonable manner within a reasonable period, and acceptance is effective upon dispatch. Even when the means chosen are "unreasonable," acceptance is effective on dispatch under the UCC 1-201(38) if it is actually received in a timely manner.

Consideration

Earlier we identified the five key ingredients in an enforceable contract: agreement, consideration, capacity, genuineness of assent, and legality of purpose. Having examined the agreement (offer/acceptance) process, we turn now to consideration. As noted earlier, consideration is the bargained-for legal value that one party agrees to pay or provide to secure the promise of another. It is what the promisor demands and receives in exchange for his or her promise. Consideration is used by the courts to distinguish a contract (enforceable) from a gratuitous promise (unenforceable). The *promisee* must suffer a *legal detriment;* that is, the promisee must give up something of value (an act or a promise) or must refrain from doing something that she or he has a legal right to do in order to enforce the promise offered by the *promisor.* Each party, then, must pay a "price" for a contract to be enforceable. In sum, consideration consists of a detriment to the promisee that is bargained for by the promisor.

The classic case that follows explores the idea of consideration and demonstrates that consideration can have legal value without involving monetary loss to the promisee.

LEGAL BRIEFCASE

Hamer v. Sidway
27 N.E. 256 (N.Y. 1891)

FACTS

In 1869 William E. Story Sr. promised his nephew, W.E. Story II, that he would pay the nephew $5,000 upon his 21st birthday if the nephew would refrain from drinking liquor, using tobacco, swearing, and playing cards or billiards for money until he reached that 21st birthday. The nephew agreed and performed his promise, but the uncle died in 1887 without paying the money, and the administrator of the estate, Sidway, declined to pay the $5,000 plus interest. The nephew had assigned (sold) his rights to the money to Louisa Hamer, who sued W.E. Story Sr.'s estate. Hamer, the plaintiff, won at the trial level, lost on appeal, and then appealed to the New York Court of Appeals.

* * * * *

Judge Parker

When the nephew arrived at the age of 21 years and on the 31st day of January 1875, he wrote to his uncle informing him that he had performed his part of the agreement and had thereby become entitled to the sum of $5,000. The uncle received the letter and a few days later and on the sixth of February, he wrote and mailed to his nephew the following letter:

Buffalo, February 6, 1875
W.E. Story, Jr.
Dear Nephew:
Your letter of the 31st came to hand all right, saying that you had lived up to the promise made to me several years ago. I have no doubt but you have, for which you shall have five thousand dollars as I promised you. I had the money in the bank the day you was 21 years old that I intend for you, and you shall have the money certain. Now, Willie I do not intend to interfere with this money in any way till I think you are capable of taking care of it and the sooner that time comes the better it will please me. I would hate very much to have you start out in some adventure that you thought all right and lose this money in one year. The first five thousand dollars that I got together cost me a heap of hard work. You would hardly believe me when I tell you that to obtain this I shoved a jackplane many a day, butchered three or four years, then came to this city, and after three months' perseverance I obtained a situation in a grocery store. I opened this store early, closed late, slept in the fourth story of the building in a room 30 by 40 feet and not a human

being in the building but myself. All this I done to live as cheap as I could to save something. I don't want you to take up with this kind of fare. I was here in the cholera season '49 and '52 and the deaths averaged 80 to 125 daily and plenty of smallpox. I wanted to go home, but Mr. Fisk, the gentleman I was working for, told me if I left then, after it got healthy he probably would not want me. I stayed. All the money I have saved I know just how I got it. It did not come to me in any mysterious way, and the reason I speak of this is that money got in this way stops longer with a fellow that gets it with hard knocks than it does when he finds it. Willie, you are 21 and you have many a thing to learn yet. This money you have earned much easier than I did besides acquiring good habits at the same time and you are quite welcome to the money; hope you will make good use of it. I was 10 long years getting this together after I was your age. Now, hoping this will be satisfactory, I stop . . .
Truly Yours,
W.E. STORY
P.S.—You can consider this money on interest.

The nephew received the letter and thereafter consented that the money should remain with his uncle in accordance with the terms and conditions of the letter. The uncle died on the 29th day of January 1887, without having paid over to his nephew any portion of the said $5,000 and interest.

* * * * *

The defendant contends that the contract was without consideration to support it, and, therefore, invalid. He asserts that the promisee by refraining from the use of liquor and tobacco was not harmed but benefited; that that which he did was best for him to do independently of his uncle's promise, and insists that it follows that unless the promisor was benefited, the contract was without consideration. A contention, which if well founded, would seem to leave open for controversy in many cases whether that which the promisee did or omitted to do was, in fact, of such benefit to him as to leave no consideration to support the enforcement of the promisor's agreement. Such a rule could not be tolerated, and is without foundation in the law.

* * * * *

"In general a waiver of any legal right at the request of another party is a sufficient consideration for a promise" (Parsons on Contracts).

Pollock, in his work on contracts, says, ". . . Consideration means not so much that one party is profiting as that the other abandons some legal right in the present or limits his legal freedom of action in the future as an inducement for the promise of the first."

Now, applying this rule to the facts before us, the promisee used tobacco, occasionally drank liquor, and had a legal right to do so. That right he abandoned for a period of years upon the strength of the promise of the testator that for such forbearance he would give him $5,000. We need not speculate on the effort which may have been required to give up the use of those stimulants. It is sufficient that he restricted his lawful freedom of action within certain prescribed limits upon the faith of his uncle's agreement, and now having fully performed the conditions imposed, it is of no moment whether such performance actually proved a benefit to the promisor, and the court will not inquire into it, but were it a proper subject of inquiry, we see nothing in this record that would permit a determination that the uncle was not benefited in a legal sense.

* * * * *

Reversed.

Questions

1. *a.* What detriment, if any, was sustained by the nephew?
   b. What benefit, if any, was secured by the uncle?
   c. As a matter of law, do we need to inquire into the uncle's benefit? Explain.

2. Lampley began work as an at-will (can be dismissed or can quit at any time) employee of Celebrity Homes in Denver, Colorado, in May 1975. On July 29, 1975, Celebrity announced a profit-sharing plan for all employees if the company reached its goals for the fiscal year, April 1,1975, to March 31, 1976. Lampley was dismissed in January 1976. Celebrity distributed its profits in May 1976. Lampley sued when she did not receive a share of the profits. Celebrity argued that its promise to share its profits was a gratuity, unsupported by consideration. Decide. Explain. See *Lampley v. Celebrity Homes*, 594 P.2d 605 (Col. Ct. App. 1979).

3. An accident in the early 1960s rendered Hoffman paraplegic. At Hoffman's invitation, Thomas lived with and provided extensive physical care for Hoffman until Hoffman's death in 2004. Thomas did not pay rent and Hoffman paid for Thomas' food, provided her with a car and cell phone and made occasional cash payments to Thomas. While never married, the couple exchanged rings in 2002 and Thomas testified that she felt they "lived as man and wife." Thomas filed suit seeking $44,625 for services rendered to Hoffman. According to the trial court, her claim was based on the theories of "express or implied contract of employment" or "unjust enrichment." Thomas lost at the trial level. How would you rule on appeal? Explain. See *In Re Estate of Hoffman*, 2006 Ia. App. LEXIS 473. [For a detailed analysis of *Hamer v. Sidway*, see **http://www.law.smu.edu/firstday/contracts/case.htm**]

Adequacy of Consideration

With certain exceptions, the courts do not, as Judge Parker indicated in the *Hamer* case, inquire into the economic value of the consideration in question. Legal sufficiency depends not on the value of the consideration but on whether the promisee suffered a detriment in some way. To hold otherwise would put the courts in the place of the market in deciding the value of transactions. We are all free to make both good and bad bargains.

On the other hand, the courts will rule that consideration is found wanting in situations of pretense or sham where the parties have clearly agreed on token or nominal consideration in an effort to present the transaction as a contract rather than a gift. Likewise, an extreme inadequacy of consideration will sometimes cause the court to question a contract on the grounds of *fraud, duress, or unconscionability* (all are discussed later in this chapter). In these instances, the agreements would be unenforceable because of a failure of consideration. These cases are uncommon, however, and the courts rarely inquire into the adequacy of consideration.

Appearance of Consideration

Some agreements appear to be accompanied by consideration, but in fact, that appearance turns out to be an illusion. Hence, if one agrees to perform a preexisting duty, consideration would be found wanting. For example, if you were to pay your neighbor $50 to keep his dog chained when outdoors and a city ordinance already requires dogs to be chained if outdoors, your promise would be unenforceable because your neighbor already had a pre-existing duty under the law to keep his dog chained. So performance of a preexisting legal duty does not constitute consideration because no legal detriment or benefit has arisen.

Similarly, preexisting duties sometimes arise from contracts. Suppose you hire a contractor to resurface the parking lot at your real estate office. You agree on a price of $12,000. With a portion of the work completed, the contractor asks you to amend the agreement to add $2,000 because the project is requiring more time than anticipated. You agree. The work is completed. Could you then legally refuse to pay the additional $2,000? The answer is yes because the contractor failed to provide consideration for the modification of your contract. He was under a preexisting duty to finish the contract; hence he did not sustain a legal detriment in the modified agreement. Note, however, that UCC section 2-209(1) provides that "an agreement modifying a contract within this Article needs no consideration to be binding."

Suppose you learn from your neighbor that your friend Ames wants to sell his house. You, as a realtor, find a buyer for the house and make all of the necessary arrangements for the sale out of regard for your friendship with Ames. Then when the transaction is complete, Ames says, "Well, this has been great of you, but I don't feel right about it. When I get my check for the sale, I'll pay you $2,000 for your hard work. I really appreciate it." What if Ames does not then pay the $2,000? Do you have recourse? No. This is a situation of *past consideration,* where the performance—arranging the sale of your friend's house—was not bargained for and was not given in exchange for the promise and thus cannot constitute consideration. In effect, the performance was a gift. Of course, past consideration is really not consideration at all. In some states, courts enforce promises to pay for benefits already received where doing so amounts to a moral obligation that must be enforced to prevent injustice.

Substitutes for Consideration

When necessary to achieve justice, the courts sometimes conclude that a contract exists even though consideration is clearly lacking. Moral obligation and quasi contract (discussed earlier) are two such instances; but the most prominent of these substitutes for consideration is the doctrine of *promissory estoppel,* in which the promisor is "stopped" from denying the existence of a contract where the promisee has detrimentally relied on that promise. Promissory estoppel requires the following:

1. A promise on which the promisor should expect the promisee to rely.
2. The promisee did justifiably rely on the promise.
3. Injustice can be avoided only by enforcing the promise.

Consider the following. You have been a part-time employee of a small fast-food chain restaurant while attending college. Upon graduation, you tell the manager of the restaurant that you think you could handle your own franchise. He says you need to get more experience and advises you to take a full-time position with the company. You do so. Everything goes well, and when you next approach the manager, he says, "If you can come up with the $50,000 and a good location, we will get you in a franchise right away. But you've gotta move on this. Maybe you better quit your job with us and concentrate on this thing." You take his advice and quit your job. You raise the $50,000 and find a vacant building to rent in a good location for a franchise. You show the building to the manager, and he agrees that it looks like a favorable location and one that can easily be converted to the company's needs. He says, "Looks like you have everything in place. If you can come up with $50,000 more we will make this thing happen." You refuse and decide to bring suit against the fast-food chain for breach of contract. The chain defends by saying that you did not provide consideration for its promise. No formal financing arrangement was ever agreed to, and you had not committed yourself to any franchising obligations. Under these circumstances you may well prevail using a promissory estoppel claim. In brief, you would argue that you had changed your position in reliance on the franchisor's promises and that relief is necessary to prevent injustice. [For a similar case see *Hoffman v. Red Owl Stores,* 133 N.W.2d 267 (Wis. S.Ct. 1965).]

Capacity

Having examined two of the required ingredients in an enforceable contract, agreement and consideration, we turn now to a third, capacity to contract. To enter a binding agreement, one must have the legal ability to do so; that is, one's mental condition and maturity must be such that the agreement was entered with understanding and in recognition of one's own interests. The three primary areas of concern are intoxication, mental impairment, and minority (infancy/youthfulness), with minority being much the more common area of dispute.

> The three primary areas of concern are intoxication, mental impairment, and minority.

Intoxication

Assume you have been drinking to celebrate your 21st birthday. You enter a contract with a friend to sell him your autographed Michael Jordan basketball card for $200. You receive the money and turn over the card. Later, when sober, you regret the deal. Will a court nullify that contract on the grounds of your intoxication? That decision depends on whether you were sufficiently intoxicated that you did not understand the nature and purpose of the contract. If the objective evidence suggests that you did not understand the transaction, the contract would be considered voidable, in which case you could probably disaffirm the contract and demand the return of the card, although courts are often not sympathetic with people who attempt to escape contracts made while intoxicated. In most states, if you recovered the card, you would be required to return the $200 to your friend.

If on recovering your sobriety, your friend argued that the contract was invalid because of your intoxication, and he demanded the return of his $200 in exchange for the card, you could then *ratify* (affirm) the contract and hold him to it. If the contract had been for one of life's *necessaries* (food, shelter, clothing, medical care, tools of one's trade, or the like), you would have been liable for the reasonable value of that necessary.

Mental Incompetence

In most cases an agreement involving a mentally incompetent person is either *void or voidable*. The transaction would be void—that is, no contract would exist—where the impaired party had been *adjudged* insane. If the impaired party was unable to understand the purpose and effect of the contract but had not been legally adjudged insane, the contract would be voidable (void in some states) at the option of the impaired party. The competent party cannot void the contract, and the impaired party would have to pay the reasonable value of any necessaries received under the contract.

Minority

Minors may complete their contracts if they wish, but they also have an absolute right to rescind most of those contracts. They may rescind until they reach adulthood and for a reasonable time thereafter. (Many states have enacted statutes forbidding minors from disaffirming some classes of contracts such as those for marriage, student loans, and life insurance.) The minor has a right of recovery for everything given up in meeting the terms of the contract. Similarly, the minor must return everything that remains in her or his possession that was received from the contract. In many states, if nothing of the bargained-for consideration remains or if its value has been depreciated, the minor has no duty to replace it but can still recover whatever she or he put into the contract. If not disaffirmed in a reasonable time after the minor reaches the age of majority, the contract is considered to be ratified, and the minor is bound to its terms. The minor is also liable for the reasonable value (not necessarily the contract price) of necessaries purchased from an adult. That is, a minor must pay the adult the reasonable value of contracted-for items such as food, clothing, shelter, medical care, basic education, and tools of the minor's trade.

> Minors may complete their contracts if they wish, but they also have an absolute right to rescind most of those contracts.

Despite the flexibility accorded to minors entering contracts, the adults who are parties to those contracts are bound to them and do not have the power to disaffirm. Hence, adults put themselves at risk when they choose to bargain with minors. As noted, in many states a minor need not make restitution if the consideration is lost, destroyed, or depreciated. On the other hand, the case that follows illustrates the growing view that minors do have some monetary obligation after disaffirming a contract.

LEGAL BRIEFCASE

Dodson v. Shrader
824 S.W.2d 545 (Tenn. S.Ct. 1992)

Justice O'Brien

In early April of 1987, Joseph Eugene Dodson, then 16 years of age, purchased a used 1984 pickup truck from Burns and Mary Shrader. The Shraders owned and operated Shrader's Auto Sales in Columbia, Tennessee. Dodson paid $4,900 in cash for the truck, using money he borrowed from his girlfriend's grandmother. At the time of the purchase there was no inquiry by the Shraders, and no misrepresentation by Dodson, concerning his minority. However, Shrader did testify that at the time he believed Dodson to be 18 or 19 years of age.

In December 1987, nine months after the date of purchase, the truck began to develop mechanical problems. A mechanic diagnosed the problem as a burnt valve, but could not be certain without inspecting the valves inside the engine. Dodson did not want, or did not have the money, to effect these repairs. He continued to drive the truck despite the mechanical problems. One month later, in January, the truck's engine "blew up" and the truck became inoperable.

Dodson parked the vehicle in the front yard at his parents' home, where he lived. He contacted the Shraders to rescind the purchase of the truck and requested a full refund. The Shraders refused to accept the tender of the truck or to give Dodson the refund requested.

Dodson then [sued] to rescind the contract and recover the amount paid for the truck. Before the circuit court could hear the case, the truck, while parked in Dodson's front yard, was struck on the left front fender by a hit-and-run driver. At the time of the circuit court trial, according to Shrader, the truck was worth only $500 due to the damage to the engine and the left front fender.

The case was heard in the circuit court in November 1988. The trial judge, based on previous common-law decisions, and under the doctrine of stare decisis, reluctantly granted the rescission. The Shraders were ordered, upon tender and delivery of the truck, to reimburse the $4,900 purchase price to Dodson. The Shraders appealed.

[T]he rule in Tennessee is in accord with the majority rule on the issue among our sister states. This rule is based on the underlying purpose of the "infancy doctrine," which is to protect minors from their lack of judgment and "from squandering their wealth through improvident contracts with crafty adults who would take advantage of them in the marketplace."

There is, however, a modern trend among the states, either by judicial action or by statute, in the approach to the problem of balancing the rights of minors against those of innocent merchants. As a result, two minority rules have developed that allow the other party to a contract with a minor to refund less than the full consideration paid in the event of rescission.

The first of these minority rules is called the "Benefit Rule." The rule holds that, upon rescission, recovery of the full purchase price is subject to a deduction for the minor's use of the merchandise. This rule recognizes that the traditional rule in regard to necessaries has been extended so far as to hold an infant bound by his contracts, where he failed to restore what he has received under them to the extent of the benefit actually derived by him from what he has received from the other party to the transaction.

The other minority rule holds that the minor's recovery of the full purchase price is subject to a deduction for the minor's "use" of the consideration he or she received under the contract, or for the "depreciation" or "deterioration" of the consideration in his or her possession.

We are impressed by the statement made by the Court of Appeals of Ohio:

> At a time when we see young persons between 18 and 21 years of age demanding and assuming more responsibilities in their daily lives; when we see such persons emancipated, married, and raising families; when we see such persons charged with the responsibility for committing crimes; when we see such persons being sued in tort claims for acts of negligence; when we see such persons subject to military service; when we see such persons engaged in business and acting in almost all other respects as an adult, it seems timely to reexamine the case law pertaining to contractual rights and responsibilities of infants to see if the law as pronounced and applied by the courts should be redefined.

* * * * *

We state the rule to be followed hereafter, in reference to a contract of a minor, to be where the minor has not been overreached in any way, and there has been no undue influence, and the contract is a fair and reasonable one, and the minor has actually paid money on the purchase price, and taken and used the article purchased; that he ought not be permitted to recover the amount actually paid, without allowing the vendor of the goods reasonable compensation for the use of, depreciation, and willful or negligent damage to the article purchased, while in his hands. If there has been any fraud or imposition on the part of the seller or if the contract is unfair, or any unfair advantage has been taken of the minor inducing him to make the purchase, then the rule does not apply. Whether there has been such an overreaching on the part of the seller, and the fair market value of the property returned, would always, in any case, be a question for the trier of fact. . . .

This rule is best adapted to modern conditions under which minors are permitted to, and do in fact, transact a great deal of business for themselves, long before they have reached the age of legal majority. Many young people work and earn money and collect it and spend it oftentimes without any oversight or restriction. The law does not question their right to buy if they have the money to pay for their purchases. It seems intolerably burdensome for everyone concerned if merchants and businesspeople cannot deal with them safely, in a fair and reasonable way.

* * * * *

We note that in this case, some nine months after the date of purchase, the truck purchased by the plaintiff began to develop mechanical problems. Plaintiff was informed of the probable nature of the difficulty, which apparently involved internal problems in the engine. He continued to drive the vehicle until the engine "blew up" and the truck became inoperable. Whether or not this involved gross negligence or intentional conduct on his part is a matter for determination at the trial level. It is not possible to determine from this record whether a counterclaim for tortious damage to the vehicle was asserted. After the first tender of the vehicle was made by plaintiff, and refused by the defendant, the truck was damaged by a hit-and-run driver while parked on plaintiff's property. The amount of that damage and the liability for that amount between the purchaser and the vendor, as well as the fair

market value of the vehicle at the time of tender, is also an issue for the jury.

[Reversed and remanded.]

Questions

1. What was the issue in this case?

2. Distinguish the two minority rules that are summarized in this case.

3. To achieve justice in contract cases involving a minor and an adult, what would you want to know about the adult's behavior toward the minor?

4. White, a 17-year-old high school sophomore, operated a trucking business, including hiring drivers, securing jobs, and so forth. He lived with his parents and received his food, clothing, and shelter from them. Valencia operated a garage and repaired White's equipment until they had a disagreement over replacement of a motor. White then disaffirmed his contract with Valencia and refused to pay what he owed. At trial the jury found that White had caused the damage to the motor, but the court held that White could disaffirm the contract and required Valencia to refund any money paid to White under the contract. Valencia appealed.

    a. Is the fact that White was in business for himself in any way relevant to the outcome of this case? Explain.

    b. Decide the case. Explain. See *Valencia v. White,* 654 P.2d 287 (Ariz. Ct. App. 1982).

Genuineness of Assent

Sometimes parties appear to have concluded a binding contract, but the courts will allow them to escape that obligation because they had not, in fact, achieved an agreement. They had achieved the appearance of agreement, but not the reality. That situation arises when the contract is the product of misrepresentation, fraud, duress, undue influence, or mistake. Ordinarily, such agreements are voidable and may be rescinded by the innocent party because of the absence of genuine assent, the fourth of five ingredients in a binding contract.

Misrepresentation and Fraud

An innocent untruth is a misrepresentation. Intentional untruths constitute fraud. In either case, a party to a contract who has been deceived may rescind the deal, and restitution may be secured if benefits were extended to the party issuing the untruth. The test for fraud is as follows:

1. Misrepresentation of a material fact.

2. The misrepresentation was intentional.

3. The injured party justifiably relied on the misrepresentation.

4. Injury resulted.

Note that the test requires a misrepresented fact. In general, misrepresented opinions are not grounds for action; but many courts are now recognizing exceptions to that rule, especially when the innocent party has relied on opinion coming from an expert.

> You are selling a house that allegedly is "haunted."

If you are selling a house that allegedly is "haunted," does your failure to reveal the ghostly presence constitute a misrepresentation? The *Stambovsky* case that follows addresses that unusual question.

LEGAL BRIEFCASE

Stambovsky v. Ackley et al.
169 A.D.2d 254 (S.Ct. N.Y., App. Div., 1st Dept. 1991)

Justice Rubin

Plaintiff, to his horror, discovered that the house he had recently contracted to purchase was widely reputed to be possessed by poltergeists, reportedly seen by defendant seller and members of her family on numerous occasions over the last nine years. Plaintiff promptly commenced this action seeking rescission of the contract of sale.

The unusual facts of this case clearly warrant a grant of equitable relief to the buyer who, as a resident of New York City, cannot be expected to have any familiarity with the folklore of the Village of Nyack. Not being a "local," plaintiff could not readily learn that the home he had contracted to purchase is haunted. Whether the source of the spectral apparitions seen by defendant seller are parapsychic or psychogenic, having reported their presence in both a national publication (*Readers' Digest*) and the local press (in 1977 and 1982, respectively), defendant is estopped to deny their existence and, as a matter of law, the house is haunted. More to the point, however, no divination is required to conclude that it is defendant's promotional efforts in publicizing her close encounters with these spirits which fostered the home's reputation in the community. In 1989, the house was included in a five-home walking tour of Nyack and described in a November 27th newspaper article as "a riverfront Victorian (with ghost)." The impact of the reputation thus created goes to the very essence of the bargain between the parties, greatly impairing both the value of the property and its potential for resale. . . .

While I agree that the real estate broker, as agent for the seller, is under no duty to disclose to a potential buyer the phantasmal reputation of the premises and that, in his pursuit of a legal remedy for fraudulent misrepresentation against the seller, plaintiff hasn't a ghost of a chance, I am nevertheless moved by the spirit of equity to allow the buyer to seek rescission of the contract of sale and recovery of his down payment.

New York law fails to recognize any remedy for damages incurred as a result of the seller's mere silence, applying instead the strict rule of caveat emptor. Therefore, the theoretical basis for granting relief, even under the extraordinary facts of this case, is elusive if not ephemeral.

From the perspective of a person in the position of plaintiff herein, a very practical problem arises with respect to the discovery of a paranormal phenomenon: "Who you gonna' call?" as a title song to the movie "Ghostbusters" asks. Applying the strict rule of caveat emptor to a contract involving a house possessed by poltergeists conjures up visions of a psychic or medium routinely accompanying the structural engineer and Terminix man on an inspection of every home subject to a contract of sale. It portends that the prudent attorney will establish an escrow account lest the subject of the transaction come back to haunt him and his client—or pray that his malpractice insurance coverage extends to supernatural disasters. In the interest of avoiding such untenable consequences, the notion that a haunting is a condition which can and should be ascertained upon reasonable inspection of the premises is a hobgoblin which should be exorcised from the body of legal precedent and laid quietly to rest.

It has been suggested by a leading authority that the ancient rule which holds that mere nondisclosure does not constitute actionable misrepresentation "finds proper application in cases where the fact undisclosed is patent, or the plaintiff has equal opportunities for obtaining information which he may be expected to utilize, or the defendant has no reason to think that he is acting under any misapprehension" (Prosser, Torts Section 106, at 696 [4th ed 1971]). However, with respect to transactions in real estate, New York adheres to the doctrine of caveat emptor and imposes no duty upon the vendor to disclose any information concerning the premises unless there is a confidential or fiduciary relationship between the parties or some conduct on the part of the seller which constitutes "active concealment."

Normally, some affirmative misrepresentation or partial disclosure is required to impose upon the seller a duty to communicate undisclosed conditions affecting the premises.

Common law is not moribund. . . . Where fairness and common sense dictate that an exception should be created, the evolution of the law should not be stifled by rigid application of a legal maxim.

The doctrine of caveat emptor requires that a buyer act prudently to assess the fitness and value of his purchase and operates to bar the purchaser who fails to exercise due care from seeking the equitable remedy of rescission. For the purposes of the instant motion to dismiss the action . . . plaintiff is entitled to every favorable inference which may reasonably be drawn from the pleadings, specifically, in this instance, that he met his obligation to conduct an inspection of the premises and a search of available public records with respect to title. It should be apparent, however, that the most meticulous inspection and the search would not reveal the presence of poltergeists at the premises or unearth the property's ghoulish reputation in the community. Therefore, there is no sound policy reason to deny plaintiff relief for failing to discover a state of affairs which the most prudent purchaser would not be expected to even contemplate.

*   *   *   *   *

Where a condition which has been created by the seller materially impairs the value of the contract and is peculiarly within the knowledge of the seller or unlikely to be discovered by a prudent purchaser exercising due care with respect to the subject transaction, nondisclosure constitutes a basis for rescission as a matter of equity. Any other outcome places upon the buyer not merely the obligation to exercise care in his purchase but rather to be omniscient with respect to any fact which may affect the bargain. No practical purpose is served by imposing such a burden upon a purchaser. To the contrary, it encourages predatory business practice. . . .

*   *   *   *   *

In the case at bar, defendant seller deliberately fostered the public belief that her home was possessed. Having undertaken to inform the public-at-large, to whom she has no legal relationship, about the supernatural occurrences on her property, she may be said to owe no less a duty to her contract vendee. . . . Where, as here, the seller not only takes unfair advantage of the buyer's ignorance but has created and perpetuated a condition about which he is unlikely to even inquire, enforcement of the contract (in whole or in part) is offensive to the court's sense of equity. Application of the remedy of rescission, within the bounds of the narrow exception to the doctrine of caveat emptor set forth herein, is entirely appropriate to

relieve the unwitting purchaser from the consequences of a most unnatural bargain.

Accordingly, the judgment of the Supreme Court, New York County (Edward H. Lehner, J.), entered April 9, 1990, which dismissed the complaint should be modified and the first cause of action seeking rescission of the contract reinstated.

DISSENT

Justice Smith (dissenting).

I would affirm the dismissal of the complaint. . . .

*   *   *   *   *

"It is settled law in New York State that the seller of real property is under no duty to speak when the parties deal at arm's length. The mere silence of the seller, without some act or conduct which deceived the purchaser, does not amount to a concealment that is actionable as a fraud. . . ."

The parties herein were represented by counsel and dealt at arm's length. . . . There is no allegation that defendants, by some specific act, other than the failure to speak deceived the plaintiff. . . .

Finally, if the doctrine of caveat emptor is to be discarded, it should be for a reason more substantive than a poltergeist. The existence of a poltergeist is no more binding upon the defendants than it is upon this court.

Based upon the foregoing, the [lower] court properly dismissed the complaint.

Questions

1. *a.* According to the court, did the defendant seller engage in a fraudulent misrepresentation in failing to disclose the "ghostly" condition of her house?
    b. The plaintiff won this case on equitable/fairness grounds. Explain the court's reasoning.
    c. Do you agree with the court's equity/fairness reasoning? Explain.
    d. Did the real estate agent engage in fraud for failing to disclose the house's haunted reputation? Explain.

2. *a.* What did the court mean by the phrase "caveat emptor?"
    b. Why did the court find for the plaintiff buyer, even though "caveat emptor" seemed to be the controlling law in this situation?
    c. Would the buyer have been successful in a misrepresentation claim if the seller had said: "This house is so peaceful. We never have any disturbances."?
    d. The defendant seller had fostered the belief that her house was haunted. Did that promotional effort by the defendant influence the court's decision making? Explain.

3. Explain dissenting Justice Smith's objection to the majority's ruling.

Toy Yoda

Former Hooters waitress Jodee Berry sued Gulf Coast Wings for not awarding a new Toyota as a prize for her victory in an April 2001 sales contest. Berry alleged that her manager told the waitresses in their Florida Hooters that the server selling the most beer would be entered in a drawing (involving other Hooters locations) with the winner receiving a new Toyota. At one point during the contest, the manager allegedly said he did not know whether the winner would receive a Toyota car, truck or van, but he did know that the winner would be required to pay registration fees. At the close of the contest, the manager told Berry that she had won. He blindfolded her and took her to the restaurant parking lot. He laughed when Berry found, not the car she expected, but a doll based on the character Yoda in the Star Wars movie (a toy Yoda). Berry did not laugh, but she did sue. The case was settled out of court. The terms of that settlement were not disclosed, but Berry's lawyer did say that she would be able to afford whatever Toyota she wanted.

Questions

1. What contract-based causes of action did Berry bring in this case?
2. Defend Hooters.
3. Make the argument that the Hooters manager never actually made an offer to the waitresses.
4. If an offer was made, how did Berry accept that offer?
5. Make the argument that the offer and acceptance, if they existed, were not supported by consideration.

Sources: Berry v. Gulf Coast Wings, Inc., Div. J (Fla. 14th Cir. Ct. July 24, 2001); and Keith A. Rowley, "You Asked for It, You Got It . . . Toy Yoda: Practical Jokes, Prizes, and Contract Law," 3 *Nevada Law Journal* 526 (2003).

Duress

Sometimes genuine assent is not secured and a contract may be rescinded because one of the parties is forced to agree. Fear lies at the heart of a duress claim. The party seeking to escape the contract must establish that a wrongful act was threatened or had occurred, causing the party to enter the contract out of fear of harm such that free will was precluded. Increasingly, courts are also setting aside contracts on the grounds of economic duress. For example, suppose you know that one of your regular customers depends on your timely delivery of steel to his factory and that he cannot expeditiously find an alternative supply. Therefore, you tell your customer that delivery will be delayed until he agrees to pay a higher price for the steel. If he agrees, the resulting contract probably could be rescinded on the grounds of economic duress.

Undue Influence

Under some circumstances, the first party to an apparent contract can escape its terms by demonstrating that the second party so dominated her will that she (the first party) did not act independently. These claims are most common in cases involving those who are old or infirm and who lose their independence of thought and action to the undue influence of a caregiver or adviser.

Mistake

Most of us, on taking a new job, operate at least for a time in fear that we will make a mistake. Assume you are new to your job and are preparing a bid that your company will submit in hopes of securing the general maintenance contract for a large office building. In preparing the bid, you inadvertently submit a final price of $50,000 rather than $500,000. What happens? Do you lose your job?

> You inadvertently submit a final price of $50,000 rather than $500,000. What happens?

In some cases, mistakes involving critical facts can be grounds for rescinding contracts. A *mutual mistake* is one in which both parties to the contract are in error about some critical fact. With exceptions, either party can rescind those contracts because genuine assent was not achieved. Your erroneous bid, however, is a *unilateral mistake;* that is, only one party to the contract made an error. The general rule is that those contracts cannot be rescinded. However, if you are able to show that the other party to the contract knew or should have known about your mistake, many courts would allow you to rescind. Certainly you would make that argument in this instance because the $50,000 bid presumably is dramatically out of line with the other bids and at odds with reasonable business expectations about the value of the contract. In cases where an error is made in drafting a contract, and both parties are unaware of the error (a mutual mistake), the courts will reform the contract rather than void it. That is, the contract will be rewritten to reflect what the parties actually intended.

$4,934 Discount on Alitalia?

The Italian national airline, Alitalia, was charging more than $5,000 for trans-Atlantic, roundtrip, business class airfares in 2006, but by mistake a fare was briefly listed online at $66.00. About the same time, Marriott was offering rooms at a New York City hotel for $24.90 when the intended price was $249.00. Alitalia honored 509 reservations at an expected cost of about $2.6 million. Marriott, however, raised the $24.90 rate to the intended $249.00. Errors of this kind happen with some frequency in the travel industry.

Questions

1. As a matter of business practice, how would you have dealt with your company's error had you been in charge at Alitalia or Marriott?

2. As a matter of law, was Alitalia or Marriott obligated to honor the low prices?

Source: Scott McCartney, "When a Fare Is Too Good to Be True," *The Wall Street Journal,* April 25, 2006, p. D5.

Legality of Purpose

Having examined agreement, consideration, capacity, and genuineness of assent, we turn now to the final requirement for the creation of a binding contract: legality of purpose (see Figure 6.2). *Illegality* refers to bargains to commit a crime or a tort (such as a deal with a coworker to embezzle funds from one's employer); but more broadly, illegality involves bargains that are forbidden by statute or violate public policy. We can identify three general categories of illegal agreements: (1) contracts that violate statutes, (2) contracts that are unconscionable, and (3) contracts that violate public policy. In general, the effect of an illegal contract is that it cannot be enforced, and the courts will not provide a remedy if its terms are unfulfilled. With exceptions, the parties to illegal deals are left where the courts find them.

FIGURE 6.2
Five Requirements of a Binding Contract

1. Agreement
2. Consideration
3. Capacity
4. Genuineness of assent
5. Legality of purpose

1. ***Contracts violating statutes.*** As noted, a contract to commit a crime or a tort is illegal and unenforceable. The states have also specified certain other agreements that are illegal. Those provisions vary from state to state, but they commonly include antigambling laws, laws forbidding the conduct of certain kinds of business on Sundays (*blue laws*), laws forbidding *usury,* and laws forbidding the practice of certain professions (law, real estate, hair care) without a license.

Who Owns the BMW?

Ryno owned Bavarian Motors in Fort Worth, Texas. In 1981 Ryno agreed to sell a 1980 BMW M-l to Tyra for $125,000. Ryno then proposed a double-or-nothing coin flip for the car. Tyra agreed and won the coin flip. Ryno then handed Tyra the keys to the car, saying, "It's yours," while handing the "German title" to the car to Tyra. On several occasions Tyra took the BMW to Ryno for servicing. The car was routinely returned to Tyra until 1982 when Ryno kept the car and sold it. Tyra sued Ryno. Who wins? Explain.

Source: Ryno v. Tyra, 752 S.W.2d 148 (Tx. Ct. App. 1988).

---

2. ***Unconscionable contracts.*** Certain agreements are so thoroughly one-sided that fairness precludes enforcing them. Problems of unconscionability often arise in situations in which the bargaining power of one of the parties is much superior to the other—where one can, in effect, "twist the arm" or otherwise take advantage of the other. Both the common law of contracts and UCC 2-302 give the courts the power to modify or refuse to enforce such deals.

> Certain agreements are so thoroughly one-sided that fairness precludes enforcing them.

3. ***Public policy.*** The courts may decline to enforce certain otherwise binding contracts because to do so would not be in the best interest of the public. For example, an agreement between the local convenience stores to charge $5.00 for a gallon of gasoline would be a restraint of trade (price fixing) and as such would be contrary to public policy and to antitrust laws (see Chapter 10) and thus would be unenforceable. Similarly, suppose as a condition of being hired for a job you must sign an agreement providing that you will not leave your employer to work for one of your employer's competitors. These *noncompete* clauses (see Chapter 12) are common and may be fully

lawful depending largely on whether the time and geographic restrictions imposed are reasonable. If unreasonable, the courts will either not enforce the clause or will alter it to achieve a fair result.

Another commonplace public policy concern is the *exculpatory clause, limited liability clause, or release.* If you participate in any potentially hazardous activity such as attending a professional hockey game, whitewater rafting, joining a school field trip, or entering an amusement park you may be required to agree to release others of any liability for harm that might befall you. If you own or manage a potentially hazardous enterprise such as a water slide, bungee tower, or even a health spa, you may try to protect yourself from litigation should a customer be hurt by including a release in the customer agreement. Often, such agreements are enforceable in the manner of any other contractual provision, but sometimes they are not. Many factors can influence that decision, including how sweeping the exculpation is, whether it was knowingly entered, and the relative bargaining power of the parties. The case that follows examines an airline contract clause limiting liability for lost luggage.

LEGAL BRIEFCASE

Hanson v. America West Airlines   544 F.Supp.2d 1038 (U.S. Dist. Ct. Central Dist. Cal. 2008)

Judge Guilford

BACKGROUND

Plaintiff David Hanson ("Plaintiff") has lost his head. More specifically, Plaintiff has lost an artistically and scientifically valuable robotic head modeled after famous science fiction author Philip K. Dick ("Head"). Dick's well-known body of work has resulted in movies—such as *Total Recall, Blade Runner, Minority Report,* and *A Scanner Darkly,* and a large group of admirers has grown following his death in Orange County, California, in 1982. His stories have questioned whether robots can be human so it seems appropriate that Plaintiff reincarnated Dick as a robot which included the Head, valued at around $750,000.

Plaintiff lost his Head on one of Defendant's planes when flying from Texas to San Francisco with a connection in Las Vegas. Plaintiff brought the Head onto the plane in a carry-on duffel bag and stored it in the overhead bin. Plaintiff fell asleep during the flight from Texas to Las Vegas, and woke up when the plane arrived in Las Vegas. On waking, Plaintiff immediately left the plane to catch his connecting flight to San Francisco. Perhaps because he had just woken up, Plaintiff lacked the total recall to remember to retrieve the Head from the overhead bin.

According to Plaintiff, as soon as he got to San Francisco, he went to the baggage counter, spoke to Defendant's employee, Leanne Miller ("Miller"), and informed her of the problem. Miller told him that the airplane with his Head was in flight, and could not be checked until it landed in Southern California. Plaintiff offered to fly to Southern California to regain his Head, but Miller told him not to do that. According to Plaintiff, he informed Miller of the importance and value of the Head, and she replied that all efforts would be made to recover the Head and that it would receive "special treatment."

Plaintiff asserts that about 45 minutes later, Miller called him with the good news that the Head had been found in Orange County. Plaintiff "remained willing" to go retrieve his Head, but Miller replied that it would be sent to San Francisco. According to Plaintiff, Miller then informed him of the special security procedures that would be taken to protect and deliver the Head. Plaintiff told Miller that Plaintiff's friend Craig Grossman would be at the airport to pick up the Head. Grossman waited for the Head at the San Francisco airport, but it never arrived and has not been found since. While hearts may be left in San Francisco, heads apparently are left in Orange County, or are simply lost or stolen.

Plaintiff sued Defendant in California state court for conversion, negligence, and involuntary bailment. Defendant removed the case to federal court, and here moves for summary judgment.

ANALYSIS

1. Contractual Liability Limitations

Defendant argues that it contractually limited its liability for loss of Plaintiff's goods. . . .

Federal common law allows a carrier to limit its liability for lost or damaged goods if the contract limiting liability offers the shipper (1) reasonable notice of the limited liability, and (2) a fair opportunity to buy higher liability.

* * * * *

If the contract states the limited liability provision and a means to avoid it, the contract is considered prima facie valid. Defendant has satisfied the elements of an enforceable limited liability provision under federal common law. The Contract of Carriage provides that "[liability of loss, delay, or damage to baggage is limited as follows unless a higher value is declared in advance and additional charges are paid." The contract later provides that the monetary limit is "USD 2,800.00 per ticketed passenger for checked baggage." More specifically for this case, the Contract of Carriage provides that Defendant "assumes no responsibility or liability for baggage, or other items, carried in the passenger compartment of the aircraft." Plaintiff admits that he was aware of the limited liability provision. Thus, Defendant provided Plaintiff with reasonable notice of limited liability and a fair opportunity to buy higher liability.

2. Plaintiff's Arguments

Plaintiff argues that Defendant is liable for the lost head because (1) there was a material deviation from the Contract of Carriage and (2) Plaintiff's discussion with Miller altered the terms of the original Contract of Carriage or created a new contract.

2.1 Material Deviation Doctrine

* * * * *

[T]he material deviation doctrine states that where a carrier effects a fundamental breach of a contract by materially deviating from the contract's terms, the carrier is liable for damage to or loss of the shipped goods. Cases have further defined the boundaries of this doctrine. For example, in *Nipponkoa Ins. Co., Ltd., v. Watkins Motor Lines, Inc.,* 431 F.Supp.2d 411 (S.D.N.Y. 2006), a carrier promised to take special measures to protect a shipment of laptop computers, including using high security locks and video surveillance. The court found that the carrier breached that promise by failing to use either high security locks or video surveillance. The court held that the carrier was responsible for the loss of the computers under the

material deviation doctrine. The court explained that the doctrine applies when a carrier breaches a "separate, risk-related promise" about the shipment of goods. The court emphasized that the agreement was specific and that the carrier deviated from the expressly agreed-upon security measures.

* * * * *

The Ninth Circuit has limited the material deviation doctrine. In *Vision Air,* for example, a carrier destroyed two trucks by using an inadequate pulley system to transport them. *Vision Air,* 155 F.3d at 1167–68. The Ninth Circuit held that even if that behavior constituted gross negligence or recklessness, it did not constitute a material deviation. "[W]e reject the notion that mere negligence may constitute an unreasonable deviation . . . we reject the notion that gross negligence or recklessness may constitute an unreasonable deviation." The court emphasized that only "more culpable misconduct" could be considered a deviation.

In the cases just discussed, the courts focused on the actual express terms of the agreement, showing that the material deviation doctrine applies only when the shipper makes a "separate, risk-related promise," and then breaches that promise.

With these boundaries, Plaintiff's argument that Defendant materially deviated from the original Contract of Carriage fails. There were no provisions in the original Contract of Carriage directly concerning transporting the Head. Indeed, the original Contract of Carriage declaimed any responsibility for carry-on baggage. Further, nothing in the original Contract of Carriage made provisions for travelers leaving baggage on the airplane. Thus, Defendant did not breach a "separate, risk-related promise" in the original Contract of Carriage, and is not liable under this theory.

2.2 Altered or New Contractual Terms and Agency Law

Plaintiff also argues that Miller either altered the terms of the original Contract of Carriage or created a new contract with Plaintiff, and that Defendant is liable under the new or altered contract.

Agents can bind their principals only if they have actual or apparent authority to do so. Actual authority may be either express or implied. If a principal specifically authorizes an agent to act, the agent has express authority to take that action. If a principle "merely states the general nature of what the agent is to do, the agent is said to have implied authority to do acts consistent with the direction."

Miller did not have express authority to contract with Plaintiff. The original Contract of Carriage provided that:

> No employee of U.S. Airways has the authority to waive, modify, or alter any provisions of these terms of

transportation or any applicable fares/charges unless authorized by a corporate officer of U.S. Airways. U.S. Airways-appointed agents and representatives are only authorized to sell tickets for air transportation on U.S. Airways pursuant to the terms of transportation and applicable fares/charges of U.S. Airways.

There is no evidence that Miller was either a corporate officer of Defendant or that she was authorized by such an officer to modify the terms of transportation. Thus, under the Contract of Carriage, Miller had no express authority either to change the terms of the contract or to create a new contract. Indeed, Miller had express authority only to "sell tickets for air transportation." Likewise, there is no evidence that Miller had implied authority.

The Contract of Carriage also leads to the conclusion that Miller had no apparent authority to change the terms of the contract or to create a new contract. "Apparent authority results when the principal does something or permits the agent to do something which reasonably leads another to believe that the agent had the authority he purported to have." *Hawaiian Paradise Park Corp.*, 414 F.2d at 756 (9th Cir. 1969). Only the acts of the principal, not of the agent, give rise to apparent authority. Plaintiff argues that Miller's station behind a desk near the baggage claim area led Plaintiff to reasonably believe that Miller had the authority to make contracts for the delivery of lost baggage. The Court disagrees.

Plaintiff is a frequent flyer and was aware of the applicable tariffs. Thus, before he lost his Head and spoke with Miller, he was aware of the tariff limiting Miller's authority. Aware of that tariff, he could not reasonably conclude, based on Miller's position behind a desk, that she suddenly had authority to contract with him.

* * * * *

Plaintiff cannot rely on representations altering the contract or creating a new contract when those representations were made by someone whose authority had been expressly limited by contract. The Court must find that Miller had neither actual nor apparent authority to either alter the Contract of Carriage or create a new contract.

2.3 Even Under the New Terms Alleged, Liability Has Not Been Established

Even if Miller had authority to alter the Contract of Carriage or create a new contract, Defendant would still not be liable for the lost Head because there is no evidence that Defendant breached the contract even under the new terms alleged. Plaintiff alleges new terms that provided for tagging and boxing the Head, informing everyone of the value, and scheduling the Head on the next flight. But Plaintiff presents no evidence that such terms were breached. Instead, Plaintiff offers theories of De-

fendant's potential conduct, such as, "[potentially informing the wrong crew of the value of the HEAD" and "[potentially informing the thief of the high value of the HEAD." These theories, while heady, are insufficient.

At best, Plaintiff's theory is that, since the Head did not arrive at its destination, Defendants must have done something wrong. This is not evidence of a breach or material deviation. Defendant may have done everything as promised, only to fall victim to a head hunting thief or other skullduggery. Alternatively, Defendant could have been negligent, and still not have committed a fundamental breach. The possibility of such negligence is "considered an inherent risk of shipping." *Information Control*, 73 Cal. App. 3d at 641. Thus, even if Plaintiff's discussion with Miller altered or created a new contract, there is no evidence establishing Defendant's liability based on breach or material deviation.

3. CONCLUSION

Philip K. Dick and other science fiction luminaries have often explored whether robots might eventually evolve to exercise freedom of choice. But there is no doubt that humans have the freedom of choice to bind themselves in mutually advantageous contractual relationships. When Plaintiff chose to enter the Contract of Carriage with Defendant he agreed, among other things, to limit Defendant's liability for lost baggage. Failing to show that he is entitled to relief from that agreement, Plaintiff is bound by the terms of that contract, which bars his state law claims.

The Court must GRANT Defendant's Motion. But it does so hoping that the android head of Mr. Dick is someday found, perhaps in an Elysian field of Orange County, Dick's homeland, choosing to dream of electric sheep.

Questions

1. As a matter of law, why did America West win this case?

2. Why was this Contract of Carriage not considered unfair and one-sided and thus unenforceable?

3. Why did America West's behavior not constitute a "material deviation" from the Contract of Carriage?

4. Ning Yan went to Gay's fitness center to use a one-week complimentary pass. On each visit he signed in on a sheet that contained a standard exculpatory clause including this language: "I also understand that Vital Power Fitness Center assumes no responsibility for any injuries and/or sicknesses incurred to me. . . ." On February 18, 1999, Yan fell from a treadmill and sustained a severe head injury. He later died from that injury. No one witnessed the fall. Yan's estate claims he struck his head against a window ledge because the treadmill was placed too close to the window. If he did strike the window ledge, who would likely win this case? Explain. See *Xu v. Gay*, 668 N.W.2d 166 (Ct. App. Mich. 2003).

PRACTICING ETHICS   2010 Gulf Oil Disaster: BP Contracts Unfair/Unconscionable?

In May 2010, British Petroleum (BP) oil company was in the midst of frantic efforts to stop the oil flowing into the Gulf of Mexico from its doomed Macondo 252 well while also trying to clean up the immense quantity that escaped after the explosion of the Deepwater Horizon drilling vessel. "Several hundred" shrimpers, oyster harvesters and others making their living from the Gulf signed contracts with BP to work as paid volunteers in the cleanup process. Among the provisions in those contracts were promises by the volunteers not to file legal claims against the oil company should they sustain damages of any kind in the cleanup process. The provisions, which many of those signing may not have fully understood, included promises not to sue in case of accident or injury and not to talk to anyone about the disaster or cleanup without BP approval. Those provisions also required a 30-day notice before pursuing legal claims against BP, even in the event of an emergency. Reportedly, BP also expected workers to add the oil giant to their personal insurance policies so that worker injuries or damages would fall to each worker's insurance rather than to BP. Commercial fisherman and United Commercial Fisherman's Association president, George Barisich, filed suit to block enforcement of the restrictive promises and U.S. District Judge Helen Berrigan ruled the offending provisions were overbroad and "unconscionable" and declared them null and void. BP and the Fisherman's Association soon reached an agreement removing the waiver language and agreeing not to enforce those provisions in contracts already signed. BP officials said the provisions were a "mistake," and they ordered the provisions removed as soon as they learned about them.

Questions

1. *a.* Were BP's protective provisions "wrong" as a matter of ethical business practice? Explain.
   b. If you were a boss or lawyer at BP, would you have included those protective provisions? Explain.

2. *a.* If you were a boss and you knew you could compel an employee to accept a pay cut in order to enhance an already healthy bottom line, would you do so? Explain.
   b. In your personal life, do you think you have made agreements with friends that were "one-sided" and "unconscionable" because of your possession of superior leverage of some kind?
   c. If so, were you "wrong" to do so. Explain.

Sources: Sabrina Canfield, "Judge Enjoins BP's Unconscionable Contract with Fishermen-Volunteers," *Courthouse News Service,* May 4, 2010, **http://www.courthousenews.com;** and Brendan Kirby, "Full Report: BP Backs Away from Controversial Oil Spill Settlement Language," May 5, 2010, **http://blog.al.com**

Part Two—Interpreting and Enforcing Contracts

We have examined the five ingredients in a binding contract: agreement, consideration, capacity, genuineness of assent, and legality of purpose. Having established those conditions, a contract may have been created, but the door to contract problems has not been closed. Contracts sometimes must fulfill writing formalities to be enforceable. Third parties may have claims against some contracts. And what happens when a party to a contract does not perform as called for by the agreement?

In Writing?

In most cases, oral contracts are fully enforceable.

Certainly a common belief is that agreements must be in writing to be enforceable; but in most cases, oral contracts are fully enforceable. The exceptions, however, are important. Oral contracts are subject to misunderstanding or to being forgotten, and fraudulent claims can readily arise from oral understandings. Consequently, our states have drawn on the English *Statute of Frauds* in specifying that the following kinds of contracts, in most cases, must be in writing to be enforceable:

1. **Collateral contract.** Assume you have just graduated from college, and you want to get started in a small printing business. You secure a bank loan on the condition that you find a creditworthy third party as a guarantor for the loan. Jacobs, a family friend, agrees with the bank to pay the debt if you fail to do so. Jacobs' promise to pay the debt must be in writing to be enforceable.

2. **The sale of land.** Broadly, land is interpreted to include the surface itself, that which is in the soil (minerals) or permanently attached to it (buildings), and growing crops when accompanying the transfer of land. Thus, if a building was permanently attached to a lot you seek for the aforementioned printing business, that building would need to be included in the written contract; but if you contracted to have a building constructed on your lot, you would not need (at least for the purposes of the Statute of Frauds) to execute a written agreement with the building contractor because you would not be contracting for an interest in land. A long-term lease (normally more than one year) for that land and building would, in most states, need to be in writing. All of these principles simply reflect the special role of land in our view of wealth and freedom.

3. **Promises that cannot be performed within one year.** This requirement springs from a concern about faulty memories, deaths, and other impediments to the satisfactory conclusion of long-term contracts. The courts have interpreted this provision narrowly, in effect saying that such a contract need not be in writing if it is *possible,* according to its terms, to perform it within one year from the day of its creation. It follows then that a contract for an indefinite period (such as an employment contract "for the balance of the employee's life") need not be in writing to be enforceable. (It is possible that the employee will die within one year.)

4. **Contracts for the sale of goods at a price of $500 or more.** With exceptions, under both the English-derived Statute of Frauds and UCC 2-201, contracts for the sale of goods (having a value of $500 or more under the UCC) must be in writing to be enforceable. Under the UCC, informal writing will suffice so long as it indicates that a contract was made, it contains a quantity term, and it was signed "by the party against whom enforcement is sought." Section 2-201 provides exceptions for certain transactions of $500 or more in goods in which a contract will be enforceable even though not in writing.

5. **Contracts in consideration of marriage.** The mutual exchange of marriage promises need not be in writing, but any contract that uses marriage as the consideration to support the contract must be in writing to be enforceable. Such contracts would include, for example, prenuptial agreements that are entered prior to marriage and serve the purpose, among others, of specifying how the couple's property will be divided in the event of a divorce. Those contracts must be in writing to be enforceable.

6. **Executor/administrator's promise.** When an individual dies, a representative is appointed to oversee the estate. A promise by that executor/administrator to pay the

estate's debts must be in writing if the payment will be made from the executor/administrator's personal funds. Thus, where the executor of an estate contracts with an auctioneer to dispose of the decedent's personal property, the executor's promise to pay the auctioneer must be in writing if the funds are to come from the executor's personal resources; the promise need not be in writing if the payment is to come from the estate.

[As we have noted, the state legislatures are considering various changes in the UCC, Article 2, including the Statute of Frauds (UCC 2-201—see the appendix) as recommended by the National Conference of Commissioners on Uniform State Laws (NCCUSL). Among the proposed changes, the $500 sale of goods standard would increase to $5,000, and electronic signatures and writings would satisfy Statute of Frauds requirements.]

Failure to Comply   A fully performed oral contract, even though not in compliance with the Statute of Frauds, will not be rescinded by the courts. However, incomplete oral contracts that fail to comply with the statute are unenforceable. If a party to an unenforceable oral contract has provided partial performance in reliance on the contract, the courts will ordinarily provide compensation under quasi-contract principles for the reasonable value of that performance. [For more on the Statute of Frauds, see **http://www.expertlaw.com/library/business/statute_of_frauds.html**]

The Parol Evidence Rule

Suppose you are the purchasing manager for a large manufacturer. You entered a written contract for 50 new personal computers. During negotiations, the seller said they would "throw in" 10 new printers if they got the computer order, but you failed to include a provision for the printers in the contract. Is your boss about to have a fit? Perhaps, because you probably will not be able to introduce evidence of that oral understanding to alter the terms of the written contract. In general, whenever a contract has been reduced to writing with the intent that the writing represents a complete and final integration of the parties' intentions, none of the parties can introduce parol evidence (oral or written words outside the "four corners" of the agreement) to add to, change, or contradict that contract when that evidence was expressed/created at the time of or prior to the writing. The written agreement is presumed to be the best evidence of the parties' intentions at the time they entered the contract. (The parol evidence rule under UCC section 2-202 is essentially the same as the common-law provisions discussed here.)

Exceptions   Parol evidence may be admissible under the following exceptional circumstances:

1. To add missing terms to an incomplete written contract.
2. To explain ambiguities in a written contract.
3. To prove circumstances that would invalidate a written contract; that is, to establish one of the grounds of mistake, fraud, illegality, and so forth explained earlier in this chapter.

E-mail a "Signed Writing?"

Stevens' employment agreement with Publicis required that any modification of the agreement was to be signed by the parties. Stevens and Bloom (representing Publicis) exchanged e-mails changing Stevens' employment duties. The parties' names were typed at the end of each e-mail.

Question

1. Does that exchange of e-mails constitute a binding agreement? Explain.

Source: Stevens v. Publicis, 854 N.Y.S.2d 690 (2008).

Third Parties

We turn now to the rights and duties of those who are not parties to a contract but hold legally recognizable interests in that contract. Those interests arise when (1) contract rights are assigned to others, (2) contract duties are delegated to others, or (3) contracts have third-party beneficiary provisions.

Assignment of Rights

Ordinarily, a party to a contract is free to transfer her or his rights under the contract to a third party. Thus, if Ames owes Jones $500 for work performed, Jones can assign that right to Smith, who can now assert her right to collect against Ames. That transfer of rights is labeled an assignment (see Figure 6.3). Jones, the party making the transfer, is the assignor; Smith, the one receiving the right, is the assignee; and Ames, the party who must perform, is the obligor. Ames, the obligor, must now perform the contract for the benefit of the assignee; that is, Ames must pay the $500 to Smith. The completed assignment then extinguishes the assignor's rights under the contract.

Some contracts are not assignable without consent of the obligor. That would be the case where the obligor's duties are materially altered by the assignment. For example, if you have a contract to serve as a personal fitness trainer for a busy chief executive officer, your contract could not be assigned without your consent to another CEO, or movie star, or the like because the highly personal and specific obligations under the contract would necessarily be materially altered with a different client.

FIGURE 6.3
Assignment of Rights

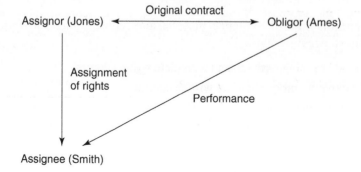

Delegation of Duties

The parties to a contract may also delegate their duties under the contract to one or more third parties. Assume Allen has secured a contract to install windows in Boyd's new office building (see Figure 6.4). Allen could delegate that duty to another contractor, Harms (although Allen would more commonly simply enter a subcontracting arrangement without actually transferring the underlying contract). A delegation of duty leaves Harms, the delegatee (the one to whom the duty is delegated), primarily responsible for performance; but Allen, the obligor/delegator, (the one who made the delegation) remains secondarily liable in case Harms, the delegatee, fails to fulfill the duty to Boyd, the obligee (the one to whom the duty is owed under both the original contract and the delegation). As with the assignment of rights, some contractual duties, particularly those of a personal service nature, cannot be delegated without consent.

FIGURE 6.4
Delegation of Duties

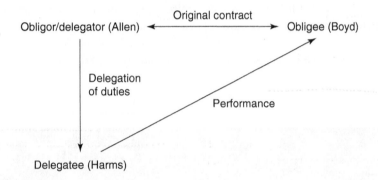

Third-Party Beneficiary Contracts

Normally, those not a party to a contract have no rights under that contract. As we have seen, however, third parties may be assigned rights or delegated duties under a contract. A third party may also enforce a contract where that contract was expressly intended to benefit the third party. An agreement of that nature is a third-party beneficiary contract. Third-party beneficiaries are of three kinds: creditor, donee, and incidental. In general, creditor and donee beneficiaries can enforce contracts made by others for their benefit; incidental beneficiaries cannot do so.

Creditor Beneficiary   Assume you decide to expand your used car business by advertising on television. Your ads appear on TV, and you owe the local station $2,000. Rather than paying the bill directly, you transfer a used car to your friend, Gleason, with the understanding that he will pay off your bill with the television station. Thus the station becomes the creditor beneficiary of the contract between you and Gleason, and the station can sue Gleason for that money if necessary while you remain secondarily responsible for the payment.

Donee Beneficiary   When the promisee's primary purpose in entering a contract is to make a gift to another, that third party is a donee beneficiary of the contract. The most common of these situations involves an ordinary life insurance policy for which the owner (the promisee) pays premiums to the life insurance company (the promisor), which is obliged to pay benefits to the third party upon the death of the promisee/policy owner. If necessary, the third-party beneficiary can sue the insurance company for payment.

Incidental Beneficiary   Often a third party receives benefit from a contract although conferring that benefit was not the contracting parties' primary purpose or intent. For example, assume a General Motors car dealer enters into a contract to buy land adjacent to your used car lot for the purpose of opening a large dealership. You would benefit immensely from the spillover effect of the large, adjacent dealership. In such a situation, you would be an incidental beneficiary of the land sale contract because that contract was not intended for your benefit. If the landowner or the GM dealer failed to perform, you, as an incidental beneficiary, would have no legal rights against either of them.

The case that follows involves a third-party claim by Gill Plumbing against its subcontractor, Jimenez. The dispute arose out of a dormitory construction contract where the general contractor, Gilbane Building, had hired Gill to do the dormitory plumbing and Gill, in turn, had hired Jimenez to install some portion of that plumbing.

LEGAL BRIEFCASE

Jimenez v. Gilbane Building Company, et al.
693 S.E.2d 126 (Ga. Ct. App. 2010)

* * * * *

Judge Adams

The background facts are that Gilbane Building Company was the general contractor for the construction of a new dormitory at Georgia Southern University. Gilbane hired Gill Plumbing as the plumbing contractor, and Gill Plumbing, in turn, hired Jose Alfredo Jimenez to perform plumbing installation work. The building was completed in July 2005, but in October, after the dormitory was occupied by students, a pipe failed causing extensive water damage to the dormitory and to some students' personal belongings. Gilbane was forced to hire Belfor USA Group, Inc. to perform remediation and repair work. Belfor's $990,060.63 bill for the services has not been paid.

Belfor filed this action against Gilbane, Gilbane filed a third-party action against Gill Plumbing, and Gill Plumbing

filed a fourth-party action against Jimenez. The parties have since been realigned. Currently, both Belfor and Gilbane have claims against Gill Plumbing, and Gill Plumbing has a third-party claim against Jimenez for the costs of the remediation and repair.

In its third-party claim, Gill Plumbing asserts that it had a written agreement with Jimenez that included an indemnity agreement, and that the damages to the dormitory resulted from negligent work performed by Jimenez. Jimenez denied that he entered into a valid and enforceable contract or an indemnity agreement with Gill Plumbing and denied the negligence. The trial court granted Gill's motion for partial summary judgment against Jimenez, finding that he was liable "for indemnification to Gill Plumbing" "in the amount, if any, of damages proven to have resulted from Mr. Jimenez's defective work." Jimenez appeals this ruling and contends that "no contract existed between Mr. Jimenez and the

indemnify = to protect against damage, loss, or injury; insure [handwritten margin note]

Appellee as a matter of law" or, at least, that there are material issues of fact regarding the contract and the indemnity agreement.

Summary judgment is proper when there is no genuine issue of material fact and the movant is entitled to judgment as a matter of law. . . .

There is no question that the parties had an oral agreement. The issue before us is whether there was an enforceable written agreement and, if so, what were the terms of that agreement. The undisputed facts show that Jimenez was hired by Gill Plumbing to perform plumbing services in the "Eagle Village" construction project at Georgia Southern University, that he performed plumbing services, and that he has been paid for the work in the amount of $167,000.

Jimenez has never worked for any company other than Gill Plumbing and the two have worked together for at least 15 years. On September 15, 2004, Jimenez signed two documents, which, Gill Plumbing contends, constitute the parties' entire written agreement; Jimenez has signed other documents for Gill Plumbing in the past. The first document is contained on one page, it is dated September 15, 2004, and it has Jimenez's typewritten name and his signature. The main body of the document is as follows:

LABOR CONTRACT
Project: Eagle Village.

Item 1	Slab	50,100.00
Item 2	Rough	66,800.00
Item 3	Set Out	50,100.00

– Weekly billing to be submitted in draw format.
   All work must be approved by Larry Pollett.

– Weekly safety meetings must be attended. Sub required to attend all jobsite agenda & safety meetings.

– Subs required to comply with all general contractor regulations & jobsite regulations

– All Subs required to provide certificate of insurance with adequate coverages per limits set by general contractor.

– Subs are required to honor subcontractor Warranty for labor & installation free of all defects for a period of

   (1) year from date of substantial completion.

– *Subs agree & abide by all terms in the attached Exhibit 'A' for insurance & indemnity.*

Total Contract Amount $167,000.00

(Emphasis supplied.) Jimenez's signature appears below the following words, which are written on the side of the above chart:

Sub-Labor

Affidavit

I certify the work for which above payment is requested has been completed according to the plans and specifications and in compliance with the terms of our contract and all labor and material bills applicable to this job have been paid to date and that Federal income, social security, and unemployment taxes have been withheld and will be paid when due on all employees employed by me on this job.

_____/s/_____ CONTRACTOR

Notably, this first document does not name Gill Plumbing anywhere, and the "affidavit" is written in the past tense as if the project had already been completed; but as of the date on the document, Jimenez's work at Eagle Village had not begun. The second document—"Exhibit A"—is two pages long, and it begins as follows:

INSURANCE AND INDEMNITY SUBCONTRACTOR AGREEMENT

The Work performed by the Subcontractor shall be at the risk of the Subcontractor exclusively. To the fullest extent permitted by law, Subcontractor shall indemnify, defend (at Subcontractor's sole expense) and hold harmless Contractor, the Owner (if different from Contractor), affiliated companies of Contractor, . . . from and against any and all claims for . . . damage to property . . . which arise or are in any way connected with the Work performed, Materials furnished, or Services provided under this Agreement by Subcontractor or its agents. . . .

The exhibit goes on to require the "Subcontractor" to obtain commercial general liability insurance in the amount of $1,000,000, and to meet other related requirements. The exhibit is signed by Jimenez on the second page over the word "Subcontractor," but it is not dated. Also, the document does not include Gill Plumbing's name anywhere. Finally, Jimenez never performed any work at Eagle Village that could be called "Set Out" as stated on page one of the document.

Jimenez contends the three-page document is not an enforceable agreement because it does not state who the other party is or mention Gill Plumbing's name; it does not include a promise by Gill Plumbing, or anyone else, to pay him; it does not specify the location or address where the work is to be performed; it leaves several terms undefined; it does not specify the time for performance; it does not direct Jimenez to perform any work at all; and although it mentions additional documents, none are attached or defined. He argues the "sub-labor affidavit" found on page one of the document

defense [handwritten margin note]

is written in the past tense, suggesting that the work was already completed when, in fact, it had not begun as of the only date indicated on the document. He also complains that the indemnification provision fails to identify who should be indemnified and that it fails to define the terms "subcontractor," "contractor," or "owner." Finally, Jimenez contends he cannot read or communicate well in English and he did not know what he signed.

In Georgia,

> The first requirement of the law relative to contracts is that there must be a meeting of the minds of the parties, and mutuality, and in order for the contract to be valid the agreement must ordinarily be expressed plainly and explicitly enough to show what the parties agreed upon. A contract cannot be enforced in any form of action if its terms are incomplete or incomprehensible.

Bagwell-Hughes, Inc. v. McConnell, 224 Ga. 659, 661–662 (164 SE2d 229) (1968). But "[a]n objection of indefiniteness may be obviated by performance on the part of one party and the acceptance of the performance by the other." *Aukerman v. Witmer,* 256 Ga. App. 211, 216 (1) (568 SE2d 123) (2002). Nevertheless, performance as a cure has its limits:

> Performance does not cure the deficiencies in an agreement that is so vague, indefinite, and uncertain "as to make it impossible for courts to determine what, if anything, was agreed upon, therefore rendering it impossible to determine whether there had been performance."

Razavi v. Shackelford, 260 Ga. App. 603, 605 (1) (580 SE2d 253) (2003).

Here, the attendant and surrounding circumstances show that Jimenez entered into an agreement with Gill Plumbing, that he performed work, and that he was paid by Gill Plumbing. The three-page document shows that the work was to be performed on the "Eagle Village" project; it stated the amount to be paid for each phase of the work; and the total equaled the amount that

Jimenez was paid for the work. And Jimenez attended weekly safety meetings. Thus, there is some evidence of performance consistent with the three-page document. But there is also evidence of performance that is inconsistent with the three-page document. Jimenez did not perform some of the work listed in the document, and the document suggests that the work had already been completed when the document was signed.

In addition, the document is ambiguous at best, and the rules of construction do not resolve the ambiguity. Jimenez is identified as the "subcontractor" in the indemnification agreement, which provides that he is to identify the "contractor" and others. Yet, the first page of the three page document identifies Jimenez as the "contractor," suggesting that he should indemnify himself. And there are two contractors who are parties to the lawsuit and other contractors on the entire project.

* * * * *

Here, among other problems, it is impossible to tell from the terms of the written document who Jimenez may have promised to indemnify, and that fact has not been made sufficiently clear by either the rules of construction or any performance under the agreement. The trial court erred by granting partial summary judgment in favor of Gill Plumbing on the purported indemnification agreement. Jury issues remain on the terms of the parties' agreement.

Judgment reversed.

Questions

1. Explain what the trial court meant in finding that Jimenez was liable "for indemnification to Gill Plumbing" "in the amount, if any, of damages proven to have resulted from Mr. Jimenez's defective work."

2. Why did the court conclude that Gill did not have an enforceable agreement with Jiminez?

3. Why did the appeals court overturn the trial court's summary judgment?

Discharge

At some point, obligations under a contract come to an end. When that moment arrives, we say the duties of the contracting parties have been discharged. In this section, we examine some of the methods of contract discharge. Discharge can occur in many ways, but the most important of these are (1) conditions, (2) performance or breach, (3) lawful excuses, (4) agreement, and (5) by operation of law.

Discharge by Conditions

Sometimes a contract is useful to one or more of the contracting parties only if some future event occurs or fails to occur. Under those circumstances, the parties may write into the contract a clause providing that performance is required only if the specified condition occurs or fails to occur. Otherwise, the duty to perform is discharged. Those conditions take three forms: conditions precedent, conditions subsequent, and conditions concurrent.

Conditions Precedent   A conditions precedent clause specifies that an event must occur before the parties to the contract are obliged to perform. Assume you are attempting to establish a business booking rock-and-roll acts for performances. You sign a deal with the rock group Passion Pit, providing for a performance "contingent upon obtaining satisfactory lease arrangements for the university field house within 14 days." If you are unable to achieve an acceptable lease, both parties are discharged from performance requirements under the contract.

> You sign a deal with the rock group Passion Pit.

Conditions Subsequent   A conditions subsequent clause excuses performance if a future event transpires. Thus, in the Passion Pit example, the band might include a clause providing that the agreement will be null and void if any member of the band is ill or otherwise unable to perform on the contracted evening. Hence in a contract with a condition subsequent the parties have bound themselves to perform unless a specified event occurs; whereas in a contract with a condition precedent the parties have no binding duties until the specified event occurs.

Conditions Concurrent   Here the contract simply specifies that the parties are to perform their duties at the same time. Each performance is dependent on the other. So if Passion Pit performs as contracted, you have a simultaneous duty to pay for the band's performance. Your duty to pay is conditioned on Passion Pit's performance and vice versa.

Express or Implied Conditions   Another way of classifying the aforementioned conditions is to treat them either as express or implied. Express conditions are those explicitly agreed to by the parties, as in the situation where you, a concert promoter, expressly conditioned performance on your ability to secure the university field house for the concert. Express conditions are often prefaced by words such as *when, if, provided,* and so forth.

Implied-in-fact conditions are not explicitly stated in the contract but are derived by the court from the conduct of the parties and the circumstances surrounding the bargain. Suppose you contract to remove snow from your neighbor's driveway during the winter. An implied-in-fact condition of your neighbor's duty to pay would be that you would complete the work within a reasonable period.

Implied-in-law conditions (also called *constructive conditions*) are those that, although not expressly provided for in the contract or not able to be reasonably inferred from the facts, the court imposes on the contract to avoid unfairness. Hence, if you contracted to put a new roof on your neighbor's house but your written contract did not include a date for payment, the court might imply a contract clause providing that your neighbor need not pay you until the job is complete.

Whose Ring?

Barry Meyer and Robyn Mitnick became engaged on August 9, 1996, at which time Barry gave Robyn a custom-designed, $19,500 engagement ring. On November 8, 1996, Barry asked Robyn to sign a prenuptial agreement, but Robyn refused. The parties agree the engagement ended at that point, but they each blame the other for the breakup. Robyn did not return the ring, and Barry sued for its return.

Questions

1. Explain each party's argument using contract principles.
2. Does it matter who was "at fault" in the breakup? Explain.
3. Who gets the ring? Explain.

Source: Meyer v. Mitnick, 625 N.W.2d 136 (Ct. App. Mich. 2001).

Discharge by Performance or by Breach of Contract

Complete performance is, of course, the normal way of discharging a contract. Failure to fully perform without a lawful excuse for that failure results in a breach of contract. The consequences of both full performance and breach of contract can be described in four parts.

Complete Performance—No Breach of Contract   Here we find the most common method of discharge—the situation in which the parties simply do precisely what the contract calls for: pay $500, provide a particular product, present the deed for a piece of land, and so on. When fully performed, a contract has been *executed.*

Substantial Performance—Nonmaterial Breach of Contract   In some cases complete performance is not achieved because of minor deviations from the agreed-on performance. Most notably in construction contracts and in many personal or professional service contracts, the courts have recognized the doctrine of substantial performance. For example, assume a contractor painted a house as agreed, except that he replaced the Benjamin Moore paint called for in the contract with a Sherwin-Williams paint of comparable quality. Assuming the variation has not materially altered the end product and assuming that the variation was not the result of bad faith, the court will enforce the contract as written, but require a deduction for any damages sustained as a consequence of the imperfect performance.

Unacceptable Performance—Material Breach of Contract   When a party falls beneath substantial performance and does not have a lawful excuse for that failure, a material breach of contract has occurred. No clear line separates substantial performance (a nonmaterial breach) from unacceptable performance (a material breach). Such decisions must be made case by case. We can say that material breaches are those that fall short of what the nonbreaching party should reasonably expect—that is, full performance in some cases and substantial performance in others. A material breach discharges the nonbreaching party's duties and permits that party to sue for damages or rescind the contract and seek restitution.

Duke University Breached Its Contract with a Student?

Andrew Giuliani (son of former New York mayor, Rudy Giuliani) was recruited by Coach Rod Myers to play golf at Duke University. Coach Myers allegedly said that Giuliani would be given "life-time access" to Duke's "state-of-the-art" training facilities when he became a Duke alum, and that he would be able to compete for the opportunity to play against the best golfers in the NCAA. Giuliani said those promises and others were instrumental in his decision to attend Duke. Giuliani alleged that Duke "promised to provide [Mr. Giuliani] with various educational services, lodging, and a right of access to the Athletic Department's Varsity program and facilities." Coach Myers unexpectedly passed away in the spring of 2007 and Coach O.D. Vincent took over. Vincent decided to cut the squad in half and announced that he was canceling Giuliani's golf eligibility. Vincent pointed to several incidents of alleged bad behavior by Giuliani. Vincent then presented Giuliani with a written agreement setting out the steps that would have allowed Giuliani to rejoin the team. Giuliani refused to sign the agreement. Giuliani then filed a breach of contract suit against Duke University and Vincent.

Questions

1. Giuliani claimed that his contractual right to play golf at Duke was based on (a) Coach Myers's oral statements and (b) Duke's Student-Athlete Handbook, the Duke Student Bulletin, the Duke Athletic Policy Manual, and the NCAA Division I Manual. Giuliani lost the case. Why did the Court reject Giuliani's contract claims?

2. Could you successfully sue your university for breach of contract if you were dismissed from school because of low grades? Explain. See, e.g., *Bissessur v. The Indiana University Board of Trustees,* 581 F.3d 599 (7th Cir. 2009).

Source: Giuliani v. Duke University, 2010 U.S. Dist. LEXIS 32691 (M.D.N.C.).

Advance Refusal to Perform—Anticipatory Breach of Contract   Sometimes one of the parties, before performance is due, indicates by word or deed that she or he will not perform. Normally an anticipatory breach (also called anticipatory repudiation) is the equivalent of a material breach, discharging the nonbreaching party from any further obligations and allowing the nonbreaching party to sue for damages, if any.

When Has a Breach of Contract Occurred? When Should the Law Intervene in a Contract?

The brief case that follows raises many claims, including breach of contract, but it also serves as an interesting test of the role of law. Should sports fans be able to secure a remedy through contract law when an event merely does not meet their expectations? The idea seems preposterous and another instance of abuse of the legal system, but consider the facts.

> Tyson spit out his mouthpiece and bit both of Holyfield's ears.

The case deals with ex-convict and former heavyweight boxing champion Mike Tyson and his famous 1997 bout with then-champion Evander Holyfield, a fight ended by disqualification in the third round when Tyson bit both of Holyfield's ears. Incensed pay-per-view customers joined in a class action seeking their money back

($50–$60 each) claiming they were "ripped off" or "scammed" by Tyson. They sued Tyson, fight promoters, and fight telecasters. A lower court dismissed the complaint for failure to state a cause of action. The plaintiffs appealed.

LEGAL BRIEFCASE

Castillo v. Tyson   701 N.Y.S. 2D 423
(N.Y. S.Ct. App. Div. 2000)

Judge Ramos

Plaintiffs claim that they were entitled to view a "legitimate heavyweight title fight" fought "in accordance with the applicable rules and regulations" of the governing boxing commission—that is, a fight that was to end either in an actual or technical knockout or by decision of the judges after 12 rounds—and that they are entitled to their money back because the fight ended in a disqualification. Many legal theories are invoked in support of this claim—breach of contract, breach of implied covenant of good faith and fair dealing, unjust enrichment, breach of express and implied warranties, tortious interference with contractual relations, "wantonness," fraud, negligent representation—none of which have merit. Plaintiffs are not in contractual privity with any of the defendants, and their claim that they are third-party beneficiaries of one or more of the contracts that defendants entered into among themselves was aptly rejected by the motion court as "contrived." Nothing in these contracts can be understood as promising a fight that did not end in a disqualification. The rules of the governing commission provide for disqualification, and it is a possibility that a fight fan can reasonably expect. Plaintiffs could not reasonably rule out such a possibility by the boxer's and promoters' public statements predicting a "sensational victory" and "the biggest fight of all time," and assuming other representations were made promising or implying a "legitimate fight," there can be no breach of warranty claim absent privity of contract between plaintiffs and defendants and also because defendants provided only a service. Nor is a claim of fraud supported by plaintiffs' allegations that the boxer's former trainer predicted that the boxer would get himself disqualified if he failed to achieve an early knockout and that the boxer came out without his mouthpiece in the beginning of the round that he was disqualified. Plaintiffs' claim for unjust enrichment was properly dismissed by the motion court on the ground that plaintiffs received what they paid for, namely,

"the right to view whatever event transpired." We have considered plaintiffs' other arguments . . . and find them unpersuasive. Affirmed.

Questions

1. Why did the court reject the plaintiffs' breach of contract claim?

2. What is unjust enrichment, and why was that claim denied by the court?

3. Defects discovered in the Michelin tires to be used by 14 of the 20 teams in a Formula One race at the Indianapolis Speedway caused those teams to withdraw prior to the start, leaving only six cars running in the race. The race was completed, but fans sued for breach of contract claiming the race was not what they had purchased tickets to see and that the race advertising had indicated that 20 cars would be racing. Decide the case. Explain. See *Bowers v. Federation Internationale de L'Automobile,* 489 F.3d 316 (7th Cir. 2007).

4. Pelullo promoted boxers and boxing matches through his company, Banner Productions. In 1999 Echols signed an agreement with Banner giving Echols a $30,000 bonus and giving Banner "the sole and exclusive right to secure all professional boxing bouts" for Echols. Banner was to provide no fewer than three bouts per year, and Echols was to be paid not less than a specified minimum amount for each fight, but the payments could be lowered or the whole agreement canceled, at Banner's option, if Echols lost a fight. Echols lost a championship bout, and Banner said it would thereafter negotiate each purse on a bout-by-bout basis. Echols continued to fight for Banner, but various disputes over purses arose, and Echols sued. Among other claims, Echols argued that the agreement was unenforceable for indefiniteness. Decide that claim. Explain. See *Echols v. Pelullo,* 377 F.3d 272 (3d Cir. 2004).

Discharge by Lawful Excuses (for Nonperformance)

Sometimes contracts are discharged lawfully even in the event of nonperformance. This can occur when performance is either impossible or impractical.

Impossibility   After agreement is reached but performance is not yet due, circumstances may be so altered that performance is a *legal impossibility.* In such situations nonperformance is excused. Impossibility here refers not simply to extreme difficulty but to objective impossibility; that is, the contracted-for performance cannot be accomplished by anyone. Notable examples of such situations are a personal service contract where the promisor has died or is incapacitated by illness, a contract where the subject of the agreement was rendered illegal by a change in the law subsequent to the agreement but prior to its performance, or a contract where an ingredient essential to performance has been destroyed and no reasonable substitutes are available. [For more on impossibility of performance, see **http://www.west.net/~smith/imposbl.htm**]

Commercial Impracticability   Akin to the doctrine of impossibility is the situation in which duties are discharged because of unforeseen events that render performance exorbitantly expensive or thoroughly impractical. Commercial impracticability is specifically provided for in UCC 2-615, which reads, "Delay in delivery or nondelivery in whole or in part by a seller . . . is not a breach of his duty under a contract for sale if performance as agreed has been made impracticable by the occurrence of a contingency the nonoccurrence of which was a basic assumption on which the contract was made. . . ."

The UCC's commercial impracticability standard is more easily established than the impossibility doctrine of the common law, but note that only exceptional and unforeseeable events fall within the impracticability excuse for nonperformance. Mere changes in market conditions do not give rise to commercial impracticability. Historically, the commercial impracticability doctrine had been applied only to transactions involving the sale of goods, but now we see courts increasingly willing to apply it to other kinds of contracts as well.

Discharge by Agreement

A contractual discharge is sometimes achieved by a new agreement arrived at after entering the original contract. These agreements take a variety of forms, but one—*accord and satisfaction*—will serve here to illustrate the general category. Parties reach an accord when they agree to a performance different from the one provided for in their contract. Performance of the accord is called satisfaction, at which point the original contract is discharged. A binding accord and satisfaction must spring from a genuine dispute between the parties, and it must include consideration as well as all of the other ingredients in a binding contract.

Discharge by Operation of Law

Under some circumstances, contractual duties are discharged by the legal system itself. Among those possibilities: (1) The contractual responsibilities of a debtor may be discharged by a bankruptcy decree. (2) Each state has a *statute of limitations* that specifies the time within which a performing party can initiate a lawsuit against a nonperforming party. For the UCC statute of limitations, see 2-725.

Remedies

We have looked at the elements of a binding contract and at those circumstances that discharge a party's duties under a contract. Now our concern is with what happens when one of the parties does not fulfill his or her contractual duties—that is, when the contract is breached. Remedies are provided in both law and in equity (see Glossary and Chapter 4).

Remedies in Law

In general, a *breach of contract* allows the nonbreaching party to sue for money damages. The general goal of remedies law is to put the parties in the position they would have occupied had the contract been fulfilled. Normally, the best available substitute for actual performance is monetary damages.

Compensatory Damages   In brief, the plaintiff in a breach of contract action is entitled to recover a sum equal to the actual damages suffered. The plaintiff is compensated for her losses by receiving a sum designed to "make her whole," to put her where she would have been had the contract not been breached.

   Sale of Goods A breach involving a sale of goods is governed by the UCC. Typically the measure of *compensatory damages* would be the difference between the contract price and the market price of the goods at the time and place the goods were to be delivered (see UCC 2-708 and 2-713). Suppose you are working for a newly established computer manufacturer, and you have contracted with the Internal Revenue Service to deliver 1,000 laptop computers at $1,500 each, although the current market price is $1,600. If you fail to make that delivery, damages could be assessed in the amount of $100,000 ($100 $\times$ 1,000), which is the additional amount the IRS would need to pay to make the substitute purchase.

Consequential Damages   The victim of a breach may be able to recover not just the direct losses from the breach but also any indirect losses that were incurred as a consequence of that breach. Such consequential damages are recoverable only if they were foreseen or were reasonably foreseeable by the breaching party. For example, if you contract for a well-known local band to play for the grand opening of your new bar and dance club and the band fails to appear, you may be able to recover damages for any lost profits that you can attribute to the band's absence. Those lost profits are a *consequence* of the breach. Of course, you will have some difficulty in specifying the profits lost and in proving that the loss was attributable to the band's failure to perform.

> The grand opening of your new bar and the band fails to appear.

Incidental Damages   The costs incurred by the nonbreaching party in arranging a substitute performance or otherwise reducing the damages sustained because of the breach are recoverable as incidental damages. They would include such items as phone calls and transportation expenses.

Nominal Damages   In some cases of breach, the court will award only an insignificant sum, perhaps 1 dollar (plus court costs), because the nonbreaching party has suffered no actual damages. The point of nominal damages is to illustrate the wrongfulness of the breach.

Punitive Damages   Sometimes when the breaching party's conduct is particularly reprehensible, the court will penalize that wrongful behavior by awarding punitive damages to the injured party. The idea is to deter such conduct in the future. Normally punitive damages cannot be awarded in breach of contract cases except when provided for by statute or when the breach is accompanied by a tort such as fraud (as where one buys a defective car having reasonably relied on the falsehoods of a salesperson).

Rescission and Restitution   In some instances, including a material breach, mistake, fraud, undue influence, and duress, the wronged party may rescind (undo) the contract. The effect of a contract rescission is to return the parties to the positions they occupied before they entered the agreement. Generally, both parties must then make restitution to each other by returning whatever goods, property, and so forth were transferred under the contract or an equivalent amount of money.

Mitigation   Obviously the law should penalize a breaching party, as we have discussed; but you may be surprised to learn that the law also imposes expectations on the victim (the nonbreaching party). Specifically, the nonbreaching party is required to take reasonable steps toward mitigation—that is, to minimize her or his damages. What happens, for example, if you are wrongfully dismissed in breach of contract from your first job after college? You are expected to mitigate your damages by seeking another job. You need not take an inferior job, nor must you disturb your life by moving to another state or community; but you must take reasonable measures to minimize your claim against your former employer.

Liquidated Damages   We have reviewed both the legal penalties for breach and the duty to mitigate damages. The law also offers the opportunity to provide some control over the penalty for breach by including in the contract a liquidated damages clause. Here you and the other party to the contract agree in advance about the measure of damages should either of you default on your duties. That clause is fully enforceable so long as it is not designed to be a penalty but rather a good faith effort to assess in advance an accurate measure of damages. A valid liquidated damages clause limits the nonbreaching party to recovery of the amount provided for in that clause.

Remedies in Equity

Where justice cannot be achieved via money damages alone, the courts will sometimes impose equitable remedies. The chief forms of equitable remedy in contract cases are specific performance, injunction, reformation, and quasi-contract.

Specific Performance   In unusual circumstances the court may order the breaching party to remedy its wrong by performing its obligations precisely as provided for in the contract. Normally that specific performance is required only where the subject matter of the contract is unique and thus cannot be adequately compensated with money. Examples of such subject matter might include a particular piece of land, an art work, or a family heirloom. By contrast, specific performance would not be available in contracts involving conventional personal property such as a television or a car unless those items were unique (such as a one-of-a-kind Rolls Royce).

Normally the courts will not grant a specific performance remedy in personal service contracts (like an agreement by a cosmetic surgeon to perform a face-lift). If the surgeon refused to perform, specific performance probably would not be ordered. The quality of the surgery likely would not be equal to what had been bargained for; courts do not want to be in the position of supervising the completion of contracts, and as a matter of public policy, we do not want to put parties, in this case, the surgeon, in a position that amounts to involuntary servitude.

Injunction   An injunction is a court order that may either require or forbid a party to perform a specified act. Injunctions are granted only under exceptional circumstances. Perhaps the most common of those are the noncompetition agreements. For example, you take a computer programming job that will afford you access to company secrets. To protect itself, the company expects you to sign an agreement specifying that you will not take employment with a competing firm for one year after departure from your employer. If you should quit and seek to work for a competitor within one year, your former employer might be able to secure an injunction preventing you from doing so until the year has passed.

Reformation   Reformation is an equitable remedy that permits the court to rewrite the contract where it imperfectly expressed the parties' true intentions. Typically such situations involve a mutual mistake or fraud. Thus, if the parties sign a contract to sell a lot in a housing development, but the contract is written with an incorrect street address for the lot, an equity court could simply correct the error in the contract.

Quasi-Contract   What happens if one party has conferred a benefit on another, but a contract has not been created because of a failure of consideration, the application of the statute of frauds, or something of the sort? To prevent unjust enrichment, the court might then imply a contract as a matter of law. For example, assume a lawn service mistakenly trims your shrubs and you watch them do so, knowing that they are supposed to be caring for your neighbor's lawn. You have not entered a contract with the lawn service, but a court might well require you to pay the reasonable value of trimming your shrubs. To do otherwise would unjustly enrich you.

PRACTICING ETHICS   Bloggers Work for Free?

Liberal journalism blog *The Huffington Post* was sued in a class action in 2011 on the grounds that the blog had failed to pay the more than 9,000 bloggers who had provided content for the blog over a period of years. In submitting copy to *The Huffington Post,* bloggers knew they would not be paid, but presumably they valued the professional/political/personal exposure afforded by publication. The lawsuit, however, claims the agreement to provide content without compensation has resulted in unjust enrichment for Huffington. AOL purchased *The Huffington Post* earlier in 2011 for $315 million. *The Huffington Post* was created in 2005 as a blog aggregator and opinion site.

Questions

1. The law aside, does *The Huffington Post* have a moral duty to compensate the bloggers who knowingly gave away their content when that content subsequently proved to be instrumental in building Huffington into a valuable property? Explain. Do you feel a duty to pay others when you are the beneficiary of "unjust enrichment?" Explain.

Source: Stephanie Francis Ward, "Huffington Post Bloggers Sue, Seeking Payment for Writing," *ABA Journal,* April 12, 2011 [**http://www.abajournal.com/news/article/huffpo_bloggers_sue_seeking_payment_for_writing/**].

Internet Exercise

Go to the ContractsProf Blog [**http://lawprofessors.typepad.com/contractsprof_blog/**] for August 17, 2010. Read about and explain the breach of contract lawsuit filed against Paris Hilton. Do a broader Internet search to update the status of the Hilton lawsuit.

Chapter Questions

1. Wardle made a standard real estate offer to buy a house owned by Kessler. The offer contained a "time is of the essence" clause specifying that the deal had to be completed on or before 11 AM on September 26, 1997. Owen then submitted a backup purchase offer for the same price as offered by Wardle. Wardle's completed contract was not delivered to Kessler until approximately 11:20 AM on September 26, so Kessler sold to Owen. Wardle then sued Kessler. Decide. Explain. See *Owen v. Kessler,* 778 N.E.2d 953 (App. Ct. Mass. 2002).

2. A Peoples Group representative interviewed Hawley in Missouri. Hawley and Peoples completed a contract (signed by Hawley in Missouri and Peoples' president in Florida) for Hawley to recruit students in Missouri to attend a Peoples college in Florida. Hawley was to be paid a commission for the students he recruited. Hawley was to be able to participate in the Peoples health and life insurance plans, and Peoples was to provide the appropriate payroll taxes for Social Security and so forth. Hawley was to maintain certain licenses and insurance coverage, to exclusively represent Peoples' interests, and to complete Peoples' training program. Hawley was never physically present in Florida. Following training, Hawley was shot and killed while attempting to make one of his first calls in Missouri. Hawley's heirs sought Florida workers' compensation. Peoples said they could not be responsible for workers' compensation payments for Hawley's heirs because Peoples and Hawley had not entered a completed, binding contract.
   a. Explain Peoples' contract argument.
   b. Did the parties achieve a binding contract? Explain. See *Peoples Group v. Hawley,* 804 So. 2d 561 (Fla. Ct. App., 1st Dist. 2002).

3. Allen M. Campbell Co. sought a contract to build houses for the U.S. Navy. Approximately one half hour before the housing bids were due, Virginia Metal Industries quoted Campbell Co. a price of $193,121 to supply the necessary doors and frames. Campbell, using the Virginia Metal quote, entered a bid and won the contract. Virginia Metal refused to supply the necessary doors, and Campbell had to secure an alternative source of supply at a price $45,562 higher than Virginia Metal's quote. Campbell sued. Explain Campbell's claim. Defend Virginia Metal. Decide. See *Allen M. Campbell Co. Inc. v. Virginia Metal Industries,* 708 F.2d 930 (4th Cir. 1983).

4. The Great Minneapolis Surplus Store placed a newspaper ad saying, "Saturday 9:00 AM sharp. 3 Brand New Fur Coats. Worth $100.00. First Come. First Served. $1 each." Lefkowitz was the first customer at the store that Saturday. He demanded a coat and indicated his readiness to pay the dollar, but the store refused saying it was a "house rule" that the coats were intended for women customers only. Lefkowitz sued. Express the issue(s) in this case. Defend Great Minneapolis. Decide. Explain. See *Lefkowitz v. Great Minneapolis Surplus Store,* 86 N.W.2d 689 (Minn. S.Ct. 1957).

5. Blette contracted with ANC in May 2008 for a one-year apartment lease at $605 per month. In February 2009, Blette complained to ANC about substandard maintenance

and other problems. Blette tendered a $752.54 check and wrote an accompanying letter saying that the payment was to settle her forthcoming March, April, and May rent minus her alleged damages. She also wrote that if the check were cashed her terms were being accepted. ANC wrote back saying it would cash the check but that her demands were unacceptable. Was Blette in breach of contract when she failed to make full payment? Explain. See *THG/Apartments Near Campus v. Deeanna Blette,* 2010 Ia. App. LEXIS 571.

6. Sherwood agreed to purchase a cow, Rose 2d of Aberlone, from Walker at a price of 5 1/2 cents per pound (about $80). The parties believed the cow to be barren. Sherwood came to Walker's farm to collect the cow, but at that point it was obvious that Rose was pregnant. Walker refused to give over the cow, which was then worth $750 to $1,000. Sherwood sued. Should he get the cow? Explain. See *Sherwood v. Walker,* 33 N.W. 919 (Mich. S.Ct. 1887).

7. Weaver leased a service station from American Oil. The lease included a clause providing that Weaver would hold American Oil harmless for any negligence by American on the premises. Weaver and an employee were burned when an American Oil employee accidentally sprayed gasoline while at Weaver's station. Weaver had one and one half years of high school education. The trial record provides no evidence that Weaver read the lease, that American's agent asked him to read it, or that Weaver's attention was drawn to the "hold harmless" clause. The clause was in fine print and contained no title heading. Is the contract enforceable against Weaver? Explain. See *Weaver v. American Oil Co.,* 276 N.E.2d 144 (Ind. S.Ct. 1971).

8. Edward Sherman wanted to sell his business, Adgraphics. He retained V.R. Brokers as an agent for the sale. On December 5, 1985, William Lyon offered $75,000 for the business. Later that day, Sherman signed a counteroffer to sell for $80,000. On December 7 at 11:35 AM Lyon signed the counteroffer, and around noon he took it to Brokers. At about 9 AM that same day, Sherman told Brokers' principal, Robert Renault, that he had decided to cancel his counteroffer. Renault told Lyon of that decision immediately before Lyon handed the signed counteroffer to Renault. Lyon then sued for breach of contract. Decide. Explain. See *Lyon v. Adgraphics,* 540 A.2d 398 (Conn. Ct. App. 1988).

9. A building was rented "for use as a saloon" under an eight-year lease. Five years thereafter the state passed a law making the sale of liquor illegal. The renter, a brewery, argued that it no longer had any duties under the contract. Was the brewery correct? Explain. See *Heart v. East Tennessee Brewing Co.,* 113 S.W. 364 (Tenn. S.Ct. 1908).

10. The La Gasse Company contracted with the City of Fort Lauderdale to renovate one of the city's swimming pools. When the job was nearly complete, vandals severely damaged the pool and most of the work had to be redone. La Gasse sought additional compensation, which the city refused. La Gasse sued, claiming that the subject matter of the contract had been destroyed, thus discharging it from responsibility. Therefore, when it repeated the work, additional compensation was warranted. Decide. Explain. See *La Gasse Pool Construction Co. v. City of Fort Lauderdale,* 288 So. 2d 273 (Fla. Ct. App., 4th Dist. 1974).

11. Preference Personnel, a North Dakota corporation, entered a contract with Peterson to help him find employment in the tax law field. The contract provided that the

employer would pay the placement fee, unless Peterson voluntarily quit within 9 days, in which case he would be responsible for the fee, which was 20 percent of one year's salary. Peterson was placed in a job with an annual salary of $60,000, but he quit after one month. Peterson refused to pay the fee, and Preference sued for breach of contract. The lower court found that Peterson breached the contract, but at the time of the contract, Preference Personnel's state-required license to operate had been allowed to lapse. The court, therefore, dismissed the Preference claim ruling that the agreement was unenforceable as a matter of public policy. Preference appealed. Rule on that appeal. Explain. See *Preference Personnel, Inc. v. Peterson,* 710 N.W.2d 383 (N.D.S.Ct. 2006).

12. Panera, the bakery/café chain, had a clause in its lease that prevented the White City Shopping Center in Shrewsbury, Massachusetts, from renting space to another sandwich shop: "Landlord agrees not to enter into a lease, . . . for a bakery or restaurant reasonably expected to have annual sales of *sandwiches* (emphasis added) greater than ten percent (10%) of its total sales . . . " Panera asked a Massachusetts Superior Court to block the Shopping Center from leasing space to a Qdoba Mexican Grill on the grounds that a lease with the Grill would violate the terms of the Panera lease. How should the Court rule? Explain. See *White City Shopping Center, LP v. PR Restaurants, LLC,* 2006 Mass. Super. LEXIS 544.

10

Torts Affecting Business

▢ Learning Objectives

In this chapter you will learn:

10-1. To compare how tort law is related to property.

10-2. To differentiate the three divisions of torts and to generate a theory of why torts are so divided.

10-3. To explain the elements of negligence and to relate these elements to the development of negligence law.

10-4. To analyze why tort litigation is so controversial in society today.

Just as contract law is the way owners exchange what they own in a property-based legal system, so also tort law is an important part of the same system. The property fence protects our use of things. It is part of what we own. But our protected use is not *infinite*. It may be *absolute* but because we live with other people and what is proper to them, we may not use things just anyway we please. We do not have a protected use of a thing if our use harms what others own, including their persons. Tort law helps define where the property fence is when it comes to our use of things. It makes our use legally wrongful and helps anyone injured by our wrongful use to get compensation, called "damages."

The word **tort** means "wrong." Legally, a tort is a civil wrong other than a breach of contract. Tort law sets limits on how people can act and use their resources so they do not violate the right

LO 10-1

*Torts are divided into intentional torts, negligence, and strict liability.

others have to their resources. If you think of property as a type of legal fence surrounding resources, then tort law defines when someone has crossed that fence wrongfully so that compensation is due to the owner.

Legal wrongs inflicted on the resources of others may be crimes as well as torts (see Chapter 12), but the law of tort itself is civil rather than criminal. The usual remedy for a tort is dollar damages. Behavior that constitutes a tort is called *tortious* behavior. One who commits a tort is a *tortfeasor*.

This chapter divides torts into three main categories: intentional torts, negligence torts, and strict liability torts. Intentional torts involve deliberate actions that cause injury. Negligence torts involve injury following a failure to use reasonable care. Strict liability torts impose legal responsibility for injury even though a liable party neither intentionally nor negligently causes the injury.

Important to torts are the concepts of duty and causation. One is not liable for another's injury unless he or she has a *duty* toward the person injured. And, of course, there is usually no liability for injury unless one has *caused* the injury. We explain these concepts under the discussion of negligence, where they are most relevant.

This chapter also covers the topic of damages. The topic concerns the business community because huge damage awards, frequently against businesses, have become common in recent years.

LO 10-2

Intent is the desire to bring about certain results.

>> Intentional Torts

An important element in the following torts is *intent,* as we are dealing with intentional torts. **Intent** is usually defined as the desire to bring about certain results. But in some circumstances the meaning is even broader, including not only desired results but also results that are "substantially likely" to result from an action. Recently, employers who knowingly exposed employees to toxic substances without warning them of the dangers have been sued for committing the intentional tort of battery. The employers did not desire their employees' injuries, but these injuries were "substantially likely" to result from the failure to warn.

The following sections explain the basic types of intentional torts. Sidebar 10.1 lists these torts.

>> *sidebar* 10.1

Types of Intentional Torts

- Assault and battery
- Intentional infliction of mental distress
- Invasion of privacy
- False imprisonment and malicious prosecution
- Trespass

- Conversion
- Defamation
- Fraud
- Common law business torts

1. ASSAULT AND BATTERY

An **assault** is the placing of another in immediate apprehension for his or her physical safety. "Apprehension" has a broader meaning than "fear." It includes the expectation that one is about to be physically injured. The person who intentionally creates such apprehension in another is guilty of the tort of assault. Many times a battery follows an assault. A **battery** is an illegal touching of another. As used here, "illegal" means that the touching is done without justification and without the consent of the person touched.

Hitting someone with a wrench causes physical injury, but as the following case illustrates, the "touching" that constitutes part of a battery need not cause physical injury.

 case 10.1 >>

HARPER v. WINSTON COUNTY
892 So.2d 346 (Ala. Sup. Ct. 2004)

Sandra Wright, the revenue commissioner of Winston County, Alabama, fired her employee, Sherry Harper. Harper sued, claiming among other things that Wright had committed an assault and battery in grabbing her and jerking her arm in trying to force her to go to Wright's office. Before trial, the court granted summary judgment in favor of Wright. The plaintiff, Harper, appealed, and the case reached the Alabama Supreme Court.

SEE, J: . . . Harper argues that the trial court erred in entering a summary judgment in favor of Wright, on Harper's assault and battery claim, because, she claims, she presented substantial evidence in support of her claim. Harper argues that Wright admits that she intentionally grabbed Harper's arm and, she asserts, Wright's grabbing of her arm was offensive. Harper states: "[Wright] jerked my arm and tried to pull me back." She argues that Alabama law does not require that Wright strike or hit her in order for a battery to occur. In response, Wright argues that she merely "took a hold of [Harper's] hand." Wright states that she did not touch Harper in an offensive manner and that she was only trying to coax Harper into stepping into her office so that they could continue their conversation away from the view of the customers and the employees of the Department. The trial court stated in its summary-judgment order that "the undisputed evidence from Sandra Wright clearly points out that the touching was not in any way harmful or offensive, but was instead done in an attempt to bring [Harper] under control."

The plaintiff in an action alleging assault and battery must prove "(1) that the defendant touched the plaintiff; (2) that the defendant intended to touch the plaintiff; and (3) that the touching was conducted in a harmful or offensive manner." In *Atmore Community Hospital*, the plaintiff presented evidence indicating that the defendant "touched her waist, rubbed against her when passing her in the hall, poked her in the armpits near the breast area, and touched her leg." The plaintiff also presented evidence indicating that "each of these touchings was intentional, was conducted with sexual overtones, and was unwelcome." We held that these factual assertions constituted substantial evidence that the defendant had committed a battery.

In *Surrency*, we stated that an actual injury to the body is not a necessary element for an assault-and-battery claim. We also stated that when the evidence as to whether a battery in fact occurred is conflicting, the question whether a battery did occur is for the jury. Quoting *Singer Sewing Machine Co.*, this Court stated:

> "To what acts will constitute a battery in a case like this, the rule is well stated by Mr. Cooley in his work on Torts. He says: 'A successful assault becomes a battery. A battery consists in an injury actually done to the person of another in an angry or revengeful or rude or insolent manner, as by spitting in the face, or in any way touching him in anger, or violently jostling him out of the way, or in doing any intentional violence to the person of another.' *The wrong here consists, not in the touching, so much as in the manner or spirit in which it is done, and the question of bodily pain is important only as affecting damages. Thus, to lay hands on another in a hostile manner is a battery, although no damage follows; but to touch another, merely to attract his attention, is no battery*

[continued]

and not unlawful. And to push gently against one, in the endeavor to make way through a crowd, is no battery; but to do so rudely and insolently is and may justify damages proportioned to the rudeness. . . ."

Alabama courts have recognized that privilege can be a defense to a plaintiff's claim that the defendant battered her. This Court has held that when a merchant suspects a customer of shoplifting, it is reasonable for the merchant's employee to use reasonable force to ensure that the suspected shoplifter is detained.

In this case, there is no question that Wright intended to touch Harper's arm; it is the "manner or spirit" in which Wright touched Harper's arm that is in dispute. Harper testified at the June 13, 2000, hearing that Wright forcefully grabbed her arm. Wright testified that she reached for Harper's arm in an attempt to lead her into her office so they could continue their discussion away from the public area. In *Surrency,* we noted that "to touch another, merely to attract his attention, is no battery and not unlawful. While it is certainly conceivable that this type of touching is all that occurred in this case, Harper presents substantial evidence to the contrary. Harper testified at her hearing that Wright "jerked" her arm. In her response to Wright's motion for a summary judgment, Harper states that Wright's touch greatly offended her and that this fact is evidenced by the fact that she filed her complaint with the Winston County Commission on May 9, 2000. In her complaint, Harper states that "[Wright] grabbed my arm and tried to force me to go with her." Reviewing the facts in the light most favorable to Harper, as this Court is required to do on an appeal from a summary judgment, we conclude that the question whether a battery occurred in this case—specifically, whether Wright touched Harper in a harmful or offensive manner—is a question of fact for the jury to decide.

We reverse the summary judgment in favor of Wright on Harper's assault-and-battery claim; and we remand this case to the trial court for proceedings consistent with this opinion.

>> CASE QUESTIONS

1. The defendant in this case did not hurt the plaintiff, Harper. Explain why the defendant might still be liable for the tort of battery.

2. Do all touchings constitute a battery? Discuss and give examples to support your conclusion.

3. In litigation what is the difference between a question of law and a question of fact? What does the Alabama Supreme Court decide in this case about whether this alleged battery is a question of law or a question of fact? Discuss.

A store manager who threatens an unpleasant customer with a wrench, for example, is guilty of assault. Actually hitting the customer with the wrench would constitute battery.

2. INTENTIONAL INFLICTION OF MENTAL DISTRESS

This tort usually requires the plaintiff to prove not only mental distress but also physical symptoms.

Intentional **infliction of mental distress** is a battery to the emotions. It arises from outrageous, intentional conduct that carries a strong probability of causing mental distress to the person at whom it is directed. Usually, one who sues on the basis of an intentional infliction of mental distress must prove that the defendant's outrageous behavior caused not only mental distress but also physical symptoms, such as headaches or sleeplessness.

The most common cases of intentional infliction of mental distress (also called *emotional distress*) have concerned employees who have been discriminated against or fired. Many such cases, however, do not involve the type of outrageous conduct necessary for the mental distress tort.

In the business world, other examples of infliction of mental distress come about from the efforts of creditors to extract payment from their debtors. Frequent, abusive, threatening phone calls by creditors might provide the basis for a claim of intentional infliction of mental distress. As torts go, this one is of fairly recent origin. It is a judge-made tort, which furnishes a good example of how the courts are becoming increasingly sensitive to the range of injuries for which compensation is appropriate. In some states, courts have gone so far as to establish liability for carelessly inflicted mental distress, such as the distress of a mother who sees her child negligently run down by a delivery truck.

3. INVASION OF PRIVACY

The tort of **invasion of privacy** is one that is still in the early stages of legal development. As the statutes and court cases recognize it, the tort at present comprises three principal invasions of personal interest. An invasion of any one of these areas of interest is sufficient to trigger liability.

Most commonly, liability will be imposed on a defendant who appropriates the plaintiff's name or likeness for his or her own use. Many advertisers and marketers have been required to pay damages to individuals when pictures of them have been used without authorization to promote products, or when their names and identities have been used without permission for promotional purposes. Before using anyone's picture or name, an advertiser must obtain a proper release from that person to avoid possible liability. See Sidebar 10.2.

> That you can recover damages for misappropriation of likeness illustrates that you own your name and likeness in certain respects.

>> *sidebar* 10.2

Privacy, Michael Jordan, and Society

Michael Jordan's name is one of the most recognizable in all of sports. Jordan has filed several lawsuits against advertisers who have used his name without permission in connection with the promotion of their products. For instance, he sued Avon for $100 million in connection with a Father's Day promotion that used his identity. Avon and Jordan settled that case. More recently, Jordan sued two Chicago-area grocery stores for using his name in order to attract customers to their stores. Sports and entertainment stars especially often sue businesses that use their identities without permission.

In general, the law considers a right to privacy as "a right to be left alone." But notice how similar a right to privacy is to the property right. Privacy, like property, is a right to exclude others from interfering with something that is privately proper to someone. Would it have been simpler if the law had developed by saying that people have *property* in their identities? Why do you think the law didn't develop this way?

Privacy concerns arose as new technologies like cameras and recorders made it easy to peer into the lives of others. The same concerns continue today with the Internet and computers. Legislatures have passed a variety of laws concerning privacy. As with the common law causes of action mentioned in this section of the text, some of the new privacy acts and statutes don't even mention the word "privacy." Chapter 18 on consumer protection covers some of the new privacy laws. In general, concern about various privacy issues illustrate how law develops to meet changing needs in society.

A second invasion of privacy is the defendant's intrusion upon the plaintiff's physical solitude. Illegal searches or invasions of home or possessions, illegal wiretapping, and persistent and unwanted telephoning can provide the basis for this invasion-of-privacy tort. In one case, a woman even recovered damages against a photographer who entered her sickroom and snapped a picture of her. Employers who enter their employees' homes without permission have also been sued successfully for invasions of privacy. If the invasion of privacy continues, it may be enjoined by the court. Jacqueline Kennedy Onassis sought and obtained an injunction that forbade a certain photographer from getting too close to her and her children. Under this tort, the invasion of physical solitude must be highly objectionable to a reasonable person.

Don't forget that the First Amendment protects you when you publish even highly personal truthful information about public officials and public figures.

The third invasion of personal interest that gives rise to the invasion-of-privacy tort is the defendant's public disclosure of highly objectionable, private information about the plaintiff. A showing of such facts can be the basis for a cause of action, even if the information is true. Thus, publishing in a newspaper that the plaintiff does not pay his or her debts has been ruled to create liability for the defendant creditor. Communicating the same facts to a credit-reporting agency or the plaintiff's employer usually does not impose liability, however. In these cases, there has been no disclosure to the public in general. Also, the news media are protected under the First Amendment when they publish information about public officials and other public figures.

4. FALSE IMPRISONMENT AND MALICIOUS PROSECUTION

One false imprisonment lawsuit arose when a tow-truck operator towed a car with the driver still in it.

Shoplifting accounts for some $18 billion a year in business losses, almost 1% of retail sales. Claims of **false imprisonment** stem most frequently in business from instances of shoplifting. This tort is the intentional unjustified confinement of a nonconsenting person. Although most states have statutes that permit merchants or their employees to detain customers suspected of shoplifting, this detention must be a reasonable one. The unnecessary use of force, lack of reasonable suspicion of shoplifting, or an unreasonable length of confinement can cause the merchant to lose the statutory privilege. The improperly detained customer is then able to sue for false imprisonment. Allegations of battery are also usually made if the customer has been touched. Not all false imprisonment lawsuits arise because of shoplifting. In one instance a KPMG employee sued for false imprisonment alleging that his manager blocked a door with a chair during a performance review and caused the employee to have to remain in the room against his will.

The tort of **malicious prosecution** is often called *false arrest*. Malicious prosecution arises from causing someone to be arrested criminally without proper grounds. It occurs, for instance, when the arrest is accomplished simply to harass someone. In Albany, New York, a jury awarded a man $200,000 for malicious prosecution. His zipper had broken, leaving his fly open, and a store security guard had him arrested for indecent exposure even after he explained that he had not noticed the problem.

5. TRESPASS

To enter another's land without consent or to remain there after being asked to leave constitutes the tort of **trespass.** A variation on the trespass tort arises when something (such as particles of pollution) is placed on another's land without consent. Although the usual civil action for trespass asks for an injunction to restrain the trespasser, the action may also ask for damages.

Union pickets walking on company property (in most instances), customers refusing to leave a store after being asked to do so, and unauthorized persons entering restricted areas are all examples of trespass. Note that trespass is often a crime as well as a tort. Intentional wrongdoing is frequently criminal.

Trespass concerns the crossing of an owner's boundaries. Today, trespass usually refers to violating the physical boundaries of an owner's land, but in legal history trespass was the legal remedy for direct injuries caused by another to one's person as well. The famous British constitutional historian Frederick Maitland wrote, "Trespass is the fertile mother of actions." By this he meant that many of our modern day causes of action in tort—like battery—come from trespass. Now do you appreciate better the connection of tort law to property in our legal system? In an important sense, we own ourselves and various things we have acquired, and those who violate our boundaries become liable to compensate us.

6. CONVERSION

Conversion is the wrongful exercise of dominion (power) and control over the personal (nonland) resources that belong to another. Conversion deprives owners of their lawful right to exclude others from such resources. The deprivation may be either temporary or permanent, but it must constitute a serious invasion of the owner's legal right. Abraham Lincoln once convinced an Illinois court that a defendant's action in riding the plaintiff's horse for 15 miles was not sufficiently serious to be a conversion since the defendant had returned the horse in good condition. The plaintiff had left the horse with the defendant to be stabled and fed.

Conversion often arises in business situations. Stealing something from an employer is conversion, as is purchasing—even innocently—something that has been stolen. Failing to return something properly acquired at the designated time, delivering something to the wrong party, and destruction or alteration of what belongs to another are all conversions when a deprivation of ownership is serious or long-lived. Even if you intend to return something, if you have converted it you are absolutely liable for any damage done to it. A warehouse operator who improperly transfers stored goods from a designated to a nondesignated warehouse is absolutely liable when a tornado destroys the goods or when a thief steals them.

7. DEFAMATION

Defamation is the publication of untrue statements about another that hold up that individual's character or reputation to contempt and ridicule. "Publication" means that the untruth must be made known to third parties. If defamation is oral, it is called **slander.** Written defamation, or defamation published over radio or television, is termed **libel.**

False accusations of dishonesty or inability to pay debts frequently bring on defamation suits in business relationships. Sometimes, such accusations arise during the course of a takeover attempt by one company of another through an offering to buy stock. In a recent instance, the chairman of one company called the chairman of a rival business "lying, deceitful, and treacherous" and charged that he "violated the standards by which decent men do business." If untrue, these remarks provide a good example of defamation of character. At one major university, a former business professor received a multimillion-dollar settlement following allegations made by university administrators that he had vandalized the new business school. The allegations cost

The reason for emphasizing how tort relates to property is to show you how our legal system has historically centered on the concept of exclusive right, which applies to your person as well as to land and other physical resources.

In one case a student drove a rental car into Mexico although the lease specifically prohibited cross-border driving. When an earthquake destroyed the car while it was parked in Mexico City, the rental company successfully sued the student for conversion.

Is it defamation of character to say that someone is gay or lesbian? How about that someone is of a different race than is correct? Is calling someone a "communist" defamatory?

In 2008, publisher Judith Reagan and her employer News Corporation settled her $100 million lawsuit against News Corporation for defaming her by saying it had fired her because she had made anti-Semitic remarks.

him a deanship at another university. Punitive or punishment damages, as well as actual damages, may be assessed in defamation cases.

Individuals are not the only ones who can sue for defamation. A corporation can also sue for defamation if untrue remarks discredit the way the corporation conducts its business. Untruthfully implying that a company's entire management is dishonest or incompetent defames the corporation.

Nearly one-third of all defamation suits are currently brought by employees against present and former employers. Often these suits arise when employers give job references on former employees who have been discharged for dishonesty. As a result, many employers will now not give job references or will do no more than verify that former employees did work for them.

There are two basic defenses to a claim of defamation. One defense is that the statements made were true. *Truth* is an absolute defense. The second defense is that the statement arose from *privileged communications*. For example, statements made by legislators, judges, attorneys, and those involved in lawsuits are privileged under many circumstances.

Defamation and the First Amendment   Because of the First Amendment, special rules regarding defamation apply to the news media. These media are not liable for the defamatory untruths they print about public officials and public figures unless plaintiffs can prove that the untruths were published with "malice" (evil intent, that is, the deliberate intent to injure) or with "reckless disregard for the truth." Public figures are those who have consciously brought themselves to public attention. See Sidebar 10.3.

>> *sidebar* 10.3

Football Coaches as Public Figures

The U.S. Supreme Court issued the "public official" standard requiring defamation plaintiffs to prove "malice" or "reckless disregard for the truth" in *New York Times v. Sullivan,* 376 U.S. 254 (1964), a case involving criticism of an Alabama police commissioner. The Court extended essentially the same standard to defamation cases against "public figures" in *Curtis Publishing Co. v. Butts,* 388 U.S. 130 (1967). The facts of this case are interesting.

The *Saturday Evening Post,* one of the nation's leading feature story magazines for many years, published a story about the University of Georgia's athletic director and former football coach Wallace ("Wally") Butts and the University of Alabama's football coach Paul ("Bear") Bryant. The *Post* alleged that in a telephone conversation overheard accidentally by an Atlanta insurance salesman, Butts told Bryant how to beat Georgia in an upcoming game. "Before the University of Georgia played the University of Alabama. . . , Wally Butts . . . gave to Bear Bryant

Georgia's plays, defensive patterns, all the significant secrets Georgia's football team possessed." The article continued, "The Georgia players, their moves analyzed and forecast like those of rats in a maze, took a frightful physical beating." Georgia lost the game, and Alabama went on to win the national championship.

Although the conversation between the two coaches may really have involved only a routine request to exchange game films, Butts ended up being forced to resign as athletic director. Both he and Bryant sued the *Post* for defamation. The coaches won their lawsuit, which was appealed to the Supreme Court.

The Court determined that the two coaches were "public figures" and that the First Amendment protected comment about them in much the same way it protected comment about public officials. However, the Court also concluded that the coaches had met their heavy burden of proof. It affirmed the judgment against the *Post.* Within a short time, the *Saturday Evening Post* went out of business.

Plaintiffs' verdicts in media defamation cases are often overturned by trial or appellate judges. In one instance a Houston investment firm, now defunct, sued *The Wall Street Journal,* claiming that a story published by the newspaper caused the firm to go out of business. Following a huge jury verdict, the trial judge threw out $200 million in damages, ruling that the firm had not proved the newspaper published certain statements with knowledge of their falsity or with reckless disregard for the truth.

Plaintiffs' verdicts in defamation cases are often overturned by appellate courts. Because of the constitutional protection given to speech and the media, appellate judges reexamine trial evidence very closely to determine whether the necessary elements of defamation had been proven.

8. FRAUD

Business managers must be alert to the intentional tort of **fraud.** A fraud is an intentional misrepresentation of a material fact that is justifiably relied upon by someone to his or her injury. An intentional misrepresentation means a lie. The lie must be of a material fact—an important one. The victim of the fraud must justifiably rely on the misrepresentation and must suffer some injury, usually a loss of money or other resource one owns.

According to a survey by the Association of Certified Fraud Examiners, U.S. companies lose an average of 6% of their profit to fraud.

Fraud applies in many different situations. Business frauds often involve the intentional misrepresentation of property or financial status. Lying about assets or liabilities in order to get credit or a loan is a fraud. Likewise, intentionally misrepresenting that land is free from hazardous waste when the seller knows that toxic chemicals are buried on the land constitutes fraud.

You can also prove fraud by giving evidence that another has harmed you by failing to disclose a material (important) hidden fact. The fraud of failure to disclose arises when the defendant is under a legal duty to disclose a fact, such as when a defendant seller knows that the foundations of a house are weakened by termites and must disclose this to the buyer.

Likewise, a defendant who has intentionally concealed an important fact and has induced reliance on it to the plaintiff's injury is liable for fraud. Following the financial collapse that began in 2007, hundreds of plaintiffs filed fraud lawsuits against banks, other financial institutions, and various of their executives based on concealment. In one such case, the former chief executive of Countrywide Financial agreed to pay $67.5 million to settle a fraud case brought by the Securities and Exchange Commission. The alleged fraud was the intentional concealment of the risks of subprime mortgages from investors in the then-largest national mortgage lender. Note that not only the common law but also many statutes regulating the financial industry provide for causes of action based on fraud.

In another concealment case, New York State filed a lawsuit based on fraud against Guidant Corporation. The complaint alleged that heart defibrillators manufactured by the company were defective and that the implanted devices had already failed in 28 patients. Further, the complaint asserted that Guidant had known of the defect for several years and concealed this information while continuing to sell the defibrillators. Said New York's former attorney general, "Concealment of negative facts that might influence a consumer to purchase another manufacturer's product is the essence of fraud."

Fraud is not only a tort but a crime as well. Do you understand the difference between torts and crimes? (See Sidebar 10.4.)

>> *sidebar* 10.4

Tort or Crime? Or Both?

Some torts are crimes and some are not. How do we make sense out of this? Crimes, which you will study in Chapter 13, generally require *intent* (also called *willfulness*). The prosecutor has to prove that the defendant intended to cross the proper boundaries (property) established by law. If the primary purpose of the state (government) is to protect people and their resources with the legal fence of property, as was thought by many framers of the Constitution, it becomes clear that most crimes, which are offenses against the proper order (property order) enforced by the government, involve the most serious and intentional crossings of the legal fences that protect people. These crossings injure or harm what belongs to people and the state punishes such harm. But people also deserve compensation because of the injury. That is where tort law comes in.

The most serious torts like assault, battery, conversion, and fraud, which are also frequently crimes, are all intentional. Accidental boundary crossings are usually not criminal unless they are extremely reckless, but when they injure what belongs to an owner, the owner can still get compensation through tort law, for example, through proof of unreasonable and careless boundary crossing called *negligence* (see Sections 11–13). Likewise, certain other accidental boundary crossings that cause injury, like the sale of a defective product, result in the person crossing the legal fence being held *strictly liable,* that is, liable even in the absence of unreasonable behavior in the crossing (see Sections 15–17). However, because these torts are unintentional, they are usually not crimes as well.

Since torts are civil and crimes are, well, criminal in nature, they have different burdens of proof, as explained in Chapter 4. The judge instructs the jury that the plaintiff must prove the tort by a preponderance of the evidence but instructs the jury in a criminal case that the prosecutor must prove the victim's intentional injury by the defendant beyond a reasonable doubt. The burdens of proof are different because to deprive criminal defendants of their freedom is considered much more serious than merely to deprive them civilly of their money. And burdens of proof exist in both civil and criminal cases because to punish a criminal defendant to protect the proper order of the state or to compensate a civil plaintiff for a wrongful boundary crossing involves the taking of something that was previously proper to defendants, whether it is their freedom, their money, or some other resource belonging to them.

Do you understand better now why the same trespass across a legal fence can be both a tort and a crime?

Additional Fraud Examples   Fraud also can be committed in the hiring process. For instance, courts have found employers liable for misrepresenting to employees about conditions at a business that later affect employment adversely. In one case, former professional football player Phil McConkey received a $10 million award because his employer misrepresented the status of merger talks with another company. McConkey lost his job the year after he was hired when the two companies merged.

Other instances of business fraud can include:

- Misrepresentation in employment. Screenwriter Benedict Fitzgerald sued actor–director Mel Gibson and his production company for defrauding him into taking a much smaller salary based on their representation that the movie budget was only $4 million–$7 million instead of the estimated $25 million–$50 million that had been actually budgeted.
- Misrepresentation about products. The tobacco industry is beginning to lose lawsuits when plaintiffs allege fraud based on the industry's claiming

for years that no tobacco consumption harm had been scientifically proved when it knew that such harm had been established. In 2008, for instance, the Oregon Supreme Court affirmed a $79.5 million punitive damage award in the fraud case of deceased smoker Jesse Williams.

- Concealment about products. Farmers and growers have received over $1 billion from DuPont in settlements based on the damage the fungicide Benlate caused various plants. DuPont allegedly committed fraud by concealing that Benlate could cause crop damage even when the company was asked about the possibility.

- Nondisclosure to third parties about home sale prices. Fannie Mae, the nation's largest investor in home loans, told lenders in 2008 that it considered certain "practices that may distort or artificially inflate" house prices to be potentially fraudulent. Fannie Mae referenced situations where home developers or builders represented that they sold homes in an area for reported high prices but in reality gave back part of the purchase price to buyers. The concern is that such practices can defraud future home buyers in that development into paying higher prices than they actually should and also mislead banks that loan money for home mortgages in the area.

The previous chapter on contracts discussed fraud as voiding a contract. But fraud is also an intentional tort, and one who is a victim of fraud can sue for damages, including punitive or punishment damages. Today many frauds, as well as other intentional torts, occur on the Internet. See Sidebar 10.5.

>> sidebar 10.5

Internet Torts

A variety of intentional torts take place on the Internet. Defamation occurs when e-mailers place messages on Listservs or public chatrooms that hold others up to "public contempt or ridicule." Intentional infliction of mental distress arises, for example, when threats are made via e-mail or websites. A jury in Oregon awarded plaintiffs over $100 million when it found that a website threatened abortion providers. When computer hackers break into company databases, trade secrets are easily misappropriated.

Perhaps the most common intentional cyber-related tort is fraud. The Federal Trade Commission has released a list of such frauds or scams that include a variety of pyramid schemes, fraudulent auctions, deceptive travel offers, sale of unmiraculous "miracle" products, health care rip-offs, phony credit card charges, and work-at-home frauds. There was even a "rebate" check sent to consumers that if cashed gave them new Internet service that could not be canceled. The FTC reports that its enforcement actions against Internet scams have risen steadily in recent years.

Fraud and Corporate Governance   Antifraud laws are a major weapon in the enforcement of good corporate governance. Much corporate misgovernance, especially by managers, arises because of misrepresentations of fact about corporate assets or liabilities. These misrepresentations usually induce investors to buy corporate stock shares at higher prices and benefit corporate managers or others inside the corporation who sell their stock. Sometimes a misrepresentation that raises the stock price obtains a bonus or other perk for managers or a loan for the corporation. Usually, a misrepresentation amounts to fraud because investors (who become owners) or lenders rely on it to their injury, that is, they lose some or all of their investment.

Many specific laws create civil and criminal liability for the fraud of corporate managers and other corporate agents. As you think about fraud, remember that it violates the principle of property. One does not acquire proper ownership by defrauding others of their resources. Fraud does not respect the equal property right of others.

9. COMMON LAW BUSINESS TORTS

The label *business torts* embraces different kinds of torts that involve intentional interference with business relations.

Injurious Falsehood   **Injurious falsehood,** sometimes called *trade disparagement,* is a common business tort. It consists of the publication of untrue statements that disparage the business owner's product or its quality. General disparagement of the plaintiff's business may also provide basis for liability. As a cause of action, injurious falsehood is similar to defamation of character. It differs, however, in that it usually applies to a product or business rather than character or reputation. The requirements of proof are also somewhat different. Defamatory remarks are presumed false unless the defendant can prove their truth. But in disparagement cases the plaintiff must establish the falsity of the defendant's statements. The plaintiff must also show actual damages arising from the untrue statements.

As an example of injurious falsehood, consider the potential harm to Procter & Gamble of the assertions that associated its former logo of moon and stars with satanism. The company threatened to sue a number of individuals. In another instance Warnaco sued Calvin Klein, alleging that Klein had made publicly disparaging remarks about how Warnaco made Calvin Klein clothing under license. The lawsuit alleged that Klein "falsely accused [Warnaco] of effectively 'counterfeiting' Calvin Klein apparel."

Intentional Interference with Contractual Relations   A second type of business tort is **intentional interference with contractual relations.** Probably the most common example of this tort involves one company raiding another for employees. If employees are under contract to an employer for a period of time, another employer cannot induce them to break their contracts. In a variation on this tort, the brokerage firm PaineWebber Group sued Morgan Stanley Dean Witter & Company over PaineWebber's merger agreement with J. C. Bradford & Company. PaineWebber claimed that Morgan Stanley pursued "a carefully planned, broadbased campaign to raid Bradford personnel and interfere with the merger agreement between PaineWebber and Bradford."

One of the most famous tort cases in history involved interference with a contract of merger. In that case a jury awarded Pennzoil over $10 billion against Texaco for persuading Getty Oil to breach an agreement of merger with Pennzoil. After Texaco filed for bankruptcy, Pennzoil accepted a settlement of around $3 billion.

> **Do** remember that you can be sued for making statements about a competitor's product that the competitor considers false.

> **Don't** induce the employees of another company to come to work for you when they are under contract to work for a period of time.

>> Negligence

The second major area of tort liability involves unreasonable behavior that causes injury. This area of tort is called **negligence.** In the United States more lawsuits allege negligence than any other single cause of action.

Negligence takes place when one who has a duty to act reasonably acts carelessly and causes injury to another. Actually, five separate elements make up negligence, and the following sections discuss these elements. Sidebar 10.6 also summarizes them. In business, negligence can occur when employees cause injury to customers or others; when those invited to a business are injured because the business fails to protect them; when products are not carefully manufactured; when services, such as accounting services, are not carefully provided; and in many other situations.

>> *sidebar* 10.6

Elements of Negligence

Existence of a duty of care owed by the defendant to the plaintiff.

Unreasonable behavior by the defendant that breaches the duty.

Causation in fact.

Proximate causation.

An actual injury.

---

10. DUTY OF CARE

A critical element of the negligence tort is **duty.** Without a duty to another person, one does not owe that person reasonable care. Accidental injuries occur daily for which people other than the victim have no responsibility, legally or otherwise.

Duty usually arises out of a person's conduct or activity. A person doing something has a duty to use reasonable care and skill around others to avoid injuring them. Whether one is driving a car or manufacturing a product, she or he has a duty not to injure others by unreasonable conduct.

Usually, a person has no duty to avoid injuring others through *nonconduct.* There is no general duty requiring a sunbather at the beach to warn a would-be surfer that a great white shark is lurking offshore, even if the sunbather has seen the fin. There is moral responsibility but no legal duty present.

When there is a special relationship between persons, the situation changes. A person in a special relationship to another may have a duty to avoid unreasonable nonconduct. A business renting surfboards at the beach would probably be liable for renting a board to a customer who was attacked by a shark if it knew the shark was nearby and failed to warn the customer. The special business relationship between the two parties creates a duty to take action and makes the business liable for its unreasonable nonconduct.

*A person doing something has a legal duty to act reasonably to avoid injuring others.

In recent years, negligence cases against businesses for nonconduct have grown dramatically. Most of these cases have involved failure to protect customers from crimes. The National Crime Prevention Institute estimates that such cases have increased tenfold since the mid-1970s.

One famous case involved the Tailhook scandal. A group of male naval aviators was sexually groping female guests as they walked down the hallway at a Hilton hotel. (Remember that an unconsented-to touching is an intentional tort.) One of the females who was sexually touched sued the Hilton hotel for negligence in knowing of the aviators' behavior and failing to protect her. A jury awarded her a total of $6.7 million against Hilton.

The extent of a business's duty to protect customers is still evolving. Note that in Case 10.2 the New Hampshire Supreme Court says that the defendant restaurant has no special relationship to the plaintiff, but still rules that it may have a duty to protect restaurant customers.

 case 10.2 >>

IANNELLI v. BURGER KING CORP.
200 N. H. Lexis 42 (N. H. Sup. Ct. 2000)

MCHUGH, J.: The plaintiffs, Nicholas and Jodiann Iannelli, individually and on behalf of their three children, brought a negligence action against the defendant, Burger King Corporation, for injuries sustained as a result of an assault at the defendant's restaurant. During the late afternoon or early evening hours of December 26, 1995, the Iannelli family went to the defendant's restaurant for the first time. Upon entering the restaurant, the Iannellis became aware of a group of teenagers consisting of five males and two females, whom they alleged were rowdy, obnoxious, loud, abusive, and using foul language. Some in the group claimed they were "hammered." Initially this group was near the ordering counter talking to an employee whom they appeared to know. The Iannellis alleged that one of the group almost bumped into Nicholas. When that fact was pointed out, the teenager exclaimed, "I don't give an F. That's his F'ing problem."

Nicholas asked his wife and children to sit down in the dining area as he ordered the food. While waiting for the food to be prepared, Nicholas joined his family at their table. The teenagers also moved into the dining area to another table. The obnoxious behavior and foul language allegedly continued. One of the Iannelli children became nervous. Nicholas then walked over to the group intending to ask them to stop swearing. As Nicholas stood two or three feet from the closest of the group, he said, "Guys, hey listen, I have three kids." Whereupon, allegedly unprovoked, one or more of the

group assaulted Nicholas by hitting him, knocking him to the ground and striking him in the head with a chair.

The plaintiffs argue that a commercial enterprise such as a restaurant has a general duty to exercise reasonable care toward its patrons, which may include a duty to safeguard against assault when circumstances provide warning signs that the safety of its patrons may be at risk. The most instructive case, given the issues presented, is *Walls v. Oxford Management Co.* In *Walls,* a tenant of an apartment complex alleged that the owner's negligent maintenance of its property allowed her to be subjected to a sexual assault in the parking lot. We held that as a general principle landlords have no duty to protect tenants from criminal attacks. In as much as landlords and tenants have a special relationship that does not exist between a commercial establishment and its guests, it follows that the same general principle of law extends to restaurants and their patrons. We recognized in *Walls,* however, that particular circumstances can give rise to such a duty. These circumstances include when the opportunity for criminal misconduct is brought about by the actions or inactions of the owner or where overriding foreseeability of such criminal activity exists.

Viewing the evidence in the light most favorable to the plaintiffs, we must decide whether the behavior of the rowdy youths could have created an unreasonable risk of injury to restaurant patrons that was foreseeable to the defendant. If the risk of injury was reasonably

[continued]

foreseeable, then a duty existed. We hold that the teenagers' unruly behavior could reasonably have been anticipated to escalate into acts that would expose patrons to an unreasonable risk of injury. The exact occurrence or precise injuries need not have been foreseen.

Viewed in a light most favorable to the plaintiffs, the evidence could support a finding that the teenagers' obnoxious behavior in the restaurant was open and notorious. Because the group was engaging in a conversation at times with a restaurant employee, it could be found that the defendant was aware of the teenagers' conduct. The near physical contact between one teenager and Nicholas Iannelli at the counter and the indifference expressed by the group member thereafter could be deemed sufficient warning to the restaurant

manager of misconduct such that it was incumbent upon him to take affirmative action to reduce the risk of injury. The plaintiffs allege that at least one other restaurant patron expressed disgust with the group's actions prior to the assault. The manager could have warned the group about their behavior or summoned the police if his warnings were not heeded.

In summary, the trial court's ruling that as a matter of law the defendant owed no duty to the plaintiffs to protect them from the assault was error. While as a general principle no such duty exists, here it could be found that the teenagers' behavior in the restaurant created a foreseeable risk of harm that the defendant unreasonably failed to alleviate. Accordingly, we **reverse and remand.**

>> CASE QUESTIONS

1. Under the decision in this case, when does a duty arise for the defendant restaurant to protect its customers?
2. What does the court suggest that the restaurant manager should have done in this case that would have satisfied the duty?
3. What do you think is the difference in this case between a "special relationship" duty and the duty of the restaurant?

Note that the duty to act reasonably also applies to professional providers, like doctors, lawyers, CPAs, architects, engineers, and others. In most negligence cases, however, the standard of reasonableness is that of a *reasonable person*. In negligence cases involving professionals, the negligence standard applied is that of the *reasonable professional*. The negligence of professionals is called *malpractice*.

As Sidebar 10.7 suggests, professional negligence is a controversial area of tort law.

11. UNREASONABLE BEHAVIOR—BREACH OF DUTY

At the core of negligence is the unreasonable behavior that breaches the duty of care that the defendant owes to the plaintiff. The problem is how do we separate reasonable behavior that causes accidental injury from unreasonable behavior that causes injury? Usually a jury determines this issue, but negligence is a mixed question of law and fact. Despite the trend for judges to let juries decide what the standard of reasonable care is, judges also continue to be involved in the definition of negligence. A well-known definition by Judge Learned Hand states that negligence is determined by "the likelihood that the defendant's conduct will injure others, taken with

A train rounds a bend but cannot stop in time to avoid running over an intoxicated person who has fallen asleep on the track. A jury is not likely to find the railroad's behavior "unreasonable."

>> *sidebar* 10.7

Medical Malpractice Crisis

Few people would disagree that physicians are extremely unhappy about the rapidly growing insurance premiums they have to pay. Some physicians have gone on strike; others have left the practice of medicine. The exact causes of the situation, however, are difficult to determine. Consider the following and make your own evaluation.

- Studies suggest between 44,000 and 98,000 people die annually from medical errors.
- A study in the *New England Journal of Medicine* found that 9 out of 10 patients who suffer disability from medical errors go uncompensated.
- In 2004 total payments for medical malpractice claims fell 8.9% nationally.
- As of 2005, 27 states have capped malpractice awards.
- In 2004 malpractice insurance costs for various medical specialties rose between 6.9% and 24.9%.

Question: what would be the impact on the cost of malpractice insurance if physicians had patients sign arbitration clauses before providing service in all but emergency cases? These clauses might provide that disputes with a physician be resolved before an arbitration board appointed by the state medical association. These clauses are currently not widely used and are specifically prohibited by several states. But under the Federal Arbitration Act, the state prohibitions are likely preempted by the federal law because medical practice has a substantial impact on interstate commerce. The Supreme Court has already ruled that law practice has such an impact, so it is likely that medical practice does as well.

Sources: *Business Week, The New York Times*, Department of Health and Human Services.

the seriousness of the injury if it happens, and balanced against the interest which he must sacrifice to avoid the risk."

Examples of Negligence Failure to exercise reasonable care can cost a company substantial sums. In one instance the licensed owner of a National Car Rental agency in Indianapolis was ordered to pay $5.5 million to a man who slipped on the floor and broke his hip. To save overtime pay the rental agency had had its floors mopped during, instead of after, normal working hours. Unaware that someone was mopping the floors behind him, the plaintiff had stepped backwards, slipped, and fallen on the wet floor.

In another case arising from unreasonable behavior, Wal-Mart Stores agreed to pay two young girls a settlement of up to $16 million. A store employee had sold the girls' father a shotgun used to kill their mother in spite of the fact that a federal form filled out by the buyer indicated that he was under a restraining order. Federal law bars those under restraining orders from purchasing guns.

Even before the terrorist attacks of 9/11, New York's World Trade Center (WTC) had been bombed. In 2005 a Manhattan jury determined that the Port Authority of New York was negligent in the earlier attack, which involved a blast from a truck filled with explosives that terrorists had driven into the public parking lot under the WTC. Six people died and over a thousand were injured. Is it an example of litigation gone wild to hold the Port Authority liable for a terrorist act? Consider that before the bombing a report commissioned by the Port Authority, which controlled the WTC parking, had specifically warned against such a bombing and recommended: "Eliminate all public parking at the World Trade Center." Citing potential loss of revenue, the Port Authority had declined to follow the report's recommendation.

Willful and Wanton Negligence   A special type of aggravated negligence is **willful and wanton negligence.** Although this does not reveal intent, it does show an extreme lack of due care. Negligent injuries inflicted by drunk drivers show willful and wanton negligence. The significance of this type of negligence is that the injured plaintiff can recover punitive damages as well as actual damages. For example, following the *Exxon Valdez* oil spill in Alaska, commercial fishers sued Exxon for damage to their livelihoods. A jury awarded substantial actual and punitive damages when it found that Exxon was willful and wanton in allowing the ship captain to be in charge of the ship when they knew he was an alcoholic.

> *Willful and wanton negligence allows an injured plaintiff to recover punitive as well as actual damages.*

In 2005 a New Jersey state court awarded a 2-year-old boy $105 million for an accident that left him permanently paralyzed from the neck down. A drunken Giants football fan had caused the accident. Before driving, the fan consumed at least 12 beers sold to him by a Giants Stadium concessionaire. The award for willful and wanton negligence against the concessionaire is the largest ever for the careless sale of alcohol. The award included $30 million in compensatory and $75 million in punitive damages.

Because employers are also liable for the intentional torts of employees in advancing the interests of their employers (see Chapter 14), employers face punitive damage awards in those instances even when they are also liable for simple negligence, or have not acted negligently at all. (See Sidebar 10.8.)

>> *sidebar* 10.8

Strip Search Hoax Costs McDonald's $6.1 Million

The caller identified himself as a police officer and told the McDonald's assistant manager that Louise Ogburn had stolen the purse of a customer who had recently left the restaurant and should be searched. For more than an hour the assistant manager and other McDonald employees detained, searched, and even committed sexual battery against Ogburn at the instruction of the caller. However, the caller was not a police officer and the call was a hoax.

Ogburn sued McDonald's and the jury awarded her a million dollars in actual damages for pain and suffering and $5 million in punitive damages against the company. To understand why McDonald's is liable, you have to understand that numerous instances of such hoaxes were known to the company involving various fast-food restaurants, yet the jury found that the company had not reasonably trained its employees such calls might be hoaxes.

If McDonald's negligence were extreme, that is, willful and wanton, that would justify the $5 million punitive damage award, but McDonald's is also liable for the intentional torts of its employees that justify awarding punitive damages. In this case the employees committed such intentional torts as false imprisonment and battery in the course of Ogburn's detention. Such detention advanced the interests of McDonald's in dealing with dishonest employees and made the intentional acts accompanying Ogburn's treatment the company's responsibility when they turned out to be wrongful.

12. CAUSATION IN FACT

Before a person is liable to another for negligent injury, the person's failure to use reasonable care must actually have "caused" the injury. This observation is not so obvious as it first appears. A motorist stops by the roadside to change a tire. Another motorist drives past carelessly and sideswipes the first as he changes the tire. What caused the accident? Was it the inattention of the second motorist or the fact that the first motorist had a flat tire? Did the argument the second motorist had with her boss before getting in the car cause the accident, or was it the decision of the first motorist to visit one more client that afternoon? In a real sense, all these things caused the accident. Chains of causation stretch out infinitely.

Still, in a negligence suit the plaintiff must prove that the defendant actually caused the injury. The courts term this **cause in fact.** In light of the many possible ways to attribute accident causation, how do courts determine if a plaintiff's lack of care, in fact, caused a certain injury? They do so very practically. Courts leave questions of cause in fact almost entirely to juries as long as the evidence reveals that a defendant's alleged carelessness could have been a substantial, material factor in bringing about an injury. Juries then make judgments about whether a defendant's behavior in fact caused the harm.

A particular problem of causation arises where the carelessness of two or more tortfeasors contributes to cause the plaintiff's injury, as when two persons are wrestling over control of the car which strikes the plaintiff. Tort law handles such cases by making each tortfeasor *jointly* and *severally* liable for the entire judgment. The plaintiff can recover only the amount of the judgment, but she or he may recover it wholly from either of the tortfeasors or get a portion of the judgment from each.

Approximately 40 states have limited joint and several liability in certain cases, for example, medical injury cases. In these states and types of cases, multiple defendants are each liable usually only for that portion of the damages juries believe they actually caused.

Many states are currently modifying the common law of torts regarding rules like that of joint and several liability.

13. PROXIMATE CAUSATION

It is not enough that a plaintiff suing for negligence prove that the defendant caused an injury in fact. The plaintiff also must establish proximate causation. **Proximate cause** is, perhaps, more accurately termed *legal cause*. It represents the proposition that those engaged in activity are legally liable only for the *foreseeable* risk that they cause.

Defining proximate causation in terms of foreseeable risk creates further problems about the meaning of the word *foreseeable*. In its application, foreseeability has come to mean that the plaintiff must have been one whom the defendant could reasonably expect to be injured by a negligent act. For example, it is reasonable to expect, thus foreseeable, that a collapsing hotel walkway should injure those on or under it. But many courts would rule as unforeseeable that someone a block away, startled upon hearing the loud crash of the walkway, should trip and stumble into the path of an oncoming car. The court would likely dismiss that person's complaint against the hotel as failing to show proximate causation.

Another application of proximate cause doctrine requires the injury to be caused *directly* by the defendant's negligence. Causes of injury that intervene

British Petroleum promised $20 billion to pay for claims arising from its oil spill in the Gulf. To date, only about a fifth of that amount has been paid out by claims adjusters. Part of the problem relates to proximate causation. How do claimants prove, for instance, that a falloff in business miles inland is directly caused by the oil spill instead of poor business practice, or for some other reason?

between the defendant's negligence and the plaintiff's injury can destroy the necessary proximate causation. Some courts, for instance, would hold that it is not foreseeable that an owner's negligence in leaving keys in a parked car should result in an intoxicated thief who steals the car, crashing and injuring another motorist. These courts would dismiss for lack of proximate cause a case brought by the motorist against the car's owner. For one of the most famous tort cases in history, see Sidebar 10.9.

>> *sidebar* 10.9

Explosion on the Long Island Railroad

Helen Palsgraf stood on the loading platform on the Long Island Railroad. Thirty feet away, two station guards were pushing a man onto a departing train when one guard dislodged an unmarked package held by the man. The package, which contained fireworks, fell to the ground with a loud explosion.

The explosion caused a heavy scale to fall on Helen Palsgraf, injuring her. She sued the railroad for the negligence of its guard and won at trial and in the appellate court. Three justices of the Court of Appeals (New York's supreme court) agreed with the lower courts: "The act [of the guard] was negligent. For its proximate consequences the defendant is liable."

However, four justices of the Court of Appeals decided that proximate causation was "foreign to the case before us." The majority ruled that what the guard did could not be considered negligence at all in relation to the plaintiff Palsgraf. The guard owed no duty to someone 30 feet away not to push a passenger—even carelessly—onto a train. The Court of Appeals reversed the damage award to the plaintiff.

The famous *Palsgraf* case illustrates the complexity of legal analysis. Question: Was it negligent for the passenger to carry fireworks in a crowded railroad station? Why didn't the plaintiff just recover damages from the passenger?

Source: *Palsgraf v. Long Island R.R.*, 162 N.E. 99 (1928).

---

14. DEFENSES TO NEGLIGENCE

There are two principal defenses to an allegation of negligence: contributory negligence and assumption of risk. Both these defenses are *affirmative defenses,* which means that the defendant must specifically raise these defenses to take advantage of them. When properly raised and proved, these defenses limit or bar the plaintiff's recovery against the defendant. The defenses are valid even though the defendant has actually been negligent.

Contributory Negligence As originally applied, the **contributory negligence** defense absolutely barred the plaintiff from recovery if the plaintiff's own fault contributed to the injury "in any degree, however slight." The trend today, however, in the great majority of states is to offset the harsh rule of contributory negligence with the doctrine of **comparative responsibility** (also called *comparative negligence* and *comparative fault*). Under comparative principles, the plaintiff's contributory negligence does not bar recovery. It merely compares the plaintiff's fault with the defendant's and reduces the damage award proportionally. For example, a jury determined damages at $3.1 million for an Atlanta plaintiff who was run over and dragged by a bus. But the jury then reduced the damage award by 20% ($620,000) on the basis that the plaintiff contributed to his own injury by failing reasonably to look out for his own safety in an area where buses come and go.

Adoption of the comparative negligence principle seems to lead to more frequent and larger awards for plaintiffs. This was the conclusion of a study by the Illinois Insurance Information Service for the year following that state's adoption of comparative negligence.

Contractual notices regarding assumption of the risk are more likely to be enforced if they prominently bring to attention the risk involved.

Assumption of Risk   If contributory negligence involves failure to use proper care for one's own safety, the **assumption-of-the-risk** defense arises from the plaintiff's knowing and willing undertaking of an activity made dangerous by the negligence of another. When professional hockey first came to this country, many spectators injured by flying hockey pucks sued and recovered for negligence. But as time went on and spectators came to realize that attending a hockey game meant that one might occasionally be exposed to flying hockey pucks, courts began to allow the defendant owners of hockey teams to assert that injured spectators had assumed the risk of injury from a speeding puck. It is important to a successful assumption-of-the-risk defense that the assumption was voluntary. Entering a hockey arena while knowing the risk of flying pucks is a voluntary assumption of the risk. However, that the injured person has really understood the risk is also significant to the assumption-of-the-risk defense. In one 2007 case, a University softball coach smacked his player in the face with a bat while demonstrating a batting grip to her. She required surgery for multiple fractures of her face and sued the coach and his employer, the university. The court denied the assumption-of-the-risk defense, asserting that it was up to the jury to determine whether the coach had acted negligently in hitting his player. The court observed that the player did not appreciate the risk of being hit by her coach with the bat.

People injured by a baseball at a baseball game or a golf ball on the golf links also usually assume the risk. Does someone assume the risk of a racing car veering off a race track and going over a barrier and into the crowd?

Courts have often ruled that people who imperil themselves while attempting to rescue their own or others' property from a risk created by the defendant have not assumed the risk voluntarily. A plaintiff who is injured while attempting to save his possessions from a fire negligently caused by the defendant is not subject to the assumption-of-the-risk defense.

Assumption of the risk may be implied from the circumstances, or it can arise from an express agreement. Many businesses attempt to relieve themselves of potential liability by having employees or customers agree contractually not to sue for negligence, that is, to assume the risk. Some of these contractual agreements are legally enforceable, but many will be struck down by the courts as being against public policy, especially where a business possesses a vastly more powerful bargaining position than does its employee or customer.

>> Strict Liability in Tort

Strict liability is a catchall phrase for the legal responsibility for injury-causing behavior that is neither intentional nor negligent. There are various types of strict liability torts, some of which are more "strict" than others. What ties them together is that they all impose legal liability, regardless of the intent or fault of the defendant. The next sections discuss these torts and tort doctrines.

15. STRICT PRODUCTS LIABILITY

A major type of strict tort liability is **strict products liability,** for the commercial sale of defective products. In most states any retail, wholesale, or manufacturing seller who sells an unreasonably dangerous defective product that causes injury to a user of the product is strictly liable. For example, if a forklift you are using at work malfunctions because of defective brakes and you run off the edge of the loading dock and are injured, you can sue the retailer, wholesaler, and manufacturer of the product for strict liability. The fact that the retailer and wholesaler may have been perfectly careful in selling the product does not matter. They are strictly liable.

Don't forget that strict products liability applies only against *commercial* sellers.

Strict products liability applies only to "commercial" sellers, those who normally sell products like the one causing injury, or who place them in the stream of commerce. Included as commercial sellers are the retailer, wholesaler, and manufacturer of a product, but also included are suppliers of defective parts and companies that assemble a defective product. Not included as a commercial seller is your next door neighbor who sells you her defective lawnmower. The neighbor may be negligent, for instance, if she knew of the defect that caused you injury and forgot to warn you about it, but she cannot be held strictly liable.

An important concept in strict products liability is that of "defect." Strict liability only applies to the sale of unreasonably dangerous *defective* products. There are two kinds of defects. **Production defects** arise when products are not manufactured to a manufacturer's own standards. Defective brakes on a new car are a good example of a production defect. Another example involves the clam chowder in which a diner found a condom, which led in 2005 to a rapid settlement between the diner and a seafood restaurant chain. **Design defects** occur when a product is manufactured according to the manufacturer's standards, but the product injures a user due to its unsafe design. Lawsuits based on design defects are common but often very controversial. Recent such lawsuits have included one against Ford that claimed Ford should have designed its vans to have a heat-venting system so children accidentally locked in the vans would be safe. Lack of adequate warnings concerning inherently dangerous products can also be considered a design defect. American Home Products settled a wrongful death lawsuit for an estimated $10 million. The lawsuit alleged that the company had not adequately warned users of its diet drug about the risks of hypertension, which had been linked to diet-drug use.

In one case, a jury found the defendant liable when its cleaning product warned users to "vent" rooms being cleaned but failed to say "vent to outside." Vapors from the product injured several people when it was used in a room with a closed circulation venting system.

In practice, strict products liability is useful in protecting those who suffer personal injury or property damage. It does not protect businesses that have economic losses due to defective products. For instance, a warehouse that loses profits because its defective forklift will not run cannot recover those lost profits under strict products liability. The warehouse would have to sue for breach of contract. However, if the forklift defect causes injury to a worker, the worker can successfully sue the forklift manufacturer for strict products liability.

Under strict products liability, contributory negligence is not a defense but assumption of the risk is. The assumption-of-the-risk defense helped protect tobacco manufacturers from health injury liability for many years. Misuse is another defense that defendants commonly raise in product liability cases. Removing safety guards from equipment is a common basis for the misuse defense. Defendants have also argued that if a product meets some federally required standard, it cannot be considered defective. Most courts, however, have ruled that federal standards only set a minimum requirement for safe design and that meeting federal standards does not automatically keep a manufacturer from being sued for strict products liability.

In recent years many states have changed or modified the rules of product liability. See Sidebar 10.10. These changes to the rules of products liability (and modifications to the rules of medical malpractice) are often known generally as "tort reform." The federal government has also enacted tort reform that applies to product liability. As of 2005, federal courts can decide any *class-action* lawsuit involving over $5 million and involving persons from different states. Federal plaintiffs in such class-action lawsuits need no longer claim the usual $75,000 jurisdictional amount.

>> *sidebar* 10.10

Tort Reform

The rapid growth of products litigation during the past two decades has brought forth many calls for "tort reform." Numerous states have changed their laws to modify the tort doctrines discussed in this section and chapter. At the federal level, comprehensive tort reform has been strongly advocated although it has not passed as of this writing. Some of the tort reforms proposed or passed by the states include:

- Permitting only negligence actions against retailers and wholesalers unless the product manufacturer is insolvent.
- Eliminating strict liability recovery for defective product design.
- Barring products liability claims against sellers if products have been altered or modified by a user.

- Providing for the presumption of reasonableness defense in product design cases in which the product meets the **state-of-the-art;** that is, the prevailing industry standards at the time of product manufacture.
- Creating a **statute of repose** that would specify a period (such as 25 years) following product sale after which plaintiffs would lose their rights to bring suits for product-related injuries.
- Reducing or eliminating punitive damage awards in most product liability cases.

Importantly, note that not all, or even most, of these reforms have been adopted by every state.

Another important development in products liability is that in nearly every state product liability case based on design defects, failures to warn adequately and testing inadequacies are now decided according to "reasonableness" standards, making these product liability cases based on the negligence. Consider the following case involving Ford Motor Company's failure to test a seatbelt sleeve.

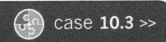

case 10.3 >>

BRANHAM v. FORD MOTOR CO.
701 S.E.2d 5 (S.C. Sup. Ct. 2010)

Hale was driving several children to her house in her Ford Bronco. No one was wearing a seatbelt. Hale admittedly took her eyes off the road and turned to the backseat to ask the children to quiet down. When she took her eyes off the road, the Bronco veered towards the shoulder of the road, and the rear right wheel left the roadway. She responded by overcorrecting to the left. Her overcorrection caused the Bronco to roll over. One of the children, Jesse Branham, was thrown from the vehicle, was severely injured, and sued Ford Motor Company and Hale. At trial, Branham did not seriously pursue the claim against Hale. The case against Ford was based on two product liability claims, one for failing to test the seatbelt sleeve, and the other a design defect claim related to the vehicle's tendency to rollover. Both of these claims were pursued in negligence and strict liability. The jury found both Ford and Hale responsible and awarded Branham $16 million in actual damages. Only Ford appeals.

KITTREDGE, J.: . . . Branham alleged Ford was negligent "in selling the Bronco II with a defective rear occupant restraint system." At trial, Branham claimed Ford was negligent and also strictly liable in failing to adequately *test* the seatbelt sleeve. The trial court dismissed the strict liability claim on the ground that the seatbelt sleeve was not as a matter of law in a defective condition unreasonably dangerous to the user at the time of manufacture. Based on this premise, Ford contends the companion negligence claim must fail, for all products liability actions, regardless of the stated theory, have common elements. "In a products liability action the plaintiff must establish three things, regardless of the theory on which he seeks recovery: (1) that he was injured by the product; (2) that the product, at the time of the accident, was in essentially the same condition as when it left the hands of the defendant; and (3) that the injury occurred because the product was in a defective condition unreasonably dangerous to the user." Ford, therefore, concludes that the negligence claim (which required Branham to prove that the seatbelt sleeve was in a defective condition unreasonably dangerous to the user) should have been dismissed. We agree.

The trial court determined as a matter of law that the seatbelt sleeve was not in a defective condition unreasonably dangerous to the user. Consequently, the absence of this common, shared element required

the dismissal of the strict liability claim *and* the companion negligence claim. The trial court erred in failing to direct a verdict as to the negligent seatbelt sleeve claim.

We next consider the "handling and stability" design defect claim in strict liability and negligence. We address Ford's two-fold argument that: (1) Branham failed to prove a reasonable alternative design pursuant to the risk-utility test; and (2) South Carolina law requires a risk-utility test in design defect cases to the exclusion of the consumer expectations test. For a plaintiff to successfully advance a design defect claim, he must show that the design of the product caused it to be "unreasonably dangerous." In South Carolina, we have traditionally employed two tests to determine whether a product was unreasonably dangerous as a result of a design defect: (1) the consumer expectations test and (2) the risk-utility test.

In *Claytor v. General Motors Corp.*, this Court phrased the consumer expectations test as follows: "The test of whether a product is or is not defective is whether the product is unreasonably dangerous to the consumer or user given the conditions and circumstances that foreseeably attend use of the product." The *Claytor* Court articulated the risk-utility test in the following manner: "[N]umerous factors must be considered when determining whether a product is unreasonably dangerous, including the usefulness and desirability of the product, the cost involved for added safety, the likelihood and potential seriousness of injury, and the obviousness of danger." In *Bragg v. Hi-Ranger, Inc.*, our court of appeals phrased the risk-utility test as follows: "[A] product is unreasonably dangerous and defective if the danger associated with the use of the product outweighs the utility of the product."

Ford contends Branham failed to present evidence of a feasible alternative design. Implicit in Ford's argument is the contention that a product may only be shown to be defective and unreasonably dangerous by way of a risk-utility test, for by its very nature, the risk-utility test requires a showing of a reasonable alternative design. Branham counters, arguing that under *Claytor* he may prove a design defect by resort to the consumer expectations test or the risk-utility test. Branham also argues that regardless of which test is required, he has met both, including evidence of a feasible alternative design. We agree with Branham's

[continued]

contention that he produced evidence of a feasible alternative design. Branham additionally points out that the jury was charged on the consumer expectations test *and* the risk-utility test.

As discussed above, Branham challenged the design of the Ford Bronco II by pointing to the MacPherson suspension as a reasonable alternative design. A former Ford vice president, Thomas Feaheny, testified that the MacPherson suspension system would have significantly increased the handling and stability of the Bronco II, making it less prone to rollovers. Branham's expert, Dr. Richardson, also noted that the MacPherson suspension system would have enhanced vehicle stability by lowering the vehicle center of gravity. There was further evidence that the desired sport utility features of the Bronco II would not have been compromised by using the MacPherson suspension. Moreover, there is evidence that use of the MacPherson suspension would not have increased costs. Whether this evidence satisfies the risk-utility test is ultimately a jury question. But it is evidence of a feasible alternative design, sufficient to survive a directed verdict motion.

While the consumer expectations test fits well in manufacturing defect cases, we do agree with Ford that the test is ill-suited in design defect cases. We hold today that the exclusive test in a products liability design case is the risk-utility test with its requirement of showing a feasible alternative design. Some form of a risk-utility test is employed by an overwhelming majority of the jurisdictions in this country. States that exclusively employ the consumer expectations test are a decided minority. By our count 35 of the 46 states that recognize strict products liability use some form of risk-utility analysis in their approach to determine whether a product is to effectively design. Four states do not recognize strict liability at all. Those four states are Delaware, Massachusetts, North Carolina, and Virginia.

We believe that in design defect cases the risk-utility test provides the best means for analyzing whether a product is designed defectively. Unlike the consumer expectations test, the focus of a risk-utility test centers upon the alleged defectively designed product. The risk-utility test provides objective factors for a trier of fact to analyze when presented with a challenge to a manufacturer's design. Conversely, we find the consumer expectations test and its focus on the consumer ill-suited to determine whether a product's design is unreasonably dangerous.

Most any product can be made more safe. Automobiles would be safer with disc brakes and steel-belted radial tires than with ordinary brakes and ordinary tires, but this does not mean that an automobile dealer would be held to have sold a defective product merely because the most safe equipment is not installed. By a like token, a bicycle is safer if equipped with lights and a bell, but the fact that one is not so equipped does not create the inference that the bicycle is defective and unreasonably dangerous. There is, of course, some danger incident to the use of any product.

In a product liability design defect action, the plaintiff must present evidence of a reasonable alternative design. The plaintiff will be required to point to a design flaw in the product and show how his alternative design would have prevented the product from being unreasonably dangerous. This presentation of an alternative design must include consideration of the costs, safety and functionality associated with the alternative design. On retrial, Branham's design defect claim will proceed under to the risk-utility test and not the consumer expectations test.

[*Reversed and remanded*]

>> CASE QUESTIONS

1. Since the injured plaintiff was not wearing a seatbelt, why is Ford being sued for failing to test the seatbelt sleeve?
2. It is often said that product liability causes of action, especially negligence and strict liability, are coming together or merging. Discuss this idea in light of the South Carolina Supreme Court's decision.
3. Is the consumer expectations test or the risk utility test more favorable to manufacturers? Explain.
4. Can Branham still win this case? Explain.

16. ULTRAHAZARDOUS ACTIVITY

In most states, the courts impose strict liability in tort for types of activities they call *ultrahazardous*. Transporting and using explosives and poisons fall under this category, as does keeping dangerous wild animals. Injuries caused from artificial storage of large quantities of liquid can also bring strict liability on the one who stores. For an example of the unusual dangers of ultrahazardous activity, see Sidebar 10.11.

Some states have analyzed fireworks-related explosions that cause accidental injury by the standard of ultrahazardous activity.

>> *sidebar* 10.11

The Great Molasses Flood

The Purity Distilling Co. had filled the enormous steel tank on the Boston hillside with two million gallons of molasses to be turned into rum. Unusually warm weather caused the molasses to expand. On January 15, 1919, with sounds like gunfire as the restraining bolts sheared, the tank exploded. A wave of hot molasses 30-feet high raced down the street toward Boston Harbor, faster than people could run, engulfing entire buildings. Before it subsided, 150 people were injured and 21 drowned. "The dead," reported the *Boston Herald*, "were like candy statues."

It took months to clean up the harbor. It took six years to resolve the 125 lawsuits that followed. The artificial storage of large quantities of liquid can be a sticky matter indeed.

Source: Anthony V. Riccio, *Portrait of an Italian-American Neighborhood* (1998).

17. OTHER STRICT LIABILITY TORTS

The majority of states impose strict liability upon tavern owners for injuries to third parties caused by their intoxicated patrons. The acts imposing this liability are called **dram shop acts.** Because of the public attention given in recent years to intoxicated drivers, there has been a tremendous increase in dram shop act cases.

Common carriers, transportation companies licensed to serve the public, are also strictly liable for damage to goods being transported by them. Common carriers, however, can limit their liability in certain instances through contractual agreement, and they are not liable for (1) acts of God, such as natural catastrophes; (2) action of an alien enemy; (3) order of public authority, such as authorities of one state barring potentially diseased fruit shipments from another state from entering their state; (4) the inherent nature of the goods, such as perishable vegetables; and (5) misconduct of the shipper, such as improper packaging.

>> Damages

LO 10-4

One legal scholar concludes that "the crucial controversy in personal injury torts today" is in the area of damages. For dramatic examples of the size of recent awards, refer to Sidebar 10.12. Juries determine the size of damage

>> *sidebar* 10.12

Highest Jury Tort Awards of 2010

EVENT CAUSING INJURY	JURY AWARD IN MILLIONS OF DOLLARS
1. Pharmaceutical products liability causing hepatitis C outbreak.	$505.1
2. Products liability for secondhand asbestos exposure to worker's laundry.	$208.8
3. Verdict against a cigarette company for providing deceased woman free cigarettes when she was a child.	$152
4. Products liability for design defect in a Ford Bronco rollover accident.	$132.5
5. Negligence verdict against a bus company to seven passengers injured or killed while riding in an unlicensed commercial van.	$124.5
6. Verdict against the world's largest law firm involving malpractice and intentional interference with business (contractual) relationships.	$103
7. Products liability against a cigarette company involving lung cancer death.	$ 90.8
8. Products liability for production defect of a carburetor in an airplane crash.	$ 89
9. Negligence in a natural gas explosion causing death at a plant.	$ 82.5
10. Cigarette products liability for lung cancer death.	$ 80

Note: Although virtually ignored in news media headlines, the damages in almost all of these large jury verdicts were reduced significantly. In some instances the judge reduced the damages as a matter of law. In other cases, appeals courts reduced damages or reversed the trial court. In many cases, however, the parties simply negotiated a reduced settlement to avoid the risk of an appeal that upheld or reversed the damages entirely. In reading about large jury verdicts, this final outcome is an important point for you to remember.

awards in most cases, but judges also play a role in damages, especially in damage instructions to the jury and in deciding whether to approve substantial damage awards.

18. COMPENSATORY DAMAGES

Most damages awarded in tort cases compensate the plaintiff for injuries suffered. The purpose of damages is to make the plaintiff whole again, at least financially. There are three major types of loss that potentially follow tort injury and are called **compensatory damages.** They are:

- Past and future medical expenses.
- Past and future economic loss (including property damage and loss of earning power).
- Past and future pain and suffering.

Compensatory damages may also be awarded for loss of limb, loss of consortium (the marriage relationship), and mental distress.

Calculation of damage awards creates significant problems. Juries frequently use state-adopted life expectancy tables and present-value discount tables to help them determine the amount of damages to award. But uncertainty about the life expectancy of injured plaintiffs and the impact of inflation often makes these tables misleading. Also, awarding damages for pain and suffering is an art rather than a science. These awards measure jury sympathy as much as they calculate compensation for any financial loss. The recent dramatic increases in the size of damage awards helps underline the problems in their calculation. One result is that many individuals and businesses are underinsured for major tort liability.

Currently, compensatory damage awards for pain and suffering are very controversial. How do you compensate injured plaintiffs for something like pain which has no market value? Many plaintiffs suffer lifelong pain or the permanent loss of vision, hearing, or mobility. No amount of damages seems large enough to compensate them, yet no amount of damages, however high, will cause their pain and suffering to stop. In 2003, President Bush called for the limitation of tort damages for pain and suffering in a case to $250,000 per person. Do you agree or disagree?

19. PUNITIVE DAMAGES

Compensatory damages are not the only kind of damages. There are also **punitive damages.** By awarding punitive damages, courts or juries punish defendants for committing intentional torts and for negligent behavior considered "gross" or "willful and wanton." The key to the award of punitive damages is the defendant's motive. Usually the motive must be "malicious," "fraudulent," or "evil." Increasingly, punitive damages are also awarded for dangerously negligent conduct that shows a conscious disregard for the interests of others. These damages punish those who commit aggravated torts and act to deter future wrongdoing. Because they make an example out of the defendant, punitive damages are sometimes called *exemplary damages.*

Presently, there is much controversy about how appropriate it is to award punitive damages against corporations for their economic activities. Especially when companies fail to warn of known danger created by their activities, or when cost-benefit decisions are made at the risk of substantial human injury, courts are upholding substantial punitive damage awards against companies. Yet consider that these damages are a windfall to the injured plaintiff who has already received compensatory damages. And instead of punishing guilty management for wrongdoing, punitive damages may end up punishing innocent shareholders by reducing their dividends.

Many court decisions also overlook a very important consideration about punitive damages. Most companies carry liability insurance policies that reimburse them for "all sums which the insured might become legally obligated to pay." This includes reimbursement for punitive damages. Instead of punishing guilty companies, punitive damages may punish other companies, which have to pay increased insurance premiums, and may punish consumers, who ultimately pay higher prices. As a matter of public policy, several states prohibit insurance from covering punitive damages, but the

Punitive or exemplary damages arise from intentional torts or extreme "willful and wanton" negligence.

"If you were to talk to foreign businesses about what scares them the most about the U.S. judicial process, they would say class actions and punitive damages."

–Carter G. Phillips, Sidney Austin Brown & Wood (law firm)

great majority of states permit such coverage. This fact severely undermines arguments for awarding punitive damages against companies for their economic activities.

Consider also that an award of punitive damages greatly resembles a criminal fine. Yet the defendant who is subject to these criminal-type damages lacks the right to be indicted by a grand jury and cannot assert the right against self-incrimination. In addition, the defendant is subject to a lower standard of proof than in a criminal case. However, defendants in tort suits have challenged awards of punitive damages on a constitutional basis. See Sidebar 10.13.

>> *sidebar* 10.13

Punitive Damage Guidelines

In 2003 the Supreme Court determined that $145 million in punitive damages in a case was unconstitutional. In *State Farm v. Campbell,* the Court decided that the large difference between punitive and compensatory damages violated due process. The Court suggested that a single-digit ratio of punitive to compensatory damages (9/1 or less) would be more constitutionally appropriate than a 145/1 ratio.

State Farm v. Campbell also reaffirmed general punitive damage guidelines from an earlier case. The Court stated, in evaluating the appropriateness of punitive damages, that courts should consider:

- "the responsibility of the defendant's conduct (how bad it was),
- the ratio of punitive to actual damages
- how the punitive damages compare with criminal or civil penalties for the same conduct."

Note that juries award punitive damages in only about 2% of litigated cases.

Finally, note that almost no other country in the world except the United States permits civil juries to award punitive damages. For instance, in 2007 an Italian court refused to enforce a $1 million award against an Italian helmet maker whose defective helmet had caused the death of a 15-year-old motorcyclist in Alabama because the award contained punitive damages. However, a few courts in other countries have enforced U.S. punitive damage awards even though courts in their own countries cannot award them.

>> Key Terms

Assault 291
Assumption-of-the-risk 308
Battery 291
Cause in fact 306
Comparative
    responsibility 307
Compensatory damages 314

Contributory negligence 307
Conversion 295
Defamation 295
Design defect 309
Dram shop act 313
Duty 301
False imprisonment 294

Fraud 297
Infliction of mental
    distress 292
Injurious falsehood 300
Intent 290
Intentional interference with
    contractual relations 300

Invasion of privacy 293
Libel 295
Malicious prosecution 294
Negligence 301
Production defect 309
Proximate cause 306

Punitive damages 315
Slander 295
State-of-the-art 310
Statute of repose 310
Strict liability 308
Strict products liability 309

Tort 289
Trespass 294
Willful and wanton
  negligence 305

>> Review Questions and Problems

Intentional Torts

1. *Assault and Battery*

   Under what theory can an employee sue her employer for merely touching her? Explain.

2. *Intentional Infliction of Mental Distress*

   In business the intentional infliction of mental distress tort has most often involved what type of situation?

3. *Invasion of Privacy*

   Explain the three principal invasions of personal interest that make up invasion of privacy.

4. *False Imprisonment and Malicious Prosecution*

   Explain the difference between false imprisonment and malicious prosecution. In what business situation does false imprisonment most frequently arise?

5. *Trespass*

   In recent months, homeowners downwind from International Cement Company have had clouds of cement dust settle on their property. Trees, shrubbery, and flowers have all been killed. The paint on houses has also been affected. Explain what tort cause of action these homeowners might pursue against International.

6. *Conversion*

   Bartley signs a storage contract with Universal Warehouses. The contract specifies that Bartley's household goods will be stored at Universal's midtown storage facility while he is out of the country on business. Later, without contacting Bartley, Universal transfers his goods to a suburban warehouse. Two days after the move, a freak flood wipes out the suburban warehouse and Bartley's goods. Is Universal liable to Bartley? Explain.

7. *Defamation*

   Acme Airlines attempts to get control of Free Fall Airways by making a public offer to buy its stock from shareholders. Free Fall's president, Joan, advises the shareholders in a letter that Acme's president, Richard, is "little better than a crook" and "can't even control his own company." Analyze the potential liability of Free Fall's president for these remarks.

8. *Fraud*

   Fraud can be used to void a contract and as a basis for intentional tort. What is the advantage to a plaintiff of suing for the tort of fraud as opposed to using fraud merely as a contractual defense?

9. *Common Law Business Torts*

   You are concerned because several of your employees have recently broken their employment contracts and left town. Investigation reveals that Sly and Company, your competitor in a nearby city, has paid bonuses to your former employees to persuade them to break their contracts. Discuss what legal steps you can take against Sly.

Negligence

10. *Duty of Care*

    (a) Do you have a duty of care to warn a stranger on the street of the potential danger of broken glass ahead?

(b) Do you have a duty to warn an employee of similar danger at a place of employment? Explain.

11. *Unreasonable Behavior—Breach of Duty*

In litigation who usually determines if the defendant's behavior is unreasonable?

12. *Causation in Fact*

(a) What does it mean to say that "chains of causation stretch out endlessly"?

(b) What is the standard used by the judge in instructing the jury about causation?

13. *Proximate Causation*

Explain the difference between proximate causation and causation in fact.

14. *Defenses to Negligence*

A jury finds Lee, the defendant, liable in a tort case. It determines that José, the plaintiff, has suffered $200,000 in damages. The jury also finds that José's own fault contributed 25% to his injuries. Under a comparative negligence instruction, what amount of damages will the jury award the plaintiff?

Strict Liability in Tort

15. *Strict Products Liability*

While driving under the influence of alcohol, Joe runs off the road and wrecks his car. As the car turns over, the protruding door latch hits the ground and the door flies open. Joe, who is not wearing his seat belt, is thrown from the car and badly hurt. Joe sues the car manufacturer, asserting that the door latch was defectively designed. Discuss the legal issues raised by these facts.

16. *Ultrahazardous Activity*

Through no one's fault, a sludge dam of the Phillips Phosphate Company breaks. Millions of gallons of sludge run off into a nearby river that empties into Pico Bay. The fishing industry in the bay area is ruined. Is Phillips Phosphate liable to the fishing industry? Explain.

17. *Other Strict Liability Torts*

Explain when common carriers are not strictly liable for damage to transported goods.

Damages

18. *Compensatory Damages*

Explain the three types of loss that give rise to compensatory damages.

19. *Punitive Damages*

During a business lunch, Bob eats salad dressing that contains almond extract. He is very allergic to nuts and suffers a severe allergic reaction. There are complications and Bob becomes almost totally paralyzed. Because Bob had instructed the restaurant waiter and the chef that he might die if he ate any nuts, he sues the restaurant for negligence. Discuss the types of damages Bob may recover.

business >> *discussions*

1. You own University Heights Apartments, a business that rents primarily to students. One evening, your tenant Sharon is attacked by an intruder who forces the lock on the sliding glass door of her ground-floor apartment. Sharon's screams attract the attention of Darryl, your resident manager, who comes to Sharon's aid. Together, he and Sharon drive the intruder off, but not before they both are badly cut by the intruder.

> Is the intruder liable for what he has done?
> Do you have legal responsibilities to Sharon and Darryl?
> What should you consider doing at your apartments?

2. You manufacture trunk locks and your major account is a large car company. When an important piece of your equipment unexpectedly breaks, you contact Mayfair, Inc., the only manufacturer of such equipment, and contract to replace it. The Mayfair sales representative assures you orally and in writing that the prepaid equipment will arrive by October 1, in time for you to complete your production for the car company. Instead, there is a union strike in the Mayfair trucking division, and the equipment does not arrive until December 1.

By December 1 the car company has made an agreement with another lock manufacturer. You threaten to sue Mayfair for their failure to deliver on time, but Mayfair reminds you of a contract term that relieves them of contractual liability because of "labor difficulties." Then you learn from a former secretary to the Mayfair sales representative that Mayfair knew that its trucking division was likely to strike. In fact the sales representative and the sales vice president had discussed whether or not to tell you of this fact and decided not to out of concern that you would not place your order.

> Has Mayfair done anything legally wrong?
> Is your legal remedy against Mayfair limited to breach of contract?
> Will you be able to get damages from Mayfair other than a refund of your prepayment? Explain.

21 Employment Laws

📋 Learning Objectives

In this chapter you will learn:

21-1. To identify major employment laws and their significance for employers and employees.

21-2. To explain the scope and limits of the employment-at-will doctrine.

21-3. To understand the limits of privacy in the workplace and the role of workers' compensation laws.

21-4. To discuss ways an employer should document employee performance in anticipation of potential employee litigation.

In addition to the employment discrimination laws detailed in Chapter 20, there are many other employment laws pertaining to the employer–employee relationship. This chapter surveys a number of important employment laws. As you read, consider how these laws contribute to the employment law framework in the United States. Most of the laws discussed are federal laws. However, it is important to understand that states and local governments may also have employment laws. One major example of this is workers' compensation laws. Each state has its own laws addressing accidental workplace injuries. Lastly, in light of the practical reality of defending against employee lawsuits, this chapter suggests ways that employers should document employee performance, so that they are prepared for potential litigation by current and former employees.

>> *sidebar* 21.1

Fair Labor Standards Act: To Pay or Not to Pay Overtime?

The number of FLSA cases is on the rise. Here are points to consider regarding overtime pay to be in compliance with the law:

- **Hourly or Salaried?** It is not uncommon for an employer to pay a salary to an employee who should be paid hourly. "Executive employees" may be paid a salary of at least $455 per week *if* (1) the employee's primary duty is managing the enterprise, or managing a customarily recognized department or subdivision of the enterprise; (2) the employee must customarily and regularly direct the work of at least two or more other full-time employees or their equivalent; (3) the employee must have the authority to hire or fire other employees, or the employee's suggestions and recommendations as to the hiring, firing, advancement, promotion, or any other change of status of other employees must be given particular weight.

- **Employee or Independent Contractor?** Because the FLSA requires employers to pay non-exempt employees overtime compensation for hours worked in excess of 40 hours per week, employers are sometimes tempted to classify these workers as "independent contractors" to avoid overtime pay.

  Although each individual's damages may not be substantial, an employer may face a FLSA collective action involving many workers who are misclassified. Workers are increasingly aware of their rights under wage and hour laws, especially when it comes to overtime pay.

  For more information see the U.S. Department of Labor, Wage and Hour Division, *FairPay Overtime Initiative,* available at www.dol.gov/whd/regs/compliance/fairpay/.

LO 21-1

>> Employment Laws

A complete review of all laws and regulations that impact how employers and employees interact is beyond our scope. The following sections address some of these laws and examine some current issues arising in many companies. Table 21.1 provides a list of some of the major employment laws and the purpose of each. Chapter 20 focused on the first category of laws, those addressing discrimination. This chapter discusses a range of employment laws from the Fair Labor Standards Act to retirement and pension laws. Chapter 22 then details labor laws, the last category in the table.

Employment laws are among the most emotionally and politically charged topics. The reason tempers flare and even violence happens is that these laws go to the heart of how business makes a profit and how people make a living.

1. MINIMUM WAGES AND MAXIMUM HOURS

The federal government regulates wages and hours through the **Fair Labor Standards Act (FLSA).** Originally enacted in 1938, the FLSA establishes a minimum wage, overtime pay, record-keeping requirements, and child labor standards. The FLSA has been repeatedly amended to keep it up to date. For example, effective May 25, 2007, the FLSA was amended to increase the federal minimum wage in three steps:

- To $5.85 per hour effective July 24, 2007.
- To $6.55 per hour effective July 24, 2008.
- To $7.25 per hour effective July 24, 2009.

table 21.1 >> Summary of Major Federal Employment Laws

Law	Purpose
Civil Rights Acts, Equal Employment Opportunity Act, Pregnancy Discrimination Act, Americans with Disabilities Act, Age Discrimination in Employment Act, and Genetic Nondiscrimination Act	• Provide national policy governing employment discrimination.
Fair Labor Standards Act (FLSA)	• Provides hourly minimum wage and maximum number of hours before overtime is owed. • Provides restrictions on child labor.
Worker Adjustment and Retraining Notification Act (WARN Act)	• Provides restrictions on plant closings and mass layoffs.
Family Medical Leave Act (FMLA)	• Provides unpaid leave to care for a newborn child, an adopted child, to care for a family member, or for serious health conditions.
Uniformed Services Employment and Reemployment Rights Act (USERRA)	• Provides reemployment rights after performing uniformed service. • Provides those serving in the military the right to be free from discrimination and retaliation based on uniformed service.
Occupational Safety and Health Act (OSHA)	• Provides standards for a safe and healthy working environment.
Social Security Act	• Provides unemployment compensation. • Provides disability benefits.
Employment Retirement Income Security Act (ERISA)	• Provides requirements for private pension plans.
Electronic Communications Privacy Act	• Provides standards to protect privacy.
Railway Labor Act, Norris-LaGuardia Act, Wagner Act, Taft-Hartley Act, and Landrum-Griffin Act	• Provide national policy for governing the union-management relationship.

Additionally, overtime pay at a rate of not less than one and one-half times the employee's regular rate of pay is required after 40 hours of work in a workweek. For example, if an employee earns $8 an hour, the overtime pay must be at least $12 per hour. Employers of "tipped employees" must pay a cash wage of at least $2.13 per hour if they claim a tip credit against their minimum wage obligation. If the employee's tips combined with the cash wage do not meet the minimum hourly wage, the employer must make up the difference (with certain conditions). Many states provide for minimum wages higher than the federal rate. Employers are legally required to pay whichever minimum wage is higher. The FLSA does not require breaks or meal periods to be given to workers. Some states, however, may require breaks or meal periods.

The highest state minimum wages: Washington at $8.02; California and Massachusetts at $8.00 per hour.

Employers should use care to properly classify workers as either "employees" or "independent contractors."

>> *sidebar* 21.2

Internship Programs under the FLSA

Individuals who participate in "for-profit" private sector internships or training programs may do so without compensation. Under what circumstances should interns be paid? According to the Department of Labor, six criteria must be applied when making the determination:

1. The internship, even though it includes actual operation of the facilities of the employer, is similar to training which would be given in an educational environment.
2. The internship experience is for the benefit of the intern.
3. The intern does not displace regular employees, but works under close supervision of existing staff.
4. The employer that provides the training derives no immediate advantage from the activities of the intern; and on occasion its operations may actually be impeded.
5. The intern is not necessarily entitled to a job at the conclusion of the internship.
6. The employer and the intern understand that the intern is not entitled to wages for the time spent in the internship.

If all of the factors listed above are met, an employment relationship *does not exist* under the FLSA, and the minimum wage and overtime provisions *do not apply* to the intern.

Source: U.S. Department of Labor, Wage and Hour Division, *Fact Sheet #71: Internship Programs Under the Fair Labor Standards Act,* April 2010, available at www.dol.gov/whd/regs/compliance/whdfs71.pdf.

Although a minimum wage and a maximum workweek of 40 hours before overtime is owed seems straightforward, there are many exceptions and factual situations complicating the general rules. In Case 21.1, the Supreme Court addresses the legal issue of how an employer is to count work hours. As you read the case, note that the courts count minutes to determine the overall amount in this "donning and doffing" case. In 2008, a Wisconsin federal court certified a similar donning/doffing class-action against Kraft Foods.

 case **21.1** >>

IBP, INC. v. ALVAREZ
546 U.S. 21 (2005)

This case actually is the consolidation of two cases. At issue in both cases is the calculation of the workday for the purposes of distinguishing between regular and overtime hours under the Fair Labor Standards Act (FLSA). Both cases involve meat processing companies and whether the employer must count the time workers spend putting on (donning) and taking off (doffing) required protective gear as a part of the workday. Also at issue are the minutes the workers walk from the locker room area to the production area. The Court analyzes the Fair Labor Standards Act and its amendment. Specifically, the Court notes that the Portal-to-Portal Act of 1947 emphasizes that the workday begins when workers engage in their principal activities. This law attempted to make it clear that employers are not

[continued]

liable to pay workers for the time they spend walking on the employers' property from a time clock to the actual workplace or for any time spent in preliminary or postliminary activities to the workers' principal working activities.

STEVENS. J.: . . . IBP, Inc. (IBP), is a large producer of fresh beef, pork, and related products. . . . All production workers must wear outer garments, hardhats, hairnets, earplugs, gloves, sleeves, aprons, leggings, and boots. Many of them, particularly those who use knives, must also wear a variety of protective equipment for their hands, arms, torsos, and legs; this gear includes chain-link metal aprons, vests, Plexiglass armguards, and special gloves. IBP requires its employees to store their equipment and tools in company locker rooms, where most of them don their protective gear.

Production workers' pay is based on the time spent cutting and bagging meat. Pay begins with the first piece of meat and ends with the last piece of meat. Since 1998, however, IBP has also paid for four minutes of clothes-changing time. In 1999, respondents, IBP employees, filed this class action to recover compensation for preproduction and postproduction work, including the time spent donning and doffing protective gear and walking between the locker rooms and the production floor before and after their assigned shifts.

After a lengthy bench trial, the District Court for the Eastern District of Washington held that donning and doffing of protective gear that was unique to the jobs at issue were compensable under the FLSA because they were integral and indispensable to the work of the employees who wore such equipment. Moreover, consistent with the continuous workday rule, the District Court concluded that, for those employees required to don and doff unique protective gear, the walking time between the locker room and the production floor was also compensable because it occurs during the workday. . . .

The District Court proceeded to apply these legal conclusions in making detailed factual findings with regard to the different groups of employees. For example, the District Court found that, under its view of what was covered by the FLSA, processing division knife users were entitled to compensation for between 12 and 14 minutes of preproduction and postproduction work, including 3.3 to 4.4 minutes of walking time. The Court of Appeals agreed with the District Court's ultimate conclusions on these issues. . . .

IBP does not challenge the holding below that . . . the donning and doffing of unique protective gear are "principal activities" under the Portal-to-Portal Act. . . . Thus,

the only question for us to decide is whether the Court of Appeals correctly rejected IBP's contention that the walking between the locker rooms and the production areas is excluded from FLSA coverage by the Portal-to-Portal Act. . . .

IBP emphasizes that our decision in *Anderson v. Mt. Clemens Pottery Co.,* 66 S. Ct. 1187, may well have been the proximate cause of the enactment of the Portal-to-Portal Act. In that case we held that the FLSA mandated compensation for the time that employees spent walking from time clocks located near the plant entrance to their respective places of work prior to the start of their productive labor. In IBP's view, Congress's forceful repudiation of that holding reflects a purpose to exclude what IBP regards as the quite similar walking time spent by respondents before and after their work slaughtering cattle and processing meat. Even if there is ambiguity in the statute, we should construe it to effectuate that important purpose.

This argument is also unpersuasive. There is a critical difference between the walking at issue in *Anderson* and the walking at issue in this case. In *Anderson* the walking preceded the employees' principal activity; it occurred before the workday began. The relevant walking in this case occurs after the workday begins and before it ends. Only if we were to endorse IBP's novel submission that an activity can be sufficiently "principal" to be compensable, but not sufficiently so to start the workday, would this case be comparable to *Anderson.* . . .

For the foregoing reasons, we hold that . . . any walking time that occurs after the beginning of the employee's first principal activity and before the end of the employee's last principal activity . . . is covered by the FLSA.

Barber Foods, Inc. (Barber), operates a poultry processing plant in Portland, Maine, that employs about 300 production workers. These employees operate six production lines and perform a variety of tasks that require different combinations of protective clothing. They are paid by the hour from the time they punch in to computerized time clocks located at the entrances to the production floor.

Petitioners are Barber employees and former employees who brought this action to recover compensation for alleged unrecorded work covered by the FLSA. Specifically, they claimed that Barber's failure to compensate them for (a) donning and doffing required protective gear and (b) the attendant walking and waiting violated the statute.

After extensive discovery, the Magistrate Judge issued a comprehensive opinion analyzing the facts

[continued]

in detail, and recommending the entry of partial summary judgment in favor of Barber. That opinion, which was later adopted by the District Court for Maine, included two critical rulings.

First, the Magistrate held that "the donning and doffing of clothing and equipment required by the defendant or by government regulation, as opposed to clothing and equipment which employees choose to wear or use at their option, is an integral part of the plaintiffs' work [and therefore are] not excluded from compensation under the Portal-to-Portal Act as preliminary or postliminary activities."

Second, the Magistrate rejected petitioners' claims for compensation for the time spent before obtaining their clothing and equipment. Such time, in the Magistrate's view, "could [not] reasonably be construed to be an integral part of employees' work activities any more than walking to the cage from which hairnets and earplugs are dispensed. . . ." Accordingly, Barber was "entitled to summary judgment on any claims based on time spent walking from the plant entrances to an employee's workstation, locker, time clock or site where clothing and equipment required to be worn on the job is to be obtained and any claims based on time spent waiting to punch in or out for such clothing or equipment." . . .

[The Court then reviews the findings of the District Court, which held for Barber, and the 1st Court of Appeals, which affirmed, saying that Barber is not responsible to pay for and count toward the FLSA maximum hours the time the workers spent waiting to put on protective gear, the time these workers spent actually putting on the protective gear, and the time these workers spent walking to the actual work site. Based on the holding in *IBP*, the Court quickly decided the 1st Circuit was wrong with respect to the time workers spent donning and doffing protective gear and walking to and from the locker room and workplace. The Court then concentrates on the issue of how to handle the time workers might spend waiting to get their protective gear.]

Petitioners also argued in the Court of Appeals that the waiting time associated with the donning and doffing of clothes was compensable. The Court of Appeals disagreed, holding that the waiting time qualified as a "preliminary or postliminary activity" and thus was excluded from FLSA coverage by the Portal-to-Portal Act. Our analysis . . . demonstrates that the Court of Appeals was incorrect with regard to the predoffing waiting time. Because doffing gear that is "integral and indispensable" to employees' work is a "principal activity" under the statute, the continuous workday rule mandates that time spent waiting to doff is not affected by the Portal-to-Portal Act and is instead covered by the FLSA.

The time spent waiting to don—time that elapses before the principal activity of donning integral and indispensable gear—presents the quite different question whether it should have the effect of advancing the time when the work-day begins. Barber argues that such predonning waiting time is explicitly covered by the Portal-to-Portal Act, which, as noted above, excludes "activities which are preliminary to or postliminary to [a] principal activity or activities" from the scope of the FLSA.

By contrast, petitioners maintain that the predonning waiting time is "integral and indispensable" to the "principal activity" of donning, and is therefore itself a principal activity. However, unlike the donning of certain types of protective gear, which is always essential if the worker is to do his job, the waiting may or may not be necessary in particular situations or for every employee. It is certainly not "integral and indispensable" in the same sense that the donning is. It does, however, always comfortably qualify as a "preliminary" activity.

We thus do not agree with petitioners that the predonning waiting time at issue in this case is a "principal activity". . . . As Barber points out, the fact that certain preshift activities are necessary for employees to engage in their principal activities does not mean that those preshift activities are "integral and indispensable" to a "principal activity." . . . For example, walking from a time clock near the factory gate to a workstation is certainly necessary for employees to begin their work, but it is indisputable that the Portal-to-Portal Act evinces Congress's intent to repudiate *Anderson's* holding that such walking time was compensable under the FLSA. We discern no limiting principle that would allow us to conclude that the waiting time in dispute here is a "principal activity," without also leading to the logical (but untenable) conclusion that the walking time at issue in *Anderson* would be a "principal activity" and would thus be unaffected by the Portal-to-Portal Act. . . .

In short, we are not persuaded that such waiting—which in this case is two steps removed from the productive activity on the assembly line—is "integral and indispensable" to a "principal activity" that identifies the time when the continuous workday begins. . . .

For the reasons stated above, we affirm the judgment of the Court of Appeals for the Ninth Circuit. We affirm in part and reverse in part the judgment of the Court of Appeals for the First Circuit, and we remand the case for further proceedings consistent with this opinion.

So ordered.

[continued]

>> CASE QUESTIONS

1. What is the split between the circuit courts that this case attempts to resolve?
2. Why are companies willing to litigate the issue of what counts and doesn't count as workday activities when so few minutes are likely involved?
3. What three holdings does the Court announce in this case?

The FLSA also sets wage, hours worked, and safety requirements for minors (individuals under age 18). The rules vary depending upon the particular age of the minor and the particular job involved. As a general rule, the FLSA sets 14 years of age as the minimum age for employment, and limits the number of hours worked by minors under the age of 16. In 2008, the FLSA was amended to increase penalties against employers who violate child labor laws. The penalties increased from $11,000 to $50,000 for each FLSA violation leading to the serious injury or death of a child worker. The increased fines are subject to doubling for repeated or willful violations.

>> *sidebar* 21.3

Break Time for Nursing Moms

The FLSA now requires break time for nursing mothers. Employers are required to provide "reasonable break time for an employee to express breast milk for her nursing child for 1 year after the child's birth each time such employee has need to express the milk."

Employers are also required to provide a functional space for expressing breast milk that is "shielded from view and free from intrusion from co-workers and the public." A bathroom, even a private one, is not a permissible location under the FLSA.

Employers with fewer than 50 employees are not subject to the FLSA break time requirement *if* compliance with the provision would impose an undue hardship.

Employers are not required to compensate nursing mothers for breaks taken for the purpose of expressing milk. However, if the employer already provides compensated breaks, an employee who uses that break time to express milk must be compensated in the same way that other employees are compensated for break time.

Source: U.S. Department of Labor, Wage and Hour Division, *Fact Sheet #73 Break Time for Nursing Mothers under the FLSA*, December 2010, available at www.dol.gov/whd/regs/compliance/whdfs73.htm.

 case **21.2** >>

KASTEN v. SAINT-GOBAIN PERFORMANCE PLASTICS CORP.
53 U.S. ___ (2011)

Petitioner Kasten brought an antiretaliation suit against his former employer, respondent (Saint-Gobain), under the Fair Labor Standards Act of 1938 *(Act), which provides minimum wage, maximum hour, and overtime pay rules; and which forbids employers "to discharge . . . any employee because such employee*

[continued]

has filed any complaint" alleging a violation of the Act, 29 U. S. C. §215(a)(3). In a related suit, the District Court found that Saint-Gobain violated the Act by placing timeclocks in a location that prevented workers from receiving credit for the time they spent donning and doffing work related protective gear.

In this suit Kasten claims that he was discharged because he orally complained to company officials about the timeclocks. The District Court granted Saint-Gobain summary judgment, concluding that the Act's antiretaliation provision did not cover oral complaints. The Seventh Circuit affirmed. Justice Breyer delivered the opinion of the Court in which Chief Justice Roberts, and Justices Kennedy, Ginsburg, Alito and Sotomayor joined. Justice Scalia filed a dissenting opinion in which Justice Thomas joined in part. Justice Kagan took no part in the consideration or decision of the case.

BREYER, J.: The Fair Labor Standards Act of 1938 (Act) sets forth employment rules concerning minimum wages, maximum hours, and overtime pay. 52 Stat. 1060, 29 U. S. C. §201 *et seq.* The Act contains an antiretaliation provision that forbids employers

> "to discharge or in any other manner discriminate against any employee because such employee has *filed any complaint* or instituted or caused to be instituted any proceeding under or related to [the Act], or has testified or is about to testify in such proceeding, or has served or is about to serve on an industry committee." §215(a)(3) (emphasis added).

We must decide whether the statutory term "filed any complaint" includes oral as well as written complaints within its scope. We conclude that it does.

I The petitioner, Kevin Kasten, brought this antiretaliation lawsuit against his former employer, Saint-Gobain Performance Plastics Corporation. Kasten says that where Kasten and other workers put on (and take off) their work-related protective gear and the area where they carry out their assigned tasks. That location prevented workers from receiving credit for the time they spent putting on and taking off their work clothes—contrary to the Act's requirements. In a related suit the District Court agreed with Kasten, finding that Saint-Gobain's "practice of not compensating . . . for time spent donning and doffing certain required protective gear and walking to work areas" violated the Act. *Kasten v. Saint-Gobain Performance Plastics Corp.*, 556 F. Supp. 2d 941, 954 (WD Wis. 2008). In this suit Kasten claims unlawful retaliation He says that Saint-Gobain discharged him because he orally complained to Saint-Gobain officials about the timeclocks.

In particular, Kasten says that he repeatedly called the unlawful timeclock location to Saint-Gobain's attention— in accordance with Saint-Gobain's internal grievance resolution procedure. See Brief for Petitioner 4 (quoting Saint-Gobain's Code of Ethics and Business Conduct as imposing upon every employee "the responsibility to report . . . suspected violations of . . . any applicable law of which he or she becomes aware"); *id.,* at 4–5 (quoting Saint-Gobain's Employee Policy Handbook as instructing employees with "questions, complaints, and problems" to "[c]ontact" their "supervisor[s] immediately" and if necessary "take the issue to the next level of management," then to the "local Human Resources Manager," then to "Human Resources" personnel at the "Regional" or "Headquarters" level).

Kasten adds that he "raised a concern" with his shift supervisor that "it was illegal for the time clocks to be where they were" because of Saint-Gobain's exclusion of "the time you come in and start doing stuff"; he told a human resources employee that "if they were to get challenged on" the location in court, "they would lose"; he told his lead operator that the location was illegal and that he "was thinking about starting a lawsuit about the placement of the time clocks"; and he told the human resources manager and the operations manager that he thought the location was illegal and that the company would "lose" in court. Record in No. 3:07–cv–00686–bbc (WD Wis.), Doc.87–3, pp. 31–34 (deposition of Kevin Kasten). This activity, Kasten concludes, led the company to discipline him and, in December 2006, to dismiss him.

Saint-Gobain presents a different version of events. It denies that Kasten made any significant complaint about the timeclock location. And it says that it dismissed Kasten simply because Kasten, after being repeatedly warned, failed to record his comings and goings on the timeclock.

For present purposes we accept Kasten's version of these contested events as valid. See *Scott v. Harris*, 550 U. S. 372, 380 (2007). That is because the District Court entered summary judgment in Saint-Gobain's favor. . . . Kasten sought certiorari. And in light of conflict among the Circuits as to whether an oral complaint is protected, we granted Kasten's petition. . . . The sole question presented is whether "an oral complaint of a violation of the Fair Labor Standards Act" is "protected conduct under the [Act's] anti-retaliation provision." Pet. for Cert. i. The Act protects employees who have "filed any complaint," 29 U. S. C. §215(a)(3), and interpretation of this phrase "depends upon reading the whole statutory text, considering the purpose and context of the statute, and consulting any precedents or authorities that inform the analysis,"

[continued]

Dolan v. *Postal Service*, 546 U. S. 481, 486 (2006). This analysis leads us to conclude that the language of the provision, considered in isolation, may be open to competing interpretations. But considering the provision in conjunction with the purpose and context leads us to conclude that only one interpretation is permissible. We begin with the text of the statute. The word "filed" has different relevant meanings in different contexts. . . .The bottom line is that the text, taken alone, cannot provide a conclusive answer to our interpretive question. The phrase "filed any complaint" might, or might not, encompass oral complaints. We must look further. . . .

Why would Congress want to limit the enforcement scheme's effectiveness by inhibiting use of the Act's complaint procedure by those who would find it difficult to reduce their complaints to writing, particularly illiterate, less educated, or overworked workers? . . . In the years prior to the passage of the Act, illiteracy rates were particularly high among the poor. . . . To limit the scope of the antiretaliation provision to the filing of written complaints would also take needed flexibility from those charged with the Act's enforcement. It could prevent Government agencies from using hotlines, interviews, and other oral methods of receiving complaints. . . . To fall within the scope of the antiretaliation provision, a complaint must be sufficiently clear and detailed for a reasonable employer to understand it, in light of both content and context, as an assertion of rights protected by the statute and a call for their protection. This standard can be met, however, by oral complaints, as well as by written ones. . . .

Second, given Congress' delegation of enforcement powers to federal administrative agencies, we also give a degree of weight to their views about the meaning of this enforcement language. . . . The Secretary of Labor has consistently held the view that the words "filed any complaint" cover oral, as well as written, complaints. . . . The EEOC has set forth a similar view in its Compliance Manual . . . These agency views are reasonable. They are consistent with the Act. . . . We conclude that the Seventh Circuit erred in determining that oral complaints cannot fall within the scope of the phrase "filed any complaint" in the Act's antiretaliation provision. We leave it to the lower courts to decide whether Kasten will be able to satisfy the Act's notice requirement. We vacate the Circuit's judgment and remand the case for further proceedings consistent with this opinion.

Reversed and remanded.

>> CASE QUESTIONS

1. What was the question before the Court?
2. What is the basis for the Court's holding?
3. Based on the facts in the case, what will Kasten need to prove his claim on remand?

2. THE WARN ACT

The Worker Adjustment and Retraining Notification Act (WARN) became law in 1989. Known as the **WARN Act,** this law requires employers to provide notice of plant closings and mass layoffs. This notice must be given in writing and be delivered at least 60 days prior to closing a work site or conducting mass layoffs. The WARN notice must be given to employees or their bargaining representatives (such as a union), the state's dislocated worker unit, and the elected chief officer of the local government impacted.

The WARN notice is required of employers with 100 or more employees. Workers who work less than half-time are not counted to determine this threshold level of 100. Employees entitled to receive the WARN notice include

The WARN notice allows impacted employees and communities some time to prepare for the negative impact of a plant closing or mass layoff.

According to the AFL-CIO, "Layoffs continue at a pace of 1.5 million impacted workers every year and almost half a million have been idled by mass layoffs in the first three months" of 2008.

those who are hourly, salaried, supervisory, and managerial. In essence all workers, even part-time, are entitled to receive the notice.

The WARN notice covers plant closings and mass layoffs involving loss of employment. Covered plant closings are defined as the shutting of an employment site resulting in a loss of employment of 50 or more employees during any 30-day period. A mass layoff requires the WARN notice if 500 or more employees lose their jobs in a 30-day period. This notice also must be given if between 50 and 499 employees are laid off if the number terminated make up at least 33 percent of the employer's workforce. Although they are entitled to receive any applicable WARN notice, less than half-time employees are not counted to reach the requirement of 50 for plant closings or the thresholds for mass layoffs. A loss of employment includes (1) termination of employment, (2) layoff exceeding 6 months, or (3) a reduction in an employee's work time of more than 50 percent in each month for six months.

The WARN notice must be provided even if the numbers in the preceding paragraph are not satisfied if there are two or more plant closings or mass layoffs in a 90-day period that when taken together satisfy the threshold numbers. The sale of a business may or may not require the WARN notice. Any required notice prior to the sale being completed is the responsibility of the seller. The buyer of the business assumes this responsibility after the date of the closing.

The penalty for failure to comply with the WARN notice is back pay to employees to cover the required 60-day period. Each day of the 60-day period that an employer fails to provide written notice to the local government can result in a $500 fine.

When an employer is replacing striking employees in large numbers, the WARN notice is not required. Employers may avoid the need to provide 60-day notice if it can show its business is faltering and to give notice of a plant closing would adversely impact its ability to get financing. Also, unforeseen business circumstances may justify a less than 60-day WARN notice for either plant closing or layoffs. Finally, natural disasters, such as storms, floods, and earthquakes, may justify a less than 60-day notice for a plant closing or mass layoff.

3. THE FAMILY AND MEDICAL LEAVE ACT

"With the Family Medical Leave Act, the United States at last joined more than 150 other countries in guaranteeing workers some time off when a baby is born or a family member is sick."

—President Bill Clinton in *My Life*

On February 5, 1993, Bill Clinton signed his first piece of legislation as president. This was the **Family and Medical Leave Act (FMLA).** While the details of this law have been called burdensome to business, it has provided eligible employees who work for covered employers to take up to 12 weeks of unpaid leave during any 12-month period if one or more of the following events occur:

- Birth and care of a newborn child of the employee.
- Placement with employee of a son or daughter for adoption or foster care.
- Care of an immediate family member with a serious health condition.
- Employee is unable to work due to a serious health condition.

The provisions relating to birth, adoption, and foster care apply to both female and male employees. Increasingly, men are opting to take leave to care for children. See Sidebar 21.4 for FMLA facts and statistics. An immediate family member is a spouse, minor child, or parent of the employee. Under the FMLA, the employee's parents in law do not qualify as an immediate family member. And the employee's children who are over 18 years old do not qualify as an immediate family member, unless that child is incapable of self-care due to a mental or physical disability that limits one or more of the major life activities as defined in the Americans with Disabilities Act. For a more thorough discussion of the ADA, see Chapter 20. In 2008, the FMLA was expanded to include leave related to a family member's military service. The law grants employees up to 26 weeks of unpaid leave to care for a family member in the military who has incurred a serious illness or injury, and allows employees to take their current 12-week FMLA leave entitlement "for any qualifying exigency" arising out of the fact that a family member is on or has been notified that he or she is being called to active duty in support of a contingency operation. The Department of Labor has the responsibility of issuing regulations related to these changes, including defining "any qualifying exigency."

The parents of a 23-year-old injured so severely in an accident that he is paralyzed are eligible for family medical leave.

On June 23, 2010, the Department of Labor announced that benefits available to parents of newborns and newly adopted children under the FMLA may apply to same-sex couples.

>> *sidebar* 21.4

FMLA: Facts and Statistics

>> WHO TAKES FMLA LEAVE?

About 62 percent of workers qualify to take leave under the FMLA.

Over 50 million people have taken FMLA leave.

>> WHY DO PEOPLE TAKE FMLA LEAVE?

To care for their own serious illness: 52 percent.

To care for a seriously ill family member: 31 percent.

To take care of a new child: 26 percent (29 percent women and 23 percent men).

>> HOW HAS FMLA IMPACTED EMPLOYERS?

98 percent of eligible employees return to work for the same employer after returning from FMLA leave.

89 percent of covered businesses report that the FMLA has a neutral or positive effect on employee morale.

90 percent of covered businesses reported that the FMLA had either a neutral or positive effect on business profitability.

Sources: *U.S. Department* of Labor's 2000 Report *Balancing the Needs of Families and Employers: Family and Medical Leave Surveys 2000 Update;* Nicole Casta's "Highlights of the 2000 U.S. Department of Labor Report: Balancing the Needs of Families and Employers: Family and Medical Leave Surveys," and the National Partnership for Women & Families' 2005 Report "Facts about the FMLA: What Does It Do, Who Uses It, and How."

Covered employers are those who employ 50 or more employees for each working day of 20 or more calendar weeks during either the current or preceding year. Eligible employees have worked for their employer for at least 12 months and have worked at least 1,250 hours during the preceding 12 months. The 12-month work period does not have to be consecutive

696 **PART 5** The Employer-Employee Relationship

To satisfy the requirement that the employer have 50 employees, all persons who work for the employer within 75 miles can be counted.

months. An employee satisfies this requirement so long as that employee has worked for the employer at least a total of 12 months. Furthermore, eligible employees must work at a location where at least 50 employees are employed.

The FMLA places a number of responsibilities on the employer. These responsibilities include notifying the employees that they are eligible for family medical leave and designating in writing when the employee has requested such leave. The employer may request a medical certification that a qualifying event has occurred in the employee's life, but the employer is not entitled to review the actual medical records of the employee.

>> *sidebar* 21.5

EEOC: Best Practices Recommendations on Work/Family Balance

As part of an ongoing attempt to avoid discrimination against workers with caregiving responsibilities, sometimes called "family responsibilities discrimination," the EEOC issued a document on best practices. Those recommendations include the following:

- Be aware of and train managers about the legal obligations that may impact decisions about the treatment of workers with caregiving responsibilities.

- Develop, disseminate, and enforce a strong EEO policy that clearly addresses the types of conduct that might constitute unlawful discrimination.

- Ensure that managers at all levels are aware of and comply with the organization's work-life policies.

- Respond to complaints of caregiver discrimination efficiently and effectively.

- Protect against retaliation.

The document also encourages employers to develop "flexible work policies," which studies have demonstrated have a "positive impact on employee engagement organizational productivity and profitability."

Case to Consider: *Chadwick v. Wellpoint, Inc.* (1st Cir. 2009), in which the court held that "unlawful sex discrimination occurs when an employer takes an adverse job action on the assumption that a woman, because she is a woman, will neglect her job responsibilities in favor of her presumed childcare responsibilities." The plaintiff in *Chadwick* was the mother of young triplets. She was passed over for promotion and the position was given to a woman with two older children. The First Circuit held that the district court erred in granting summary judgment in favor of the employer and, accordingly, reversed and remanded the case for further proceedings.

Source: EEOC, *Employer Best Practices for Workers with Caregiving Responsibilities*, 2009, available at www.eeoc.gov/policy/docs/caregiver-best-practices.html.

Once family medical leave is granted, the employer must keep the employee's job available for when the leave is up and the employee returns to work. In essence, the employee who qualifies for family medical leave is not supposed to be disadvantaged by the fact that the leave was taken. For example, if the employer gives a bonus for perfect attendance, the employee on family medical leave should be awarded this bonus, assuming perfect attendance other than the leave period. If a bonus is based on the amount of sales, the FMLA does not require the employer to award sales that the employee would have made if not on family medical leave.

Employees who believe they have been denied their rights under the FMLA can sue the employer in federal district court for equitable and monetary damages. Such an employee may sue for reinstatement or may seek damages or both.

>> *sidebar* 21.6

Are States Immune from Certain FMLA Claims?

>> CASE TO WATCH: *COLEMAN V. MARYLAND COURT OF APPEALS*

On June 27, 2011, the U.S. Supreme Court granted certiorari in this case to decide whether a State can be sued under the Family Medical Leave Act where the employee is seeking leave due to his or her own serious health condition.

Key Facts: Daniel Coleman was an employee of the Maryland Court of Appeals for six years. In August 2007, he sent a letter requesting sick leave for a documented medical condition. The request was denied and Mr. Coleman was given an ultimatum: resign or be terminated. In this complaint, Mr. Coleman claimed that his FMLA leave was denied in retaliation for his complaints of wrongdoing in the office.

Procedural History: The District Court granted defendants' motion to dismiss, including plaintiffs'

FMLA claims, holding that "the FMLA's self-care provisions did not validly abrogate Eleventh Amendment immunity." The Fourth Circuit affirmed.

Explanation: The Eleventh Amendment of the U.S. Constitution bars claims in federal court against an unconsenting state and any governmental units that are arms of the state unless Congress has abrogated immunity. To do so, Congress must make clear its intent to abrogate and must act in accordance with a valid exercise of power. The Supreme Court's decision should address whether a State can be sued under the FMLA in cases involving self-care.

For ongoing information about this case and official documents, see www.scotusblog.com/case-files/cases/coleman-v-maryland-court-of-appeals/.

---

4. UNIFORMED SERVICES EMPLOYMENT AND REEMPLOYMENT RIGHTS ACT

The **Uniformed Services Employment and Reemployment Rights Act (USERRA)** protects the rights of individuals who voluntarily or involuntarily leave employment positions to undertake military service or certain types of service in the National Disaster Medical System. Specifically, USERRA provides reemployment rights following a period of service if:

- The individual held a civilian job
- The employee informed the employer that he/she was leaving the job for service in the uniformed services
- The period of service did not exceed five years (with exceptions)
- The release from service was under "honorable conditions"
- The individual reports back to the civilian employer in a timely manner or submits a timely application for reemployment

An international survey of 173 countries revealed that the United States is only one of four countries that does not guarantee any paid leave for new mothers. The other countries are Liberia, Papua New Guinea, and Swaziland. Source: Project on Global Working Families' 2007 Report "Work, Family, and Equity Index."

Those eligible to be reemployed must be restored to the job and receive benefits that would have been attained had there not been an absence due to military service. USERRA protects those performing uniformed service from discrimination in:

- Initial employment
- Reemployment
- Retention in employment
- Promotion
- Any benefit of employment

Employers may not retaliate against anyone assisting in the enforcement of USERRA rights, even if that person has no service connection.

USERRA also contains health insurance provisions. Covered individuals who leave a job to perform military service have the right to elect to continue existing employer-based health plan coverage for up to 24 months. For those who do not elect to continue coverage, they have the right to be reinstated in the employer's health plan when reemployed, generally without any waiting periods or exclusions (except for service connected illnesses or injuries). Federal law required employers to notify employees of their rights under USERRA, including by displaying government notices.

>> sidebar 21.7

Rand Study: Invisible Wounds of War

Rand, a non-profit global think tank, conducted a study of U.S troops to determine the effects of their service. Since October 2001, approximately 1.64 million U.S. troops have been deployed for operations in Iraq and Afghanistan. The study assessed the post-deployment health-related needs. Major findings:

- About 19 percent of returning veterans report symptoms consistent with a diagnosis of post-traumatic stress disorder (PTSD) or depression.
- About 20 percent reported having suffered a probably traumatic brain injury while deployed.
- Only about half of those who need treatment for PTSD and depression actually seek it, and slightly more than half of those who receive treatment get care that meets minimal clinical standards.

- Concerns about confidentiality and career issues were major reasons why many veterans did not seek treatment.
- Removing such barriers to care and delivering treatment supported by scientific evidence can improve recovery rates and reduce societal costs.

Taking into consideration these issues, the U.S. Department of Labor issued *Hiring Veterans: A Step-by-Step Toolkit for Employers* to help employers working with transitioning service members. The guide includes information about available resources and developing effective strategies to hire veterans.

Source: Rand, *Invisible Wounds of War: Psychological and Cognitive Injuries, Their Consequences, and Services to Assist Recovery*, 2008, available at www.rand.org/health/feature/forty/invisible_wounds.html.

case 21.3 >>

STAUB v. PROCTOR HOSPITAL
562 U.S. ___ (2011)

This case contains a reference to the Seventeenth Century fable, "The Monkey and the Cat" by French poet Jean de la Fontine. In that fable, a monkey persuades an unsuspecting cat to extract some chestnuts from a fire. The monkey absconds with the nuts, leaving the cat with only a burnt paw. Under the cat's paw theory of liability, an employer may be held liable when a biased non-decision maker (the monkey) influences an unbiased decision maker (the cat) to take action he or she would not otherwise take.

While employed as an angiography technician by respondent Proctor Hospital, petitioner Staub was a member of the United States Army Reserve. Both his immediate supervisor (Mulally) and Mulally's supervisor (Korenchuk) were hostile to his military obligations. Mulally gave Staub disciplinary warning, which included a directive requiring Staub to report to her or Korenchuk when his cases were completed. After receiving a report from Korenchuk that Staub had violated the Corrective Action, Proctor's vice president of human resources (Buck) reviewed Staub's personnel file and decided to fire him. Staub filed a grievance, claiming that Mulally had fabricated the allegation underlying the warning out of hostility toward his military obligations, but Buck adhered to her decision. Staub sued Proctor under the Uniformed Services Employment and Reemployment Rights Act of 1994 (USERRA). He contended not that Buck was motivated by hostility to his military obligations, but that Mulally and Korenchuk were, and that their actions influenced Buck's decision. A jury found Proctor liable and awarded Staub damages, but the Seventh Circuit reversed, holding that Proctor was entitled to judgment as a matter of law because the decision maker had relied on more than Mulally's and Korenchuk's advice in making her decision. The U.S. Supreme Court unanimously reversed. Justice Kagan did not take part in the decision.

SCALIA, J.: We consider the circumstances under which an employer may be held liable for employment discrimination based on the discriminatory animus of an employee who influenced, but did not make, the ultimate employment decision.

Petitioner Vincent Staub worked as an angiography technician for respondent Proctor Hospital until 2004, when he was fired. Staub and Proctor hotly dispute the facts surrounding the firing, but because a jury found for Staub in his claim of employment discrimination against Proctor, we describe the facts viewed in the light most favorable to him. While employed by Proctor, Staub was a member of the United States Army Reserve, which required him to attend drill one weekend per month and to train full time for two to three weeks a year. Both Janice Mulally, Staub's immediate supervisor, and Michael Korenchuk, Mulally's supervisor, were hostile to Staub's military obligations. . . .

On April 2, 2004, Angie Day, Staub's co-worker, complained to Linda Buck, Proctor's vice president of human resources, and Garrett McGowan, Proctor's chief operating officer, about Staub's frequent unavailability and abruptness. McGowan directed Korenchuk and Buck to create a plan that would solve Staub's "availability' problems." But three weeks later, before they had time to do so, Korenchuk informed Buck that Staub had left his desk without informing a supervisor, in violation of the January Corrective Action. Staub now contends this accusation was false: he had left Korenchuk a voicemail notification that he was leaving his desk. Buck relied on Korenchuk's accusation, however, and after reviewing Staub's personnel file, she decided to fire him. The termination notice stated that Staub had ignored the directive issued in the January 2004 Corrective Action.

Staub challenged his firing through Proctor's grievance process, claiming that Mulally had fabricated the allegation underlying the Corrective Action out of hostility toward his military obligations. Buck did not follow up with Mulally about this claim. After discussing the matter with another personnel officer, Buck adhered to her decision.

Staub sued Proctor under the Uniformed Services Employment and Reemployment Rights Act of 1994, 38 U. S. C. §4301 et seq., claiming that his discharge was motivated by hostility to his obligations as a military reservist. His contention was not that Buck had any such hostility but that Mulally and Korenchuk did, and that their actions influenced Buck's ultimate employment decision. A jury found that Staub's "military status was a motivating factor in [Proctor's] decision to discharge him," App. 68a, and awarded $57,640 in damages.

The Seventh Circuit reversed, holding that Proctor was entitled to judgment as a matter of law. 560 F. 3d 647. The court observed that Staub had brought a "'cat's

[continued]

paw' case," meaning that he sought to hold his employer liable for the animus of a supervisor who was not charged with making the ultimate employment decision. . . . Here, however, Staub is seeking to hold liable not Mulally and Korenchuk, but their employer. Perhaps, therefore, the discriminatory motive of one of the employer's agents (Mulally or Korenchuk) can be aggregated with the act of another agent (Buck) to impose liability on Proctor. . . . Thus, if the employer's investigation results in an adverse action for reasons unrelated to the supervisor's original biased action (by the terms of USERRA it is the employer's burden to establish that), then the employer will not be liable. But the supervisor's biased report may remain a causal factor if the independent investigation takes it into account without determining that the adverse action was, apart from the supervisor's recommendation, entirely justified. We are aware of no principle in tort or agency law under which an employer's mere conduct of an independent investigation has a claim-preclusive effect. Nor do we think the independent investigation somehow relieves the employer of "fault." The employer is at fault because one of its agents committed an action based on discriminatory animus that was intended to cause, and did in fact cause, an adverse employment decision. . . . motivated by antimilitary animus that is intended by the supervisor to cause an adverse employment action, and if that act is a proximate cause of the ultimate employment action, then the employer is liable under USERRA . . . Applying our analysis to the facts of this case, it is clear that the Seventh Circuit's judgment must be reversed. Both Mulally and Korenchuk were acting within the scope of their employment when they took the actions that allegedly caused Buck to fire Staub. A "reprimand . . . for workplace failings" constitutes conduct within the scope of an agent's employment. *Faragher* v. *Boca Raton,* 524 U.S. 775, 798–799 (1998). As the Seventh Circuit recognized, there was evidence that Mulally's and Korenchuk's actions were motivated by hostility toward Staub's military obligations. There was also evidence that Mulally's and Korenchuk's actions were causal factors underlying Buck's decision to fire Staub. Buck's termination notice expressly stated that Staub was terminated because he had "ignored" the directive in the Corrective Action. Finally, there was evidence that both Mulally and Korenchuk had the specific intent to cause Staub to be terminated. Mulally stated she was trying to "get rid of" Staub, and Korenchuk was aware that Mulally was "out to get" Staub. Moreover, Korenchuk informed Buck, Proctor's personnel officer responsible for terminating employees, of Staub's alleged noncompliance with Mulally's Corrective Action, and Buck fired Staub immediately thereafter; a reasonable jury could infer that Korenchuk intended that Staub be fired. The Seventh Circuit therefore erred in holding that Proctor was entitled to judgment as a matter of law.

It is less clear whether the jury's verdict should be reinstated or whether Proctor is entitled to a new trial. The jury instruction did not hew precisely to the rule we adopt today; it required only that the jury find that "military status was a motivating factor in [Proctor's] decision to discharge him." App. 68a. Whether the variance between the instruction and our rule was harmless error or should mandate a new trial is a matter the Seventh Circuit may consider in the first instance.

Reversed and Remanded.

>> CASE QUESTIONS

1. How does the "cat's paw" theory of liability apply to this case?
2. What is the Court's rationale for reversing the Seventh Circuit?
3. Could the rationale in this case be applied to Title VII cases?

5. OCCUPATIONAL SAFETY AND HEALTH ADMINISTRATION

Occupational Safety and Health Administration (OSHA) has jurisdiction over complaints about hazardous conditions in the workplace. Employers are required to comply with OSHA standards to furnish a workplace free

>> *sidebar* 21.8

New OSHA Crowd Management Safety Guidelines

In 2008, a temporary maintenance worker was pushed to the ground and suffocated to death after approximately 2,000 holiday shoppers broke through Walmart's glass doors. The shoppers were racing to buy sharply discounted televisions, computers and other gifts. OSHA filed a citation against Walmart, alleging that it did not furnish a workplace "free from recognizable hazard" that were likely to cause death or serious physical harm to an employee due to "crowd crush." Walmart was fined $7,000 and was required to take steps to correct the hazard. Although the fine is *de minimus* for Walmart, concerned about the ramifications for future crowd-attracting events, the retailer appealed. The fine was upheld on appeal.

As a result of this incident, OSHA issued *Crowd Control Guidelines* in November 2010. The detailed guidelines address steps to be taken during planning,

pre-event setup, the sales event and in emergency situations. Considerations include staffing plans, emergency contacts, training workers in crowd management, using barricades or ropes with adequate breaks or turns, using wristbands, tickets or an Internet lottery for "hot items," and ensuring adequate communication between employees, customers, and emergency personnel.

Specific measures implemented by Walmart include issuing tickets for hot items, placing employees on platforms to direct customers, using steel barriers in zig-zag patters in front to the store to guide customers into the store in an orderly fashion—avoiding a shoving and crushing mass trying to enter the store.

For more about OSHA's new rules, see *Crowd Control Guidelines* at www.osha.gov/OshDoc/data_General_Facts/Crowd_Control.pdf.

from recognized hazards. Employees have the right to request an OSHA inspection if they believe that there are unsafe and unhealthful conditions in the workplace. Employees making complaints who are subjected to retaliation or discrimination by their employers may also file a complaint with OSHA. There is no private cause of action under OSHA, which means that an employee cannot sue an employer for damages based on an OSHA violation.

OSHA investigates a wide variety of workplace hazards. For example, following the deaths of 20 workers in 2008 in construction accidents in New York City, OSHA is sending inspectors there in an effort to increase safety and improve working conditions. OSHA inspectors will examine cranes and high-rise construction sites. In addition to the inspections, OSHA sent notices to employers' insurance and workers' compensation carriers. Citations involving training violations at unionized sites will also be sent to the unions representing workers and to their training funds. The U.S. House Education and Labor Committee is reviewing the sufficiency of OSHA's construction enforcement. OSHA is also investigating The Atlanta Ballet following the fall of a 17-year-old dancer wearing a panda costume during a performance of "The Nutcracker" at the Fox Theater in Atlanta. The dancer, who fell about 12 feet into the empty orchestra pit, suffered serious injuries, requiring spinal surgery. OSHA conducted over 38,000 inspections in 2006.

>> *sidebar* 21.9

OSHA's Severe Violator Enforcement Program

Under the Obama administration, OSHA is increasing its focus on enforcing safe workplaces. One significant step was releasing the Severe Violator Enforcement Program (SVEP) draft directive to concentrate resources on "inspecting employers who have demonstrated indifference" to their OSHA obligations "by willful, repeated, or failure-to-abate violations." If an employer engages in this behavior in one of the following four areas, it is at risk for being placed in the SVEP:

1. Fatality and/or catastrophic situations, such as three or more hospitalizations or the death of an employee
2. Non-fatality and/or catastrophic situations in which the employer has exposed the employee to one of the most severe workplace hazards, including "high gravity serious violations" such as fall hazards, combustible dust hazards and lead hazards
3. Hazards due to the potential release of a highly hazardous chemical
4. Any violation that is deemed "egregious" under current OSHA regulations

The SVEP casts a wide enforcement net, applying to employers of all sizes.

Source: OSHA, Severe Violator Enforcement Program Directive, available at www.osha.gov/dep/svep-directive.pdf.

6. PENSION PLANS AND HEALTH CARE

In 1974, Congress passed and President Nixon signed the Employee Retirement Income Security Act (ERISA). This law attempts to protect employees whose employers have voluntary pension plans. These protections include disclosure of information about the management of and fiduciary relationships within the plan. Since ERISA, the federal government has enacted a number of other laws directed at protecting employees' health care. Among these laws are Consolidated Omnibus Budget Reconciliation Act (COBRA), which was passed in 1986, and provides that employees can continue to purchase health insurance even after their employment is terminated. The Health Insurance Portability and Accountability Act (HIPAA) became law in 1996 and protects employees who have preexisting health conditions when they change jobs.

For more details about these laws, visit www.dol.gov/dol/topic/health-plans/erisa.htm#content

During the early part of this century, we have seen a new crisis arising. This involves businesses who are changing their defined-benefit retirement plans to private individual accounts, such as 401(k) plans. A number of companies have gone into bankruptcy and have sought permission to cancel retirement plans. It appears a very real competitive advantage is to be a new company that is not burdened by large pension plans obligations. For example, many of the legacy airlines, such as Delta, United, and Northwest, have gone into and come out of bankruptcy in the hope that they will be competitive with newer airlines, which do not have the large obligation of paying the pensions of thousands of retirees. Sidebar 21.10 provides detail of a major company's changes in pension plans.

7. LIMITATIONS ON EMPLOYMENT AT WILL

Historically, unless employees contracted for a definite period of employment (such as for one year), employers were able to discharge them without cause at any time. This is called the **employment-at-will doctrine.**

During the 1930s, employers began to lose this absolute right to discharge employees whenever they desired. The Labor-Management Relations Act prohibited employers from firing employees for union activities. Now, many federal laws limit employers in their right to terminate employees. Table 21.2 provides a listing of some of these laws. Some states also prohibit employers

table 21.2 >> Federal Statutes Limiting Employment-at-Will Doctrine

Statute	Limitation on Employee Discharge
Labor-Management Relations Act	Prohibits discharge for union activity or for filing charges under the act.
Fair Labor Standards Act	Forbids discharge for exercising rights guaranteed by minimum-wage and overtime provisions of the act.
Occupational Safety and Health Act	Prohibits discharge for exercising rights under the act.
Civil Rights Act	Makes illegal discharge based on race, sex, color, religion, or national origin.
Age Discrimination in Employment Act	Forbids age-based discharge of employees over age 40.
Employee Retirement Income Security Act	Prohibits discharge to prevent employees from getting vested pension rights.
Clean Air Act	Prevents discharge of employees who cooperate in proceedings against an employer for violation of the act.
Clean Water Act	Prevents discharge of employees who cooperate in proceedings against an employer for violation of the act.
Consumer Credit Protection Act	Prohibits discharge of employees due to garnishment of wages for any one indebtedness.
Judiciary and Judicial Procedure Act	Forbids discharge of employees for service on federal grand or petit juries.

by statute from discharging employees for certain reasons, such as for refusing to take lie detector examinations.

Courts, too, have begun limiting the at-will doctrine. Under contract theory, several courts have stated that at-will employment contracts (which are not written and are little more than an agreement to pay for work performed) contain an implied promise of good faith and fair dealing by the employer.

Other courts have ruled that the employer's publication of an employee handbook can change the nature of at-will employment. They have held the employer liable for breach of contract for discharging an employee in violation of statements made in the handbook about discharge procedures.

Many contract and tort exceptions to employment at will have involved one of three types of employer behavior:

Do understand that any commitments stated in an employee handbook are viewed by courts as a contractual promise by the employer.

- Discharge of employee for performance of an important public obligation, such as jury duty.
- Discharge of employee for reporting employer's alleged violations of law (whistleblowing). The recent financial reform legislation, Dodd-Frank, includes financial incentives to blow the whistle for a broad range of wrongdoing from securities and accounting fraud to bribery allegations. (See Sidebar 21.11 for information about IRS whistleblowers.)
- Discharge of employee for exercising statutory rights.

>> *sidebar* 21.11

IRS Whistleblowers Rewards Program

In 2006, the IRS amended its whistleblower statute to encourage the reporting of tax fraud perpetrated by individuals and corporations. Pursuant to 26 U.S.C. §7623, whistleblowers have an enforceable right to a reward when they report significant tax violations. A person who provides information regarding tax law violations under the IRS Whistleblower Law is known as a whistleblower. To be eligible to recover compensation from the IRS, a person must bring information to the Internal Revenue Service's attention. The whistleblower may receive compensation only from monies actually collected based on the information provided.

Under the IRS Whistleblower Reform Law, a person can receive a reward of between 15 percent and 30 percent of the total collected proceeds (including penalties, interest, additions to tax, and additional amounts). If the IRS moves forward with an administrative or judicial action based on information brought by a whistleblower, the whistleblower is eligible to receive at least 15 percent and up to a cap of 30 percent of the recovery, depending on the whistleblower's contribution to the prosecution

of the action. The IRS may give awards of lesser amounts under certain circumstances (i.e., when the fraud has already been publicly disclosed and the whistleblower is not an original source).

>> WHAT ARE THE MOST COMMON TAX FRAUD SCHEMES?

- Failing to report income earned in a foreign stock exchange.
- Participating in bogus income tax shelters.
- Hiding or transferring assets or income out of the United States.
- Overstating deductions.
- Making false entries in books and records.
- Claiming personal expenses as business expenses.
- Claiming false deductions.
- Underreporting tip income.
- Paying employees in cash.
- Keeping two sets of books.

Most of the cases that limit at-will employment state that the employer has violated *public policy.* What does it mean to say that an employer has violated public policy? Is it a court's way of saying that most people no longer support the employer's right to do what it did?

Limitations on discrimination and employment at will evidence a growing concern for the rights of employees in their jobs and may suggest a trend that could lead to some type of broad, legally guaranteed job security. In recent years, unions have also increasingly focused on job-security issues in their bargaining with employers.

>> *sidebar* 21.12

Privacy, Technology and Social Media

Technology and social media are raising ongoing issues about privacy in the workplace. Both employers and employees are dealing with how to navigate these issues. Here are a few examples:

- The U.S. Supreme Court unanimously found that notwithstanding a city policy officer's reasonable expectation of privacy in text messages received on a pager provided by the City, the City did not violate his privacy rights under the Fourth Amendment by reviewing transcripts of those text messages. In this case, many of the messages were not work related and were sexually explicit. (*City of Ontario v. Quon,* 560 U.S. __ (2010).)

- Employers may review an applicant's Facebook, MySpace, or LinkedIn pages to learn more about potential employees during the recruitment and hiring process.

- Many employers now have documented policies pertaining to their employees' use of social media sites while on the job.

- When using social media sites, employers must use care not to base a decision on something learned that cannot legally be used to make an employment decision.

---

8. WORKERS' PRIVACY

Individual privacy is such an important part of individual freedom that both legal and ethical questions regarding privacy are bound to multiply in the computer age. While debate continues concerning the need for further federal privacy legislation, many states have passed their own privacy-related statutes. Several states guarantee workers access to their job personnel files and restrict disclosure of personal information to third parties.

Concerns for individual privacy also contributed to passage of the Electronic Communications Privacy Act of 1986 and the 1988 Employee Polygraph Protection Act. Under this latter federal law, private employers generally are forbidden from using lie detector tests while screening job applicants. Current employees may not be tested randomly but may be tested as a result of a specific incident or activity that causes economic injury or loss to an employer's business. The act permits private security companies to test job applicants and allows companies that manufacture or sell controlled substances to test both job applicants and current employees. The Labor Department may seek fines of up to $10,000 against employers who violate the act. Employees are also authorized to sue employers for violating the act.

Don't rely on an expectation of privacy in the workplace; employers may monitor e-mail systems they provide.

Another important privacy concern involves drug testing. At present there is no uniform law regarding the drug testing of employees. Many private companies conduct such testing. However, some states have placed some limits on a private company's right to test for drugs.

Public employees are protected from some drug testing by the Fourth Amendment's prohibition against *unreasonable* searches. However, exactly when drug tests are unreasonable is subject to much debate in the courts. In general, public employees may be tested when there is a proper suspicion that employees are using illegal drugs that impair working ability or violate employment rules. Courts have also upheld drug testing as part of required annual medical exams.

> *Unlike the U.S., workers in other jurisdictions, such as the European Union, enjoy a much higher expectation of privacy in the workplace.*

>> *sidebar* 21.13

Is There Any Reasonable Expectation of Privacy in the Workplace?

There is very little expectation of privacy in the American workplace. For example, of the employers surveyed:

- 73 percent monitored e-mail messages.
- 66 percent monitored Web surfing.
- 48 percent monitored with video surveillance.
- 45 percent monitored keystrokes and keyboard time.
- 43 percent monitored computer files.

Of those employers, a number reported firing employees for violating policies regarding use of the Internet (30 percent), e-mail (28 percent), or phones (6 percent).

Source: 2007 Electronic Monitoring & Surveillance Survey (released February 2008) by the American Management Association and The ePolicy Institute.

9. WORKER'S COMPENSATION ACTS

In Chapter 10, you learned about torts. What happens, however, if a worker is injured at work? Around the turn of the century, the tort system was largely replaced in the workplace by a series of workers' compensation acts. These statutes were enacted at both the state and federal level, and they imposed a type of strict liability on employers for accidental workplace injuries suffered by their employees. The clear purpose of these statues was to remove financial losses of injury from workers and redistribute them onto employers and ultimately onto society.

> *Even if an employee's contributory negligence or assumption of risk leads to an accidental injury, the employee still receives workers' compensation.*

History **Workers' compensation** laws are state statutes designed to protect employees and their families from the risks of accidental injury, death, or disease resulting from their employment. They were passed because the common law did not give adequate protection to employees from the hazards of their work. At common law, anyone was liable in tort for damages resulting from injuries caused to another as a proximate result of negligence. If an employer acted unreasonably and his or her carelessness was the proximate cause of physical injury suffered by an employee, the latter could sue and recover damages from the employer. However, the common law also provided the employer with the means of escaping this tort liability in most cases through three defenses:

> *Remember workers' compensation is a form of insurance required by the states.*

> *If you are injured at work, report the accident immediately.*

- Assumption of the risk
- Contributory negligence
- The fellow-servant rule

For example, assume that the employer knowingly instructed workers to operate dangerous machinery not equipped with any safety devices, even though it realized injury to them was likely. A worker had his arm mangled when it was caught in the gears of one of these machines. Even though the employer was negligent in permitting this hazardous condition to persist, if the worker was aware of the dangers that existed, he would be unable to recover damages because he knowingly *assumed the risk* of his injury. In addition, if the injury were caused by *contributory negligence* of the employee as well as the negligence of the employer, the action was defeated. And, if the injury occurred because of the negligence of another employee, the negligent employee, rather than the employer, was liable because of the *fellow-servant rule.*

The English Parliament passed a workers' compensation statute in 1897. Today all states have such legislation, modeled to a greater or lesser degree on the English act. These laws vary a great deal from state to state as to the industries subject to them, the employees they cover, the nature of the injuries or diseases that are compensable, the rates of compensation, and the means of administration. In spite of wide variances in the laws of the states in this area, certain general observations can be made about them.

The System   State workers' compensation statutes provide a system to pay workers or their families if the worker is accidentally killed or injured or incurs an occupational disease while employed. To be compensable, the death, illness, or injury must arise out of and in the course of the employment. Under these acts, the negligence or fault of the employer in causing an on-the-job injury is not an issue. Instead, these laws recognize the fact of life that a certain number of injuries, deaths, and diseases are bound to occur in a modern industrial society as a result of the attempts of businesses and their employees to provide the goods and services demanded by the consuming public. This view leads to the conclusion that it is fairer for the consuming public to bear the cost of such mishaps rather than to impose it on injured workers.

Workers' compensation laws create strict liability for employers of accidentally injured workers. Liability exists regardless of lack of negligence or fault, provided the necessary association between the injuries and the business of the employer is present. The three defenses the employer had at common law are eliminated. The employers, treating the costs of these injuries as part of the costs of production, pass them on to the consumers who created the demand for the product or service being furnished.

Workers' compensation acts give covered employees the right to certain cash payments for their loss of income due to accidental, on-the-job injuries. In the event of a married employee's death, benefits are provided for the surviving spouse and minor children. The amount of such awards usually is subject to a stated maximum and is calculated by using a percentage of the wages of the employee. If the employee suffers permanent, partial disability, most states provide compensation both for injuries that are scheduled in the statute and those that are nonscheduled. As an example of the former, a worker who loses a hand might be awarded 100 weeks of compensation at $95 per week. Besides scheduling specific compensation for certain specific injuries, most acts also provide compensation for nonscheduled ones based upon the earning power the employee lost due to his or her injury. In addition to the above payments, all statutes provide for medical benefits.

In some states, employers have a choice of covering their workers' compensation risk with insurance or of being self-insured (that is, paying all claims directly) if they can demonstrate their capability to do so. Approximately 20 percent of compensation benefits are paid by self-insurers. In other states, employers pay into a state fund used to compensate workers entitled to benefits. In these states, the amounts of the payments are based on the size of the payroll and the experience of the employer in having claims filed against the system by its employees. Workers' compensation laws are usually administered exclusively by an administrative agency called the industrial commission or board, which has quasi-judicial powers. Of course, the ruling of such boards is subject to review by the courts of the jurisdiction in the same manner as the actions of other administrative agencies.

Tests for Determining Compensation   The tests for determining whether an employer must pay workers' compensation to an employee are simply:

1. Was the injury accidental?
2. Did the injury arise out of and in the course of employment?

Because workers' compensation laws benefit workers, courts interpret them liberally to favor workers. In recent years, cases have tended to expand employers' liability. For instance, courts have held that heart attacks (as well as other common ailments in which the employee has had either a preexisting disease or a physical condition likely to lead to the disease) are compensable as "accidental injuries." One ruling approved an award to a purchasing agent who became mentally ill because she was exposed to unusual work, stresses, and strains.

Her "nerve-racking" job involved a business whose sales grew over sixfold in 10 years. Factors contributing to her "accidental injury" included harsh criticism by her supervisor and long hours of work. Likewise, the courts have been liberal in upholding awards that have been challenged on the grounds that the injury did not arise "out of and in the course of employment." Courts routinely support compensation awards for almost any accidental injury that employees suffer while traveling for their employers. A Minnesota Supreme Court decision upheld a lower court award of compensation to a bus driver. On a layover during a trip, the driver had been shot accidentally in a tavern parking lot following a night on the town.

Exclusive Remedy Rule   Recently, some courts have been liberal in their interpretations of the **exclusive remedy rule.** This rule, which is written into all compensation statutes, states that an employee's sole remedy against an employer for workplace injury or illness shall be workers' compensation. In the past few years, courts in several important jurisdictions have created exceptions to this rule. Note that these exceptions recognize in part that workers' compensation laws do not adequately compensate badly injured workers.

Since workers' compensation laws apply only to accidentally injured workers, the exclusive remedy rule does not protect employers who intentionally injure workers. But the issue arises as to how "intentional" such an injury has to be. What if an employer knowingly exposes employees to a chemical that may cause illness in some employees over a long term?

The Future of State Workers' Compensation   Currently, many problems confront the state workers' compensation system. Fifty separate non-uniform acts make up the system. Many acts exclude from coverage groups such as farmworkers, government employees, and employees of small businesses. Many state legislatures have enacted changes in their compensation laws. However, states that have broadened coverage and increased benefits have greatly boosted the cost of doing business within their borders. This discourages new businesses from locating within these states and encourages those already there to move out.

In the last decade, workers' compensation payments have tripled. Many workers exaggerate their injuries to get compensation. At the same time, compensation payments to seriously injured workers are often inadequate, and this has led to attempts to get around the exclusive remedy rule.

As our national economy moves from a manufacturing to a service emphasis, the nature of injuries suffered under workers' compensation programs begins to change. In particular, the number of mental stress claims rises. The National Council on Compensation Insurance states that these claims have increased fivefold in the past few years. Problems of proving (or disproving) mental stress claims bring new concerns for the workers' compensation system.

A major problem concerns slowly developing occupational diseases. Many toxic chemicals cause cancer and other diseases only after workers have been exposed to them over many years. Often it is difficult or impossible for workers or their survivors to recover workers' compensation for such diseases. One solution to the problems confronting the workers' compensation system would be federal reform. Those advocating such reform have put forth several plans, but Congress has shown little inclination so far to adopt a uniform federal act.

>> *sidebar* 21.14

Workplace Issues Related to Medical Marijuana

The use of medical marijuana is raising a range of workplace issues. Sixteen states and the District of Columbia have statutes decriminalizing the use of marijuana for medical purposes. This is creating a range of questions for employers in those states:

- Are random drug tests problematic under the Americans with Disabilities Act?
- Employers have a "general duty" to provide a safe workplace under OSHA, so can they terminate a worker who tests positive for THC?

- How do these laws affect an employers' obligations under the federal Drug-Free Workplace Act of 1988 if they are receiving federal contracts?
- If a employees are legally using medical marijuana outside of the workplace, yet tests positive at work, can they be fired?

This is an evolving area of the law and one that employers need to be mindful of as they make decisions involving workers who are using medical marijuana.

---

10. EMPLOYMENT ELIGIBILITY VERIFICATION

In accordance with the federal Immigration Reform and Control Act of 1986 ("IRCA"), all U.S. employers must complete and retain Form I-9 **Employment Eligibility Verification** forms for each individual they hire in the United

States. Both citizens and noncitizens must complete the form. The employer is required to examine the employment eligibility and identify document(s) an employee presents to determine whether the document(s) reasonably appear to be "genuine." Acceptable documents that establish both identity and employment authorization include:

- U.S. Passport or U.S. Passport Card
- Permanent Resident Card or Alien Registration Receipt Card
- Foreign passport that contains a temporary I-551 stamp or temporary I-551 printed notation on a machine-readable visa
- An Employment Authorization document that contains a photograph

If none of these documents are available, a worker may use a combination of documents specified by federal law. Employers must use care to determine that the documents appear genuine, but not to go overboard and be liable for "document abuse" or discriminatory practices related to verification. The U.S. Citizen and Immigration Services broadly categorizes document abuse into four categories:

1. Improperly requesting that employees produce more documents than are required by Form I-9 to establish the employee's identity and employment authorization
2. Improperly requesting that employees present a particular document, such as a "green card," to establish identity and/or employment authorization
3. Improperly rejecting documents that reasonably appear to be genuine and to relate to the employee presenting them
4. Improperly treating groups of applicants differently when completing Form I-9, such as requiring certain groups of employees who look or sound "foreign" to present particular documents to the employer

The completed forms must be retained by the employer either for three years after the date of hire or for one year after employment is terminated, whichever is later.

>> *sidebar* 21.15

Arizona Law on Hiring Foreign Workers Is Upheld

By a 5-3 vote, the U.S. Supreme Court ruled in *Chamber of Commerce v. Whiting*, 563 U.S. ___ (2011) that the federal Immigration Reform and Control Act (IRCA) law does *not* pre-empt the Arizona statute that penalizes employers who knowingly hire unauthorized foreign workers. The Legal Arizona Workers Act provides that the licenses of state employers that knowingly or intentionally employ unauthorized aliens may be, and in certain circumstances must be, suspended or revoked. The law also requires all Arizona employers to use E-Verify, an Internet-based system that provides instant verification of work authorization.

The U.S. Chamber of Commerce, along with various business and civil rights organizations, challenged the Arizona law. The Court reasoned that Arizona's licensing law falls well within the confines of the authority Congress chose to leave to the States and therefore is not expressly preempted.

11. EMPLOYEE LAWSUITS

LO 21-4

Despite the presence of many examples of the employer's violating an employment law, most employers strive to obey the law. They still risk lawsuits, however, including many brought by unsatisfactory employees who have been disciplined, denied promotion, or discharged. How can employers protect themselves from unjustified employee lawsuits?

One important protection against unjustified employee lawsuits is an established system of adequate documentation. Sometimes called the **paper fortress,** this documentation consists of job descriptions, personnel manuals, and employee personnel files.

Before handing anyone an employment application, the employer should insist that the potential candidate carefully study a job description. A well-written job description will help potential applicants eliminate themselves from job situations for which they lack interest or qualification, thus preventing employers from having to dismiss them later and risking lawsuits.

Once a new employee is hired, the employer should give the employee a personnel manual. This manual should include information about employee benefits and should also outline work rules and job requirements. The employer should go over the manual with the employee and answer any questions. Clear identification of employer expectations and policies helps provide a defense against employee lawsuits if subsequent discipline or discharge of the employee becomes necessary. The employer should ask that the employee sign a form indicating receipt of the manual and an understanding of the employer's explanation of its contents.

The employer should enter this form, with all other documentation relevant to an employee's work history, into the employee's personnel file. Regular written evaluations of employee performance should also be entered into the personnel file. A chronological record of unsatisfactory work performance is a very useful defense against unjustified lawsuits following discipline, denial of promotion, or discharge.

Another piece of documentation that helps justify employer decisions is the written warning. Anytime an employee breaks a work rule or performs unsatisfactorily, the employer should issue the employee a written warning and place a duplicate in the personnel file. The warning should explain specifically what work rule the employee violated. In addition, employers should either have an employee sign that he or she has received a written warning or else note in the personnel file that the employee has received a copy of it. The employer should also give the employee the opportunity to place a letter of explanation in the personnel file.

Laws discussed in this chapter and the next one should not prevent employers from discharging unsatisfactory employees. In an actual termination conversation, however, the employer should provide the employee with specific reasons for discharge, taken from the personnel file. Detailed documentation is vital in successfully responding to unjustified employee lawsuits. Even better is to prevent them in the first place through the development, enforcement, and review of company policies that promote legal compliance.

See Sidebar 21.16 for practical suggestions for employers to prevent employee lawsuits.

Taking any disciplinary action without documentation fails to build the record for increased sanctions in the future.

>> *sidebar* 21.16

What Can Employers Do to Avoid Employment Litigation?

There are a number of steps that employers can take to avoid employment litigation, including:

- Implementing workplace policies and procedures, and training employees to understand the rules and apply them consistently. The policies should cover how to prevent sexual harassment and other forms of discrimination and how to report the same.
- Conducting regular candid performance evaluations, with clear feedback to employees.
- Investigating all complaints thoroughly, never taking any adverse action against persons making honest complaint.

- Documenting all employee incidents, including disciplinary issues and other problems, in each employee's personnel file.
- Being fair and objective when dealing with employees. Being upfront and honest about action taken in the workplace, including termination, helps employees understand the rationale for the action.

Keep these practical suggestions in mind as you study discrimination in Chapter 20, and realize how many workers could potentially assert one or more discrimination claims against their employer.

>> Key Terms

Employment Eligibility
    Verification 709
Employment-at-will doctrine 703
Exclusive Remedy Rule 708
Fair Labor Standards Act
    (FLSA) 686

Family and Medical Leave Act
    (FMLA) 694
Occupational Safety and
    Health Administration
    (OSHA) 700
Paper fortress 711

Uniformed Services
    Employment and
    Reemployment Rights Act
    (USERRA) 697
WARN Act 693
Workers' Compensation 706

>> Review Questions and Problems

Employment Laws

1. *Minimum Wages and Maximum Hours*
   (a) What federal law establishes the minimum wage and the hours in a work week?
   (b) What is the minimum wage and what is considered the maximum work week?
   (c) What is required regarding overtime compensation or time off?

2. *The WARN Act*
   To show your understanding of the WARN notice, answer these questions:
   (a) Who are the covered employers?
   (b) What format is required for a WARN notice?
   (c) When must the WARN notice be given?
   (d) To whom must the WARN notice be delivered?

3. *The Family and Medical Leave Act*
   In the sixth month of her pregnancy, Suzanne was advised by her doctors to slow down the hectic pace of her consulting career. Upon this advice, Suzanne requested and was granted by

her employer 12 weeks of medical leave. During the tenth week of this leave, Suzanne had a healthy baby. How much family leave is Suzanne entitled to take under the FMLA to care for her newborn?

4. *Uniformed Services Employment and Reemployment Rights Act*

   Robert left his position as commercial airline pilot to undertake his duties in the Marine Reserves for a tour of duty in Iraq. When he returns home a year later, his employer apologetically tells him that they filled his position during his absence and they "will call" when something comes available. They also express concern about his ability to fly commercial jets because he has not flown in the last year. What legal recourse does Robert have, if any?

5. *Occupational Safety and Health Administration*

   Larry, a machine operator, is concerned that the cardboard baler he is working on should have a safety shield to protect his arms from the moving parts. He is also worried that if he reports his concerns, he will be put on the night shift. What should he do? Does he have any protection if he reports the issue?

6. *Pension Plans and Health Care*

   Why has the aging of the "baby boom" generation put so much pressure on the financial stability of historically successful companies?

7. *Limitations on Employment at Will*

   Terry was hired as an assistant manager by the Assurance Manufacturing Company. There was no specific time period related to Terry's employment. During Terry's first day at work, the personnel director of Assurance gave Terry a copy of the employee's handbook. In this handbook, Assurance stated that no employee would be terminated without a justifiable explanation. Five months after beginning work at Assurance, Terry was notified that after an additional two weeks there would be no further job for Terry at Assurance. When Terry asked why this termination was occurring, the personnel director told Terry, "Under state law no reason for termination has to be given. In essence, you are an employee only for as long as Assurance desires." What is the best argument Terry can make that the employment-at-will doctrine is not applicable in this situation? Explain.

8. *Workers' Privacy*

   John Hancock Life Insurance Company instructed its employees to create passwords to protect their e-mail accounts. Employees also were told to create personal folders for messages they send and receive. After a company investigation, Nancy and Joanne were terminated as John Hancock employees for using their e-mail accounts to send sexually explicit messages. These employees sued John Hancock for wrongful discharge on the basis that the company's investigation had violated their rights of privacy. Was John Hancock entitled to examine these employees' e-mail accounts?

9. *Workers' Compensation Acts*

   If Sam fails to wear a hard hat, as required by Super Construction, Inc., his employer, and is injured by a falling hammer, can he recover workers' compensation from Super Construction, Inc.? Your answer should explain the basis for recovering workers' compensation.

10. *Employment Eligibility Verification*

    Sophia's Glam Designs needs to hire 100 new workers to manufacture a new line of back-to-school outfits. The company received hundreds of applications for the positions. Simone, Sophia's Glam Designs Human Resources Manager, requires all new hires to complete an I-9 and to produce a valid passport or green card to prove employment eligibility. When one worker attempts to use a combination of a Georgia driver's license and a social security card, Simone refuses to accept the documents. Because of the large amount of workers hired, she wants to use documents she feels comfortable verifying and streamline the documentation process. Is this permissible?

11. *Employee Lawsuits*
   (a) What is meant by the phrase "paper fortress"?
   (b) How does maintaining a paper fortress aid the employer when the employee claims unfair treatment?

business >> *discussions*

1. You just had one of those days—exciting and overwhelming. As your company's director of human relations, you have dealt with an employee asking how much leave he can take when his wife has their first baby next month. A phone call from the company's CFO involved discussions of potential layoffs in order to "make the budget." A group of employees came to meet with you, and they indicated they were talking with union organizers as a way to combat the company's policy of monitoring phone calls and e-mail messages. Another group of employees expressed their feelings that they were not being paid for all the time they worked.

Before heading home, you take a few minutes to reflect and ask yourself the following questions:

How is the workday calculated?
What legal requirements have to be met before layoffs can occur?
What is the company's responsibility to educate employees about their rights under the Family and Medical Leave Act?
Can your company properly monitor its employees' phone calls and e-mail messages?

20

Discrimination in Employment

☐ Learning Objectives

In this chapter you will learn:

20-1. To discuss the general provisions of Title VII, enforcement procedures, and the differences between disparate treatment and disparate impact.

20-2. To understand the specific kinds of discrimination prohibited by Title VII.

20-3. To discuss employment practices that may be challenged.

20-4. To apply other federal statutes protecting against employment discrimination.

20-5. To realize that state laws may offer additional protection against workplace discrimination.

Laws prohibiting discrimination exist at both the federal and state levels. The opening sections of the chapter focus on antidiscrimination laws at the federal level. Title VII of the Civil Rights Act of 1964 (including its amendments) is the principal such law. It prohibits certain discrimination based on race, sex, color, religion, and national origin. Next, employment practices that may be challenged as discriminatory are considered. Other antidiscrimination laws covered are the Civil Rights Act of 1866 (referred to as Section 1981), the Age Discrimination in Employment Act, Americans with Disabilities Act, the Genetic Information Nondiscrimination Act and the Uniformed Services Employment and Reemployment Act. The chapter concludes with a discussion of trends in employment discrimination litigation and a section on employment discrimination, corporate governance, and the broad sense of property.

>> The Civil Rights Act of 1964

"That all men are created equal" was one of the "self-evident" truths recognized by the Founding Fathers in the Declaration of Independence. However, equality among all our citizens clearly has been an ideal rather than a fact. The Constitution itself recognizes slavery by saying that slaves should count as "three fifths of all other Persons" for determining population in House of Representatives elections. And of course, that all *men* are created equal says nothing about women, who did not even get a constitutionally guaranteed right to vote until 1920.

Nowhere have effects of inequality and discrimination been felt more acutely than in the area of job opportunity. Historically, common law permitted employers to hire and fire virtually at will, unless restrained by contract or statute. Under this system, white males came to dominate the job market in their ability to gain employment and their salaries and wages.

Although the Civil Rights Act of 1866 contains a provision that plaintiffs now widely use in employment discrimination cases, such use is relatively recent. Passage of labor law in the 1920s and 1930s marks the first significant federal limitation on the relatively unrestricted right of employers to hire and fire. Then, in connection with the war effort, President Franklin D. Roosevelt issued executive orders in 1941 and 1943 requiring a clause prohibiting racial discrimination in all federal contracts with private contractors. Subsequent executive orders in the 1950s established committees to investigate complaints of racial discrimination against such contractors. Affirmative action requirements on federal contracts followed from executive orders of the 1960s.

The most important statute eliminating discriminatory employment practices, however, is the federal Civil Rights Act of 1964, as amended by the Equal Employment Opportunity Act of 1972, the Pregnancy Discrimination Act of 1978, and the Civil Rights Act of 1991.

> Historically, common law permitted employers to hire and fire at will. At-will employment still applies today unless modified by legislation.

1. GENERAL PROVISIONS

The provisions of Title VII of the Civil Rights Act of 1964 apply to employers with 15 or more employees, labor unions, and certain other employers. The major purpose of these laws is to eliminate job discrimination based on race, color, religion, sex, or national origin. Discrimination for any of these reasons is a violation of the law, except that employers, employment agencies, and labor unions can discriminate on the basis of religion, sex, or national origin where these are **bona fide occupational qualifications (BFOQs)** reasonably necessary to normal business operations. Title VII also permits discrimination if it results unintentionally from a seniority or merit system.

The types of employer action in which discrimination is prohibited include:

- Discharge.
- Refusal to hire.
- Compensation.
- Terms, conditions, or privileges of employment.

Employment *agencies* are prohibited from either *failing to refer* or from *actually referring* an individual for employment on the basis of race, color,

> **Don't** forget that a defense to intentional discrimination is that such discrimination is a BFOQ.

> According to the Seventh Circuit Court of Appeals, denial of overtime can constitute an adverse employment action sufficient to trigger Title VII.

religion, sex, or national origin. This prohibition differs from the law binding *employers,* where it is unlawful only to fail or refuse to hire on discriminatory grounds—the affirmative act of hiring for a discriminatory reason is apparently not illegal. For example, assume that a contractor with a government contract seeks a qualified African American engineer and requests an employment agency to refer one. The agency complies with the request. Unless a white applicant was discriminated against, the employer likely did not break the law; but the employment agency, by referring on the basis of color, unquestionably *did* violate Title VII.

Employers, unions, and employment agencies are prohibited from discriminating against an employee, applicant, or union member because he or she has made a charge, testified, or participated in an investigation or hearing under the act or otherwise opposed any unlawful practice.

Note that regarding general hiring, referrals, advertising, and admissions to training or apprenticeship programs, Title VII allows discrimination only on the basis of religion, sex, or national origin and only where these considerations are bona fide occupational qualifications. For example, it is legal for a Baptist church to refuse to engage a Lutheran minister. EEOC guidelines on sex discrimination consider sex to be a bona fide occupational qualification, for example, where it is necessary for authenticity or genuineness in hiring an actor or actress. The omission of *race* and *color* from this exception must mean that Congress does not feel these two factors are ever bona fide occupational qualifications.

> Discriminating in employment on the basis of race or color can almost never be a BFOQ.

Additional exemptions exist with respect to laws creating preferential treatment for veterans and hiring based on professionally developed ability tests that are not designed or intended to be used to discriminate. Such tests must bear a relationship to the job for which they are administered, however.

2. ENFORCEMENT PROCEDURES

The Civil Rights Act of 1964 created the Equal Employment Opportunity Commission (EEOC). This agency has the primary responsibility of enforcing the provisions of the act. The EEOC is composed of five members, not more than three of whom may be members of the same political party. They are appointed by the president, with the advice and consent of the Senate, and serve a five-year term. In the course of its investigations, the EEOC has broad authority to hold hearings, obtain evidence, and subpoena and examine witnesses under oath.

Under the Equal Employment Opportunity Act of 1972, the EEOC can file a civil suit in federal district court and represent a person charging a violation of the act. However, it must first exhaust efforts to settle the claim. Remedies that may be obtained in such an action include reinstatement with back pay for the victim of an illegal discrimination and injunctions against future violations of the act by the defendant. See Figure 20.1 for a breakdown of charges received by the EEOC.

> "[M]ajor American businesses have made clear that the skills needed in today's increasingly global marketplace can only be developed through exposure to widely diverse people, cultures, ideas, and viewpoints."
>
> **–Justice Sandra Day O'Connor,** *Grutter v. Bollinger,* **539 U.S. 306, 330 (2003)**

The 1991 Amendments In 1991 Congress amended the Civil Rights Act to allow the recovery of compensatory and punitive damages of up to $300,000 per person. These damages are in addition to other remedies such as job reinstatement (depending on the size of the employer) and back pay or front pay. Compensatory damages include damages for the pain and suffering of discrimination. Punitive damages are appropriate whenever discrimination

> Under Title VII, a plaintiff can recover up to $300,000 in punitive and compensatory damages for *intentional* discrimination. Back pay damages can further add to that amount.

Figure 20.1 *What Kinds of Claims Are Being Filed with the EEOC?*

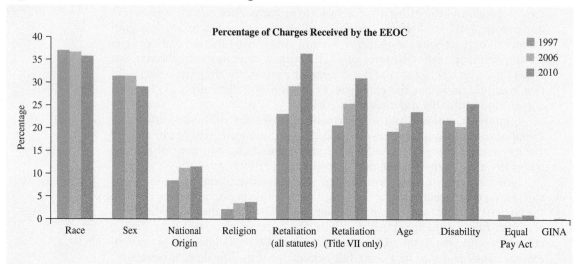

In 1997, the EEOC received 80,680 total charges, in 2006, it received 75,768 charges, and in 2010, it received 99,922 charges.

Source: EEOC Charge Statistics FY1997–2010, www.eeoc.gov/eeoc/statistics/enforcement/charges.cfm.

occurs with "malice or with reckless or callous indifference to the federally protected rights of others." The 1991 amendments allow compensatory and punitive damages *only* when employers are guilty of *intentional* discrimination.

In enacting Title VII of the Civil Rights Act of 1964, Congress made it clear that it did not intend to preempt states' fair employment laws. Where state agencies begin discrimination proceedings, the EEOC must wait 60 days before it starts action. Furthermore, if a state law provides relief to a discrimination charge, the EEOC must notify the appropriate state officials and wait 60 days before continuing action.

An employee must file charges of illegal discrimination with the EEOC within 180 days after notice of the unlawful practice. If the employee first filed in a timely fashion with a state fair employment practices commission, the law extends the time for filing with the EEOC to 300 days.

Do remember that the three types of cases permitted under Title VII are for (1) disparate treatment, (2) disparate impact, and (3) retaliation.

Winning a Title VII Civil Action To win a Title VII civil action, a plaintiff must initially show that steps taken by the employer likely had an illegally discriminatory basis, such as race. Generally, the plaintiff must prove either disparate (unequal) treatment or disparate impact. In proving **disparate treatment,** the plaintiff must convince the court that the employer *intentionally* discriminated against the plaintiff. If discrimination is a substantial or motivating factor, an employer's practice is illegal even though other factors (such as customer preference) also contributed. Even if the plaintiff proves disparate treatment, the defendant can win by showing that all or substantially all members of the plaintiff's class *cannot* perform the duties of the job. This defense is the BFOQ defense mentioned in Section 1 of this chapter.

In a **disparate impact** case the plaintiff must prove that the employer's practices or policies had a discriminatory effect on a group protected by Title VII. The employer can defeat the plaintiff's claim by proving the

business necessity defense. This defense requires that the employer prove that the practices or policies used are job related and based on business necessity. However, the plaintiff can still establish a violation by showing that other policies would serve the legitimate interests of business necessity without having undesirable discriminatory effects.

A third type of discrimination case concerns **retaliation.** It is illegal for employers to retaliate against employees for making discrimination charges, giving testimony in a discrimination case, or in any way participating in a discrimination investigation. Such retaliation discrimination involves employers taking "adverse employment actions" against employees, such as firing employees or transferring them to less desirable jobs.

What are ways a company can avoid retaliation claims? As illustrated in Figure 20.1, retaliation claims are on the rise. There are a number of steps an employer can take to address allegations of discrimination without triggering a retaliation claim:

- Treat complaints seriously as soon as they are made.

- Investigate the complaint.

- Be sure managers and other employees know and follow the company's policies on discrimination, including harassment.

- Follow-up with the complainant, including explaining how the company will address the problem.

- Create an atmosphere in which the complainant and others with information feel comfortable coming forward with information or other complaints.

- Never take adverse action against a complainant or witnesses, based on information obtained in the investigation.

These straightforward steps go a long way to create an atmosphere of fairness and head off additional claims based on retaliation.

Before the 1991 Civil Rights Act amendments, employees or the EEOC sometimes claimed that proving racial or gender statistical imbalances in a workforce established illegal discrimination. They claimed that such imbalances showed illegal discrimination, much like disparate impact discrimination, even in the absence of proof of an employer's discriminatory intent. However, the 1991 amendments state that the showing of a statistically imbalanced workforce is not enough *in itself* to establish a violation of Title VII.

> If an employee who complains about discrimination is transferred to the night shift, even without a loss of pay, he may have a claim for retaliation under Title VII. *Burlington Northern and Santa Fe Railroad Co. v. White,* 548 U.S. 53 (2007).

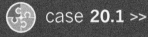 case **20.1** >>

THOMPSON v. NORTH AMERICAN STAINLESS, LP
562 U.S. __ (2011)

After petitioner Thompson's fiancée, Miriam Regalado, filed a sex discrimination charge with the Equal Employment Opportunity Commission (EEOC) against their employer, respondent North American Stainless (NAS), NAS fired Thompson. He filed his *own charge and a subsequent suit under Title VII of the Civil Rights Act, claiming that NAS fired him to retaliate against Regalado for filing her charge. The District Court granted NAS summary judgment on the ground that third-party retaliation claims were not*

[continued]

permitted by Title VII, which prohibits discrimination against an employee "because he has made a [Title VII] charge." The en banc Sixth Circuit affirmed, reasoning that Thompson was not entitled to sue NAS for retaliation because he had not engaged in any activity protected by the statute. By a vote of 8-0, the Supreme Court overturned the Court of Appeals. (Justice Kagan took no part in the consideration of the case.)

SCALIA, J.: Until 2003, both petitioner Eric Thompson and his fiancée, Miriam Regalado, were employees of respondent North American Stainless (NAS). In February 2003, the Equal Employment Opportunity Commission (EEOC) notified NAS that Regalado had filed a charge alleging sex discrimination. Three weeks later, NAS fired Thompson.

Thompson then filed a charge with the EEOC. After conciliation efforts proved unsuccessful, he sued NAS in the United States District Court for the Eastern District of Kentucky under Title VII of the Civil Rights Act of 1964, 78 Stat. 253, 42 U. S. C. §2000e *et seq.*, claiming that NAS had fired him in order to retaliate against Regalado for filing her charge with the EEOC. The District Court granted summary judgment to NAS, concluding that Title VII "does not permit third party retaliation claims." 435 F. Supp. 2d 633, 639 (ED Ky. 2006). After a panel of the Sixth Circuit reversed the District Court, the Sixth Circuit granted rehearing en banc and affirmed by a 10-to-6 vote. 567 F. 3d 804 (2009). The court reasoned that because Thompson did not "engag[e] in any statutorily protected activity, either on his own behalf or on behalf of Miriam Regalado," he "is not included in the class of persons for whom Congress created a retaliation cause of action." . . .

Title VII provides that "[i]t shall be an unlawful employment practice for an employer to discriminate against any of his employees . . . because he has made a charge" under Title VII. 42 U. S. C. §2000e–3(a). The statute permits "a person claiming to be aggrieved" to file a charge with the EEOC alleging that the employer committed an unlawful employment practice, and, if the EEOC declines to sue the employer, it permits a civil action to "be brought . . . by the person claiming to be aggrieved . . . by the alleged unlawful employment practice." §2000e–5(b), (f)(1). It is undisputed that Regalado's filing of a charge with the EEOC was protected conduct under Title VII. In the procedural posture of this case, we are also required to assume that NAS fired Thompson in order to retaliate against Regalado for filing a charge of discrimination. This case therefore presents two questions: First, did NAS's firing of Thompson constitute unlawful retaliation? And second, if it did, does Title VII grant Thompson a cause of action?

With regard to the first question, we have little difficulty concluding that if the facts alleged by Thompson are true, then NAS's firing of Thompson violated Title VII. In *Burlington N. & S. F. R. Co. v. White,* 548 U. S. 53 (2006), we held that Title VII's antiretaliation provision must be construed to cover a broad range of employer conduct. We reached that conclusion by contrasting the text of Title VII's antiretaliation provision with its substantive antidiscrimination provision. . . . Title VII's antiretaliation provision prohibits any employer action that "well might have dissuaded a reasonable worker from making or supporting a charge of discrimination." *Id.,* at 68 (internal quotation marks omitted). We think it obvious that a reasonable worker might be dissuaded from engaging in protected activity if she knew that her fiancé would be fired. Indeed, NAS does not dispute that Thompson's firing meets the standard set forth in *Burlington.* Tr. of Oral Arg. 30. NAS raises the concern, however, that prohibiting reprisals against third parties will lead to difficult line-drawing problems concerning the types of relationships entitled to protection. Perhaps retaliating against an employee by firing his fiancée would dissuade the employee from engaging in protected activity, but what about firing an employee's girlfriend, close friend, or trusted co-worker? . . .

Although we acknowledge the force of this point, we do not think it justifies a categorical rule that third-party reprisals do not violate Title VII. As explained above, we adopted a broad standard in *Burlington* because Title VII's antiretaliation provision is worded broadly. We think there is no textual basis for making an exception to it for third-party reprisals, and a preference for clear rules cannot justify departing from statutory text. We must also decline to identify a fixed class of relationships for which third-party reprisals are unlawful. We expect that firing a close family member will almost always meet the *Burlington* standard, and inflicting a milder reprisal on a mere acquaintance will almost never do so, but beyond that we are reluctant to generalize. . . .

The more difficult question in this case is whether Thompson may sue NAS for its alleged violation of Title VII. The statute provides that "a civil action may be brought . . . by the person claiming to be aggrieved." ". . . to be aggrieved" to bring "a civil action." It is arguable that the aggrievement referred to is nothing more than the minimal Article III standing, which consists of injury in fact caused by the defendant and remediable by the court. See *Lujan* v. *Defenders of Wildlife,* 504 U. S. 555, 560–561 (1992). But Thompson's claim undoubtedly meets those requirements, so if that is indeed all that aggrievement consists of, he may sue. . . .

We hold that the term "aggrieved" in Title VII incorporates this test, enabling suit by any plaintiff with

[continued]

an interest "arguably [sought] to be protected by the statutes," *National Credit Union Admin. v. First Nat. Bank & Trust Co.,* 522 U. S. 479, 495 (1998) (internal quotation marks omitted), while excluding plaintiffs who might technically be injured in an Article III sense but whose interests are unrelated to the statutory prohibitions in Title VII. Applying that test here, we conclude that Thompson falls within the zone of interests protected by Title VII. Thompson was an employee of NAS, and the purpose of Title VII is to protect employees from their employers' unlawful actions. Moreover,

accepting the facts as alleged, Thompson is not an accidental victim of the retaliation—collateral damage, so to speak, of the employer's unlawful act. To the contrary, injuring him was the employer's intended means of harming Regalado. Hurting him was the unlawful act by which the employer punished her. In those circumstances, we think Thompson well within the zone of interests sought to be protected by Title VII. He is a person aggrieved with standing to sue.

Reversed and remanded.

>> CASE QUESTIONS

1. What are the key facts of this case?
2. What were the two issues before the Supreme Court?
3. What did the Court decide? What is the rationale for the decisions?

3. DISCRIMINATION ON THE BASIS OF RACE OR COLOR

LO 20-2

The integration of African Americans into the mainstream of American society is the primary objective of the Civil Rights Act of 1964. Title VII, which deals with employment practices, is the key legal regulation for achieving this goal. Without equal employment opportunities, African Americans can hardly enjoy other guaranteed rights, such as access to public accommodations.

Title VII prohibits discriminatory employment practices based on race or color that involve *recruiting, hiring,* and *promotion* of employees. Of course, intentional discrimination in these matters is illegal, but, as previously stated, policies with disparate impact are also forbidden. Such discrimination arises from an employer's policies or practices that apply equally to everyone but that discriminate in greater proportion against minorities and have no relation to job qualification.

Examples of disparate impact on race include:

- Using personnel tests that have no substantial relation to job qualification, which have the effect of screening out minorities.
- Denying employment to unwed mothers, when minorities have a higher rate of illegitimate births than whites.
- Refusing to hire people because of a poor credit rating, when minorities are disproportionately affected.
- Giving hiring priority to relatives of present employees, when minorities are underrepresented in the workforce.

Often at issue in disparate impact cases is whether a discriminatory policy or practice relates to job qualification. Courts require proof, not mere assertion, of job relatedness before upholding an employer's discriminatory personnel test or other practice.

Lockheed Martin settled a race discrimination and retaliation lawsuit for $2.5 million in 2008. The case alleged a racially hostile work environment at several job sites, including threats of lynching and the use of the "N-word."

The law also prohibits discrimination in *employment conditions* and *benefits*. EEOC decisions have found such practices as the following to be violations:

- Permitting racial insults in the work situation.
- Maintaining all-white or all-black crews for no demonstrable reasons.
- Providing better housing for whites than blacks.
- Granting higher average Christmas bonuses to whites than blacks for reasons that were not persuasive to the commission.

>> *sidebar* 20.1

Hithon v. Tyson Foods, Inc.: The Use of the Word "Boy"

John Hithon and Anthony Ash, African American men, worked at a Tyson Foods plant in Alabama. When two supervisor positions opened up, they were passed over for promotion and two white men from other plants were hired. Believing that the failure to be promoted resulted from racial prejudice, Hithon and Ash filed an employment discrimination claim against their employer.

As part of their case, the plaintiffs produced evidence that their white boss used the term "boy" when referring to them. Is the use of the term *boy* racially discriminatory?

In 2002, an Alabama jury awarded Hithon and Ash $250,000 each in compensatory damages and $1.5 million in punitive damages. After a magistrate overruled the jury's verdict, Hilton and Ash appealed. On appeal, the 11th Circuit determined that an adult African American man being called "boy" alone was

not discriminatory unless it was preceded by "black" or "white."

The U.S. Supreme Court unanimously reversed the 11th Circuit's decision, stating:

> Although it is true that the disputed word will not always be evidence of racial animus, it does not follow that the term, standing alone, is always benign . . . The speaker's meaning may depend on various factors including context, inflection, tone of voice, local custom and historical usage.

Thereafter, another Alabama jury found in favor of Hithon, awarding him $35,000 in back pay, $300,000 in compensatory damages for his mental anguish and $1 million in punitives. The District Court vacated the punitive damage award. Both sides appealed. On appeal, the 11th Circuit voted 2-1 entering a judgment in favor of Tyson Foods. The majority said that the evidence did not support Hithon's argument.

Researchers revealed racial bias in hiring based on an applicant's name. The study tracked response rates to resumes sent to 1,300 help-wanted ads. The authors found that white-sounding names (such as Anne, Emily, Allison, Neil, Todd, and Matthew) are 50 percent more likely to get called for an initial interview than applicants with African American-sounding names (such as Tamika, Latoya, Latonya, Tyrone, Tremayne, and Rasheed). Additionally, race affects the degree to which applicants benefit from having more experience and credentials. The study showed that white applicants with higher-quality resumes received 30 percent more callbacks than whites with lower-quality resumes. By contract, African American applicants experienced only 9 percent more callbacks for the same improvement in credentials.

It is important to appreciate that Title VII prohibits employment discrimination against members of all races. In one recent case, a federal court jury awarded a white senior air traffic official $500,000 in damages against the Federal Aviation Administration. The official charged the FAA had demoted

The State of New York has outlawed the display of a noose as a threat, punishable by up to four years in prison.

him and replaced him with an African American following complaints that blacks were underrepresented in senior management levels. Note that this case did not involve affirmative action.

case 20.2 >>

RICCI v. DESTEFANO
557 U.S.__ (2009)

New Haven, Conn. (City), uses objective examinations to identify those firefighters best qualified for promotion. When the results of such an exam to fill vacant lieutenant and captain positions showed that white candidates had outperformed minority candidates, a rancorous public debate ensued. Confronted with arguments both for and against certifying the test results—and threats of a lawsuit either way—the City threw out the results based on the statistical racial disparity. Petitioners, white and Hispanic firefighters who passed the exams but were denied a chance at promotions by the City's refusal to certify the test results, sued the City and respondent officials, alleging that discarding the test results discriminated against them based on their race in violation of, inter alia, Title VII of the Civil Rights Act of 1964. The defendants responded that had they certified the test results, they could have faced Title VII liability for adopting a practice having a disparate impact on minority firefighters. The District Court granted summary judgment for the defendants, and the Second Circuit affirmed. Justice Sotomayor was on the Second Circuit at the time of that decision. Justice Kennedy wrote the majority opinion in which Chief Justice Roberts, and Justices Scalia, Thomas and Alito joined.

Justice Ginsburg filed a dissenting opinion in which Justices Stevens, Souter and Breyer joined. In her dissent, Justice Ginsburg notes that firefighting is "a profession in which the legacy of racial discrimination casts an especially long shadow" and that the facts of this case should be assessed "against this backdrop of entrenched inequality."

KENNEDY, J.: In the fire department of New Haven, Connecticut—as in emergency-service agencies throughout the Nation—firefighters prize their promotion to and within the officer ranks. An agency's officers command respect within the department and in the whole community; and, of course, added responsibilities command increased salary and benefits. Aware of the

intense competition for promotions, New Haven, like many cities, relies on objective examinations to identify the best-qualified candidates. In 2003, 118 New Haven firefighters took examinations to qualify for promotion to the rank of lieutenant or captain. Promotion examinations in New Haven (or City) were infrequent, so the stakes were high. The results would determine which firefighters would be considered for promotions during the next two years, and the order in which they would be considered. Many firefighters studied for months, at considerable personal and financial cost.

When the examination results showed that white candidates had outperformed minority candidates, the mayor and other local politicians opened a public debate that turned rancorous. Some firefighters argued the tests should be discarded because the results showed the tests to be discriminatory. They threatened a discrimination lawsuit if the City made promotions based on the tests. Other firefighters said the exams were neutral and fair. And they, in turn, threatened a discrimination lawsuit if the City, relying on the statistical racial disparity, ignored the test results and denied promotions to the candidates who had performed well. In the end the City took the side of those who protested the test results. It threw out the examinations.

Certain white and Hispanic firefighters who likely would have been promoted based on their good test performance sued the City and some of its officials. Theirs is the suit now before us. The suit alleges that, by discarding the test results, the City and the named officials discriminated against the plaintiffs based on their race, in violation of both Title VII of the Civil Rights Act of 1964, 78 Stat. 253, as amended, 42 U. S. C. §2000e *et seq.*, and the Equal Protection Clause of the Fourteenth Amendment. The City and the officials defended their actions, arguing that if they had certified the results, they could have faced liability under Title VII for adopting a practice that had a disparate

[continued]

impact on the minority firefighters. The District Court granted summary judgment for the defendants, and the Court of Appeals affirmed.

We conclude that race-based action like the City's in this case is impermissible under Title VII unless the employer can demonstrate a strong basis in evidence that, had it not taken the action, it would have been liable under the disparate-impact statute. The respondents, we further determine, cannot meet that threshold standard. As a result, the City's action in discarding the tests was a violation of Title VII. In light of our ruling under the statutes, we need not reach the question whether respondents' actions may have violated the Equal Protection Clause. . . .

Title VII of the Civil Rights Act of 1964, 42 U. S. C.§2000e *et seq.,* as amended, prohibits employment discrimination on the basis of race, color, religion, sex, or national origin. Title VII prohibits both intentional discrimination (known as "disparate treatment") as well as, in some cases, practices that are not intended to discriminate but in fact have a disproportionately adverse effect on minorities (known as "disparate impact"). . . . The Civil Rights Act of 1964 did not include an express prohibition on policies or practices that produce a disparate impact. But in *Griggs* v. *Duke Power Co.,* 401 U. S. 424 (1971), the Court interpreted the Act to prohibit, in some cases, employers' facially neutral practices that, in fact, are "discriminatory in operation." *Id.,* at 431. The *Griggs* Court stated that the "touchstone" for disparate impact liability is the lack of "business necessity": "If an employment practice which operates to exclude [minorities] cannot be shown to be related to job performance, the practice is prohibited." . . . Twenty years after *Griggs,* the Civil Rights Act of 1991, 105 Stat. 1071, was enacted. The Act included a provision codifying the prohibition on disparate-impact discrimination. That provision is now in force along with the disparate-treatment section already noted. Under the disparate-impact statute, a plaintiff establishes a prima facie violation by showing that an employer uses "a particular employment practice that causes a disparate impact on the basis of race, color, religion, sex, or national origin." 42 U. S. C. §2000e–2(k)(1)(A)(i). An employer may defend against liability by demonstrating that the practice is "job related for the position in question and consistent with business necessity." *Ibid.* Even if the employer meets that burden, however, a plaintiff may still succeed by showing that the employer refuses to adopt an available alternative employment practice that has less disparate impact and serves the employer's legitimate needs. . . . Petitioners allege that when the CSB refused to certify the captain and lieutenant exam results based on the race of the successful

candidates, it discriminated against them in violation of Title VII's disparate-treatment provision. The City counters that its decision was permissible because the tests "appear[ed] to violate Title VII's disparate impact provisions." . . . The same interests are at work in the interplay between the disparate-treatment and disparate-impact provisions of Title VII. Congress has imposed liability on employers for unintentional discrimination in order to rid the workplace of "practices that are fair in form, but discriminatory in operation." *Griggs, supra,* at 431. But it has also prohibited employers from taking adverse employment actions "because of" race. §2000e–2(a)(1). Applying the strong-basis-in-evidence standard to Title VII gives effect to both the disparate-treatment and disparate-impact provisions, allowing violations of one in the name of compliance with the other only in certain, narrow circumstances. The standard leaves ample room for employers' voluntary compliance efforts, which are essential to the statutory scheme and to Congress's efforts to eradicate workplace discrimination. See *Firefighters, supra,* at 515. And the standard appropriately constrains employers' discretion in making race-based decisions: It limits that discretion to cases in which there is a strong basis in evidence of disparate-impact liability, but it is not so restrictive that it allows employers to act only when there is a provable, actual violation.

Resolving the statutory conflict in this way allows the disparate-impact prohibition to work in a manner that is consistent with other provisions of Title VII, including the prohibition on adjusting employment-related test scores on the basis of race. . . . The racial adverse impact here was significant, and petitioners do not dispute that the City was faced with a prima facie case of disparate-impact liability. On the captain exam, the pass rate for white candidates was 64 percent but was 37.5 percent for both black and Hispanic candidates. On the lieutenant exam, the pass rate for white candidates was 58.1 percent; for black candidates, 31.6 percent; and for Hispanic candidates, 20 percent. The pass rates of minorities, which were approximately one half the pass rates for white candidates, fall well below the 80-percent standard set by the EEOC to implement the disparate-impact provision of Title VII. . . .

There is no genuine dispute that the examinations were job-related and consistent with business necessity. . . . On the record before us, there is no genuine dispute that the City lacked a strong basis in evidence to believe it would face disparate-impact liability if it certified the examination results. In other words, there is no evidence—let alone the required strong basis in evidence—that the tests were flawed because they were not job-related or because other, equally valid

[continued]

and less discriminatory tests were available to the City. Fear of litigation alone cannot justify an employer's reliance on race to the detriment of individuals who passed the examinations and qualified for promotions. The City's discarding the test results was impermissible under Title VII, and summary judgment is appropriate for petitioners on their disparate-treatment claim. . . . Many of the candidates had studied for months, at considerable personal and financial expense, and thus the injury caused by the City's reliance on raw racial statistics at the end of the process was all the more severe. Confronted with arguments both for and against certifying the test results—and threats of a lawsuit either way—the City was required to make a difficult inquiry. But its hearings produced no strong evidence of a disparate-impact violation, and the City was not entitled to disregard the tests based solely on the racial disparity in the results.

Reversed.

>> CASE QUESTIONS

1. Explain how the case involved both issues of disparate treatment and disparate impact?
2. If you were representing the City of New Haven, would you have certified the test results? Why or why not?
3. What is the basis for the Supreme Court's holding?

>> *sidebar* 20.2

Abercrombie & Fitch's $40 Million Diversity Lesson

In 2005, Abercrombie & Fitch (A&F) settled a discrimination lawsuit with over 10,000 class members. The suit alleged hiring discrimination against Latino, African American, and Asian American applicants. The checks ranged from several hundred to several thousand dollars each, totaling $40 million. The settlement agreement also requires A&F to:

- Set "benchmarks" (*not* quotas) for hiring and promotion of women, Latinos, African Americans, and Asian Americans.
- Stop targeting fraternities, sororities, or specific colleges for recruitment.
- Hire 25 recruiters who will focus on seeking women and minority employees.
- Implement a new internal complaint procedure.
- Create marketing materials reflecting diversity.

What is A&F saying about diversity now? According to Mike Jeffries, A&F's Chairman and CEO, "Diversity and inclusion are key to our organization's success."

In 2011, Abercrombie was sued again for discrimination. This time, a Muslim woman claims that she was fired for refusing to remove her hijab at work.

4. DISCRIMINATION ON THE BASIS OF NATIONAL ORIGIN

Title VII's prohibition against national origin discrimination protects various ethnic groups in the workplace. In a recent case, the court ruled that Title VII had been violated when a bakery employee of Iranian descent was called "Ayatollah" in the workplace by the assistant manager and other employees. After he complained, he was fired. In 2005, the EEOC reported that employees of Middle Eastern descent had filed almost a thousand

Approximately 1.2 million Americans are of Middle Eastern or Arab descent, according to the U.S. Census.

discrimination complaints against employers since the terrorist bombings of in September 11, 2001.

Don't forget that a policy requiring employees to speak English will violate Title VII as disparate impact unless it is justified by *business necessity*.

Discrimination concerning the speaking of a native language frequently causes national-origin lawsuits under Title VII. For instance, courts have ruled illegal an employer's rule against speaking Spanish during work hours when the employer could not show a business need to understand all conversations between Hispanic employees. On the other hand, some courts have held that if jobs require contact with the public, a requirement that employees speak some English may be a business necessity.

Direct foreign investment in the United States has doubled and redoubled in recent years. This increasing investment has presented some unusual issues of employment discrimination law. For instance, many commercial treaties with foreign countries give foreign companies operating in the United States the right to hire executive-level employees "of their choice." Does this mean that foreign companies in the United States can discriminate as to their managerial employees on a basis forbidden under Title VII? The Supreme Court has partially resolved this issue by ruling that the civil rights law applied to a Japanese company that did business through a subsidiary incorporated in this country.

>> *sidebar* 20.3

National Origin Discrimination: Problematic Ethnic Slurs

  The EEOC brought a lawsuit on behalf of Mexican immigrant workers at Sam's Club who claimed they were harassed about their national origin *by a co-worker who is Mexican American.* Among the allegations:

- At least nine female workers of Mexican descent and one woman married to a Mexican were subjected to ethnic slurs and derogatory remarks.
- The insults were made on a "near daily" basis, including being called "f----n' wetbacks" and references to Mexicans only being good to clean the harasser's home.

- The harasser also threatened to report three of the victims to immigration authorities, despite their legal status.
- The victims complained about the hostile work environment but this "only intensified the harassment and led to intimidation."

  Wal-Mart Stores agreed to pay $440,000 to settle this case.

Source: EEOC Press Release, Wal-Mart to Pay $440,000 to Settle EEOC Suit for Harassment of Latinos, April 14, 2011, www.eeoc.gov/eeoc/newsroom/release/4-14-11.cfm

---

5. DISCRIMINATION ON THE BASIS OF RELIGION

Note that religious corporations, associations, or societies can discriminate in all their employment practices on the basis of religion, but not on the basis of race, color, sex, or national origin. Other employers cannot discriminate on the basis of religion in employment practices, and they must make reasonable accommodation to the religious needs of their employees if it does not result in undue hardship to them.

In one case the Supreme Court let stand a lower court ruling that employees cannot be required to pay union dues if they have religious objections to unions. The case determined that a union violated Title VII by forcing a company to fire a Seventh Day Adventist who did not comply with a collective bargaining agreement term that all employees must pay union dues. The union argued unsuccessfully that it had made reasonable accommodation to the worker's religious beliefs by offering to give any dues paid by him to charity. However, in another case the Supreme Court ruled that a company rightfully fired an employee who refused to work on Saturdays due to religious belief. The Court said that the company did not have to burden other employees by making them work Saturdays.

A growing source of religious discrimination lawsuits concerns employees who for religious reasons refuse to perform some task required by the employer. For example, in one case a vegetarian bus driver refused to distribute hamburger coupons on his bus, asserting religious beliefs. When his employer fired him, he sued. The parties settled the case for $50,000. Note that even if an employer wins such a lawsuit, it can be extremely expensive to defend.

As mentioned earlier, since the 9/11 bombings religious discrimination against Muslim employees has risen steeply. In 2003 the EEOC settled a complaint by four Muslim machine operators against Stockton Steel of California for $1.1 million. The four operators claimed they were given the worst jobs, ridiculed during their prayers, and called names like "camel jockey" and "raghead."

UPS paid $46,000 to settle a religious discrimination case for failing to accommodate the Rastafarian religious beliefs of an employee whose religious beliefs prohibited him from cutting his hair or shaving his beard to comply with UPS policy.

In the case of employees of Arab descent, note the close connection between national origin discrimination and religious discrimination.

>> *sidebar* 20.4

Workplace Discrimination Against Muslims

About 25 percent of the religious discrimination claims filed with the EEOC are brought by Muslims, even though Muslims make up only 2 percent of the U.S. population. Complaints include:

- Somali immigrants working at a meatpacking company who were cursed for being Muslim; had blood, meat, and bones thrown at them; and were interrupted during prayer breaks.
- Dress policies forbidding headwear, prohibiting Muslim women from wearing headscarves, also called hijabs.
- Name-calling, including: "terrorist," "Osama," "camel jockey," and "towel head."

What steps should employers take to accommodate Muslims in the workplace? If it will not cause undue hardship, employers should consider allowing the following kinds of accommodations:

- Prayer breaks with the understanding that Muslims pray five times a day for approximately five to 15 minutes.
- Headscarves for women if they do not create a safety issue.
- Facial Hair for men.
- Vacation days for religious holidays such as *Eid al-Fitr* and *Eid al-Adha*.

Overall, as is the case with any form of illegal discrimination, employers should be vigilant and take action to ensure that the workplace is free from discriminatory animus.

6. DISCRIMINATION ON THE BASIS OF SEX

Historically, states have enacted many laws designed supposedly to protect women. For example, many states by statute have prohibited the employment of women in certain occupations such as those that require lifting heavy objects. Others have barred women from working during the night or more than a given number of hours per week or day. A federal district court held that a California state law that required rest periods for women only was in violation of Title VII. Some statutes prohibit employing women for a specified time after childbirth. Under EEOC guidelines, such statutes are not a defense to a charge of illegal sex discrimination and do not provide an employer with a bona fide occupational qualification in hiring standards. Other EEOC guidelines forbid employers:

- To classify jobs as male or female.
- To advertise in help-wanted columns that are designated male or female, unless sex is a bona fide job qualification.

Query: Could Victoria's Secret stores legally hire only women for certain positions?

Similarly, employers may not have separate male and female seniority lists.

Whether sex is a bona fide occupational qualification (and discrimination is thus legal) has been raised in several cases. The courts have tended to consider this exception narrowly. In the following instances involving hiring policy, *no* bona fide occupational qualification was found to exist:

- A rule requiring airline stewardesses, but not stewards, to be single.
- A policy of hiring only females as flight cabin attendants.
- A rule against hiring females with preschool-age children, but not against hiring males with such children.
- A telephone company policy against hiring females as switchers because of the alleged heavy lifting involved on the job.

In the telephone company case, the court held that for a bona fide occupational qualification to exist, there must be "reasonable cause to believe, that is, a factual basis for believing, that all or substantially all women would be unable to perform safely and efficiently the duties of the job involved." The Supreme Court has indicated that for such a qualification to exist, sex must be provably relevant to job performance.

Other examples of illegal sex discrimination include:

- Refusing to hire a female newscaster because "news coming from a woman sounds like gossip."
- Allowing women to retire at age 50, but requiring men to wait until age 55.
- Failing to promote women to overseas positions because foreign clients were reluctant to do business with women.

The much-talked about Hooters restaurant case involved a lawsuit filed by men in Illinois and Maryland who were denied jobs. Hooters paid $3.75 million to settle the lawsuit. The settlement allows Hooters to continue employing voluptuous and scantily clad female "Hooters Girls," but they must create and fill a few other support jobs, like bartenders and hosts, without regard to gender.

The largest gender discrimination case was brought as a class action against Wal-Mart and Sam's Club. In 2011, the U.S. Supreme Court refused to certify the class. For more information about this case, see Case 4.2 in Chapter 4.

>> *sidebar* 20.5

Gender Bias in Corporate America

Here are some examples of gender bias cases brought by women against major U.S. firms:

- **Novartis Pharmaceuticals Corp.**—After finding discrimination against women employees in pay, promotion and pregnancy policies, a New York jury awarded the plaintiffs $3,367,250 in compensatory damages and $250 million in punitive damages. In his closing argument, the plaintiffs' lawyer told the jury that the evidence proved that Novartis "tolerated a culture of sexism, a boys' club atmosphere." Novartis subsequently settled the remaining gender bias claims, agreeing to a settlement of approximately $152.5 million to current and former female sales representatives.

- **Morgan Stanley**—In 2004, the firm agreed to pay $54 million to settle a gender discrimination suit brought by a former bond saleswoman.

- **Goldman Sachs Group, Inc.**—Three former female employees have sued Goldman Sachs in 2010, alleging "systemic" violations of female employees' rights, including allegations of excluding women from golf outings and other work-related social events, push-up contests, and retaliation after complaining about being groped by a male colleague after an outing at a topless bar. The suit alleges that the decentralized structure gives managers "unchecked discretion" in assigning pay and responsibilities.

- **Citigroup**—Six current and former female employees sued Citigroup alleging that it engages in "pervasive discrimination and retaliation" against female employees during the 2008 layoffs. Calling the firm an "outdated 'boys' club,'" it allegedly systematically discriminates against women at all levels.

Sexual Harassment   A common type of illegal sex discrimination in the workplace is **sexual harassment.** The typical sexual harassment case involves a plaintiff who has been promised benefits or threatened with loss if she or he does not give sexual favors to an employment supervisor. Such a case is also called a *quid pro quo* (this for that) case. Under Title VII and agency law, an employer is liable for this sex discrimination.

Another type of sexual harassment is the **hostile work environment,** one in which co-workers make offensive sexual comments or propositions, engage in suggestive touching, show nude pictures, or draw sexual graffiti. The Supreme Court in *Meritor Savings Bank v. Vinson* ruled that Title VII prohibits "an offensive or hostile working environment," even when no economic loss occurs. By so ruling, the Court acknowledged that the work environment itself is a condition of employment covered by Title VII.

The Supreme Court also addressed the hostile work environment issue in *Harris v. Forklift Systems, Inc.* Specifically, the Court was asked to determine whether, before a person could sue under Title VII, a hostile work environment had "to seriously affect [his or her] psychological well-being" or "cause injury." The Court ruled that illegal sexual harassment goes beyond that which causes "injury." It includes any harassment reasonably perceived as "hostile and abusive."

Is all sexually offensive conduct between employees illegal? The answer is no, although an employee's company may choose to forbid and punish all

Think of sexual harassment discrimination in terms of (1) quid pro quo cases and (2) hostile work environment cases.

Well-known talk show hosts Maury Povich and Bill O'Reilly both have been accused of sexual harassment in multimillion-dollar lawsuits. O'Reilly settled the case for an undisclosed amount.

such conduct. In 2005 the Supreme Court in *Clarke County School District v. Breeden* summarized when offensive sexual conduct becomes illegal:

> [S]exual harassment is actionable under Title VII only if it is so severe or pervasive as to alter the conditions of the victim's employment and create an abusive working environment.

The Court continued:

> Workplace conduct is not measured in isolation; instead, whether an environment is sufficiently hostile or abusive must be judged by looking at all the circumstances, including the frequency of the discriminatory conduct; its severity; whether it is physically threatening or humiliating, or a mere offensive utterance; and whether it unreasonably interferes with an employee's work performance.

16.4% of all sexual harassment claims—or 2,094 claims—were filed by men in 2009.

It is not uncommon for a discrimination lawsuit to involve multiple kinds of claims. A good example of this is a recent case against Cracker Barrel, in which the restaurant agreed to pay $2 million to settle a lawsuit alleging sexual harassment, racial harassment, and retaliation by 51 current or former employees. On behalf of the workers, the EEOC alleged that male co-workers and managers subjected female workers to unwelcome and offensive sexual comments and touching. According to the EEOC, "Black employees said that they experienced racially charged language in the workplace, including 'spear chucking porch monkey,' 'you people,' and the 'n-word.'" In addition to the monetary settlement, Cracker Barrel must train all employees in its stores about harassment.

>> *sidebar* 20.6

Vulgar Workplace Language & Sexual Harassment

Can vulgar language, *even if it is not specifically directed at an individual,* be actionable as sexual harassment under Title VII? Yes—according to the 11th Circuit Court of Appeals. The plaintiff, Ingrid Reeves, worked at a sales company, C.H. Robinson. Reeves alleged that she was subjected to hearing her male co-workers call other women names such as "b***h," "wh**e" and "c**t" on a daily basis. She also claimed that there were repeated vulgar discussions about female body parts and a pornographic image of a woman in the office. Reeves complained to her co-workers, her supervisor, and top company executives, but the offensive conduct was "accepted and tolerated."

According to the 11th Circuit, "if Reeves's account is to be believed, C.H. Robinson's workplace was more than a rough environment—indiscriminately vulgar, profane, and sexual. Instead, a just reasonably could find that it was a workplace that exposed Reeves to disadvantageous terms or conditions of employment to which members of the other sex were not exposed." Moreover, the court stated that it was no defense to assert "that the workplace may have been vulgar and sexually degrading before Reeves arrived."

For more information, see, *Reeves v. C.H. Robinson Worldwide, Inc.,* 07-10270 (11th Cir. Jan. 20, 2010), available at www.ca11.uscourts.gov/opinions/ops/200710270op2.pdf.

Employer's Defense to Hostile Environment   Is an employer always liable when fellow employees create a hostile environment based on gender? The answer is that the employer is not always legally responsible for a hostile environment. The employer may have a defense. Courts have ruled that an employer is liable to a plaintiff employee for a hostile working environment created by fellow employees only when the employer knows of the problem and fails to take prompt and reasonable steps to correct it, such as by moving the harassers away from the plaintiff employee. The employer can defend itself by proving the employer exercised reasonable care to prevent and correct promptly any sexually harassing behavior, and the plaintiff employee unreasonably failed to take advantage of any preventive or corrective opportunities provided by the employer.

Remember Title VII says that an employer is liable for discriminatory practices only if an employee files a complaint concerning them with the EEOC within 180 days of their happening (within 300 days if the employee has first filed with a state fair employment practices commission). Employers are liable for acts that occurred before 180 days of EEOC filing if they are part of a single hostile environment that continued within the 180-day period.

Pregnancy Discrimination Act The Pregnancy Discrimination Act amended the Civil Rights Act in 1978. Under it, employers can no longer discriminate against women workers who become pregnant or give birth. Thus, employers with health or disability plans must cover pregnancy, childbirth, and related medical conditions in the same manner as other conditions are covered. The law covers unmarried as well as married pregnant women. It also states that an employer cannot force a pregnant woman to stop working until her baby is born, provided she is still capable of performing her duties properly. And the employer cannot specify how long a leave of absence must be taken after childbirth. Coverage for abortion is not required by the statute unless an employee carries to term and her life is endangered or she develops medical complications because of an abortion. If a woman undergoes an abortion, though, all other benefits provided for employees, such as sick leave, must be provided to her.

Note that sex discrimination applies to discrimination against men as well as women. For example, under the Pregnancy Discrimination Act the Supreme Court ruled unlawful an employer's health insurance plan that covered the pregnancies of female employees but did not cover the pregnancies of male employees' wives.

> **Don't** forget that employers are liable if plaintiffs prove quid pro quo harassment. But employers may have a defense to hostile environment harassment.

> Men as well as women may be subject to illegal sex discrimination.

>> *sidebar* 20.7

Pregnancy Discrimination: Claims on the Rise

The EEOC reports that pregnancy-related claims are consistently increasing:

YEAR	CLAIMS RECEIVED
1997	3977
2000	4160
2003	4649
2007	5587
2010	6119

What does a woman need to bring a successful claim? She must prove that her pregnancy or her status as a mother motivated the employer's adverse action.

In 2007, the EEOC sued Bloomberg LP, the news and financial services company, alleging discrimination against women who became pregnant and took maternity leave. The complaint alleges that Bloomberg engaged in a pattern of demoting and reducing the pay of women after they were pregnant. Other allegations included that some women were subjected to stereotyping about their abilities to do work while they were tending to family and caregiver responsibilities.

For more information, see www.eeoc.gov/types/pregnancy.html.

According to the census statistics, women earned 77 cents on the male dollar in 2008. April 20th is now Equal Pay Day in the U.S. to highlight awareness of this ongoing discrepancy.

Equal Pay Act   Historically, employers have paid female employees less than males, even when they held the same jobs. In 1964, women earned only 59 cents for every dollar earned by males. By 2008, female employees earned just 77 cents for every dollar earned by males.

Federal legislation prohibits sex discrimination in employment compensation under both Title VII and the Equal Pay Act of 1963. Administered by the EEOC, the Equal Pay Act prohibits an employer from discriminating on the basis of sex in the payment of wages for equal work performed. For jobs to be equal, they must require "equal skill, effort, and responsibility" and must be performed "under similar working conditions." Discrimination is allowed if it arises from a seniority system, a merit system, a piecework production system, or any factor other than sex.

The focus of Equal Pay Act cases is whether the male and female jobs being compared involve "equal" work. Courts have recognized that *equal* does not mean *identical;* it means *substantially* equal. Thus, courts have ruled "equal" the work of male barbers and female beauticians and of male tailors and female seamstresses. Differences in male and female job descriptions will not totally protect employers against charges of equal-pay infractions. The courts have held that "substantially equal" work done on different machines would require the employer to compensate male and female employees equally.

One court ruled that an employer could pay male physician assistants more than female nurses because the physician assistants had administrative duties that nurses did not have to perform.

The Supreme Court has ruled that discriminatory male and female pay differences can also be illegal under Title VII. In *County of Washington v. Gunther,* the Court decided that plaintiffs can use evidence of such pay differences to help prove intentional sex discrimination, even when the work performed is not substantially equal. Relying on the *Gunther* case, at least one lower court has held that women must be paid equally with men who perform comparable work. A federal district court ruled that the state of Washington discriminated against secretaries (mostly women) by paying them less than maintenance and other personnel (mostly men). However, the **comparable worth** theory is highly controversial, and other courts have not agreed with the theory. Equal Pay Act cases tend to rely heavily on statistical analysis of disparities.

In a landmark Equal Pay Act decision, *Ledbetter v. Goodyear Tire & Rubber Co., Inc.* (2007), a sharply divided Supreme Court rejected the pro-employee paycheck-accrual theory of pay discrimination previously accepted by many courts. Simply stated, employees must file an EEOC charge within 180 or 300 days (depending on their state) after each discriminatory pay decision or forever lose their claim. For more details about the controversial *Ledbetter* case, see Sidebar 20.8.

Examples of successful Equal Pay Act cases include one against Wal-Mart and another against the New York Corrections Department. In the first case, a pharmacist who claimed Wal-Mart fired her after asking to be paid the same as her male colleagues won nearly a $2 million award against Wal-Mart. Wal-Mart argued that it fired the pharmacist for leaving the pharmacy unattended and allowing a technician to use her computer security code to issue prescriptions, including a fraudulent prescription for a painkiller. Countering this argument, the pharmacist argued that the prescription incident

>> *sidebar* 20.8

Did the Supreme Court Get It Wrong? Fallout Over the *Ledbetter* Case

Lilly Ledbetter worked for Goodyear for nearly 20 years. During that time, Ledbetter and other salaried employees received or were denied raises based on their supervisors' evaluation of their performance. Near the end of her tenure at Goodyear, Ledbetter discovered that her pay was significantly less—as much as 40 percent less—than her male counterparts. Ledbetter then filed a charge with the EEOC.

>> PROCEDURAL HISTORY

The district court allowed Ledbetter to present evidence of her entire 19-year career at Goodyear. A jury found in her favor, awarding both compensatory and punitive damages. The Eleventh Circuit reversed and the Supreme Court (5–4) affirmed the decision that a Title VII pay discrimination claim cannot be based on any pay decision that occurred outside of the EEOC charging period.

>> DISSENTING VIEWS

Justice Ruth Bader Ginsberg wrote a spirited dissent (joined by Justices Stevens, Souter, and Breyer) arguing that "[p]ay disparities often occur . . . in small increments" and "cause to suspect that discrimination is at work develops only over time." She continued, asserting that discriminatory disparities in pay, like hostile work environment claims, rest not on "one particular paycheck, but on 'the cumulative effect of individual acts.'" Incensed about the majority opinion, Justice Ginsberg read her dissent aloud from the bench.

>> LEGISLATIVE RESPONSE

The first piece of legislation President Obama signed into law was the Lilly Ledbetter Fair Pay Act of 2009. The Ledbetter Act extends the time for employees to bring gender discrimination claims challenging pay or promotion decision.

---

took place 18 months before her termination and more severe infractions by her male counterparts were unpunished. In the second case, the EEOC settled an Equal Pay Act suit against the New York Department of Corrections for nearly $1 million. The EEOC alleged that female employees were receiving less benefits than their male counterparts.

Sexual Orientation Discrimination   Title VII does not prohibit discrimination against employees based on their sexual orientation, or whether they are gay, lesbian, bisexual, transgendered, or heterosexual. The word *sex* in Title VII refers only to gender, whether someone is female or male. A quarter of the states, however, and numerous cities do forbid discrimination based on sexual orientation, and Congress could amend Title VII to protect employees from such discrimination. Already, thousands of companies ranging from American Express, Coca-Cola, and J. P. Morgan Chase Bank to Ford, General Motors, and Chrysler, offer domestic partner benefits to all employees without regard to sexual orientation.

Although the House of Representatives voted 235–184 to pass the Employment Non-Discrimination Act of 2007, banning employment discrimination on the basis of sexual orientation, it has not yet become federal law. See Sidebar 20.9 for other developments in sexual orientation laws and protections.

>> *sidebar* 20.9

Sexual Orientation Discrimination: State and Local Laws

Although there is no federal protection prohibiting sexual orientation in the workplace based on sexual orientation, many private employers—especially those who operate in many states—have company policies prohibiting sexual orientation discrimination. Consider these facts and legal developments:

- The majority of Fortune 500 companies provide health insurance for domestic partners of their employees.
- According to Human Rights Campaign, a gay political group, more than 7,000 employers offer domestic partner benefits.
- *State laws.* Twenty states and the District of Columbia have laws that currently prohibit sexual orientation discrimination in private employment:

California, Colorado, Connecticut, Hawaii, Illinois, Iowa, Maine, Maryland, Massachusetts, Minnesota, Nevada, New Hampshire, New Jersey, New Mexico, New York, Oregon, Rhode Island, Vermont, Washington, and Wisconsin. Some of these states also specifically prohibit discrimination based on gender identity.

- *Local laws.* More than 180 cities and counties nationwide prohibit sexual orientation discrimination in at least some workplaces.

For more information and a state-by-state list of antidiscrimination laws, including city and county ordinances, see the Lambda Legal Defense and Education Fund website at www.lambdalegal.org.

>> Employment Practices That May Be Challenged

In studying the Civil Rights Act, we can usefully consider several specific employment practices that employees or job applicants may challenge as discriminatory. These practices include:

- Setting testing and educational requirements.
- Having height and weight requirements for physical labor.
- Maintaining appearance requirements.
- Practicing affirmative action.
- Using seniority systems.

The following sections take a close look at these practices.

7. QUESTIONNAIRES, INTERVIEWS, TESTING, AND EDUCATIONAL REQUIREMENTS

Employers have used a number of tools to help them find the right person for the right job. Among these tools are questionnaires, interviews, references, minimum educational requirements (such as a high school diploma), and personnel tests. However, employers must be extremely careful not to use tools that illegally discriminate. For example, Rent-A-Center, a Dallas-based appliance-rental company, agreed to pay more than $2 million in damages to more than 1,200 job applicants and employees who were asked questions about their sex lives and religious views in a 500-item true-false questionnaire. Plaintiffs claimed the questionnaire discriminated illegally on the basis of gender and religion and that it violated their privacy.

Interviews can also discriminate illegally, and personnel interviewers must be well trained. One study indicated that interviewers can be biased even if they are not aware of it. The study showed that the interviewers tended to select males over females for sales positions because the interviewers *subconsciously* related sales success with height, and males are on the average taller than females. References may not be so reliable, either. A previous employer's letter may reflect personal biases against an applicant that were not related to job performance.

At the other extreme, an employer may give a poor employee a top recommendation because of sympathy or fear of a lawsuit in case the letter is somehow obtained by the employee. Advocates of personnel tests in the selection process feel they are very valuable in weeding out the wrong persons for a job and picking the right ones. They believe reliance on test results eliminates biases that interviewers or former employers who give references may have.

Tests, however, can have a *disparate impact* on job applicants, discriminating on the basis of race, sex, color, religion, or national origin. Setting educational standards such as requiring a high school diploma for employment can also have a disparate impact. To avoid discrimination challenges, employers must make sure that all testing and educational requirements are job related and necessary for the business.

> Most employment practices that discriminate illegally do so because of their disparate impact.

In the past, some employers have "race normed" employment tests. *Race norming* is the practice of setting two different cutoff test scores for employment based on race or one of the other Title VII categories. For example, on a race-normed test, the minimum score for employment of white job applicants might be set at 75 out of 100. For minority applicants, the minimum score might be set at 65. *The Civil Rights Act amendments of 1991 specifically prohibit the race norming of employment tests.*

> **Don't** forget that for employers to race-norm employment tests violates Title VII.

8. HEIGHT AND WEIGHT REQUIREMENTS

Minimum or maximum height or weight job requirements apply equally to all job applicants, but if they have the effect of screening out applicants on the basis of race, national origin, or sex, the employer must demonstrate that such requirements are validly related to the ability to perform the work in question. For example, maximum size standards would be permissible, even if they favored women over men, if the available work space were too small to permit large persons to perform the duties of the job properly. Most size requirements have dictated minimum heights or weights, often based on a stereotyped assumption that a certain amount of strength that smaller persons might not have probably was necessary for the work. In one case, a 5-foot, 5-inch, 130-pound Hispanic won a suit against a police department on the basis that the department's 5-foot, 8-inch minimum height requirement discriminated against Hispanics, who often are shorter than that standard. He was later hired when he passed the department's physical agility examination, which included dragging a 150-pound body 75 feet and scaling a 6-foot wall.

9. APPEARANCE REQUIREMENTS

Walt Disney World has detailed instructions for employees on "The Disney Look," including eyewear, body piercing, earlobe expansion, facial hair, fingernails, hear length, and sideburns. The goal is to look "friendly, approachable, and knowledgeable."

Employers often have set grooming standards for their employees. Those regulating hair length of males or prohibiting beards or mustaches have been among the most common. Undoubtedly, motivation for these rules stems from the feeling of the employer that the image it projects to the public through its employees will be adversely affected if their appearance is not "proper." It is unclear whether appearance requirements are legal or illegal, since there have been rulings both ways. However, in 2000 the EEOC filed a lawsuit in Atlanta against FedEx Corporation for firing a bearded delivery driver who refused to shave in violation of a company policy that permitted beards only when medically necessary. The driver's Islamic beliefs required males to wear beards, and the lawsuit alleged that FedEx's policy constituted religious discrimination.

The burden of proof in a disparate impact case requires the employer to prove that appearance is a business necessity.

In another case, a black employee argued that he was wrongfully fired for breaking a company rule prohibiting beards. Dermatologists testified that the plaintiff had a condition called "razor bumps" (which occurs when the tightly curled facial hairs of black men become ingrown from shaving) and that the only known cure was for him not to shave. Although the federal appeals court found that the plaintiff was prejudiced by the employer's regulation, it held in favor of the company, ruling that its *slight racial impact* was justified by the *business necessity* it served. A conflicting opinion in still another case upheld an employee's right to wear a beard because of razor bumps.

10. AFFIRMATIVE ACTION PROGRAMS AND REVERSE DISCRIMINATION

Since the 1940s, a series of presidential executive orders have promoted nondiscrimination and **affirmative action** by employers who contract with the federal government. The authority for these orders rests with the president's executive power to control the granting of federal contracts. As a condition to obtaining such contracts, employers must agree contractually to take affirmative action to avoid unlawful discrimination in recruitment, employment, promotion, training, rate of compensation, and layoff of workers.

It is not unusual for an employment ad to state that the company is an "affirmative action/ equal opportunity employer." Some ads also state: "Women and underrepresented minorities are encouraged to apply."

The affirmative action requirement means that federally contracting employers must actively recruit members of minority groups being underused in the workforce. That is, employers must hire members of these groups when there are fewer minority workers in a given job category than one could reasonably expect, considering their availability. In many instances, employers must develop written affirmative action plans and set goals and timetables for bringing minority (or female) workforces up to their percentages in the available labor pool.

The Labor Department administers executive orders through its Office of Federal Contract Compliance Programs (OFCCP). The OFCCP can terminate federal contracts with employers who do not comply with its guidelines and can make them ineligible for any future federal business. For instance, it required Uniroyal, Inc., to give its female employees an estimated $18 million in back pay to compensate for past employment discrimination. The alternative was elimination of $36 million of existing federal contracts and ineligibility for future federal business.

The Labor Department has eased OFCCP regulations on 75 percent of the firms that do business with the federal government. Firms with fewer than 250 employees and federal contracts of under $1 million no longer must prepare written affirmative action plans for hiring women and minorities. The OFCCP has also begun to limit its use of back pay awards to specific individuals who can show an actual loss due to violation of OFCCP guidelines.

Private Employer Affirmative Action Not all affirmative action programs arise under federal contracting rules. Courts also impose affirmative action on private employers to overcome a history of prior discrimination. Sometimes private employers voluntarily adopt affirmative action or agree to it with unions. These affirmative action programs can give rise to claims of **reverse discrimination** when minorities or women with lower qualifications or less seniority than white males are given preference in employment or training. Even though such programs are intended to remedy the effects of present or past discrimination or other barriers to equal employment opportunity, white males have argued that the law does not permit employers to discriminate against *them* on the basis of race or sex any more than it allows discrimination against minorities or women.

In *United Steelworkers of America v. Weber,* the Supreme Court ruled legal under Title VII a voluntary affirmative action plan between an employer and a union. The plan required that at least 50 percent of certain new work trainees be black. The Court noted that the plan did not require that white employees be fired or excluded altogether from advancement. It was only a temporary measure to eliminate actual racial imbalance in the workforce.

Note the difference between taking affirmative action and setting a "quota." Affirmative action is taken to help correct historic workforce imbalances and usually has target goals that are pursued for a limited time. On the other hand, quotas set rigid standards for various groups, such as that 50 percent of the workforce must be female. The 1991 Civil Rights Act amendments prohibit the setting of quotas in employment.

The EEOC has issued guidelines intended to protect employers who set up affirmative action plans. These guidelines indicate that Title VII is not violated if an employer determines that there is a reasonable basis for concluding that such a plan is appropriate and the employer takes *reasonable* affirmative action. For example, if an employer discovers that it has a job category where one might expect to find more women and minorities employed than are actually in its workforce, the employer has a reasonable basis for affirmative action.

In *Adarand Constructors, Inc. v. Pena,* the Supreme Court emphasized that government-imposed affirmative action plans are subject to *strict judicial scrutiny* under equal protection guaranteed by the Fifth and Fourteenth Amendments. To be constitutional, such plans must now be supported by a *compelling interest.* The *Adarand* decision will make it constitutionally difficult to justify some government-imposed affirmative action plans. Much litigation has followed that tests the constitutionality of various plans.

In California voters approved the controversial Proposition 209. In relevant part it says that "the state shall not discriminate against, or grant preferential treatment to, any individual or group on the basis of race, sex, color, ethnicity, or national origin in the operation of public employment,

Do remember that the justification for affirmative action is the historic discrimination against protected groups.

In 2005, a federal jury found that the New Orleans district attorney discriminated against 43 white employees by firing them and replacing them with African Americans.

Voluntary affirmative action plans by private employers *may* violate Title VII but do *not* violate constitutional equal protection because they are not "state action."

public education, or public contracting." The Supreme Court refused to hear an appeal from a lower court decision that upheld Proposition 209 against constitutional challenge and the assertion it violated federal civil rights law. Although Proposition 209 *does not* affect private employer affirmative action plans required by federal law, it does illustrate the current opposition that many Americans have to affirmative action. Polls show that almost three-fourths of the general population disapproves of affirmative action. Nearly 50 percent of African Americans also oppose it.

11. SENIORITY SYSTEMS

> Title VII specifically allows employers to adopt seniority systems even when they may operate to discriminate against protected groups.

Seniority systems give priority to those employees who have worked longer for a particular employer or in a particular line of employment of the employer. Employers may institute seniority systems on their own, but in a union shop they are usually the result of collective bargaining. Their terms are spelled out in the agreement between the company and the union. Seniority systems often determine the calculation of vacation, pension, and other fringe benefits. They also control many employment decisions such as the order in which employees may choose shifts or qualify for promotions or transfers to different jobs. They also are used to select the persons to be laid off when an employer is reducing its labor force. As a result of seniority, the last hired are usually the first fired. Decisions based on seniority have been challenged in recent years as violating the laws relating to equal employment opportunity. Challenges often arose when recently hired members of minority groups were laid off during periods of economic downturn. Firms with successful affirmative action programs often lost most of their minority employees.

Section 703(h) of the Civil Rights Act of 1964 provides that, in spite of other provisions in the act, it is not an unlawful employment practice for an employer to apply different employment standards under a bona fide (good-faith) seniority system if the differences are not the result of an *intention* to discriminate. In *Memphis Fire Dept. v. Stotts* the Supreme Court ruled that discrimination resulting from application of a seniority system was lawful even when it affected minorities hired or promoted by affirmative action.

>> Other Statutes and Discrimination in Employment

Although the Civil Rights Act of 1964 is the most widely used antidiscrimination statute, there are other important antidiscrimination laws. They include the Civil Rights Act of 1866, the Age Discrimination in Employment Act, the Americans with Disabilities Act, and various state and local laws. The following sections examine these laws.

12. CIVIL RIGHTS ACT OF 1866

An important federal law that complements Title VII of the 1964 Civil Rights Act is the Civil Rights Act of 1866. One provision of that act, known as **Section 1981** (referring to its U.S. Code designation, 42 U.S.C. §1981), provides that "all persons . . . shall have the same right to make and enforce contracts . . . as enjoyed by white citizens." Since union memberships and employment relationships involve contracts, Section 1981 bans racial discrimination in these areas.

The courts have interpreted Section 1981 as giving a private plaintiff most of the same protections against racial discrimination that the 1964 Civil Rights Act provides. In addition, there are at least two advantages to the plaintiff who files a suit based on Section 1981. First, there are no procedural requirements for bringing such a suit, whereas there are a number of fairly complex requirements plaintiffs must follow before bringing a private suit under Title VII. For instance, before a plaintiff can file a lawsuit against an employer, the plaintiff must file charges of discrimination with the EEOC and obtain a notice of right to sue from the agency. By using Section 1981, a plaintiff can immediately sue an employer in federal court without first going through the EEOC.

Unlimited Damages   A second advantage to Section 1981 is that under it the courts can award unlimited compensatory and punitive damages. There are no capped limits as there are under Title VII. As a practical matter, parties alleging racial discrimination usually sue under both Section 1981 and Title VII.

Note that Section 1981 does not cover discrimination based on sex, religion, national origin, age, or handicap. As interpreted by the courts, this section applies only to *racial* discrimination. However, what is race? The Supreme Court has held that being of Arabic or Jewish ancestry constitutes "race" as protected by Section 1981. The Court stated that when the law was passed in the nineteenth century, the concept of race was much broader than it is today. Race then included the descendants of a particular "family, tribe, people, or nation." Has the Court opened the door for a white job applicant to sue a black employer for discrimination under Section 1981?

In *Patterson v. McLean,* the Supreme Court interpreted Section 1981 to apply only to the actual hiring or firing of employees based on race. Under this interpretation, Section 1981 did not offer protection against discrimination such as a hostile working environment. But the Civil Rights Act amendments of 1991 redefined Section 1981 to include protection against discrimination in "enjoyment of all benefits, privileges, terms and conditions of the contractual relationship." Thus Section 1981 now also protects against hostile environment discrimination. In 2008, the Supreme Court also extended Section 1981 to claims of retaliation for complaining about race discrimination.

13. DISCRIMINATION ON THE BASIS OF AGE

The workforce is "graying." The U.S. Census Bureau projects that by 2010 over 51 percent of the workforce will be 40 years of age or older. As percentages of older workers rise in coming years, so will the increase in complaints about age discrimination.

Neither the Civil Rights Act nor the Equal Employment Opportunity Act forbids discrimination based on age. However, the Age Discrimination in Employment Act (ADEA) does. It prohibits employment discrimination

---

Denny's restaurants have been repeatedly sued for black customers claiming Denny's violated their civil rights. Denny's has paid more than $54 million to settle the lawsuits.

Don't forget that Section 1981 is why racial discrimination is subject to damages far in excess of the $300,000 limit imposed on individuals under Title VII.

Under Section 1981, "race" includes ethnic or national groups.

"Age bias is still a persistent problem in the 21st century workplace."

–Spencer H. Lewis, EEOC district director

against employees ages 40 and older, and it prohibits the mandatory retirement of these employees. Only certain executives and high policymakers of private companies can be forced into early retirement. Specifically, "bona fide" executives and high-level policy makers age 65 and older who are entitled to receive annual retirement benefits of at least $44,000 a year are subject to mandatory retirement policies. The ADEA applies to employers with 20 or more employees. The ADEA also invalidates retirement plans and labor contracts that violate the law.

Types of Age Discrimination   The ADEA recognizes both disparate treatment and disparate impact discrimination. The Supreme Court has upheld a jury's finding of disparate treatment in an age discrimination case. The employer had said the employee "was so old [he] must have come over on the Mayflower" and that he "was too damn old to do his job." When the employer later fired the employee, the jury found for the employee in spite of the employer's assertion that it had fired the employee for reasons other than age.

The Supreme Court has also stated that the ADEA recognizes disparate impact in age discrimination cases. The city of Jackson, Mississippi, had awarded pay raises to junior ranks of police officers that were substantially higher than the pay raises given to more senior ranks. These raises had the impact of discriminating on the basis of age. Older officers received lower pay raises because they were mostly in senior ranks.

However, the Supreme Court stated that disparate impact alone did not prove illegality under the ADEA. The city of Jackson was merely attempting to match the salaries offered to junior officers in nearby cities, which was a "reasonable factor other than age." See Sidebar 20.10 for an example of illegal mandatory retirement policy.

Employer Defenses in ADEA Cases   The employer defenses to age discrimination, disparate treatment, and disparate impact differ slightly from the defense in Title VII cases.

For instance, under the ADEA age is seldom recognized as the basis for a bona fide occupational qualification. It is recognized that as people grow older, their physical strength, agility, reflexes, hearing, and vision tend to diminish in quality. However, this generally provides no legal reason for discriminating against older persons as a class. Although courts will uphold job-related physical requirements if they apply on a case-by-case basis, they frequently find as illegal those policies that prohibit the hiring of persons beyond a maximum age or that establish a maximum age beyond which employees are forced to retire for physical reasons. Thus, one court ruled that a mandatory retirement age of 65 was illegally discriminatory as applied to the job of district fire chief. In an exception to the general rule, one court has ruled that age can be a BFOQ in a case where the airlines imposed a maximum age for hiring new pilots. The court observed that the Federal Aviation Administration mandated a retirement age for pilots.

The ADEA also does not require the employer to prove a "business necessity" in order to successfully defend an age discrimination case of disparate impact. All the employer need do is establish that a "reasonable factor other than age" accounted for the discriminatory impact. Further, unlike under Title VII, the employer's defense of a reasonable factor other than age cannot be

Willful violations of the ADEA allow courts to impose double damage awards against employers.

defeated by the employee's showing of a less discriminatory way of achieving the employer's purpose.

Remedies under the ADEA   Courts have disagreed on whether remedies for violation of the ADEA include, in addition to reinstatement and wages lost, damages for the psychological trauma of being fired or forced to resign illegally. One federal district court awarded $200,000 to a victim of age discrimination who was an inventor and scientist, for the psychological and physical effects suffered from being forced into early retirement at age 60. Also awarded were out-of-pocket costs of $60,000 and attorneys' fees of $65,000. Note that *willful* violations of the act permit discrimination victims to be awarded *double damages*.

Note an important exception to this general rule about remedies under the ADEA. In accordance with the Supreme Court case *Kimel v. Florida Board of Regents* (2000), a plaintiff cannot recover money damages against a state entity. State law, however, may offer additional remedies for age discrimination perpetrated by a state.

>> *sidebar* 20.10

Did You Read the Law? A Law Firm Runs Afoul of the ADEA

The EEOC filed a lawsuit against Sidley Austin Brown & Wood ("Sidley Austin"), a major Chicago-based international law firm, alleging that it violated the ADEA when it selected 32 "partners" for expulsion from the firm on account of their age or forced them to retire.

After over two years of litigation, Sidley Austin agreed to pay $27.5 million to the former partners. The firm also agreed to refrain from "terminating,

expelling, retiring, reducing the compensation of or otherwise adversely changing the partnership status of any partner because of age" or "maintaining any formal or informal policy or practice requiring retirement as a partner or requiring permission to continue as a partner once the partner has reached a certain age."

Source: EEOC Press Releases.

---

14. DISCRIMINATION ON THE BASIS OF DISABILITIES

According to a Harris poll, two-thirds of all disabled Americans between the ages of 16 and 64 are not working, even though most of them want to work. To help those with disabilities obtain work, Congress in 1990 passed the Americans with Disabilities Act (ADA). Thereafter, the U.S. Supreme Court rendered a number of employer–friendly decisions restricting the scope of the ADA's protection. Responding to criticism that the U.S. Supreme Court unreasonably restricted the ADA's scope, Congress passed the ADA Amendments Act of 2008, effective January 1, 2009 and, in 2011, the EEOC released its final regulations. The ADA is now expanded to protect a broader group of individuals.

To prevent disability discrimination, the ADA prohibits employers from requiring a preemployment medical examination or asking questions about the job applicant's medical history. Only after a job offer has been extended

It is now easier to establish a "disability" within the definition of the ADA and employers need to be prepared to make reasonable accommodations.

can the employer condition employment on the employee's responses to *job related* medical questions.

The ADA prohibits employer discrimination against job applicants or employees based on (1) their having a disability, (2) their having a disability in the past, or (3) their being *regarded as* having a disability. The ADA defines **disability** as "any physical or mental impairment that substantially limits one or more of an individual's major life activities." "Substantially limits" now requires a lower degree of limitation than was previously applied by the courts.

"Physical and mental impairment" includes physical disorders and conditions, disease, disfigurement, amputation affecting a vital body system, psychological disorders, mental retardation, mental illness, and learning disabilities. An individual can demonstrate that he or she is "regarded as" having a disability by establishing that he or she has been subjected to an action prohibited by the ADA "because of an actual or perceived physical or mental impairment whether or not the impairment limits or is perceived to limit a major life activity."

"Major life activities" include such activities as "caring for oneself, performing manual tasks, seeing, hearing, eating, sleeping, walking, standing, lifting, bending, speaking, breathing, learning, reading, concentrating, thinking, communicating and working." The definition also includes the operation of any major body function, including functions of the immune system, normal cell growth, and digestive, bowel, bladder, neurological, brain, respiratory, circulatory, endocrine, and reproductive functions. The determination of whether an impairment substantially limits a major life activity must be made without regard to the "ameliorative effects of mitigating measures"—that is, individuals who use medications, artificial limbs, or hearing aids qualify for protection under the ADA, even though those measures may overcome the limiting effects of an impairment. (Ordinary eyeglasses and contact lenses are specifically excluded from this list by the amendments to the ADA.) The ADA also states that an individual with an impairment that is "transitory and minor," defined as having an actual or expected duration of six months or less, does not fall under the ADA. However, individuals with impairments that are episodic or in remission, such as epilepsy, diabetes, or cancer are not barred from coverage under the ADA.

Not included by the ADA as protected disabilities are homosexuality, sexual behavior disorders, compulsive gambling, kleptomania, and disorders resulting from *current* drug or alcohol use. The emphasis on current drug or alcohol use means that employees who have successfully recovered or are successfully recovering from drug or alcohol disabilities are protected from employment discrimination.

The ADA prohibits employers of 15 or more employees (also unions with 15 or more members and employment agencies) from discriminating against the qualified disabled with respect to hiring, advancement, termination, compensation, training, or other terms, conditions, or privileges of employment. **Qualified disabled** are defined as those with a disability who, with or without reasonable accommodation, can perform the essential functions of a particular job position. Employers must make reasonable accommodation only for the *qualified* disabled.

The concept of "disability" includes mental disabilities and diseases as well as physical impairment.

Impairments, such as cancer, that are substantially limiting when active remain so despite being in remission.

According to the American Bar Association's *Mental & Physical Disability Law Reporter,* employers prevailed in 94.5 percent of 327 disability discrimination cases decided in federal courts across the United States in 2002.

Individuals with HIV or AIDS are protected by the ADA. Persons who are discriminated against because they are regarded as being HIV-positive are also protected.

Reasonable Accommodation under the ADA The ADA does not require employers to hire the unqualified disabled, but they must make reasonable accommodation so qualified disabled employees can succeed in the workplace. **Reasonable accommodation** is the process of adjusting a job or work environment to fit the needs of disabled employees. It may include:

- Making the work facilities accessible and usable to disabled employees.
- Restructuring jobs or modifying work schedules.
- Purchasing or modifying necessary equipment for use by the disabled.
- Providing appropriate training materials or assistance modified to fit the needs of disabled employees.

Note that an employer need make only reasonable accommodation for disabled employees. The employer can plead *undue hardship,* defined as "an action requiring significant difficulty or expense," as a reason for not accommodating the needs of disabled employees. The ADA specifies that in evaluating undue hardship, the cost of the accommodation, the resources of the employer, the size of the employer, and the nature of the employer's business be considered.

Businesses must reasonably accommodate not only *employees* for their disabilities under the ADA but also customers and others who use public facilities such as hotels, restaurants, theaters, schools (even private ones), most places of entertainment, offices providing services, and other establishments doing business with the public. The Supreme Court ruled that the Professional Golf Association had to accommodate golfer Casey Martin, who suffered a walking disability because of a circulatory disorder, by allowing him to use a golf cart in PGA tournaments. The Court held (1) that PGA tournaments were open to any member of the public who paid a qualifying fee and participated successfully in a qualifying tournament and (2) that accommodating Casey Martin by allowing him to use a golf cart while other golfers walked a tournament course did not "fundamentally alter the nature" of PGA tournament events.

>> *sidebar* 20.11

Chipotle Mexican Grill: Must Accommodate Disabled Patrons

The ADA prohibits discrimination in employment and in public accommodations. Maurizio Antoninetti, a patron of the Chipotle Mexican Grill, complained that a 45-inch barrier at Chipotle restaurants blocked his view of the counter, preventing him from inspecting each dish, choosing his order, and watching it be prepared.

Chipotle argued that it accommodated the needs of customers in wheelchairs by bringing them spoonfuls of their preferred dish for inspection before ordering.

This fell short of being adequate. The Ninth Circuit Court of Appeals held that the barrier "subjects disabled customers to a disadvantage that non-disabled customers do not suffer." The U.S. Supreme Court denied certiorari. Chipotle is retrofitting its restaurants with new counters to eliminate concerns regarding wheelchair accessibility.

The remedies under the ADA are basically the same remedies available under Title VII.

Remedies under the ADA   Remedies under the ADA are basically the same remedies available under the Civil Rights Act, including hiring, reinstatement, back pay, injunctive relief, and compensatory and punitive damages. As with the Civil Rights Act, a plaintiff must first seek administration remedies with the EEOC. Compensatory and punitive damages are not available for policies that mere have disparate impact. They are available for intentional discrimination and for other employer actions such as failing to make reasonable accommodation for known job applicant or employee disabilities.

The ADA replaces the Rehabilitation Act of 1973 as the primary federal law protecting the disabled. However, the Rehabilitation Act, which applies only to employers doing business with the government under a federal contract for $2,500 or more, still requires that such employers have a qualified affirmative action program for hiring and promoting the disabled.

15. GENETIC DISCRIMINATION

The **Genetic Information Nondiscrimination Act (GINA),** effective November 2009, prohibits covered employers from firing, refusing to hire, or otherwise discriminating against individuals on the basis of their genetic information, and from discriminating against employees and applicants on the basis of a family member's genetic information. Genetic information includes information about an individual's genetic tests; genetic information about genetic tests of an individual's family members; information about the manifestation of a disease or disorder in an individual's family history; request for or receipt of genetic services; and genetic information of a fetus and the genetic information of any embryo held by the individual or a family member.

"Covered employers" is defined as all employers subject to Title VII. The act further prohibits the limitation, segregation, or classification of employees in such a way "that would deprive or tend to deprive any employee of employment opportunities or otherwise adversely affect the status of the employee as an employee, because of genetic information with respect to the employee."

Under GINA, it is unlawful for an employer to "request, require, or purchase genetic information with respect to an employee or the family member of an employee," with limited exceptions.

GINA also has ramifications for group health plans and health insurance companies. Although many states have already enacted similar legislation, GINA establishes a federal baseline for protection against employment discrimination based on genetic information.

In November 2010, the EEOC published final regulations implementing Title II of GINA, which protects applicants for employment, current employees, former employees, apprentices, trainees and labor organization members against discrimination based on their genetic information. The EEOC regulations, which became effective on January 11, 2011, are intended to:

- Prohibit the use of genetic information in employment decisions
- Restrict employers from requesting, requiring, or purchasing genetic information

- Require that genetic information be maintained as a confidential medical records and place strict limits on the disclosure of genetic information
- Provide remedies for individuals whose genetic information is acquired, used or disclosed in violation of GINA

Tests that are considered to be "genetic tests" under GINA include:

- Tests that might determine if a person is genetically disposed to breast cancer, colon cancer or Huntington's Disease
- Amniocentesis and newborn screening
- Carrier screening for cystic fibrosis, sickle cell anemia, spinal muscular dystrophy, and fragile X syndrome
- DNA testing to detect genetic markers associated with ancestry information

>> sidebar 20.12

Protecting Against Inadvertent Acquisition of Medical Information in Violation of GINA

Employers should incorporate the following language into FMLA and other forms to establish a defense to any claim that it wrongfully obtained genetic information in response to an otherwise lawful request for medical information:

The Genetic Information Nondiscrimination Act of 2008 (GINA) prohibits employers and other entities covered by GINA Title II from requesting or requiring genetic information of an individual or family member of the individual, except as specifically allowed by this law. To comply with this law, we are asking

that you not provide any genetic information when responding to this request for medical information. 'Genetic information' as defined by GINA, includes an individual's family medical history, the results of an individual's or family member's genetic tests, the fact that an individual or an individual's family member sought or received genetic services, and genetic information of a fetus carried by an individual or an individual's family member or an embryo lawfully held by an individual or family member receiving assistive reproductive services.

16. DISCRIMINATION IN GETTING AND KEEPING HEALTH INSURANCE

A new act prohibits group health plans and health insurance issuers from discriminating against employees based on certain factors. The Health Insurance Portability and Accountability Act (HIPAA) forbids group plans and issuers from excluding an employee from insurance coverage or requiring different premiums based on the employee's health status, medical condition or history, genetic information, or disability.

The act primarily prevents discrimination against individual employees in small businesses. Before the act, individual employees with an illness like cancer or a genetic condition like sickle cell anemia were sometimes denied coverage in a new health plan. The small size of the plan deterred insurers from covering individual employees whose medical condition might produce large claims. The act denies insurers the right to discriminate on this basis. It also guarantees that insured employees who leave their old employer and join a new employer are not denied health insurance. As of this writing, the exact meanings of many HIPAA provisions are still unclear.

Note, however, that the act only applies to prevent discrimination in group health insurance plans. It does not apply to individuals who purchase individual health insurance. Congress is considering legislation to extend HIPAA's antidiscrimination provisions to individual insurance. Behind HIPAA and proposals for new legislation is the concern that new forms of genetic testing will allow insurers and employers to identify and discriminate against individuals who may in the future develop certain medical conditions.

17. OTHER FEDERAL LEGISLATION

Other federal legislation dealing with employment discrimination includes the National Labor Relations Act of 1936. The National Labor Relations Board has ruled that appeals to racial prejudice in a collective bargaining representation election constitute an unfair labor practice. The NLRB has also revoked the certification of unions that practice discriminatory admission or representation policies. Additionally, employers have an obligation to bargain with certified unions over matters of employment discrimination. Such matters are considered "terms and conditions of employment" and are thus mandatory bargaining issues.

Finally, various other federal agencies may prohibit discriminatory employment practices under their authorizing statutes. The Federal Communications Commission, for example, has prohibited employment discrimination by its licensees (radio and TV stations) and has required the submission of affirmative action plans as a condition of license renewal.

18. STATE ANTIDISCRIMINATION LAWS

LO 20-5

State antidiscrimination laws may permit discrimination lawsuits against employers of fewer than 15 employees, the minimum number for a lawsuit under federal Title VII.

According to a study by the Rudd Center at Yale University, discrimination against overweight people, particularly women, is as common as racial discrimination.

Federal laws concerning equal employment opportunity specifically permit state laws imposing additional duties and liabilities. In recent years, fair employment practices legislation has been introduced and passed by many state legislatures. When the federal Equal Employment Opportunity Act became effective, 40 states had such laws, but their provisions varied considerably. A typical state act makes it an unfair employment practice for any employer to refuse to hire or otherwise discriminate against any individual because of his or her race, color, religion, national origin, or ancestry. If employment agencies or labor organizations discriminate against an individual in any way because of one of these reasons, they are also guilty of an unfair employment practice. State acts usually set up an administrative body, generally known as the Fair Employment Practices Commission, which has the power to make rules and regulations and hear and decide charges of violations filed by complainants.

State antidiscrimination laws sometimes protect categories of persons not protected by federal law. For example, some protect persons from employment discrimination based on weight.

As discussed earlier, state and local law may prohibit sexual orientation discrimination in the workplace (see Sidebar 20.9). Other state and local laws prohibit employment discrimination based on weight (e.g., Michigan; Santa Cruz and San Francisco, California; and Washington DC). Michigan's antidiscrimination discrimination law also includes height and weight.

State law may also supplement Title VII, offering remedies to victims of sexual harassment. In New York, for example, former Knicks team executive Anucha Browne Sanders sued the owner of the New York Knicks and Madison Square Garden for discrimination using Title VII, as well as New York State Human Rights Law, New York Executive Law §296, and the Administrative Code of the City of New York §8-107, which prohibit unlawful discriminatory practices. After hearing testimony about crude racial and sexual insults and unwanted advances from coach Isiah Thomas, a jury awarded Sanders $11.6 million.

As indicated in Chapter 10 on torts, discrimination plaintiffs can also sue employers under various state common law causes of action, like negligence, assault, battery, intentional infliction of mental distress, invasion of privacy, and defamation. Under common law, plaintiffs may be able to receive unlimited compensatory and punitive damages, and greater numbers of plaintiffs seem to be suing under common law. In Las Vegas a jury awarded over $5 million against the Hilton Hotel and in favor of a plaintiff who had been sexually groped at an aviators' Tailhook convention. The jury determined that the hotel had been negligent in failing to provide adequate security.

> **Do** remember that discrimination lawsuits can be based on multiple causes of action, including common law ones.

19. TRENDS IN EMPLOYMENT DISCRIMINATION AND LITIGATION

Several current trends in employment discrimination and litigation will require close attention from managers in the coming years. These trends highlight the fact that the workforce is increasingly diverse and that new managers must be alert to the full impact of antidiscrimination laws. They also show the effects of new technology.

Surge in Private Lawsuits   Private lawsuits alleging discrimination in employment surged in recent years, more than tripling. Several factors account for the rapid increase. The 1991 revision of the Civil Rights Act to support punitive and compensatory damages has encouraged employees to sue their employers. The passage of the Americans with Disabilities Act has led to a new area of discrimination lawsuits, and some 50 million Americans, according to a conservative estimate, may legally qualify as disabled. Finally, as the large generation of baby boomers ages in the workforce, more lawsuits arise under the Age Discrimination in Employment Act. In the new century, these trends continue, making it ever more important for business managers to understand the law prohibiting discrimination in employment. See Sidebar 20.13 for an interesting study about female CEOs.

>> *sidebar* 20.13

Is It Important to Investors If the CEO Is a Man or a Woman?

The clear answer is, unfortunately, "Yes" according to a study by Lyda Bigelow and Judi McLean Parks at the Olin School of Business, Washington University in St. Louis.

Bigelow and McLean Parks created a prospectus for a fictitious company about to go public, along with a set of qualifications for the company's CEO. To determine if gender played a role in the decision, they gave half of the potential investors information with a female CEO and the other half a male CEO—the qualifications, however, were the same. Only the name and gender were different. They then asked individuals with a background in finance to consider investing in the company.

The researchers found that the CEO's gender clearly affected potential investors. For example, the study showed that the participants were inclined to invest up to three times more with the company with the male CEO. Executive compensation was also an issue. The participants in the study indicated that they would pay the female CEO 14 percent less than her male counterpart.

Perhaps even more disturbing, female CEOs were evaluated more harshly in other very subjective categories. Although the only difference given in the study was gender, participants deemed female CEOs as less competent leaders in a variety of realms, including handling a crisis and dealing with the company's board of directors.

Overall, the study showed that participants viewed male CEOs as more favorable representatives of the company in the public eye.

Source: *U.S. News and World Report,* www.usnews.com/usnews/ biztech/articles/060508/8investment_bias.htm.

Arbitration in Employment Discrimination Disputes Arbitration is usually cheaper, quicker, and less public than litigation. Accustomed to using arbitration clauses in contracts with customers and suppliers, many employers also have begun placing arbitration clauses in employment contracts and personnel handbooks. These clauses require arbitration in employment discrimination disputes and with other employment controversies.

The Federal Arbitration Act (see Chapter 5) prefers arbitration over litigation, but that act may not apply to certain employment contracts. The EEOC has issued a policy statement concluding that "agreements that mandate binding arbitration of discrimination claims as a condition of employment are contrary to the fundamental principles" of antidiscrimination laws.

However, without specifically discussing the EEOC's policy statement, the Supreme Court has upheld arbitration clauses in certain employment discrimination cases. In *Circuit City Stores, Inc. v. Adams,* 532 U.S. 105 (2001), the Supreme Court decided that the Federal Arbitration Act did not prohibit enforceability of the following arbitration provision, which an employee had signed in his job application:

> I agree that I will settle any and all previously unasserted claims, disputes or controversies arising out of or relating to my application or candidacy for employment, employment and/or cessation of employment with Circuit City, *exclusively* by final and binding *arbitration* before a neutral arbitrator. By way of example only, such claims include claims under federal, state, and local statutory or common law, such as the Age Discrimination in Employment Act, Title VII of the Civil Rights Act of 1964, as amended, including the amendments of the Civil Rights Act of 1991, the Americans with Disabilities Act, the law of contract and the law of tort.

Congress may ultimately decide whether binding arbitration as a condition of working for an employer is an acceptable part of the employment contract. In the meantime, employers who wish to have employment disputes, including discrimination disputes, arbitrated should consider the following:

- Paying employees separately from the employment contract to sign arbitration agreements.
- Ensuring that arbitration agreements allow for the same range of remedies contained in the antidiscrimination laws.
- Allowing limited discovery in arbitration, which traditionally has no discovery process.
- Permitting employees to participate in selecting neutral, knowledgeable professional arbitrators instead of using an industry arbitration panel.
- Not requiring the employee to pay arbitration fees and costs.

These steps should go far toward eliminating many of the objections to the arbitration of employment discrimination disputes.

Proper arbitration agreements should continue to be considered as a business response to discrimination in employment disputes. Interestingly, at least one study has found that employees alleging discrimination win more often before arbitration panels than before juries and only two-thirds of the time.

Insuring against Employment Discrimination Claims

Employers commonly insure against many potential liabilities. However, the general liability policies carried by many businesses, which cover bodily injury and property damage, often do not insure against intentional torts. Intent is a key element in many employment discrimination claims. In addition, general policies may not cover the back pay or damages for mental anguish that many discrimination plaintiffs seek. As a result, employers are beginning to ask for and get employment practices liability insurance, a type of insurance aimed specifically at discrimination claims.

Even with the availability of the new insurance, not all types of employment discrimination can be insured against in every state. States like New York and California do not permit companies to insure against "intentional acts." Disparate treatment discrimination is an example of such an act. Similarly, some states do not permit companies to insure against punitive damages that can arise in intentional violations of Title VII. Managers should also be aware that what the new policies cover and what they exclude vary widely.

> Insurance policies are more likely to insure against disparate impact claims rather than disparate treatment claims. Do you understand why?

concept >> *summary*

Illegal Employment Practices

Unless bona fide occupational qualifications or business necessity can be proved, federal law prohibits recruiting, hiring, promoting, and other employment practices that involve disparate treatment or produce a disparate impact on the basis of:

- Race or color.
- National origin.
- Religion.

- Sex.
- Test scores and educational requirements.
- Height and weight.
- Appearance.
- Age.
- Disabilities.

>> Key Terms

Affirmative action 666
Bona fide occupational
   qualifications (BFOQs) 646
Business necessity defense 649
Comparable worth 662
Disability 672
Disparate impact 648

Disparate treatment 648
Genetic Information
   Nondiscrimination Act
   (GINA) 674
Hostile work environment 659
Qualified disabled 672

Reasonable
   accommodation 673
Retaliation 649
Reverse discrimination 667
Section 1981 668
Seniority system 668
Sexual harassment 659

>> Review Questions and Problems

The Civil Rights Act of 1964

1. *General Provisions*

   Martel, a competent male secretary to the president of ICU, was fired because the new president of the company believed it is more appropriate to have a female secretary.

   (a) Has a violation of the law occurred?

   (b) Assume that a violation of the law has occurred and Martel decided to take an extended vacation after he was fired. Upon his return seven months later, Martel filed suit in federal district court against ICU, charging illegal discrimination under the Civil Rights Act of 1964. What remedies will be available to him under the act?

2. *Enforcement Procedures*

   Muscles-Are-You, Inc., a bodybuilding spa targeted primarily toward male bodybuilders, refused to hire a woman for the position of executive director. The spa's management stated that the executive director must have a "macho" image to relate well with the spa's customers. Discuss whether it is likely that the spa has violated Title VII.

3. *Discrimination on the Basis of Race or Color*

   Does Title VII prohibit employment discrimination against members of all races? Explain.

4. *Discrimination on the Basis of National Origin*

   Ace Tennis Co. hires only employees who speak English. Does this policy illegally discriminate against Hispanic job applicants who speak only Spanish? Discuss.

5. *Discrimination on the Basis of Religion*

   Ortega, an employee of ABC, Inc., recently joined a church that forbids working on Saturdays, Sundays, and Mondays. Ortega requested that his employer change his work schedule from eight-hour days, Monday through Friday, to ten-hour days, Tuesday through Friday. Ortega's request was refused because the employer is in operation only eight hours per day, five days a week. After a month during which Ortega failed to work on Mondays, he was fired. The employer stated that "only a full-time employee would be acceptable" for Ortega's position. What are Ortega's legal rights, if any?

6. *Discrimination on the Basis of Sex*

   A male supervisor at Star Company made repeated offensive sexual remarks to female employees. The employees complained to higher management, which ignored the complaints. If the company does not discharge or otherwise penalize the employee, has it violated Title VII? Discuss.

Employment Practices That May Be Challenged

7. *Questionnaires, Interviews, Testing, and Educational Requirements*

   Jennings Company, which manufactures sophisticated electronic equipment, hires its assembly employees on the basis of applicants' scores on a standardized mathematics aptitude test. It has been shown that those who score higher on the test almost always perform better on the job. However, it has also been demonstrated that the use of the test in hiring employees has the effect of excluding African Americans and other minority groups. Is this practice of the Jennings Company prohibited by the Civil Rights Act of 1964?

8. *Height and Weight Requirements*

   (a) An employer hires job applicants to wait tables in the Executive Heights Restaurant only if they are over 6 feet tall. Does this policy likely violate Title VII? Explain.

   (b) If a class of job applicants under 6 feet sues the employer, will it likely get compensatory and punitive damages? Explain.

9. *Appearance Requirements*

   Silicon Products requires all male employees to wear their hair "off the collar." Does this policy violate Title VII? Discuss.

10. *Affirmative Action Programs and Reverse Discrimination*

    Kartel, Inc., found that historically African Americans had been significantly underrepresented in its workforce. It decided to remedy the situation and place African Americans in 50 percent of all new job openings. Discuss the legality of Kartel's action.

11. *Seniority Systems*

    Are seniority systems in the workplace legal under Title VII if in fact they discriminate on the basis of gender or race? Explain.

Other Statutes and Discrimination in Employment

12. *Civil Rights Act of 1866*

    When is it an advantage for a plaintiff to use Section 1981 as the basis for discrimination litigation as contrasted with using Title VII?

13. *Discrimination on the Basis of Age*

    Cantrell, the controller of Xylec's, Inc., was forced to retire at age 58 due to a general company policy. Although Cantrell has a company pension of $50,000 per year, she believes that her lifestyle will soon be hampered due to inflation, since the pension provides for no cost-of-living increases. What are Cantrell's rights, if any?

14. *Discrimination on the Basis of Disabilities*

    Ralph is a systems analyst for the Silicon Corporation, a major defense contractor. When Ralph's co-workers learn that he has AIDS, six of them quit work immediately. Fearing that additional resignations will delay production, the company discharges Ralph. Discuss whether or not the company acted legally.

15. *Genetic Discrimination*

    Amy learns that she has the "breast cancer gene." Devastated, she shares the news with her supervisor. A few days later, Amy receives a harsh employment evaluation—the first of her career—criticizing her handling of a client matter. Two weeks later, Amy is fired. Amy cannot understand how she went from being a model employee with strong performance reviews to unemployed in such a short time. Does she have any claim against her employer?

16. *Discrimination in Getting and Keeping Health Insurance*

    Why does Title VII not apply to preventing discrimination in the getting and keeping of health insurance?

17. *Other Federal Legislation*

    Do employers have an obligation to negotiate with groups of employees over issues of discrimination? Explain.

18. *State Antidiscrimination Laws*

    Explain how state antidiscrimination laws protect workers in situations where federal laws do not.

19. *Trends in Employment Discrimination and Litigation*

    Can arbitration agreements be used to keep employees from litigating discrimination issues? Discuss.

business >> *discussions*

1. When Maria Suarez got her new job, she was happy. As an oil rigger, she would make enough money to support herself and her two children. But after a week of working with a primarily male crew, her happiness was gone. Her co-workers were the reason. At first the men made unwelcome comments about her body. Then sexual graffiti mentioning her name appeared. When she came to work one morning a nude female picture was pinned to one of the rigs. Her name had been scrawled across the bottom. Maria complained to the crew foreman, who referred her to the site manager. "Let's ignore it for a while," he told Maria. "It's just good fun. The men are testing you. You've got to fit in."

What are Maria's legal rights in this situation?
What would you do if you were the site manager?
Do you think Maria should just try to "fit in"?

2. Delivery Quik, Inc., delivers packages to small retail stores from a central distribution point in a major metropolitan area. Drivers both load and unload their packages, some of which weigh close to 100 pounds. Although equipment helps the drivers in their tasks, there is still considerable lifting necessary. Delivery Quik has a policy that drivers must stand at least 6 feet tall and weigh no less than 180 pounds. All drivers must retire at age 45 and have at least a high school education.

Does the height, weight, age, and education policy discriminate illegally?
How would you change the policy?
If your customers prefer male drivers, does their preference mean that the company can hire only males as drivers?

CHAPTER FOUR

The American Legal System

After completing this chapter, students will be able to:

1. Describe the importance of law to private enterprise.

2. Compare and contrast the objectives of law in society.

3. Differentiate the elements of a case brief.

4. Distinguish between substantive and procedural law.

5. Differentiate constitutional law, case law, and statutory law.

6. Compare and contrast civil and criminal law.

7. Describe the elements of the basic court system structure.

8. Explain the purposes of subject matter and personal jurisdiction as requirements for a court's power to hear a dispute.

9. Describe the typical steps in the civil trial process.

10. Distinguish trials and appeals.

11. Identify dispute resolution alternatives to trials.

Introduction

Presumably we can agree that some business behavior is bad for America. This text examines what should be done to change that behavior. The fundamental options in the United States have been fourfold: Let the market "regulate" the behavior; leave the problem to the individual decision maker's own ethical dictates; pass a law; or rely on some combination of the market, ethics, and law. Market regulation was discussed in Chapter 1. Self-regulation through ethics was explored in Chapters 2 and 3. This chapter begins the discussion of the legal regulation of business with a brief outline of the

American legal system. We will also look at alternative conflict resolution processes such as negotiation, mediation, and arbitration that do not resort to the legal system. We begin by reminding ourselves of the indispensable role of law in fostering business practice.

Law and the Market　Whatever we may think about lawyers, judges and America's dispute resolution methods, the crucial role of a reliable legal system in fostering and maintaining capitalism is indisputable. The following law review excerpt explains.

READING　The Importance of Law to the Private Enterprise System

Deb Ballam

Nobel economist Frederich von Hayek describes the theoretical importance of law to private enterprise. According to Hayek, law that secures property rights in modern society is a prerequisite to private enterprise. Without the order of law enforcing private property ownership and facilitating the transfer of property rights, business enterprise in a complex, heterogeneous culture is simply infeasible.

The importance of law to the conduct of private enterprise is evident in economic developments in . . . the Republic of China. In moving from state-controlled to private enterprise, [China] faced substantial difficulties arising from the lack of a legal system that would secure property ownership and the contractual transfer of property rights.

. . . China's economy has grown steadily in recent years. Minxin Pei, a political scientist at Princeton University, explains law's contribution to that growth: "Legal reform has become one of the most important institutional changes in China since the late 1970s. . . . Within China, the changing legal institutions have begun to play an increasingly important role in governing economic activities, resolving civil disputes, enforcing law and order, and setting the boundaries between the power of the state and the autonomy of society. . . ."

Of course, the importance of law to private enterprise goes far beyond its initial support as an institutional framework guaranteeing ownership rights. As the market system grows more complex both nationally and internationally, the legal recognition of promise keeping becomes increasingly

significant in facilitating business. A condition for emerging economies entering international trade is learning how to keep promises to strangers, and whether enforced through litigation or arbitration, promise keeping in business requires the ordering presence of contract law.

In a democracy, law is important to business for another reason quite separate from its function in establishing ownership rights and facilitating promise keeping necessary to their transfer: It provides the formal expression of democratic social will. That expression implicates private enterprise in a plethora of ways, including regulation of the environment, employment laws, securities regulation, consumer protection statutes, and product liability. As contemporary society becomes increasingly diverse, law grows, not diminishes, in its importance to private enterprise; and in spite of valid concerns about the impact of law on efficiency, future business managers will need to know more, not less, about how law affects business operations. No evidence suggests any other conclusion.

Source: Deb Ballam, quoting from "The Importance of Law to the Private Enterprise System," *The American Legal Studies in Business Task Force Report* by O. Lee Reed. *American Business Law Journal* 36, no. 1 (Fall 1998), p. ix. Reprinted by permission.

Questions

1. *a.* Do you expect to see greater reliance on law as our society becomes increasingly complex?
   b. Can you think of any meaningful substitutes for law as we now practice it? Explain.

Part One—Legal Foundations

Objectives of the Law

Americans differ dramatically in their views of the role the law should play in contemporary life. For some, the courts and the police primarily act as obstructions to personal freedom and to a fully efficient marketplace. Others seek much more law to ensure that everyone is cared for who is in need and everyone is sheltered from wrongdoers. We are in constant conflict about the law's precise path in our lives, but most of us can agree on some foundational expectations for a fair, efficient legal system. Certainly we expect the law to *maintain order* in our diverse, rapidly changing society. Of course, we rely on law to peacefully, fairly, and intelligently *resolve conflict.* Perhaps less obvious, but no less important, the law serves to *preserve dominant values.* Americans differ about core values, but we have reached a workable accord about our most fundamental beliefs. Some of those, such as freedom of speech, press, and religion, are guaranteed by our Bill of Rights, thus setting a steady foundation for an enduring nation. We can see that the law is a vital force in *guaranteeing freedom.* (But freedom can be confusing: Are you free to smoke wherever you wish, or do I have a right to smoke-free air?)

Justice

Broadly, we count on the law to *achieve and preserve justice.* The pursuit of justice often relies on honorable, efficient government. The World Justice Project's 2010 "Rule of Law Index" ranks governmental quality by such measures as access to justice, clear and stable laws, open government, and limited corruption. Among the 35 countries studied, Sweden and The Netherlands ranked particularly well. In most categories, the United States ranked near the bottom of the 11 high-income nations studied.[1] Perhaps the study is correct in the sense that America still has abundant room for improvement. Nonetheless, Americans can properly be proud of a long struggle to build a more just society for all. Efforts, for example, to curb discrimination, guarantee due process, reduce violence, protect those in need, maintain order and security, build fair, efficient regulatory systems and respect the rights of all are central practices in an extraordinarily complex and rapidly evolving American culture. As you read this chapter, ask yourself repeatedly, "Does this rule (this procedure, this case) contribute to the search for justice?" In the end, all legal studies must involve the search for justice. [For a daily update of legal news, see **http://www.law.com**]

> All legal studies must involve the search for justice.

Question

In 2010, a New York City lower court judge ruled that a four-year-old girl can be sued for negligence. According to *The New York Times,* the young girl was riding her bicycle with training wheels on a Manhattan sidewalk. She joined in a race against a five-year-old boy during which the children struck an 87-year-old woman who suffered a hip injury requiring surgery. The woman died three months later of unrelated causes. Both children were under the supervision of their mothers.

The girl's attorney argued that she was too young to be responsible for negligent actions and that she was not engaging in an adult activity at the time of the injury. The judge cited cases dating back to 1928 in concluding that the girl could be sued. The judge noted that children under the age of four are conclusively presumed to be incapable of negligence, but he was unwilling to extend that presumption to the girl who was three months shy of her fifth birthday. (The other child and his mother did not seek dismissal of the negligence action against them.)

As a matter of justice, do you think a four-year-old child should be the subject of a negligence action? Explain. See Alan Feuer, "4-Year-Old Can Be Sued, Judge Rules in Bike Case," *The New York Times,* October 28, 2010 [**http://www.nytimes.com/**].

Too Many Rules in Britain?

All societies struggle to find the proper balance between personal freedom and legal intervention. Great Britain created its antisocial behavior orders (ASBOs) in 1998 to discourage "loutish," conduct involving minor offenses. The government's Antisocial Behavior Action Plan is designed to address everyday headaches from "nuisance neighbors" to begging to graffiti. The orders have been used to ban thousands of people, some as young as 10, from associating with certain people or engaging in activities as varied as shouting, swearing, spray-painting, playing loud music, and walking down certain streets. Breaching an order is a crime, potentially punishable by time in prison. The ASBOs have also reached unusual situations including a woman whose noisy sex disturbed her neighbors, a 60-year-old man who was banned from dressing as a schoolgirl, and a militant atheist who was banned from taking religiously offensive material (e.g., images of religious figures in sexual poses) in a public place. One official summed up the frustration that led to the ASBOs:

> We are not talking about high jinks from a few mischievous youngsters—we are talking about yobs whose persistent criminal activity, intimidation and plain disregard for others are making our city centres a no-go area.

In 2010 after a change in government, British Home Secretary Theresa May said that it was time to review the system: "We need to make anti-social behavior what it once was—abnormal and something to stand up to . . . rather than frequent and tolerated." The opposition Labor Party, however, said that the ASBOs had made a "huge contribution" to curbing crime.

Question

Do we need more rules, perhaps something like ASBOs, to regulate obnoxious, annoying behavior in America? Explain.

Sources: Jill Lawless, Associated Press, "Britain Tries to Rein in Louts with Bans on Misbehavior," *The Des Moines Register,* September 1, 2004, p. 5A; Philip Johnston, "Blair's Asbo Is Failing to Tame a Hard Core of Offenders," *The Daily Telegraph (London),* December 7, 2006, p. 12 (News); and "Time to 'Move Beyond' Asbos, Says Home Secretary May," BBC News, July 28, 2010 [**http://www.bbc.co.uk/news/**].

Primary Sources of Law

United States law is a vast and constantly growing, mutating body of rules and reason. That law is derived from four primary sources: constitutions, statutes, regulations, and cases (called the *common law* or judge-made law).

Constitutions

These are the supreme expressions of law at both the federal and state levels of government. All other law is subordinate to federal constitutional law. Among other things, constitutions prescribe the general structure of governments and provide protection for individual rights. Chapters 5 and 8 give extensive attention to the U.S. Constitution and the Bill of Rights.

Statutes

These are laws that are adopted by legislative bodies, particularly congress and the state legislatures. City councils enact statutes that usually are called *ordinances*. Legislators and the statutes they enact shape the policy direction of American law. Of course, legislators are not free of constraints. Federal legislation cannot conflict with the U.S. Constitution, and state legislation cannot violate either federal law or the constitutions of that state and the nation.

Regulations

Administrative agencies include such bodies as the Federal Trade Commission and the Securities and Exchange Commission at the federal level, and a Public Service Commission (to regulate utilities) and a Human Rights Commission (to address discrimination problems) at the state level. These agencies have the specialized expertise to carry out much of the day-to-day business of government. Among other duties, they produce and oversee regulations that add the details needed to implement the broader mandates provided by federal and state statutes. (For more detail, see Chapter 8.)

Common Law (Also Called Case Law or Judge-Made Law)

Our case law has its roots in the early English king's courts, where rules of law gradually developed out of a series of individual dispute resolutions. That body of law, the common law, was imported to America where it is has grown and evolved as the courts address the constantly changing legal requirements of our complex society.

The development of English common law and American judicial decisions into a just, ordered package is attributable in large measure to reliance on the doctrine of *stare decisis* (let the decision stand). That is, judges endeavor to follow the precedents established by previous decisions. Following precedent, however, is not mandatory. As societal beliefs change, so does the law. For example, a U.S. Supreme Court decision approving racially separate but equal education was eventually overruled by a Supreme Court decision mandating integrated schools. Nonetheless, the principle of stare decisis is generally adhered to because of its beneficial effect. It offers the wisdom of the past and enhances efficiency by eliminating the need for resolving every case as though it were the first of its kind. Stare decisis affords stability and predictability to the law.

The Case Law: Locating and Analyzing

To prepare for the *Nichols* case, which follows, a bit of practical guidance should be useful. The study of law is founded largely on the analysis of judicial opinions. Except for the federal level and a few states, trial court decisions are filed locally for public inspection rather than being published. Appellate (appeals court) opinions, on the other hand, are generally published in volumes called *reports*. State court opinions are found in the reports of that state, and in a regional reporter series published by West Publishing Company that divides the United States into units, such as South Eastern (S.E.) and Pacific (P.).

Within the appropriate reporter, the cases are cited by case name, volume, reporter name, and page number. For example, *Nichols v. Niesen,* 746 N.W.2d 220 (Wisc. S. Ct. 2008) means that the opinion will be found in volume 746 of the North Western Reporter, 2nd series, at page 220 and that the decision was reached in 2008 by the Wisconsin Supreme Court. Federal court decisions are found in several reporters, including the *Federal Reporter* and the *United States Supreme Court Reports.* In practice, of course, those cases can most readily be found via a standard search engine or in online databases such as LexisNexis and Westlaw. [For broad databases of law topics, see **http://www.findlaw.com,http://www.yahoo.com/government/law or www.justia.com**]

Briefing the Case

Most students find the preparation of *case briefs* (outlines or digests) to be helpful in mastering the law. A brief should evolve into the form that best suits the individual student's needs. The following approach should be a useful starting point:

1. Parties   Identify the plaintiff and the defendant at the trial level. At the appeals level, identify the appellant (the party bringing the appeal; Nichols, in this instance) and the appellee (the other party on appeal; Niesen, in this instance).

2. Facts   Summarize only those facts critical to the outcome of the case.

3. Procedure   How did the case reach this court? Who won in the lower court(s)?

4. Issue   Note the central question or questions on which the case turns.

5. Holding   How did the court resolve the issue(s)? Who won?

6. Reasoning   Explain the logic that supported the court's decision.

LEGAL BRIEFCASE — Nichols v. Niesen
746 N.W.2d 220 (Wisc. S. Ct. 2008)

Justice N. Patrick Crooks

The court of appeals allowed the claim of Shannon, Lee, Brooke, and Brittney Nichols (the Nichols) to proceed against the Niesens for common-law negligence. The Nichols claimed that the Niesens were social hosts, who did not provide any alcoholic beverages to underage guests, but allegedly were aware that minors were on their property consuming alcoholic beverages. After leaving the Niesens' premises, one of these guests allegedly caused injuries while driving intoxicated. The circuit court had granted the Niesens' . . . motion to dismiss the Nichols' complaint, after concluding that the complaint failed to state a claim in common-law negligence. The primary issue upon review is whether a claim for common-law negli-

gence should be permitted against social hosts under these circumstances.

I

On June 5, 2004, the Nichols were in a motor vehicle on County Trunk Highway J in Columbia County, Wisconsin, when that vehicle was struck by another motor vehicle, driven by Beth Carr (Carr), which had crossed the highway's center line. The Nichols alleged that the accident was caused by Carr's "failure to properly manage and control the vehicle she was operating, due in part to the voluntary ingestion by her of intoxicating beverages." As a result of the accident, Shannon Nichols "suffered very severe personal injuries," and Brittney, Brooke, and Lee Nichols "suffered injuries requiring medical care and treatment."

On the night of June 4, 2004, and into the early morning of June 5, 2004, the Nichols alleged that "a large gathering of underage high school students" congregated and consumed alcohol at the premises controlled by the Niesens. . . . [T]he Nichols alleged that "the Niesens were aware that the minors on their property were consuming alcohol." The Nichols did not allege that the Niesens knew, in advance, that the students would be consuming alcohol. The Nichols contended that the Niesens "had a duty to supervise and monitor the activities on their property" and that they were negligent because they failed to do so.

The Nichols contended that the consumption of alcohol by Carr was a substantial factor in causing the accident. Defendant Michael Shumate (Shumate), "or one or more adult residents of his household[,]" not the Niesens, was alleged to have provided the alcohol that was consumed by Carr on the Niesens' property. There was no allegation that Shumate was at the Niesens' property.

II (OMITTED-ED.)

III

On review, the Nichols claim that the Niesens' conduct was negligent, and that it was reasonably foreseeable that someone drinking on the Niesens' property would cause an accident. . . .

[T]he Niesens argue that knowledge of someone drinking on one's premises does not create a foreseeable risk of harm to others, and that public policy issues preclude liability in cases such as this one. The Niesens argue that the court of appeals created a new basis of liability for social hosts in Wisconsin. They argue that social hosts have never been held liable in Wisconsin solely because they were aware that an underage person had been consuming alcohol. To allow the court of appeals' decision to stand would mean that liability would apply to any social hosts who knew of underage drinking, regardless of where the alcohol was possessed or consumed, which would lead to liability with no sensible stopping point. The Niesens argue that they had limited involvement with the party outside of their alleged knowledge of underage drinking at the party, and, as a result, they should not be held liable. To hold social hosts liable in such circumstances would place an unreasonable burden on social hosts. The Niesens argue that a reasonable person would not foresee that knowledge of some unidentified underage person drinking would create an unreasonable risk to others. Rather, a reasonable person would conclude that any such risk was created by the provider of the alcohol and the underage drinker. The Niesens contend that, because they played no role in procuring or furnishing the alcohol, a negligence analysis should not be applied to their actions in this matter. Finally, the Niesens argue that the legislature, not the judiciary, is the branch of Wisconsin's government that should impose any new liability on social hosts who do not provide alcoholic beverages to underage guests.

Whether the Nichols' complaint states a claim for common-law negligence depends on whether they sufficiently pled facts, which if proven true, would establish all four required elements of an actionable negligence claim. First, the plaintiff must establish "'the existence of a duty of care on the part of the defendant. . . .'" Second, the plaintiff must establish that the defendant breached that duty of care. Third, the plaintiff must establish "'a causal connection between the defendant's breach of the duty of care and the plaintiffs injury. . . .'" Fourth, the plaintiff must establish that he or she suffered an actual loss or damage that resulted from the breach.

* * * * *

The court of appeals framed the issue for the first element of the test for common-law negligence as "whether the Niesens owed a duty to refrain from knowingly permitting minors to consume alcohol on their property, thus enabling them, including Carr, to drive away from their property while intoxicated." As a result, the court held that the first factor had been met because "it was reasonably foreseeable that permitting underage high school students to illegally drink alcohol on the Niesens' property would result in harm to some person or something," and because the Nichols had adequately "alleged the Niesens had a duty to refrain from knowingly permitting underage high school students from engaging in illegal alcohol consumption on their property."

[T]he court of appeals also determined that the Nichols had appropriately alleged the second factor of an actionable common-law negligence claim, which is that the Niesens had breached a duty of care that they owed to the Nichols. The court stated, "Because the Nichols' complaint alleges the Niesens knowingly permitted and failed to supervise underage alcohol consumption on their property, it alleges 'a breach of their duty to exercise ordinary care.'" . . .

The court also held that the Nichols had established the third factor of a common-law negligence claim by showing "'a causal connection between the defendant's breach of the duty of care and the plaintiff's injury. . . .'" That court stated, "The Nichols have sufficiently alleged that the Niesens' permitting underage alcohol consumption on their property was a substantial factor in causing the automobile accident that resulted in their injuries."

The court of appeals further held that the Nichols had appropriately alleged the fourth factor of a common-law negligence claim, that they had suffered an actual loss or damage that resulted from the Niesens' breach. . . .

For purposes of our public policy analysis, we will assume, without deciding, that the court of appeals was correct in holding that the Nichols had stated a common-law negligence claim. [E]ven if a plaintiff adequately establishes all four elements of a common-law negligence claim, Wisconsin courts have "reserved the right to deny the existence of a negligence claim based on public policy reasons...." As a result, "even if all the elements for a claim of negligence are proved, or liability for negligent conduct is assumed by the court, the court nonetheless may preclude liability based on public policy factors." This is so because "'negligence and liability are distinct concepts.'"

In turning to our analysis of the public policy factors that bear on the Nichols' common-law negligence claim against the Niesens, it is instructive to note what is not alleged by the Nichols. The Nichols do not allege that the Niesens provided alcohol to Carr, that the Niesens were aware that Carr (specifically) was consuming alcoholic beverages, that the Niesens knew or should have known that Carr was intoxicated, or that the Niesens knew or should have known that Carr was not able to drive her motor vehicle safely at the time of the accident We note that there also is no allegation by the Nichols that the Niesens aided, agreed to assist, or attempted to aid Carr or any other person in the procurement or consumption of alcohol on premises under their control. There also are no allegations that the Niesens knew in advance that any underage individuals would be drinking.

* * * * *

If one or more of the public policy "factors so dictates, the court may refuse to impose liability in a case."

The first public policy factor upon which recovery against a negligent tortfeasor may be denied is when "the injury is too remote from the negligence...."

The second public policy factor upon which recovery against a negligent tortfeasor may be denied is when "the injury is too wholly out of proportion to the tortfeasor's culpability...."

The third public policy factor upon which recovery against a negligent tortfeasor may be denied is when "in retrospect it appears too highly extraordinary that the negligence should have brought about the harm...."

The fourth public policy factor upon which recovery against a negligent tortfeasor may be denied is when "allowing recovery would place too unreasonable a burden upon the tortfeasor...."

The fifth public policy factor upon which recovery against a negligent tortfeasor may be denied is when "allowing recovery would be too likely to open the way to fraudulent claims...."

The sixth, and here perhaps the most significant, public policy factor upon which recovery against a negligent tortfeasor

may be denied is when "allowing recovery would have no sensible or just stopping point...."

* * * * *

Here, the Niesens and their insurer argue that there would be no sensible or just stopping point if the court of appeals' decision stands. They claim that the decision of the court of appeals would put tort law on the path of strict liability for anyone who owns property in Wisconsin, and who knows even scant details of an underage person consuming alcohol on the property under his or her control. They argue that the next step, beyond such a proposed expansion in common-law negligence liability, may be to include in the framework of liability not just social hosts but anyone who knows that an underage person was drinking on property that is not even under their control, or to include anyone, not just property owners, who knows that any underage individual has had too much to drink.

We note that there is no allegation by the Nichols here that the Niesens knew Carr was intoxicated, impaired, or unable to safely drive a vehicle. The Niesens argue that they could not have foreseen that people coming onto their property, who already had broken the law before they arrived, would break the law again after leaving. The Niesens could not reasonably have foreseen that an underage guest who they were not specifically aware was intoxicated, and who arrived at the premises under their control with alcohol purchased elsewhere, would cause foreseeable harm to others.

We agree with the Niesens ... that allowing recovery here would have no sensible or just stopping point.

* * * * *

If the Nichols' claim were allowed to proceed, the expansion of liability might also include liability for parents who allegedly should have known that drinking would occur on their property while they were absent, based on the proclivities of teenagers in a given area to consume alcohol. Imposing such liability would be only a short step away from imposing strict liability upon property owners for any underage drinking that occurs on property under their control. As Judge David G. Deininger stated in his dissent in the court of appeals, "if liability is permitted to extend to parents and property owners who fail to 'supervise and monitor the activities on their property,'" as the Nichols contend of the Niesens, "then parents or other owners of property occupied by sixteen- to twenty-year-olds" would "be well-advised to never leave home, or if they must, to ensure that all underage persons go elsewhere as well...." As a result, even assuming that the Nichols had pled a viable claim for common-law negligence against the Niesens using the four-factor test, we are satisfied that the Nichols' claim should be barred on public policy considerations, since allowing recovery here would have no sensible or just stopping point.

* * * * *

Liability has never been applied to conduct like that of the Niesens, and liability has required active, direct and affirmative acts, such as the provision of alcohol. Neither the legislature nor this court has expanded liability to social hosts who have not provided alcohol to minors. The legislature is the appropriate governmental branch to expand liability if it desires to do so. As a result for the reasons stated herein, we reverse the court of appeals, and hold that such an expansion of liability should come from the legislature, if it is to occur at all.

* * * * *

Questions

1. Explain the Nichols' legal claim.

2. *a.* Who won this case and why?
   b. Do you agree with the Court's decision and its reasoning? Explain.

3. Moos consumed alcohol at a party hosted by the Graffs and Hausmons. Allegedly, Moos left the party in an intoxicated condition and was involved in an accident that resulted in an injury to another driver, Beard.
   a. Are the social hosts, the Graffs and Hausmons, liable (along with Moos) for Beard's injuries? Explain.
   b. Should they be liable? Explain. See *Graff, Graff, Hausmon and Hausmon v. Beard and Beard*, 858 S.W.2d 918 (Texas S. Ct. 1993).

4. Nichols, age 26, and Dobler, a minor, were guests at Maldonado's party. Dobler was served alcohol and, while intoxicated, repeatedly hit Nichols with a hammer. Nichols sued Maldanado for negligence in serving alcohol to a minor. The jury found for Nichols. Maldanado appealed. How would you rule on that appeal? Explain. See *Nichols v. Dobler*, 655 N.W.2d 787 (Mich. Ct. App. 2002).

5. Richard Paul Dube suffered serious injuries when the vehicle he was driving was struck head-on by a vehicle being driven in the wrong direction on a Massachusetts highway by Ravindra Bhoge. Bhoge had earlier in the evening consumed a number of drinks with three friends at a bar. Bhoge and his friends met regularly on Fridays after work to drink at local bars. Each person took turns paying the bill, or on some occasions, payment would be equally divided. On the night of the accident Bhoge drank enough that the trial judge inferred that Bhoge's intoxication would have been apparent. Bhoge's three friends said they saw nothing to indicate that Bhoge was impaired, although Bhoge had left his coat behind in the bar on a particularly cold evening, and he was outside the bar for 45 minutes prior to his departure. Bhoge indicated to his friends that he was "okay" as they all prepared to leave in their vehicles. Dube sued Bhoge's three friends claiming they were social hosts and were negligent in permitting Bhoge to continue drinking. How would you rule on Dube's claim? Explain. See *Dube v. Lanphear & Others*, 868 N.E.2d 619 (2007). [For the National Center for State Courts, see **http://www.ncsconline.org/**]

Classifications of Law

We can divide the law into some categories that will help us better understand the many legal domains and processes.

Substantive and Procedural Law

Substantive laws create, define, and regulate legal rights and obligations. Thus, for example, the federal Civil Rights Act of 1964 forbids discrimination in employment and other matters (see Chapter 13).

Procedural law embraces the systems and methods available to enforce the rights specified in the substantive law. So procedural law includes the judicial system and the rules by which it operates. Questions of where to hear a case, what evidence to admit, and which decisions can be appealed fall within the procedural domain. [For a "collaboratively built, freely available legal dictionary and encyclopedia," see **http://topics.law.cornell.edu/wex**]

Law and Equity

Following the Norman conquest of England in 1066, a system of king's courts was established in which the king's representatives settled disputes. Those representatives were empowered to provide remedies of land, money, or personal property. The king's courts became known as *courts of law,* and the remedies were labeled *remedies of law.* Some litigants, however, sought compensation other than the three provided. They took their pleas to the king.

Typically the chancellor, an aide to the king, would hear these petitions and, guided by the standard of fairness, could grant a remedy (such as an injunction or specific performance—see the glossary of legal terms in the back of the book) specifically appropriate to the case. The chancellors' decisions accumulated over time such that a new body of remedies—and with it a new court system, known as *courts of equity*—evolved. Both court systems were adopted in the United States following the American Revolution, but today actions at law and equity are typically heard in the same court.

Public Law and Private Law

Public law deals with the relationship between government and the citizens. Constitutional, criminal, and administrative law (relating to such bodies as the Federal Trade Commission) fall in the public law category. *Private law* regulates the legal relationship among individuals. Contracts, agency, and commercial paper are traditional business law topics in the private category.

Civil Law and Criminal Law

The legislature or other lawmaking body normally specifies that new legislation is either *civil* or *criminal* or both. Broadly, all legislation not specifically labeled criminal law falls in the civil law category. *Civil law* addresses the legal rights and duties arising among individuals, organizations such as corporations, and governments. Thus, for example, a person might sue a company raising a civil law claim of breach of contract. *Criminal law,* on the other hand, involves wrongs against the general welfare as formulated in specific criminal statutes. Murder and theft are, of course, criminal wrongs because society has forbidden those acts in specific legislative enactments. (For a brief discussion of business and white-collar crime and the federal sentencing guidelines, see Chapter 2.)

Crimes   Crimes are of three kinds. In general, *felonies* are more serious crimes, such as murder, rape, and robbery. They are typically punishable by death or by imprisonment in a federal or state penitentiary for more than one year. In general, *misdemeanors* are less serious crimes, such as petty theft, disorderly conduct, and traffic offenses. They are typically punishable by fine or by imprisonment for no more than one year. *Treason* is the special situation in which one levies war against the United States or gives aid and comfort to its enemies.

Elements of a Crime   In a broad sense, crimes consist of two elements: (1) a wrongful act or omission (*actus reus*) and (2) evil intent (*mens rea*). Thus, an individual who pockets a pen and leaves the store without paying for it may be charged with petty theft. The accused may defend, however, by arguing that he or she merely absentmindedly and unintentionally slipped the pen in a pocket after picking it off the shelf to consider its merits. Intent is a state of mind, so the jury or judge must reach a determination from the objective facts as to what the accused's state of mind must have been.

Criminal Procedure   In general, criminal procedure following an arrest, and an initial appearance before a magistrate, (and in some cases a preliminary hearing) is structured as follows: For misdemeanor cases, prosecutors typically file what is called an *information,* a formal expression of the charges. The information may be reviewed by a magistrate before issuance. For felony cases, the process begins with the prosecuting officials either filing an information or seeking an *indictment* by bringing their charges before a grand jury of citizens to determine whether the charges have sufficient merit to justify a trial.

After an indictment or information, the individual is brought before the court for *arraignment,* where the charges are read and a plea is entered. If the individual pleads not guilty, he or she will go to trial, where guilt must be established *beyond a reasonable doubt.* In a criminal trial, the burden of proof is on the state. The defendant is, of course, presumed innocent and is entitled to a jury trial, but she or he may choose to have the case decided by the judge alone. If found guilty, the defendant can, among other possibilities, seek a new trial or appeal errors in the prosecution. If found innocent, the defendant may, if necessary, invoke the doctrine of *double jeopardy* under which a person cannot be prosecuted twice in the same tribunal for the same criminal offense. [For an extensive criminal justice database, see **http://www.ncjrs.gov/**]

Miranda Warnings

The 1966 *Miranda v. Arizona* U.S. Supreme Court decision provided that a suspect in police custody must be told:

> You have the right to remain silent. Anything you say can and will be used against you in a court of law. You have the right to an attorney. If you cannot afford an attorney, one will be appointed for you.

If warnings are not properly provided, any statements made by the suspect and any evidence derived from those statements cannot subsequently be used in court. The warnings are highly controversial, and the current Supreme Court appears to be inclined to relax the *Miranda* requirements.

Michigan police informed a suspect, Van Thompkins, of his Fifth Amendment rights against self-incrimination including the right to remain silent. Thompkins said he understood, but he did not say he wanted the questioning to stop or that he wanted a lawyer. Rather, he sat through two hours and 45 minutes of questioning without speaking until an officer asked: "Do you pray to God to forgive you for shooting that boy down?" Thompkins said, "Yes." He did not speak further, and he did not sign a confession. He was later convicted of murder, that verdict being based largely on his one-word reply. The U.S. 6th Circuit Court of Appeals overturned the conviction, ruling that the use of the incriminating answer violated Thompkins's Fifth Amendment rights, as defined and required by *Miranda.*

The case, *Berghuis v. Thompkins,* then reached the U.S. Supreme Court in 2010 where the Court chipped away at the *Miranda* requirements in a 5–4 reversal of the

Court of Appeals ruling. The Court said, "A suspect who has received and understood the *Miranda* warnings and has not invoked his *Miranda* rights waives the right to remain silent by making an uncoerced statement to the police." The Court's decision requires a criminal suspect to explicitly and unambiguously tell the police he or she wants to remain silent. Merely remaining silent had previously been treated as an invocation of the right to remain silent, but the Court's *Thompkins* ruling changed that practice and, in the view of critics, ill advisedly diminished rights previously guaranteed to defendants.

The Supreme Court further relaxed the Miranda requirements in two other 2010 decisions (*Florida v. Powell* and *Maryland v. Shatzer*), but in 2011, the Court strengthened *Miranda* protection for young people when it ruled that the police must consider the age of a suspect in deciding whether *Miranda* warnings must be issued. In *J.D.B. v. North Carolina,* a 13-year-old Chapel Hill, North Carolina student confessed to a pair of home break-ins during a half hour of questioning by police officers and school administrators in a middle school conference room. The warnings were not issued and J.D.B. was not permitted to call his grandmother, who was his guardian. The state, however, claimed J.D.B. was not in custody and therefore the warnings were not required. In general, a suspect is considered not to have been in custody if a "reasonable person" under the circumstances would have felt free to leave. The North Carolina courts ruled that J.D.B. was not in custody, but the U.S. Supreme Court held that the police must consider the suspect's age when deciding if custody has been achieved such that the warnings are required. The case was returned to North Carolina to determine whether J.D.B., given his age, was in custody during the questioning.

Questions

1. Do you think Thompkins's response, "Yes." to the police inquiry should have been admissible in court against him? Explain.

2. In general, do you think the *Miranda* warnings offer too much protection for criminal suspects? Explain.

Sources: Berghuis v. Thompkins, 130 S. Ct. 2250 (2010), *Florida v. Powell,* 130 S. Ct. 1195 (2010), *J.D.B. v. North Carolina,* 2011 U.S. LEXIS 4557, *Maryland v. Shatzer,* 130 S. Ct. 1213 (2010), *Miranda v. Arizona,* 86 S. Ct. 1602 (1966); Jesse J. Holland, "Miranda Warning Rights Trimmed Bit by Bit by High Court," *Christian Science Monitor,* August 2, 2010 [**http://www.csmonitor.com/**]; and David Savage, "Supreme Court Backs Off Strict Enforcement of Miranda Rights," *latimes.com* [**latimes.com/news/la-na-court-miranda-20100602,0,2431552.story**].

PRACTICING ETHICS   When Sex Becomes Rape

On December 13, 2003, J. L., an 18-year-old female attending community college in Maryland, drove Maouloud Baby, then 16, and his friend, Michael Wilson, 15, to a residential area. Wilson allegedly had sex with J.L. while Baby waited outside of the car. According to court records, Baby then said it was his turn and asked J.L.: "Are you going to let me hit that?" He also said, "I don't want to rape you." J.L. testified in court that she agreed to sex "as long as he stops when I tell him to." When asked if she felt she had a choice about agreeing to sex, J.L. testified: "Not really. I don't know. Something just clicked off and I just did whatever they said." According to J.L.'s testimony, Baby commenced intercourse, but J.L. told him to stop because he was hurting her. Baby, however, continued the sexual intercourse for "five or so" seconds, according to J.L. Baby testified that he believed J.L. had given him permission to have sex with her, and he said that he stopped when she wanted him to do so. After Baby withdrew from J.L., the trio drove to a local McDonald's where J.L. gave her phone number to Baby, at his request, and where Wilson hugged her. J.L. then went shopping for a time and thereafter went to a friend's house where she explained what happened to her friend's mother, who then called the police.[2] Prosecutors attributed J.L.'s delayed disclosure to rape trauma.

Wilson pleaded guilty to second-degree rape and was sentenced to 18 months in prison. Baby was convicted of first-degree rape, among other offenses. He was sentenced to 15 years imprisonment, with all but five years suspended, and five years probation upon his release. Baby appealed, and the conviction was reversed, but upon further appeal, Maryland's highest court ruled that a woman has a right to revoke consent during intercourse, and a man who fails to comply with that altered decision can be charged with rape.[3] Eight state courts have now concluded that consent can be withdrawn after intercourse has commenced, and Illinois passed a statute to that effect. North Carolina law explicitly provides that rape cannot occur once permission is given.

Questions

1. The law aside, was J.L. morally wronged by Baby? Explain.

2. In your view, does rape occur if permission is withdrawn and sexual intercourse continues? Explain.

3. Was Baby morally wronged by J.L.'s rape charge? Explain.

Questions—Part One

1. Jonathan Rauch argued that America is making a mistake in allowing what he calls Hidden Law to be replaced by what he calls Bureaucratic Legalism. Hidden Law refers to unwritten social codes, whereas Bureaucratic Legalism refers to state-provided due process for every problem. Thus, universities formerly expected insults and epithets among students to be resolved via informal modes such as apologies, while today many universities have written codes forbidding offensive or discriminatory verbal conduct. Similarly, four kindergarten students in New Jersey were suspended from school for three days because they were observed "shooting" each other with their fingers serving as guns.

    a. Should we leave campus insults and school-yard finger "shootings" to the Hidden Law? Explain.

    b. Can you think of other examples where we have gradually replaced Hidden Law with Bureaucratic Legalism?

    c. Rauch argued that the breakdown of one Hidden Law, the rule that a man must marry a woman whom he has impregnated, may be "the most far-reaching social change of our era." Do you agree? Explain. See George Will, "Penalizing These Kids Is Zero Tolerance at a Ridiculous Extreme," *The Des Moines Register,* December 27, 2000, p. 11A.

2. A number of nations, including The Netherlands and Germany, have "legalized" and regulated prostitution for safety.

    a. Should the United States do the same? For a discussion of this issue, see Emily Bazelon, "Why Is Prostitution Illegal?" *Slate,* March 10, 2008 [**http://www.slate.com/id/2186243/**].

b. Should we remove criminal penalties from all of the so-called victimless crimes including vagrancy, pornography, and gambling? Should we regulate those practices in any way? Explain.

3. In 2010, *The Wall Street Journal* reported that Pennsylvania had become the 21st state to consider legislation prohibiting the practice of "sexting" (cell phone transmission of nude photos of themselves and other risqué material) by minors.[4]

   a. What objections would you raise to a criminal law forbidding sexting by minors?

   b. Is this an area where the government should simply refrain from intervention? Explain.

4. A Rhode Island man pleaded guilty to child molestation. As an alternative to imprisonment and as a condition of his probation, the judge ordered him to purchase a newspaper ad displaying his picture, identifying himself as a sex offender, and encouraging others to seek assistance. One Florida judge has sentenced hundreds of shoplifters to carrying in public a sign that reads: "I stole from this store." Constitutional law expert Jonathan Turley says "creative sentencing" is growing, a trend he disapproves of and regards as a strategy for entertaining the public more than deterring crime.[5]

   a. What objections would a defendant's lawyer raise to these public humiliation punishments?

   b. Would you impose a "humiliation sentence" if you were the judge? Explain.

Part Two—The Judicial Process

Most disputes are settled without resort to litigation, but when agreement cannot be reached, we can turn to the courts—a highly technical and sophisticated dispute resolution mechanism.

State Court Systems

While state court systems vary substantially, a general pattern can be summarized. As shown in Figure 4.1, at the base of the court pyramid in most states is a trial court of general jurisdiction, commonly labeled a *district court* or a *superior court.* Most trials—both civil and criminal—arising out of state law are heard here, but certain classes of cases are reserved to courts of limited subject-matter jurisdiction or to various state administrative agencies (such as the state public utilities commission and the workers' compensation board). Family, small claims, juvenile, and traffic courts are examples of trial courts with limited jurisdiction. At the top of the judicial pyramid in all states is a court of appeals, ordinarily labeled the *supreme court.* A number of states also provide for an intermediate court of appeals located in the hierarchy between the trial courts and the highest appeals court.

FIGURE 4.1 **State and Federal Court Systems**

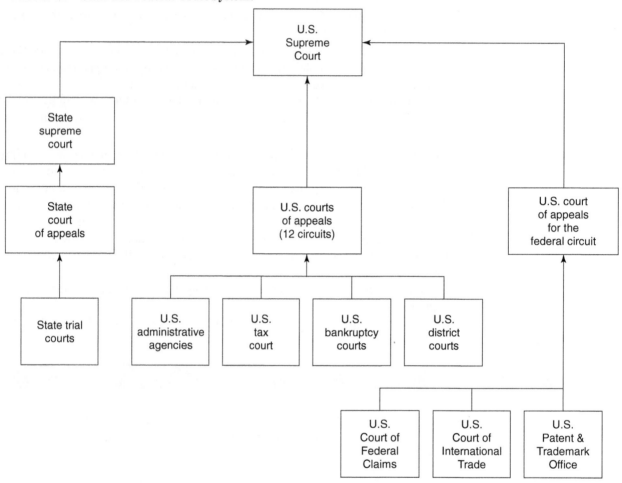

Federal Court System

District Courts

The Constitution provides for a Supreme Court and such inferior courts as Congress shall authorize. Pursuant to that authority, Congress has established at least one district court for each state and territory. The 94 district courts serve as the foundation of the federal judicial system. These are trial courts where witnesses are heard and questions of law and fact are resolved. Most federal cases begin in the district courts or in a federal administrative agency (such as the Federal Communications Commission). Congress has also provided for several courts of limited jurisdiction, including the U.S. Tax Court and the U.S. Court of International Trade.

[For access to all federal court web sites, see the Federal Judicial Center at **http://www.fjc.gov**]

Courts of Appeals

Congress has divided the United States geographically into 11 judicial circuits and the District of Columbia and has established a court of appeals for each. Those courts hear appeals from the district courts within their circuit and review decisions and enforce orders of the various federal administrative agencies. In addition, the U.S. Court of Appeals for the Federal Circuit hears, among others, all patent appeals and all appeals from the U.S. Court of Federal Claims (monetary claims against the United States).

Supreme Court

The Supreme Court consists of nine justices. Those justices (along with the federal district and appeals court judges) are appointed for life by the president and confirmed by the Senate. Almost all of the Supreme Court's work consists of reviewing lower court decisions, principally from the courts of appeal with a small number from state high courts. Virtually all parties seeking Supreme Court review must petition the Court for a *writ of certiorari,* which commands the lower court to forward the trial records to the Court.

Decisions regarding those petitions are entirely discretionary with the Court. Typically it will hear those cases that will assist in resolving conflicting courts of appeal decisions, as well as those that raise questions of special significance about the Constitution or the national welfare. Petitions to the Supreme Court have grown steadily over the years and now total approximately 8,000 cases per year. Formal, written opinions, however, are issued in only about 70 to 90 cases, a decline from, for example, 175 in 1986. Thus, in terms of numbers alone, the Court has backed away from its more activist approach of the 1960s, 1970s, and 1980s.

Critics

Questions of "judicial activism," the liberal/conservative balance on the Supreme Court, the politics of the justices, and the justices' deference to big business interests have made the Court a target for criticism. Citing scholarly studies, *The New York Times* in 2010 said the current Supreme Court under Chief Justice John Roberts is "the most conservative in decades."[6] Journalist E.J. Dionne, Jr. has written about the "Court's Defense of the Powerful:"

> The current Supreme Court is "the most conservative in decades."

> The United States Supreme Court now sees its central task as comforting the already comfortable and afflicting those already afflicted.[7]

More specifically, the current Court is accused of being particularly friendly to business interests and free market values. (Remember the *Citizens United* election law decision we discussed in Chapter 2.) After five full terms, the Roberts Court had ruled for business interests in 61 percent of the relevant decisions, as contrasted with a 42 percent average by all courts since 1953.[8] On the other hand, several decisions in late 2010 and early 2011 supported fired workers, expanded antidiscrimination law, and ruled against the Chamber of Commerce position in four of the five cases the Chamber addressed.[9]

Ideological Rulings?

We want to believe that the Supreme Court reaches its decisions in a rational, objective fashion relying on the commands of the Constitution and precedent to maintain a consistent, fair, orderly judicial system free of political influence. The facts, however, reveal a Supreme Court that is often divided along what appear to be ideological lines. During the Roberts era, decisions have frequently been reached by 5–4 margins with a clear and substantially consistent division between conservative and liberal justices. Analysis of voting patterns shows that four of the six most conservative justices of the 44 justices who have served the Court since 1938 are sitting on the Court now.[10] A recent study by the Brookings Institution provides "striking evidence of a relationship between the political party of the appointing president and judicial voting patterns."[11] Critics say that those conservative ideological inclinations have led the Roberts Court to at times abandon traditional judicial restraint and decide issues that were broader than required by the case before it.[12]

Of course, public respect for the fairness and the rationality of Supreme Court decisions could be undermined if they come to be viewed as the product of liberal or conservative political/ideological views, rather than dispassionate, lawyerly analysis. Perhaps we should be concerned that a decreasing number of high courts around the world are citing U.S. Supreme Court decisions. Declining respect for Supreme Court rulings would undermine the rule of law in America and perhaps threaten democracy itself.[13] One response to these worries is a resurgence of interest in establishing term limits for justices. A prominent current proposal, for example, would fulfill the Constitution's requirement of lifetime appointment for justices by moving justices to some kind of senior role at the Court after 18 years on the bench.[14] [For an overview of the Supreme Court, see **http://www.supremecourtus.gov/**]

Jurisdiction

A plaintiff may not simply proceed to trial at the court of his or her preference. The plaintiff must go to a court with *jurisdiction*—that is, a court with the necessary power and authority to hear the dispute. The court must have jurisdiction over both the subject matter and the persons (or, in some instances, the property) involved in the case.

Subject-Matter Jurisdiction

Subject-matter jurisdiction imposes bounds on the classes of cases a court may hear. The legislation or constitution creating the court will normally specify that court's jurisdictional authority. State courts of general jurisdiction, for example, may hear most types of cases, but a criminal court or probate court is limited in the subject matter it may hear.

The outer bounds of federal jurisdiction are specified in the Constitution, while Congress has further particularized that issue by statute. Essentially, the federal district courts may hear two types of cases: (1) those involving a federal question and (2) those involving diversity of citizenship and more than $75,000.

Federal question jurisdiction exists in any suit where the plaintiff's claim is based on the U.S. Constitution, a U.S. treaty, or a federal statute. Thus litigants can bring cases to the federal courts involving, for example, the federal antitrust statutes, federal criminal laws, constitutional issues such as freedom of the press, and federal tax questions. Federal question jurisdiction does not require an amount in controversy exceeding $75,000. Furthermore, federal and state courts have *concurrent jurisdiction* for some federal questions. Thus, some federal question cases are decided in state courts applying federal law. Federal courts can also hear cases involving state laws. Congress has accorded the federal courts exclusive jurisdiction over certain subjects, including federal criminal laws, bankruptcy, and copyrights.

Under *diversity jurisdiction,* federal district courts may hear cases involving more than $75,000 where the plaintiff(s) and the defendant(s) are citizens of different states. (Corporations are treated as citizens both of their state of incorporation and the state in which their principal place of business is located.) Diversity cases may also be heard in state courts, but plaintiffs frequently prefer to bring their actions in federal courts. The quality of the federal judiciary is generally believed to be superior to that of the states, and the federal courts are considered less likely to be influenced by local bias.

Personal Jurisdiction

Judicial authority over the person is known as *in personam jurisdiction.* In general, a state court's powers are limited to the bounds of the state. Broadly, we can say that state court jurisdiction can be established in three ways: (1) When the defendant is a resident of the state, a summons may be served at that residence. (2) When the defendant is not a resident, a summons may be personally served should he or she be physically present in the state. (3) Most states have legislated "long-arm" statutes that allow a state or federal court to secure jurisdiction against an out-of-state party where the defendant has committed a tort in the state or where the defendant is conducting business in the state. Hence, in an auto accident in Ohio involving both an Ohio resident and a Kentucky resident, the Ohio resident may sue in Ohio and use the long-arm statute to achieve service of process over the defendant living in Kentucky.

A state court may also acquire jurisdiction via an *in rem action.* In that instance the defendant may be a nonresident, but his or her property, which must be the subject of the suit, must be located within the state.

The following case involves a dispute about the commercial use of the name of celebrated actor and former California governor, Arnold Schwarzenegger.

LEGAL BRIEFCASE

Arnold Schwarzenegger v. Fred Martin Motor Company
374 F. 3d 797 (9th Cir. 2004)

Circuit Judge Fletcher

Arnold Schwarzenegger, an internationally known movie star and, currently, the governor of California, appeals the district court's dismissal of his suit against Fred Martin Motor Company ("Fred Martin"), an Ohio car dealership, for lack of personal jurisdiction. Fred Martin had run a series of five full-page color advertisements in the *Akron Beacon Journal,* a locally circulated Ohio newspaper. Each advertisement included a small photograph of Schwarzenegger, portrayed as the "Terminator," without his permission. Schwarzenegger brought suit in California, alleging that these unauthorized uses of his image infringed his right of publicity. We affirm the district court's dismissal for lack of personal jurisdiction.

I. BACKGROUND

Schwarzenegger is a resident of California. When Schwarzenegger brought this suit, he was a private citizen and movie star, best known for his roles as a muscle-bound hero of action films and distinctive Austrian accent. As explained in his complaint, Schwarzenegger was generally cast as the lead character in so-called star-driven films. One of Schwarzenegger's most popular and readily recognizable film roles is that of the title character in "The Terminator" (1984). . . .

Fred Martin is an automobile dealership incorporated under the laws of Ohio and located in Barberton, Ohio, a few miles southwest of Akron. There is no evidence in the record that Fred Martin has any operations or employees in California, has ever advertised in California, or has ever sold a car to anyone in California. Fred Martin maintains an Internet website that is available for viewing in California and, for that matter, from any Internet cafe in Istanbul, Bangkok, or anywhere else in the world.

In early 2002, Fred Martin engaged defendant Zimmerman & Partners Advertising, Inc. ("Zimmerman") to design and place a full-page color advertisement in the *Akron Beacon Journal*, a local Akron-based newspaper. The advertisement ran in the *Akron Beacon Journal* five times in April 2002. Most of the advertisement consists of small photographs and descriptions of various cars available for purchase or lease from Fred Martin. Just below a large-font promise that Fred Martin "WON'T BE BEAT," the advertisement includes a small, but clearly recognizable photograph of Schwarzenegger as the Terminator. A "bubble quotation," like those found in comic strips, is drawn next to Schwarzenegger's mouth, reading, "Arnold says: 'Terminate EARLY at Fred Martin!'" This part of the advertisement refers to a special offer from Fred Martin to customers, inviting them to close out their current leases before the expected termination date, and to buy or lease a new car from Fred Martin.

Neither Fred Martin nor Zimmerman ever sought or received Schwarzenegger's permission to use his photograph in the advertisement. Schwarzenegger states in his complaint that, had such a request been made, it would have been refused. The advertisement, as far as the record reveals, was never circulated outside of Ohio.

Schwarzenegger brought suit against Fred Martin and Zimmerman in Los Angeles County Superior Court alleging six state law causes of action arising out of the unauthorized use of his image in the advertisement. He claims that the defendants caused him financial harm in that the use of his photograph to endorse Fred Martin "diminishes his hard earned reputation as a major motion picture star, and risks the potential for overexposure of his image to the public, thereby potentially diminishing the compensation he would otherwise garner from his career as a major motion picture star." According to Schwarzenegger's complaint, his compensation as the lead actor in star-driven films was based on his ability to draw crowds to the box office, and his ability to do so depended in part on the scarcity of his image. According to his complaint, if Schwarzenegger's image were to become ubiquitous—in advertisements and on television, for example—the movie-going public would be less likely to spend their money to see his films, and his compensation would diminish accordingly. Therefore, Schwarzenegger maintains, it is vital for him to avoid "over-saturation of his image." According to his complaint, he has steadfastly refused to endorse any products in the United States, despite being offered substantial sums to do so.

Defendants removed the action to federal district court in California, and Fred Martin moved to dismiss the complaint for lack of personal jurisdiction. The district court granted Fred Martin's motion, and Schwarzenegger appealed.

II. PERSONAL JURISDICTION

For a court to exercise personal jurisdiction over a nonresident defendant, that defendant must have at least "minimum contacts" with the relevant forum such that the exercise of jurisdiction "does not offend traditional notions of fair play and substantial justice." *International Shoe Co. v. Washington,* 326 U.S. 310, 316. (1945)

A. General Jurisdiction

Schwarzenegger argues, quite implausibly, that California has general personal jurisdiction over Fred Martin. For general jurisdiction to exist over a nonresident defendant such as Fred Martin, the defendant must engage in "continuous and systematic general business contacts," *Helicopteros Nacionales de Colombia, S.A. v. Hall,* 466 U.S. 408 (1984) that "approximate physical presence" in the forum state. *Bancroft & Masters,* 223 F. 3d at 1086. This is an exacting standard, as it should be, because a finding of general jurisdiction permits a defendant to be haled into court in the forum state to answer for any of its activities anywhere in the world.

Schwarzenegger contends that Fred Martin's contacts with California are so extensive that it is subject to general jurisdiction. He points to the following contacts: Fred Martin regularly purchases Asian-made automobiles that are imported by California entities. However, in purchasing these automobiles, Fred Martin dealt directly with representatives in Illinois and New Jersey, but never dealt directly with the California-based importers. Some of Fred Martin's sales contracts with its automobile suppliers include a choice-of-law provision specifying California law. In addition, Fred Martin regularly retains the services of a California-based direct-mail marketing company; has hired a sales training company, incorporated in California, for consulting services; and maintains an Internet website accessible by anyone capable of using the Internet, including people living in California.

These contacts fall well short of the "continuous and systematic" contacts that the Supreme Court and this court have held to constitute sufficient "presence" to warrant general jurisdiction. Schwarzenegger has therefore failed to establish a prima facie case of general jurisdiction.

B. Specific Jurisdiction

Alternatively, Schwarzenegger argues that Fred Martin has sufficient "minimum contacts" with California arising from, or related to, its actions in creating and distributing the advertisement such that the forum may assert specific personal jurisdiction. We have established a three-prong test for analyzing a claim of specific personal jurisdiction:

(1) The nonresident defendant must purposefully direct his activities or consummate some transaction with the forum or resident thereof; or perform some act by which he purposefully avails himself of the privilege of conducting activities in the forum, thereby invoking the benefits and protections of its laws;

(2) the claim must be one which arises out of or relates to the defendant's forum-related activities; and

(3) the exercise of jurisdiction must comport with fair play and substantial justice, i.e., it must be reasonable.

The plaintiff bears the burden of satisfying the first two prongs of the test. If the plaintiff fails to satisfy either of these prongs, personal jurisdiction is not established in the forum state. If the plaintiff succeeds in satisfying both of the first two prongs, the burden then shifts to the defendant to "present a compelling case" that the exercise of jurisdiction would not be reasonable. For the reasons that follow, we hold that Schwarzenegger has failed to satisfy the first prong.

1. Purposeful Availment or Direction Generally

Under the first prong of our three-part specific jurisdiction test, Schwarzenegger must establish that Fred Martin either purposefully availed itself of the privilege of conducting activities in California, or purposefully directed its activities toward California.

* * * * *

A showing that a defendant purposefully availed himself of the privilege of doing business in a forum state typically consists of evidence of the defendant's actions in the forum, such as executing or performing a contract there. By taking such actions, a defendant "purposefully avails itself of the privilege of conducting activities within the forum State, thus invoking the benefits and protections of its laws." *Hanson v. Denckla,* 357 U.S. 235, 253 (1958). In return for these "benefits and protections," a defendant must—as a quid pro quo—"submit to the burdens of litigation in that forum." *Burger King,* 471 U.S. at 476.

A showing that a defendant purposefully directed his conduct toward a forum state, by contrast, usually consists of evidence of the defendant's actions outside the forum state that are directed at the forum, such as the distribution in the forum state of goods originating elsewhere.

2. Purposeful Direction

Schwarzenegger does not point to any conduct by Fred Martin in California related to the advertisement that would be readily susceptible to a purposeful availment analysis. Rather, the conduct of which Schwarzenegger complains—the unauthorized inclusion of the photograph in the advertisement and its distribution in the Akron Beacon Journal—took place in Ohio, not California. Fred Martin received no benefit, privilege, or protection from California in connection with the advertisement, and the traditional quid pro quo justification for finding purposeful availment thus does not apply. Therefore, to the extent that Fred Martin's conduct might justify the exercise of personal jurisdiction in California, that conduct must have been purposefully directed at California.

* * * * *

Here, Fred Martin's intentional act—the creation and publication of the advertisement—was expressly aimed at Ohio rather than California. The purpose of the advertisement was to entice Ohioans to buy or lease cars from Fred Martin and, in particular, to "terminate" their current car leases. The advertisement was never circulated in California, and Fred Martin had no reason to believe that any Californians would see it and pay a visit to the dealership. Fred Martin certainly had no reason to believe that a Californian had a current car lease with Fred Martin that could be "terminated" as recommended in the advertisement. It may be true that Fred Martin's intentional act eventually caused harm to Schwarzenegger in California and Fred Martin may have known that Schwarzenegger lived in California. But this does not confer jurisdiction, for Fred Martin's express aim was local. We therefore conclude that the advertisement was not expressly aimed at California.

CONCLUSION

We hold that Schwarzenegger has established neither general nor specific jurisdiction over Fred Martin in California. Schwarzenegger has not shown that Fred Martin has "continuous and systematic general business contacts," Helicopteros, 466 U.S. at 416, that "approximate physical presence" in California, Bancroft & Masters, 223 F. 3d at 1086, such that it can be sued there for any act it has committed anywhere in the world. Further, while Schwarzenegger has made out a prima facie case that Fred Martin committed intentional acts that may have caused harm to Schwarzenegger in California, he has not made out a prima facie case that Fred Martin expressly aimed its acts at California.

Affirmed.

AFTERWORD

Schwarzenegger's claim was settled out of court in 2004 when the Fred Martin Motor Company issued a written apology and agreed to pay a "substantial" sum to Arnold's All-Stars, an after-school program founded by Schwarzenegger.

Questions

1. Explain Schwarzenegger's complaint.

2. Why was Schwarzenegger unable to sue Fred Martin in California?

3. The Robinsons filed a product liability suit in an Oklahoma state court to recover for injuries sustained in an automobile accident in Oklahoma. The auto had been purchased in New York from the defendant, World-Wide Volkswagen Corp. Oklahoma's long-arm statute was used in an attempt to secure jurisdiction over the defendant. World-Wide conducted no business in Oklahoma. Nor did it solicit business there.

   a. Build an argument to support the claim of jurisdiction for the Oklahoma court.

   b. Decide. See *World-Wide Volkswagen Corp. v. Woodson*, 100 S. Ct. 559 (1980).

4. Burger King conducted a franchise, fast-food operation from its Miami, Florida, headquarters. John Rudzewicz and a partner, both residents of Michigan, secured a Burger King franchise in Michigan. Subsequently, the franchisees allegedly fell behind in payments, and after negotiations failed, Burger King ordered the franchisees to vacate the premises. They declined to do so, and continued to operate the franchise. Burger King brought suit in a federal district court in Florida. The defendant franchisees argued that the Florida court did not have personal jurisdiction over them because they were Michigan residents and because the claim did not arise in Florida. However, the district court found the defendants to be subject to the Florida long-arm statute, which extends jurisdiction to "[a]ny person, whether or not a citizen or resident of this state" who, "[b]reach[es] a contract in this state by failing to perform acts required by the contract to be performed in this state." The franchise contract provided for governance of the relationship by Florida law. Policy was set in Miami, although day-to-day supervision was managed through various district offices. The case ultimately reached the U.S. Supreme Court.

   a. What constitutional argument would you raise on behalf of the defendant franchisees?

   b. Decide. See *Burger King Corp. v. Rudzewicz*, 471 U.S. 462 (1985).

Venue

Once jurisdictional authority—that is, the power to hear the case—is established, the proper *venue* (geographic location within the court system) comes into question. Ordinarily, a case will be heard by the court geographically closest to the incident or property in question or to where the parties reside. Sometimes one of the parties may seek a *change of venue* based on considerations such as unfavorable pretrial publicity or the pursuit of a more favorable legal climate. The importance of venue is evident in a 2010 decision forcing Los Angeles-based Occidental Petroleum to defend itself in an environmental dispute in California rather than in Peru where the conflict emerged. Members of the

The Achuar tribe, indigenous to the Amazon rain forest, brought a class action in Los Angeles.

Achuar tribe, indigenous to the Amazon rain forest, brought a class action in Los Angeles against Occidental alleging the oil company dumped millions of gallons of waste water into their rivers and contaminated their land with waste.[15] A California federal district court dismissed the Achuar claim, but the 9th Circuit U.S. Court of Appeals reversed the district court. The appeals court ruled, among other things, that Occidental had failed to demonstrate that Peru was the more convenient forum for the lawsuit.[16] The Achuar plaintiffs want the case tried in California, in part, because the Peruvian courts have a history of favoring corporate interests in conflicts with natives. At this writing, the case is expected to go forward in Los Angeles.

Standing to Sue

All who wish to bring a claim before a court will not be permitted to do so. To receive the court's attention, the litigant must demonstrate *standing to sue*. That is, the person must show that her or his interest in the outcome of the controversy is sufficiently direct and substantial as to justify the court's consideration. The litigant must show that she or he is personally suffering, or will be suffering, injury. Mere interest in the problem at hand is insufficient to grant standing to sue. We all suffer injustices. We all have complaints in life. But have we suffered an injury to a legally protected right or interest? That is the question in the *Mayer* case that arose out of "Spygate," an alleged National Football League cheating scandal.[17]

LEGAL BRIEFCASE

Mayer v. Bill Belichick; The New England Patriots; National Football League

605 F. 3d 223 (3d Cir. 2010); Cert. Den. 2011 U.S. LEXIS 2027

FACTS

In an episode popularly known as "Spygate," an employee of the New England Patriots National Football League team was caught videotaping New York Jets' sideline signals, in violation of NFL rules, during a 2007 game with the Jets. The taping was later discovered to have been part of an illicit taping program that reportedly had been ongoing since the 2000 season. The NFL penalized the Patriots and their coach, Bill Belichick.

Mayer sued on behalf of himself and a class of Jets season ticketholders claiming the improper conduct violated the contractual expectations and rights of the ticketholders who had paid to observe an honest football game played in conformance with the rules. Mayer lost at trial where the federal district court ruled that he had failed to demonstrate an actionable injury; that is, he was unable to show the court that the facts he asserted could support a right to relief under the law. Put another way, he did not have standing to sue. Mayer then appealed to the Third Circuit Federal Court of Appeals.

Circuit Judge Cowen

(I-III OMITTED-ED.)

IV

The District Court, while noting that Mayer alleged numerous theories of liability in this case, appropriately turned to the following dispositive question: namely, whether or not he stated an actionable injury (or, in other words, a legally protected right or interest) arising out of the alleged "dishonest" videotaping program undertaken by the Patriots and the NFL team's head coach.

* * * * *

Initially, we consider how tickets to sporting and other entertainment events have been treated in the past. New Jersey has generally followed a so-called "license" approach[1]....

Although it did not use the specific term "license," the ticket stub provided by the Patriots nevertheless appears consistent with this traditional approach. For example, it unambiguously stated that "[t]his ticket only grants entry into the stadium and a spectator seat for the specified NFL game." The stub further made clear that the Jets and the owners of the stadium retain sole discretion to refuse admission or to eject a ticket-holder.... Given that Mayer was never barred or expelled from any game at Giants Stadium, much more is needed to establish a cognizable right, interest, or injury....

Mayer possessed either a license or, at best, a contractual right to enter Giants Stadium and to have a seat from which to watch a professional football game. In the clear language of the ticket stub, "[t]his ticket only grants entry into the stadium and a spectator seat for the specified NFL game." Mayer actually was allowed to enter the stadium and witnessed the "specified NFL game[s]" between the Jets and Patriots. He thereby suffered no cognizable injury to a legally protected right or interest.

Accordingly, we need not, and do not decide, whether a ticket-holder possesses nothing more than a license to enter and view whatever event, if any, happens to transpire. Here, Mayer undeniably saw *football* games played by two *NFL* teams. This therefore is not a case where, for example, the game or games were cancelled, strike replacement players were used, or the professional football teams themselves did

[1] A license, for our purposes, is generally defined as "[a] permission ... to commit some act that would otherwise be unlawful; esp., an agreement that it is lawful for the licensee to enter the licensor's land to do some act that would otherwise be illegal, such as hunting game." *Black's Law Dictionary* 1002 (9th ed. 2009).

something nonsensical or absurd, such as deciding to play basketball.

* * * * *

Furthermore, we do recognize that Mayer alleged that he was the victim, not of mere poor performance by a team or its players, but of a team's ongoing acts of dishonesty or cheating in violation of the express rules of the game. Nevertheless, there are any number of often complicated rules and standards applicable to a variety of sports, including professional football. It appears uncontested that players often commit intentional rule infractions in order to obtain an advantage over the course of the game.... Mayer further does not appear to contest the fact that a team is evidently permitted by the rules to engage in a wide variety of arguably "dishonest" conduct to uncover an opponent's signals. For example, a team is apparently free to take advantage of the knowledge that a newly hired player or coach takes with him after leaving his former team, and it may even have personnel on the sidelines who try to pick up the opposing team's signals with the assistance of lip-reading, binoculars, note-taking, and other devices. In addition, even Mayer acknowledged in his amended complaint that "[t]eams are allowed to have a limited number of their own videographers on the sideline during the game."

In fact, the NFL's own commissioner did ultimately take action here. He found that the Patriots and Belichick were guilty of violating the applicable NFL rules, imposed sanctions in the form of fines and the loss of draft picks, and rather harshly characterized the whole episode as a calculated attempt to avoid well-established rules designed to encourage fair play and honest competition. At least in this specific context, it is not the role of judges and juries to be second-guessing the decision taken by a professional sports league purportedly enforcing its *own* rules....

This Court refuses to countenance a course of action that would only further burden already limited judicial resources and force professional sports organizations and related individuals to expend money, time, and resources to defend against such litigation....

In conclusion, this Court will affirm the dismissal of Mayer's amended complaint. Again, it bears repeating that our reasoning here is limited to the unusual and even unique circumstances presented by this appeal. We do not condone the conduct on the part of the Patriots and the team's head coach, and we likewise refrain from assessing whether the NFL's sanctions (and its alleged destruction of the videotapes themselves) were otherwise appropriate. We further recognize that professional football, like other professional sports, is a multi-billion dollar business. In turn, ticket-holders and other fans may have legitimate issues with the manner in which they are treated. . . . Significantly, our ruling also does not leave Mayer and other ticket-holders without any recourse. Instead, fans could speak out against the Patriots, their coach, and the NFL itself. In fact, they could even go so far as to refuse to purchase tickets or NFL-related merchandise. However, the one thing they *cannot* do is bring a legal action in a court of law.

Affirmed.

Questions

1. *a.* Why did Mayer lose this case?
   b. Do you think he should have won?

2. According to the Court, under what circumstances might a plaintiff conceivably have an actionable claim involving a sports event gone wrong?

3. To some extent, the Court's decision was influenced by a decision to protect the judicial system from a flood of litigation. Explain what kinds of legal claims might have been filed if this Court had found that the plaintiff, Mayer, had stated an actionable injury.

Class Actions

In some instances, multiple plaintiffs may join together to represent themselves and all others who are similarly situated to file a single lawsuit alleging similar harm arising from the same, or substantially the same, wrong. The high cost of litigation, the great uncertainty of victory and the likelihood of small individual recoveries have made the class action a very useful tool for plaintiffs. Of course, the class action also enhances judicial efficiency by bringing many claims together in one case.

An important U.S. Supreme Court ruling in the *Wal-Mart Stores v. Dukes* case looks to have sharply reduced the usefulness of the class action in some–perhaps many–business disputes. A small group of current and former Walmart employees sued the company for sex discrimination on behalf of a nationwide class of 1.5 million female employees. Walmart challenged the class action certification, but the plaintiffs prevailed in the lower courts. The U.S. Supreme Court, however, ruled 9-0 in June 2011 that the case did not meet the technical requirements of federal class action procedural rules. Then in a 5-4 portion of the ruling, the Court held that the claims against Walmart did not share enough common elements to tie together the millions of employment decisions affecting women at Walmart. As a matter of company policy, discretion over pay and promotions rested with local managers at the 4,000 or so company stores thus undercutting the plantiffs' claims of a unified national policy or common standard for evaluating workers. The plaintiffs failed to identify a specific employment practice that tied all of their claims together.[18]

Current Walmart female employees and former employees can proceed with the case individually or in store-wide or perhaps regional classes, but that task will be extremely expensive, time-consuming and emotionally wrenching. The 5-4 portion of the decision may discourage other class actions in employment law cases and perhaps in other areas of law as well.

[For a *Today* show account of the *Dukes* ruling, see **http://www.msnbc.msn.com/id/43468398/ns/business-personal_finance/t/wal-mart-ruling-raises-bar-class-actions/**].

The Civil Trial Process

Civil procedure varies by jurisdiction. The following generalizations merely typify the process. (See Figure 4.2.) [For a vast "catalog" of law on the Internet, see **http://www. catalaw.com**]

Pleadings

Pleadings are the documents by which each party sets his or her initial case before the court. A civil action begins when the plaintiff files his or her first pleading, which is labeled a *complaint.* The complaint specifies (1) the parties to the suit, (2) evidence as to the court's jurisdiction in the case, (3) a statement of the facts, and (4) a prayer for relief (a remedy).

The complaint is filed with the clerk of court and a summons is issued, directing the defendant to appear in court to answer the claims alleged against him or her. A sheriff or some other official attempts to personally deliver the summons to the defendant. If personal delivery cannot be achieved, the summons may be left with a responsible party at the defendant's residence. Failing that, other modes of delivery are permissible, including a mailing. Publication of a notice in a newspaper will, in some instances, constitute good service of process. Ordinarily, a copy of the complaint accompanies the summons, so the defendant is apprised of the nature of the claim.

FIGURE 4.2   **Stages of a Lawsuit**

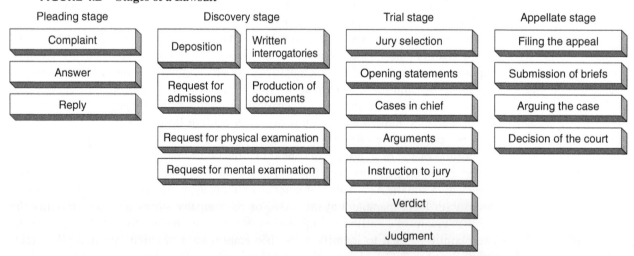

The defendant has several options. He or she may do nothing, but failure to respond may result in a *default judgment* in favor of the plaintiff. The defendant may choose to respond by filing a *demurrer* or a *motion to dismiss,* the essence of which is to argue that even if the plaintiff's recitation of the facts is accurate, a claim on which relief can be granted has not been stated.

Alternatively, the defendant may file with the court an initial pleading, called an *answer,* wherein the defendant enters a denial by setting out his or her version of the facts and law, or in which the defendant simply concedes the validity of the plaintiff's position. The answer may also contain an *affirmative defense,* such as the statute of limitations or the statute of frauds that would bar the plaintiff's claim. The defendant's answer might include a *counterclaim* or *cross-claim.* A counterclaim is the defendant's assertion of a claim of action against the plaintiff. A cross-claim is the defendant's assertion of a claim of action against a codefendant. In some states, these would be labeled *cross-complaints.* In the event of a counterclaim or the assertion of new facts in the answer, the plaintiff will respond with a *reply.* The complaint, answer, reply, and their components are the pleadings that serve to give notice, clarify the issues, and limit the dimensions of the litigation. [For a summary of "Famous Trials" in history, see **http://law2.umkc.edu/faculty/projects/ ftrials/ftrials.htm**]

Motions

As necessary during and after the filing of the pleadings, either party may file motions with the court. For example, a party may move to clarify a pleading or to strike a portion deemed unnecessary. Of special importance is a *motion for a judgment on the pleadings* or a *motion for summary judgment.* In a motion for a judgment on the pleadings, either party simply asks the judge to reach a decision based on the information in the pleadings. The judge will do so only if the defendant's answer constitutes an admission of the accuracy of the plaintiff's claim, or if the plaintiff's claim clearly has no foundation in law.

In a motion for a summary judgment, the party filing the motion is claiming that no facts are in dispute. Therefore, the judge may make a ruling about the law without taking the case to trial. In a summary judgment hearing, the court can look beyond the pleadings to hear evidence from affidavits, depositions, and so on. These motions avoid the time and expense of trial.

Discovery

Discovery is the primary information-gathering stage in the pretrial process. That information clarifies the trial issues, promotes pretrial settlements, and helps prevent surprises at the trial, among other things. Discovery may consist of *depositions* (recorded, sworn testimony in preparation for trial), physical and mental examinations, answers to written questions (*interrogatories*), requests for access to documents and property to inspect them prior to trial, and *admissions* (agreement by the parties to stipulated issues of fact or law prior to trial).

The era of electronic communication and storage has added important new expectations and burdens to the discovery process by requiring that litigants exchange all relevant electronically stored information (ESI) during the discovery phase. Individuals and companies must be able to produce ESI from all sources, including e-mail, files, scanned handwritten notes, stored records, voice mail, fax data, instant messages, spreadsheets, videos, PowerPoint presentations, and so on.

Pretrial Conference

Either party may request, and many courts require, a pretrial meeting involving the attorneys, the judge, and occasionally the parties. Usually following discovery, the conference is designed to plan the course of the trial in the interests of efficiency and justice. The participants seek to define the issues and settle the dispute in advance of trial. If no settlement is reached, a trial date is set.

The Judge and Jury

The federal Constitution and most state constitutions provide for the right to a jury trial in a civil case (excepting equity actions). Some states place dollar minimums on that guarantee. At the federal level and in most states, unless one of the parties requests a jury, the judge alone will hear the case and decide all questions of law and fact. If the case is tried before a jury, that body will resolve questions of fact, but all questions of law will be resolved by the judge who will also instruct the jury as to the law governing the case.

Jurors are selected from a jury pool composed of a cross section of the community. A panel is drawn from that pool. The individuals in that panel are questioned by the judge, by the attorneys, or by all to determine if any individual is prejudiced about the case such that he or she could not reach an objective decision on the merits. The questioning process is called *voir dire.*

From an attorney's point of view, jury selection is often not so much a matter of finding jurors without bias as it is a matter of identifying those jurors who are most likely to reach a decision favorable to one's client. To that end, elaborate mechanisms and strategies have been employed—particularly in criminal trials—to identify desirable jurors. For example, sophisticated, computer-assisted surveys of the trial community have been conducted to develop objective evidence by which to identify jurors who would not admit to racial prejudice but whose "profile" suggests the likelihood of such prejudice.

After questioning, the attorneys may *challenge for cause,* arguing to the judge that the individual cannot exercise the necessary objectivity of judgment. Attorneys are also afforded a limited number of *peremptory challenges,* by which the attorney can have a potential juror dismissed without the judge's concurrence and without offering a reason. Peremptory challenges may not be used to reject jurors on the basis of race or gender.

Facebook the Jury Pool

Social media, such as Facebook, MySpace, and Twitter, can be a valuable source of information to attorneys as they try to shape the composition of juries. Information that might not be revealed in voir dire sometimes comes to light online. Jury consultant Amber Yearwood in San Francisco discovered online that a member of a jury pool was highly opinionated and often dispensed medical and sex advice, a personality not well suited to the client's cause. The prospective juror was dismissed.

Source: Ana Campoy and Ashby Jones, "Searching for Details Online, Lawyers Facebook the Jury," *The New York Times,* February 22, 2011, p. A2.

Misleading the Jury?

The case that follows examines allegations of trial misconduct by the plaintiff's attorney in an apparent effort to prejudice the jury.

LEGAL BRIEFCASE

Minichiello v. Supper Club
296 A.D.2d 350 (S. Ct. N.Y., App. Div., 1st Dept. 2002)

Judges Buckley, Rosenberger, Lerner, Rubin, Marlow

[P]laintiff alleges that he was verbally and physically abused by defendants because of his sexual orientation and then wrongfully discharged when he refused to voluntarily relinquish his position at the Supper Club.

The Supper Club is a dining and dancing establishment operated by defendant, Edison Associates, L.P. (hereinafter Edison), a limited partnership. Defendant Martin Theising is a partner in Edison and defendant Andre Cortez is the general manager of The Supper Club and is responsible for its day-to-day operations. Defendant Oliver Hoffman was an independent consultant to The Supper Club.

In November 1992, plaintiff was hired as The Supper Club's late night manager initially responsible for its disco and later for its cabaret until he was discharged in July 1995. Plaintiff alleges in his complaint, that during the course of his employment, he was repeatedly subjected to humiliation and to discriminatory epithets regarding his sexual orientation and that, two weeks before he was discharged, he was physically held down by Hoffman and another individual while Cortez threatened to cut off his ponytail with a pair of scissors.

After a lengthy trial, the jury found that plaintiff had been subjected to a hostile work environment and had been discharged because of his sexual orientation and that Cortez had committed assault and battery. The jury awarded $160,000 in lost wages, finding that plaintiff could not have mitigated his damages. It further awarded $8,000,000 for past pain, suffering, and emotional distress and $2,000,000 for such future damages. The jury also awarded punitive damages of $1,000,000 against The Supper Club, $54,000 against Cortez and $2,200,000 against Theising with respect to the discrimination claims.

Defendants contend that the damages awarded were so grossly excessive as to be the result of passion and prejudice born of plaintiff's counsel's misconduct and judicial error, that a mere reduction of the awards would not be an adequate remedy.

"When misconduct of counsel in interrogation or summation so violates the rights of the other party to the litigation that extraneous matters beyond the proper scope of the trial may have substantially influenced or been determinative of the outcome, such breaches of the rules will not be condoned." (*Kohlmann v. City of New York*, 8 AD2d 598, 598.) Although evidence of hostility and harassment to other minorities may be relevant to a claim of a hostile work environment based on sexual orientation, the cumulative effect of the many irrelevant and highly prejudicial comments made by plaintiff's counsel in the course of this trial only served to incite the jury's passion and sympathy and effectively prevented a fair and dispassionate consideration of the evidence. Plaintiff's counsel referred to Theising, a German national with an apparent accent, as someone who exhibited an "attitude of hatred" and made forced analogies to Nazi Germany and the Holocaust. While the issue of this case was sexual orientation discrimination, plaintiff's counsel presented to the jury inappropriate matters involving African Americans, Latinos, and Jews that went far beyond any permissible boundaries and served no other purpose than to incite the jury's passions. Similarly, plaintiff's counsel elicited testimony about an alleged physical attack by an assistant to Cortez on an employee dying of AIDS and extensive testimony from several witnesses regarding the consumption of alcoholic beverages by Cortez, Hoffman, and Theising which was highly prejudicial with little or no probative value.

We find that the aggregate effect of such comments and conduct of plaintiff's counsel, which cannot be characterized as inadvertent or harmless, inflamed the jury's passion and sympathy to such an extent as to render the resulting judgment meaningless. . . .

The trial court erred in refusing to allow defendants to introduce evidence that no other employees were treated abusively . . . and in denying defendants' requested jury charge on mitigation. Likewise, . . . the trial court made a number of demeaning comments in the presence of the jury demonstrating a marked antipathy toward defense counsel which, in light of the totality of circumstances at trial, warrant a new trial.

Were this Court not to reverse and remand for a new trial for the reasons stated above, we would have nevertheless reversed on the issue of damages. The jury's grossly excessive compensatory and punitive damages awards totaling approximately $20,000,000 have no rational basis. . . . [Reversed. Remanded to "a different justice."]

Questions

1. *a.* Why did this appeals court reverse the decision of the lower court?

   b. Why was the case remanded to "a different justice"?

2. Did this decision conclude that the plaintiff had not been a victim of sexual harassment, wrongful dismissal, or the like? Explain.

3. According to this appeals court, what errors were made by the judge at trial?

Eminem Inspires Judicial Rap

A Michigan trial judge dismissed a 2003 defamation claim by DeAngelo Bailey against rapper Eminem. Bailey claimed that Eminem falsely depicted him as a bully in a song called "Brain Damage." The song's lyrics recount a childhood attack when Bailey allegedly beat up Marshall Mathers (Eminem). Perhaps inspired by the famous rapper, the judge added a rap footnote to her 13-page opinion. A portion follows:

Mr. Bailey complains that his rep is trash/so he's seeking compensation in the form of cash/Bailey thinks he's entitled to some monetary gain/Because Eminem used his name in vain.

The lyrics are stories no one would take as fact/they're an exaggeration of a childish act. It is therefore this Court's ultimate position/that Eminem is entitled to summary disposition.

The Michigan Court of Appeals affirmed the trial court decision.

Sources: "Eminem Delivered Favorable Verdict by Rap-Lovin' Judge" [**http://www.chartattack.com/ damn/2003/10/2106.cfm**]; *Bailey v. Mathers,* No. 252123, 2005 WL 857242 (Michigan Ct. App., April 14, 2005).

The Trial

The trial begins with opening statements by the attorneys. Each is expected to outline what he or she intends to prove. The plaintiff, bearing the burden of proof, then presents evidence, which may include both testimony and physical evidence, such as documents and photos. Those are called *exhibits.*

The plaintiff's attorney secures testimony from his or her own witnesses via questioning labeled *direct examination.* After the plaintiff's attorney completes direct examination of a witness, the defense attorney may question that witness in a process labeled *cross-examination. Redirect* and *recross* may then follow. After all of the plaintiff's witnesses have been questioned, the plaintiff rests his or her case.

At this stage, the defense may make a motion for a *directed verdict,* arguing, in essence, that the plaintiff has offered insufficient evidence to justify relief, so time and expense may be saved by terminating the trial. Understandably, the judge considers the motion in the light most favorable to the plaintiff. Such motions ordinarily fail, and the trial goes forward with the defendant's presentation of evidence.

At the completion of the defendant's case, both parties may be permitted to offer *rebuttal* evidence, and either party may move for a directed verdict. Barring a directed verdict, the case goes forward, with each party making a closing argument. When the trial is by jury, the judge must instruct the jurors as to the law to be applied to the case. The attorneys often submit their views of the proper instructions. In most civil cases, a verdict for the plaintiff must be supported by a *preponderance of the evidence* (more likely than not). After deliberation, the verdict of the jury is rendered, and a judgment is entered by the court. [For a company providing a virtual jury in advance of trial, see **http://www.virtualjury.com**]

Experts

In this highly technological and scientific era, one of the biggest dilemmas facing judges and juries is the weight to give to expert testimony. Very often, in cases such as medical malpractice and product liability (see Chapter 7), the testimony of experts is decisive to the outcome; but that testimony varies wildly in its reliability and credibility. The golfing case that follows investigates the theme of experience as a qualification for expert testimony.

LEGAL BRIEFCASE

Nickles v. Schild
617 N.W.2d 659 (S. D. S. Ct. 2000)

Justice Gilbertson

Larry Nickles, the guardian of Mark Nickles, appeals the trial court's admission of expert testimony.

FACTS

On May 5, 1996, Jay Schild (Schild), Mark Nickles and Schild's younger brother drove to the Human Services Golf Course in Yankton, South Dakota, to play golf. All three boys were minors. Both Nickles and Schild had previously received golf instructions and had been taught some golfing rules.

After playing five holes, Schild and Nickles proceeded to the next tee box. Schild's younger brother was still on the fifth hole green retrieving his ball, which Nickles had knocked a short distance from the green. Schild proceeded to tee up his ball at the front center of the tee box and was preparing to hit his next drive. In the meantime, Nickles moved off the tee box approximately 10 feet and was facing the previous green watching Schild's brother. Schild, who had seen Nickles walk off the tee box, stepped back from his ball and took three practice swings. On the third practice swing, Schild hit Nickles in the head, fracturing his skull and permanently injuring his left eye.

Guardian (sic) commenced a personal injury action against Schild for damages sustained as a result of Schild's negligence and failure to exercise reasonable care in swinging his golf club. Schild denied he was negligent and claimed that Nickles was contributory (sic) negligent and assumed the risk of his injuries. During trial, Schild called Robert Boldus as an expert witness. Boldus was a former member of the Professional Golfer's (sic) Association and golf professional at Fox Run Golf Course in Yankton, South Dakota. Boldus had often given golfing lessons to junior golfers while at Fox Run.

Schild asked Boldus whether "as a golf professional," he had "formed any opinions as to what had happened in this case?" Nickles immediately requested permission to briefly interrogate Boldus for purposes of objecting to his opinion. During this interrogation, the following discussion occurred:

Q: (Nickles's attorney): Mr. Boldus, as a professional golfer, a member of PGA or based upon your experience, have you had any training in evaluating liability or standards of care required in golf liability cases?

A: (Boldus): No, I haven't.

Nickles then objected to the opinion by Boldus regarding standards of care or the ultimate issue. The trial judge overruled Nickles's objection and allowed Boldus to give his opinion:

Q: (Schild's attorney): And could you tell the jury what opinions you have come to?

A: (Boldus): In my opinion it was an accident. But one of the players moved, and when you're in your preshot routine if you move, you back away from the ball six inches to a foot or one step, and then you take your practice swings. My opinion, somehow Mark Nickles had moved in the way of the swing and got hit.

Q: (Schild's attorney): In your opinion did [Schild] violate any standards of care?

A: (Boldus): No.

The jury returned a verdict in favor of Schild. Nickles appealed, raising the following issue:

Whether the trial court abused its discretion by permitting expert testimony from Boldus.

* * * * *

DECISION

* * * * *

[A]n expert is not limited to testifying only upon those areas in which he or she has received formal training. Rather, when giving an opinion, an expert is allowed to draw upon all the knowledge, skill, or experience that he or she has accumulated.

[W]hile Boldus may not have had any formal classroom "training" in the applicable liability standards, it is clear Boldus was no novice at the game of golf. He was a former member of the PGA and a golf professional at Fox Run Golf Course in Yankton. While at Fox Run, he had often given golf lessons to junior golfers, which included golf etiquette and safety. He had even previously given golf lessons to Nickles. By any of these methods of acquiring the appropriate expertise or combination thereof, he could have qualified himself as an expert to testify as to "what happened."

It is quite clear from the testimony of Boldus and his vitae that he did have an opinion on the standards of care required in golf and the expertise to give such an opinion. The following testimony regarding the standard of care applicable to the game of golf was elicited from Boldus during direct testimony:

Q: When someone has addressed the ball and stepped back and they're doing their practice swings, what is the person's duty when they're doing those practice swings?

A: Well, basically there's nothing stated that says that you have to look around. You should be, when you begin your preshot routine, prior to taking your practice swings you should look and kind of [get] an idea where people are at so they are out of your way so you can take a swing. Once you begin your practice swings I think it's a duty of the other person to stay out of the way.

Q: So once, right before you start your preshot routine is when you have the duty to check what's going around?

A: Yes.

Q: And then as you start your preshot routine then it's the duty of those around you to become aware that that's what you're going to do, to watch?

A: Yes.

* * * * *

Boldus merely described, in his opinion, "what happened in this case" and that Schild's actions did not violate any standard of care concerning the game of golf. He did not invade the province of the jury as Nickles suggests. Boldus did not testify as to the ultimate issue of negligence. In fact, Boldus did not discuss the issue of liability at all until he was asked upon cross-examination, "but one party is liable, aren't they?" Boldus responded, "I wouldn't—yah—I don't know about liable, but somebody [is responsible for that]."

Nickles' objection as to the qualifications of Boldus goes in part to formal training concerning the issue of ultimate liability. The ultimate liability of one of the parties is not the same as standard of care. One can violate a standard of care and still not be held liable. There could be further potential questions of contributory negligence, assumption of the risk, financial responsibility of a minor and/or his parents, questions of duty to supervise a minor and the like, all of which can have a decisive effect on liability and which clearly are outside the expertise of a golf pro and his knowledge of golf standards of care. Boldus did not testify as to any of these issues; his testimony was limited to describing the standard of care for the game of golf.

Affirmed.

DISSENT

Justice Sabers

I dissent.

I write specially to point out that the majority opinion misses the point—not once, but several times.

Whether Boldus was qualified as an expert witness is immaterial. The point is that under the pretense of being an expert witness, Boldus cannot testify as a fact witness. He was not present at the scene. He does not know what happened. Only fact witnesses can testify "as to what happened?" Therefore, under these circumstances it was totally improper for Boldus to testify to his opinion "as to what happened in this case."

Questions

1. What were Nickles's objections to the expert, Boldus's, testimony?

2. What objection was raised by the dissenting Justice Sabers?

3. Do you agree with the expert, Boldus, that once a golfer has properly started the preshot routine the duty of care shifts to those around the golfer to be aware of what is happening and to keep themselves out of harm's way? Explain.

4. Dodge slipped leaving work and claimed that she suffered knee, ankle, and back injuries. Dodge sued the workplace cleaning service, but she provided no expert testimony to establish that the fall caused the injuries. Rather Dodge provided her own explanation of the fall and resulting injuries. Did the trial court err in admitting Dodge's lay person testimony? Explain, See *Dodge-Farrar v. American Cleaning Services Co.,* 54 P. 3d 954 (Ida. Ct. App. 2002).

Post-Trial Motions

The losing party may seek a *judgment notwithstanding the verdict (judgment n.o.v)* on the grounds that the jury's decision was clearly inconsistent with the law or the evidence. Such motions are rarely granted. The judge is also empowered to enter a judgment n.o.v on his or her own initiative.

Either party may also move for a new trial. The winning party might do so on the grounds that the remedy provided was inferior to that warranted by the evidence. The losing party commonly claims an error of law to support a motion for a new trial. Other possible grounds for a new trial include jury misconduct or new evidence.

Appeals

After the judgment is rendered, either party may appeal the decision to a higher court. The winner may do so if he or she feels the remedy is inadequate. Ordinarily, of course, the losing party brings the appeal. As noted, the appealing party is the *appellant* or the *petitioner,* while the other party is the *appellee* or *respondent.* The appeals court does not try the case again. In theory, at least, its consideration is limited to mistakes of law at the trial level. The appellant will argue, for example, that a jury instruction was erroneous or that the judge erred in failing to grant a motion to strike testimony alleged to have been prejudicial. The appeals court does not hear new evidence. Its decision is based on the trial record, materials filed by the opposing attorneys, and oral arguments.

The appellate court announces its judgment and ordinarily explains that decision in an accompanying document labeled an *opinion.* (Most of the cases in this text are appellate court opinions.) If no error is found, the lower court decision is *affirmed.* In finding prejudicial error, the appellate court may simply *reverse* (overrule) the lower court. Or the judgment may be to *reverse and remand,* wherein the lower court is overruled and the case must be tried again in accordance with the law as articulated in the appeals court opinion. After the decision of the intermediate appellate court, a further appeal may be sought at the highest court of the jurisdiction. Most of those petitions are denied.

Questions—Part Two

1. What are the purposes and uses of the concept of jurisdiction? Why do we limit the courts to which a claim can be taken?

2. Law cases often read like soap operas even as they reveal important truths. A woman and man, each married to others, had engaged in a long-term love affair. The woman's husband died, and she pleaded with her paramour to leave his New York home to visit her in Florida. She affirmed her love for the man. They made arrangements to meet in Miami, but on his arrival at the airport he was served a summons informing him that he was being sued. His Florida "lover" sought $500,000 for money allegedly loaned to him and for seduction inspired by a promise of marriage.
   a. Does the Florida court have proper jurisdiction over him?
   b. What if he had voluntarily come to Florida on vacation? See *Wyman v. Newhouse,* 93 F.2d 313 (2d Cir. 1937).

3. Sea Pines, a privately owned suburban community on Hilton Head Island, South Carolina, was designated a wildlife sanctuary by the state legislature. After study, the

state Department of Natural Resources decided to issue permits to allow limited deer hunting on the land to reduce overpopulation. Various environmental groups challenged the issuance of the permits. What defense would you expect the state to offer in court? Explain. See *Sea Pines Ass'n for Protection of Wildlife v. South Carolina Dept. of Natural Resources,* 550 S.E. 2d 287 (S.C. S. Ct. 2001).

Part Three—Criticism and Alternatives

Criticism

To many Americans, our system of justice is neither systematic nor just. With more than 1.1 million lawyers in a population of over 310 million people, critics argue that excessive, unproductive litigation is inevitable.

Too Many Lawyers and Lawsuits?

Many lawsuits are less a search for justice and more a pursuit of big dollars for attorneys, the critics claim. Former Enron CEO Jeffrey Skilling was found guilty in 2006 of fraud, conspiracy and other crimes in his trial involving the 2001 collapse of Enron, the Texas energy giant. The Enron bankruptcy cost thousands of jobs, more than $60 billion in Enron stock and more than $2 billion in employee pension funds. Skilling was sentenced to 24 years in prison. Skilling's lawyer, Daniel Petrocelli, billed his services at nearly $800 per hour. Petrocelli represented Skilling for a total of five years in various civil suits, testimony before government agencies, and so on. Petrocelli said that Skilling's criminal defense required a team of 12 lawyers, five paralegals, and many temporary staffers. The total legal bill: $70 million.[19] As one attorney later quipped: "What would he have been paid if he had won?"[20] Some five years later at this writing, Skilling is in jail after his latest appeal failed. Presumably the legal bills continue to mount. Are extraordinary legal bills a symptom of a troubled legal system?

> The total legal bill: $70 million. As one attorney later quipped: "What would he have been paid if he had won?"

Legal critic Philip K. Howard argues that we need fewer lawsuits, fewer rules, and greater personal responsibility. He thinks we feel powerless in the face of rules:

> Ordinary choices–by teachers, doctors, officials, managers, even volunteers—are paralyzed by legal self-consciousness. Did you check the rules? Who will be responsible if there is an accident? . . . We have become a culture of rule followers, trained to frame every solution in terms of existing law or possible legal risk. . . . [21]

Even Supreme Court Justice Antonin Scalia has argued that we have too many lawyers:

> Lawyers don't dig ditches or build buildings. When a society requires such a large number of its best minds to conduct the unproductive enterprise of the law, something is wrong with the legal system.[22]

Polling results suggest that Americans have deep reservations about our legal system, but they also recognize its indispensable role in maintaining a just society. U.S. Chamber of Commerce polling, for example, shows that nine of 10 Americans believe we have too many frivolous or unfair lawsuits, that 84 percent of Americans say that meritless lawsuits clog the justice process and that 75 percent of Americans believe our justice system is most beneficial to lawyers themselves.[23] At the same time, a 2007 national poll by the American Association for Justice (formerly the American Trial Lawyers Association) found more concern about corporate abuse than about lawyers and the legal system. In identifying "extremely serious" problems facing the nation, only 34 percent of those polled cited "trial lawyers making too much money when they successfully represent a client in a lawsuit," and 24 percent cited "victims in cases involving personal injury or medical malpractice receiving too much money from juries."[24] "Corporations giving huge salaries and bonuses to CEOs, while cutting the jobs and benefits of employees" topped the list of problems, having been cited by 64 percent of those polled.[25] Broadly, those polled favored careful oversight of corporate conduct:

> They (the poll respondents) tell us that making sure corporations are held accountable when their actions harm consumers, employees, or communities (70 percent) should be a much higher priority for the civil justice system than limiting the amount of compensation that juries can award for pain and suffering "so that lawsuits do not cause as big a burden on our economy" (25 percent). Similarly, they give priority to holding corporations accountable (61 percent) over "reducing the number of frivolous lawsuits" and penalizing those who file them (32 percent).[26]

> **Nine of 10 Americans believe we have too many frivolous lawsuits.**

The Corporate Perspective

The legal system plays an invaluable role in facilitating and stabilizing commercial practice, but for corporate America the law is also a source of significant expense and abundant frustration. As one expert explained, dealing with legal responsibilities and problems has become a central ingredient in management practice:

> Only a few decades ago, the law was peripheral to the core activities of doing business. When I became a business lawyer in the late 1950s, for example, our involvement was generally limited to forming a corporation or partnership for a client, providing for the investment capital, doing a lease for an office or factory, and maybe handling a key contract with a CEO or a major supplier. . . . Today the law can affect almost every action a manager takes. It has moved closer to the core activities of conducting business and succeeding in a red-hot, competitive environment. More people now have "rights" they can assert against your company, so you face claims from employees, consumers, competitors, and the government. Consequently, today's manager needs to know something about employment law, discrimination claims, sexual harassment rules, product safety issues, the rules of advertising and competition, antitrust rules, environmental law, the value of intellectual property, and more.[27]

[For a site dedicated to laughing at lawyers, see **http://www.power-of-attorneys.com/**] [For a critique of the American legal system, see the U.S. Chamber Institute for Legal Reform (an affiliate of the U.S. Chamber of Commerce) at **http://www.facesoflawsuitabuse.com/**]

Pants: Abusing the Legal System?

Washington, DC administrative law judge, Roy Pearson, attracted the attention of journalists from around the world by suing his neighborhood laundry for $54 million, down from an earlier claim of $67 million, over the alleged loss of the pants belonging to his $1,000 suit. Pearson thought he was entitled to $18,000 per day for each day the pants were missing over a period of nearly four years. Owners Soo and Jin Chung of Custom Cleaners attempted to give Pearson a pair of pants they said were the missing item, but he said the ones offered were not his. Pearson brought claims of mental suffering, inconvenience, discomfort, and fraud (based on the "Satisfaction Guaranteed" sign at Custom Cleaners). Along the way, Pearson had rejected settlement offers that reached $12,000. The Chungs won an easy trial victory with the court concluding that Pearson was unable to prove the pants offered to him were not his and that the "Satisfaction Guaranteed" sign did not require the Chungs to satisfy a customer's unreasonable demands. Pearson was ordered to pay the Chungs' court costs, and the legal fees for the Chungs' defense were covered by contributions. The Chung's dry cleaner went out of business. Pearson subsequently failed in his bid to be reappointed to his judge's position. He sued for wrongful discharge and lost at the federal district court and then appealed to the federal court of appeals where he also lost.

Sources: Henri E. Cauvin, "Court Rules for Cleaners in $54 Million Pants Suit," *The Washington Post,* June 26, 2007, p. A01; and "'Pants Judge' Roy Pearson Strikes Out in Court," *The Wall Street Journal,* May 27, 2010 [**http://blogs.wsj.com/law/**].

Criticized in America; Embraced Abroad

Highly criticized at home, the American legal system, nonetheless, has received a respectful endorsement around the globe. American-style litigation has followed American-style capitalism, and its variants, to all corners of the world. An unexpected consequence of globalization is the remarkable growth in lawyers and lawsuits in many other countries. Consider Japan, a nation that once disdained America's litigation "mania."

Japan   Globalization has changed Japan's traditionally cooperative corporate culture. Historically, the Japanese government maintained quiet order in the cartel-bound, clubby private sector, but the pressure of global competition has provoked increased friction, and lawsuits have soared in a culture that prefers working things out quietly. For most of its post–World War II era, Japan had not felt the need for lawyers, and their numbers today remain among the smallest in the world, but at 29,000 in total, Japanese lawyers have increased by 68 percent since 2000 and from 2004 to 2009 lawsuits increased by 73 percent (totaling 235,509).[28] Regardless of the growth of lawyers, the Japanese legal system remains resistant to legal pressures particularly as applied to manufacturers such as Toyota. *The Wall Street Journal* noted Japan's restrained response to Toyota's many recent vehicle recall problems:

> Over in Japan, meanwhile, pressure on the company is perhaps a bit less intense than it is in the U.S. That's because in Japan, Toyota is largely shielded from lawsuits and regulatory action by rules and customs more deferential to manufacturers.[29]

Furthermore, Japanese courts seldom award punitive damages, and class actions are uncommon, but *BusinessWeek* reports that Japan may need a stronger legal system:

> Despite the changes, it is unlikely Japan will ever fully embrace the kind of legal conflict common in the U.S. . . . But a more sophisticated, and contentious, legal system may be just what the country needs in order to keep its economic overhaul on track.[30]

PRACTICING ETHICS   Private Law for Walmart?

A portion of Walmart's Ethical Standards Program demands employee welfare throughout its vast supply chain:

> We do not own, operate, or manage any factories. Instead, we purchase merchandise from suppliers located in more than 60 countries. Our Ethical Standards team is dedicated to verifying that these supplier factories are in compliance with our Standards for Suppliers. These standards cover compliance with local and national laws and regulations governing compensation, hours of labor, forced/prison labor, underage labor, discrimination, freedom of association and collective bargaining, health and safety, environment, and the right of audit by Walmart Stores, Inc.[31]

Law professor Larry Cata Backer argues that Walmart and other global giants are effectively legislating their own private law in the form of contract and business relationships and ethics standards governing product quality, working conditions and similar matters. Walmart's Standards for Suppliers are the core of its global governance system that, according to Backer, is "an important emerging phenomenon: the development of efficient systems of private law making by nongovernmental organizations that sometimes supplement, and sometimes displace traditional legal systems."[32] Working with the media, nongovernmental organizations (NGOs), consumers, and investors, Walmart and other multinationals, Backer argues, are beginning to build independent mechanisms for efficient regulation of economic behavior on a global scale that may lead to systems of law beyond governments and moderated largely by stakeholders.[33]

Question

1. Should we welcome and encourage the development of a private law system enforced through contractual and ethical standards by giant multinationals, or should we be concerned that strengthened, strictly enforced private law arrangements would place too much authority in the hands of already powerful organizations? Explain.

On the Other Hand—Litigation as a Last Resort

Almost everyone seems to be unhappy about lawyers and lawsuits, but at the same time Americans expect lawyers and the courts to settle disputes, preserve freedom and justice and correct problems not satisfactorily addressed by the market, legislatures and regulators. Feeling threatened by abusive bosses, corporate fraud, dangerous drugs, defective products, environmental decline, and so on, Americans count on the justice system to protect our pecuniary interests as well as the personal freedom and democracy we prize. Lawyers and the courts often are the only available weapons to right what we believe to be a wrong. So the frustration many feel about exploding litigation may be attributable to us as much as to greedy lawyers. Furthermore, laws and lawyers are central to economic efficiency. Lawyers devise the rules, processes, and structures that permit capitalism to operate effectively. As we have read, the balance of the world is coming to recognize that law and lawyers are prerequisites to economic stability and progress.

Fewer Trials   Whatever we may feel about lawyers and the justice system, the simple fact, as reported by *BusinessWeek,* is that federal civil trials have declined in recent years:

> Around the country, plenty of lawsuits are getting filed, but fewer and fewer are going to trial. The civil trial is one of the most iconic American institutions, a time-honored forum where disputes over injuries, divorces, and all manner of business disasters are resolved. Yet rising legal costs, decreasing judicial tolerance for weak lawsuits, and the surging use of alternative dispute resolution (ADR) are combining to make courtroom showdowns exceptional occurrences.[34]

According to *BusinessWeek,* civil suits filed in federal district courts in the past 40 years soared from 66,144 to 259,541, but the number of those that eventually went to trial fell to a new low of 3,555 in 2006, down from a peak of 12,018 in 1984.[35] Likewise, in the 21 states with available data, the number of civil jury trials fell 40 percent from 1976 to 2004.[36] Trials often are an inefficient way of resolving disputes so these numbers may be considered very good news. On the other hand, trials are visible affirmations of the indispensability of justice, and they provide the careful reasoning and precedents that identify impermissible behavior.

> Trials often are an inefficient way of resolving disputes.

PRACTICING ETHICS   Declining Access to Lawyers?

One of the reasons for the declining number of trials, despite increasing disputes, may be difficulty in affording a lawyer in civil suits. *The New York Times* and other publications have reported an increasing number of cases going forward with one of the parties serving as a "do-it-yourself" lawyer.[37] Pursuing a claim in a federal district court costs an average of $15,000 with more complicated cases involving scientific evidence often reaching $100,000.[38] Indeed, *The New York Times* reports that expense has become such a hurdle that lawsuits have become investment vehicles: "Large banks, hedge funds and private investors hungry for new and lucrative opportunities are bankrolling other people's lawsuits, pumping hundreds of millions of dollars into medical malpractice claims, divorce battles and class actions against corporations. . . ."[39] Lawsuit investments nationwide are estimated to exceed $1 billion at any given time, and some of those lawsuits are actually initiated and controlled by the investors.[40]

One result is that some litigants appear to be victimized by lawsuit lenders in a lightly regulated industry where interest rates "often exceed 100 percent per year."[41]

Litigants who go it alone may find help on the Internet. Illinois, for example, established Illinois Legal Aid Online to provide introductory education and access to online conversations with volunteer law students.[42] However, with serious matters such as bankruptcy, eviction, and employment rights at stake, experts are concerned that the legal system is failing many Americans.

Question

1. While indigent criminal defendants are assured the right to counsel under American law, the same is not assured in civil disputes. Do you think we must begin to close the "justice gap" by providing taxpayer-funded legal aid for indigents in serious civil cases such as housing, health care, and child custody? Explain.

Reform: Judicial Efficiency

Governments, businesses, lawyers, judges—all are frustrated with the expense and inefficiency of our overburdened judicial system. Some small businesses are now buying legal services insurance or prepaid legal services for a flat monthly fee.

Some cities have taken novel approaches to adjudication such as business courts that hear only commercial claims, thus allowing jurists to become very efficient in handling contract problems, shareholder claims, and the like. Those systems are variations on the small claims courts that have long proven effective in settling minor disputes.

Small Claims Courts

Suppose you move out of your apartment and your landlord refuses to return your $500 damage deposit even though the rooms are spotless. Hiring a lawyer doesn't make good financial sense and is beyond your means anyway, but a small claims court may provide an effective solution.

Small claims courts, for the most part, resolve relatively minor disputes, like your landlord-tenant problem. A wide range of problems, such as divorce or bankruptcy, cannot be litigated in small claims courts. Maximum recoveries vary from place to place but typically range from a few thousand dollars up to $7,500 or so. To prepare for a small claims case, the key is developing and presenting to the judge as much credible evidence as possible. If you can present witnesses on your behalf, do so, but if not, clearly written memos expressing what the witnesses would have said may be acceptable to the judge. You need not hire a lawyer, but in most states you may do so if you wish. Should the small claims litigation not work out well for you, an appeal is permitted in many states.[43]

Alternative Dispute Resolution (ADR)

Businesses, in particular, are increasingly looking outside the judicial system for dispute resolution strategies. Dot-com entrepreneurs are developing interesting new online mechanisms for conveniently addressing Internet-based disputes. Networks of human mediators, dispute resolution software, and PayPal dispute resolution are among the online methods of settling problems outside of court.

Cybersettle is an online system for resolving insurance disputes, often of the fender-bender or slip-and-fall variety. The parties log on to Cybersettle and type in their monetary demands or offers. The system works 24 hours a day, 7 days a week. The computer compares the bids, round by round. When those numbers come within a predetermined range, the two sides are notified that a settlement has been achieved. If necessary, a telephone facilitator may join the process to help reach the final sum to be paid. Cybersettle has patented its system and says it has settled over 200,000 transactions and has facilitated over $1.8 billion in settlements. [See **http://www.cybersettle.com/pub/**] Critics say some Internet legal resources such as **http://www.whocanisue.com/,** a highly-advertised Web site that matches potential clients with lawyers, may degrade the legal profession and serve primarily to generate litigation.[44]

What Is ADR? alternative dispute resolution.

Of course, any form of negotiation and settlement would constitute an alternative to litigation, but mediation and arbitration are the most prominent of the substitutes. Given the expense, frustration, and risk of lawsuits, we are seeing increasing imagination in building other ADR options including private trials and minitrials. [For many ADR links, see **www.hg.org/adr.html**]

Mediation

Mediation introduces a neutral third party into the resolution process. Ideally, the parties devise their own solution, with the mediator as a facilitator, not a decision maker. Even if the mediator proposes a solution, it will likely be in the nature of a compromise, not a determination of right and wrong. The bottom line is that only the disputing parties can adopt any particular outcome. The mediator may aid the parties in a number of ways, such as opening up communication between them.

Arbitration

In *arbitration* a neutral third party is given the power to determine a binding resolution of the dispute. Depending on the situation, the resolution may be either a compromise solution or a determination of the rights of the parties and a win–lose solution. Even in the latter case, however, arbitration may be quicker and less costly than a trial, and the arbitrator may be an expert in the subject area of the dispute instead of a generalist, as a judge would be. Arbitration is procedurally more formal than mediation, with the presentation of proofs and arguments by the parties, but less formal than court adjudication.

The arbitrator's decision ordinarily is legally binding and final, although an increasing but still small number of arbitration decisions are reaching court.[45]

[For a brief overview of mediation and arbitration see **http://www.youtube.com/watch?v=KLdia39awl0**] (The final two characters in this URL are a lowercase l, as in law, and zero.)

Private Trials

"Rent-a-Judge"

A number of states now permit mutually-agreed-on private trials, sometimes labeled "rent-a-judge." Normally a third party such as a mediation firm makes the necessary arrangements, including hiring a retired judge and jurors. The proceedings are conducted much as in a courtroom. Because the parties are paying, however, the process normally moves along more rapidly, and the proceeding may be conducted in private. Appeals to the formal judicial system are provided for in some states. Critics question the fairness of the private system and wonder if it will further erode faith in public trials, but the time and money saved can be quite substantial.

Mini-trials

In recent years, some corporations have agreed to settle their disputes by holding informal hearings that clarify the facts and the issues that would emerge if the dispute were litigated. In the mini-trial, each organization presents its version of the case to a panel of senior executives from each organization. The trial is presided over by a neutral third party who may be expected to issue a nonbinding opinion as to the likely result were the case to be litigated. The executives then meet to attempt to negotiate a settlement. The neutral third party sometimes facilitates that discussion. Mini-trials are voluntary and nonbinding, but if an agreement is reached, the parties can formalize it by entering a settlement contract.

ADR Assessed

ADR mechanisms generally have been sustained in the courts. ADR—particularly arbitration—is often the required dispute-resolution mechanism for employee complaints such as discrimination or harassment. Mandatory arbitration clauses are often included in consumer transactions involving loans, credit cards, cable service, auto warranties, brokerage accounts, insurance and more. Ordinarily, ADR costs less and is resolved more quickly than litigation. ADR is less formal and less adversarial than the judicial process. Furthermore, the parties have more control over the proceedings in that they can choose the facilitator, they can choose when and where the dispute will be heard, and they can keep the dispute private if they wish. Despite those strengths, alternative dispute resolution has some limitations when compared with litigation.

A new study of nearly 4,000 employee arbitration cases found an employee win rate of only 21.4 percent, a lower result than in litigation. In arbitration cases won by employees, the median recovery was $36,500 and the mean was $109,858 both of which are substantially lower than awards reported from litigation. On the other hand, arbitration, on average, was both quicker and less expensive than litigation.[46]

A 2011 U.S. Supreme Court decision makes arbitration less functional for consumers by allowing businesses to continue their commonplace practice of requiring arbitration of disputes but forbidding class action arbitration (and litigation) thus compelling consumers to individually arbitrate alleged wrongdoing. In that case, Vincent and Liza Concepcion complained that AT&T Mobility charged them $30.22 in sales tax and other fees for what was advertised as a "free" phone. They sought class action status for themselves and others, but the 5-4 Supreme Court ruling denied that possibility and left the Concepcions and others similarly aggrieved to file individual claims for very small amounts of money.[47] The case that follows examines whether a mandatory arbitration clause in a travel agency contract to climb Mount Kilimanjaro was unconscionable under California law.

> AT&T Mobility charged them $30.22 for a "free" phone.

Lhotka v. Geographic Expeditions
181 Cal. App. 4th 816 (2010)
(Petition for review denied *Lhotka v. Geographic Expeditions*, 2010 Cal. LEXIS 3320 [Cal. S. Ct.])[48]

LEGAL BRIEFCASE

Judge Siggins

Geographic Expeditions, Inc. (GeoEx), appeals from an order denying its motion to compel arbitration of a wrongful death action brought by the survivors of one of its clients who died on a Mount Kilimanjaro hiking expedition. . . .

BACKGROUND

Jason Lhotka was 37 years old when he died of an altitude-related illness while on a GeoEx expedition up Mount Kilimanjaro with his mother, plaintiff Sandra Menefee. GeoEx's limitation of liability and release form, which both Lhotka and Menefee signed as a requirement of participating in the expedition, provided that each of them released GeoEx from all liability in connection with the trek and waived any claims for liability "to the maximum extent permitted by law." The release also required that the parties would submit any disputes between themselves first to mediation and then to binding arbitration. It reads: "I understand that all Trip Applications are subject to acceptance by GeoEx in San Francisco, California, USA. I agree that in the unlikely event a dispute of any kind arises between me and GeoEx, the following conditions will apply: (a) the dispute will be submitted to a neutral third-party mediator in San Francisco, California, with both parties splitting equally the cost of such mediator. If the dispute cannot be resolved through mediation, then (b) the dispute will be submitted for binding arbitration to the American Arbitration Association in San Francisco, California; (c) the dispute will be governed by California law; and (d) the maximum amount of recovery to which I will be entitled under any and all circumstances will be the sum of the land and air cost of my trip with GeoEx. I agree that this is a fair and reasonable limitation on the damages, of any sort whatsoever, that I may suffer. I agree to fully indemnify GeoEx for all of its costs (including attorneys' fees) if I commence an action or claim against GeoEx based upon claims I have previously released or waived by signing this release." Menefee paid $16,831 for herself and Lhotka to go on the trip.

A letter from GeoEx president James Sano that accompanied the limitation of liability and release explained that the form was mandatory and that, on this point, "our lawyers, insurance carriers and medical consultants give us no discretion. A signed, unmodified release form is required before any traveler may join one of our trips. Ultimately, we believe that you should choose your travel company based on its track record, not what you are asked to sign. . . . My review of other travel companies' release forms suggests that our forms are not a whole lot different from theirs."

After her son's death, Menefee sued GeoEx for wrongful death and alleged various theories of liability including fraud, gross negligence and recklessness, and intentional infliction of emotional distress. GeoEx moved to compel arbitration.

The trial court found the arbitration provision was unconscionable and on that basis denied the motion.

*   *   *   *   *

This appeal timely followed.

DISCUSSION

The question . . . posed here[is] whether the agreement to arbitrate is unconscionable and, therefore, unenforceable.

*   *   *   *   *

II. Unconscionability (I omitted-Ed.)
(1) We turn first to GeoEx's contention that the court erred when it found the arbitration agreement unconscionable. . . .

"[U]nconscionability has generally been recognized to include an absence of meaningful choice on the part of one of the parties together with contract terms which are unreasonably favorable to the other party.' Phrased another way, unconscionability has both a 'procedural' and a 'substantive'

element." The procedural element requires oppression or surprise. Oppression occurs where a contract involves lack of negotiation and meaningful choice, surprise where the allegedly unconscionable provision is hidden within a prolix printed form. The substantive element concerns whether a contractual provision reallocates risks in an objectively unreasonable or unexpected manner.' Under this approach, both the procedural and substantive elements must be met before a contract or term will be deemed unconscionable. Both, however, need not be present to the same degree. A sliding scale is applied so that 'the more substantively oppressive the contract term, the less evidence of procedural unconscionability is required to come to the conclusion that the term is unenforceable, and vice versa.'" . . .

A. Procedural Unconscionability

*   *   *   *   *

GeoEx led plaintiffs to understand not only that its terms and conditions were nonnegotiable, but that plaintiffs would encounter the same requirements with any other travel company. This is a sufficient basis for us to conclude plaintiffs lacked bargaining power.

GeoEx also contends its terms were not oppressive . . . because Menefee and Lhotka could have simply decided not to trek up Mount Kilimanjaro. It argues that contracts for recreational activities can *never* be unconscionably oppressive because, unlike agreements for necessities such as medical care or employment, a consumer of recreational activities *always* has the option of foregoing the activity. . . .
(2) While the nonessential nature of recreational activities is a factor to be taken into account in assessing whether a contract is oppressive, it is not necessarily the dispositive factor.

*   *   *   *   *

(3) Here, certainly, plaintiffs could have chosen not to sign on with the expedition. That option, like any availability of market alternatives, is relevant to the existence, and degree, of oppression. . . .

But we must also consider the other circumstances surrounding the execution of the agreement. . . .

GeoEx presented its terms as both nonnegotiable and *no different than what plaintiffs would find with any other provider* Under these circumstances, plaintiffs made a sufficient showing to establish at least a minimal level of oppression to justify a finding of procedural unconscionability.

B. Substantive Unconscionability

With the "sliding scale" rule firmly in mind, we address whether the substantive unconscionability of the GeoEx contract warrants the trial court's ruling.

The arbitration provision in GeoEx's release is . . . one-sided. . . . It guaranteed that plaintiffs could not possibly obtain anything approaching full recompense for their harm by limiting any recovery they could obtain to the amount they paid GeoEx for their trip. In addition to a limit on their recovery plaintiffs, residents of Colorado, were required to mediate and arbitrate in San Francisco—all but guaranteeing both that GeoEx would never be out more than the amount plaintiffs had paid for their trip, and that any recovery plaintiffs might obtain would be devoured by the expense they incur in pursing their remedy. The release also required plaintiffs to indemnify GeoEx for its costs and attorney fees for defending any claims covered by the release of liability form. Notably, there is no reciprocal limitation on damages or indemnification obligations imposed on GeoEx. Rather than providing a neutral forum for dispute resolution, GeoEx's arbitration scheme provides a potent disincentive for an aggrieved client to pursue any claim, in any forum—and may well guarantee that GeoEx wins even if it loses. Absent reasonable justification for this arrangement—and none is apparent— we agree with the trial court that the arbitration clause is so one-sided as to be substantively unconscionable.

Affirmed.

Questions

1. Why was the Lhotka/Geographic Expeditions agreement to arbitrate ruled unconscionable?

2. Differentiate procedural and substantive unconscionability.

3. Kalliope and David Valchine entered court-ordered mediation to try to resolve the problems that had led them to seek a divorce. Lawyers represented both Kalliope and David at mediation. The mediation led to a marital settlement agreement between Kalliope and David. One month later, Kalliope sought to set aside the agreement, arguing that she had been coerced by her husband, her husband's attorney, and the mediator. Kalliope testified that the mediator threatened to report her to the judge for being uncooperative in refusing to sign a reasonable settlement offer. She claimed that the mediator also told her that she could sign the agreement and then object to its provisions at the final hearing. See *Kalliope Vitakis-Valchine v. David L. Valchine*, 793 So.2d 1094 (Fla. App. 4th Dist. 2001); 34 So.3d 17 (Fla. App. 4th Dist. 2010).

   Should the settlement be set aside? Explain.

4. Is an arbitration clause as a condition of employment a fair method of alternate dispute resolution, if entered knowingly and voluntarily? Explain.

5. In an effort to reduce legal expenses, some major banks and other businesses follow policies providing that all customer complaints will be subject to arbitration. Is mandatory arbitration fair to consumers? Explain.

Internet Exercise

Go to the "2010 U.S. Chamber of Commerce State Liability Systems Ranking Study," at [**www.instituteforlegalreform.com/lawsuit-climate.html**]. Check your state's ranking according to the study; then click on the Key Issues button to read experts' views about the most important legal problems facing state policy makers. Then for links to some critiques of the Chamber study go to [**http://viztac.com/general/challenge-to-validity-of-annual-u-s-chamber-of-commerce-state-liability-systems-ranking-study**].

Chapter Questions

1. Economist Stephen Magee argues that one way to strengthen the American economy would be to close the law schools:

   > Every time you turn out one law school graduate, you've got a 40-year problem on your hands, he says. These guys run around and generate a lot of spurious conflict. They're like heat-seeking missiles.[49]

   Comment.

2. Professor and criminal justice expert Morgan O. Reynolds argues that sterner punishment has led to reduced crime in the United States:

This reflects a broader pattern: As our crime rates have fallen, serious crime rates in England have risen substantially, as a recent study from the U.S. Bureau of Justice Statistics found. For example, victim surveys show that

- The English robbery rate was about half the U.S. rate in 1981 but was 40 percent higher than America's in 1995.
- The English assault rate was slightly higher than America's in 1981 but more than double by 1995.
- The English burglary rate was half America's in 1981 but nearly double by 1995.

Why these dramatic increases in English crime rates, while Americans' lives and property grew safer? The obvious explanation has been too often downplayed or ignored: The United States has instituted tougher, more predictable punishment for crime. The study's authors attribute the trends they note to the increasing conviction rates and longer sentences meted out in the United States versus the decreasing conviction rates and softer sentences in England and Wales. English conviction rates for rape, burglary, assault, and auto theft have plunged by half or more since 1981, while the likelihood of serving prison time for committing a serious violent crime or a burglary has increased substantially in the United States.[50]

a. Do you agree that harsher and more certain punishment will reduce criminal behavior?

b. Do "root causes" such as being born out of wedlock affect criminal behavior? Explain.

3. Crowley, who became intoxicated at a postrace party on McRoberts's boat, was driving after the party and caused a multicar accident that resulted in serious injuries to Culver, who was driving one of the other vehicles. Culver's passenger was killed, and Crowley was later convicted of reckless homicide. Culver sued McRoberts for negligence. Crowley's drinking took place in the galley of McRoberts's 40-foot boat. McRoberts did not provide the liquor and McRoberts, who was busy with recording race results, was not aware of how much drinking Crowley had done. The Indiana Dram Shop statute provided that "it is unlawful for a person to sell, barter, deliver, or give away an alcoholic beverage to another person who is in a state of intoxication if the person knows that the other person is intoxicated." Expert testimony and a blood alcohol reading suggested that Crowley may have been visibly drunk, but several witnesses on the boat said they did not observe visible signs of intoxication. Did McRoberts violate the Indiana Dram Shop law, and was McRoberts negligent in failing to properly supervise Crowley? Explain. See *Culver v. McRoberts,* 192 F.3d 1095 (7th Cir. 1999).

4. Dubuque, Iowa's City Council and mayor in 2011 enacted a parental responsibility ordinance providing that: "A failure by a parent to exercise reasonable control over the parent's minor which causes the minor to commit an unlawful act is a violation . . ." The ordinance is directed to derelict parents whose negligence or indifference facilitates criminal behavior by children and leads to big investments of police time in simply locating parents. A violation initially results in a warning with increasing fines (or parenting classes) for violations thereafter. The city's plan is to provide resources to aid parents who are in violation of the ordinance.

The city has indicated that "reasonable control" means doing what the average person would do.[51]

a. What objections would you raise to this ordinance?

b. Do you think a parent would violate the reasonable control standard if his/her child failed to come home from the movies by the hour agreed on, but the parent then made an effort to find the child? Explain.

c. Is the ordinance a good idea in your judgment? Explain.

5. After drinking at the Elks Lodge, Dionne was escorted to a taxi where the driver, Grader, was told to take Dionne home because he had too much to drink. Dionne would not give Grader directions to his home and then told Grader to take him to another bar. Dionne paid his fare and went into the second bar, and later that bar summoned the same cab to take Dionne home. On this occasion, Dionne told Grader to take him to a convenience store. Dionne conducted his business there with no overt signs of intoxication. He then returned to the cab and asked to be driven back to the Elks Lodge. Grader deposited Dionne at the Elks Lodge and watched as Dionne passed by his own car in the parking lot. Grader heard other voices in the lot, assumed Dionne would be fine, and resumed his work. Later that evening Dionne died in a single-car accident. His blood-alcohol level was .25. The facts are not clear as to whether Dionne drank more after leaving Grader's cab. The taxi service was sued for negligence for not taking Dionne home. How would you rule on that negligence claim? Explain. See *Mastriano v. Blyer*, 779 A.2d 951 (Sup. Jud. Ct. Maine 2001).

6. A letter to *The Wall Street Journal:*

> The problems with our legal system go much deeper than irresponsible plaintiffs, amoral lawyers, and inept juries. The trouble is, our system of checks and balances has been corrupted; 100 percent of the executive, 100 percent of the judicial, and 43 percent of the legislative branches have been taken over by one group—lawyers.
>
> The Constitution charges Congress to ordain and establish the courts. It is no wonder it has created a system that maximizes the incomes of its own kind. The system is rigged to drag out cases that are billed by the hour, or to find moochers and looters willing to bring huge civil suits against productive citizens and corporations in front of dumbed-down juries.[52]

Do you agree? Explain.

7. In your opinion are attractive criminal defendants likely to receive more favorable treatment in the courts than similarly situated but less attractive defendants? Explain.

8. According to Warren Avis, founder of Avis Rent-a-Car,

> We've reached a point in this country where, in many instances, power has become more important than justice—not a matter of who is right, but of who has the most money, time, and the largest battery of lawyers to drag a case through the courts.[53]

a. Should the rich be entitled to better legal representation, just as they have access to better food, better medical care, better education, and so on? Explain.

b. Should we employ a nationwide legal services program sufficient to guarantee competent legal aid to all? Explain.

9. Peremptory challenges may not constitutionally be used to exclude a potential juror from a trial on racial or gender grounds.
   a. Must a criminal jury reflect the ethnic or racial diversity of the community? Explain. See *Powers v. Ohio,* 111 S. Ct. 1364 (1991).
   b. Could potential jurors lawfully be rejected on the basis of their place of residence? Explain. See *U.S. v. Bishop,* 959 F.2d 820 (9th Cir. 1992).

10. French journalist Alain Clement offered a partial explanation for Americans' increasing reliance on lawsuits to resolve conflicts:

    > Diverse causes explain the growth of the contentious mood in America. One could be called the devaluing of the future. In 1911, the Russian political scientist Moise Ostrgorski wrote, "Confident of the future, Americans manifest a remarkable endurance to an unhappy present, a submissive patience that is willing to bargain about not only civic rights, but even the rights of man."[54]

    a. What does Clement mean?
    b. How do you explain our increased reliance on litigation?

11. In 1982, a security guard was murdered during a robbery of a south Chicago McDonald's. Alton Logan was sentenced to life in prison for that murder. At the same time, two Chicago public defenders, Dale Coventry and Jamie Kunz, were representing Andrew Wilson, who was accused of murdering two police officers. Based on a tip, Coventry and Kunz suspected that Wilson was the actual murderer in the McDonald's case. They questioned Wilson who admitted that he, not Logan, was the murderer. Because of their duties under the attorney-client privilege, Coventry and Kunz felt they could not reveal what they knew. Logan, therefore, went to prison an innocent man, they believed. The public defenders decided to write the story in a notarized affidavit and lock it in a box in case something should happen that would allow them to reveal what they knew. When Wilson died in prison of natural causes in 2008, Coventry and Kunz revealed their client's confession. After 26 years, Logan was released from prison. He was granted a certificate of innocence in 2009, and at this writing, he is suing various police officers for framing him.[55]
    a. Why does the legal profession expect lawyers to keep secret their clients' confidential communications?
    b. Had you been Coventry and Kunz, would you have revealed what you knew in order to immediately secure justice for Logan? Explain.

12. On July 5, 1884, four sailors were cast away from their ship in a storm 1,600 miles from the Cape of Good Hope. Their lifeboat contained neither water nor much food. On the 20th day of their ordeal, Dudley and Stevens, without the assistance or agreement of Brooks, cut the throat of the fourth sailor, a 17- or 18-year-old boy. They had not eaten since day 12. Water had been available only occasionally. At the time of the death, the men were probably about 1,000 miles from land. Prior to his death, the boy was lying helplessly in the bottom of the boat. The three surviving sailors ate the boy's remains for four days, at which point they were rescued by a passing boat. They were in a seriously weakened condition.
    a. Were Dudley and Stevens guilty of murder? Explain.
    b. Should Brooks have been charged with a crime for eating the boy's flesh? Explain. See *The Queen v. Dudley and Stephens,* 14 Queen's Bench Division 273 (1884).

13. Tompkins was a citizen of Pennsylvania. While walking on a railroad footpath in that state, he was struck by an object protruding from a passing freight train owned by the Erie Railroad Company, a New York corporation. Tompkins, by virtue of diversity of citizenship, filed a negligence suit against Erie in a New York federal court. Erie argued for the application of Pennsylvania common law, in which case Tompkins would have been treated as a trespasser. Tompkins argued that the absence of a Pennsylvania statute addressing the topic meant that federal common law had to be applied to the case. Should the federal court apply the relevant Pennsylvania state law, or should the court be free to exercise its independent judgment about what the common law of the state is or should be? See *Erie Railroad v. Tompkins,* 304 U.S. 64 (1938).

14. China is rapidly training lawyers and moving toward a more Western approach to judicial systems. The following quote describes China's historic view of dispute resolution:

    > Most Chinese persons engage in a large variety of economic and social activities and resolve disputes involved in those activities without coming in contact with the formal legal system. As in Japan, litigation in a court of law is not considered a normal way to resolve a dispute. Custom and extrajudicial dispute-settling mechanisms are utilized not only by private parties but by public entities. Decisions declaring someone right and someone wrong are not a desirable goal. Settlements and compromises are preferable. Even in court, Chinese litigants generally do not obtain a clear defeat or victory.[56]

    In your view, would China be better off in the contemporary world to retain its traditional means of conflict settlement or should it continue its turn toward Western-style litigation? Explain.

15. Boschetto, a California resident, bought a 1964 Ford Galaxie 500XL advertised on eBay from Hansing, a Wisconsin resident. Hansing said the car was in excellent condition, including an "R code" classification. After delivery to California, Boschetto discovered many problems including the fact that the car was not an "R code." The parties could not reach an out-of-court settlement so Boschetto sued. Hansing moved for dismissal of the claim on the grounds of lack of personal jurisdiction. Does the fact that the transaction was conducted via eBay satisfy the jurisdictional requirement? Explain. See *Boschetto v. Hansing,* 539 F.3d 1011 (9th Cir. 2008); cert. den. *Boschetto v. Hansing,* 129 S. Ct. 1318 (2009).

16. University of Chicago law professor Richard Epstein pointed out how quickly Americans turn to legal remedies rather than relying on informal social customs (negotiation, neighborhood groups, simply accepting small losses and disturbances rather than fighting about them) to resolve conflicts. In your view, why are social customs often ineffective in settling disputes in this country? Explain.

17. Judicial reform advocates often argue that the United States should adopt the English rule providing that the losing party in a lawsuit must pay the reasonable litigation expenses of the winner.
    a. In brief, what are the strengths and weaknesses of the English rule?
    b. Would you favor it? Explain. See "Loser Pays, Everyone Wins," *The Wall Street Journal,* December 15, 2010 [**http://online.wsj.com/**].

18. Plaintiff Jonathan Gold was hired to work at defendant Deutsche Bank after completing his MBA degree at New York University. Before beginning employment, Gold signed

various documents, including Form U-4 that the National Association of Securities Dealers (NASD) required all registered representatives to sign. Form U-4 provided for arbitration for all employment disputes. Gold was fired after working about one year. He then filed suit claiming sexual harassment based on his sexual orientation. Deutsche Bank moved to compel arbitration. Gold resisted arbitration arguing, among other things, that Form U-4 was too difficult to understand and that it raised questions in his mind. Gold also showed that Deutsche Bank had certified that it provided Gold with the relevant NASD rules when it had not. Was Gold required to submit his claim to arbitration? Explain. See *Gold v. Deutsche Aktiengesellschaft,* 365 F.3d 144 (2d Cir. 2004); cert. den. *Gold v. Deutsche Aktiengesellschaft,* 543 U.S. 874 (2004).

Notes

1. AFP, "Sweden Tops Government Ranking—While US Lags," *Swedish Wire,* October 14, 2010 [**http://www.swedishwire.com/**].
2. *Maouloud Baby v. State of Maryland,* 916 A.2d 410 (Md. Ct. Special App. 2007).
3. *State of Maryland v. Maouloud Baby,* 2008 Md. LEXIS 190 (Md. Ct. of Appeals).
4. "Pennsylvania Latest State to Consider Criminalizing Teen 'Sexting'," *The Wall Street Journal,* August 3, 2010 [**http://blogs.wsj.com/**].
5. *Orlando Sentinel,* "More U.S. Judges Impose Creative Punishments," *The Des Moines Register,* October 29, 2010, p. 10A.
6. Adam Liptak, "Court Under Roberts Is Most Conservative in Decades," *The New York Times,* July 24, 2010 [**http://www.nytimes.com**].
7. E.J. Dionne, Jr., "The Supreme Court's Defense of the Powerful," *The Washington Post,* June 29, 2011 [**http://www.washingtonpost.com/**].
8. Adam Liptak, "Justices Offer Receptive Ear to Business Interests," *The New York Times,* December 18, 2010 [**http://www.nytimes.com/**].
9. David G. Savage, "Justices Have Been Siding with Workers, Underdogs," *latimes.com,* March 13, 2011 [**latimes.com/news/nationworld/nation/la-na-court-unanimous-20110313,0,4601488.story**].
10. Liptak, "Court Under Roberts," [**http://www.nytimes.com**].
11. John C. Henry, "Do You Know Who Works Here? They Can Change Your Life," *AARP.org/Bulletin,* November 2010, p. 26.
12. Editorial, "Our Constitutional Court," *The New York Times,* November 22, 2010 [**http://www.nytimes.com/**].
13. Lincoln Caplan, "A Judge's Warning about the Legitimacy of the Supreme Court," *The New York Times,* September 26, 2010 [**http://www.nytimes.com/**].
14. Robert Barnes, "Legal Experts Propose Limiting Justices' Powers, Terms," *The Washington Post,* February 23, 2009, p. A15.
15. Editorial, "Case Against Oxy Hits Home," *latimes.com,* December 10, 2010 [**latimes.com/news/opinion/opinionla-la-ed-peru-20101210,0,2576676.story**].
16. *Carijano v. Occidental Petroleum,* 626 F.3d 1137(9th Cir. 2010).
17. For an archive of "Spygate" articles, see "Spygate," *The New York Times,* July 12, 2011 [**http://topics.nytimes.com/**].
18. *Wal-Mart Stores v. Dukes,* 2011 U.S. LEXIS 4567.
19. Christopher Palmeri, "One of Them Is Still Laughing," *BusinessWeek,* October 30, 2006, p. 13.

20. Ibid.

21. Philip K. Howard, "How Modern Law Makes Us Powerless," *The Wall Street Journal*, January 26, 2009 [**http://online.wsj.com/**].

22. Lyric Wallwork Winik, "Are There Too Many Lawyers?" *Parade*, September 14, 2008, p. 9.

23. John O'Brien, "Poll: Voters Not Worried about Tort Reform," *LegalNewsline.com*, July 12, 2007 [**http://www.legalnewsline.com/news/197868-poll-voters-not-worried-about-tort-reform**].

24. Ibid.

25. Peter Hart Research Associates, Inc., "Civil Justice Issues and the 2008 Election," July 11, 2007 [**http://www.atla.org/pressroom/CJSPollMemo.pdf**].

26. Ibid.

27. Milton Bordwin, "Your Company and the Law," *Management Review*, January 2000, p. 58.

28. "Toyota Lawsuits Not So Big in Japan, but that Might Be Changing," *The Wall Street Journal*, February 23, 2010 [**http://blogs.wsj.com/law/2010/**].

29. Ibid.

30. Ian Rowley and Kenji Hall, "Lawyers Wanted. No, Really," *BusinessWeek*, April 3, 2006, p. 46.

31. "Becoming a Wal-Mart or Sam's Club Supplier" [**http://www.walmartstores.com/Files/Supplier_GettingStarted.pdf**].

32. Larry Cata Backer, "Economic Globalization and the Rise of Efficient Systems of Global Private Lawmaking: Wal-Mart as Global Legislator," 39 *Connecticut Law Review* 1741 (2007).

33. Ibid.

34. Michael Orey, "The Vanishing Trial," *BusinessWeek*, April 30, 2007, p. 38.

35. Ibid.

36. Ibid.

37. John T. Broderick Jr. and Ronald M. George, "A Nation of Do-It-Yourself Lawyers," *The New York Times*, January 2, 2010 [**http://www.nytimes.com/**].

38. Binyamin Appelbaum, "Investors Put Money on Lawsuits to Get Payouts," *The New York Times*, November 14, 2010 [**http://www.nytimes.com**].

39. Ibid.

40. Ibid.

41. Binyamin Appelbaum, "Lawsuit Loans Add New Risk for the Injured," *The New York Times*, January 16, 2011 [**http://www.nytimes.com/**].

42. John Keilman, "Litigants Become Their Own Lawyers," *Los Angeles Times*, August 10, 2009 [**http://www.latimes.com/**].

43. This paragraph is derived from "Small Claims Court FAQ," NOLO [**http://www.nolo.com**].

44. Missy Diaz, "Lawyers Are Divided over WhoCanISue.com," *latimes.com*, October 11, 2009 [**http://www.latimes.com/**].

45. "Arbitration: Increasingly, It's Not Over until the Vacatur Motion Fails," *The Wall Street Journal*, February 14, 2011 [**http://blogs.wsj.com/**].

46. Alexander J.S. Colvin, "An Empirical Study of Employment Arbitration: Case Outcomes and Processes," *Journal of Empirical Legal Studies* 8, Issue 1, (March 2011), p. 1.

47. *AT&T Mobility v. Vincent Concepcion*, 2011 U.S. LEXIS 3367.

48. See related proceedings *Geographic Expeditions, Inc. v. Lhotka*, 2010 U.S. LEXIS 6305.

49. "An Economist Out to Be Sued," *Los Angeles Times,* October 8, 1990, p. D1.

50. Morgan O. Reynolds, "Europe Surpasses America—in Crime," *The Wall Street Journal,* October 16, 1998, p. A14.

51. Dubuque, Iowa Ordinance No. 28-11, March 21, 2011 and Andy Piper, "Police: Ordinance Will ID Derelict Parents," *Dubuque Telegraph Herald,* March 23, 2011 [**http://www.thonline.com/article.cfm?id=315715**].

52. Darrell Dusina, "Lawyers, Everywhere," *The Wall Street Journal,* November 23, 1998, p. A23.

53. Warren Avis, "Court before Justice," *The New York Times,* July 21, 1978, p. 25.

54. Alain Clement, "Judges, Lawyers Are the Ruling Class in U.S. Society," *The Washington Post,* August 22, 1980, p. A25.

55. Associated Press, "Illinois Man Imprisoned for 26 Years Declared Innocent," *Springfield State Journal-Register,* April 17, 2009 [**http://www.sj-r.com/**] and "26-Year Secret Kept Innocent Man in Prison," "60 Minutes," March 8, 2008 [**http://truthinjustice.org/alton-logan.htm**].

56. Percy Luney, "Traditions and Foreign Influences: Systems of Law in China and Japan," *Law and Contemporary Problems* 52 (Spring 1989), pp. 129, 136.

11

Intellectual Property

⬜ Learning Objectives

In this chapter you learn:

11-1. To recognize why intellectual property is so important to our economic system and explain how it creates incentives for investment.

11-2. To identify the type of information that is protected by trade secret law and characterize circumstances that constitute misappropriation.

11-3. To list the requirements for a valid patent and recognize important issues in the enforcement of patents.

11-4. To categorize source indicators as trademark types and to differentiate between trademark dilution and infringement.

11-5. To define copyright protection and fair use limitations.

11-6. To describe the basic elements of the international system for protecting intellectual property rights.

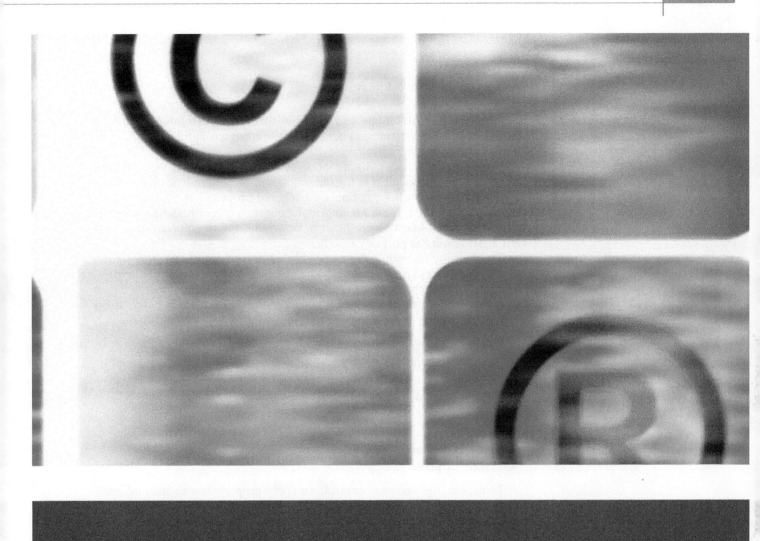

In reading the previous chapters, you should have come to understand that the essence of "property" is a certain system of law. **Property** establishes a relationship of legal exclusion between an owner and other people regarding limited resources. It makes a particular resource like a new discovery legally "proper" to the owner rather than someone else.

The concept of ownership is easiest to understand in the context of something physical. You can readily intuit what it means to own a plot of land surrounded by a fence or an automobile, and laws that protect such ownership seem natural. Of course, it is a mistake to think that you can always know the exact boundaries of what is legally proper to you. Your property includes the legal uses of what you own, and the full extent of these uses is frequently unclear. By using what you own, you will at some point collide with the equal right of others to what they own. It is the job of both common law and statutory tort law to determine when you cross the boundary separating your proper use from wrongful injury to what belongs legally to others.

If defining boundaries is a daunting task in the tangible world, consider how much more difficult it is for the intangible. Should individuals or firms be permitted to own information as if it were property? If so, how do we determine the limits? These are important questions, because when property boundaries are unknown or difficult to determine and to enforce, much concern arises about the property system.

The decision to permit the ownership of information is not theoretical. Modern businesses count on the advantage of controlling inventions, expressions, marks, designs and business secrets like marketing plans or a list of customers. The different kinds of intangible, mostly knowledge-based assets that businesses may possess include the following:

- Employee skills and talents
- Production designs, inventions, and technologies
- Processes and methods of business operation
- Reports, manuals, and databases
- Relationships with customers and suppliers and brand identity
- Software
- New product or service research
- Marketing plans

To provide the necessary control, we apply property law to such information through rights like trade secrets, patents, trademarks, and copyrights. Today, intellectual property represents protection of some of the most valuable resources that businesses have. However, against this backdrop of economic significance, we continue to explore the proper boundaries of information ownership.

>> *sidebar* 11.1

The Increasing Importance of Intellectual Property

Knowledge assets are perhaps the most valuable resources of modern businesses. How to make things, how to do things, where to get things, how to sell things, how to buy things, and how to manage people are all vitally important to businesses. To some extent, knowledge assets can be protected by property, and property enables businesses to capture or realize the value of these assets.

Although it is impossible to know the exact value of intellectual property owned by a firm at any given time, there is a general consensus that it constitutes an ever-greater percentage of firm assets.

The information economy, in which some successful businesses never produce a single physical product, has increased the importance of intangible information. In addition, the business community has become more aware of the advantages of intellectual property ownership. Firms are seeking portfolios that are striking in their breadth and diversity. Sports teams and universities vigorously protect trademarks. Social networking services like Facebook even own patents. In the modern business world, it is critical to understand the basics of intellectual property just to compete.

This chapter begins by considering the justification for intellectual property. It then explores the importance of knowledge assets to businesses, followed by the major forms of intellectual property: trade secrets, patents, trademarks, and copyrights. It concludes by reviewing the international legal environment and examining how intellectual property serves the common good.

1. THE JUSTIFICATION FOR INTELLECTUAL PROPERTY   LO 11-1

The justification for **intellectual property** is the same as for the private property system generally. Property relationships are believed to be more productive in allocating scarce resources and producing new ones than legal relationships that merely divide resources equally.

Abraham Lincoln said that intellectual property couples "the fuel of interest with the fire of genius." He was referring to how an exclusive right to what you acquire and produce gives incentive to create new things, new ways of doing things, and new invention generally. The framers of the U.S. Constitution made sure that Congress could protect intellectual property. Article 1, Section 8, of the Constitution grants Congress the power "[t]o promote the Progress of Science and useful Arts, by securing for limited Times to Authors and Inventors the exclusive Right to their respective Writings and Discoveries." Note that the justification for "securing" an "exclusive Right" is "[t]o promote the Progress of Science [knowledge and creativity] and the useful Arts [inventions]." The Constitution recognizes that exclusive property boundaries promote, or give incentive to, the business production of what people need and want. However, the Constitution also ensures that after "limited Times" defined by Congress, the resources of new expression and invention, which were formerly exclusive to "Authors and Inventors," will be freely available to everyone.

2. INTELLECTUAL PROPERTY AND COMPETITION

The basic economic system of intellectual property is grounded in the idea of incentives. We give firms and individuals the ability to secure property rights if they produce certain types of information. Those property rights provide exclusivity that can lead to market advantages such as the ability to charge premium prices or utilize customer recognition. The possibility of economic return on investment encourages firms and individuals to create more information than they otherwise would.

Conversely, without intellectual property, the pace of creative research and development (R&D) in business would slow dramatically. R&D is expensive. If businesses have to finance R&D and then compete against others who quickly copy the resulting new invention, the businesses paying for R&D will be at a competitive disadvantage.

Countering the benefits of intellectual property protection are certain costs. Property rights in information reduce competition (at least temporarily) that could otherwise increase availability and keep prices low for consumers. Intellectual property systems presume that the long-term benefits of increased information and investment are greater than the short-term costs.

Is intellectual property protection necessary for the production of *all* information? Intuitively, you know this is not true. An artist may paint simply to express herself without any notion of making a profit or excluding others from the work. A university scientist may investigate the mechanism of disease for the notoriety of discovery and the desire to benefit humanity. A blogger may write a post solely for the satisfaction of knowing that it will be shared widely and many people will read it. It is fair to say that intellectual property is believed to *incrementally increase* the production of information and investment over that which would normally occur. Society obtains this benefit in exchange for allowing some information to be controlled through property. The great debate regarding our intellectual property laws is whether they are truly calibrated to provide a net benefit to society.

>> *sidebar* 11.2

The Open Source Alternative

You may have heard of information products like software being distributed under an open source model. This means that the information is shared freely, and individuals and firms are able to build upon it outside of the strict control of the creator. Open source models of information development have been particularly successful in networked communities as exist across the Internet. Some believe that it is a better alternative than intellectual property or contract for producing certain types of information.

Note that open source products are not necessarily divorced from intellectual property rights.

For example, open source software is often offered accompanied by a license that sets certain use limitations. The purpose of the license may be to ensure continued open access and to prevent unauthorized commercialization, which is usually not a property-centric goal. Yet, these open access provisions may be enforced through intellectual property. Failure to adhere to the terms constitutes infringement.

Source: Yochai Benkler, *Coase's Penguin, or, Linux and* The Nature of the Firm, 112 Yale L.J. 369 (2002).

---

3. CAPTURING INTELLECTUAL PROPERTY

The protections of property often do not apply automatically to ownership of intangible knowledge resources. Depending on the type of information, you may be required to undertake certain steps to protect the time, effort, and money spent in developing knowledge in order to transform it into valuable intangible assets. Some intellectual property forms have very strict deadlines for asserting rights or other formal requirements. The failure to follow the rules may mean that information that could have been captured is instead dedicated to the public domain, meaning that anyone can use it. In general, once information is in the public domain, an intellectual property right cannot be applied to recapture it. Firms that do not have an intellectual property strategy in place risk losing valuable assets.

The sections that follow describe the forms of property that protect knowledge-based intangible business resources. Some general principles are conveyed, that can guide you in finding more detailed information. This chapter concludes by examining the right of property and the common good.

LO 11-2   >> **Trade Secrets**

One of the most common ways of asserting property in knowledge-based intangible business resources is through the trade secret. Trade secret law developed in the common law industrial revolutions of the 1800s. Before this time, the relationship of confidence and trust between skilled artisans (craftspersons) and their apprentices protected what the artisans knew from harmful competition by their former apprentices. But the 1800s brought large factories to the economy. The employees of these factories were not apprentices and at first were free to take their employers' knowledge, leave employment, and compete against their former employers. Trade secret law arose to protect the employers' valuable knowledge. It also facilitated economic development by making employers willing to hire employees who might come into contact with the employers' knowledge.

A **trade secret** is any form of knowledge or information that (1) has economic value from not being generally known to, or readily ascertainable by proper means by, others and (2) has been the subject of reasonable efforts by the owner to maintain secrecy. To violate another's trade secret rights, one must misappropriate the information. This is an important distinction from intellectual property rights that make one liable simply for unauthorized use. The majority of states have adopted the Uniform Trade Secrets Act (UTSA), but some states continue to rely on common law protection. The UTSA does not differ substantially from common law. Let us now examine the two elements of a trade secret.

> "More than ever before, information is what gives businesses their competitive edge, and they want to make sure that inside dope on products and services doesn't walk out the door."
>
> *–BusinessWeek,* **November 12, 2007, p. 76.**

4. ESTABLISHING THE EXISTENCE OF A TRADE SECRET

As described above, businesses may possess many different forms of valuable knowledge. It may be financial, technical, scientific, economic, or engineering knowledge. When a business has spent time, effort, or money in training skills, preparing materials, making plans, or developing relationships with customers and suppliers, the business may wish that its competitors not have access to this knowledge. However, not all of this knowledge is covered by the law of trade secrets. To protect information as a trade secret, the information must actually be secret, and the business must take *reasonable measures* to keep it so.

A first step in protecting trade secrets is to identify confidential knowledge-based resources. It is useful for all businesses to conduct a *trade secret audit*, which simply lists all the valuable forms of information possessed by the business, including formulas, plans, reports, manuals, research, and knowledge of customers and suppliers. Interestingly, multiple businesses may have trade secret property in substantially the same knowledge. For example, they may each have customer lists that overlap with many of the same names. As long as there are actual or potential competitors who are not aware of all the customer names, the knowledge still has economic value. It has not become general public knowledge just because multiple competitors have overlapping lists.

Trade secret audits help you identify the valuable information that a business produces.

Having identified potential trade secrets, a business must next assert its property by preserving secrecy. Reasonable measures to preserve secrecy over valuable knowledge resources include physically locking away formulas, research results, blueprints, and various written plans. In the era of e-mail and the Internet, companies routinely protect computer-stored knowledge with protective "firewalls" and encryption to keep hackers from obtaining access. Some companies maintain two different computer systems in order to protect proprietary (owned) knowledge, one connected to the Internet and one networked only internally. Employees use the internal network to send messages about matters that are not for public consumption. To protect trade secrets from outsiders, companies often also carefully regulate who can visit the business and what areas of the business visitors can see. Visitors are sometimes required to sign agreements not to disclose to the public what they see and learn in a company they visit.

Business customers, suppliers, and repair technicians—in addition to visitors—may also have access to knowledge that a company values and protects. Like visitors, these parties may also be asked to sign nondisclosure agreements (contracts). As long as a company takes such reasonable measures to prevent the public dissemination of trade secrets, it does not lose its property in knowledge-based resources merely because customers, suppliers, repair technicians, or even visitors come into contact with the secrets.

Establishing the existence of a trade secret is a critical step in controlling valuable knowledge resources. The failure to maintain secrecy, or to prove that the knowledge was secret in the first place, can mean that competitors may be able to access it. Case 11.1 is an illustration of this fundamental requirement.

 case **11.1** >>

NATIONWIDE MUTUAL INSURANCE CO v. MORTENSEN
606 F.3d 22 (2d Cir. 2010)

The file that an insurance company keeps for a customer includes valuable information about the customer's history that informs pricing and policy options. If a competitor obtains that information, it can offer an alternate policy and take away business. Although customer files have economic value, it is essentially the customer's information. That customer can repeat it to anyone else without breaching a duty of confidentiality. Therefore, courts have been reluctant to characterize customer files as a trade secret. However, is a secret created when a company incorporates this information into a secure computer system?

PARKER, J: When each defendant began to work as a Nationwide insurance agent, he or she signed an identical, standard-form contract with Nationwide called an Agent's Agreement. By the terms of the contract, each defendant's relationship with the company was that of an exclusive agent and "independent contractor." Initially, the agents were given a large number of policyholder files of preexisting Nationwide customers. From then on, they serviced these customers and solicited new ones. In the course of this work, they maintained physical policyholder files containing

information relevant to the customers' insurance needs, including documentation that they received from both the customers and Nationwide . . .

The agents also used Nationwide's Agency Office Automation ("AOA") computer system, which they were required to lease from Nationwide. This database linked them with Nationwide's central computers, permitting them to access insurance quotes in real-time, and it gathered and sorted the information collected in the policyholder files. The AOA system was password-protected. . . .

In late 1999 and early 2000, the defendants terminated their agency relationships with Nationwide. In the months leading up to the terminations, they met with representatives of other insurance companies to discuss possible employment. During these meetings, they allegedly shared with the companies information contained in Nationwide's policyholder files concerning prices, computer print-outs of policyholder information from the AOA computer system ("screen prints"), and copies of documents they received from Nationwide relating to their sales and commissions. After terminating the Agent's Agreement, they began to compete with Nationwide by selling policies issued by its competitors. . . .

[continued]

On learning of the defendants' activities, Nation-wide filed this suit in diversity, contending that the agents had violated numerous provisions of Connecti-cut law . . .

Nationwide's primary claim is that the policyholder files retained by the departing agents constitute trade secrets protected by [the Connecticut Uniform Trade Secrets Act (CUTSA)]. . . . While customer lists are within the scope of CUTSA, a number of courts have noted that such materials often lie "on the periphery of the law of trade secrets and unfair competition." . . .

Importantly, although Nationwide contested the agents' right to all of the policyholder files and infor-mation in the litigation below, on appeal it focuses exclusively on print-outs that the agents took from the AOA computer system. This strategy was designed, presumably, to strengthen Nationwide's argument that the screen-prints represent proprietary or confidential information [because a significant number of courts have rejected the argument that the agents' policy-holder files themselves qualify as trade secrets]. The shift in focus, however, seriously undercuts Nation-wide's argument. We must conclude, as a result, that Nationwide's claims with respect to the physical pol-icyholder files have been waived on appeal. . . . Yet at the same time, the company nowhere shows that the AOA screen-prints contain substantially different information from the physical policyholder files. . . .

It is difficult to understand, then, how the screen-prints could be protected as trade secrets when this information could be easily obtained from the physical policyholder files themselves.

In order to qualify as a trade secret, materials can-not be "readily ascertainable by proper means" from another source. . . . The record offers little basis for concluding that the information in the AOA screen-prints was materially different from that contained in the files themselves. . . . On appeal, Nationwide points to no evidence suggesting otherwise. In fact, it is undis-puted that the agents generally entered information into the AOA database directly from the physical files maintained at their offices. At most, the AOA database condensed this information into an organized format and permitted an agent to generate Nationwide quotes based on a policyholder's data in real-time. But, at bottom, a screen-print was an electronic compila-tion of information readily available in the very same office. Simply because the AOA information existed in a different, better-protected format than the physi-cal folders does not elevate it to trade secret status. It is not the medium that matters here, but whether the information itself was adequately protected—and it was not. Because this same information was readily available from another source, it does not qualify as a trade secret as a matter of law. The district court's dismissal is affirmed. . . .

>> CASE QUESTIONS

1. Why was this case tried in federal court rather than in state court?
2. What did the court determine about the trade secret status of the screen-print files?
3. Could Nationwide possess any confidential information regarding its customers, outside of the policyholder files?
4. Can you imagine any other ways that Nationwide could have limited competition from its agents?

5. DEMONSTRATING MISAPPROPRIATION

To be liable in a trade secret case, a defendant must have misappropriated the information in question. Misappropriation obviously occurs when one improperly acquires secret information through burglary, espionage or com-puter hacking. However, misappropriation also occurs when one discloses information that one was under a duty to keep secret, even if the original acquisition was proper. Such a duty may arise from an employment relation-ship or a contractual agreement. Additionally, if one acquires a secret from another who has a duty to maintain secrecy, and one knows of that duty, mis-appropriation has occurred.

Importantly, independent creation does *not* constitute misappropriation. If, through your own effort, you are able to recreate the same information that another considers to be a trade secret, no misappropriation has occurred. In addition, reverse engineering a secret by looking at a product and figuring out how it works or how it is formulated is not misappropriation. An exception to this principle would be if one contractually agreed to keep the information secret.

The fact that secrets can get out through normal product marketing is an important limitation on trade secret rights. For that reason, as discussed below, a patent may provide better protection for a valuable invention embodied in a product, assuming the stringent requirements can be met. On the other hand, if the valuable information relates to processes or techniques that will not be disclosed when a product or service is sold, trade secret rights may be a viable, relatively inexpensive, and long-lived option.

> **Do** remember the role of contractual confidentiality agreements and do not compete agreements in preserving trade secrets.

Employee Mobility and Trade Secrets Businesses have to take reasonable measures to protect trade secrets even from employees. Employees may leave an employer and use the knowledge they have gained to compete against their former employer, or they may go to work for their former employer's competitors.

Increasingly, employers require employees to sign confidentiality contracts promising not to disclose what they learn in confidence in the workplace. This promise, however, applies only to knowledge that is unknown publicly and amounts to trade secrets. Additionally, not all states presume that former employees are likely to disclose confidential information in a new position. This creates difficulty in establishing misappropriation. Because it may be difficult to establish all of the elements of a trade secret case employers frequently take the additional step of having employees agree not to compete against them if the employees leave their employment.

The law states that employers can enforce agreements (or contractual "covenants") not to compete only when there is a "valid business purpose" for the contract. Generally, this means that employers are protecting trade secrets, or, at least protecting their investment in the training of their employees, which itself can be a trade secret. The laws of unfair competition limit the extent to which employers can prevent employees from competing against them. The contracts and antitrust chapters discuss these limitations in greater detail. You should appreciate, however, how businesses use contracts to ensure recognition of property over intangible resources.

6. CIVIL ENFORCEMENT OF TRADE SECRETS

> The wrongful taking of any kind of intellectual property is called *misappropriation* or *infringement*.

The owner of a trade secret may go into court and get an injunction to prevent others—often former employees—from divulging or using a trade secret. An **injunction** is an order by a judge either to do something or to refrain from doing something. In the case of trade secrets, the injunction orders those who have *misappropriated* the trade secret to refrain from using it or telling others about it. In rare instances the injunction may also order that one delay in taking a new job.

Trade secret owners can also obtain damages against those who misappropriate trade secrets. In 2011, a California jury awarded St. Jude Medical, Inc., $2.3 billion in a dispute against a former employee and rival medical device company, Nervicon. The employee allegedly left St. Jude with documents related to a crystal oscillator, and used the document to help Nervicon create the same device.

7. CRIMINAL ENFORCEMENT OF TRADE SECRETS

In addition to civil enforcement of trade secret boundaries, criminal prosecution can also result from misappropriation of trade secrets. Although various state laws make intentional trade secret misappropriation a crime, the primary criminal prosecutions today result under the federal Economic Espionage Act (EEA). The act makes it a crime to steal (intentionally misappropriate) trade secrets and provides for fines and up to 10 years' imprisonment for individuals and up to a $5 million fine for organizations.

Although one provision of the EEA makes one liable for misappropriation to benefit a foreign government—the act that usually comes to mind when we think of espionage—the law also has a provision that relates to common trade secret theft. The Coca-Cola case in Sidebar 11.3 is an example of an Economic Espionage Act criminal prosecution.

>> *sidebar* 11.3

Soda Secrets

The Coca-Cola Company considers the formula for its namesake drink, also known as Coke, to be a valuable secret. Even though it was created over 100 years ago, the company refuses to disclose the original formula and continues to undertake measures to maintain its secrecy. Through various reformulations, the basic recipe remains confidential according to the company.

However, is it possible to discern the formula for Coca-Cola from a purchased bottle? Science provides the means for characterizing the various elements of chemical compounds, and one would assume that such techniques could be applied to a soft drink to learn its composition. Absent a contract, patent, or employee relationship, this type of reverse engineering does not violate the law. In fact, over the years, several people have claimed to be in possession of the secret formula for Coca-Cola through disclosure or reverse engineering, including the host of the radio program *This American Life* in 2011. Without a confirmation from the Coca-Cola Company, it is difficult to know for certain how accurate such claims are.

Regardless of whether the actual formula for Coca-Cola is known outside the company, it is certainly true that Coca-Cola can possess protectable trade secrets on newer products. In 2007, a jury convicted a former Coca-Cola secretary for conspiring with others to steal secrets for products in development and sell them to rival Pepsi for $1.5 million. She was sentenced to eight years in prison. The scheme came to light when Pepsi informed the FBI that it received an offer to obtain Coca-Cola's product secrets.

Sources: Robbie Brow & Kim Severson, "Recipe for Coke? One More to Add to the File," *The New York Times*, Feb. 19, 2011; "Ex-Secretary Gets 8-Year Term in Coca-Cola Secrets Case," The Associated Press, May 24, 2007.

The following sections discuss other types of intellectual property and the boundaries they establish.

>> *sidebar* 11.4

Federal Government Intellectual Property Enforcement

Although private parties carry out much enforcement of state and federal intellectual property laws, governments also play an important role. In particular, the federal government prosecutes criminal cases involving copyright infringement (referred to as piracy in some cases), trademark infringement (also known as counterfeiting in some cases), and trade secret misappropriation. In 2008, the Prioritizing Resources and Organization for Intellectual Property Act (PRO IP Act) became law, creating a new position for coordinating federal agency intellectual property enforcement known as the Intellectual

Property Enforcement Coordinator (IPEC). Agencies that enforce the nations intellectual property laws include the Department of Justice, through its Computer Crime and Intellectual Property Section (CCIPS), the Federal Bureau of Investigation (FBI), and Customs and Border Protection, as well as many others. CCIPS conducts the actual prosecution of intellectual property cases, and a significant amount of information on its work and the relevant laws can be found at www.cybercrime.gov.

Source: PRO IP Act, Pub. L. No. 110-403 (2008).

>> Patent Law

Patents have existed for hundreds of years as property rights, but the term has not always been associated with a new idea. Historically, a patent was any legal monopoly openly issued by the government. In some cases, European monarchs sold "letters of patent" for large sums of money in order to give private persons sole control over such things as the operation of toll roads, river ferries, and profits. However, patents were associated with invention at least as early as the 1400s. The Venetian Patent Act of 1474 is generally considered to be the world's first patent statute for the purpose of rewarding new ideas. Many of its basic principles for protecting inventions are present in modern patent law.

Today, a **patent** is firmly associated with an inventive act, and conveys a right to exclude others from making, using selling or importing the covered invention. The Constitution authorizes Congress to create patents, and Congress has passed numerous laws affecting exclusive patent right, which, of course, is property. Since colonial times, the United States has been a world leader in establishing patent law. Many of the constitutional framers were interested in technology and new invention, and during the Constitutional Convention in Philadelphia, the framers apparently took time off one afternoon to watch a newly invented steamboat cruising on the Delaware River.

In 1790, Thomas Jefferson helped draft the first federal patent law, and he personally invented numerous new devices and ways of doing things. Abraham Lincoln, however, was the first American president to patent an invention. In 1849 he applied for a patent on a system of air chambers to help boats float in shallow water. The disclosure begins:

To all whom it may concern:

Be it known that I, Abraham Lincoln, of Springfield, in the County of Sangamon, in the State of Illinois, have invented a new and improved manner of combining adjustable buoyant air chambers with a steamboat or other vessel for the purpose of enabling their draught of water [how deep the boat sinks in the water] to be readily lessened to enable them to pass over bars, or through shallow water, without discharging their cargoes. . . .

Many other famous Americans have held patents. For an example, see Sidebar 11.5.

>> *sidebar* 11.5

A Famous Writer's Love Affair with Patents

Mark Twain is best known as one of America's most famous writers. His single most profitable property right, however, came not from any of his books but from a 1873 patent issued on a self-pasting scrapbook. In part, his books were not so profitable because of inadequate enforcement of property law (copyright) to protect their copying and sale.

So fond was Mark Twain of patent law that he wrote about it in *A Connecticut Yankee in King Author's Court* (1889). In the book the main character, Hank

Morgan, gets in a barroom brawl and is knocked out. When he wakes up, he is in the time of King Arthur. By predicting a solar eclipse, he gains the king's favor and is appointed the king's "perpetual minister and executive." He later explains:

> [T]he very first official thing I did in my administration—and it was on the very first day of it too—was to start a patent office; for I knew that a country without a patent office and good patent laws was just a crab, and couldn't travel any way but sideways or backways.

---

8. OBTAINING A PATENT

A patent is an exclusive right created by statute and conveyed by the U.S. Patent and Trademark Office (PTO) for a limited period of time. This property applies to inventions, which are new applications of information.

Don't forget that patents apply for only a limited period of time.

Patent Type It is important to understand that there are actually three types of patents granted by the PTO, each with their own distinct subject matter (See Figure 11.1).

An easy way to remember the distinction between a utility patent and a design patent is that the former applies to useful, functional inventions. Such inventions are what most of us think of when we see the word "patent."

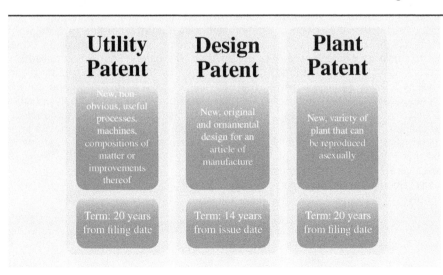

Figure 11.1 *Types of Patents*

Utility Patent	Design Patent	Plant Patent
New, non-obvious, useful processes, machines, compositions of matter or improvements thereof	New, original and ornamental design for an article of manufacture	New, variety of plant that can be reproduced asexually
Term: 20 years from filing date	Term: 14 years from issue date	Term: 20 years from filing date

On the other hand, design patents apply to the appearance of an article of manufacture, unrelated to its function. They cover subject matter more similar to copyrights (discussed later in this chapter). Plant patents apply to new varieties of asexually reproduced plants. However, it is important to understand that many inventions related to plants may also be protected as utility patents. For example, one or more utility patent rights often cover genetically modified plants. Therefore, just because the subject matter is a plant, the relevant property right is not necessarily a plant patent.

In 2010, the U.S. Patent and Trademark Office received 520,277 patent applications, which is approximately double that received in 1998.

To obtain a patent, an inventor must pay a filing fee and file an application with the PTO. In the case of a utility patent the application must in words and drawings (1) explain how to make and use the basic invention; (2) show why the invention is different from *prior art,* that is, from all previous and related inventions or state of knowledge; and (3) precisely detail the subject matter that the inventor regards as the invention (called *claims*). The PTO assigns a *patent examiner* to consider the application, and there is usually a great deal of communication between the examiner and the applicant over the adequacy of the application's explanations, the scope of the proposed patent (exactly what the patent applies to), and whether the invention even qualifies at all for a patent. The applicant can amend the application, and the process can take several years from start to finish.

In 2011, the President signed into law the *America Invents Act,* the first substantial revision to U.S. patent law since 1999. Among the law's many changes is the eventual switch from a first-to-invent system to a first-inventor-to-file system. This means that, in a contest between two inventors claiming the same patentable idea, the first to get to the patent office will win. On the other hand, the law increases the ability of companies to keep some internal

>> *sidebar* 11.6

Should Utility Patents Always be Presumed Valid?

As noted above, utility patents issue only after a substantial analysis by a professional PTO Examiner. Following such scrutiny, it seems reasonable to give some degree of credit to the process. Patent law accomplishes this by establishing a higher burden of proof for a defendant who wishes to challenge a patent. According to this principle, courts have determined that proof of invalidity must be made by "clear and convincing evidence" instead of the "preponderance of the evidence" standard that exists in most civil cases. This makes it more likely that a patent will be upheld in court.

An increased burden makes sense if the PTO fully considered every issue that the defendant attempts to raise in court. However, what if the defendant finds new evidence of invalidity? Should the clear and convincing standard still apply?

The Supreme Court recently considered this issue in *Microsoft Corp. v. i4i LTD. Partnership*. The case involved software code patented by i4i that Microsoft allegedly incorporated into its word processing software without permission. Microsoft argued that i4i's patent was invalid based on facts not considered by the PTO, even though these facts did not rise to the level of "clear and convincing." The Supreme Court rejected Microsoft's position and decided that clear and convincing evidence of invalidity is necessary in all cases to eliminate an issued patent. The case ensures that utility patents remain strong property rights.

Source: Microsoft Corp. v. i4i LTD. Partnership, 131 S.Ct. 2238 (June 9, 2011)

processes secret and avoid infringing another's patent through "prior user rights." Other provisions in the law are expected to make the patent examination process more efficient, particularly by giving the PTO more control over its funding.

9. PATENTABLE SUBJECT MATTER

After the PTO issues a patent, the patent owner may choose to maintain its exclusivity in the invention. Alternatively, the patentee may license others. However, if another infringes the patent by making, using, selling, or importing the invention without permission, the patent owner may have to defend its property. When the patent owner threatens a lawsuit, it is common for the alleged infringer to respond by attacking the validity of the patent. Validity can be challenged in court or the PTO. If the patent is found invalid, the alleged infringer will win. A finding that a patent is completely invalid in one case is very significant, as it renders the patent invalid against all future defendants, essentially eliminating it.

A process is a way of doing something through a series of operations.

Attacking the "subject matter" of a patent is one common way of testing the validity of a patent. Although not unlimited, the subject matter for a potential patent is quite broad. This is particularly true for utility patents. In *Diamond v. Chakrabarty*, 447 U.S. 303 (1980), the Supreme Court ruled that a scientist could cover with a utility patent a genetically modified bacterium that ate hydrocarbons found in oil spills. The Court said, "Congress is free to amend §101 [the subject matter section of the general patent law] so as to exclude from patent protection organisms produced by genetic engineering. . . . Or it may choose to craft a statute specifically designed for such living things. But until Congress takes such action, the language of §101 fairly embraces the respondent's invention." In an example of such congressional action, the 2011 revisions to the patent act explicitly preclude patents covering humans.

One of the most controversial areas of potentially patentable subject matter concerns "processes." What is a process? Is a computer program a process? Are ways of doing business a process? Mere ideas are not a patentable process. Nor are mathematical algorithms or formulas like $E = mc^2$ that express truths about the universe. Historically, business methods like double-entry bookkeeping were considered unpatentable, but they are after all processes, methods for doing things.

In *State Street Bank and Trust Co. v. Signature Financial Group, Inc.*, 149 F.3d 1360 (1998), a federal circuit court that considers all patent appeals from district courts upheld the patent on a data processing system that allowed an administrator to monitor and record the financial information flow and make all calculations necessary for maintaining a mutual fund investment partnership. Following this case, thousands of patents were filed on business-related processes. Subsequently, that court narrowed its ruling asserting that a claim involving mental processes or algorithms is patentable subject matter only if it is tied to a machine or involves the transformation of a physical object. This rule called into question the validity of issued business method patents, and some believed that it could have impacted software as well. In the following case, the Supreme Court considered the viability of "machine or transformation" rule.

case 11.2 >>

BILSKI v. KAPPOS
130 S. Ct. 3218 (2010)

KENNEDY, J: . . . Petitioners' application seeks patent protection for a claimed invention that explains how buyers and sellers of commodities in the energy market can protect, or hedge, against the risk of price changes. The key claims are claims 1 and 4. . . . Claim 1 consists of the following steps:

> "(a) initiating a series of transactions between said commodity provider and consumers of said commodity wherein said consumers purchase said commodity at a fixed rate based upon historical averages, said fixed rate corresponding to a risk position of said consumers;
>
> "(b) identifying market participants for said commodity having a counter-risk position to said consumers; and
>
> "(c) initiating a series of transactions between said commodity provider and said market participants at a second fixed rate such that said series of market participant transactions balances the risk position of said series of consumer transactions." . . .

The patent examiner rejected petitioners' application, explaining that it "'is not implemented on a specific apparatus and merely manipulates [an] abstract idea and solves a purely mathematical problem without any limitation to a practical application, therefore, the invention is not directed to the technological arts.'" . . . The Board of Patent Appeals and Interferences affirmed, concluding that the application involved only mental steps that do not transform physical matter and was directed to an abstract idea. . . .

Section 101 . . . specifies four independent categories of inventions or discoveries that are eligible for protection: processes, machines, manufactures, and compositions of matter. "In choosing such expansive terms . . . modified by the comprehensive 'any,' Congress plainly contemplated that the patent laws would be given wide scope." . . . Congress took this permissive approach to patent eligibility to ensure that "'ingenuity should receive a liberal encouragement.'" *Id.*, at 308-309, 100 S. Ct. 2204, 65 L. Ed. 2d 144 (quoting 5 Writings of Thomas Jefferson 75-76 (H. Washington ed. 1871)).

The Court's precedents provide three specific exceptions to §101's broad patent-eligibility principles: "laws of nature, physical phenomena, and abstract ideas." . . . While these exceptions are not required by the statutory text, they are consistent with the notion that a patentable process must be "new and useful." . . .

The §101 patent-eligibility inquiry is only a threshold test. Even if an invention qualifies as a process, machine, manufacture, or composition of matter, in order to receive the Patent Act's protection the claimed invention must also satisfy "the conditions and requirements of this title." §101. Those requirements include that the invention be novel, see §102, nonobvious, see §103, and fully and particularly described, see §112.

The present case involves an invention that is claimed to be a "process" under §101. . . .

Under the Court of Appeals' formulation, an invention is a "process" only if: "(1) it is tied to a particular machine or apparatus, or (2) it transforms a particular article into a different state or thing." 545 F.3d at 954. This Court has "more than once cautioned that courts 'should not read into the patent laws limitations and conditions which the legislature has not expressed.'" . . .

Any suggestion in this Court's case law that the Patent Act's terms deviate from their ordinary meaning has only been an explanation for the exceptions for laws of nature, physical phenomena, and abstract ideas. . . . This Court has not indicated that the existence of these well-established exceptions gives the Judiciary *carte blanche* to impose other limitations that are inconsistent with the text and the statute's purpose and design. Concerns about attempts to call any form of human activity a "process" can be met by making sure the claim meets the requirements of §101.

Adopting the machine-or-transformation test as the sole test for what constitutes a "process" (as opposed to just an important and useful clue) violates these statutory interpretation principles. . . .

Section 101 similarly precludes the broad contention that the term "process" categorically excludes business methods. . . .

The term "method," which is within §100(b)'s definition of "process," at least as a textual matter and before consulting other limitations in the Patent Act and this Court's precedents, may include at least some methods of doing business. . . . The Court is unaware of any argument that the "'ordinary, contemporary, common meaning,'" . . . , of "method" excludes business methods. Nor is it clear how far a prohibition on business method patents would reach, and whether it would exclude technologies for conducting a business more efficiently. . . .

Even though petitioners' application is not categorically outside of §101 under the two broad and atextual approaches the Court rejects today, that does not mean

[continued]

it is a "process" under §101. Petitioners seek to patent both the concept of hedging risk and the application of that concept to energy markets. App. 19-20. Rather than adopting categorical rules that might have wide-ranging and unforeseen impacts, the Court resolves this case narrowly on the basis of this Court's decisions in *Benson, Flook,* and *Diehr,* which show that petitioners' claims are not patentable processes because they are attempts to patent abstract ideas. Indeed, all members of the Court agree that the patent application at issue here falls outside of §101 because it claims an abstract idea. . . .

Today, the Court once again declines to impose limitations on the Patent Act that are inconsistent with the Act's text. The patent application here can be rejected under our precedents on the unpatentability of abstract ideas. The Court, therefore, need not define further what constitutes a patentable "process," beyond pointing to the definition of that term provided in §100(b) and looking to the guideposts in *Benson, Flook,* and *Diehr.*

And nothing in today's opinion should be read as endorsing interpretations of §101 that the Court of Appeals for the Federal Circuit has used in the past. See, *e.g., State Street,* 149 F.3d at 1373; *AT&T Corp.,* 172 F.3d at 1357. It may be that the Court of Appeals thought it needed to make the machine-or-transformation test exclusive precisely because its case law had not adequately identified less extreme means of restricting business method patents, including (but not limited to) application of our opinions in *Benson, Flook,* and *Diehr.* In disapproving an exclusive machine-or-transformation test, we by no means foreclose the Federal Circuit's development of other limiting criteria that further the purposes of the Patent Act and are not inconsistent with its text.

The judgment of the Court of Appeals is affirmed.

10. NOVELTY, NONOBVIOUSNESS, AND UTILITY

To be patentable, it is not enough for something to be appropriate subject matter. An invention must also have certain characteristics. Namely, it must be novel, nonobvious, and useful. An alleged infringer can always defend against an infringement lawsuit by proving that the patent is invalid because the invention is previously known, obvious, or lacks utility.

> Perhaps the most common way of challenging a patent's validity is to claim that the "invention" is obvious to someone with knowledge in the field.

The characteristic of novelty indicates that something is new and different from the prior art (the previous state of knowledge in the field). The test is met when no single piece of prior art meets all of the elements of an invention's claims. However, under patent law even if an invention is otherwise new, it fails the novelty test if it has been described in a publication, sold, or put to public use more than one year before a patent application on it is filed (the one-year grace period). This limitation exists even if it is the inventor who undertakes such actions. The 2011 revisions to the law apply the one-year grace period only to an inventor's publication, use or sale; activity by others before a patent is filed preclude patentability, even within a year. Note that many countries have no grace period at all.

Nonobviousness refers to the ability of an invention to produce surprising or unexpected results; that is, results not anticipated by prior art. The nonobviousness standard is measured in relation to someone who has ordinary skill in the prior art. For instance, to be patentable a computer hardware invention would need to be nonobvious to an ordinary computer engineer. Importantly, obviousness is assessed as of the date of the application as opposed to later in the litigation. Courts are careful to avoid "highlight" bias, which is the tendency to see any invention as obvious after it is revealed and its significance is known.

Patent litigation over the obviousness of an invention is typically very subjective with each side to the lawsuit producing experts who disagree. Ultimately it is up to the court to determine the state of knowledge existing when the inventor filed the application and whether the invention is nonobvious. See Sidebar 11.7.

>> *sidebar* 11.7

The Determination of Obviousness

A problem of the patent system is that a single manufactured item like an automobile may have hundreds of patents applying to various parts. Any time an improvement is made on a part by manufacturer X, there is always the possibility that a current patent holder Y will sue claiming infringement. X often responds that Y's patent claim is invalid because it was obvious. If Y's patent claim is obvious, then the fact that X based its new improvement on technology covered by Y's claim is not patent infringement because the patent is invalid.

The Supreme Court faced this situation in *KSR International Co. v. Teleflex, Inc.*, 127 S. Ct. 1727 (2007), a case involving Teleflex's accusation that KSR infringed its patent by adding a new electronic sensor to an adjustable automobile accelerator pedal. Teleflex believed it had a patent that covered the use of electronic sensors along with adjustable automobile accelerator pedals, a combination that did not exist in the prior art. KSR responded by asserting that the patent claim was invalid because the technology of attaching the electronic sensor to the pedal was obvious. In its decision favoring KSR, the Supreme Court rejected a prior decision by the United States Court of Appeals for the Federal Circuit, which deals with patents. That prior case decided that a patent claim is only proved obvious when some specific reference like a journal article prior to the patent in question teaches, suggests or motivates one of ordinary skill to create the claimed invention (in this case suggesting the attaching of the electronic sensor to an adjustable automobile accelerator pedal prior to the Teleflex patent).

Instead, the Supreme Court observed that a variety of factors could lead a court to conclude legally that a patent was invalid for obviousness. Importantly, the Court said, "We build and create by bringing to the tangible and palpable reality around us new works based on instinct, simple logic, ordinary inferences, extraordinary ideas, and sometimes even genius. These advances, once part of our shared knowledge, define a new threshold for which innovation starts once more. And as progress beginning from higher levels of achievement is expected in the normal course, the results of ordinary innovation are not the subject of exclusive rights under the patent laws. Were it otherwise patents might stifle, rather than promote, the progress of useful arts."

What the Supreme Court has done is to make it somewhat easier to challenge the validity of patents by arguing that patent claims are obvious and that new improvements in technology or designs do not violate patents in the old technology or designs.

Except for patents issued on designs or plants, an invention to be valid must have utility, that is, it must do something useful. Suppose that Acme Laboratory scientists invent a new chemical compound. Until the compound has a use, say, ridding pets of fleas, Acme will be unable to get a utility patent on it. Usefulness was the issue in *Diamond v. Diehr*, 450 U.S. 175 (1981), the first Supreme Court decision to recognize a patent on computer software. The Court stated that the software involved controlled the timing for curing rubber and thus was useful. Since this case, the mathematical algorithms contained in computer software have been patentable if they do something in the real world.

Computer software code has long been copyrightable. The importance of patenting software as opposed to just copyrighting is that the copyright protects only the actual programming code and the look and feel of the program; it does not cover the functionality, which can be copied using different code. But if you patent the actions of the software, you may have a legal monopoly over the way the computer does something, such as controlling rubber curing. Merely changing the code will not keep someone from infringing a patent.

11. PATENT ENFORCEMENT

As the U.S. Constitution specifies, the property represented by patents runs for limited duration. Statutes limit utility patents and plant patents to 20 years from the filing date, and design patents to 14 years from the issue date. When a patent expires, the invention is in the public domain, and others may use it without limitation. Remember that when the patent expires, it is easy to use the invention since the patent application explains exactly how the invention works, including drawings of its construction. The explicit purpose of patent law is to make inventions public following the limited period of legal property right. For the duration of a patent, the owner can sue those who infringe on it. If successful, the owner can get an injunction prohibiting future infringement, damages, including triple damages for willful infringement.

Complicating the business environment for patents is the fact that they can overlap. Simply owning one is not a license to produce a product or service. A fundamental concept in patent law is that patents only convey the right to exclude others from making, using, selling, and importing the invention. They do not include the right to use the invention. At first glance, the latter point may seem counterintuitive. Can you really own a patent and have no right to make a product that is covered by it? The answer, surprisingly, is yes, and the key to understanding it is to realize that multiple intellectual property rights can cover the same article. There is often more than one patent to a product.

Consider an average cell phone. Imagine that you own a patent that covers touch screen technology, enabling you to open programs and type by placing your fingers on the screen. Now, imagine that your friend owns a patent on technology that allows a phone to switch between hardware buttons and a touch screen. Add another friend who has a patent and perhaps a copyright that cover the phone's operating system (See Figure 11.2). Even though you

*When a patent expires, the patent is in the *public domain,* and others may use it without limitation.

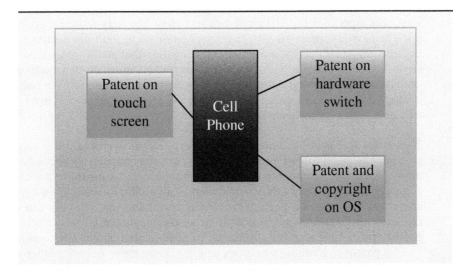

Figure 11.2
Overlapping Intellectual Property Rights

338   **PART 3** Legal Foundations for Business

The consequences of patent infringement can be high, with two recent cases involving jury awards of over $1 billion. Such awards are often reduced on appeal, but still amount to millions in damages.

own a patent that covers part of a cell phone, you cannot produce the cell phone with the characteristics above without using the rights of others. In reality, of course, cell phones are covered by hundreds of patents as well as other rights. Many licenses are required to produce a single phone. This situation exists to varying degrees with other products.

12. CURRENT ISSUES IN PATENT LAW

What property protects is not always clear. As a patent is an application of property, what patents protect are not always clear. Even when what patents protect is quite certain, the question arises as to whether a property monopoly is appropriate. Consider the following issues.

Some non-practicing patent entities have quite large portfolios, raising concerns on their impact on the marketplace. For example, a company called Intellectual Ventures is reported to own more than 30,000 patents.

Patent Trolls As described above, patents may overlap to cover a single product, and in some fields the number overlapping rights can be quite large. This makes it difficult to identify and license all of the patents one might infringe. The ambiguity provides an opportunity for one who purchases a patent right simply to sue existing companies, because the damages (from trial or settlement) can be great and the risk to the patent owners relatively small. Out of the belief that such non-practicing patent owners are nothing more than a toll-taker on a bridge, they have been widely referred to as "patent trolls." The pejorative term suggests that non-producing patent owners do not contribute as much to the innovation environment compared to the costs imposed by their enforcement.

As a counter to the patent troll rhetoric, one might consider the fact that non-practicing entities are exercising a legitimate right under their property grant. Patents do not require their owners to actually make and sell an invention. This concept is similar to land property, wherein one may own a plot land but decide not to build anything. However, the overlapping nature of intellectual property sets the stage for greater conflict than with non-producing landowners.

Companies that believe they are disproportionately impacted by troll-like behavior, such as consumer electronics firms, have pushed for reforms. At least two aspects of the 2011 reforms to patent law may reduce troll behavior. The new law prevents patent owners from suing multiple parties merely because they infringe the same patent, a change that makes litigation more expensive for trolls. Going forward, patent owners must show a common set of facts or a case arising out of the same occurrence to join multiple parties in a suit. Additionally, business method patents, as described above, are subject to a new review proceeding if litigated.

"It's a measure of the deeply dysfunctional U.S. patent system that the most sophisticated technology companies have been reduced to investing in patents to defend themselves from one another."

L. Gordon Crovitz in the *Wall Street Journal*, August 22, 2011.

Patenting Genes Another controversial issue surrounding patent law concerns the patenting of human genes. In part, the controversy arises because many people do not understand what a gene is or what it means to patent one. A gene is a sequence of DNA that occupies a specific location on a chromosome and determines a particular inherited characteristic. Patents can cover the sequence of DNA itself, similar to other chemical compounds. Worldwide, patent offices have received thousands of gene-related patent applications.

To patent a human gene does not mean that the patent holder owns some part of you. Only when the gene has been isolated and purified in a way that can be put to use can someone patent it. Still, many believe that one should not be able to patent basic knowledge about specific genes. They argue that there should be a common use of this knowledge and that its production does not depend on the same incentives that justify other types of patents.

A recent challenge to gene patents has arisen in the context of genes useful for detecting breast cancer. A company called Myriad owns patents covering natural mutations of genes, BRCA1 and BRCA2, that are strongly correlated with breast cancer. Concerned scientists in concert with advocacy groups like the American Civil Liberties Union (ACLU) sued to have the patents declared invalid. To the surprise of many, a federal district court in New York ruled that such gene patents are in fact not patentable subject matter, as they are not materially different from DNA that exists in nature. *Assoc. for Molecular Pathology v. U.S. Patent & Trademark Off.*, 702 F. Supp. 2d 181 (S.D.N.Y. 2010). The decision was largely overturned on appeal by a federal circuit court in July of 2011, but it may be further appealed and eventually reach the U.S. Supreme Court. The outcome of the dispute is extremely important to industries that rely on gene patents, like biotechnology, pharmaceuticals, and even universities.

>> Trademark Law

For thousands of years, people have used marks on what they produce to represent the origin of goods and services. Pottery from ancient Greece, Rome and China often bears the mark of its maker. The same is true for ancient building materials like brick and tile. Today, we generally call such marks **trademarks** and when they indicate a specific producer, the law protects them against use by others.

Trademarks are a form of intellectual property. Like patents you can register them with the PTO, and also like patents, trademarks are some of the most valuable properties that businesses own. McDonald's golden arches, the Nike "swoosh," Coca-Cola, Sony, Facebook, Amazon.com, the Colonel, Exxon, Kodak, Kleenex, the Olympic rings, Rolex, Levi's—the list of famous trademarks is almost endless, but always recognizable.

Although registration systems exist at the federal and state level, it is important to understand that trademark rights come from *use* of the mark in association with goods or services. One can have rights in an unregistered trademark, and even sue for infringement. You cannot presume that, simply because a mark is unregistered, it is open for use in your field. However, this is not to say that registration is irrelevant. Particularly at the federal level under the Lanham Act, registration conveys important advantages. Therefore, it is advisable for a business to pursue a federal trademark registration for its source indicating marks whenever possible.

Recognizability or *distinctiveness* is the function of trademarks. In a world cluttered with stimulation, information, and advertising, trademarks pierce through the clutter and let people know that the goods or services represented are "the real thing"—that they come from one source. They are an information property, exclusively distinguishing the reputation and goodwill of a particular business from that of all other businesses. Trademarks protect

According to a 2010 study by *Interbrand,* the four most valuable brands belong to Coca-Cola, IBM, Microsoft, and Google both businesses and consumers from confusion regarding who makes or provides what. As one recent Federal Court of Appeals case observed:

> Trademarks are designed to inform potential buyers who makes the goods on sale. Knowledge of origin may convey information about a product's attributes and quality, and consistent attribution of origin is vital when vendors reputations matter. Without a way to know who makes what reputations cannot be created and evaluated, and the process of competition will be less effective. *Top Tobacco, L.P. v. North Atlantic Operating Co., 509 F. 3d 380, 381 (7th Cir. 2007)*

Trademark infringement, which may involve intentional use of the owner's mark or an accidental design of one's own mark too similarly to another's, is a major business problem, especially in the Digital Age when often the only point of contact people have with a goods or service provider is a computer screen.

13. TYPES OF TRADEMARKS

Although state law protects trademarks, this chapter focuses on the federal protection given trademarks by the Lanham Act of 1946. The Lanham Act protects the following marks used to represent a product, service, or organization:

- Trademark—any mark, word, picture, or design that attaches to goods to indicate their source.
- Service mark—a mark associated with a service, for example, LinkedIn.
- Certification mark—a mark used by someone other than the owner to certify the quality, point of origin, or other characteristics of goods or services, for example, the Good Housekeeping Seal of Approval.
- Collective mark—a mark representing membership in a certain organization or association, for example, the National Football League logo.

For convenience, all of these marks will be referred to as trademarks.

>> sidebar 11.8

Brands vs. Trademarks

In a marketing class you may have heard the term "brand" used quite frequently. However, in law, the term "trademark" is used. Do these terms have the same meaning, and are they completely interchangeable?

The terms have a long history of association. Branding as a means of marking animals to designate ownership could be considered the original form of trademark. And its modern use related to marking products is derived by analogy to this ancient practice. The term "brand" actually comes from the Anglo-Saxon verb that means "to burn."

In the modern business context, a mark, symbol, or picture that someone refers to as a brand would also qualify in almost all cases as a trademark. A brand is a marketing concept that invokes a corporate strategy to capture a family of products or services in a readily identifiable manner. A trademark is the legal designation given to a mark that serves as a source identifier. It may not be as broad as a brand. Consider, for example, the different models of cars sold under the Ford brand. Each model name likely qualifies as a trademark itself, but may not be considered a separate brand. It is probably fair to say that most brands are trademarks, but not all trademarks are brands.

Source: Sidney A. Diamond, "The Historical Development of Trademarks," 65 *Trademark Reporter* 265 (1975).

Trade Dress Similar to trademarks, and also protected by the Lanham Act, is trade dress. **Trade dress** refers to a color or shape associated with a product or service. The red color scheme of Coca-Cola when associated with the general design of Coca-Cola labeling constitutes trade dress. Trade dress protection prevents Coca-Cola competitors from designing a shape that resembles "Coca-Cola" and attaching the characteristic Coke red to the design in such a way as to confuse potential Coke customers about what they are getting. Trade dress also includes distinctive store decorating motifs (e.g., McDonald's) or package shapes and colors.

The distinctive "wasp-shaped" Coca-Cola bottle is part of its trade dress.

An important trade dress case is *Two Pesos, Inc. v. Taco Cabana, Inc.,* 505 U.S. 763 (1992). In that case the Supreme Court defined trade dress as "the total image and overall appearance" of a business. The Court upheld a decision that Two Pesos had violated Taco Cabana's trade dress. The Court stated that "trade dress [in this case] may include the shape and general appearance of the exterior of the restaurant, the identifying sign, the interior kitchen floor plan, the décor, the menu, the equipment used to serve food, the servers' uniforms and other features reflecting on the total image of the restaurant." The law protects trade dress from being copied as long as it is distinctive. If it is distinctive and registered, the law protects it even without proof that the public has come to identify the trade dress with a specific source.

14. TRADEMARK REGISTRATION

If one wishes to register a trademark with the PTO, one must use the mark in interstate commerce. Posting the trademark on an Internet website in association with a product or service meets this qualification. Alternatively, an intent-to-use application may be filed, followed by an amended application when actual use begins.

To be registerable, a trademark must be distinctive. The PTO will deny registration in the following circumstances:

- If the mark is the same or similar to a mark currently used on similar related goods, for example, a computer company's cherry mark that resembles the apple mark of Apple Inc.

- If the mark contains certain prohibited or reserved names or designs, including the U.S. flag, other governmental symbols, immoral names or symbols, the names or likenesses of living persons without their consent, and the names or likenesses of deceased American presidents without the permission of their spouses.

- If the mark merely describes a product or service, for example, "Fast Food" for a restaurant franchise.

- If the mark is generic and represents a product or service, for example, "cell phone" for a wireless communication company.

Note that a mark that is descriptive or generic in one context may be unique and distinctive in another. "Apple" appears to be an arbitrary term in the context of consumer electronics because it easily distinguishes the source of one company's products and services from another's. However, it would not be registerable for a fruit stand that sells apples.

As part of the trademark application process, the PTO places a proposed mark in the *Official Gazette,* which gives existing mark owners notice and allows them to object that the proposed mark is similar to their own. If existing mark owners object to the proposed mark's registration, the PTO holds a hearing to resolve the objection and, possibly, to deny registration. Finally, if the PTO determines the mark acceptable, it registers the mark on the *Principal Register.* This registration provides notice of official trademark registration status.

Unlike a patent, which specifies a limited property duration, the trademark enjoys a potentially unlimited protection period. But after six years the trademark owner must notify the PTO that the trademark is still in use. Currently, every 10 years the owner must renew the trademark registration.

The attempt to register certain descriptive terms, or a person's name, presents a special problem. Generally, the PTO will not accept a person's name or a descriptive term for protection on the *Principal Register.* However, there is a process by which a name or descriptive term can achieve full trademark status and protection. If it is listed on the PTO's *Supplemental Register* for five years *and* acquires a secondary meaning, it can then be transferred to the *Principal Register* for full protection.

Secondary meaning refers to a public meaning that is different from its meaning as a person's name or as a descriptive term, a public meaning that makes the name or term distinctive. In the public mind, "Ford" now refers to an automobile rather than a person, "Levi" means jeans rather than a family, and "Disney" refers to a specific entertainment company rather than its founder.

15. TRADEMARK ENFORCEMENT

Trademark law protects the trademark's owner from having the mark used in an unauthorized way. Using a mark that is confusingly similar to the trademark owner's mark violates the law. The standard for liability is proof that a defendant's use has created a "likelihood of confusion" with the plaintiff's trademark. To make this determination, courts use a multi-factored test that considers elements such as the defendant's intent and proof of actual consumer confusion. The law establishes both civil and criminal trademark violation.

Civil violation of a trademark (or a patent) is termed **infringement.** The violator infringes on the trademark's property right through an unintentional or a willful unauthorized use, misappropriating the goodwill and reputation that the trademark represents and confusing the public about the identity of the user. Remedies for civil infringement include a variety of damages, injunctions, prohibiting future infringement, and orders to destroy infringing products in anyone's possession.

The following case illustrates the application of the likelihood of confusion test as well as the extent to which unregistered trade dress can serve as a protectable mark.

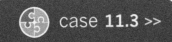

case 11.3 >>

LOUISIANA STATE UNIVERSITY v. SMACK APPAREL CO.
550 F.3d 465 (5th Cir. 2008)

REAVLEY, J: . . . The plaintiffs are Louisiana State University (LSU), the University of Oklahoma (OU), Ohio State University (OSU), the University of Southern California (USC), and Collegiate Licensing Company (CLC), which is the official licensing agent for the schools. . . . Each university has adopted a particular two-color scheme as its school colors (purple and gold for LSU, crimson and creme for OU, scarlet and gray for OSU, and cardinal and gold for USC). The Universities have used their respective color combinations for over one hundred years, and the color schemes are immediately recognizable to those who are familiar with the Universities. The schools use these color schemes in many areas associated with university life, including on campus signs and buildings, on printed brochures, journals, and magazines, and on materials sent to potential donors. The Universities also use the color schemes extensively in connection with their athletic programs, particularly on team uniforms, resulting in wide-spread recognition of the colors among college sports fans. Each university operates a successful collegiate football program, and the respective football teams have appeared on numerous occasions in nationally televised football games that have been viewed by millions of people.

The schools also grant licenses for retail sales of products, including t-shirts, that bear the university colors and trademarks. In recent years, the total annual sales volume of products bearing the school colors along with other identifying marks has exceeded $ 93 million for all the Universities combined. The Universities hold registered trademarks in their respective names and commonly used initials. They do not, however, possess registered trademarks in their color schemes.

Smack Apparel Company is located in Tampa, Florida. Since 1998 Smack has manufactured t-shirts targeted toward fans of college sports teams, and it uses school colors and printed messages associated with the Universities on its shirts. Smack sells some of the shirts over the Internet, but most are sold wholesale to retailers and t-shirt vendors. The shirts frequently appear alongside those that have been officially licensed by the Universities. The instant case involves six of Smack's t-shirt designs that concern the appearance of the OU and LSU football teams in the 2004 Sugar Bowl in New Orleans, Louisiana, and the number of national championships previously won by OSU and USC. . . .

The Universities claimed that Smack's products are similar to and competed with goods sold or licensed by the Universities and are sold directly alongside merchandise authorized by the plaintiffs at or near events referenced in the shirts. In this way, according to the Universities, the sale of Smack's products is likely to deceive, confuse, and mislead consumers into believing that Smack's products are produced, authorized, or associated with the plaintiff Universities. The Universities sought injunctive relief, lost profits, damages, costs, and attorneys' fees. . . .

To prevail on their trademark infringement claim, the plaintiffs must show two things. First, they must establish ownership in a legally protectible mark, and second, they must show infringement by demonstrating a likelihood of confusion.

The Lanham Act provides that a trademark may be "any word, name, symbol, or device, or any combination thereof" that is used or intended to be used "to identify and distinguish" a person's goods "from those manufactured or sold by others and to indicate the source of the goods, even if that source is unknown."[15] A mark need not be registered in order to obtain protection because "[o]wnership of trademarks is established by use, not by registration." . . .

The parties correctly agree that a color scheme can be protected as a trademark when it has acquired secondary meaning and is non-functional. . . . Although the parties discuss color at length in their briefs, the Universities do not claim that every instance in which their team colors appear violates their respective trademarks. Instead, the claimed trademark is in the colors on merchandise that combines other identifying indicia referring to the Universities. . . .

Secondary meaning "occurs when, 'in the minds of the public, the primary significance of a [mark] is to identify the source of the product rather than the product itself.'" . . .

The record shows that the Universities have been using their color combinations since the late 1800s. The color schemes appear on all manner of materials, including brochures, media guides, and alumni materials associated with the Universities. Significantly, each university features the color schemes on

[continued]

merchandise, especially apparel connected with school sports teams, and such prominent display supports a finding of secondary meaning. . . . The record also shows that sales of licensed products combining the color schemes with other references to the Universities annually exceed the tens of millions of dollars. As for advertising, the district court held that the Universities "advertise items with their school colors in almost every conceivable manner . . ." . . . Furthermore, the district court correctly observed that the school color schemes have been referenced multiple times in newspapers and magazines and that the schools also frequently refer to themselves using the colors. . . . Given the longstanding use of the color scheme marks and their prominent display on merchandise, in addition to the well-known nature of the colors as shorthand for the schools themselves and Smack's intentional use of the colors and other references, there is no genuine issue of fact that when viewed in the context of t-shirts or other apparel, the marks at issue here have acquired the secondary meaning of identifying the Universities in the minds of consumers as the source or sponsor of the products rather than identifying the products themselves.

We think this conclusion is consistent with the importance generally placed on sports team logos and colors by the public. We have previously noted, although not in the context of secondary meaning, that team emblems and symbols are sold because they serve to identify particular teams, organizations, or entities with which people wish to identify. . . . We think this desire by consumers to associate with a particular university supports the conclusion that team colors and logos are, in the minds of the fans and other consumers, source indicators of team-related apparel. By associating the color and other indicia with the university, the fans perceive the university as the source or sponsor of the goods because they want to associate with that source. . . .

Once a plaintiff shows ownership in a protectible trademark, he must next show that the defendant's use of the mark "creates a likelihood of confusion in the minds of potential customers as to the 'source, affiliation, or sponsorship'" of the product at issue. . . . "Likelihood of confusion is synonymous with a probability of confusion, which is more than a mere possibility of confusion." When assessing the likelihood of confusion, we consider a nonexhaustive list of so-called "digits of confusion," including: "(1) the type of mark allegedly infringed, (2) the similarity between the two marks, (3) the similarity of the products or services, (4) the identity of the retail outlets and purchasers, (5) the identity of the advertising media used, (6) the defendant's intent, and (7) any evidence of actual confusion." . . . Courts also consider (8) the degree of care exercised by potential purchasers. . . . No single factor is dispositive, and a finding of a likelihood of confusion need not be supported by a majority of the factors. . . .

After reviewing the record, we conclude that there is no genuine issue of fact that Smack's use of the Universities' color schemes and other identifying indicia creates a likelihood of confusion as to the source, affiliation, or sponsorship of the t-shirts. . . . [T]he digits of confusion—particularly the overwhelming similarity of the marks and the defendant's intent to profit from the Universities' reputation—compel this conclusion. This is so, we have noted, because Smack's use of the Universities' colors and indicia is designed to create the illusion of affiliation with the Universities and essentially obtain a "free ride" by profiting from confusion among the fans of the Universities' football teams who desire to show support for and affiliation with those teams. . . . This creation of a link in the consumer's mind between the t-shirts and the Universities and the intent to directly profit therefrom results in "an unmistakable aura of deception" and likelihood of confusion. . . .

We hold that given the record in this case and the digits of confusion analysis discussed above—including the overwhelming similarity between the defendant's t-shirts and the Universities' licensed products, and the defendant's admitted intent to create an association with the plaintiffs and to influence consumers in calling the plaintiffs to mind—that the inescapable conclusion is that many consumers would likely be confused and believe that Smack's t-shirts were sponsored or endorsed by the Universities. The Universities exercise stringent control over the use of their marks on apparel through their licensing program. It is also undisputed that the Universities annually sell millions of dollars worth of licensed apparel. We further recognize the public's indisputable desire to associate with college sports teams by wearing team-related apparel. We are not persuaded that simply because some consumers might not care whether Smack's shirts are officially licensed the likelihood of confusion is negated. Whether or not a consumer *cares* about official sponsorship is a different question from whether that consumer would likely *believe* the product is officially sponsored. For the foregoing reasons, we conclude that a likelihood of confusion connecting the presence of the Universities' marks and the Universities' themselves was demonstrated in this case.

[continued]

>> CASE QUESTIONS

1. Describe what the universities were seeking to protect as a trademark or trade dress.
2. What evidence supported that the trademarks in question had "secondary meaning"?
3. What factors (or digits) did the court consider most important in its analysis?
4. What could Smack do if it wished to continue selling clothing with the universities' marks?

Trademark owners must be vigilant in protecting their marks because if a trademark becomes **generic,** if it loses its distinctiveness, it also loses its status as a protected trademark. A trademark is most likely to become generic (1) when an owner does not defend against unauthorized use and (2) when the public becomes confused as to whether a term refers to a particular product/service or refers to a general class of products/services. Due to concern that its famous trademark not become generic, Coca-Cola seeks to prevent trademark infringement by employees at soda fountains who without comment give customers other colas when asked for a "Coke." Employers are warned to advise employees to specify that another cola will be substituted if Coke is not available.

As Table 11.1 illustrates, a number of trademarks have been lost because the public came to think of them as generic terms.

To win a trademark infringement lawsuit, a defendant will usually present one of three basic defenses: (1) the mark is not distinctive, (2) there is

Don't forget what it means for a trademark to become **generic.**

---

table 11.1 >> Trademarks Lost Due to Generic Use

The following generic terms were once trademarks:

Aspirin	Lite Beer
Cellophane	Refrigerator
Cola	Thermos
Escalator	Zipper

To ensure that its well-known trademark not be lost to generic use, the Xerox Corporation spent millions of dollars advertising to the public that *xerox* is a registered trademark and that the term should not be used as a verb (to "xerox" a copy) or as a noun (a "xerox").

Note that a term that is generic in one country may be protectable in another. For example, the term "aspirin" is a protected trademark of Bayer AG in many countries, including Canada.

> The use of trademarked names in this textbook is a "fair use."

little chance of the public's being confused by use of a term trademarked by someone else, or (3) the use is a "fair use." In arguing the first defense, the defendant maintains that the mark is descriptive or generic and that the PTO should not have protected it in the first instance. Alternatively, the defendant argues that the mark has become generic since its trademarking and that it now stands for a class of items. Note that a court can declare a mark invalid even if the PTO accepted registration.

The second defense argues that there is little chance of public confusion over two uses of the same mark. For example, the public is not likely confused between the Ford automobile and the Ford Modeling Agency. But the confusion defense does not always work. In 2010, a federal district court awarded the owners of the Rolls-Royce trademark $2 million against a defendant calling itself "Rolls-Royce USA" for willful infringement in the context of clothing such as t-shirts. Despite the fact that the trademark owners primarily manufacture airplane engines and automobiles, not clothing, confusion was established.

The third defense raised in trademark infringement lawsuits is that of fair use. *Fair use* of a registered trademark is allowed by the Lanham Act and relates to a discussion, criticism, or parody of the trademark, the product, or its owner, for example, in the news media, on the Internet, or in a textbook. The courts have been explicit that the use of a rival's trademark in comparative advertising is also a fair use. You can legally advertise the results of a study that show your product to be superior to a competitor's, even if you mention the competitor's trademarked product by name.

Criminal trademark penalties apply to those who manufacture or traffic in *counterfeit* trademarked products, products such as imitation "Rolex" watches or "Levi" jeans. What makes counterfeiting criminal is the deliberate intent to pass off, or *palm off,* fake products as real by attaching an unauthorized trademark.

> "The International Chamber of Commerce estimates that the value of counterfeit and pirated products worldwide is about $600 billion, and projects that figure to double by 2015."
>
> –Elizabeth Holmes in *the Wall Street Journal,* June 30, 2011

Trademarks and the Internet   Cyber technology and the Internet produce a combination of old and new trademark issues. One new issue concerns the relationship between a website domain name registered with the Internet Corporation for Assigned Names and Numbers (ICANN) and a trademark registered with the Patent and Trademark Office. There have been numerous instances in which people attempt to register domain names containing well-known trademarks that did not belong to them. Generally, it is a violation of trademark law to use another's registered mark in your domain name. Further, the Anticyber-squatting Consumer Protection Act of 1999 provides a remedy of statutory damages and transfer of a *famous* trademark domain name to its owner if it was registered in "bad faith." As an alternative to litigation, a trademark owner can pursue an arbitration against an improper domain name registrant. ICANN, an international organization that administers the Internet's addressing system, has a formal dispute resolution policy. ICANN has the authority to cancel or transfer the registration of the losing party.

16. TRADEMARK DILUTION

In 1995, Congress passed the Federal Trademark Dilution Act. This law prohibits you from using a mark the same as or similar to another's "famous" trademark so as to dilute its significance, reputation, and goodwill. Even if an owner of a famous trademark cannot prove that the public is confused by another's use of a similar mark (called a "junior" mark), the owner of the "senior" famous trademark can still get an injunction prohibiting further use of the junior mark on the basis of **trademark dilution.** The court also has discretion to award the owner the infringer's profits, actual damages, and attorney's fees if the infringer "willfully intended to trade on the owner's reputation or to cause dilution of the famous mark."

In 2006, Congress passed the Trademark Dilution Revision Act, which established that dilution exists when a defendant creates a "likelihood of dilution." The law was designed, in part, to overrule an earlier Supreme Court decision, *Mosely v. V. Secret Catalogue, Inc.,* which set a higher standard of actual dilution. Thus, it is now slightly easier to win a dilution case.

> Remember: only the owners of famous marks can prevail under the Federal Trademark Dilution Act.

>> Copyright Law

LO 11-5

Like patent, **copyright** gives those who have this property a monopoly over the right to exclude others from copying and marketing for a limited period of time. Unlike patent, copyright deals with original *expression* rather than invention. The importance of copyright began with the development of the printing press in the early 1400s, but the first copyright law was the Statute of Anne, enacted in England in 1710. In the United States copyright is authorized in the Constitution, and Congress has revised copyright several times. Until the late 1800s, however, the United States did not recognize foreign copyright laws as they protected the works of foreign authors. As a result, U.S. publishers felt free to publish the works of foreign authors without permission or the payment of fees called *royalties.*

Today the United States has joined most other countries in international agreements, such as the Berne Convention, in protecting the copyright of other nations, but once again copyright has come to a turning point in the road. Digital technology makes it ever easier to copy not only printed material, but music, movies, and software as well. No longer is a large business necessary to copy and distribute copyrighted materials illegally. Individuals can copy materials quickly and almost without cost and send them around the world in a blink of an eye. As you read the following sections on copyright law, keep in mind the new digital age you have entered.

17. COPYRIGHT OWNERSHIP

Copyright law grants property in certain creative expressions that keeps others from reproducing it without the owner's permission. The copyright attaches not to an idea or to facts but to the original *expression* of an idea or facts. Three criteria are necessary for copyright protection to occur:

- A work must be original. It must be created, not copied. Facts are not original, though collections of facts may be, depending on the selection and arrangement.
- The work must be fixed in a tangible medium of expression like a book, canvas, compact disk, hard drive, or flash memory.
- The work must show some creative expression. For example, the Supreme Court ruled in *Feist Publications, Inc. v. Rural Telephone Service Co.,* 499 U.S. 340 (1991), that the mere effort and alphabetic arrangement of names that went into a telephone directory's white pages was insufficiently creative to warrant a copyright.

Copyright laws protect authors rather than inventors. An author creates works of a literary, dramatic, musical, graphic, choreographic, audio, or visual nature. Ranging from printed material to photographs to records and motion pictures, these works receive automatic federal protection under the Copyright Act of 1976 from the moment the author creates them. Importantly, no registration is required to obtain a copyright under federal law. Additionally, notice—for example, a copyright symbol or the word "copyrighted"—is also *not* required. For that reason, businesses are often advised to assume that a work created by another is copyrighted, no matter if it appears freely available without notice.

Companies can be considered authors under copyright law. In fact, when an employee creates a work within the scope of their employment, the employer is automatically the owner and author. This type of work is called a "work-for-hire." It eliminates the need for companies to negotiate the rights to letters, documents, web pages, etc., that employees produce in the course of every day work.

The copyright allows the holder to control the reproduction, display, distribution, and performance of a protected work. The copyright runs for the author's lifetime, plus 70 additional years for an individual, and 95 years from publication or 120 years from creation for a work by a company. Congress has occasionally extended the term for copyrights in existence. The last time was in 1998 under the Copyright Term Extension Act, which added 20 years to the term.

18. COPYRIGHT PROTECTION

An important part of what copyright holders own is a limited resource in the market for their music or other expressions. That means the object of their property right is the market itself.

Although copyright protection attaches at the moment a work is created, an action for copyright infringement cannot be begun unless the author has properly registered the work with the Copyright Office. Unless the work was registered within three months of publication, a copyright owner can obtain statutory damages only if the work is registered before a defendant's infringement. The author may also be able to obtain actual damages, attorney's fees and the infringer's profits. Illegally reproduced copies may also be seized, and willful copyright violations can be a criminal offense.

The Copyright Act specifies that a fair use of copyrighted materials is not an infringement of the owner's property. **Fair use** includes copying for "criticism, comment, news reporting, teaching (including multiple copies for classroom use), scholarship, or research." In determining whether a particular use is a fair one, a court will consider

- The purpose and character of the use, including whether such use is for commercial or nonprofit educational purposes.
- The nature of the copyrighted work.
- The amount and substantiality of the portion used in relation to the copyrighted work as a whole.
- The effect of the use upon the potential market for the copyrighted work.

The determination of a fair use in light of these factors is made on a case-by-case basis. In Case 11.4, the Supreme Court considers whether one song makes a fair use of a previous song's copyrighted lyrics. The fair use being considered concerns *parody*, a form of expression that criticizes by poking fun at something through exaggeration.

case 11.4 >>

CAMPBELL v. ACUFF-ROSE MUSIC, INC.
510 U.S. 569 (1994)

The rap group 2 Live Crew recorded and sold a commercial parody of Roy Orbison's copyrighted song "Oh Pretty Woman." Acuff-Rose Music, Inc., the copyright holder, sued the 2 Live Crew members after nearly a quarter million copies of the recording had been sold. The case came before the Supreme Court after the court of appeals decided that 2 Live Crew's parody had taken too much of "Oh Pretty Woman" to be protected as a fair use.

SOUTER, J: It is uncontested here that 2 Live Crew's song would be an infringement of AcuffRose's rights in "Oh Pretty Woman," under the Copyright Act of 1976, but for a finding of fair use through parody. From the infancy of copyright protection, some opportunity for fair use of copyrighted materials has been thought necessary to fulfill copyright's very purpose, "to promote the Progress of Science and useful Arts. . . ." For as Justice Story explained, "in truth, in literature, in science and in art, there are, and can be, few, if any, things, which in an abstract sense, are strictly new and original throughout. Every book in literature, science and art, borrows, and must necessarily borrow, and use much which was well known and used before."

The first factor in a fair use enquiry is "the purpose and character of the use, including whether such use is of a commercial nature or is for nonprofit educational purposes." The enquiry here may be guided by looking to whether the use is for criticism, or comment, or news reporting, and the like. The central purpose of this investigation is to see, in Justice Story's words, whether the new work merely "supersede[s] the objects" of the original creation, or instead adds something new, with a further purpose or different character, altering the first with new expression, meaning, or message; it asks, in other words, whether and to what extent the new work is "transformative." Although such transformative use is not absolutely necessary for a finding of fair use, the goal of copyright, to promote science and the arts, is generally furthered by the creation of transformative works. Such works thus lie at the heart of the fair use doctrine's guarantee of breathing space within the confines of copyright, and the more transformative the new work, the less will be the significance of other factors, like commercialism, that may weigh against a finding of fair use.

The second statutory factor, "the nature of the copyrighted work," calls for recognition that some works are closer to the core of intended copyright protection than others, with one consequence that fair use is more difficult to establish when the former works are copied. We agree with both the District Court and the Court of Appeals that the Orbison original's creative expression for public dissemination falls within the core of the copyright's protective purposes. This fact, however, is not much help in this case, or ever likely to help much in separating the fair use sheep from the infringing goats in a parody case, since parodies almost invariably copy publicly known, expressive works.

The third factor asks whether "the amount and substantiality of the portion used in relation to the copyrighted work as a whole" are reasonable in relation to the purpose of the copying. The District Court considered the song's parodic purpose in finding that 2 Live Crew had not helped themselves overmuch. The Court of Appeals disagreed, stating that "while it may not be inappropriate to find that no more was taken than necessary, the copying was qualitatively substantial. . . . We conclude that taking the heart of the original and making it the heart of a new work was to purloin a substantial portion of the essence of the original."

Suffice it to say here that, as to the lyrics, we fail to see how the copying can be excessive in relation to its parodic purpose, even if the portion taken is the original's "heart." As to the music, we express no opinion whether repetition of the bass riff is excessive copying, and we remand to permit evaluation of the amount taken, in light of the song's parodic purpose and character, its transformative elements, and considerations of the potential for market substitution sketched more fully below.

The fourth fair use factor is "the effect of the use upon the potential market for or value of the copyrighted work." It requires courts to consider not only the extent of market harm caused by the particular actions of the alleged infringer, but also "whether unrestricted and widespread conduct of the sort engaged in by the defendant . . . would result in a substantially adverse impact on the potential market" for the original. The enquiry "must take account not only of harm to the original but also of harm to the market for derivative works."

[continued]

Although 2 Live Crew submitted uncontroverted affidavits on the question of market harm to the original, neither they, nor Acuff-Rose, introduced evidence or affidavits addressing the likely effect of 2 Live Crew's parodic rap song on the market for a nonparody, rap version of "Oh Pretty Woman." And while Acuff-Rose would have us find evidence of a rap market in the very facts that 2 Live Crew recorded a rap parody of "Oh Pretty Woman" and another rap group sought a license to record a rap derivative, there was no evidence that a potential rap market was harmed in any way by 2 Live Crew's parody, rap version.

It was error for the Court of Appeals to conclude that the commercial nature of 2 Live Crew's parody of "Pretty Woman" rendered it presumptively unfair. No such evidentiary presumption is available to address either the first factor, the character and purpose of the use, or the fourth, market harm, in determining whether a transformative use, such as parody, is a fair one. The court also erred in holding that 2 Live Crew had necessarily copied excessively from the Orbison original, considering the parodic purpose of the use. We therefore reverse the judgment of the Court of Appeals and remand the case for further proceedings consistent with this opinion.

Reversed and remanded.

19. COPYRIGHT IN THE DIGITAL AGE

Under copyright law it is illegal not only to make copies that violate the law but also to assist others in doing so. When copyright holders challenged certain programs that assisted file sharing of materials—mostly, copyrighted music—one case went to the Supreme Court. In *Metro-Goldwyn-Mayer Studios v. Grokster*, 125 S. Ct. 2764 (2005), the Court asserted: "We hold that one who distributes a device with the object of promoting its use to infringe copyright, as shown by clear expression or other affirmative steps taken to foster infringement, is liable for the resulting acts of infringement by third parties." In addition to inducing others to infringe, one can be liable for materially contributing to another's infringement with knowledge of the infringement. Obtaining financial benefit with the ability to supervise the infringement also makes one vicariously liable.

International piracy of copyrighted material is a major problem, but international enforcement efforts are improving slowly.

Criminal prosecutions and civil lawsuits for "file sharing" copyrighted material over the Internet continue. The motion picture and recording industries have been particularly active over the years in pursuing individuals for file sharing. Some excuse file sharing by saying that intellectual property does not diminish the way that tangible property does when someone misappropriates it. But consider this: property is a legal right to exclude, not a physical thing, and the object of a property copyright includes the reproduction of music for commercial profit. The holder of a copyright owns the right to market what is copyrighted, and the market resource is diminished for the copyright owner when file sharers misappropriate music. In the early years of this century, the volume of sales for copyrighted music has declined significantly, largely due to misappropriation.

20. DIGITAL MILLENNIUM COPYRIGHT ACT

Because copyrighted property is easily misappropriated over the Internet, Congress passed a law in 1998 that prohibits certain activities leading to copyright violation. The Digital Millennium Copyright Act (DMCA) makes illegal the effort to get around (circumvent) devices used by copyright owners to keep their works from being infringed. In particular, the act prevents the production, marketing, or sales of a product or service designed to circumvent technological protections of computer software, videos, and compact disks. The act also prevents circumvention of access protections for such products. It further provides a safe-harbor for Internet service providers, protecting them from liability (1) for illegal copies that pass temporarily through their systems and (2) for permanent illegal copies stored in their systems, for example, at a website, if the service provider removes the offending material upon request of a copyright owner. Finally, the act relieves service providers from liability for unintentionally linking to a website that contains infringing materials.

>> *sidebar* 11.9

Knowledge of Users' Infringing Activity

Internet service provides (ISPs), which include companies that provide Internet access as well as those that host content like videos, have protection against claims of contributory infringement so long as they act to address copyright owner claims. For hosting services, the DMCA requires content removal when a copyright owner provides notice. However, ISPs may be obligated to act even before a copyright owner notifies them. Under the act, actual knowledge of infringing works posted by users requires action. Additionally, knowledge of facts or circumstances from which infringement is apparent requires that an ISP remove the infringing content.

When do facts and circumstances make infringement apparent? Is a general knowledge that some users post infringing content enough? This question was addressed in the recent case *Viacom Intern. Inc. v. YouTube, Inc.,* 718 F. Supp. 2d 514 (S.D.N.Y. 2010). Viacom contended that YouTube was aware of infringing activity on its service and did not work sufficiently to eliminate it. The court rejected that argument, stating "Mere knowledge of prevalence of such activity in general is not enough." The court found that YouTube was protected by the DMCA's safe harbor provisions.

Violations of the DMCA permit civil remedies, including injunction, actual damages, and statutory damages. A court can assess triple damages against a repeat offender. Willful circumvention for financial gain can also result in up to 10 years' imprisonment.

>> International Intellectual Property Rights

LO 11-6

To this point, this chapter has presented the basic rules of U.S. intellectual property rights. You may be aware that you can obtain similar rights in other countries. Is such protection automatic once you have protection in the U.S.? Is there an international system for protecting intellectual property? These are essential questions for any modern business. As commerce becomes global, the protection of intellectual property internationally is increasingly important.

There are in fact no fully international intellectual property rights, *per se*. Local or regional law controls the creation and ownership of patents, copyrights, trademarks and trade secrets. However, there are international standards that most industrialized nations have agreed to uphold. The most important source for standards is an international treaty known as the Trade-Related Aspects of Intellectual Property Agreement (TRIPS). This agreement was formed in 1994 as part of the treaty that created the World Trade Organization (WTO). The United States has been a member since the agreement's inception, and was a major force is drafting its provisions. TRIPS requires that member countries provide protection for all of the forms of intellectual property discussed in this chapter. In addition, it sets forth baseline rules for that protection in terms of subject matter, procedure, and enforcement. By virtue of the TRIPS agreement, businesses can count on being able to obtain similar protection for intellectual property in other countries. However, differences in the manner in which counties comply with TRIPS require that companies exercise due care in pursuing international rights.

In addition to substantive protection, international treaties exist that can facilitate filing for rights in several countries at the same time. In the context of patents, there is the Patent Cooperation Treaty (PCT), which allows an applicant to obtain a preliminary international examination and then pursue final rights in multiple countries at the same time. Similarly, trademark owners can pursue rights in several countries at the same time through the Madrid System for International Registration of Marks. Because members of the Berne Convention, described above, are not required to undertake any formalities to obtain copyright protection, no international filing system is necessary. Members agree to provide rights if similar rights are obtained in an author's home country.

In order to monitor and administer certain aspects of international intellectual property agreements, countries have provided authority to certain independent international organizations. The most important two organizations are the WTO and the World Intellectual Property Organization (WIPO). The WTO administers the TRIPS agreement, including the settlement of disputes concerning its interpretation. The WIPO administers the PCT and Madrid System in addition to many other international intellectual property treaties. Both organizations provide much useful information to businesses, and it is worth consulting their respective web resources before pursuing international protection.

>> A Conclusion about Intellectual Property

Intellectual property, like property itself, serves the common good. The U.S. Constitution points this out in Article 1, Section 8, by asserting that the purpose for Congress granting "to authors and inventors the exclusive right to their respective writings and discoveries" is to promote the progress of science and business, which society believes promotes the common good. The framers of the Constitution believed, as do modern economists, that property, including intellectual property, gives incentive for private production of goods and services, which benefits not only the owners providing goods and services, but also to the overall wealth of society.

A property system is only as effective as the mechanism for enforcing it. Without adequate enforcement, a property system cannot function for the common good, and enforcement relies upon more than laws and courts. It depends also on the attitudes of people toward legitimacy of the property. Without social recognition of the exclusive legal fences that are at the heart of the property system and without adequate enforcement of property, the system cannot provide the incentive necessary for private productive effort.

Increasingly, we live in a global society, and the information that is the resource of intellectual property moves easily across national borders. This means that the enforcement of intellectual property is something important to all nations that are part of the global trading system.

>> Key Terms

Copyright 347	Injunction 328	Trade dress 341
Fair use 348	Intellectual property 323	Trademark 339
Generic 345	Patent 330	Trademark dilution 347
Infringement 342	Property 321	Trade secret 325

>> Review Questions and Problems

1. *The Justification for Intellectual Property*
   (a) What is the purpose of patents and copyrights as identified in the Constitution?
   (b) Explain the claim that the pace of research and development of new products would slow if intellectual property right did not protect it.

2. Intellectual Property and Competition
   (a) Explain the balance between intellectual property's rights of exclusion and competition.
   (b) Articulate alternatives to intellectual property for encouraging information creation.

3. Capturing Intellectual Property
   Explain the assertion that businesses can lose rights if they do not diligently assess and pursue intellectual property protection.

Trade Secrets

4. *Trade Secret: Taking Reasonable Measures to Keep the Secret*
   (a) How do trade secrets differ from other applications of property?
   (b) Discuss several ways of preserving trade secrets.

5. Demonstrating Misappropriation
   What types of actions constitute misappropriation under trade secret law?

6. *Trade Secret: Civil Enforcement*
   What are the remedies available for the civil enforcement of trade secrets?

7. *Trade Secret: Criminal Enforcement*
   Why has criminal misappropriation of trade secrets become an issue of greater concern in recent years?

Patent Law

8. *Obtaining a Patent*
   Describe the process for obtaining a patent.

9. *Patentable Subject Matter*
   Through long, expensive research you determine that both a bowling ball and a feather fall at the rate of 32 feet per second in a vacuum. Can you patent this knowledge? Explain.

10. *Nonobviousness, Novelty, and Usefulness*

    (a) Imagine that you discover a long-ignored cure for headaches in an old U.S. medical journal from the 1800s, and you apply for a patent. Explain why a patent examiner would likely reject your application.

    (b) Discuss the patent requirement of nonobviousness.

11. *Patent Enforcement*

    Is it possible for two utility patents owned by different people to cover the same product? Explain.

12. *Current Issues in Patent Law*

    (a) Discuss the propriety of entities that acquire and assert patents but make no product.

    (b) You discover a specific human gene that determines male pattern baldness. Explain what it means to say that you can patent this gene.

Trademark Law

13. *Types of Trademarks*

    Name four types of marks that are often called "trademarks."

14. *Trademark Registration*

    (a) Can you register the name "Fast Food" as a trademark? Explain.

    (b) Under what conditions can you *not* register a mark?

15. *Trademark Enforcement*

    Do you ever "google" something on the Internet? Is the company Google in danger of losing its name as a trademark? Explain.

16. *Trademark Dilution*

    Articulate an example that would constitute trademark dilution, but not infringement. Can you come up with one that constitutes infringement but not dilution?

Copyright Law

17. *Copyright Ownership*

    (a) If you spend the time and effort necessary to alphabetize the names of the students at your school and list their e-mail addresses, can you copyright a printed version? Explain.

    (b) Explain the rights a company has to the works created by its employees.

18. *Copyright Protection*

    Imagine that you are making a presentation to a class on the occurrence of product advertising in film. You display a short clip of a recent film to illustrate your point. Explain how one would argue that this use constitutes a "fair use" of the copyrighted material.

19. *Copyright in the Digital Age*

    Explain why digital copies of works create greater difficulties in controlling infringement.

20. *Digital Millennium Copyright Act*

    Are file-hosting sites like YouTube liable for infringing videos posted by their users?

business >> *discussions*

1. Colonel Cars, Inc., plans to introduce a new speaker complex in the steering wheels of its automobiles. It believes the change will revolutionize the drivers' music-listening enjoyment. The company is also preparing an advertising campaign around the improved listening experience. Both the new steering-wheel speakers and the ad campaign are carefully kept secrets. But Colonel Cars's vice president for marketing is hired by European Motor Works (EMW) to be the president of its international division. Before Colonel Cars can begin its advertising, EMW comes out with an ad campaign centered on—you guessed it—speakers in the steering wheels of its new model cars.

What is "property"?
Can a company have property in its marketing plans the way you can have property in your car?
Can EMW use Colonel Car's marketing plans without permission?

12   International Law

□ Learning Objectives

In this chapter you will learn:

12-1. To understand the legal risk inherent in international transactions, including the requirements of the Foreign Corrupt Practices Act.

12-2. To identify the basic sources of international law and major institutions.

12-3. To consider the importance of free trade agreements on the global economy.

12-4. To grasp the basic methods of transacting international business.

12-5. To realize the complexity of resolving international disputes.

The risks of engaging in global transactions are apparent in the news on a daily basis. From increased prosecutions for bribery to lawsuits involving global operations, the international marketplace is fraught with potential legal issues.

The collapse of Lehman Brothers during the fall of 2008, illustrates the interconnectedness of international business. Lehman's bankruptcy triggered a "cash crunch" around the world, precipitating losses and accelerating the demise of other businesses. The U.S. laws and regulations governing financial institutions immediately were subjected to international scrutiny.

Law is fundamental to business in the United States and throughout the globe. As American businesses become increasingly global in a very competitive international marketplace, some understanding of legal issues in this context is essential. Throughout this text, the importance of *the rule of law* is emphasized. This concept is particularly important for companies doing business abroad. Property rights and contracts must be enforced to minimize risk in international transactions.

The United States enters into treaties and trade agreements to govern competition and the way goods and technology are sold from one country to the next. Every country is interested in developing rules that make its products and services more competitive in the global market. Nation-states and corporations alike are protected by a mutual respect for property and contractual rights.

The goal of American trade policy is to open markets throughout the world. The idea is to create new opportunities for business and also higher living standards. The United States is a party to many trade agreements and is continually negotiating new ones to further open markets to free trade. National economies rely on their ability to export products and services abroad to create jobs and economic growth at home. Companies likewise are continually looking for productive ways to expand their international business. Overall, however, the United States has a huge trade deficit because it buys more than it sells abroad. At the end of 2010, the trade deficit was $497.8 billion. For a chart of the top trading partners with the United States, see Figure 12.1.

This chapter discusses the risks of global trade, with increased emphasis on the pressure for bribes. It then provides a basic understanding about international law and organizations that affect trade, including major trade agreements. Next, it provides an overview of methods of transacting international business and concludes with ways of resolving international disputes. Overall, this chapter should help you understand the issues affecting business in the international landscape.

> "Travel is fatal to prejudice, bigotry, and narrow-mindedness ... Broad, wholesome, charitable views of men and things cannot be acquired by vegetating in one little corner of the earth all one's lifetime."
>
> **– Mark Twain, American humorist (1857)**

Figure 12.1 *Top Ten Trading Partners with the United States*

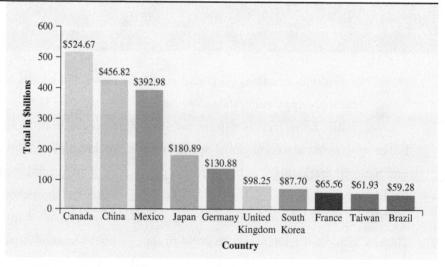

Source: U.S. Census Bureau Statistics for 2010

>> Risks Involved in International Trade

LO 12-1

Because international trade means dealing with different legal systems, cultures, and ways of doing business, there are a number of risks involved. For example, when a firm expends globally, a host of potential risks and concerns are raised, such as:

- What U.S. laws have an "extraterritorial" reach?
- Are property rights enforced?
- Will foreign courts uphold the validity of contracts?
- Is intellectual property protected or is it vulnerable to infringement?
- Are there export or import restrictions on the firm's products?
- Are there risks associated with political instability and/or war?
- What international trade agreements will affect the firm's expansion?
- What national laws (e.g., labor and environmental) affect the firm?
- How should language and cultural differences be bridged?

See Sidebar 12.1 as an example of problems that can arise with outsourcing manufacturing. This section addresses specific concerns about pressures for bribes, expropriation and nationalization, and export controls.

>> *sidebar* 12.1

Problems with Outsourcing in China: Mattel's Massive Toy Recall

In 2007, Mattel, Inc., recalled over 10 million toys manufactured in China. What was at issue? Lead paint and tiny magnets presented safety hazards for children. At least one U.S. child died and 19 others required surgery after swallowing magnets in the toys. The recall included some of Mattel's most popular toys, including Barbie, Dora, Thomas the Train, Polly Pocket, and *Cars* movie items. The over $33 billion U.S. toy industry heavily relies on manufacturing in China for approximately 80 percent of its toys.

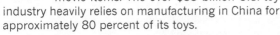

>> **PRACTICAL CONSIDERATIONS FOR BUSINESS**

Who is responsible?

What is the best way to address the problem?

Should there be tighter consumer standards?

How can companies better control outsourced manufacturing?

---

1. PRESSURES FOR BRIBES

Following widespread disclosure of scandalous payments by domestic firms to officials of foreign government, Congress enacted the **Foreign Corrupt Practices Act (FCPA)** in 1977. The law is designed to stop bribery of foreign officials and to prohibit U.S. citizens and companies from making payments to foreign officials whose duties are not "essentially ministerial or clerical" for the purpose of obtaining business. Since 2009, FCPA enforcement increased substantially. Any company trading on a U.S. stock exchange can be prosecuted for FCPA violations.

This statute has two principal requirements:

1. Financial records and accounts must be kept "which, in reasonable detail, accurately and fairly reflect the transactions and dispositions of assets" of the business.
2. The business must "devise and maintain a system of internal accounting controls sufficient to provide reasonable assurances" that transactions are being carried out in accordance with management's authorization.

These provisions are intended to correct the previously widespread practice of accounting for bribes as commission payments, payments for services, or other normal business expenses and then illegally deducting the payments on income tax returns.

Many legal observers criticized the FCPA for creating a significantly chilling effect on U.S. companies seeking business in many developing countries where under-the-table payments to government officials are an accepted practice. Indeed, many civil servants in other nations are expected to supplement their salaries in this manner. The U.S. prohibition of such payments is perceived as an attempt to impose U.S. standards of morality in other parts of the world, and it has caused resentment and discrimination against U.S. businesses. Moreover, the FCPA arguably puts U.S. firms at a competitive disadvantage with businesses in other countries that are not operating under similar constraints.

>> *sidebar* 12.2

Turning Back the Tide of Corruption

An international group known as Transparency International generates the Corruption Perceptions Index annually. It ranks 178 countries according to perception of corruption in the public sector. This global coalition against corruption measures perceptions as a reliable measure of the degree of corruption of a country. Here is a sampling of countries from the 2010 report:

Denmark, New Zealand and Singapore tied for #1
Canada #6
Germany #15

United States #22
China #78
Mexico #96
Iraq #175
Afghanistan #176
Myanmar #177
Somalia #178
#1 = least corrupt #178 = most corrupt

Source: Transparency International Corruption Perceptions Index, www.transparency.org

---

As a result of intensive lobbying by the U.S. business community, Congress amended the FCPA in 1988 in an effort to eliminate ambiguity and uncertainty over what constitutes improper conduct. Although the law still

table 12.1 >> FCPA: Legal or Permissible Payments

The following payments are permissible under the FCPA:

"Facilitating," "expediting," or "grease" payments for "routine government action." Examples include obtaining permits, licenses, or other official documents; processing governmental papers (e.g., visas and work orders); providing police protection; loading and unloading cargo; and scheduling inspections associated with contract performance or transit of goods across country.

Any payments permitted under the written laws of the foreign country.

Travel expenses of a foreign official for the purpose of demonstrating a product or for performing a contractual obligation.

prohibits bribery and corruption, the amendments establish clearer standards for firms to follow in overseas operations. The amendments limit criminal liability for violations of accounting standards to those who "knowingly" circumvent accounting controls or falsify records of corporate payments and transactions. The amendments also clarify the level of detail required in such record keeping and should improve compliance by businesses and enforcement by the government. Moreover, under the new law otherwise prohibited payments to foreign officials may be defended if they were legal under the written laws of the host country or if they cover "reasonable and bona fide" expenses associated with the promotion of the product and the completion of the contract (see Table 12.1).

The FCPA also prohibits corrupt payments through intermediaries. It is unlawful to make a payment to a third party, while knowing that all or a portion of the payment will go directly or indirectly to a foreign official. The term *knowing* includes conscious disregard and deliberate indifference. Additionally, the antibribery provisions of the FCPA apply to foreign firms and persons who take action in furtherance of a corrupt payment while in the United States.

Criminal penalties may be imposed for violations of the FCPA: corporations and other business entities are subject to a fine of up to $2,000,000; officers, directors, stockholders, employees, and agents are subject to a fine of up to $100,000 and imprisonment for up to five years. Fines imposed on individuals may *not* be paid by their employer or principal. The attorney general or the SEC, as appropriate, may also bring a civil action for fines against any firm, as well as any officer, director, employee, or agent of a firm or stockholder acting on behalf of the firm who violates the antibribery provisions. The conduct that violates the antibribery provisions of the FCPA may also give rise to a private cause of action for treble damages under the Racketeer Influenced and Corrupt Organizations Act (RICO). For example, a RICO action could be brought by a competitor who alleges that the bribery caused the defendant to obtain a foreign contract. See Sidebar 12.3 for examples of successful FCPA prosecutions.

Payment of a bribe in violation of the FCPA can buy you jail time.

>> *sidebar* 12.3

FCPA Prosecutions: U.S. Government Success Stories

Siemens AG paid a record-breaking $800 million for FCPA violations. The total consisted of a $450 million fine to the Department of Justice and $350 million in disgorgement of profits to the Securities and Exchange Commission. Siemens allegedly violated the FCPA by paying $1.36 billion in bribes around the world in connection with obtaining contracts. According to the prosecution, the corruption implicated all levels of management, including senior management, and involved elaborate payment schemes and off-book accounts to conceal payments. The Department of Justice described the level of corruption at Siemens as a "pattern of bribery" that was "unprecedented in scale and geographic reach."

>> OTHER RECENT PROSECUTIONS

Daimler paid a $93.6 million fine and $91.4 million fine for disgorgement of profits. The company and its subsidiaries allegedly made hundreds of improper payments in at least 22 countries, including China and Russia.

Johnson & Johnson agreed to pay $70 million to settle civil and criminal bribery charges involving bribes

paid to public doctors and public hospital administrators in Greece, Poland, and Romania.

Baker Hughes paid $44 million following accusations that the company used bribes to win an oil fields contract in Kazakhstan.

IBM agreed to pay $10 million to settle civil bribery charges involving payments by more than 100 employees of a subsidiaries and joint ventures in Asia.

Tyson Foods, Inc., paid $5.2 million in criminal and civil penalties to resolve FCPA allegations involving meat inspectors employed by the Mexican government.

Antonio Perez, a former controller of a Florida-based telecommunications company, pleaded guilty to conspiring to commit FCPA violations and money laundering in connection with payments made to Telecommunications D'Haiti. He was sentenced to two years in prison, to serve an additional two years of supervised release following his prison term, and to forfeit $36,375.

concept >> *summary*

Risks Involved in International Trade

1. The Foreign Corrupt Practices Act seeks to stop the bribery of foreign government officials.
2. Expropriation and nationalization are risks involved in international business.
3. Expert controls seek to balance national security interests against global trade.

2. EXPROPRIATION AND NATIONALIZATION

Creeping expropriation is a series of acts, such as taxes, regulation, or other changes in law that have an expropriatory effect, reducing or eliminating foreign investments.

If a domestic firm is involved in a foreign country to the extent of locating assets there (whether through branches, subsidiaries, joint ventures, or otherwise), it may be subject to the ultimate legal and political risk of international business activity—expropriation. **Expropriation,** as used in the context of international law, is the seizure of foreign-owned property by a government. When the owners are not fairly compensated, the expropriation is also considered to be a *confiscation* of property. Usually, the expropriating government also assumes ownership of the property, so the process includes

nationalization as well. In the United States, the counterpart of expropriation is called the *power of eminent domain.*

This power of a government to take private property is regarded as inherent; yet it is subject to restraints upon its exercise. The U.S. Constitution (as well as the constitutions and laws of most nations) prohibits the government from seizing private property except for "public purposes" and upon the payment of "just compensation."

However, the extent of such protection varies widely. Treaties (or other agreements) between the United States and other countries provide additional protection against uncompensated takings of property. It is customary for international law to recognize the right of governments to expropriate the property of foreigners only when accompanied by "prompt, adequate, and effective compensation." This so-called modern traditional theory is accepted by most nations as the international standard and requires full compensation to the investor including fair market value as a going concern. See Sidebar 12.4 for an example of nationalization.

>> *sidebar* 12.4

ExxonMobil Corp. v. Petróleos de Venezuela: Chavez and Nationalization of the Oil Industry

 Venezuelan President Hugo Chavez nationalized the last privately run oil fields in the country in 2007. The government took over four oil projects run by some of the world's biggest petroleum companies, including Exxon Mobil Corp. In his announcement of the takeover, Chavez told cheering workers that foreign oil companies damaged Venezuela's national interests and that reclaiming them represented an historic victory.

Exxon is not taking the loss without a fight. Exxon brought an action against state-owned Petróleos de Venezuela (PDVSA) in the United States. In early 2008, Exxon won a $315 million freeze of PDVSA's assets, as well as a ruling blocking PDVSA's transactions with Britain and the Netherlands, affecting as much as $12 billion in assets. Ultimately, what compensation will Exxon receive for the loss of its assets in Venezuela? Will other foreign oil companies whose assets were nationalized in Venezuela be compensated? The matter is far from resolved and has far-reaching political implications.

Chavez is also taking steps to nationalize utilities, the telecommunications industry, and the Venezuelan subsidiary of Mexican cement company Cemex SEB.

3. EXPORT CONTROLS

Another risk involved in doing business abroad is **export controls** placed on the sale of U.S. strategic products and technology abroad. Controlling the export of such items has been the cornerstone of Western policy since the conclusion of World War II. Most of the attention was focused on preventing the acquisition of technology by the former Soviet Union and its allies. However, since the end of the Cold War the policy rationale behind export controls has been drawn into question, with many Western countries contending they should be eliminated to increase trading opportunities with Russia, China, Eastern Europe, and the Middle East. Indeed, the Coordinating Committee for Multilateral Export Controls (COCOM), an organization created by the major Western nations (including the United States, Europe, and Japan) to control exports, came to an end in 1994.

Exports from the United States to countries such as Cuba, Iran, Libya, North Korea, Sudan, and Syria are restricted.

Query: Should the U.S. lift its trade embargo with Cuba? The EU agreed to lift its sanctions against Cuba in June 2008.

Since that time, a new organization supported by 33 countries, known as the Wassanaar Arrangement, has come into existence to help control the spread of both military and dual-use technology to unstable areas of the world. Participating nations seek, through their national policies, to ensure that transfer of conventional arms and strategic goods and technologies do not destabilize regional and international security. The 2002 plenary meeting of the Wassanaar Arrangement, held in Vienna, resulted in several significant initiatives to combat terrorism. The member countries agreed on several measures aimed at intensifying cooperation to prevent terrorist groups and individuals from acquiring arms and strategic goods and technologies.

The U.S. export control system currently is regulated by the Department of State and the Department of Commerce under authority provided by the Export Administration Act and the Arms Export Control Act. The Department of Defense also plays a key role in determining the technology to be controlled as does the U.S. Customs Service in the enforcement of the controls. Significant criminal and administrative sanctions may be imposed upon corporations and individuals convicted of violating the law.

>> *sidebar* 12.5

Export Control Reform

The Comprehensive Iran Sanctions, Accountability, and Divestment Act of 2010 makes significant improvements for the nation's export enforcement authorities. This law harmonizes the different maximum export control criminal penalties under four different statutes. It also permanently restores the Department of Commerce's export enforcement authorities.

On November 9, 2010, the President signed Executive Order 13558, establishing an Export Enforcement Coordination Center (EECC) among the Departments of State, the Treasury, Defense, Justice, Commerce, Energy, and Homeland Security, as well as elements of the Intelligence Community. The Department of Homeland Security will administer the EECC. The EECC is designed to:

• Prevent conflicts in criminal and administrative enforcement operations and coordination of industry enforcement outreach activity.

• Provide a conduit between federal law enforcement agencies and the U.S. intelligence community.

• Serve as the primary point of contact between enforcement agencies and export licensing agencies for enforcement and licensing matters.

• Resolve interagency conflicts not settled in the field.

• Establish governmentwide statistical tracking capabilities for U.S. export enforcement activities.

The goal of this reform is to harmonize business practices and processes across the export enforcement agencies.

Source: www.export.gov/ecr/eg_main_027618.asp

According to the U.S. Export Control and Related Border Security Assistance (EXBS) Program, exporters should be aware of the following "red flags":

• *A customer* is reluctant to provide end-use/user information; is willing to pay cash for high-value shipments; has little background in the relevant business; declines normal warranty/service/installation; or orders products incompatible with the business.

- *A shipment* involves a private intermediary in a major weapons sale; shipments are directed to entities with no connection to the buyer; requests for packing are inconsistent with the normal mode of shipping; or circuitous or illogical routing.
- *The end-user* requests equipment inconsistent with inventory; spare parts in excess of projected needs; the end-use is at variance with standard practices; a middleman from a third country places the order; or the end-user refuses to state whether the goods are for domestic use, export, or re-export.

In 2000, the U.S. government extended the Export Administration Act and raised the penalties for violators. The export control agenda for the twenty-first century remains focused on maintaining national security and reducing the proliferation of weapons, while also facilitating U.S. competitiveness in the global economy.

The successful prosecution of two leading American aerospace companies, Hughes Electronics and Boeing Satellite Systems, illustrates the government's commitment to vigorous export control to prevent harmful proliferation of weapons. The companies paid a record $32 million in penalties to settle charges in connection with 123 alleged violations of export control laws regarding the transfer of rocket and satellite data to China.

However, the future of the U.S. system remains in doubt with many proposals pending in Congress to reform and limit the current export control system. Over the past several years, these controls have become an extremely controversial topic in the international business community. Export controls make successful business deals more difficult because foreign buyers may be reluctant to trade with a U.S. firm due to the red tape involved in obtaining governmental approval as compared with Europe or Japan.

>> *sidebar* 12.6

Twenty-First Century Pirates

 According to the International Maritime Bureau, in 2010, pirates hijacked 53 ships worldwide and took 1,181 hostages in 445 attacks—a 10 percent rise from 2009. Most of the hijackings occurred in the Gulf of Aden. A study by One Earth Future estimates that maritime piracy costs between $7 and $12 billion a year. In early 2011, Somali pirates were still holding 31 ships and over 700 crewmembers. Other violent attacks were reported in the South China Sea off of Indonesia, Bangladesh, and Nigeria.

Sources: "Pirates Seized Record 1,181 Hostages in 2010," *Report BBC News* (Jan. 1, 2011) and One Earth Future at www.oneearthfuture.org/.

>> International Law and Organizations

What is "international law"? Inasmuch as there is no "world government" or "world legislature," international law is not created the same way as domestic law. International law is found in a variety of sources, including U.S. domestic law, national laws of other countries, international agreements, treaties, and even in what is called "customary international law." Customary international law involves principles that are widely practiced and acknowledged by many civilized nations to be law.

In the landmark case of *The Paquette Habana* (1900), the United States Supreme Court held that "[i]nternational law is part of our law, and must be ascertained and administered by the courts of justice of appropriate jurisdiction as often as questions of right depending upon it are duly presented for their determination."

International organizations, such as the United Nations, the World Trade Organization, and the European Union, directly impact international business transactions. Agreements entered into by the United States, including the Convention on the International Sale of Goods, the North American Free Trade Agreement, and the Dominican Republic-Central American Free Trade Agreement also affect the global sale of goods. These agreements facilitate trade and minimize risk for business.

>> *sidebar* 12.7

What Are Corporate Codes of Conduct?

Corporate codes of conduct are policy statements adopted by companies to define ethical standards for their conduct. These are completely voluntary, often addressing topics such as:

- Forced labor.
- Child labor.
- Discrimination.
- Health and safety of workers.
- Freedom of association and collective bargaining.
- Hours of work, wages, benefits, and overtime compensation.
- Working conditions.
- Environmental issues.
- Monitoring and enforcement of the code of conduct.

Recognizing that there are different legal and cultural environments around the world, companies often develop a code of conduct to establish a foundation for their standards in international business. Seeking to promote global corporate citizenship, the United Nations developed the Global Compact, a voluntary code of conduct supported by companies and organizations around the world. For a list of participants, see www.globalcompact.org. Many major corporations engaging in global operations, including Microsoft, GAP, Inc., and Cisco Systems, Inc., also have supplier or vendor codes of conduct. These codes allow companies to set standards for their suppliers and vendors consistent with the companies' mission and values.

LO 12-2

4. SOURCES OF INTERNATIONAL LAW

What are the principles or rules of international law that apply to a particular contract or dispute? Generally, international law is classified as either **public international law** or **private international law.** Public international law examines relationships between nations and uses rules that are binding on all countries in the international community. Private international law examines relationships created by commercial transactions and utilizes international agreements, as well as the laws of nations to resolve business disputes. Business managers are primarily concerned with private international law issues.

Public International Law Article 38 of the Statute of the **International Court of Justice (ICJ)** is the traditional place for ascertaining what is public international law. However, in contrast to what you learned in Chapter 1 regarding U.S. cases, the decisions made by the ICJ, the World Court, do not create binding rules of law or precedent in future cases.

The ICJ is the judicial branch of the United Nations and sits at The Hague in the Netherlands. It consists of 15 judges representing all of the world's major legal systems. The judges are elected by the U.N. General Assembly and the Security Council after having been nominated by national groups, not governments. No more than one judge may be a national of any country.

The ICJ has not been a major force in settling disputes since it began functioning in 1946. The ICJ renders, on average, only one contested decision per year and one advisory opinion every two years. There has been widespread reluctance to resort to the ICJ as a forum for resolving international disputes for several reasons. First, only countries have access to the Court. Private parties or corporations may not directly present claims before the Court. No device exists under U.S. law by which a firm or individual can compel the U.S. government to press a claim on its behalf before the ICJ. Furthermore, only countries that have submitted to the Court's jurisdiction may be parties, since there is no compulsory process for forcing a country to come before the Court. A country may choose to accept the Court's jurisdiction only when the use of the Court may suit its own interests. Moreover, the ICJ has no enforcement authority and must rely on diplomacy or economic sanctions against countries that breach international law. For these reasons, infractions of international law often are settled through diplomacy or arbitration, rather than by the presentation of formal charges to the ICJ.

Of course, deciding whether international law has been violated is often a very difficult question. Article 38 sets forth the following order of importance for determining what is international law in a given case:

> The Court, whose function is to decide in accordance with international law such disputes as are submitted to it, shall apply:
>
> a. *International Conventions*, whether general or particular, establishing rules expressly recognized by the contesting states;
>
> b. *International Custom*, as evidence of a general practice accepted as law;
>
> c. *The General Principles of Law* recognized by civilized nations;
>
> d. *Judicial Decisions and the Teachings of the Most Highly Qualified Publicists* of various nations, as subsidiary means for the determination of rules of law.

International Conventions are similar to legislation or statutes and represent formal agreements between nations. International Custom describes common legal practices followed by nations in working with each other over a long period of time. General Principles of Law may be found in national rules common to the countries in a dispute. Finally, Judicial Decisions and Teachings, although not binding, may be used for guidance in resolving a dispute. See Sidebar 12.8 for an example of an ICJ decision and the interplay with U.S. courts.

The ICJ's hearings are open to the public, unless one of the parties asks for the proceedings to be *in camera* or the Court so decides. The hearings take place in the Great Hall of Justice in the Peace Palace, in The Hague.

>> *sidebar* 12.8

Medellin v. Texas (2008): The U.S. Supreme Court and the International Court of Justice (ICJ)

What is the effect of an ICJ judgment in the United States? In a 6–3 ruling, the U.S. Supreme Court held that President Bush went too far when he decreed that the states must abide by a 2004 decision by the ICJ. The ICJ found that several dozen Mexican citizens sentenced to death in the United States had not been given the assistance of Mexican diplomats that they were entitled to under the Vienna Convention.

The case in question involved Jose Medellin, a onetime Houston gang member who took part in the rape and murder of two teenaged girls. After he was arrested, and read his Miranda Rights, Medellin confessed to the crimes, including revealing particularly egregious details. The conviction was challenged because law enforcement authorities failed to inform him of his right under the Vienna Convention.

In the majority opinion, Chief Justice Roberts states that neither the defendant nor his supporters "have identified a single nation that treats ICJ judgments as binding in domestic courts." In response, Mexico has asked the ICJ to declare that the United States "must provide review and reconsideration of the convictions and sentences" consistent with its 2004 decision.

Do include choice of law and forum selection clauses in all international contracts.

Eight UN Millennium Development Goals:

1. Eradicate extreme poverty and hunger.
2. Achieve universal primary education.
3. Promote gender equality and empower women.
4. Reduce child mortality.
5. Improve maternal health.
6. Combat HIV/AIDS, malaria, and other diseases.
7. Ensure environmental sustainability.
8. Develop a global partnership for development.

Private International Law Private international law is represented by the laws of individual nations and the multilateral agreements developed between nations to provide mutual understanding and some degree of continuity to international business transactions. Even in purely domestic business deals, the law is rarely predictable or certain. When different national laws, languages, practices, and cultures are added to the transaction, the situation can become very unstable for international business.

International law can be complicated and a single business transaction can involve several companies in different nations. For example, a contract dispute between a Chinese manufacturer, an American wholesaler, and a Canadian retailer could potentially involve the law of all three countries. Which law controls? The answer could affect the outcome of the case. Determining which nation's court may hear the case can be difficult. For this reason, most international contracts contain choice of law and forum provisions to eliminate this uncertainty.

5. INTERNATIONAL ORGANIZATIONS

Several international organizations play important roles in the development of political, economic, and legal rules for the conduct of international business. The two primary organizations are the United Nations and the World Trade Organization. Additionally, the European Union plays an important role in international trade.

United Nations Established after World War II, the **United Nations** has grown considerably from the 51 founding nations. Almost every country in the world is a member today. The Charter of the United Nations sets forth as its primary goal "to save succeeding generations from the scourge of war" and, to that end, authorizes "collective measures for the prevention and removal of threats to the peace, and for the suppression of acts of aggression or other breaches of the peace."

The General Assembly is composed of every nation represented in the United Nations and permits each country to cast one vote. The real power in the United Nations rests in the Security Council, which is composed of 15 member states. The Security Council has the power to authorize military action and to sever diplomatic relations with other nations. The five permanent members of the Council (United States, Russia, China, France, and United Kingdom) have veto power over any action proposed in the Council. France and Russia used the threat of a veto in 2003 to force the United States to go forward with the war in Iraq without clear United Nations' authority. Although the United States contended that its authority for war came from previously passed UN resolutions regarding Iraq, the U.S. government was disturbed by the veto threat. The failure of the United Nations to dictate the resolution of the U.S.-Iraq conflict created serious questions about the future authority and role of the United Nations in international conflicts.

A number of organizations affiliated with the United Nations have authority over activities that directly affect international business. The United Nations Commission on International Trade Law (UNCITRAL) was created in 1966 to develop standardized commercial practices and agreements. One of the documents drafted by UNCITRAL is the Convention on the International Sale of Goods, which is discussed in more detail later in this chapter. UNCITRAL has no authority to force any country to adopt any of the conventions or agreements that it proposes. The United Nations Conference on Trade and Development (UNCTAD) deals with international trade reform and the redistribution of income through trading with developing countries. UNCTAD drafted both the Transfer of Technology Code and the Restrictive Business Practices Code, which are largely ignored by most nations.

At the Bretton Woods Conference of 1944, two important institutions were also created under the auspices of the United Nations. The **International Monetary Fund (IMF)** encourages international trade by maintaining stable foreign exchange rates and works closely with commercial banks to promote orderly exchange policies with members. The **World Bank** promotes economic development in poor countries by making loans to finance necessary development projects and programs.

For more information about current projects at the World Bank and IMF, see www.worldbank.org/ and www.imf.org/.

> "The human spirit is indomitable. Each individual matters. The seeds of policies and innovations planted today can influence tomorrow. And free men and women can move the world."
>
> **–Robert B. Zoellick, president of the World Bank Group (2008)**

World Trade Organization   Every nation has the right to establish its own trading policies and has its own national interests at stake when dealing with other nations. Ultimately, after years of economic conflict, many countries concluded that their own interests could be served best by liberalizing trade through reduced tariffs and free markets. The **General Agreement on Tariffs and Trade (GATT)** was originally signed by 23 countries after World War II and represented the determination of a war-weary world to open trade and end the protection of domestic industries. Since GATT was created in 1948, it has undergone eight major revisions, including the 1994 Uruguay Round, which culminated in the creation of the **World Trade Organization (WTO)** as an umbrella organization to regulate world trade. The 1994 agreement was signed by 125 countries.

The WTO is an international organization which, as its primary purpose, seeks to resolve trade disputes between member nations. The WTO administers the GATT but does not have the authority to regulate world trade in any manner it desires. The WTO expects nations to avoid unilateral trade wars and rely on GATT dispute settlement procedures to avert conflict. At the heart of the 1994 Uruguay Round are several enduring GATT principles:

1. Nondiscrimination (treating all member countries equally with respect to trade).
2. National treatment (countries not favoring their domestic products over imported products.
3. Elimination of trade barriers (reducing tariffs and other restrictions in foreign products).

Under the WTO, existing tariffs are reduced and the agreement extends GATT rules to new areas such as agricultural products and service industries. The WTO further restricts tariffs on textiles, apparel, and forest products. It also requires countries to upgrade their intellectual property laws to protect patents and copyrights and to guard against the piracy of items such as computer software and videotapes.

Another important aspect of the WTO is the **Agreement on Trade-Related Aspects of Intellectual Property Rights (TRIPS),** including trade in counterfeit goods. Recognizing that there are widely different standards for the protection of intellectual property, as well as a lack of a multilateral framework of rules for dealing with counterfeit goods, the WTO directly addressed this issue with TRIPS. This agreement discusses the applicability of GATT principles and those of relevant international property agreements in an effort to strengthen the protection of intellectual property in the international sphere.

The WTO has the power to hear disputes involving member states. The United States has been involved in a number of disputes. For example, the United States brought an action against the European Union claiming that the Europeanwide restrictions on genetically modified food violate WTO rules. Additionally, the United States brought a successful challenge against Mexico; the WTO held that Mexico's beverage tax on soft drinks made with imported sweeteners is discriminatory. Under the beverage tax, soft drinks made with cane sugar are tax exempt. Because the beverage tax discriminates against U.S. products, it is contrary to WTO rules.

If a nation does not comply with a WTO ruling, the organization has the power to impose sanctions. Like any international institution, compliance by the most powerful trading nations is necessary to give the WTO credibility.

The WTO faces opposition from antiglobalization protesters. There are many reasons to support the WTO and the important role it plays in trade. Concerns, however, are raised by opponents who are concerned about human rights, environmental, and labor issues. Tensions between developed and developing nations are hindering negotiations to cut tariffs. Overall, the future of the WTO is uncertain. The cooperation of member states is critical to its success in liberalizing trade.

The European Union   The European Union is an economic and political partnership between 27 democratic European countries. In 1957, six

> The WTO is the only global international trade organization dealing with the rules of trade between nations.

table 12.2 >> Twenty-Seven European Union Member States	

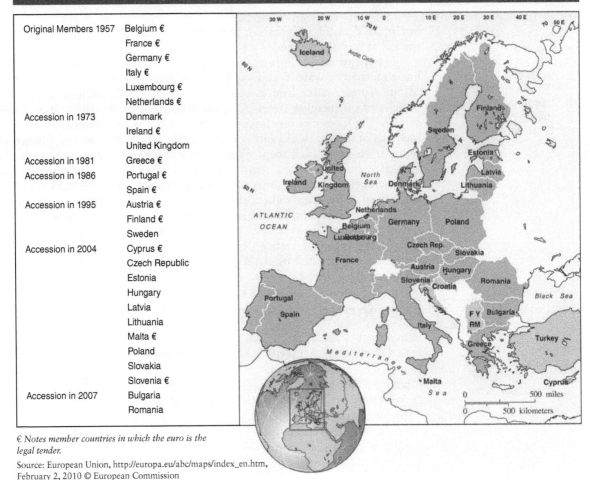

Original Members 1957	Belgium €
	France €
	Germany €
	Italy €
	Luxembourg €
	Netherlands €
Accession in 1973	Denmark
	Ireland €
	United Kingdom
Accession in 1981	Greece €
Accession in 1986	Portugal €
	Spain €
Accession in 1995	Austria €
	Finland €
	Sweden
Accession in 2004	Cyprus €
	Czech Republic
	Estonia
	Hungary
	Latvia
	Lithuania
	Malta €
	Poland
	Slovakia
	Slovenia €
Accession in 2007	Bulgaria
	Romania

€ Notes member countries in which the euro is the legal tender.

Source: European Union, http://europa.eu/abc/maps/index_en.htm, February 2, 2010 © European Commission

European countries, Belgium, France, Germany, Luxembourg, and the Netherlands signed the Treaty of Rome, creating the European Community. Six successive enlargements created the **European Union (EU)**, as it is known today. See Table 12.2 for a complete list of states, accession dates, and those countries using the euro as legal tender. Negotiations are ongoing with Croatia, the Republic of Macedonia, and Turkey about possible membership in the EU.

Europe's mission in the twenty-first century is to:

- Provide peace, prosperity, and stability for its peoples.
- Overcome the divisions on the continent.
- Ensure that its people live in safety.
- Promote balanced economic and social development.
- Meet the challenges of globalization and preserve the diversity of the peoples of Europe.

- Uphold the values that Europeans share, such as sustainable development and a sound environment, respect for human rights, and the social market economy.

For more detailed information about these goals, see the official website of the EU at http://europa.eu.

The major institutions of the EU are the Council of Ministers, the Commission, the Parliament, and the Court of Justice. The Council is composed of one representative from each member state. The Council coordinates the policies of the member states in a variety of areas from economics to foreign affairs. The Commission consists of individuals who represent the will and interests of the entire EU, rather than specific national concerns. Elected representatives from each member state compose the Parliament, which plays an active role in drafting legislation that has an impact on the daily lives of its citizens. The Parliament, for example, has addressed environmental protection, consumer rights, equal opportunities, transport, and the free movement of workers, capital, services, and goods. Parliament also has joint power with the Council over the annual budget of the European Union. Finally, the Court of Justice decides the nature and parameters of EU law. Justices are appointed by the Council, and each member state has a justice seated on the Court.

The aims of the European Union are: "Peace, prosperity and freedom for its 495 million citizens—in a fairer, safer world."

LO 12-3

6. MAJOR AGREEMENTS AFFECTING TRADE

In addition to the international institutions discussed in this chapter, a number of international agreements also facilitate trade.

The U.S. Trade Representative is a Cabinet member who serves as the president's principal trade adviser, negotiator, and spokesperson on trade issues. See www.ustr.gov for current trade news.

Convention on the International Sale of Goods   The **Convention on the International Sale of Goods (CISG)** outlines standard international practices for the sale of goods. It took several years to develop, and represents many compromises among nations that follow a variety of practices in the area of contracts. Effective in 1988, it has been adopted by the United States and most of the other countries that engage in large quantities of international trade. The CISG represents the cumulative work of over 60 nations and international groups and is widely accepted around the globe.

The CISG applies to contracts for the commercial sale of goods (consumer sales for personal, family, or household use are excluded) between parties whose businesses are located in different nations, provided that those nations have adopted the convention. If a commercial seller or buyer in the United States, for example, contracts for the sale of goods with a company located in another country that also has adopted the CISG, the convention and not the U.S. Uniform Commercial Code (UCC) applies to the transaction.

Under the CISG, a significant degree of freedom is provided for the individual parties in an international contract. The parties may negotiate contract terms as they deem fit for their business practices and may, if desired, even opt out of the CISG entirely. One of the most interesting provisions in the CISG includes a rule that contracts for the sale of goods need not be in writing. The

"We must continue to open markets if we want our exports to grow. . . . Open markets create higher paying jobs and help support the prosperity of American workers, farmers, and entrepreneurs."

–Susan C. Schwab, U.S. Trade Representative (2008)

CISG also provides that in contract negotiations an acceptance that contains new provisions that do not materially alter the terms of the offer becomes part of the contract, unless the offeror promptly objects to the change. The CISG sets forth the fundamental elements that will materially alter a contract such as price, payment, quality, and quantity of the goods, place and time of delivery of goods, provisions related to one party's liability to the other, and methods for settling disputes. Since international transactions typically involve sophisticated parties, the CISG also makes it easier to disclaim warranties on goods than under traditional U.S. law. The CISG does not resolve all areas of contract law; parties are still subject to local laws and customs, which makes international agreements complex and tricky to negotiate.

North American Free Trade Agreement   The passage of the **North American Free Trade Agreement (NAFTA)** in 1993 set in motion increased trade and foreign investment and opportunities for economic growth in the United States, Mexico, and Canada. Free trade is at the core of NAFTA, through the reduction and eventual elimination of tariffs and other barriers to business between these three countries. NAFTA also provides for a dispute settlement mechanism that makes it easier to resolve trade disputes between the three countries. Based upon concerns that cheap labor and poor environmental controls might cause U.S. firms to relocate to Mexico, side agreements also were reached to improve labor rights and environmental protection in Mexico. Since its enactment, NAFTA has expanded shipments of U.S. goods to Mexico and Canada, as well as Mexican and Canadian exports to the United States.

Central America-Dominican Republic Free Trade Agreement   Similar to NAFTA, the passage of the **Central America-Dominican Republic Free Trade Agreement (CAFTA-DR)** in 2005 opened up many opportunities for business in Central America. CAFTA-DR is a comprehensive trade agreement between Costa Rica, El Salvador, Guatemala, Honduras, Nicaragua, the Dominican Republic, and the United States. This agreement is designed to eliminate the barriers on products trades between the member countries. Prior to CAFTA-DR, many exports of American goods to Central America faced high tariffs. This trade agreement is a step to create a fairer playing field for American exports.

> Jimmy Carter supported the passage of CAFTA-DR as a "chance to reinforce democracies in the region."

Recent Free Trade Agreements   The United States is continually seeking opportunities to open global trade. In October 2011, Congress passed free trade agreements for three key markets: Colombia, Panama, and South Korea. The agreement with Colombia was the most controversial. According to the U.S. Trade Representative's office, this agreement is important (1) To open a significant new export market; (2) to level the playing field for American business, farmers, ranchers, and workers; (3) to strengthen peace, democracy, freedom, and reform; (4) to promote economic growth and poverty reduction; and (5) to anchor longstanding ties with a vital regional ally. Opponents to the Colombia agreement argued that the agreement does not contain adequate provisions to address labor concerns and human rights violations, including violence against union members.

concept >> *summary*

International Law and Organizations

1. International law is classified as either public or private.
2. The International Court of Justice is the traditional place for determining public international law.
3. The World Trade Organization regulates world trade for member nations.

4. The Convention on the International Sale of Goods governs international practices for the sale of goods.
5. The European Union has evolved into the most important economic force in Europe.
6. The North American Free Trade Agreement has substantially expanded trade with Mexico and Canada.

>> *sidebar* 12.9

Philip Morris: Restrictions Affecting Their Global Business

With more and more anti-smoking laws in the United States and general public opposition to smoking, global markets are increasingly important to tobacco giant Philip Morris. What kinds of issues does it face abroad?

- Limits on cigarette advertising in Britain
- More detailed health warnings in South America
- Higher cigarette taxes in the Philippines and Mexico
- Prohibitions on store displays in Ireland and Norway
- The World Health Organization Framework Convention on Tobacco Control, a public health treaty ratified by 171 nations

- Mandatory health warnings that cover 80 percent of cigarette packages in Uruguay

Alleging that its tobacco regulations are excessive, Philip Morris sued the government of Uruguay. Philip Morris also brought an action against Brazil, arguing that the images the government wants to put on cigarette packages "vilify" tobacco companies.

Sources: Duff Wilson, "Cigarette Giants in Global Fight on Tighter Rules," *The New York Times* (Nov. 13, 2010); World Health Organization Framework Convention on Tobacco Control, www.who.int/fctc/en/.

LO 12-4

>> Methods of Transacting International Business

A U.S. business that wants to engage in international trade is presented with an almost limitless array of possibilities. Choosing a method of doing business in foreign countries not only requires understanding the factors normally involved in selecting an organization and operating a business domestically but also demands an appreciation of the international trade perspective. Depending upon the country, type of export, and amount of export involved in a particular transaction, international trade may involve direct foreign sales, licensing agreements, franchise agreements, or direct foreign investment.

7. FOREIGN SALES

The most common approach for a manufacturer to use when trying to enter foreign markets is to sell goods directly to buyers located in other countries. However, with foreign sales, increased uncertainty over the ability to enforce the buyer's promise to pay for goods often requires that more complex arrangements for payment be made than with the usual domestic sale. International sales involve many risky legal issues. Commonly, an **irrevocable letter of credit** is used to ensure payment. Transactions using such a letter involve, in addition to a seller and buyer, an *issuing bank* in the buyer's country. The buyer obtains a commitment from the bank to advance (pay) a specified amount (i.e., the price of the goods) upon receipt, from the carrier, of a **bill of lading,** stating that the goods have been shipped. The issuing bank's commitment to pay is given, not to the seller directly, but to a *confirming bank* located in the United States from which the seller obtains payment. The confirming bank forwards the bill of lading to the issuing bank in order to obtain reimbursement of the funds that have been paid to the seller. The issuing bank releases the bill of lading to the buyer after it has been paid, and with the bill of lading the buyer is able to obtain the goods from the carrier. Use of a letter of credit in the transaction thus reduces the uncertainties involved. The buyer need not pay the seller for goods prior to shipment, and the seller can obtain payment for the goods immediately upon shipment.

There is no room in documentary transactions for substantial performance. All of the duties and responsibilities of parties must be evaluated based upon the documents tendered, and these documents must comply *strictly* with the letter of credit. The tradition and purpose of the letter of credit in international transactions is demonstrated in Case 12.1, where the issue of notice became the central issue for the court.

> **Do** learn more about the traditions, culture, and etiquette of a host nation before you travel, including business card protocol.

 case **12.1** >>

VOEST-ALPINE TRADING USA v. BANK OF CHINA
288 F. 3d 262 (5th Cir. 2002)

Jiangyin Foreign Trade Corporation ("JFTC"), a Chinese company, agreed to purchase 1,000 metric tons of styrene monomer from Voest-Alpine Trading USA Corporation ("Voest-Alpine"), an American company. At Voest-Alpine's insistence, JFTC obtained a letter of credit from the Bank of China for the purchase price of $1.2 million. The letter of credit provided for payment to Voest-Alpine after it delivered the monomer and presented several designated documents to the Bank of China. By the time Voest-Alpine was ready to ship its product, the market price of styrene monomer had dropped significantly from the original contract price. JFTC asked for a price concession, but Voest-Alpine
refused. After shipping the monomer to JFTC, Voest-Alpine presented the documents specified in the letter of credit to Texas Commerce Bank ("TCB"), which would forward the documents to the Bank of China. TCB noted several discrepancies between what Voest-Alpine presented and what the letter of credit required. Because it did not believe any of the discrepancies would warrant refusal to pay, Voest-Alpine instructed TCB to present the documents to the Bank of China "on approval," meaning that JFTC would be asked to waive the problems.

The Bank of China received the documents. The bank notified TCB that the documents contained

[continued]

several discrepancies and that it would contact JFTC about acceptance. On August 15, 1995, TCB, acting on behalf of Voest-Alpine, responded that the alleged discrepancies were not adequate grounds for dishonoring the letter of credit and demanded payment. On August 19, the Bank of China reiterated its position that the documents were insufficient and stated: "Now the discrepant documents may have us refuse to take up the documents according to article 14(B) of UCP 500." JFTC refused to waive the discrepancies, and the Bank of China returned the documents to TCB on September 18, 1995.

CLEMENT, J.: Voest-Alpine filed the instant action for payment on the letter of credit.

The Bank of China's primary contention on appeal is that the district court erroneously concluded that the bank failed to provide proper notice of refusal to Voest-Alpine. In order to reject payment on a letter of credit, an issuing bank must give notice of refusal to the beneficiary no later than the close of the seventh banking day following the day of receipt of the [presentation] documents. If the Bank of China did not provide timely notice, it must honor the letter of credit despite any questions as to Voest-Alpine's compliance.

The Bank of China received Voest-Alpine's documents on August 9. Since August 12 and 13 were Chinese banking holidays, the deadline for giving notice of dishonor was August 18. The Bank of China's only communication before the deadline was its telex of August 11. Accordingly, the issue is whether that telex provided notice of refusal. The bank's August 11 telex stated:

> Upon checking documents, we note the following discrepancy:
>
> 1. Late presentation.
> 2. Beneficiary's name is differ (*sic*) from L/C.
> 3. B/L should be presented in three originals (*sic*) i/o duplicate, triplicate.
> 4. Inv. P/L. and cert. Of origin not showing "original."
> 5. The date of surver (*sic*) report later than B/L date.
> 6. Wrong L/C no. in fax copy.
> 7. Wrong destination in cert. Of origin and beneficiary's cert.
>
> We are contacting the applicant for acceptance of the relative discrepancy. Holding documents at your risk and disposal.

The district court found that the telex failed to provide notice of refusal because (1) the bank did not explicitly state that it was rejecting the documents; (2) the bank's statement that it would contact JFTC about accepting the documents despite the discrepancies holds open the possibility of acceptance upon waiver and indicates that the Bank of China has not

refused the documents; and (3) the Bank of China did not even mention refusal until its August 19 telex in which it wrote: "Now the discrepant documents may have us refuse to take up the documents according to article 14(B) of UCP 500." In light of these circumstances, the district court concluded that the August 11 telex was merely a status report, the bank would not reject the documents until after it consulted JFTC, and the bank did not raise the possibility of refusing payment on the letter of credit until August 19. Accordingly, the district court held that the Bank of China forfeited its right to refuse the documents and was obligated to pay Voest-Alpine.

We find ample evidence supporting the district court's decision. The court's determination that the August 11 telex did not reject the letter of credit is based primarily on the Bank of China's offer to obtain waiver from JFTC. The offer to solicit a waiver, the district court reasoned, suggests that the documents had not in fact been refused but might be accepted after consultation with JFTC. In reaching this conclusion, the district court relied heavily on the testimony of Voest-Alpine's expert witness on international standard banking practices. [The expert] testified that the bank's telex would have given adequate notice had it not contained the waiver clause. The waiver clause, he explained, deviated from the norm and introduced an ambiguity that converted what might otherwise have been a notice of refusal into nothing more than a status report. Faced with this evidence, the district court correctly decided that the Bank of China noted discrepancies in the documents, and, instead of rejecting the letter of credit outright, contacted JFTC for waiver.

Viewed in the context of standard international banking practices, the Bank of China's notice of refusal was clearly deficient. The bank failed to use the standard language for refusal, failed to comply with generally accepted trade usages, and created ambiguity by offering to contact JFTC about waiver, thus leaving open the possibility that the allegedly discrepant documents might have been accepted at a future date. Accordingly, the district court properly found that the August 11 telex was not an adequate notice of refusal. Since we agree with the district court that the bank failed to provide timely notice, we need not reach the question of whether the alleged discrepancies warranted refusal.

The Bank of China failed to provide Voest-Alpine with adequate notice that it was refusing payment on the letter of credit. Without a valid excuse for nonpayment, the bank is liable for the full amount of the letter of credit and for VoestAlpine's legal fees. Accordingly, we affirm the judgment of the district court.

Affirmed.

[continued]

>> CASE QUESTIONS

1. Why is the issue of "timely notice" so important in the case?
2. What is the primary importance of a letter of credit?
3. Why did the court rule against Bank of China?

8. LICENSES OR FRANCHISES

In appropriate circumstances, a domestic firm may choose to grant a foreign firm the means to produce and sell its product. The typical method for controlling these transfers of information is the **license** or **franchise** contract. In this manner, intangible property rights, such as patents, copyrights, trademarks, or manufacturing processes, are transferred in exchange for royalties in the foreign country. A licensing arrangement allows the international business to enter a foreign market without any direct foreign investment. Licensing often is used as a transitional technique for firms expanding international operations since the risks are greater than with foreign sales but considerably less than with direct foreign investment. Licensing and franchise agreements also must follow the local laws where they operate.

Licensing technology or the sale of a product to a foreign firm is a way to expand the company's market without the need for substantial capital. The foreign firm may agree to this arrangement because it lacks sufficient research and development capability or the management skills or marketing strategies to promote the product alone. Of course, as with all international trade agreements, there is some level of risk. The licensor must take care to restrict the use of the product or technology to agreed-upon geographic areas and must take adequate steps to protect the confidential information that is licensed to the foreign firm so that third parties cannot exploit it.

Each day, McDonald's serves an average of 64 million customers worldwide.

Subway is one of the fastest growing franchises with over 34,000 restaurants in 97 countries.

9. DIRECT FOREIGN INVESTMENT

As a business increases its level of international trade, it may find that creation of a **foreign subsidiary** is necessary. Most countries will permit a foreign firm to conduct business only if a national (individual or firm) of the host country is designated as its legal representative. Since this designation may create difficulties in control and result in unnecessary expense, the usual practice for multinational corporations is to create a foreign subsidiary in the host country. The form of subsidiary most closely resembling a U.S. corporation is known as a *société anonyme (S.A.)* or, in German-speaking countries, an *Aktiengesellschaft (AG)*. Other forms of subsidiaries may also exist that have characteristics of limited liability of the owners and fewer formalities in their creation and operation.

Creation of a foreign subsidiary may pose considerable risk to the domestic parent firm by subjecting it to foreign laws and the jurisdiction of foreign courts. An industrial accident in Bhopal, India, where hundreds of people were killed and thousands injured as a result of toxic gas leaks from a chemical plant, resulted in lawsuits against both the Indian subsidiary corporation and Union Carbide, the parent firm in the United States. Union Carbide agreed to pay more than $450 million to settle outstanding claims and compensate the victims of the disaster.

In many instances, however, the only legal or political means a firm has to invest directly in a foreign country is to engage in a **joint venture** with an entity from that host country. A host country's participant may be a private enterprise or, especially in developing countries, a government agency or government-owned corporation. Many foreign countries favor joint ventures because they allow local individuals and firms to participate in the benefits of economic growth and decrease the risk of foreign domination of local industry. Many of the developing countries require that the local partner have majority equity control of the venture and also insist on joint ventures with government participation.

>> *sidebar* 12.10

Chiquita Brands International: Payments to Death Squads for "Protection"

Chiquita Brands International pled guilty to doing business with the United Self-Defense Forces of Colombia (UAC), a right-wing paramilitary group in Colombia. Prosecutors said the banana company made $1.7 million in "protection payments" to this death squad, which is reportedly responsible for some of Colombia's worst massacres. In 2001, the U.S. State Department declared that UAC was an "international terrorist group," making it a violation of U.S. law to conduct business with the group. To settle the charges, Chiquita paid $25 million, arguing that it had no choice but to pay protection money to prevent the UAC from turning death squads loose on its banana workers.

Families of over 350 people thought to have been killed by UAC are suing Chiquita in U.S. federal court seeking $7.86 billion in civil damages. The families claim that Chiquita aided and abetted terrorism, war crimes, and crimes against humanity because of its financial support of UAC. In May 2011, the seven pending lawsuits were consolidated into one action involving allegations of over 4,000 killings of Colombian nationals. In June 2011, the federal judge in Florida overseeing the litigation denied Chiquita's motion to dismiss some of the claims brought under the ATCA and Torture Victim Protection Act. The judge rejected Chiquita's argument that the case should be dismissed because it could have foreign policy implications.

Colombia's attorney general has also threatened to seek extradition of eight Chiquita executives to face criminal prosecution.

LO 12-5 ## >> Resolving International Disputes

International law can be complicated, and a single business transaction may involve several companies in different nations. For example, a contract dispute between a Chinese manufacturer, an American wholesaler, and a Canadian retailer could potentially involve the law of all three countries. Which law controls? What jurisdiction has the power to resolve the dispute? The answers to these questions could affect the outcome of the case. As such, most international contracts contain choice of law and forum provisions to eliminate this uncertainty. This section addresses the limitations on suing foreign governments in the United States, issues raised when suing foreign firms in the United States, and international arbitration options.

10. ALIEN TORT CLAIMS ACT

The **Alien Tort Claims Act (ATCA),** enacted in 1789, grants jurisdiction to U.S. federal district courts over "any civil action by an alien for a tort only, committed in violation of the law of nations or a treaty of the United States." For nearly 200 years, the law lapsed into obscurity. In the last 20 years, however, it has been revived in a number of human rights contexts, including claims brought against U.S. global companies. An essential aspect of a successful claim under the ATCA is to demonstrate that the acts committed violate the law of nations. This prompts many unanswered legal questions in the international labor context. What constitutes the "law of nations"? In general, the law of nations is embodied in international agreements, treaties, and conventions. ATCA actions have been alleged against many U.S. companies, including Bridgestone, Chevron, Del Monte, Drummond Company, Dyncorp, ExxonMobil, Gap, Inc., Texaco, Inc., Unocal Corp., Wal-Mart, and, most recently, Yahoo. Claims typically involve allegations of forced labor, but may also include other human rights abuses such as murder, rape, torture, unlawful detention, and kidnapping. It is not unusual for these cases to also allege that acts were committed by paramilitaries hired by the company.

> The ATCA is viewed by some as a way to hold U.S. companies responsible for their participation in human rights abuses abroad.

 case 12.2 >>

KIOBEL v. ROYAL DUTCH PETROLEUM, CO.
621 F.3d 111 (2nd Cir. 2010)

Nigerian residents filed a class action under the Alien Tort Claims Act (ATCA) or Alien Tort Stature (ATS) alleging that Dutch, British and Nigerian corporations engaged in oil exploration and production aided and abetted the Nigerian government in committing human rights abuses in violation of the law of nations. In 2004, the U.S. Supreme Court endeavored to clarify the scope of the ATCA. In his opinion, Justice Souter stated "judicial power should be exercised on the understanding that the door is still ajar subject to vigilant door-keeping, and thus open to a narrow class of international norms today." (542 U.S. 692, 729). Relying on the Sosa decision, defendants moved to dismiss this action. In September 2006, the District Court dismissed plaintiffs' claims for aiding and abetting property destruction; forced exile; extrajudicial killing; and violations of the rights to life, liberty, security and association. The District Court reasoned that customary international law did not define those violations with the particularity required by Sosa. The District Court denied defendants' motion to dismiss with respect to the remaining claims of aiding and abetting arbitrary arrest and detention' crime against humanity; and torture or cruel, inhuman, and degrading treatment. The District Court certified its entire order for interlocutory appeal.

JOSÉ A. CABRANES, CIRCUIT JUDGE: Once again we consider a case brought under the Alien Tort Statute ("ATS"), 28 U.S.C. §1350,FN1 a jurisdictional provision unlike any other in American law and of a kind apparently unknown to any other legal system in the world. Passed by the first Congress in 1789, the ATS lay largely dormant for over 170 years. Judge Friendly called it a "legal Lohengrin"—"no one seems to know whence it came." Then, in 1980, the statute was given new life, when our Court first recognized in *Filartiga v. Pena-Irala* that the ATS provides jurisdiction over (1) tort actions, (2) brought by aliens (only), (3) for violations of the law of nations (also called "customary international law" including, as a general matter, war crimes and crimes against humanity-crimes in which the perpetrator can be called "*hostis humani generis,* an enemy of all mankind." . . .

[continued]

Because appellate review of ATS suits has been so uncommon, there remain a number of unresolved issues lurking in our ATS jurisprudence—issues that we have simply had no occasion to address in the handful of cases we have decided in the thirty years since the revival of the ATS. This case involves one such unresolved issue: Does the jurisdiction granted by the ATS extend to civil actions brought against corporations under the law of nations? . . .

Plaintiffs are residents of Nigeria who claim that Dutch, British, and Nigerian corporations engaged in oil exploration and production aided and abetted the Nigerian government in committing violations of the law of nations. They seek damages under the ATS, and thus their suit may proceed only if the ATS provides jurisdiction over tort actions brought against corporations under customary international law. A legal culture long accustomed to imposing liability on corporations may, at first blush, assume that corporations must be subject to tort liability under the ATS, just as corporations are generally liable in tort under our domestic law (what international law calls "municipal law"). But the substantive law that determines our jurisdiction under the ATS is neither the domestic law of the United States nor the domestic law of any other country. By conferring subject matter jurisdiction over a limited number of offenses defined by *customary international law,* the ATS requires federal courts to look beyond rules of domestic law—however well-established they may be—to examine the specific and universally accepted rules that the nations of the world treat as binding *in their dealings with one another.* . . .

Accordingly, absent a relevant treaty of the United States-and none is relied on here-we must ask whether a plaintiff bringing an ATS suit against a corporation has alleged a violation of customary international law. The singular achievement of international law since the Second World War has come in the area of human rights, where the subjects of customary international law—*i.e.,* those with international rights, duties, and liabilities-now include not merely *states,* but also *individuals.* This principle was most famously applied by the International Military Tribunal at Nuremberg. . . .

From the beginning, however, the principle of individual liability for violations of international law has been limited to natural persons—not "juridical" persons such as corporations-because the moral responsibility for a crime so heinous and unbounded as to rise to the level of an "international crime" has rested solely with the individual men and women who have perpetrated it. . . .

In short, because customary international law imposes individual liability for a limited number of international crimes—including war crimes, crimes against humanity (such as genocide), and torture—we have held that the ATS provides jurisdiction over claims in tort against individuals who are alleged to have committed such crimes. As we explain in detail below, however, customary international law has steadfastly rejected the notion of corporate liability for international crimes, and no international tribunal has ever held a corporation liable for a violation of the law of nations. We must conclude, therefore, that insofar as plaintiffs bring claims under the ATS against corporations, plaintiffs fail to allege violations of the law of nations, and plaintiffs' claims fall outside the limited jurisdiction provided by the ATS. We emphasize that the question before us is not whether corporations are "immune" from suit under the ATS: That formulation improperly assumes that there is a norm imposing liability in the first place. Rather, the question before us, as the Supreme Court has explained, "is whether international law extends the scope of liability for a violation of a given norm to the perpetrator being sued, if the defendant is a private actor such as a corporation or individual." Looking to international law, we find a jurisprudence, first set forth in Nuremberg and repeated by every international tribunal of which we are aware, that offenses against the law of nations (*i.e.,* customary international law) for violations of human rights can be charged against States and against individual men and women but not against juridical persons such as corporations. As a result, although customary international law has sometimes extended the scope of liability for a violation of a given norm to individuals, it has *never* extended the scope of liability to a corporation. . . .

Accordingly, insofar as plaintiffs in this action seek to hold only corporations liable for their conduct in Nigeria (as opposed to individuals within those corporations), and only under the ATS, their claims must be dismissed for lack of subject matter jurisdiction. . . .

Conclusion

The ATS provides federal district courts jurisdiction over a tort, brought by an alien only, alleging a "violation of the law of nations or a treaty of the United States." 28 U.S.C. §1350. When an ATS suit is brought under the "law of nations," also known as "customary international law," jurisdiction is limited to those cases alleging a violation of an international norm that is "specific, universal, and obligatory." *Sosa v. Alvarez-Machain,* 542 U.S. 692, 732, 124 S.Ct. 2739, 159 L.Ed.2d 718 (2004). . . .

To summarize, we hold as follows:

(1) Since *Filartiga,* which in 1980 marked the advent of the modern era of litigation for violations of human rights under the Alien Tort

[continued]

Statute, all of our precedents—and the Supreme Court's decision in *Sosa,* 542 U.S. at 732 n. 20 require us to look to international law to determine whether a particular class of defendant, such as corporations, can be liable under the Alien Tort Statute for alleged violations of the law of nations.

(2) The concept of corporate liability for violations of customary international law has not achieved universal recognition or acceptance as a norm in the relations of States with each other. . . . Inasmuch as plaintiffs assert claims against corporations only, their complaint must be dismissed for lack of subject matter jurisdiction.

>> CASE QUESTIONS

1. What kinds of claims can be brought under the Alien Tort Statute?
2. Why does the Second Circuit reject imposing liability on corporations?
3. What are the ramifications of the decision?

11. SUING FOREIGN GOVERNMENTS IN THE UNITED STATES

The doctrine of **sovereign immunity** provides that a foreign sovereign is immune from suit in the United States. Under the doctrine of sovereign immunity, the foreign sovereign claims to be immune from suit entirely based on its status as a state.

Until approximately 1952, this notion was absolute. From 1952 until 1976, U.S. courts adhered to a *restrictive theory* under which immunity existed with regard to sovereign or public acts but not with regard to private or commercial acts. In 1976, Congress enacted the **Foreign Sovereign Immunities Act (FSIA),** which codifies this restrictive theory and rejects immunity for *commercial acts* carried on in the United States or having direct effects in this country.

The Supreme Court held that the doctrine should not be extended to foreign governments acting in a commercial capacity and "should not be extended to include the repudiation of a purely commercial obligation owed by a foreign sovereign or by one of its commercial instrumentalities." This interpretation recognizes that governments also may act in a private or commercial capacity and, when doing so, will be subjected to the same rules of law as are applicable to private individuals. A nationalization of assets, however, probably will be considered an act in the "public interest" and immune from suit under the FSIA.

Sovereignty is defined as the supreme, absolute, and uncontrollable power by which any state is governed.

12. SUING FOREIGN FIRMS IN THE UNITED STATES

As foreign products and technology are imported into the United States, disputes may arise over either the terms of contract or the performance of the goods. To sue a foreign firm in the United States, the Supreme Court held that the plaintiff must establish "minimum contacts" between the foreign defendant and the forum court. The plaintiff must demonstrate that exercise of

Although punitive damages may be awarded in U.S. courts against a foreign company doing business in the United States, it may be difficult or impossible to enforce the award in the company's home country. Outside of the United States, very few countries allow punitive damage awards, which are viewed as a "peculiarity of American law."

personal jurisdiction over the defendant "does not offend traditional notions of fair play and substantial justice."

Once the plaintiff decides to sue in the United States, he or she also must comply with the terms of the Hague Service Convention when serving the foreign defendant notice of the lawsuit. The Hague Service Convention is a treaty that was formulated "to provide a simpler way to serve process abroad, to assure that defendants sued in foreign jurisdictions would receive actual and timely notice of suit, and to facilitate proof of service abroad." Many countries, including the United States, follow this convention. The primary requirement of the agreement is to require each nation to establish a central authority to process requests for service of documents from other countries. After the central authority receives the request in proper form, it must serve the documents by a method prescribed by the internal law of the receiving state or by a method designated by the requester and compatible with the law.

>> *sidebar* 12.11

The Reach of U.S. Law: *Spector v. Norwegian Cruise Line, Ltd.* 545 U.S. 119 (2005)

Issue: Whether foreign-flagged cruise ships serving U.S. ports must comply with the public accommodations provisions in Title III of the Americans with Disabilities Act.

Key Facts: Disabled plaintiffs and their companions alleged that physical barriers on the Norwegian Cruise Line Ltd. (NCL) ships denied them access to various equipment, programs, and facilities on the ships. They sought injunctive relief

requiring NCL to remove certain barriers that obstructed their access to the ships' facilities.

Procedural History: The district court found that foreign-flagged cruise ships *are* subject to the ADA. The Fifth Circuit Court of Appeals *reversed.*

Outcome: The U.S. Supreme Court reversed, holding that Title III of the ADA is applicable to foreign-flag cruise ships in U.S. waters.

In Case 12.3, the court considers a lawsuit against a foreign firm over whether U.S. employment laws can be imposed on its domestic employees. Also, see Sidebar 12.11 for another example of the reach of U.S. law.

---

 case 12.3 >>

MORELLI v. CEDEL
141 F. 3d 39 (2d Cir. 1998)

CUDAHY, J.: This appeal requires us to decide whether the domestic employees of certain foreign corporations are protected under the Age Discrimination and Employment Act of 1967 (the ADEA), and, if so, whether a foreign corporation's foreign employees are counted for the purpose of determining whether the corporation has enough employees to be subject to the ADEA. We answer both questions in the affirmative.

[continued]

After the defendant fired the plaintiff, the plaintiff sued the defendant. The plaintiff's amended complaint asserted that the defendant violated the ADEA, the Employment Retirement Security Act (ERISA), and New York State's Human Rights Law. The district court dismissed the complaint on the grounds that the defendant was not subject to the ADEA.

As alleged in the complaint, the facts relevant to this appeal are as follows. The plaintiff, Ida Morelli, was born on April 11, 1939. The defendant is a Luxembourg bank. On or about June 29, 1984, the defendant hired the plaintiff to work in its New York office. On or about February 26, 1993, the plaintiff became an assistant to Dennis Sabourin, a manager in the defendant's New York office. Mr. Sabourin summoned the then 54-year-old plaintiff to his office on January 18, 1994, handed her a separation agreement, and insisted that she sign it.

Under the terms of the separation agreement, the plaintiff would resign, effective April 30, 1994. She would continue to receive her salary and benefits until the effective date of her resignation, but she would be relieved of her duties as an employee, effective immediately. Both the defendant and the employee would renounce all claims arising out of "their past working relationship." Mr. Sabourin told the plaintiff that she would receive the three months' severance pay, medical coverage for three months, and her pension only on the condition that she sign the agreement on the spot. The plaintiff had never seen the separation agreement before and had no warning that she was going to be asked to resign. But in the face of Mr. Sabourin's ultimatum, she did sign the agreement immediately and returned it to him. The defendant, however, never provided her with a pension distribution.

The ADEA was enacted to prevent arbitrary discrimination by employers on the basis of age. In order to determine whether the defendant is subject to the ADEA, we must first determine whether the ADEA generally protects the employees of a branch of a foreign employer located in the United States.

[T]he ADEA provides that the prohibitions of [the ADEA] shall not apply where the employer is a foreign person not controlled by an American employer. At a minimum, this provision means that the ADEA does not apply to the foreign operations of foreign employers—unless there is an American employer behind the scenes. An absolutely literal reading of [the statute] might suggest that the ADEA also does not apply to the domestic operations of foreign employers. But the plain language is not necessarily decisive if it is inconsistent with Congress' clearly expressed legislative purpose. Congress' purpose was not to exempt the domestic workplaces of foreign employers from the ADEA's prohibition of age discrimination. . . .

We have previously concluded that even when a foreign employer operating in the United States can invoke a Friendship, Commerce and Navigation treaty to justify employing its own nationals, this does not give the employer license to violate American laws prohibiting discrimination in employment. Although the Supreme Court vacated our judgment in that case on the grounds that the defendant could not invoke the treaty, the Court observed that "the highest level of protection afforded by commercial treaties" to foreign corporations operating in the United States is generally no more than "equal treatment with domestic corporations." Here equal treatment would require that antidiscrimination rules apply to foreign enterprises' U.S. branches, since defending personnel decisions is a fact of business life in contemporary America and is a burden that the domestic competitors of foreign enterprise have been required to shoulder. Also, U.S. subsidiaries of foreign corporations are generally subject to U.S. antidiscrimination laws, and, absent treaty protection—not an issue in this case—a U.S. branch of a foreign corporation is not entitled to an immunity not enjoyed by such subsidiaries.

Cedel will still not be subject to the ADEA by virtue of its U.S. operations unless Cedel is an "employer" under the ADEA. A business must have at least twenty "employees" to be an "employer." Cedel maintains that, in the case of foreign employers, only domestic employees should be counted. The district court agreed, and, since Cedel had fewer than 20 employees in its U.S. branch, the court granted Cedel's motion to dismiss for lack of subject matter jurisdiction without considering the number of Cedel's overseas employees.

The district court reasoned that the overseas employees of foreign employers should not be counted because they are not protected by the ADEA. But there is no requirement that an employee be protected by the ADEA to be counted; an enumeration, for the purpose of ADEA coverage of an employer, includes employees under age 40, who are also unprotected. The nose count of employees relates to the scale of the employer rather than to the extent of protection.

Cedel contends that because it has fewer than 20 employees in the United States, it is the equivalent of a small U.S. employer. This is implausible with respect to compliance and litigation costs; their impact on Cedel is better gauged by its worldwide employment. Cedel would not appear to be any more a boutique operation in the United States than would a business with ten employees each in offices in, say, Alaska and Florida, which would be subject to the ADEA. Further, a U.S. corporation with many foreign employees but

[continued]

fewer than 20 domestic ones would certainly be subject to the ADEA.

Accordingly, in determining whether Cedel satisfies the ADEA's 20-employee threshold, employees cannot be ignored merely because they work overseas.

We therefore vacate the judgment on the plaintiff's ADEA count.

So ordered.

>> CASE QUESTIONS

1. What is the purpose behind the ADEA?
2. How did the court find that the ADEA covered a U.S. branch of a foreign employer?
3. Why did the court count foreign employees of the firm in determining whether the employer was subject to the ADEA?

>> *sidebar* 12.12

Chevron and Texaco in Ecuador: $18 Billion Judgment

In February 2011, an Ecuadorian court in Lago Agrio rendered an $18 billion judgment against Chevron for alleged environmental damage. Chevron's subsidiary, Texaco Petroleum Co. (TexPet), conducted oil operations in Chevron. Chevron claims that TexPet fully remediated its share of environmental impacts arising from oil production and that any remaining environmental issues are the responsibility of Ecuador's state-owned oil company, Petroecuador.

Chevron is appealing the Ecuadorian verdict on the grounds that it "lacks scientific merit and that it ignores overwhelming evidence of fraud and corruption." Chevron also claims that it was not afforded due process in Ecuador.

>> SUBSEQUENT EVENTS

- Southern District of New York Judge Lewis Kaplan issued a preliminary injunction "enjoining and restraining" the plaintiffs from enforcing the ruling anywhere in the world.
- An International Tribunal from the Permanent Court of Arbitration in The Hague ordered Ecuador to suspend the enforcement or recognition of the judgment.
- Chevron filed a Racketeer Influenced and Corrupt Organizations Act against Steven Donziger (the plaintiffs' lead U.S. lawyer), Ecuadorian lawyer Pablo Fajardo, environmental activist Luis Yanza, and three organizations, including Amazon Watch.

The documentary *Crude* presents the controversial story of the environmental damage and the ensuing complicated litigation.

13. INTERNATIONAL ARBITRATION

International businesses now are focusing on the need for new methods of resolving international commercial disputes and, as a result, are frequently resorting to the use of arbitration. The advantages of arbitration in domestic transactions, previously discussed in Chapter 5, are more pronounced in international transactions where differences in languages and legal systems make litigation costs still more costly.

The United Nations Convention on the Recognition and Enforcement of Foreign Arbitral Awards of 1958 (New York Convention), adopted in more than 50 countries, encourages the use of arbitration in commercial agreements made by companies in the signatory countries. Under the New York Convention it is easier to compel arbitration, where previously agreed upon by the parties, and to enforce the arbitrator's award once a decision is reached.

Once the parties to an international transaction agree to arbitrate disputes between them, the U.S. courts are reluctant to disturb that agreement. In the case of *Mitsubishi Motors v. Soler Chrysler-Plymouth* (1985) the Supreme Court upheld an international agreement even where it required the parties to arbitrate all disputes, including federal antitrust claims. The Court decided that the international character of the undertaking required enforcement of the arbitration clause even as to the antitrust claims normally heard in a U.S. court.

There are many advantages to arbitrating international disputes. The arbitration process likely will be more streamlined and easier for the parties to understand than litigating the dispute in a foreign court. Moreover, the parties can avoid the unwanted publicity that often results in open court proceedings. Finally, the parties can agree, before the dispute even arises, on a neutral and objective third party to act as the arbitrator. Several organizations, such as the International Chamber of Commerce in Paris and the Court of International Arbitration in London, provide arbitration services for international disputes.

China International Economic and Trade Arbitration Commission

The China International Economic and Trade Arbitration Commission (CIETAC) is a permanent arbitration institution established to resolve economic and trade disputes arising in China. The parties must agree in writing to submit their dispute for arbitration. Here is a sample arbitration clause recommended by CIETAC:

> Any dispute arising from or in connection with this Contract shall be submitted to CIETAC for arbitration, which shall be conducted in accordance with the Commission's arbitration rules in effect at the time of applying for arbitration. The arbitral always is final and binding upon both parties.

Frequently, the parties will also stipulate the location of the arbitration; the language of the proceeding; the number of arbitrators; the nationality of the arbitrators; the method of selecting the arbitrators; and the law governing the contract. For more information, including a current list of arbitrators and their areas of expertise, see www.cietac.org.

The World Intellectual Property Organization: Arbitration and Mediation Center

The World Intellectual Property Organization (WIPO) Arbitration and Mediation Center hears cases involving domain name disputes and cybersquatting. The Uniform Domain Name Dispute Resolution Policy (UDRP) went into effect in 1999. Since that time, over 8,350 disputes involving 127 countries and some 16,000 domain names have been handled by the WIPO.

Many UDRP cases involve high-value, well-known brands. In fact, cases involving most of the 100 largest international brands by value have been heard by the WIPO. Well-known individuals, including Madonna, Julia Roberts, Eminem, Pamela Anderson, J K Rowling, Morgan Freeman, and Lance Armstrong have used the WIPO's services. For more information about WIPO cases, see www.wipo.int.

>> Key Terms

Agreement on Trade-Related Aspects of Intellectual Property Rights (TRIPS) 370

Alien Tort Claims Act (ATCA) 379

Bill of lading 375

Central America-Dominican Republic Free Trade Agreement (CAFTA-DR) 373

Convention on the International Sale of Goods (CISG) 372

European Union (EU) 371

Export controls 363

Expropriation 362

Foreign Corrupt Practices Act (FCPA) 359

Foreign Sovereign Immunities Act (FSIA) 381

Foreign subsidiary 377

Franchise 377

General Agreement on Tariffs and Trade (GATT) 369

International Court of Justice (ICJ) 367

International Monetary Fund (IMF) 369

Irrevocable letter of credit 375

Joint venture 378

License 377

Nationalization 363

North American Free Trade Agreement (NAFTA) 373

Private international law 366

Public international law 366

Sovereign immunity 381

United Nations 368

World Bank 369

World Trade Organization (WTO) 369

>> Review Questions and Problems

Risks Involved in International Trade

1. *Pressures for Bribes*

   XYZ Company, a U.S. firm, is seeking to obtain business in Indonesia. XYZ learns that one of its major competitors, a German firm, is offering a key Indonesian governmental official a trip around the world for choosing their firm in the transaction. Can XYZ report this bribe to the Department of Justice and have the German firm prosecuted under the Foreign Corrupt Practices Act?

2. *Expropriation and Nationalization*

   Explain the "modern traditional theory" of compensation related to the taking of private property by a foreign government.

3. *Export Controls*

   (a) Why is the future of export controls in doubt?

   (b) What are some of the dangers associated with having an inadequate export control regime as nations combat terrorism?

International Law and Organizations

4. *Sources of International Law*

   (a) What are the essential differences between the International Court of Justice and the U.S. Supreme Court?

   (b) How does the ICJ determine international law?

5. *International Organizations*

   (a) What are the three major principles of the World Trade Organization?

   (b) Has adherence to those principles improved international trade?

   (c) Describe the organization of the European Union.

   (d) How is it similar to the structure of the government of the United States?

6. *Major Agreements Affecting Trade*

   (a) How does the CISG facilitate international sales of goods?

   (b) How do free trade agreements, such as NAFTA and CAFTA-DR, benefit U.S. businesses?

Methods of Transacting International Business

7. *Foreign Sales*

   BMW, a German buyer, opens an irrevocable letter of credit in favor of Goodyear, an American seller, for the purchase of tires on BMW automobiles. BMW confirms the letter of credit with Goodyear's bank in New York, JPMorgan Chase. How will the seller obtain payment?

8. *Licenses or Franchises*
   (a) How should a licensor protect its investment in a foreign country?
   (b) Is licensing a less risky approach for the seller than direct foreign investment?
9. *Direct Foreign Investment*
   What are the advantages and disadvantages of a joint venture with a foreign firm?

Resolving International Disputes

10. *Alien Tort Claims Act*
    Several citizens of Colombia filed an action in the U.S. against Super Bananas, a U.S. company that owns the banana plantation where the individuals worked. In their complaint, the plaintiffs allege that they were threatened, beaten and tortured by Super Banana's security guards when they tried to unionize. Do they have an actionable claim under the ATCA?

11. *Suing Foreign Governments in the United States*
    Belgium arrests an American citizen, while he is visiting Brussels, on suspicion that he is an international drug smuggler. After a thorough investigation, Belgium realizes that it has arrested the wrong person. Can the American citizen successfully sue Belgium in the United States for false arrest?

12. *Suing Foreign Firms in the United States*
    What is the primary requirement of the Hague Service Convention and how does it help a plaintiff when filing a lawsuit?

13. *International Arbitration*
    Why are arbitration clauses in international agreements favored by the courts and likely to be enforced when conflicts arise between the contracting parties?

business >> *discussions*

1. XYZ Company is a U.S. firm that makes communication software used in a variety of consumer goods manufactured and sold in the United States. XYZ recently learned that one of the manufacturing firms it supplies, ABC Company, is exporting finished goods to a country where U.S. goods and component parts are prohibited because of numerous conflicts with the U.S. government.

Does XYZ have any moral or legal responsibility in this case?
How should XYZ protect itself under these circumstances?
Should American business practices be impacted by conflicts between governments?

2. Hello-Hello is a U.S. telecommunications company with global operations. Sophia is an assistant vice president of Hello-Hello. She is dispatched to China to handle two situations. First, a shipment of 500 cases of cell phones is stalled in customs. She is assigned the task of getting the goods out of customs and into retail stores. Sophia learns through the grapevine that customs officials expect $5 (U.S. per case) to help "speed things along." Second, she is instructed by her boss to do "whatever is necessary" to secure cell tower permits from local officials in two outlying areas. A local agent suggests that she give him $500,000 in cash so they can get to know the officials better. When Sophia asks him what the money will be used for, he tells her that he wants to take them out to dinner, maybe on a weekend outing in the city, and that he generally needs "flexibility."

Should Sophia call the home office to ask for advice?
If her boss says to pay the money, should she do it?
What potential legal problems are presented by the payments?

>> *appendix IV*

>> Selected Sections of Article 2 of Uniform Commercial Code

§2-104. Definitions: "Merchant"; "Between Merchants"; "Financing Agency."

(1) **"Merchant"** means a person who deals in goods of the kind or otherwise by his occupation holds himself out as having knowledge or skill peculiar to the practices or goods involved in the transaction or to whom such knowledge or skill may be attributed by his employment of an agent or broker or other intermediary who by his occupation holds himself out as having such knowledge or skill.

(3) **"Between Merchants"** means in any transaction with respect to which both parties are chargeable with the knowledge or skill of merchants.

§2-201. Formal Requirements; Statute of Frauds.

(1) Except as otherwise provided in this section a contract for the sale of goods for the price of $500 or more is not enforceable by way of action or defense unless there is some writing sufficient to indicate that a contract for sale has been made between the parties and signed by the party against whom enforcement is sought or by his authorized agent or broker. A writing is not insufficient because it omits or incorrectly states a term agreed upon but the contract is not enforceable under this paragraph beyond the quantity of goods shown in such writing.

(2) Between merchants if within a reasonable time a writing in confirmation of the contract and sufficient against the sender is received and the party receiving it has reason to know its contents, it satisfies the requirements of subsection (1) against such party unless written notice of objection to its contents is given within 10 days after it is received.

(3) A contract which does not satisfy the requirements of subsection (1) but which is valid in other respects is enforceable

- (a) if the goods are to be specially manufactured for the buyer and are not suitable for sale

to others in the ordinary course of the seller's business and the seller, before notice of repudiation is received and under circumstances which reasonably indicate that the goods are for the buyer, has made either a substantial beginning of their manufacture or commitments for their procurement; or

- (b) if the party against whom enforcement is sought admits in his pleading, testimony or otherwise in court that a contract for sale was made, but the contract is not enforceable under this provision beyond the quantity of goods admitted; or
- (c) with respect to goods for which payment has been made and accepted or which have been received and accepted (Sec. 2-606).

§2-205. Firm Offers.

An offer by a merchant to buy or sell goods in a signed writing which by its terms gives assurance that it will be held open is not revocable, for lack of consideration, during the time stated or if no time is stated for a reasonable time, but in no event may such period of irrevocability exceed three months; but any such term of assurance on a form supplied by the offeree must be separately signed by the offeror.

§2-206. Offer and Acceptance in Formation of Contract.

(1) Unless otherwise unambiguously indicated by the language or circumstances

- (a) an offer to make a contract shall be construed as inviting acceptance in any manner and by any medium reasonable in the circumstances;
- (b) an order or other offer to buy goods for prompt or current shipment shall be construed as inviting acceptance either by a prompt promise to ship or by the prompt or current shipment of conforming or non-conforming goods, but such a shipment of non-conforming goods does not constitute an acceptance if the seller seasonably notifies the buyer that the shipment is offered only as an accommodation to the buyer.

(2) Where the beginning of a requested performance is a reasonable mode of acceptance an offeror who is not notified of acceptance within a reasonable time may treat the offer as having lapsed before acceptance.

§2-207. Additional Terms in Acceptance or Confirmation.

(1) A definite and seasonable expression of acceptance or a written confirmation which is sent within a reasonable time operates as an acceptance even though it states terms additional to or different from those offered or agreed upon, unless acceptance is expressly made conditional on assent to the additional or different terms.

(2) The additional terms are to be construed as proposals for addition to the contract. Between merchants such terms become part of the contract unless:

- (a) the offer expressly limits acceptance to the terms of the offer;
- (b) they materially alter it; or
- (c) notification of objection to them has already been given or is given within a reasonable time after notice of them is received.

(3) Conduct by both parties which recognizes the existence of a contract is sufficient to establish a contract for sale although the writings of the parties do not otherwise establish a contract. In such case the terms of the particular contract consist of those terms on which the writings of the parties agree, together with any supplementary terms incorporated under any other provisions of this Act.

§2-209. Modification, Rescission and Waiver.

(1) An agreement modifying a contract within this Article needs no consideration to be binding.

(2) A signed agreement which excludes modification or rescission except by a signed writing cannot be otherwise modified or rescinded, but except as between merchants such a requirement on a form supplied by the merchant must be separately signed by the other party.

(3) The requirements of the statute of frauds section of this Article (Section 2-201) must be satisfied if the contract as modified is within its provisions.

(4) Although an attempt at modification or rescission does not satisfy the requirements of subsection (2) or (3) it can operate as a waiver.

(5) A party who has made a waiver affecting an executory portion of the contract may retract the waiver by reasonable notification received by the other party that strict performance will be required of any term waived, unless the retraction would be unjust in view of a material change of position in reliance on the waiver.

§2-210. Delegation of Performance; Assignment of Rights.

(1) A party may perform his duty through a delegate unless otherwise agreed or unless the other party has a substantial interest in having his original promisor perform or control the acts required by the contract. No delegation of performance relieves the party delegating of any duty to perform or any liability for breach.

(2) Unless otherwise agreed all rights of either seller or buyer can be assigned except where the assignment would materially change the duty of the other party, or increase materially the burden or risk imposed on him by his contract, or impair materially his chance of obtaining return performance. A right to damages for breach of the whole contract or a right arising out of the assignor's due performance of his entire obligation can be assigned despite agreement otherwise.

(3) Unless the circumstances indicate the contrary a prohibition of assignment of "the contract" is to be construed as barring only the delegation to the assignee of the assignor's performance.

(4) An assignment of "the contract" or of "all my rights under the contract" or an assignment in similar general terms is an assignment of rights and unless the language or the circumstances (as in an assignment for security) indicate the contrary, it is a delegation of performance of the duties of the assignor and its acceptance by the assignee constitutes a promise by him to perform those duties.

This promise is enforceable by either the assignor or the other party to the original contract.

(5) The other party may treat any assignment which delegates performance as creating reasonable grounds for insecurity and may without prejudice to his rights against the assignor demand assurances from the assignee (Section 2-609).

§2-301. General Obligations of Parties. The obligation of the seller is to transfer and deliver and that of the buyer is to accept and pay in accordance with the contract.

§2-302. Unconscionable contract or Clause.

(1) If the court as a matter of law finds the contract or any clause of the contract to have been unconscionable at the time it was made the court may refuse to enforce the contract, or it may enforce the remainder

of the contract without the unconscionable clause, or it may so limit the application of any unconscionable clause as to avoid any unconscionable result.

(2) When it is claimed or appears to the court that the contract or any clause thereof may be unconscionable the parties shall be afforded a reasonable opportunity to present evidence as to its commercial setting, purpose and effect to aid the court in making the determination.

§2-305. Open Price Term.

(1) The parties if they so intend can conclude a contract for sale even though the price is not settled. In such a case the price is a reasonable price at the time for delivery if

- (a) nothing is said as to price; or
- (b) the price is left to be agreed by the parties and they fail to agree; or
- (c) the price is to be fixed in terms of some agreed market or other standard as set or recorded by a third person or agency and it is not so set or recorded.

(2) A price to be fixed by the seller or by the buyer means a price for him to fix in good faith.

(3) When a price left to be fixed otherwise than by agreement of the parties fails to be fixed through fault of one party the other may at his option treat the contract as cancelled or himself fix a reasonable price.

(4) Where, however, the parties intend not to be bound unless the price be fixed or agreed and it is not fixed or agreed there is no contract. In such a case the buyer must return any goods already received or if unable so to do must pay their reasonable value at the time of delivery and the seller must return any portion of the price paid on account.

§2-306. Output, Requirements and Exclusive Dealings.

(1) A term which measures the quantity by the output of the seller or the requirements of the buyer means such actual output or requirements as may occur in good faith, except that no quantity unreasonably disproportionate to any stated estimate or in the absence of a stated estimate to any normal or otherwise comparable prior output or requirements may be tendered or demanded.

(2) A lawful agreement by either the seller or the buyer for exclusive dealing in the kind of goods concerned imposes unless otherwise agreed an obligation by the seller to use best efforts to supply the goods and by the buyer to use best efforts to promote their sale.

§2-307. Delivery in Single Lot or Several Lots.
Unless otherwise agreed all goods called for by a contract for sale must be tendered in a single delivery and payment is due only on such tender but where the circumstances give either party the right to make or demand delivery in lots the price if it can be apportioned may be demanded for each lot.

§2-308. Absence of Specified Place for Delivery.
Unless otherwise agreed

- (a) the place for delivery of goods is the seller's place of business or if he has none his residence; but
- (b) in a contract for sale of identified goods which to the knowledge of the parties at the time of contracting are in some other place, that place is the place for their delivery; and
- (c) documents of title may be delivered through customary banking channels.

§2-310. Open Time for Payment or Running of Credit; Authority to Ship Under Reservation.
Unless otherwise agreed

- (a) payment is due at the time and place at which the buyer is to receive the goods even though the place of shipment is the place of delivery; and
- (b) if the seller is authorized to send the goods he may ship them under reservation, and may tender the documents of title, but the buyer may inspect the goods after their arrival before payment is due unless such inspection is inconsistent with the terms of the contract (Section 2-513); and
- (c) if delivery is authorized and made by way of documents of title otherwise than by subsection (b) then payment is due at the time and place at which the buyer is to receive the documents regardless of where the goods are to be received; and
- (d) where the seller is required or authorized to ship the goods on credit the credit period runs from the time of shipment but post-dating the invoice or delaying its dispatch will correspondingly delay the starting of the credit period.

§2-503. Manner of Seller's Tender of Delivery.

(1) Tender of delivery requires that the seller put and hold conforming goods at the buyer's disposition and give the buyer any notification reasonably necessary to

enable him to take delivery. The manner, time and place for tender are determined by the agreement and this Article, and in particular

- (a) tender must be at a reasonable hour, and if it is of goods they must be kept available for the period reasonably necessary to enable the buyer to take possession; but

- (b) unless otherwise agreed the buyer must furnish facilities reasonably suited to the receipt of the goods.

(2) Where the case is within the next section respecting shipment tender requires that the seller comply with its provisions.

(3) Where the seller is required to deliver at a particular destination tender requires that he comply with subsection (1) and also in any appropriate case tender documents as described in subsections (4) and (5) of this section.

(4) Where goods are in the possession of a bailee and are to be delivered without being moved

- (a) tender requires that the seller either tender a negotiable document of title covering such goods or procure acknowledgment by the bailee of the buyer's right to possession of the goods; but

- (b) tender to the buyer of a non-negotiable document of title or of a written direction to the bailee to deliver is sufficient tender unless the buyer seasonably objects, and receipt by the bailee of notification of the buyer's rights fixes those rights as against the bailee and all third persons; but risk of loss of the goods and of any failure by the bailee to honor the non-negotiable document of title or to obey the direction remains on the seller until the buyer has had a reasonable time to present the document or direction, and a refusal by the bailee to honor the document or to obey the direction defeats the tender.

(5) Where the contract requires the seller to deliver documents

- (a) he must tender all such documents in correct form, except as provided in this Article with respect to bills of lading in a set (subsection (2) of Section 2-323); and

- (b) tender through customary banking channels is sufficient and dishonor of a draft accompanying the documents constitutes non-acceptance or rejection.

§2-504. Shipment by Seller. Where

the seller is required or authorized to send the goods to the buyer and the contract does not require him to deliver them at a particular destination, then unless otherwise agreed he must

- (a) put the goods in the possession of such a carrier and make such a contract for their transportation as may be reasonable having regard to the nature of the goods and other circumstances of the case; and

- (b) obtain and promptly deliver or tender in due form any document necessary to enable the buyer to obtain possession of the goods or otherwise required by the agreement or by usage of trade; and

- (c) promptly notify the buyer of the shipment.

Failure to notify the buyer under paragraph (c) or to make a proper contract under paragraph (a) is a ground for rejection only if material delay or loss ensues.

§2-507. Effect of Seller's Tender; Delivery on Condition.

(1) Tender of delivery is a condition to the buyer's duty to accept the goods and, unless otherwise agreed, to his duty to pay for them. Tender entitles the seller to acceptance of the goods and to payment according to the contract.

(2) Where payment is due and demanded on the delivery to the buyer of goods or documents of title, his right as against the seller to retain or dispose of them is conditional upon his making the payment due.

§2-509. Risk of Loss in the Absence of Breach.

(1) Where the contract requires or authorizes the seller to ship the goods by carrier

- (a) if it does not require him to deliver them at a particular destination, the risk of loss passes to the buyer when the goods are duly delivered to the carrier even though the shipment is under reservation (Section 2-505); but

- (b) if it does require him to deliver them at a particular destination and the goods are there duly tendered while in the possession of the carrier, the risk of loss passes to the buyer when the goods are there duly so tendered as to enable the buyer to take delivery.

(2) Where the goods are held by a bailee to be delivered without being moved, the risk of loss passes to the buyer

- (a) on his receipt of a negotiable document of title covering the goods; or

- (b) on acknowledgment by the bailee of the buyer's right to possession of the goods; or

- (c) after his receipt of a non-negotiable document of title or other written direction to deliver, as provided in subsection (4)(b) of Section 2-503.

(3) In any case not within subsection (1) or (2), the risk of loss passes to the buyer on his receipt of the goods if the seller is a merchant; otherwise the risk passes to the buyer on tender of delivery.

(4) The provisions of this section are subject to contrary agreement of the parties and to the provisions of this Article on sale on approval (Section 2-327) and on effect of breach on risk of loss (Section 2-510).

§2-510. Effect of Breach on Risk of Loss.

(1) Where a tender or delivery of goods so fails to conform to the contract as to give a right of rejection the risk of their loss remains on the seller until cure or acceptance.

(2) Where the buyer rightfully revokes acceptance he may to the extent of any deficiency in his effective insurance coverage treat the risk of loss as having rested on the seller from the beginning.

(3) Where the buyer as to conforming goods already identified to the contract for sale repudiates or is otherwise in breach before risk of their loss has passed to him, the seller may to the extent of any deficiency in his effective insurance coverage treat the risk of loss as resting on the buyer for a commercially reasonable time.

§2-511. Tender of Payment by Buyer; Payment by Check.

(1) Unless otherwise agreed tender of payment is a condition to the seller's duty to tender and complete any delivery.

(2) Tender of payment is sufficient when made by any means or in any manner current in the ordinary course of business unless the seller demands payment in legal tender and gives any extension of time reasonably necessary to procure it.

(3) Subject to the provisions of this Act on the effect of an instrument on an obligation (Section 3-802), payment by check is conditional and is defeated as between the parties by dishonor of the check on due presentment.

§2-615. Excuse by Failure of Presupposed Conditions. Except so far as a seller may have assumed a greater obligation and subject to the preceding section on substituted performance:

- (a) Delay in delivery or non-delivery in whole or in part by a seller who complies with paragraphs (b) and (c) is not a breach of his duty under a contract for sale if performance as agreed has been made impracticable by the occurrence of a contingency the non-occurrence of which was a basic assumption on which the contract was made or by compliance in good faith with any applicable foreign or domestic governmental regulation or order whether or not it later proves to be invalid.
- (b) Where the causes mentioned in paragraph (a) affect only a part of the seller's capacity to perform, he must allocate production and deliveries among his customers but may at his option include regular customers not then under contract as well as his own requirements for further manufacture. He may so allocate in any manner which is fair and reasonable.
- (c) The seller must notify the buyer seasonably that there will be delay or non-delivery and, when allocation is required under paragraph (b), of the estimated quota thus made available for the buyer.

§2-703. Seller's Remedies in General.

Where the buyer wrongfully rejects or revokes acceptance of goods or fails to make a payment due on or before delivery or repudiates with respect to a part or the whole, then with respect to any goods directly affected and; if the breach is of the whole contract (Section 2-612), then also with respect to the whole undelivered balance, the aggrieved seller may

- (a) withhold delivery of such goods;
- (b) stop delivery by any bailee as hereafter provided (Section 2-705);
- (c) proceed under the next section respecting goods still unidentified to the contract;
- (d) resell and recover damages as hereafter provided (Section 2-706);
- (e) recover damages for non-acceptance (Section 2-708) or in a proper case the price (Section 2-709);
- (f) cancel.

§2-711. Buyer's Remedies in General; Buyer's Security Interest in Rejected Goods.

(1) Where the seller fails to make delivery or repudiates or the buyer rightfully rejects or justifiably revokes acceptance then with respect to any goods

involved, and with respect to the whole if the breach goes to the whole contract (Section 2-612), the buyer may cancel and whether or not he has done so may in addition to recovering so much of the price as has been paid

- (a) "cover" and have damages under the next section as to all the goods affected whether or not they have been identified to the contract; or
- (b) recover damages for non-delivery as provided in this Article (Section 2-713).

(2) Where the seller fails to deliver or repudiates the buyer may also

- (a) if the goods have been identified recover them as provided in this Article (Section 2-502); or
- (b) in a proper case obtain specific performance or replevy the goods as provided in this Article (Section 2-716).

(3) On rightful rejection or justifiable revocation of acceptance a buyer has a security interest in goods in his possession or control for any payments made on their price and any expenses reasonably incurred in their inspection, receipt, transportation, care and custody and may hold such goods and resell them in like manner as an aggrieved seller (Section 2-706).

§2-725. *Statute of Limitations in Contracts for Sale.*

(1) An action for breach of any contract for sale must be commenced within four years after the cause of action has accrued. By the original agreement the parties may reduce the period of limitation to not less than one year but may not extend it.

(2) A cause of action accrues when the breach occurs, regardless of the aggrieved party's lack of knowledge of the breach. A breach of warranty occurs when tender of delivery is made, except that where a warranty explicitly extends to future performance of the goods and discovery of the breach must await the time of such performance the cause of action accrues when the breach is or should have been discovered.

(3) Where an action commenced within the time limited by subsection (1) is so terminated as to leave available a remedy by another action for the same breach such other action may be commenced after the expiration of the time limited and within six months after the termination of the first action unless the termination resulted from voluntary discontinuance or from dismissal for failure or neglect to prosecute.

(4) This section does not alter the law on tolling of the statute of limitations nor does it apply to causes of action which have accrued before this Act becomes effective.

>> *appendix V*

>> Selected Sections of the Sarbanes-Oxley Act of 2002

TITLE I—PUBLIC COMPANY ACCOUNTING OVERSIGHT BOARD

Sec. 101. Establishment; Administrative Provisions.

(a) Establishment of Board.—There is established the Public Company Accounting Oversight Board, to oversee the audit of public companies that are subject to the securities laws, and related matters, in order to protect the interests of investors and further the public interest in the preparation of informative, accurate, and independent audit reports for companies the securities of which are sold to, and held by and for, public investors. The Board shall be a body corporate, operate as a nonprofit corporation, and have succession until dissolved by an Act of Congress.

(c) Duties of the Board.—The Board shall, subject to action by the Commission under section 107, and once a determination is made by the Commission under subsection (d) of this section—

(1) register public accounting firms that prepare audit reports for issuers, in accordance with section 102;

(2) establish or adopt, or both, by rule, auditing, quality control, ethics, independence, and other standards relating to the preparation of audit reports for issuers, in accordance with section 103;

(3) conduct inspections of registered public accounting firms, in accordance with section 104 and the rules of the Board;

(4) conduct investigations and disciplinary proceedings concerning, and impose appropriate sanctions where justified upon, registered public accounting firms and associated persons of such firms, in accordance with section 105;

(5) perform such other duties or functions as the Board (or the Commission, by rule or order) determines are necessary or appropriate to promote high professional standards among, and improve the quality of audit services offered by, registered public accounting firms and associated persons thereof, or otherwise to carry out this Act, in order to protect investors, or to further the public interest;

(6) enforce compliance with this Act, the rules of the Board, professional standards, and the securities laws relating to the preparation and issuance of audit reports and the obligations and liabilities of accountants with respect thereto, by registered public accounting firms and associated persons thereof; and

(7) set the budget and manage the operations of the Board and the staff of the Board.

(h) Annual Report to the Commission.—The Board shall submit an annual report (including its audited financial statements) to the Commission, and the Commission shall transmit a copy of that report to the Committee on Banking, Housing, and Urban Affairs of the Senate, and the Committee on Financial Services of the House of Representatives, not later than 30 days after the date of receipt of that report by the Commission.

Sec. 107. Commission Oversight of The Board.

(a) General Oversight Responsibility.—The Commission shall have oversight and enforcement authority over the Board, as provided in this Act. . . .

TITLE II—AUDITOR INDEPENDENCE

Sec. 203. Audit Partner Rotation.

(j) Audit Partner Rotation.—It shall be unlawful for a registered public accounting firm to provide audit services to an issuer if the lead (or coordinating) audit partner (having primary responsibility for the audit), or the audit partner responsible for reviewing the audit, has performed audit services for that issuer in each of the 5 previous fiscal years of that issuer.

Sec. 204. Auditor Reports to Audit Committees.

(k) Reports to Audit Committees.—Each registered public accounting firm that performs for any issuer any audit required by this title shall timely report to the audit committee of the issuer—

(1) all critical accounting policies and practices to be used;

(2) all alternative treatments of financial information within generally accepted accounting principles that have been discussed with management officials of the

issuer, ramifications of the use of such alternative disclosures and treatments, and the treatment preferred by the registered public accounting firm; and

(3) other material written communications between the registered public accounting firm and the management of the issuer, such as any management letter or schedule of unadjusted differences.

TITLE III—CORPORATE RESPONSIBILITY

Sec. 302. Corporate Responsibility for Financial Reports.

(a) Regulations Required.—The Commission shall, by rule, require, for each company filing periodic reports under section 13(a) or 15(d) of the Securities Exchange Act of 1934, that the principal executive officer or officers and the principal financial officer or officers, or persons performing similar functions, certify in each annual or quarterly report filed or submitted under either such section of such Act that—

(1) the signing officer has reviewed the report;

(2) based on the officer's knowledge, the report does not contain any untrue statement of a material fact or omit to state a material fact necessary in order to make the statements made, in light of the circumstances under which such statements were made, not misleading;

(3) based on such officer's knowledge, the financial statements, and other financial information included in the report, fairly present in all material respects the financial condition and results of operations of the issuer as of, and for, the periods presented in the report;

(4) the signing officers—

(A) are responsible for establishing and maintaining internal controls;

(B) have designed such internal controls to ensure that material information relating to the issuer and its consolidated subsidiaries is made known to such officers by others within those entities, particularly during the period in which the periodic reports are being prepared;

(C) have evaluated the effectiveness of the issuer's internal controls as of a date within 90 days prior to the report; and

(D) have presented in the report their conclusions about the effectiveness of their internal controls based on their evaluation as of that date;

(5) the signing officers have disclosed to the issuer's auditors and the audit committee of the board of directors (or persons fulfilling the equivalent function)—

(A) all significant deficiencies in the design or operation of internal controls which could adversely affect the issuer's ability to record, process, summarize, and report financial data and have identified for the issuer's auditors any material weaknesses in internal controls; and

(B) any fraud, whether or not material, that involves management or other employees who have a significant role in the issuer's internal controls; and

(6) the signing officers have indicated in the report whether or not there were significant changes in internal controls or in other factors that could significantly affect internal controls subsequent to the date of their evaluation, including any corrective actions with regard to significant deficiencies and material weaknesses.

(b) Foreign Reincorporations Have No Effect.—Nothing in this section 302 shall be interpreted or applied in any way to allow any issuer to lessen the legal force of the statement required under this section 302, by an issuer having reincorporated or having engaged in any other transaction that resulted in the transfer of the corporate domicile or offices of the issuer from inside the United States to outside of the United States.

(c) Deadline.—The rules required by subsection (a) shall be effective not later than 30 days after the date of enactment of this Act.

Sec. 303. Improper Influence on Conduct of Audits.

(a) Rules To Prohibit.—It shall be unlawful, in contravention of such rules or regulations as the Commission shall prescribe as necessary and appropriate in the public interest or for the protection of investors, for any officer or director of an issuer, or any other person acting under the direction thereof, to take any action to fraudulently influence, coerce, manipulate, or mislead any independent public or certified accountant engaged in the performance of an audit of the financial statements of that issuer for the purpose of rendering such financial statements materially misleading.

Sec. 304. Forfeiture of Certain Bonuses and Profits.

(a) Additional Compensation Prior to Noncompliance With Commission Financial Reporting Requirements.—If an issuer is required to prepare an accounting restatement due to the material noncompliance of the issuer, as a result of misconduct, with

any financial reporting requirement under the securities laws, the chief executive officer and chief financial officer of the issuer shall reimburse the issuer for—

(1) any bonus or other incentive-based or equity-based compensation received by that person from the issuer during the 12-month period following the first public issuance or filing with the Commission (whichever first occurs) of the financial document embodying such financial reporting requirement; and (2) any profits realized from the sale of securities of the issuer during that 12-month period.

Sec. 306. Insider Trades During Pension Fund Blackout Periods.

(a) Prohibition of Insider Trading During Pension Fund Blackout Periods.—

(1) IN GENERAL.—Except to the extent otherwise provided by rule of the Commission pursuant to paragraph (3), it shall be unlawful for any director or executive officer of an issuer of any equity security (other than an exempted security), directly or indirectly, to purchase, sell, or otherwise acquire or transfer any equity security of the issuer (other than an exempted security) during any blackout period with respect to such equity security if such director or officer acquires such equity security in connection with his or her service or employment as a director or executive officer.

(2) REMEDY.—

(A) IN GENERAL.—Any profit realized by a director or executive officer referred to in paragraph (1) from any purchase, sale, or other acquisition or transfer in violation of this subsection shall inure to and be recoverable by the issuer, irrespective of any intention on the part of such director or executive officer in entering into the transaction.

(B) ACTIONS TO RECOVER PROFITS.—An action to recover profits in accordance with this subsection may be instituted at law or in equity in any court of competent jurisdiction by the issuer, or by the owner of any security of the issuer in the name and in behalf of the issuer if the issuer fails or refuses to bring such action within 60 days after the date of request, or fails diligently to prosecute the action thereafter, except that no such suit shall be brought more than 2 years after the date on which such profit was realized.

(3) CIVIL PENALTIES FOR FAILURE TO PROVIDE NOTICE.—(7) The Secretary may assess a civil penalty against a plan administrator of up to $100 a day from the date of the plan administrator's failure or refusal to provide notice to participants and beneficiaries in accordance with section 101(i). For purposes of this paragraph, each violation with respect to any single participant or beneficiary shall be treated as a separate violation.

TITLE IV—ENHANCED FINANCIAL DISCLOSURES

Sec. 404. Management Assessment of Internal Controls.

*(a) Rules Required.—*The Commission shall prescribe rules requiring each annual report required by section 13(a) or 15(d) of the Securities Exchange Act of 1934 to contain an internal control report, which shall—

(1) state the responsibility of management for establishing and maintaining an adequate internal control structure and procedures for financial reporting; and

(2) contain an assessment, as of the end of the most recent fiscal year of the issuer, of the effectiveness of the internal control structure and procedures of the issuer for financial reporting.

(b) Internal Control Evaluation and Reporting.—With respect to the internal control assessment required by subsection (a), each registered public accounting firm that prepares or issues the audit report for the issuer shall attest to, and report on, the assessment made by the management of the issuer. An attestation made under this subsection shall be made in accordance with standards for attestation engagements issued or adopted by the Board. Any such attestation shall not be the subject of a separate engagement.

Sec. 407. Disclosure of Audit Committee Financial Expert.

*(a) Rules Defining "Financial Expert".—*The Commission shall issue rules, as necessary or appropriate in the public interest and consistent with the protection of investors, to require each issuer, together with periodic reports required pursuant to sections 13(a) and 15(d) of the Securities Exchange Act of 1934, to disclose whether or not, and if not, the reasons therefor, the audit committee of that issuer is comprised of at least 1 member who is a financial expert, as such term is defined by the Commission.

*(b) Considerations.—*In defining the term "financial expert" for purposes of subsection (a), the Commission shall consider whether a person has, through

education and experience as a public accountant or auditor or a principal financial officer, comptroller, or principal accounting officer of an issuer, or from a position involving the performance of similar functions—

(1) an understanding of generally accepted accounting principles and financial statements;

(2) experience in—

(A) the preparation or auditing of financial statements of generally comparable issuers; and

(B) the application of such principles in connection with the accounting for estimates, accruals, and reserves;

(3) experience with internal accounting controls; and

(4) an understanding of audit committee functions.

TITLE VIII—CORPORATE AND CRIMINAL FRAUD ACCOUNTABILITY

Sec. 801. Short Title. This title may be cited as the "Corporate and Criminal Fraud Accountability Act of 2002".

Sec. 804. Statute of Limitations for Securities Fraud. . . . [A] private right of action that involves a claim of fraud, deceit, manipulation, or contrivance in contravention of a regulatory requirement concerning the securities laws . . . may be brought not later than the earlier of—

(1) 2 years after the discovery of the facts constituting the violation; or

(2) 5 years after such violation.

Sec. 806. Protection for Employees of Publicly Traded Companies Who Provide Evidence of Fraud.

(a) Whistleblower Protection for Employees of Publicly Traded Companies.—No company with a class of securities registered under section 12 of the Securities Exchange Act of 1934 or that is required to file reports under . . . the Securities Exchange Act of 1934 or any officer, employee, contractor, subcontractor, or agent of such company, may discharge, demote, suspend, threaten, harass, or in any other manner discriminate against an employee in the terms and conditions of employment because of any lawful act done by the employee—

(1) to provide information, cause information to be provided, or otherwise assist in an investigation regarding any conduct which the employee reasonably believes constitutes a violation of . . . any rule or regulation of the Securities and Exchange Commission, or any provision of Federal law relating to fraud against shareholders, when the information or assistance is provided to or the investigation is conducted by—

(A) a Federal regulatory or law enforcement agency;

(B) any Member of Congress or any committee of Congress; or

(C) a person with supervisory authority over the employee (or such other person working for the employer who has the authority to investigate, discover, or terminate misconduct); or

(2) to file, cause to be filed, testify, participate in, or otherwise assist in a proceeding filed or about to be filed (with any knowledge of the employer) relating to an alleged violation of . . . any rule or regulation of the Securities and Exchange Commission, or any provision of Federal law relating to fraud against shareholders.

Sec. 807. Criminal Penalties for Defrauding Shareholders of Publicly Traded Companies.

(a) In General—Chapter 63 of title 18, United States Code, is amended by adding at the end the following:

" §1348. Securities fraud

"Whoever knowingly executes, or attempts to execute. a scheme or artifice—

"(1) to defraud any person in connection with any security of an issuer with a class of securities registered under section 12 of the Securities Exchange Act of 1934 or that is required to file reports under section 15(d) of the Securities Exchange Act of 1934; or

"(2) to obtain, by means of false or fraudulent pretenses, representations, or promises, any money or property in connection with the purchase or sale of any security of an issuer with a class of securities registered under section 12 of the Securities Exchange Act of 1934 or that is required to file reports under section 15(d) of the Securities Exchange Act of 1934 shall be fined under this title, or imprisoned not more than 25 years, or both."

TITLE IX—WHITE-COLLAR CRIME PENALTY ENHANCEMENTS

Sec. 903. Criminal Penalties for Mail and Wire Fraud.

(a) Mail Fraud.—Section 1341 of title 18, United States Code, is amended by striking "five" and inserting "20".

(b) Wire Fraud.—Section 1343 of title 18, United States Code, is amended by striking "five" and inserting "20".

TITLE XI—CORPORATE FRAUD ACCOUNTABILITY

Sec. 1106. Increased Criminal Penalties Under Securities Exchange Act of 1934.

Section 32(a) of the Securities Exchange Act of 1934 is amended—

(1) by striking "$1,000,000, or imprisoned not more than 10 years" and inserting "$5,000,000, or imprisoned not more than 20 years"; and

(2) by striking "$2,500,000" and inserting "$25,000,000".

Sec. 1107. Retaliation Against Informants.

(a) In General.—Section 1513 of title 18, United States Code, is amended by adding at the end the following:

"(e) Whoever knowingly, with the intent to retaliate, takes any action harmful to any person, including interference with the lawful employment or livelihood of any person, for providing to a law enforcement officer any truthful information relating to the commission or possible commission of any Federal offense, shall be fined under this title or imprisoned not more than 10 years, or both."

>> appendix VI

>> Selected Sections of Securities Act of 1933

Section 6—Registration of Securities and Signing of Registration Statement

a. Any security may be registered with the Commission under the terms and conditions hereinafter providd, by filing a registration statement in triplicate, at least one of which shall be signed by each issuer, its principal executive officer or officers, its principal financial officer, its comptroller or principal accounting officer, and the majority of its board of directors or persons performing similar functions (or, if there is no board of directors or persons performing similar functions, by the majority of the persons or board having the power of management of the issuer) . . .

Section 11—Civil Liabilities on Account of False Registration Statement

a. In case any part of the registration statement, when such part became effective, contained an untrue statement of a material fact or omitted to state a material fact required to be stated therein or necessary to make the statements therein not misleading, any person acquiring such security (unless it is proved that at the time of such acquisition he knew of such untruth or omission) may, either at law or in equity, in any court of competent jurisdiction, sue—

1. every person who signed the registration statement;

2. every person who was a director of (or person performing similar functions) or partner in the issuer at the time of the filing of the part of the registration statement with respect to which his liability is asserted;

3. every person who, with his consent, is named in the registration statement as being or about to become a director, person performing similar functions, or partner;

4. every accountant, engineer, or appraiser, or any person whose profession gives authority to a

statement made by him, who has with his consent been named as having prepared or certified any part of the registration statement, or as having prepared or certified any report or valuation which is used in connection with the registration statement, with respect to the statement in such registration statement, report, or valuation, which purports to have been prepared or certified by him;

5. every underwriter with respect to such security.

Section 12—Civil Liabilities Arising in Connection with Prospectuses and Communications

a. **In General.** Any person who—

1. offers or sells a security in violation of section 5, or

2. offers or sells a security . . . by the use of any means or instruments of transportation or communication in interstate commerce or of the mails, by means of a prospectus or oral communication, which includes an untrue statement of a material fact or omits to state a material fact necessary in order to make the statements, in the light of the circumstances under which they were made, not misleading (the purchaser not knowing of such untruth or omission), and who shall not sustain the burden of proof that he did not know, and in the exercise of reasonable care could not have known, of such untruth or omission, shall be liable, subject to subsection (b), to the person purchasing such security from him, who may sue either at law or in equity in any court of competent jurisdiction, to recover the consideration paid for such security with interest thereon, less the amount of any income received thereon, upon the tender of such security, or for damages if he no longer owns the security.

b. **Loss Causation.** In an action described in subsection (a)(2), if the person who offered or sold such security proves that any portion or all of the amount recoverable under subsection (a)(2) represents other than the depreciation in value of the subject security resulting from such part of the prospectus or oral communication, with respect to which the liability of that person is asserted, not being true or omitting to state a material fact required to be stated therein or necessary to make the statement not misleading, then such portion or amount, as the case may be, shall not be recoverable.

Section 17—Fraudulent Interstate Transactions

a. It shall be unlawful for any person in the offer or sale of any securities by the use of any means or instruments of transportation or communication in interstate commerce or by the use of the mails, directly or indirectly—

1. to employ any device, scheme, or artifice to defraud, or

2. to obtain money or property by means of any untrue statement of a material fact or any omission to state a material fact necessary in order to make the statements made, in the light of the circumstances under which they were made, not misleading, or

3. to engage in any transaction, practice, or course of business which operates or would operate as a fraud or deceit upon the purchaser.

b. It shall be unlawful for any person, by the use of any means or instruments of transportation or communication in interstate commerce or by the use of the mails, to publish, give publicity to, or circulate any notice, circular, advertisement, newspaper, article, letter, investment service, or communication which, though not purporting to offer a security for sale, describes such security for a consideration received or to be received, directly or indirectly, from an issuer, underwriter, or dealer, without fully disclosing the receipt, whether past or prospective, of such consideration and the amount thereof.

Section 24—Penalties.

Any person who willfully violates any of the provisions of this title, or the rules and regulations promulgated by the Commission under authority thereof, or any person who willfully, in a registration statement filed under this title, makes any untrue statement of a material fact or omits to state any material fact required to be stated therein or necessary to make the statements therein not misleading, shall upon conviction be fined not more than $10,000 or imprisoned not more than five years, or both.

>> *appendix VII*

>> Selected Sections of Securities Exchange Act of 1934

Section 4—Securities and Exchange Commission

1. There is hereby established a Securities and Exchange Commission (hereinafter referred to as the "Commission") to be composed of five commissioners to be appointed by the President by and with the advice and consent of the Senate. Not more than three of such commissioners shall be members of the same political party, and in making appointments members of different political parties shall be appointed alternately as nearly as may be practicable. No commissioner shall engage in any other business, vocation, or employment than that of serving as commissioner, nor shall any commissioner participate, directly or indirectly, in any stock-market operations or transactions of a character subject to regulation by the Commission pursuant to this title. Each commissioner shall hold office for a term of five years and until his successor is appointed and has qualified . . .

Section 10—Regulation of the Use of Manipulative and Deceptive Devices.

It shall be unlawful for any person, directly or indirectly, by the use of any means or instrumentality of interstate commerce or of the mails, or of any facility of any national securities exchange—

b. To use or employ, in connection with the purchase or sale of any security registered on a national securities exchange or any security not so registered, any manipulative or deceptive device or any securities-based swap agreement . . ., or contrivance in contravention of such rules and regulations as the Commission may prescribe as necessary or appropriate in the public interest or for the protection of investors.

Section 16—Directors, Officers, and Principal Stockholders

a. DISCLOSURES REQUIRED.—

(1) *Directors, officers, and principal stockholders required to file.*—Every person who is directly or indirectly the beneficial owner of more than 10 percent of any class of any equity security (other than an exempted security) which is registered pursuant to section 12, or who is a director or an officer of the issuer of such security, shall file the statements required by this subsection with the Commission (and, if such security is registered on a national securities exchange, also with the exchange).

(2) TIME OF FILING.—The statements required by this subsection shall be filed—

(A) at the time of the registration of such security on a national securities exchange or by the effective date of a registration statement filed pursuant to section 12(g);

(B) within 10 days after he or she becomes such beneficial owner, director, or officer;

(C) if there has been a change in such ownership, or if such person shall have purchased or sold a security- based swap agreement . . . involving such equity security, before the end of the second business day following the day on which the subject transaction has been executed, or at such other time as the Commission shall establish, by rule, in any case in which the Commission determines that such 2-day period is not feasible.

(3) CONTENTS OF STATEMENTS.—A statement filed—

(A) under subparagraph (A) or (B) of paragraph (2) shall contain a statement of the amount of all equity securities of such issuer of which the filing person is the beneficial owner; and

(B) under subparagraph (C) of such paragraph shall indicate ownership by the filing person at the date of filing, any such changes in such ownership, and such purchases and sales of the security-based swap agreements as have occurred since the most recent such filing under such subparagraph.

(4) ELECTRONIC FILING AND AVAILABILITY. — Beginning not later than 1 year after the date of enactment of the Sarbanes-Oxley Act of 2002—

(A) a statement filed under subparagraph (C) of paragraph (2) shall be filed electronically;

(B) the Commission shall provide each such statement on a publicly accessible Internet site not later than the end of the business day following that filing; and

(C) the issuer (if the issuer maintains a corporate website) shall provide that statement on that corporate website, not later than the end of the business day following that filing.

Section 18—Liability for Misleading Statements

a. Any person who shall make or cause to be made any statement in any application, report, or document filed pursuant to this title or any rule or regulation thereunder or any undertaking contained in a registration statement . . ., which statement was at the time and in the light of the circumstances under which it was made false or misleading with respect to any material fact, shall be liable to any person (not knowing that such statement was false or misleading) who, in reliance upon such statement, shall have purchased or sold a security at a price which was affected by such statement, for damages caused by such reliance, unless the person sued shall prove that he acted in good faith and had no knowledge that such statement was false or misleading. A person seeking to enforce such liability may sue at law or in equity in any court of competent jurisdiction. In any such suit the court may, in its discretion, require an undertaking for the payment of the costs of such suit, and assess reasonable costs, including reasonable attorneys' fees, against either party litigant.

b. Every person who becomes liable to make payment under this section may recover contribution as in cases of contract from any person who, if joined in the original suit, would have been liable to make the same payment.

c. No action shall be maintained to enforce any liability created under this section unless brought within one year after the discovery of the facts constituting the cause of action and within three years after such cause of action accrued.

Section 32—Penalties

a. Any person who willfully violates any provision of this chapter . . . or any rule or regulation thereunder the violation of which is made unlawful or the observance of which is required under the terms of this chapter, or any person who willfully and knowingly makes, or causes to be made, any statement in any application, report, or document required to be filed under this chapter or any rule or regulation thereunder or any undertaking contained in a registration statement . . . or by any self-regulatory organization in connection with an application for membership or participation therein or to become associated with a member thereof, which statement was false or misleading with respect to any material fact, shall upon conviction be fined not more than $5,000,000, or imprisoned not more than 20 years, or both, except that when such person is a person other than a natural person, a fine not exceeding $25,000,000 may be imposed; but no person shall be subject to imprisonment under this section for the violation of any rule or regulation if he proves that he had no knowledge of such rule or regulation.